THE VOCATION OF TH

RELIGION, MARRIAGE, AND FAMILY

Series Editors

Don S. Browning
John Witte Jr.

The Vocation of the Child

Edited by

Patrick McKinley Brennan

WILLIAM B. EERDMANS PUBLISHING COMPANY
GRAND RAPIDS, MICHIGAN / CAMBRIDGE, U.K.

Published 2008 by
Wm. B. Eerdmans Publishing Co.
2140 Oak Industrial Drive N.E., Grand Rapids, Michigan 49505 /
P.O. Box 163, Cambridge CB3 9PU U.K.

Printed and bound in Great Britain by
Marston Book Services Limited, Didcot

13 12 11 10 09 08   7 6 5 4 3 2 1

Library of Congress Cataloging-in-Publication Data

The vocation of the child / edited by Patrick McKinley Brennan.
    p.   cm. — (Religion, marriage, and family)
Includes bibliographical references.
ISBN 978-0-8028-6240-2 (pbk.: alk. paper)
1. Children (Christian theology)   I. Brennan, Patrick M., 1966-

BT705.V63   2008
233 — dc22

2008026252

www.eerdmans.com

Contents

Series Foreword

The Religion, Marriage, and Family series has a complex history. It is also the product of some synergism. The books in the first phase evolved from a research project located at the University of Chicago and supported by a generous grant from the Division of Religion of the Lilly Endowment. The books in this new phase of the series will come from more recent research projects located in the Center for the Study of Law and Religion in the School of Law of Emory University.

This second phase of the series will include books from two of this Center's projects, both supported by generous grants from The Pew Charitable Trusts and Emory University. The first project was called Sex, Marriage, and Family in the Religions of the Book and began with an Emory University faculty seminar in 2001. The second project was called The Child in Law, Religion, and Society and also was initiated by a semester-long Emory faculty seminar that met during the autumn of 2003.

Although the first phase of the Religion, Marriage, and Family series primarily examined Christian perspectives on the family, it also included books on theological views of children. In this second phase, family in the broad sense is still in the picture but an even greater emphasis on children will be evident. The Chicago projects and the Emory projects have enjoyed a profitable synergistic relationship. Legal historian John Witte, director of the two Emory projects, worked with practical theologian Don Browning on the Chicago initiatives. Later, Browning worked with Witte on the research at Emory. Historian Martin Marty joined Witte and Browning and led the 2003 seminar on childhood.

Some of the coming books in the Religion, Marriage, and Family series will be written or edited by Emory faculty members who participated in the two seminars of 2001 and 2003. But authors in this new phase also will come from other universities and academic settings. They will be scholars, however, who have been in conversation with the Emory projects.

This series intends to go beyond the sentimentality, political manipulation, and ungrounded assertions that characterize so much of the contemporary debate over marriage, family, and children. In all cases, they will be books probing the depths of resources in Christianity and the other Abrahamic religions for understanding, renewing, and in some respects redefining current views of marriage, family, and children. The series will continue its investigation of parenthood and children, work and family, responsible fatherhood and motherhood, and equality in the family. It will study the responsibility of the major professions such as law, medicine, and education in promoting and protecting sound families and healthy children. It will analyze the respective roles of church, market, state, legislature, and court in supporting marriages, families, children, and parents.

The editors of this series hope to develop a thoughtful and accessible new literature for colleges, seminaries, churches, other religious institutions, and probing laypersons. In this post-9/11 era, we are all learning that issues pertaining to families, marriage, and children are not just idiosyncratic preoccupations of the United States; they have become worldwide concerns as modernization, globalization, changing values, emerging poverty, changing gender roles, and colliding religious traditions are disrupting families and challenging us to think anew about what it means to be husbands, wives, parents, and children.

DON S. BROWNING *and* JOHN WITTE, JR.

Acknowledgments

The idea for this study arose in the meandering but insistent course of a season-after-season conversation between John Coons and John Witte, Jr., about the shortcomings of much contemporary discourse concerning the child. In this area, as in so many other areas of social concern, rights-talk has a tendency to occupy the field, with the result that people of good will can by misadventure reduce the child to the status of a junior rights-bearer. Christians have a long tradition of affirming the rights of children, to be sure, but Christians have more to say about the child than that he or she just "has rights." Jesus set the standard when he warned his followers, "unless . . . you become like little children, you shall not enter the kingdom of heaven" (Matt. 18:3). Christians have it on good authority to look to the child.

Increasingly convinced that an interdisciplinary and Christian study of the *calling* of the child held the promise of providing a new focus for contemporary discussion of child and family, Coons and Witte decided to enlist help. Witte and Coons had collaborated before, and Coons and I had collaborated extensively on a range of projects. In his capacity as director of the Center for the Study of Law and Religion at Emory University, Witte asked Coons and me to codirect a project on "The Vocation of the Child." The concept of vocation is at once a term of art in Christian theology and a loose, umbrella term of heuristic utility.

With the Center's support, as well as funding from the Templeton Foundation, a dozen leading scholars met at Emory in the fall of 2005 to share research and ideas about the moral and spiritual calling of the child. The disciplines of history, education, spirituality, theology, philosophy, ethics, and law were represented; the scholars from these disciplines spoke variously from the Catholic tradition, several Protestant denominations, and Orthodoxy. Following the fall meeting, decisions were taken about the architecture of the emergent volume, and additional scholars were invited to join the project in order to address topics or themes that the group identified as in need of further development. The editorial aim was to assure that the study be broad, rigorous, and provocative, but by no means exhaustive. Limits of space ensured that many Christian perspectives would remain unmentioned. What Islamic, Jewish, Native American, and other non-Christian religious traditions can add to a discussion of the vocation of the child is a question that has not been asked in this study.

This volume on the vocation of the child took final form as the fifteen contributors pursued questions in their respective areas of expertise, under the watchful eye of cross-disciplinary dialogue. As the introduction explains, there emerged as a central, unifying theme of the book the nature and extent of a child's moral or spiritual vulnerability. One way of putting this vital question is this: Can adults help or hinder a child's vocation to become and to be a moral, spiritual person? The Christian voices collected in conversation here disagree in interesting ways about the answer to this question, but those fifteen voices agree among themselves that attention to the vocation of the child opens up fertile fields of inquiry that remain untouched when the focus remains, as it so often does, on the rights, duties, or privileges of the child. This study of the vocation of the child adds a new dimension to the burgeoning literature on children's spiritual and moral formation.

In my editing work I have enjoyed the superb assistance of Villanova law students Lindsay Bish, Roman Galas, Erin Galbally, Christine Green, Sean Philbin, and John Wagner. I bear the six of them a great debt of thanks. Villanova law student William Weiss deserves the lion's share of the credit for producing the index. Villanova Dean Mark Sargent and Associate Deans John Gotanda, Doris Brogan, and William James provided the necessary material resources and other support, and to them too I am thankful. At Emory, Anita Mann, April Bogle, and Amy Wheeler provided their customary expert assistance. At Villanova, Amy Spare, with the help of her colleagues, provided professional, prompt, and creative library assistance. Terri LaVerghetta provided secretarial assistance in the early phases of the project. I owe a special thanks to Susan Coady, who brought the project to completion. For her able, apt, and cheerful secretarial assistance, I am most grateful.

As the work on this volume progressed, I became ever more persuaded that our society desperately needs the Christian religion's insights into the human and spiritual phenomenon of the child — needs, more specifically, to be invited to grapple with what the child is and what the child is called to become. It has been a privilege and pleasure to collaborate with so many distinguished and passionate students of the child's place in society and in God's plan of salvation. For making the study possible, I am deeply grateful to John Witte. For asking and persisting in the questions that led Witte to pursue a study of the vocation of the child, I join many others in abiding gratitude to the estimable Jack Coons, whose words at the end of his earlier collaboration with Witte should stand at the beginning of this collaborative work:

> The family is for most of us the primary medium of moral expression. The parent experiences the child as both an audience and as a message to the world. In a faith echo of the divine, children are the most important Word most of us will utter.

These acknowledgments would not be complete without a special word of thanks to my friend and colleague Michael Moreland, whose comments on the introduction and thoughts on the project as a whole were invaluable. I look forward to the day when we can co-teach that course on *Brideshead Revisited*. My wife Jaime, equally a lover of *The Sacred and Profane Memories of Captain Charles Ryder,* has my deepest gratitude, for things visible and for things invisible. She saw right away who was up to what in the story Charles tells, and how the "twitch upon the thread" works. Finally, I dedicate this book to the memory of Brother R. Columban, F.S.C. (1914-2008). Though he preferred Trollope to Waugh, he was the first to instruct me, in both word and deed, concerning the mysteries of vocation. Brother Columban brought joy to my youth, to my adolescence, to my 20s, to my 30s, and, at length of days, to my early 40s. We laughed together and prayed together for twenty-nine years. It is fitting that this study should include a chapter, by another of Brother Columban's students, on the theology of childhood of St. John Baptist de la Salle. For seventy-five years, Brother Columban every day answered the call to follow in the pathway of the Patron of Teachers of Youth, and he lived that vocation inspired by the words of reminder that always adorned the wall of his spartan room: *Servite Domino in Laetitia.*

Patrick McKinley Brennan
Philadelphia, Pennsylvania

Permissions

The editor and publisher gratefully acknowledge permission to include material from the following sources:

Contributors

Patrick McKinley Brennan is Professor of Law and the John F. Scarpa Chair in Catholic Legal Studies at Villanova University School of Law. Professor Brennan earned his B.A. in philosophy from Yale College, his M.A. in philosophy from the University of Toronto, and his J.D. from the University of California, Berkeley, School of Law. Professor Brennan has written nearly forty articles and book chapters, authored *By Nature Equal: The Anatomy of a Western Insight* (1999) (with Coons), and edited *Civilizing Authority: Society, State, and Church* (2007).

Marcia J. Bunge is Professor of Humanities and Theology at Christ College, the Honors College of Valparaiso University. Professor Bunge earned her B.A. in English and music from St. Olaf College and her M.A. in divinity and Ph.D. in religion and literature from the University of Chicago. The author of dozens of articles and book chapters, Professor Bunge has edited five books, including *Children and Childhood: Biblical Perspectives and Children* (2008), *Childhood in World Religions: Classic Texts of Judaism, Christianity, Islam, Hinduism, Buddhism, and Confucianism* (2008), and *The Child in Christian Thought* (2001).

John E. Coons is Robert L. Bridges Professor of Law, Emeritus, at the University of California, Berkeley, School of Law. Professor Coons received his B.A. from the University of Minnesota, Duluth, and his J.D. from Northwestern University. In addition to many articles and book chapters, Professor Coons has written *By Nature Equal: The Anatomy of a Western Insight* (1999) (with Brennan), *Making School Choice Work for All Families* (1999) (with Steve Sugarman), *Scholarships for Children* (1992) (with Sugarman), *Education by Choice* (1978) (with Sugarman), and *Private Wealth and Public Education* (with William Clune and Sugarman).

Charles L. Glenn is Professor and Chairman of Administration Training and Policy in the School of Education at Boston University. Professor Glenn received his B.A. and Ed.D. from Harvard University and his Ph.D. from Boston University. Professor Glenn's publications are extensive. They include *The Myth of the Common School* (1988, 2002), *The Ambiguous Embrace: Government and Faith-Based Schools and Social Agencies* (2000), and *Balancing Freedom, Autonomy, and Accountability in Education* (2004) (with De Groof).

Heather M. Good earned her J.D. and M.T.S. from Emory University. Ms. Good served as a law clerk to the Honorable Edward Carnes on the United States Court of Appeals for the Eleventh Circuit. She is an associate at Crowell Moring in Washington, D.C.

Vigen Guroian is Professor of Religious Studies in Orthodox Christianity at the University of Virginia. Professor Guroian received his B.A. from the University of Virginia and his Ph.D. in theology from Drew University. Professor Guroian is the author of more than 150 articles and nine books. His most recent books are *The Fragrance of God* (2006) and *Rallying the Really Human Things: The Moral Imagination in Politics, Literature, and Everyday Life* (2005)

William Harmless, S.J., is Professor of Theology at Creighton University. Professor Harmless was awarded his B.A. in English from Rice University, his M.Div. from Weston School of Theology, and his Ph.D. in Religion and Education from Boston College. Among Father Harmless's many publications are *Mystics* (2007), *Desert Christians: An Introduction to the Literature of Early Monasticism* and *Mystics* (2004), and *Augustine and the Catechumenate* (1995).

Anthony J. Kelly, C.Ss.R., is Professor of Theology at the Australian Catholic University and is a member of the International Theological Commission. Father Kelly completed his doctoral and postdoctoral studies in Rome, Toronto, and Paris, earning his doctorate in theology from the Anselmianum. In addition to numerous articles and other books, Professor Kelly is the author of *Eschatology and Hope* (2006) and a coauthor of *Experiencing God in the Gospel of John* (2003) (with Moloney).

Bonnie J. Miller-McLemore is the E. Rhodes and Leona B. Carpenter Professor of Pastoral Theology and Counseling at the Graduate Department of Religion at Vanderbilt University. Professor Miller-McLemore received her B.A. from Kalamazoo University and both her M.A. and Ph.D. from the University of Chicago. Professor Miller-McLemore is the author of many articles and book chapters and seven books, including *Children in American Religions* (2008), *In the Midst of Chaos: Care of Children as Spiritual Practice* (2006), and *Let the Children Come: Reimagining Childhood from a Christian Perspective* (2003).

Charles J. Reid, Jr., is Professor of Law at the University of St. Thomas School of Law. Professor Reid received his B.A. in Latin, classics, and history from the University of Wisconsin-Milwaukee, his Ph.D. in the history of medieval law from Cornell University, and his J.D. and J.C.L. from the Catholic University of America. In addition to many articles, book chapters, and other publications, Professor Reid is the author of *Power over the Body, Equality in the Family: Rights and Domestic Relations in Medieval Canon Law* (2004).

Philip L. Reynolds is Aquinas Professor of Historical Theology in the Candler School of Theology at Emory University. Dr. Reynolds received his B.A. from the University of Oxford and his Ph.D. from the University of Toronto. In addition to many articles and other publications, Professor Reynolds is the author of *Food and Body* (1999) and *Marriage in the Western Church* (1994). In addition, Professor Reynolds has published *To Have and to Hold: Marrying and Its Documentation in Western Christendom, 400-1600* (2003) (with John Witte, Jr.).

Elmer John Thiessen is Professor Emeritus at Medicine Hat College. Professor Thiessen earned his M.A. in philosophy from McMaster University and his Ph.D. from the University of Waterloo. Professor Thiessen has published dozens of articles and book chapters and authored *In Defence of Religious Schools and Colleges* (2003) and *Teaching for Commitment* (1993).

George Van Grieken, F.S.C., is Director of Vocation Ministry for the San Francisco Province of the De La Salle Christian Brothers. He received an M.A. in theology from St. Mary's College in California and a Ph.D. in religious education from Boston College. Brother George is the author of *Touching the Hearts of Students: Characteristics of a Lasallian School* (1999).

Robert K. Vischer is Associate Professor of Law at the University of St. Thomas School of Law (Minnesota). Professor Vischer earned his B.A. from the University of New Orleans and his J.D. from Harvard Law School. Professor Vischer has published articles on a range of topics including conscience, subsidiarity, and pluralism.

William Werpehowski is Professor of Christian Ethics and Director at the Center for Peace and Justice Education at Villanova University. Professor Werpehowski received his B.A. in religion from Princeton University and his Ph.D. in religious ethics from Yale University. The author of dozens of articles and book chapters, Professor Werpehowski has also coedited *The Oxford Handbook of Theological Ethics* (2007) (with Gilbert Meilaender) and published *American Protestant Ethics and the Legacy of H. Richard Niebuhr* (2002).

John Witte, Jr., is the Jonas Robitscher Professor of Law and director of the Center for the Study of Law and Religion at Emory University School of Law. Professor Witte received his B.A. from Calvin College and his J.D. from Harvard University. Professor Witte has published more than 150 articles, ten journal symposia, and twenty-two books. Among his most recent books are *The Reformation of Rights: Law, Religion, and Human Rights in Early Modern Calvinism* (2008) and *Christianity and Law: An Introduction* (2008) (with Frank Alexander).

Introduction

Patrick McKinley Brennan

I. Of Fate, Luck, and Vocation

Out-of-wedlock births in the United States, long on the rise, now account for a near record 40 percent of the babies born. While such births have historically been associated with teenage mothers, in 2005 the birthrate of unwed teenage mothers dropped while that of unwed women in their twenties rose.[1] *On any given day* in 2005 in the United States, 3,879 babies were born to unmarried mothers.[2] In addition, the number of unmarried-couple households with children has risen precipitously in recent years; fewer than 200,000 in 1970, it surpassed 1.7 million in 2005.[3] Anyone giving such statistics conscientious attention will wonder and worry about the children involved.

Other statistics, about the daily lives of some of the most vulnerable among us, raise additional cause for concern. In 2005 in the United States, more than twelve million children — that is, nearly 17 percent of the child population — lived in households where there was low or very low "food security."[4] Because

1. "Babies Born to Singles Are at Record: Nearly 4 in 10," *New York Times,* November 22, 2006.

2. 2005 Children's Defense Fund Action Council, "Did Your Members of Congress Protect Children?" Nonpartisan Congressional Scorecard, 2006.

3. "Babies Born to Singles Are at Record."

4. U.S. Department of Agriculture, *Household Food Security in the United States,* 2005, Economic Research Report, no. 29. A U.S. household is "food secure" if the household has "consistent, dependable access to enough food for active, healthy living" (iv). A household experiences food insecurity when its access to food "is limited by a lack of money and other resources." Although children are usually shielded in a situation of food scarcity, on a typical day in 2005, children in 32,000 to 43,000 households experienced disrupted eating patterns and a reduction in food intake (v). In 2006, 17 million children received a free or reduced-price lunch through the National School Lunch Program and 8 million children received a free or reduced-price

1

data about exactly how food gets shared around a table of hungry mouths are understandably impossible to produce, one can only speculate about the exact number of children who go to bed hungry on a given night.

Other facts are easier to come by, but not easy to forget. *On any given day* in 2005 in the United States, 2,447 babies were born into poverty, and 2,482 children were confirmed as abused or neglected.[5] It is estimated that 1 million to 1.6 million children in the United States are likely to experience homelessness over the course of a year.[6] One study estimates that 39 percent of the homeless population are children. Again, anyone attending to such statistics will worry about the children.

Many people, perhaps including a good number of Christians, will frame their worry in terms of the *fate* of the children. Fate is a word Christians use only provisionally, however. They speak the word-sound, all right, but, as Saint Augustine said of some converts who continued to rue their "luck," they must believe in their heart that the revelation of the providence of a personal, loving God supplants the randomness of an ungoverned cosmic lottery. Quite simply, Christians ask what God wills for them and calls them to; they seek their *vocation*. And, because they believe in faith that no person exceeds God's providence, they affirm that every person is called by name, that *every* person has a vocation.[7] They even go so far as to inquire into the vocation *of the child*.

And so they ask, what is the vocation of children born to single mothers or unwed couples? How does it fare vis-à-vis the vocation of children born to parents bound together in married love? What is the providential "fate" of babies who do not know the vowed love of two parents? What is the destiny of babies born in poverty? Of children who grow up in squalor?

The measurable effects of poverty and other forms of neglect confirm the child's vulnerability.[8] But is a person's *vocation*, because it is from God, *invul-*

---

breakfast through the National School Breakfast Program. U.S. Department of Agriculture, Food and Nutrition Service Program Data, as of December 22, 2006. In contrast, only 1.9 million children participated in the Summer Food Service Program during the peak month of July.

5. 2005 Children's Defense Fund Action Council, "Did Your Members of Congress Protect Children?"

6. National Alliance to End Homelessness, "Fundamental Issues to Prevent and End Youth Homelessness," Youth Homelessness Series, Brief No. 1, May 2006. Homeless families, comprised of an adult with one or more children, make up 34 percent of homeless people found in homeless assistance programs. Maggie McCarty, *Homelessness: Recent Statistics, Targeted Federal Programs, and Recent Legislation,* Congressional Research Service, May 31, 2005.

7. On "vocation" as a contested but uniting Christian concept, see William A. Placher, *Callings: Twenty Centuries of Christian Wisdom on Vocation* (Grand Rapids: Eerdmans, 2005).

8. See, e.g., T. Berry Bazelton and Stanley I. Greenspan, *The Irreducible Needs of Children: What Every Child Must Have to Grow, Learn, and Flourish* (Cambridge, Mass.: Perseus, 2000).

nerable? Are we adults capable of squandering our children's vocations? Alternatively, can we help them discover and realize their vocations?

The belief that a person has a vocation can supply a reason to others to help that person find and embrace it. Differently conceived, the belief that everyone has a vocation can court apathy or detachment, if only at an unconscious level. The agnostic saying has it that "There is a reason for everything." It is obvious that very young children are, in almost every respect, helpless to help themselves. According to the seminal chapter by John Coons (chapter 3), however, the *vocation* of even the youngest (rational) children is wholly in their own hands. Coons's provocative thesis draws on Christian philosophy and theology, but even more on moral sentiments that are widely shared, in order to identify within the vulnerable child a core *self* that stands invulnerable, infallibly called by God. Without licensing adults to neglect their dependents, Coons attempts a proleptic rescue of the true vocation of the child — a feat to which we return repeatedly below.

Shifting the focus from the consequences of a child's being born either out of wedlock or in poverty, what about the "fate" of children adopted or artificially conceived by lesbian or gay couples? What do these rapidly changing social norms mean for the children involved? Today, all but eight states permit adoption by gays and lesbians. All but two states permit gays and lesbians to serve as foster parents. However, as of 2008, only six states permit gay couples to enter into marriage or civil unions. Meanwhile, as many as nine million children in the United States have a gay or lesbian parent, and approximately a quarter of all lesbian or gay couples are raising children.[9]

These children have an experience that is importantly different from the one that has been both normal and normative. Would anyone suggest, though, that these children have a vocation that is categorically compromised, as compared to that of children born to a heterosexual mother in traditional marriage in which the parents stay together and share the parenting responsibilities? The social science shows that children reared by homosexual parents are more likely to be homosexual as adults.[10] Readers will draw different conclusions about the significance of this phenomenon.

Another social force that shapes our children is schooling. In the United States, primary and secondary schools of the "public" sort are funded on the basis of property taxes. The result is that children in rich or prosperous districts attend commendable schools, while children in poorer districts are conscripted

9. Richard E. Redding, "It's Really about Sex: Same-Sex Marriage, Lesbigay Parenting, and the Psychology of Disgust," *Duke Journal of Gender Law and Policy* 15 (2008): 127. On file with author.

10. For a survey of the social science literature on the effects on children of growing up in gay or lesbian households, see Redding, "It's Really about Sex."

by schools that range from threadbare to threatening. An exception to the rule for children from poor districts depends on scholarships, voucher programs, or charter schools that allow access to the educational opportunities that are the ordinary option of the children of rich and upper-middle-class parents.

Is it not worth wondering what this educational disparity means for the vocation of the children who live it? Are the children playing and praying together at Portsmouth Abbey better equipped to discern and embrace their vocation than those smoking cigarettes in the bathroom or crack in the alley, undetected by the disaffected and disenchanted staff? God calls, but who can hear?

And then there are the approximately two million children involved, on an annual basis, in prostitution and pornography. Not to mention the nearly six million in forced and bonded labor. As well as the 300,000 engaged in armed conflict.[11] What of their vocation? To what, and by whom, are *they* called?

Without risking hyperbole, one can say that the visible situation of the child today frequently is grim. Even in the generally prosperous and comparatively educated United States, some children flourish, but strikingly many, and not just the victims of prostitution or pornography, lack what many agree is necessary to a healthy upbringing and a bright, or at least promising, future.

"No child left behind"? That is not what happens in the world we see. But what of the child's vocation from God? Can it possibly be safe from worldly depredation, as Coons hopes? Can Christians, along with others, *plausibly* regard it as invulnerable?

II. An Ironic Reversal

It is widely acknowledged that the twentieth century was the most violent in human history. As our capacity to destroy one another grew exponentially, our willingness to care for our fellow humans suffered in proportion. Alongside quantum leaps in science and medicine, we witness a growing degradation of the human person in war, widening poverty, devastating disease, and every conceivable social malady.

This growing human capacity for self-destruction has led to an arresting, though easily overlooked, reversal, of which this study, of the vocation of the child, might be seen as a manifestation. "It is no longer the human which takes charge of defending the divine," Jacques Maritain observed in 1965, "but the di-

---

11. International Labour Organization, "Every Child Counts: New Global Estimates on Child Labour," *Statistical Information and Monitoring Programme on Child Labour* (Geneva, 2006).

vine which offers itself to defend the human (if the latter does not refuse the aid offered)."[12] The trend Maritain recognized was only in its infancy in 1965. Today, with ever greater frequency and fervency, Christians are coming together, both denominationally and ecumenically, to remind the forgetful that it does not fall to us humans, least of all as a right enforceable at law, "to define one's concept of existence, of meaning, of the universe, and of the mystery of human life."[13] Christians are testifying that it falls to us, rather, to seek to discover the divine plan for human life, a plan that includes peace, respect, justice, and treatment consistent with human dignity. In a word, it includes recognition of and response to the vocation of every person, if we do not "refuse the aid offered."

Christian efforts to defend the human have had among their targets war, violence, starvation — social surds of which no known historical epoch has been innocent. Increasingly, though, Christians have also lent support to defending the divinely ordained but thoroughly human institutions of marriage and family. Once virtually unquestioned and almost everywhere supported, today marriage and family are insulted and undermined. It is even suggested that they are optional. For example, one scholar avers that "The law," alone, "creates the family, and things could not be otherwise."[14] What the positive law has created solely of its own power, it can de-create — thus raising the hard-to-imagine possibility of a family-less world. Christians, in concert with others, answer by reminding humanity of what would have seemed obvious to our forebears: "The law no more 'creates' the family than the Rule Against Perpetuities 'creates' dirt."[15]

Though the efforts of Christians on behalf of the family necessarily have had children among their intended and actual beneficiaries, Christians have also come directly to the defense of the child. For, although the child is at home in the family, the child is by no means reducible to it. Children are needful of additional, and specific, defense. In a tradition that has oscillated between regarding children as "priceless" gems and as a source of cheap labor, as gifts from God and as mouths to feed, as models of innocence and pictures of wickedness, the child wants understanding.[16] Is the child "like the young of some domestic

---

12. Jacques Maritain, *The Peasant of the Garonne* (New York: Holt, Rinehart and Winston, 1968), 4.

13. *Planned Parenthood v. Casey,* 505 US 833, 851 (1992).

14. James G. Dwyer, "Spiritual Treatment Exemptions to Child Medical Neglect Laws: What We Outsiders Should Think," *Notre Dame Law Review* 76, no. 1 (2000): 167.

15. Richard W. Garnett, "Taking Pierce Seriously: The Family, Religious Education, and Harm to Children," *Notre Dame Law Review* 76, no. 1 (2000): 114 n. 29.

16. For a survey of centuries of societal attitudes toward children, see Linda A. Pollock, *Forgotten Children: Parent-Child Relations from 1500 to 1900* (New York: Cambridge University Press, 1983).

pet in need of habit training, . . . [or] like the seed which should be allowed to grow naturally,"[17] or like some third thing? Appreciating the child for what she is, in both her vulnerability and her promise, may even lead, moreover, to a renewed appreciation of what family itself is for.

The youngest and most defenseless among us, children have always been at risk of abandonment, of exposure, of abuse, of neglect. However, in a new world order in which it is the putative power for self-definition that is revered, children, along with the aged and disabled, become vulnerable in a novel way. Unable to speak on behalf of himself or herself, the child can be defined away, into spans of time or into systems, by enterprising or eloquent elders. For an example of the latter de-creating act, one might consider the analysis of Harvard philosopher John Searle:

> It would be tricky to try to define the notion of system, but the simple intuitive idea is that systems are collections of particles where the spatio-temporal boundaries of the system are set by causal relations. . . . Babies, elephants, and mountain ranges . . . are examples of systems.[18]

Not called by name, they may not be called at all. And so we might ask, with Joseph Vining, "whence comes any real reluctance in total theorists," those who see it all as system, "to treat the child like the young song sparrow, deafening him, keeping him in silence, isolating him, sacrificing him, and cutting his brain into slices?"[19] Christians coming to the defense of the human see openings, not system; callings, not cuttings; vocations, not brains for vats. Anthony Kelly, C.Ss.R (chapter 8), puts it this way: "[T]he child is conceived," in the flesh, "as an irreducible 'other,'" (220) and it is our task — as parents, aunts and uncles, neighbors, fellow citizens, fellow Christians — to understand the child, to care for him, and of course to love him. But how? Perhaps by understanding what the child is *called to.*

The recent book *The Child in Christian Thought* provided "a critical examination of past [Christian] theological perspectives on children in order to strengthen ethical and theological reflection on children today to contribute to the current academic and broader public discussion on children."[20] The present volume pursues a cognate goal, but by asking an intentionally unexpected ques-

---

17. Hugh Cunningham, *Children and Childhood in Western Society Since 1500*, 2nd ed. (Harlow, England: Pearson-Longman, 2005), 202.

18. John Searle, *The Rediscovery of Mind* (Cambridge: MIT Press, 1992), 86-87 (quoted in Joseph Vining, *The Song Sparrow and the Child* [Notre Dame, Ind.: University of Notre Dame Press, 2004], 8).

19. Vining, *The Song Sparrow,* 114.

20. Marcia J. Bunge, ed., *The Child in Christian Thought* (Grand Rapids: Eerdmans, 2001), 7.

tion: "What is the vocation of the child?" Centuries of reflection on the duties and rights of children, decades of modern international pronouncements of the rights of children, several generations of American debate about the intersection of the "right to life" and the "right to choose" have made timely a fresh focus on an ancient Christian question. Christians are heard to claim that every human person has a "vocation." But what of the young person, the child? What can it mean for him or her, who can neither get a real job nor be ordained to ministry, to have a "vocation"?

Some of the work of this volume is historical; an understanding of the child is not ours to invent from scratch. Much of the work is philosophical and theological; the child continues to demand much of our efforts to say and spell out what nature and grace make possible. There is also what Anthony Kelly calls "phenomenological" work to be done, for, as Kelly observes, the child is a phenomenon, one of what Jean-Luc Marion understood as "saturated phenomena." We need not romanticize or idealize the child when we observe that he or she is a gift, and

> an open-ended, transformative event. It is no *fait accompli* in terms of assignable causes and predictable effects, but an event overflowing into the constitution of the family, society and even world history. . . . (220)

As he goes deeper and deeper into his own phenomenology of the child, Kelly is finally led to ask whether the phenomenon of the child "call[s] the church itself to a new kind of thinking" (222). Together and each in its own way, the fifteen chapters of this study of the vocation of the child, while drawing on the traditional categories of rights, duties, responsibilities, and so forth, also invite a new kind of thinking. Wielding control of food, sacraments, schools, shelters, discipline, and violence, we adults have to decide where the child "is to be put,"[21] and knowing what it is for a child to have a vocation will help both us and the child, whom we, necessarily, "put."

III. The Splendor of Vocation

In *Brideshead Revisited: The Sacred and Profane Memoirs of Captain Charles Ryder*,[22] English novelist Evelyn Waugh (1903-1966) uses the narrative voice of

21. Vining, *The Song Sparrow*, 152.

22. Evelyn Waugh, *Brideshead Revisited: The Sacred and Profane Memoirs of Captain Charles Ryder* (London: Little, Brown, 1944; New York: Knopf, 1993). Citations are to the Knopf edition.

Charles Ryder to chronicle the life of the fabulously rich Flyte family and those who come into contact with them during the second quarter of the twentieth century. The Flytes, though very English, are all of them Catholic, each in a puzzlingly peculiar but perhaps profound way. Drawn into the Flyte family by its charm, Ryder, a confirmed agnostic, is at first patronizing toward the varieties of the family members' religious experience. The Flytes do say, and do, some remarkable things in the name of their Catholic religion. Over time, though, Ryder's contempt matures into curiosity. The unanticipated deathbed repentance of the long-lost Flyte family patriarch, Lord Marchmain, who spent most of his adult life in flight (with a mistress) from his scrupulously pious wife, is the beginning of Charles Ryder's conversion to the Catholic faith.

Along the way, Charles is taken by, but pities, the zealous and guileless Cordelia, the youngest Flyte, who hopes she has a vocation, as she blurts out over dinner with Charles at the Ritz Grill.

> "I hope I've got a vocation."
> "I don't know what that means."
> "It means you can be a nun. If you haven't a vocation, it's no good however much you want to be; and if you have a vocation, you can't get away from it, however much you hate it. Bridey thinks he has a vocation and hasn't. I used to think Sebastian had and hated it — but I don't know now. Everything has changed so much suddenly."[23]

Bridey, or Brideshead, the eldest of the four Flyte children, supercilious and greedy, half hoped for a vocation to the priesthood. He fades from the story, and is disinherited, after marrying Mrs. Musprat, a widow whose late husband he knew thanks to their common interest in matchboxes. Cordelia, meeting up with Charles years after their dinner at the Ritz, inquires, "When you met me last night did you think, 'Poor Cordelia, such an engaging child, grown up a plain and pious spinster, full of good works'? Did you think 'thwarted'?"[24] Though Cordelia shows the wear of her work in the war prison-camps in Spain, she does not speak a word of dissatisfaction about anything. Charles answers Cordelia's questions in the affirmative, but then goes on to doubt his first impression because of what, in the interim, he learns from Cordelia about her brother Sebastian, whom they both loved.

Sebastian, the most conspicuous man of his year at Oxford, by reason of his physical beauty and ostentatious behavior, dies in obscurity in North Africa, an alcoholic in flight from his overbearing family, but even more from his own

---

23. Waugh, *Brideshead Revisited*, 201.
24. Waugh, *Brideshead Revisited*, 279.

weakness of will. So far as the reader is given to speculate, Sebastian's last days are spent on the fringes of a monastery, living devoutly and serving the community, except for the occasional several days' bout of drinking. When Charles suggests to Cordelia that Sebastian's last days were not "what one would have foretold," and goes on to console himself with the thought that at least Sebastian "doesn't suffer," Cordelia replies, "Oh, yes, I think he does. One can have no idea what the suffering may be, to be maimed as he is — no dignity, no power of will. No one is ever holy without suffering."[25] People such as Sebastian, Cordelia believes, "are very near and dear to God."[26]

Before his own conversion, Charles naturally sees Sebastian as thwarted, full stop. Cordelia, who in her youth equated vocation with a call to priesthood or the nunnery, teaches Charles that beautiful, willful Sebastian was not without a vocation. No one is without a vocation.

Vocation, as Waugh understands it, is a call to a "single, peculiar act of service," some unique act "which only we can do and for which we were each created." It refers to "a particular task for each individual soul, which the individual is free to accept or decline at will and whose ultimate destiny is determined by his response to God's vocation."[27] God's call is a person's vocation. For all the Flyte family's religiosity, and for all the family members' varied decencies, it is only Sebastian the drunkard whom the reader is invited to regard as holy. Yet, by Waugh's lights, each person has a unique work to do, a singular life to lead, a particular person to become and be. This is his "vocation" because God calls him to it.

The case of Sebastian Flyte illustrates a risk to those taking Evelyn Waugh's measure of vocation, especially as it may touch children. Sebastian's suffering was real, his objective circumstances wretched. The tradition of worrying that Christians will try to rationalize circumstances that they should seek to improve is venerable, if checkered; even Christians are heard to say "everything happens for a reason." If Sebastian was holy, "very near . . . to God," still, the suffering, which Charles was inclined to blink, asks to be accounted for. Cordelia makes it a condition of Sebastian's holiness.[28]

The young Cordelia's limiting "vocation" to God's calling a person to holy

25. Waugh, *Brideshead Revisited*, 279.

26. Waugh, *Brideshead Revisited*, 278.

27. Douglas Lane Patey, *The Life of Evelyn Waugh: A Critical Biography* (Oxford: Blackwell, 2001), 296.

28. For a concise statement of Waugh's theological conviction that suffering is at the heart of God's call of every person to holiness, see George Weigel's introduction to Evelyn Waugh's novel *Helena*, about the vocation of the mother of the emperor Constantine. George Weigel, introduction to *Helena*, by Evelyn Waugh (Chicago: Loyola Press, 2005), xiii-xvii.

orders or religious life has its contemporary echoes in some Catholic quarters. The common conception today, however, continues the theological turn begun when Martin Luther and then other reformers taught that every person has a vocation, which may include (but is not exhausted by) the work we do in the world. Quoting John Henry Newman, William Werpehowski (chapter 2) reminds us that "in truth we are not called only once, but many times; all through our life Christ is calling us" (53), and what he is calling us to, Werpehowski continues in his own voice, is to "become a self" (71) — a particular, engaged, relational son or daughter of Christ. This latter, distinguishable understanding of vocation depends on God's "little" callings to us, day by day and hour by hour, throughout our life, but on a whole lot more, as well. It might depend on the education we receive. It might even depend on incorporation into the body of Christ through baptism.

Werpehowski warns that, when it comes to the idea of the vocation *of the child,* there is a danger "of the self-deception it can foster among those who care for children in societies like our own, and may thus inflict damage in its name" (54). "Yet it is dangerous in a second, salutary sense," Werpehowski continues, "for the notion properly considered imperils that same partly willed, partial blindness through its challenge, through its *calling us out,* truthfully to see real children as they may be called by God." Coons's thesis potentially implicates both of the dangers identified by Werpehowski, a point to which we shall return.

Vigen Guroian (chapter 4), speaking from the perspective of Orthodox Christianity, develops an understanding of childhood in terms of "office" rather than "vocation." In dialogue with Werpehowski, Guroian considers the risk of taking an excessively particularistic approach to Christian vocation. We are (also) called to certain *kinds* of relations, Guroian explains. Office bespeaks the work a child is to do in the categorical relations he assumes, both as son or daughter and as member of the family and the community. "The essence of being a child," Guroian explains, "is to act responsibly toward one's parents, family, and the larger community. . . . The offices of child and of parent are reciprocal and inextricably related to one another. Each, however, has its own set of virtues" (105). And, because it necessarily will be adult parents who catalogue the virtues of childhood for the children they believe to be called to sonship, the dangers identified by Werpehowski are again, if differently, implicated.

Working from within the Lutheran tradition but with her eye on the whole Christian tradition of reflection on vocation, Marcia Bunge (chapter 1) develops a theology of vocation that, unlike many others, refuses to leave the child out. Observing that even many capacious understandings of vocation have supposed that God starts calling people when and if they become adults, Bunge turns to Scripture to identify the specific tasks and relationships to which God calls the child. Bunge finds that children have work to do *in the present;* they have "offices" to fulfill, and these include learning the faith and modeling it for adults. Of especial salience, in light of the question whether the child's vocation is invulnerable, is Bunge's reminder of Luther's admonition about the social and personal wages of failing to educate the child: "[I]n the sight of God none among the outward sins so heavily burdens the world and merits such severe punishment as this very sin which we commit against children by not educating them" (37).

IV. The (Central) Question of "Moral Luck"

Luther is not alone in recking what impoverished education might mean for children themselves. Surveying the contemporary scene, Coons gives voice to a common concern that the involuntary assignments that punctuate childhood — whether to the squalor and neglect of a ghetto school or to the opulence of a too-clever-by-half suburban prep school that has given up teaching the Golden Rule — can arrange a child's moral tragedy. Does the child with impoverished skills for seeking the good, whether obtained at Sterling Academy or in the ghetto, necessarily suffer a "vocation" to moral mediocrity or tragedy? Raising one's eyes from the terrestrial to the celestial, a second question arises: Is the ill-instructed, untutored child — the child who does not know the first thing about the faith — destined not to seek, and therefore not to find, the *summum bonum,* and therefore to end up with a "vocation" to damnation?

Modern sensibilities regard this eventuality as unlikely, but the questions are worth asking. Many of the giants on whose shoulders we stand, both pagan and Christian, regard correct knowledge, either of the good or of the faith, as a necessary condition either for moral achievement or for salvation, and they do not exempt the little ones.

In answer to the first question, eudaemonist (or virtue-theoretic) moral theorists offer notoriously bleak news. For Aristotle, to pick the leading example, human goodness just *is* the life of virtue according to a rational principle. Children, if they are lucky, are in training for the good life; without apt training and other luck, goodness is simply impossible, no matter one's good intentions, best efforts, or most ardent imprecations. By the eudaemonist's lights, life is a cosmic (but not comical) variation on what the lawyers call "strict liability." Either luck and effort (which, if you can make it, is again thanks to luck) combine to make yours a happy life, or they do not. In a word, bad biology, or standing in the wrong place at the wrong time, can be a person's *moral* death knell. Aristotle saw no alternative. In order to capture the "powerful strain of thought that centers on a feeling of ultimate and outrageous absurdity in the idea that achievement of highest kind of moral worth should depend on natural capacities, unequally and fortuitously distributed,"[29] Bernard Williams coined the oxymoron "moral luck."[30]

Williams had adults in mind, but the *locus classicus* of the phenomenon is the child. Adults, we might suppose, can help themselves overcome some of nature's unequal distributions. But if little children are captives of a cosmic lottery, to whom can they turn?

Williams's world, like Aristotle's, does not include a providential God who could, conceivably, perform a rescue, as by grace. Williams found no way out of the eudaemonist's prison. Some people are involuntarily the stuff of tragedy, that genre perfected by the Greeks and never surpassed. Coons, though, remains resolutely more hopeful, especially for the rescue of children.

It is Coons's conviction that the Aristotle-Williams report is not the last word. Refusing to let morality pivot on the unchosen fulcrum of biology or other luck, Coons distinguishes two *kinds* of good. One kind is all the goods the eudaemonist might mention — health, wisdom, friendship, Athenian citizenship, and so forth. This kind of good Coons designates "second good," in order to distinguish it from "first good." The latter, according to Coons, is "self-perfection," moral goodness par excellence: it crowns the act of seeking or trying for second, nonmoral goods. In sum, first good rewards the simple, though not necessarily easy, decision to seek second goods. The thesis, then, is that involuntary failure to realize or instantiate second goods does not imperil first good. If this be true, highest human achievement has been made invulnerable to luck and the eudaemonist's dilemma.

According to Coons, first good is *equally* available to all rational actors because, *in fact,* from the first dawn of rationality, every child is conscious of an obligation to seek second goods. So long as the child manages rationality, first good is within his grasp, because every rational child has *equal* awareness of the obligation to seek second goods. The "prize" (78) of self-perfection awaits anyone who performs the search, no matter the poverty of his ability or the paucity of his success in determining and instantiating particular goods. The *vocation* of the rational child is to seek second goods. According to Coons, no rational child is left out. The rational child's vocation is secure notwithstanding the poverty, of whatever kind, encamped about him.

29. Bernard Williams, "The Idea of Equality," in *Problems of the Self* (Cambridge: Cambridge University Press, 1973), 230.

30. Bernard Williams, "Moral Luck," in *Moral Luck,* ed. Daniel Statman (New York: SUNY Press, 1992), 35.

So Coons claims. But has the eudaemonist's sting *in fact* been withdrawn? Has the specter of moral luck been successfully dissolved? The thesis is that the division of the good into first and second, combined with rational humans' equal access to first good, rescues the child from the eudaemonist lottery. Is the thesis correct? Does every rational person have a plenary awareness of a primordial obligation to seek second goods? Is the good divisible? Are children morally safe wherever they happen to be assigned?

If one is asking Immanuel Kant, the answer is a clear yes. Indeed, according to Bernard Williams, Kant's philosophy

> contains the working out to the very end of that thought, a thought which in less thoroughgoing forms marks the greatest difference between moral ideas influenced by Christianity, and those of the ancient [Greek] world. It is this thought, that moral worth must be separated from any natural advantage whatsoever, which, consistently pursued by Kant, leads to the conclusion that the source of moral thought and action must be located outside the empirically conditioned self.[31]

Writing in 1960, Arthur Adkins asserted that "[W]e are all Kantians now."[32] More recently, Roger Sullivan opined that "The Kantian view or something closely akin to it seems clearly to be the way many people think about morality even today, particularly those reared in the Judeo-Christian tradition. Kant often says what they themselves would say about their moral life, were they to articulate it."[33] Coons's voice can sound like Everyman's.

Many of the authors of this volume, however, along with those whom they study and engage, deny the Kantian premises that lurk largely unnamed in the shadows of Coons's bifurcation of the good.[34] Kant had his Pietistic reasons for making the human good a purely formal category,[35] to be sure, but, as a group, and *pace* the late Bernard Williams, the leading Christian thinkers have resisted the temptation to consider human goodness as disembodied.

Thomas Aquinas's paradigm of childhood, as developed by Philip Reynolds (chapter 6), posits that the work of the child is to grow old enough to be able "to acquire knowledge and virtue" (187). According to Reynolds,

31. Williams, "The Idea of Equality," 228.

32. Arthur W. H. Adkins, *Merit and Responsibility: A Study in Greek Values* (Oxford: Oxford University Press, 1960), 2.

33. Roger J. Sullivan, *Immanuel Kant's Moral Theory* (Cambridge: Cambridge University Press, 1989), xiii.

34. Cf. Coons, "Luck, Obedience, and the Vocation of Childhood," 76-79 below, n. 10.

35. Patrick McKinley Brennan, "Arguing for Human Equality," *Journal of Law and Religion* 18, no. 1 (2002): 132.

"Thomas consistently characterizes childhood in terms of deficiency and imperfection" (175). Reynolds explains that, for Aquinas, if the child has a "vocation," it is the modest but indispensable one of developing over time into an adult who is sober enough to become virtuous. Aquinas is, then, what Coons terms a "gnostic," because he holds, with Aristotle (and Williams), that action that makes a person good depends on action informed by correct knowledge, and the child, even the prodigy, is just beginning to acquire the necessary knowledge. Aquinas displays not the least concern if God predestines some to salvation and others to perdition:

> Neither on this account can there be said to be injustice in God, if He prepares unequal lots for not unequal things. This would be altogether contrary to the notion of justice, if the effect of predestination were granted as a debt, and not gratuitously. In things which are given gratuitously a person can give more or less, just as he pleases (provided he deprives nobody of his due), without any infringement of justice.[36]

Is it possible to romanticize a childhood from which the possibility of (first) goodness is absent?

Aquinas need not have the last word, of course, notwithstanding his canonical status in the Catholic tradition. If what Reynolds refers to as the "biological child" (164-67) does not prevail in the work of the twentieth century's leading Thomist philosopher, Jacques Maritain (1882-1973), it is not because the good has been bifurcated and a purely formal goodness given priority, at least not quite. As the present author (chapter 7) argues, it is because what exceeds the natural human good has entered and transformed it, namely, grace. Reacting against the moral elitism of the Greek eudaemonist, Maritain explains:

> The great novelty introduced by Christianity is this appeal to all, to free men and slaves, to the ignorant and the cultivated, adolescents and old men, a call to perfection which no effort of nature can attain but which is given by grace and consists in love, and from which therefore no one is excluded except by his own refusal.[37]

Maritain appreciates the importance of the development of the biological child and also evinces keen insight into the natural psychological life and development of children and adolescents. Maritain's theology of grace, however, ani-

---

36. Aquinas, *Summa Theologica* I, q. 23, art. 5, reply 3.
37. Jacques Maritain, *Moral Philosophy: An Historical and Critical Survey of the Great Systems* (New York: Charles Scribner's Sons, 1964), 85.

mated by appreciation that "God wills that all men be saved" (1 Tim. 2:4), teaches that even — or, rather, exemplarily — the child can satisfy the universal human vocation to choose the good *qua* good and (at least implicitly) God. According to Maritain, grace makes possible an act of which bare human nature would be incapable, and this act, "the first act of freedom," is, "in a moral sense, an absolute beginning." To make it, with its possibility of divine reward, is the vocation of the child, at least of those chosen children who are "lucky" enough to get baptized, another point to which we shall return.

The conviction that children are capable of, and called to, an act of freedom stakes out a claim against those who, with John Searle, would dissolve children into systems. Among those who join forces with the reducers-to-system are stage and developmental psychologists who, as Guroian elucidates, postulate that children *must* develop in a certain way, after the manner of the oak sapling that necessarily must become an oak tree with a particular shape and type of foliage (107-9). *Pace* the postmodernist social-constructionists at the other end of the spectrum, children do, like oaks, have an essence or nature — human nature, we call it. But, as our cognitional and volitional abilities come alive, we humans become capable, first as children, of freedom. As Guroian explains, "Who we are and what we may become does not depend solely upon natural processes" (112). Freedom is ours, and most Christian teachers believe that, in order to exercise that freedom as they ought, children will need education.

While the Coons thesis downplays the importance of education, by limiting its significance to "second good," most theorists and others, including elected officials and voters, sense that education plays a critical, if not virtually decisive, role in determining whether a child can know and realize his vocation. Much of the implicit theorizing about the vocation *vel non* of the child occurs in the ongoing debate about, and idiom of, education and rights thereto.

V. Schooling, Open Futures, and the Rights of the Child

"The annual crop of infants is a potential invasion of barbarians." Hardly anyone would dispute this claim. Nor would one find much disagreement with Bernard Lonergan's further observation that "education may be conceived as the first line of defense,"[38] both of society and of the individual infants themselves. However,

---

38. *Collected Works of Bernard Lonergan,* vol. 10, *Topics in Education: The Cincinnati Lectures of 1959 on the Philosophy of Education,* ed. Robert M. Doran and Frederick E. Crowe (Toronto: University of Toronto Press, 1959), 59.

to consider the proper aims of education of children is to enter a minefield. The present investigation of the vocation of the child goes forward against a politico-philosophical background that is, as Robert Vischer (chapter 15) observes, a "culture war cacophony" in which "no battle front is more stridently contested than the socialization and value-inculcation of children" (408).

The limit case is the argument of philosopher Joel Feinberg, according to which children have a right to an "open future,"[39] "one in which they, rather than their parents, choose the orienting principles by which they will guide their lives."[40] If most theorists and citizens stop short of advocating a contentless childhood in hope of a future that is entirely of the child's invention, mainstream thought continues to worry the question about the extent to which adults can rule over children, and on what basis they so rule. Children need nurture and education, but who is to provide either or both, and who is to police the providing? Increasingly, the answer is "the state" — even if, as observed above, "the state" provides unequal educational opportunities for children who are equally children.

The chapters by Charles Glenn, Elmer Thiessen, George Van Grieken, F.S.C., and Robert Vischer, along with several others, argue on behalf of children, by arguing, to varying degrees, on behalf of parents and church. Without denying the right of state or civil society to advance the common good, they redirect attention to the child and those who by nature are ordinarily best positioned to know and care for her. They do so against a background that increasingly imagines that the dream child will be almost self-made. They all affirm that the child's vocation includes learning.

The United Nations Convention on the Rights of the Child, adopted by the U.N. General Assembly in 1989 (and later ratified by every nation in the world, including the Vatican, but excepting Somalia and the United States), embodies the emergent, if not yet dominant, understanding of the concept of the child that vies with Christian conceptions for implementation in social policy and law. Vischer notes that the Declaration posits not only traditional "protection rights" — to property, to physical care and security, and to procedural due process — but also "choice rights." These latter rights, traditionally reserved to adults, "grant individuals the authority to make affirmative and legally binding decisions, such as voting, marrying, making contracts, exercising religious pref-

39. Joel Feinberg, "The Child's Right to an Open Future," in *Whose Child? Children's Rights, Parental Authority, and State Power,* ed. William Aiken and Hugh LaFollette (Totowa, N.J.: Littlefield, Adams, 1980), 124.

40. Shelley Burtt, "The Proper Scope of Parental Authority: Why We Don't Owe Children an 'Open Future,'" in *Nomos,* vol. 44, *Child, Family, and State,* ed. Stephen Macedo and Iris Marion Young (New York: New York University Press, 2003), 245.

erences, or choosing whether or how to be educated" (413).[41] Article 17 of the Convention, for example, requires states to "ensure that the child has access to information and material from a diversity of national and international sources, especially those aimed at the promotion of his or her social, spiritual, and moral well-being and physical and mental health."

The idea that parents *must* provide "diverse" reading material is perhaps disturbing enough, but Vischer goes on to observe that in the Convention, the provision of "choice rights" to children combines with another doctrine to situate the primary determinations regarding the child's education even further away from the traditional locus. Article 3 provides that "[i]n all actions concerning children whether undertaken by public or private social welfare institutions, courts of law, administrative authorities, or legislative bodies, the best interests of the child shall be a primary consideration" (414). "Best interests" are hard to quarrel with, but here the rub comes from the fact that states, rather than parents, are empowered to determine them. According to Vischer, the Convention, by its own description and aspiration, seeks to drive a wedge between parent and child. According to the description offered by the U.N. itself, the Convention "promotes a 'new concept of separate rights for children with the Government accepting responsibility [for] protecting the child from the power of parents'" (414).

What do Christians say in response? Is the vocation of the child to be supplied by the state? Thwarted by the state? Who decides what the child will become?

Charles Glenn (chapter 12) tells the story of "who decides what the child will become," from Plato to the present (327). In their philosophizing, Plato and then Aristotle assigned the state a significant role in educating children. In the course of history, however, it took until the modern period, beginning in the eighteenth and nineteenth centuries and coming to term in the twentieth, for the state and its schools to grow to be regarded as possessing ultimate authority over the shaping of children. Glenn shows how the philosophers of enlightenment of the eighteenth century had great ambitions for the state to use education to make people better — and, of course, one should start early. But, for squeezing parents out, Glenn fingers above all the professionalization of education, as by John Dewey and other reformers. Vocation fits awkwardly in John Dewey's classroom.

Religious schools, too, felt the squeeze, such that the United States Supreme Court was moved to insist, in the 1925 case *Pierce v. Society of the Sisters,* that "the child is not the mere creature of the state."[42] The American legal public

---

41. Quoting Bruce C. Hafen and Jonathan O. Hafen, "Abandoning Children to Their Autonomy: The United Nations Convention on the Rights of the Child," *Harvard International Law Journal* 37 (1996).

42. *Pierce v. Society of the Sisters,* 268 US 510, 535 (1925).

was not the only body that needed reminding, apparently, because Pope Pius XI's 1939 encyclical letter *Divini illius magistri,* "On Christian Education," addressed to hierarchs as well as to "all the faithful of the Catholic world," took the truly extraordinary step of commending the *Pierce* court for recognizing and giving effect to the "incontestable right of the family" to bring up and educate children: "it is not in the competence of the State," the pope explained, adverting to *Pierce,* "to fix any uniform standard of education by forcing children to receive education exclusively in public schools."[43]

Elmer John Thiessen (chapter 14) highlights the vocation of the child to be a learner and, along with this vocation, the correlative "primacy of parental rights and responsibilities to help their children to learn" (397). For Thiessen, there is no avoiding that children are not capable of fulfilling their vocation without help. Nor, according to Thiessen, is the help they need the provision of a childhood analogue of a liberal-arts course catalogue. As one scholar has explained in opposing Feinberg's and other liberals' pleas to keep children's options open, the liberal position misjudges and generally underestimates what children need. Children do not need to pluck values from a tree, come the age of majority. They need to become persons or selves, and that is not a project for another day. As Thiessen elaborates, the time of childhood consists of socialization, initiation, and absorption. Otherwise, children wither on the vine of life.

Thiessen joins Coons in arguing that the young learner's responsibility is to subordinate himself to adult guides, and that ordinarily a child's own parents will be the best, though not necessarily good, guides. Parents ordinarily love their children, and are, therefore, in the best position to discern and look out for their best interests. Parents' authority thus comes from their *presumptive* capacity to meet children's impressive needs for education and enculturation. Coons concedes that "Children get born to adults who have rather different ideas about the good; and it is the ideas of particular parents that the child will hear. Call this providence; call it luck" (95). Obviously, it should matter which of the two you believe it to be. Thiessen is in accord: "Young children are not in a position to choose who influences or teaches them. They are stuck with 'fate' if you will, or a 'divine lottery' if you prefer religious language" (385).

VI. Education, Salvation, and Other Rights of the Child

Many of those who embrace Christian "religious language," although they affirm that parents ordinarily hold the first right and responsibility to educate

43. Pope Pius XI, *Divini illius magistri,* no. 37 (1939).

their children, are not content to leave it entirely to parents to ensure that children can fulfill their vocation. Almost no one imagines that parents alone have a legitimate claim on deciding who the child will become. Believing that the child's education may have some bearing on the fate of his eternal soul, the church has been at hand to coordinate with parents. Charles Glenn shows how, in the wake of the Reformation, schooling became a priority in Protestant territories. Everyone was expected to read the Bible for himself, and church, state, and family cooperated in countless combinations to alter the probabilities in favor of biblical literacy. If medieval Christianity was largely content with a peasant population that lacked access to written bearers of tradition, for the Counter-Reformation the task was to ensure that the faithful receive the right, not the rebellious, doctrine. Seminary education was reformed, and new orders were founded to be what Glenn describes as "internal missionaries" (336).

The mission of one of the Catholic orders mentioned by Glenn receives extended elaboration and analysis in the chapter herein by George Van Grieken, F.S.C. (chapter 13). It is the Institute of the Brothers of the Christian Schools, more commonly known as the Christian Brothers, founded by Saint John Baptist de La Salle (1651-1719) in Rheims, France, in 1681. The Brothers stepped in to educate poor children, youngsters neglected by family, state, civil society, and even church. La Salle's order continues its mission around the globe today, and in 1950 the Catholic Church recognized La Salle as the patron of all teachers of youth, a recognition of La Salle's theology of the child.

La Salle does not use the term "vocation," but his writings everywhere radiate a visionary Christian understanding of the calling of children. According to La Salle, Van Grieken explains, "[t]heir 'vocation' is to grow into the mature fulfillment of who they are, and they are to do so in concert with their educational progress and with the guidance of 'older brothers,' their teachers" (363). La Salle combined a strong judgment of the spiritual reality of the child with an equally strong judgment that the child's spiritual development, which by no means would be automatic, required practical assistance.

The insights of Thiessen and Coons, that children are principally learners whose success depends on docility to a worthy older navigator, find support in La Salle's theology. La Salle, however, professed that children's salvation may depend on their coming to knowledge of and faith in Christian truth, and how, La Salle reasoned, can God will that all people be saved and come to knowledge of the truth, as Saint Paul teaches (1 Tim. 2:4), if children lack teachers?[44] La Salle's missionary zeal derives from his theological judgment that, for aught

---

44. See Patrick McKinley Brennan, "Harmonizing Plural Societies: The Case of Lasallians, Families, Schools — and the Poor," *Journal of Catholic Legal Studies* 45 (2006): 131, 144.

that appears, a child's vocation to faith and salvation can be thwarted by not being educated.

Would Christians, then, say that children have a "right," a *natural* right, to education? The answer, for most or all Christians today, is yes, and it issues from a long tradition of recognizing that children have — and should have enforced on their behalf, if necessary — *rights*. The second half of the twentieth century is conspicuous for its proliferation of declarations of rights, including on behalf of the child, such as the Convention. However, rights, understood as something claimable and enforceable through legal or other social mechanisms, have a long history, including for the child.

The medieval canonists incrementally but aggressively overturned the doctrines of Roman law and custom that had long permitted infanticide, exposure, and abandonment, in favor of enforceable rights of children to life, support, and education. As Charles Reid (chapter 9) demonstrates, even children born out of wedlock might have enforceable rights against their father. In addition to recognizing the natural rights of the youngest and most vulnerable, the medieval canonists affirmed the rights of older children to marry and to make religious vows. The canonists also insisted upon the right of children to inherit from their parents, a doctrine anathema to the Anglo-American freedom of the testator to do as he pleases. Claims of natural right, though not reducible to or interchangeable with the claim that a person has a vocation, do seem to reveal what people regard the rights-holders as called to do, or to have done for them.

These Christian claims of rights, which run in favor of children, are not confined to history. The current *Code of Canon Law* (1983), for example, sets out, as a matter of the law of the Catholic Church, that "parents have the most grave duty and the primary right to care as best they can for the physical, social, cultural, moral, and religious education of their offspring."[45] In a world in which the Convention on the Rights of the Child would set the child "free" on the basis of a right to an "open future," the canonical tradition continues to teach that Christian children have "a right to a *Christian* education."[46] Commentary on this canon, Canon 217, states that satisfaction of this right is *necessary* if children are to be able to cooperate with God's salvific will.[47] Is God's salvific will for individuals vulnerable to more than their own, personal choice to flout it? Can God save those who cannot, as opposed to will not, cooperate

---

45. Canon 1136.

46. Canon 217 (italics added).

47. See John P. Beal, James A. Coriden, and Thomas J. Green, eds., *New Commentary on the Code of Canon Law* (New York: Paulist, 2000), 273.

with his will? In the next section we introduce the vocation of children who die before the age of reason and without baptism.

VII. Baptism, Limbo, and Hope

Among the reasons Christians have for trying to understand the child is the one Christ gave in the Gospel according to Mark: "Amen I say to you: Whoever does not receive the Kingdom of God like a child will not enter into it" (Mark 10:15). The eminent Catholic theologian Hans Urs von Balthasar has argued that Christ's treatment of the child is intended to contradict the view — which Balthasar associates with the Jews, Romans, and Greeks — according to which "childhood [is] a stage on the way to fullness of humanity."[48] For Jesus, Balthasar explains, the "zone or dimension in which the child lives reveals . . . itself as a sphere of original wholeness and health, and it may even be said to contain an element of holiness, since at first the child cannot yet distinguish between parental and divine love."[49] Balthasar's contemporary, the German Jesuit theologian Karl Rahner (1904-84), while also insistent that childhood is not a stage of incompletion on the way to wholeness, stopped short of attributing innocence to children. According to Rahner, "[c]hildhood is openness. Human childhood is infinite openness."[50] It is possible to make this affirmation, according to Rahner, because "Christianity knows that the child and his origins are indeed encompassed by the love of God through the pledge of that grace which, in God's will to save all mankind, comes in all cases and to every man from God in Christ Jesus."[51]

Neither Balthasar nor Rahner is infallible, of course, and it was another, and very different, fallible but brilliant mind that shaped much Christian speculation about the vocation of the child, some of which speculation verged on the dogmatic. "The great luminary of the western world is, as we know, St. Augustine," wrote John Henry Newman; "he, no infallible teacher, has formed the intellect of Europe."[52] And Europe was not the limit.

With respect to children, the crying children whom mothers hastened to

48. Hans Urs von Balthasar, *Unless You Become Like This Child,* trans. Erasmo Leiva-Merikakis (San Francisco: Ignatius, 1988), 12.

49. Balthasar, *Unless You Become,* 12.

50. Karl Rahner, "Ideas for a Theology of Childhood," in *Theological Investigations,* vol. 8 (New York: Herder and Herder, 1971), 33, 48. See Werpehowski, "In Search of Real Children," 64n.36 below.

51. Rahner, "Ideas," 39.

52. John Henry Newman, *Apologia* (London: Fontana, 1959), 296.

church to have baptized, Saint Augustine taught that mothers did well to run, not walk, to the baptismal font. As William Harmless, S.J. (chapter 5), demonstrates, Augustine regarded original sin as a disease whose cure was "Christ the physician" operating through the waters of baptism. According to Augustine, "[S]ince infants are as yet held debt-bound by no sin from their own lives, then it must be the disease of original sin that is cured in them, cured by that grace of his which makes them healthy through the bath of rebirth."[53] Harmless shows that, according to Augustine, children's eternal vocation was radically contingent upon their being healed by Christ. There was no "middle place" for those who committed no personal sin but died without forgiveness of original sin; it was either heaven or hell. Baptism was, in Augustine's judgment, the required way of being healed. It is for good reason the mother runs to church with her infant.

Not all Christians have shared Augustine's judgment. As the chapter by Vischer makes clear, members of the evangelical tradition (like Baptists and Methodists) deny that baptism works an "ontological change" that is necessary for salvation. Baptism symbolizes a spiritual rebirth that occurs exclusively through a conversion experience, something that is out of the parents' hands. The covenantal tradition (such as the Reformed and Presbyterian churches), for its part, also denies that baptism is necessary if one is to be saved, but baptism is of more than symbolic value. Baptism brings the child into grace that has already been imparted to the community through the covenant. Children of the covenant have a "right" to baptism, a sign and seal of God's promise of salvation (425).

Does the Catholic tradition still share Augustine's judgment that baptism is necessary? "Sixteen hundred years have passed, and the [Catholic] Church has come to offer hope to the distressed mother in another way" than baptism, writes Anthony Kelly. Kelly continues by quoting section 1261 of the *Catechism of the Catholic Church* (1994) as follows:

> As regards children who have died without baptism, the Church can only entrust them to the mercy of God, as she does in her funeral rites for them. Indeed the great mercy of God who desires all men to be saved, and Jesus' tenderness toward children which caused him to say, "Let the children come to me, do not hinder them" (Mk 10:14) allow us to hope that there is a way of salvation for children who have died without baptism.

One strand of the tradition, exemplified in this volume by Jacques Maritain, has supposed that the most that can be hoped for as concerns unbaptized infants is a sweet repose in "Limbo." The doctrine of Limbo, while never defined

---

53. Quoted by Harmless, "Christ the Pediatrician," 139 below.

by the church, long enjoyed the support of leading theologians down through the centuries, as Kelly shows. But, as Kelly also shows, "as theology reflected further on such scriptural texts as 1 Timothy 2:4, Vatican II opened the door for the development of hope" (231). The Council had this to say:

> All this holds true not only for Christians, but for all people of good will in whose hearts grace is invisibly active. For since Christ died for all (Rom 8:32), and since all are in fact called to one and the same destiny which is divine, we must hold that the Holy Spirit offers to all the possibility of being made participants, in a way known only to God, in the paschal mystery.[54]

At the time this introduction was being written, it was rumored that the International Theological Commission would conclude that the hypothesis of Limbo should be definitively rejected by the magisterium of the Catholic Church. This is some of the "new kind of thinking" to which Kelly believes the child has called the Catholic Church. The conclusions to which the Commission in fact later came are full of hope for all children.

So, Catholic theology has become more hopeful about the vocation of the not-small number of children who die without baptism. But, as Kelly adds, the "question as to the fate of unbaptized infants dying without baptism must seem to many as marginal, to say the least, given the enormity of the evils and oppression facing the human race." However, Kelly continues, "the death of a child means a grief beyond tears and a heart left to its own silence. There is no joy of accomplishment; and the promise of a new life can never be kept. Unless," Kelly continues, "through baptism" (225). And Catholics can now hope that God does not limit it to the ways that are manifest.

Like other Christian parents, grieving Catholic parents now have the consolation of the theological hope that their child, too, has a vocation in Christ. It was the specter of moral death through bad "moral luck" that moved Coons to look for an opening for "first good," especially for God's children. Is it possible "in a way known only to God"? Coons devoutly reminds us "never [to] scoff at fears for dead children," acknowledging that "[his] own answer leaves room for anxiety." Kelly's conclusion includes this: "What faith knows about God invites us in its every lineament to leave to God what is necessarily beyond human determination. A grieving parent can find no other consolation" (239). There will be more to say about the vocation of dying children in the concluding section, but first there is more to say about the work of living children.

---

54. *Gaudium et spes,* in *Vatican Council II: The Conciliar and Post Conciliar Documents* (Boston: St. Paul Editions, 1980), no. 22 (discussed in Kelly, "Hope for Unbaptized Infants," 238 below).

VIII. The Work of Childhood

Adults seeking communion with God have the example of Christ's adult life to study and imitate. Thomas à Kempis, the author of the second-most-published book in history, *The Imitation of Christ,* could meditate on the particulars of how Jesus lived from age thirty until age thirty-three. Those who would shape children's living — and perhaps their vocation? — lack such a model, however.

Christ's childhood is largely hidden from us. Though the Scriptures relate that the child Jesus grew in wisdom and that the grace of God was upon him, they include no particulars about the holy family's life in Nazareth. The lone pericope with any detail about the life of Jesus as a youth concerns his disappearance from his mother Mary and stepfather Joseph as they were going home from Jerusalem to Nazareth. When they returned to Jerusalem, discovered the child Jesus teaching in the temple, and asked the child why he had so grieved them by disappearing, he answered, "Did you not know that I must be about my Father's business?"[55] The Greek that is usually translated as "business" could as well be rendered in English as "things" or, even more colloquially, "stuff."

Our lone, sure glimpse into the life of the holy family reveals a boy who had received from the Father things to do, and was doing them. Without supposing that the twelve-year-old Messiah already enjoyed a fully adult consciousness of the work he had been sent and was called to perform, or suggesting that anyone else's work is terribly like his, we can observe that the child Jesus recognized both the authority of his parents on earth and the exigency of doing the will of his Father, who is the Father of all and who desires all people to be saved. The Gospel of Luke records that Jesus' earthly parents did not understand the meaning of what he spoke to them in Jerusalem, and that he returned with them to Nazareth where he was "obedient" to them, "and grew in wisdom, age, and grace, before both God and man" (2:50-52). Reflecting on the Christ child's admonition to Mary and Joseph that he must be about his Father's work, Balthasar observes "the truth that, even as one who has been sent out, he never ceases to repose in the bosom and will of the Father."[56] The one who would imitate the child Jesus would seek to do the will of the Father.

Abounding in both number and usage over the centuries, and parallel to the *Imitation of Christ* for adults, was a historical medium for teaching the du-

---

55. Of the four canonical Gospels, only Luke records this incident. A version of it is also included in the apocryphal *Gospel of Thomas.* See Kurt Aland, *Synopsis Quatuour Evangeliorum, editio tertia decima revisa* (Stuttgart: Deutsche Bibelgesellschaft, 1985), 18-19.

56. Balthasar, *Unless You Become,* 34.

ties and vocation of the child. Popular among both Protestants and Catholics from the fourteenth century through the nineteenth, this now largely neglected genre, explored in the chapter by John Witte, Jr., and Heather Good (chapter 10), provides concrete insight into what premodern children were taught by their parents and others about their vocation. These Christian teachers did not imagine that a person's early years are to be a time of idleness or uselessness, a fault Bonnie Miller-McClemore (chapter 11) finds with some modern accounts of childhood. Like La Salle, the authors of the manuals discern a deep connection between children's comportment and their ability to discover and embrace their "vocation," a term of art that carries freight in some of the manuals.

The authors of the hundred-plus household manuals sampled by Witte and Good instruct children that they have duties, the first of which, stated in the first commandment of the first table, is to love, worship, and revere God, and from this follows, in the first commandment of the second table, the duty to love and honor parents. The manualists also identified a second duty of the child to *be* loved by their parents, guardians, and others. While this duty to be loved was occasionally described in some later manuals as a "right" of the child, such usage was controversial, and the overwhelming emphasis rested on the vocation of the child, the child's duty to love and be loved.

In its emphasis on the scriptural statements, along with the practicalities, of the child's vocation both to love parents and to be loved *by* parents, the manualist tradition finds a contemporary echo in Marcia Bunge's voice. Bunge emphasizes that it is the child's vocation to love and honor his or her parents, but also to disobey parents if ultimate loyalty to God requires it (42-45). Bunge discerns in the child's vocation to be absolutely obedient to God a *limit* on parental and other adult authority. It would be gravely wrong for parents or others to divert or deflect children from their calling to obey God. The child's dependence on, and the child's duty to obey, his or her parents, Bunge explains, drawing on the insights of Dietrich Bonhoeffer, coexist with the child's responsibility to discern and act on his or her vocation to be obedient to God. Without undermining the seriousness of the child's vocation, Bunge also brings out that childhood is, in part, a time to play. Miller-McLemore asks poignantly: "Doesn't the imperative to 'become like children' (Matthew 18:3) have something essential to do with prizing playfulness as a part of rejoicing in God's love?"[57]

Childhood is a time to begin discerning the difference between what is real and what is imagined, what will work and what will not work. Children can be fed *Alice in Wonderland,* and thereby be made to believe it. "[T]he land of

---

57. Bonnie J. Miller-McLemore, *In the Midst of Chaos: Caring for Children as Spiritual Practice* (San Francisco: Wiley, 2007), 150.

'seeming truth,'" as Maritain calls it,[58] is no place to live, however. The wondering by which children come to distinguish the true from the imagined, though perhaps natural, is not automatic. Its conditions include being called *by being loved.* "It does not suffice for us simply to exist," observes philosopher Joseph Pieper. While each of us is lovable by virtue of our being created and loved by God, that is, by our simply existing, each of us also needs to be loved by another person if we are to rise above the level of mere existence. The necessary "being loved" means being called out of our pure interiority into relationships of mutuality, Pieper explains: "Being created by God actually does not suffice, it would seem; the fact of creation needs continuation and perfection by the creative power of human love."[59] If this is so, the reader may again wonder whether Coons's hypothesis of a supervening "first good" that is in no way contingent on love received, is imperiled. Does a child who goes unloved have a "chance" to seek second good?

It would be a common mistake to idealize or romanticize these relations of mutuality by which children are called out of their interiority. As a matter of fact, they begin squarely in the lap of the family (or its substitute), where, as Miller-McLemore argues, children make demands but demands are also made of children (319-20). Just as children are not to be indentured, so they are not to be put on a shelf. Unlike cans, children do not have a shelf life. They are called, along with the rest of us, to build up the common good, which begins at home:

> [W]hen viewed from the perspective of Christian vocation, children are not an investment or achievement from which one expects a return. They are not slaves to adult bidding. They are a gift which one hopes will flourish. Part of that flourishing involves work, but work of a different sort, done in the best of circumstances for the good of creation and its redemption. Christian theology encourages us to consider children's call to contribute to the common good around them. In the most immediate sense the family comprises the first exposure to a life-long practice of meeting communal obligations and caring for the common good. (322)

Miller-McLemore notes the possibility that a reinvigorated understanding of the vocation of the child might in turn reinvigorate a just division of labor within the family, rendering work, love, and play, all three of them, tasks that men, women, and children share, rather than tasks parceled out on the basis of

---

58. Jacques Maritain, *Redeeming the Time,* trans. Harry Lorin Binsse (London: Centenary Press, 1946), 203.

59. Joseph Pieper, *Faith, Hope, Love* (San Francisco: Ignatius, 1986), 171, 174. I owe this citation to H. David Baer.

gender or age. Children are not to be lost and submerged within the family, but neither are they to be imagined into a splendid isolation that is, ironically but perversely, subhuman.

Miller-McLemore's call for realism about the earthen crucible of vocation in the family reinforces "a hard, but enduring, lesson" (290) that Witte and Good educe from the manuals, and to which other authors in this volume testify, as well. The lesson is that the duties of love by and for a child, while mutually dependent, are not mutually conditional. Parents' failures do not absolve — but rather increase — the child's duties to parents. "A Christian child must fulfill her duties to God, including the duty to honor and love her father and mother, even if the parents are undeserving" (291). As Witte and Good go on to register, "[t]his traditional teaching goes entirely against modern views that children are less culpable for their personal failures when they suffer from poor parenting" (291). It is unalterably the vocation of the child to love God and parents, and, as a condition of doing so, to overcome whatever obstacles providence throws in their way. The theme of invulnerability combines with that of unalterability, but awkwardly.

In *The Spiritual Life of Children*, Robert Coles quotes the following statement from a fifth-grader in Lawrence, Massachusetts: "I'm like I am now, but I could change when I grow up. You never know who you'll be until you get to that age when you're all grown. But God must know all the time."[60] The child assumes she will have time to grow up, and "change." Some pages later, Coles recalls a conversation with Dorothy Day:

> In many ways I feel I'm the same person now that I was when I was a girl of nine, maybe, or ten, or eleven. You look surprised! I thought you folks [psychiatrists] believe we're "made," once and for all, in childhood. . . . Some of the things I asked then — asked my parents, my friends, and a lot of the time myself — I'm still asking myself now, forty or fifty or sixty years later! I don't think it's any different with my daughter, or with the many children I've known during my life; they all want to know why they are here, and what's ahead as they get older — heaven, hell, nothing at all, or as Tamar once said to me, "Mother, will it be the cemetery, and that's the end?" A natural question. I'd call it her spiritual side expressing itself — and we, as parents, should take notice![61]

These chapters on the vocation of the child constitute a taking notice, a taking in hand the child whose vocation "calls us out," as Werpehowski signaled it has

---

60. Robert Coles, *The Spiritual Life of Children* (Boston: Houghton Mifflin, 1990), 310.
61. Coles, *Spiritual Life of Children*, 329.

the potential to do. God knows all the time who we are going to become, and the (Catholic) Church's "new kind of thinking" offers hope for children who lose the way, hope to those who love them, and, yes, hope to those who fail to love them as they ought.

In the Gospel of Luke, Jesus assures his followers that "nothing will hurt you" (10:19). This passage can hardly be given a literal reading, as Jesus was plainly aware that the flesh is fragile (Luke 21:16). "Nevertheless," Timothy Jackson observes, "[J]esus appears to subscribe to a kind of *spiritual* invulnerability."[62] But is it true that those whom we neglect, abuse, or even torture are spiritually untouched, because untouchable? Jackson continues: "Spiritual invulnerability has been a very attractive doctrine to many Christians, and it has often gone hand-in-hand with an insistence on radical individual responsibility."[63] For those in charge, it becomes an ever more attractive doctrine in a world of radical individualists whose sense of responsibility is on the wane. For children, the prospect that they are spiritually invulnerable cuts both ways, perhaps to the quick. "[T]he divine . . . offers itself to defend the human (if the latter does not refuse the aid offered)." Though called by God, and endowed with a vocation, little children are powerless to accept the aid on their own.

---

62. Timothy P. Jackson, *Love Disconsoled: Meditations on Christian Charity* (Princeton: Princeton University Press, 1999), 145.

63. Jackson, *Love Disconsoled*, 145.

I. The Vocation, Calling, or Office of a Child

1. The Vocation of the Child: Theological Perspectives on the Particular and Paradoxical Roles and Responsibilities of Children

Marcia J. Bunge

Although "vocation" or "calling" is an ancient religious term, it is used in contemporary culture and the church in a number of ways when speaking about aims and goals in life. For example, some people today speak about their occupation or profession as a "vocation" or "calling." In the past, only so-called service professions, such as teaching or medicine, were understood as callings, but today many popular books explore the service dimension of other professions, such as business or law, and speak about them, too, as callings. Others think of vocation or calling more specifically as entering the priesthood or ordained ministry or becoming a monk or a nun. Seminary students sometimes say, for example, they received "the call," and brochures for many seminaries use the words "called to ministry" or "called to the religious life." This is particularly true among Roman Catholics, even though many Catholic theologians are trying to change this misconception of calling. But Protestants, too, sometimes think of vocation or calling primarily in relation to ordained ministry. Still others speak about vocation or calling more generally as finding a sense of self-fulfillment and purpose in life. They understand calling to be what one does, whether paid or not, to find wholeness and personal meaning and happiness. They might say, for example, that they work for a living and to pay the bills but that their hobby or "avocation" is their true vocation or calling in life.

All three of these common ways of speaking of vocation leave out children, and from a Christian theological perspective, all three of them are too narrow. Within the Christian tradition, "vocation" or "calling" is a rich concept that embraces far more than the adult world of paid work, ordained ministry, or personal fulfillment. Most Christian theologians and ethicists, regardless of their particular denominations, claim that the concept of vocation, rightly understood, addresses our deepest human longings for purpose and meaning in life and encompasses the totality of our lives. Although Christians have certainly interpreted "vocation" and "calling" in various ways, central to many of these interpretations is the notion that God is calling us to a life centered in Christ and to ways in which we meaningfully participate in and contribute to God's work in the world. Thus, "vocation" is a term that applies to everyone — regardless of gender, race, class, or age.

The understanding of "vocation" as a religious term that applies to everyone was emphasized during the Reformation. Since that time, Protestants have often stated in various ways that all people have a "vocation" or "calling" in two senses.[1] On the one hand, they are all called to follow Christ and to love God and to love and serve the neighbor, especially those in need.[2] This is their common vocation or calling: it is, as some Protestants have said, a "general" or "spiritual" vocation that all Christians share. It is the call to discipleship and to unity with Christ. On the other hand, people are also called by God to particular "vocations": to specific "offices," "stations," or "places of responsibility" in which they use their gifts and talents to serve the well-being of others, whether at home, at work, at church, or in civic life. They serve others in particular ways, for example, as spouses and parents, doctors and lawyers, pastors and deacons, or politicians and soldiers. This is sometimes called their "particular" or "external" vocation.

Even though vocation understood in this twofold way refers to how all people, in various ways, are called to unity with Christ and to contribute in specific ways to the welfare of the community, most Christians, and even most Christian theologians and ethicists, do not discuss the particular vocation of the child. This is the case, in part, because very few theologians and ethicists speak about children at all. Most of them have neither struggled directly in their work with issues regarding children nor sought to articulate sound theological understandings of children themselves. Certainly, they have devoted significant attention to many issues related to children, such as abortion, human sexuality, gender relations, contraception, reproductive technology, marriage, and the family. However, they have not developed sophisticated teachings about fundamental subjects regarding children themselves, such as the nature and status of children; parental obligations to them; the role of church and state in protecting children; the role of children in religious communities; the moral and spiritual formation of children; the role of children in the faith maturation of adults; adoption; or children's rights and responsibilities. Contemporary

---

1. William C. Placher, ed., *Callings: Twenty Centuries of Christian Wisdom on Vocation* (Grand Rapids: Eerdmans, 2005), 206. Placher's book is an excellent introduction to various understandings of vocation in the history of Christianity.

2. This sense of calling is built on Jesus' command to his followers to "love the Lord your God with all your heart, and with all your soul, and with all your mind, and with all your strength" and to "love your neighbor as yourself" (Mark 12:30-31; Matt. 22:37-39; Luke 10:27-28).

theologians and ethicists have tended to consider such issues as "beneath" the work of serious scholars and theologians and as a fitting area of inquiry only for pastoral counselors and religious educators — or something only for Sunday school teachers or youth directors.

Thus, in general, theological discourse in many Christian traditions has been dominated by simplistic and ambivalent views of children and young people that diminish their complexity and integrity, fostering, in turn, narrow understandings of adult-child relationships. For example, some Christians today and in the past have tended to view children primarily as ignorant, sinful, or defiant, thereby restricting their view of adult-child relationships to instruction, discipline, and punishment. Other Christians have perceived children mainly as innocent (almost angelic), thereby enjoying children yet often underestimating adult responsibilities of helping them develop morally and spiritually. These kinds of simplistic conceptions of children in the church inform and reflect other widely held perceptions about children also found in contemporary culture. We tend to depict infants and young children as pure and innocent beings whom we adore and teenagers as hidden and dark creatures whom we must fear. Children who are twelve or thirteen fall somewhere in the middle, and thus in cases of juvenile crime, we have public debates about whether they are victims of abuse or fully conscious criminals.

Unfortunately, these kinds of simplistic views of children also affect our treatment of them in both society and religious communities, and in many ways we treat children as almost subhuman. For example, in the United States, every person over sixty-five years of age has health care, but nine million children do not. Most affluent children have access to a good education, but many poor children must often attend inadequate or even dangerous schools. Furthermore, many children, regardless of their economic situation, suffer neglect and abuse and struggle with drug and alcohol abuse, suicide and depression, and lack of sexual boundaries.[3] Around the world, one child every three seconds dies of hunger or a preventable disease, and many poor children are being used as cheap laborers or soldiers. According to the International Justice Mission in Washington, D.C., more than a million children a year are forced into child prostitution.[4]

---

3. For more information about the situation of children, see the following Web sites: United States Census Bureau (census.gov); Children's Defense Fund (childrensdefense.org); United Nations Children's Fund (unicef.org); and National Center for Children in Poverty (nccp.org).

4. Gary A. Haugen, *Good News about Injustice: A Witness of Courage in a Hurting World* (Downers Grove, Ill.: InterVarsity, 1999), 42. For more about the situation of sexually exploited children, see, for example, Gary A. Haugen with Gregg Hunter, *Terrify No More* (Nashville: W. Publishing Group, 2005).

In a global economy, scholars also wonder about the effects of technology, the media, and market pressures on rich and poor children alike.

In the church, perhaps the most alarming example of injustice to children is that they have been sexually abused, and reputations of priests, pastors, and bishops have taken priority over child safety. However, children are neglected or treated unjustly in many far more subtle ways in their congregations and homes. For example, although sound religious education programs do exist, many congregations offer weak religious education programs and fail to emphasize the importance of parents in faith development. The curricula of many programs are theologically weak and uninteresting to children, and they assume children themselves have no questions, ideas, or spiritual experiences. Programs for children and youth are often underfunded, and leaders for them are difficult to recruit and retain. Furthermore, there is little coordinated effort between the church and the home in terms of a child's spiritual formation. Many parents don't even know what their children are learning in their congregation's educational programs, and parents are also not given the sense that they are primarily responsible for the faith formation of their children.

This chapter addresses some of the challenges facing children today by exploring the notion of vocation in relation to children. Since theological understandings of vocation take into account large questions of meaning and purpose in life, and since they also value the particular roles and responsibilities in which individuals carry out their specific callings, exploring the vocation of the child is a particularly rich and fruitful way to challenge common and often narrow conceptions of children; to deepen our understanding of who children are and the significant roles they play in families and community life; and to strengthen our commitment to children in our own various and specific callings in life.

This chapter explores the vocation of the child first by outlining more fully a theological understanding of vocation that includes children (part 1) and then by examining the particular duties and responsibilities of the vocation of a child that are emphasized in the Christian tradition (part 2). The chapter finds that although the vocation of the child is a neglected theme in both church and society, a sound theological understanding of vocation can and should include children. In addition, the Bible and the tradition emphasize that the specific vocation of the child contains at least eight almost paradoxical elements. Each of these elements is built on a complex theological understanding of the nature of children, and each one is coupled with corresponding duties and responsibilities of parents and other caring adults. By examining these eight elements, we discover that a robust understanding of the vocation of the child must be built on a vibrant theological understanding of children themselves. Furthermore, a sound theological understanding of the vocation of the child has many practical implications for strengthening our commitment to and treatment of children in the church and both nationally and internationally. Since each person on earth is or was a child, and since aspects of a child's vocation are lifelong because we continue to be the children of our parents even when we are adults, an exploration of the vocation of the child sheds light on fundamental social roles and responsibilities not only of young children but also of adult children.

Although the chapter articulates a particular theological understanding of vocation that is broad and deep enough to include children by building primarily on Martin Luther's view of vocation, it illustrates the possibility of critically retrieving the concept of vocation from various strands of the Christian tradition in ways that honor the dignity and complexity of children and their roles and responsibilities in the community.

Part 1: Building on Insights from Martin Luther to Articulate a Concept of Vocation That Includes Children

Although theologians and ethicists today have neglected the vocation of the child, some theologians in the past have reflected deeply on the central tasks and responsibilities of children, and they have incorporated the child into their views of vocation or calling as a whole. One of these theologians, who also significantly shaped Protestant ideas about vocation, was Martin Luther, the sixteenth-century German reformer.[5] In his view of vocation or calling, he emphasizes that all believers are called to love God and to love and serve the neighbor.[6] They are called to express their faith in works of love and service within the church and the broader culture.[7] This is their common vocation or calling.

Although Luther claims all believers share this common Christian calling, he also emphasizes that they honorably carry it out in a wide variety of specific "vocations" in specific "stations" or "places of responsibility" in which they serve the well-being of others, whether at home, at work, at church, or in civic life. Thus, for Luther, they carry out specific vocations, for example, not only in their particular professions as doctors, lawyers, or pastors but also in domestic life in

---

5. For an excellent discussion of Luther's view of vocation, see Douglas Schuurman, *Vocation: Discerning Our Callings in Life* (Grand Rapids: Eerdmans, 2004).

6. This sense of calling is built on Jesus' command to his followers to "love the Lord your God with all your heart, and with all your soul, and with all your mind, and with all your strength" and to "love your neighbor as yourself" (Mark 12:30-31; Matt. 22:34-40; Luke 10:25-28).

7. As Luther wrote, "Faith is truly active through love, that is, it finds expression in works of the freest service, cheerfully and lovingly done. . . ." "The Freedom of a Christian," in *Martin Luther's Basic Theological Writings*, ed. Timothy Lull (Minneapolis: Fortress, 1989), 617.

their roles as parents, spouses, sons and daughters, aunts and uncles, and friends. For Luther, all these varied and specific callings are ways in which Christians carry out the general calling to follow Christ and to love and serve others.

Furthermore, according to Luther, all work that benefits the community holds equal religious value. As he states in his treatise *To the Christian Nobility:*

> [T]here is no true, basic difference between laymen and priests, princes and bishops, between religious and secular, except for the sake of office and work, but not for the sake of status. They are all of the spiritual estate, all are truly priests, bishops, and popes. But they do not all have the same work to do. . . . Further, everyone must benefit and serve every other by means of his own work or office so that in this way many kinds of work may be done for the bodily and spiritual welfare of the community, just as all the members of the body serve one another.[8]

Thus, a priest or pastor does not have a "higher calling" than a teacher or parent. All roles and positions that serve the neighbor and benefit the community are equally sacred and worthy callings.

Given Luther's view of vocation, he believes that everyone has a calling, including children. Everyone has "roles" or "offices" whether given or chosen, for in addition to our professional roles and duties, even our social and familial relationships are places into which God calls us to serve God and the neighbor. Thus, children, teenagers, and college students have a calling here and now — even before they get a job or land a career. Whatever their age, they already have certain duties, roles, and responsibilities that benefit the family and the community.

This robust theology of vocation is closely intertwined with Luther's views of education: not only his support of schooling and a solid liberal arts education for all children but also his emphasis on religious education and the faith formation of children and young people. Luther supported formal education and schools because he was convinced that well-educated citizens would serve both church and society. For him, government-supported schools were necessary so that everyone could not only read and interpret Scripture but also gain the skills and knowledge necessary to be good citizens. Excellent schools help develop the gifts of young people so that they can live out their particular vocations and take up particular roles or offices that serve others and contribute to the common good. As he stated in his appeal to city governments to establish schools, "A city's best and greatest welfare, safety, and strength consist rather in its having many able, learned, wise, honorable, and well-educated

---

8. Martin Luther, *Luther's Works,* vol. 44, ed. James Atkinson and Helmut T. Lehmann (Philadelphia: Fortress, 1955-86), 129-30.

citizens."[9] According to Luther, "[I]n the sight of God none among the outward sins so heavily burdens the world and merits such severe punishment as this very sin which we commit against the children by not educating them."[10]

Thus, Luther and his friend and colleague Philipp Melanchthon were strong public advocates for universal schooling, the liberal arts, and educational reform. At a time when formal education was viewed as unnecessary for most children and educational opportunities were limited primarily to the nobility, to boys, or to those entering monasteries, Luther and Melanchthon recommended that all children, including girls and the poor, be given a basic education. Furthermore, Luther and Melanchthon recommended a broad liberal arts program for schools and universities that reflected the humanist reforms of the day. Thus, their education program included reading, writing, history, theology, philosophy, languages, mathematics, the natural sciences, and training in the arts, music, and poetry.

Through their initiatives, Luther and Melanchthon prompted several reforms that influenced German schools and universities at that time and still today, including public education for all children. Many Lutherans after the Reformation have also been leaders in educational policy and reform, and they have a long history of establishing schools and colleges to educate young people for service in church and society. For example, August Hermann Francke in the eighteenth century established a vast set of institutions to serve children, including an orphanage, schools for rich and poor alike, and the first German pediatric hospital. Norwegian, German, Danish, and Swedish Lutherans who settled in the United States also created several schools, colleges, and seminaries. Lutherans in the United States today continue to support a network of educational institutions, including over thirty colleges and universities.

Luther's view of vocation also influenced his emphasis on faith formation of children and young people both in congregations and in the home. He believed that those who are baptized should understand their faith and live it out in daily life. Although he believed that pastors and congregations should certainly help children and young people learn about their faith, he stressed that children must also be taught the faith at home by their parents.

Given his emphasis on faith formation and his expansive view of vocation that included both professional and familial roles and relationships, Luther reflected seriously on the central tasks and responsibilities of parenting. Al-

9. Luther, "To the Councilmen of All Cities in Germany That They Establish and Maintain Christian Schools," in *Luther's Works*, vol. 45, ed. Walther I. Brandt and Helmut T. Lehmann (Philadelphia: Fortress, 1955-86), 356.

10. Luther, "To the Councilmen," 45:353.

though he knew that parenting can be a difficult task and is often considered an insignificant and even distasteful job, he believed parenting is a serious and divine calling that is "adorned with divine approval as with the costliest gold and jewels."[11] In one often-quoted passage, he says the following:

> Now you tell me, when a father goes ahead and washes diapers or performs some other mean task for his child, and someone ridicules him as an effeminate fool — though that father is acting in the spirit just described and in Christian faith — my dear fellow you tell me, which of the two is most keenly ridiculing the other? God, with all his angels and creatures, is smiling — not because that father is washing diapers, but because he is doing so in Christian faith.[12]

Luther further underscored the importance of parenting by claiming:

> Most certainly father and mother are apostles, bishops, and priests to their children, for it is they who make them acquainted with the gospel. In short, there is no greater or nobler authority on earth than that of parents over their children, for this authority is both spiritual and temporal.[13]

According to Luther, as priests and bishops to their children, parents have a twofold task: to nurture the faith of their children and to help them develop their gifts to serve others.[14] He also helped parents in this task by preaching about parenting and by writing the *Small Catechism,* which was intended for use in the home.

Followers of Luther also spoke meaningfully about the sacred task of parenting. Francke, for example, claimed that the primary goal of parents is to help children live out their vocation. They are to help children grow in faith, empowering them to use their gifts and talents to love and serve God and the neighbor and to contribute to the common good.[15]

11. Luther, "Estate of Marriage," in *Luther's Works,* 45:39.

12. Luther, "Estate of Marriage," 45:40.

13. Luther, "Estate of Marriage," 45:46.

14. For a full discussion of Luther's views on parenting, see, for example: "The Child in Luther's Theology: 'For What Purpose Do We Older Folks Exist, Other Than to Care for . . . the Young?'" by Jane E. Strohl in *The Child in Christian Thought,* ed. Marcia Bunge (Grand Rapids: Eerdmans, 2001), 134-59; William Lazareth, *Luther on the Christian Home: An Application of the Social Ethics of the Reformation* (Philadelphia: Muhlenberg, 1969); F. V. N. Painter, *Luther on Education* (The Lutheran Publication Society, 1889); and Gerald Strauss, *Luther's House of Learning* (Baltimore: Johns Hopkins University Press, 1978).

15. See Marcia Bunge, "Education and the Child in Eighteenth-Century German Pietism: Perspectives from the Work of A. H. Francke," in *The Child in Christian Thought,* 247-78.

Amidst their recommendations for parenting, Luther and his followers recognized an important paradox. They believed that faith comes through God's grace and God's activity. They were not as certain as some theologians that good parenting and a proper upbringing result in faith. Nevertheless, by providing very specific guidelines about the goals and task of parenting, they believed that nurturing faith in children is an urgent task and that faith results largely from the diligent work of parents.[16]

Even though there is more to say about Luther's view of vocation, a Lutheran understanding of vocation provides a solid theological foundation for speaking about the vocation of the child. Overall, the concept invites people of all ages to reflect on a number of issues, such as: our service to the needs of the neighbor; our unique gifts and talents; how to strengthen and to develop them; our multiple duties in various spheres of life; the relation between faith and learning; our relationship to God; and God's love for and care of the world. Furthermore, a Lutheran concept of vocation deeply integrates faith and learning and provides theological grounding for strong educational opportunities for all so that everyone can use their gifts to serve the neighbor and contribute to the common good. The concept of vocation also informs the need for faith formation of children and young people at church and in the home.

Clearly, theological understandings of vocation and calling vary amidst the diverse strands of the Christian tradition, and Lutherans themselves have interpreted the doctrine of vocation in a variety of ways. Furthermore, Luther was certainly a man of his own time, and elements of his views of children, women, education, and parenting cannot be appropriated uncritically into an interpretation of vocation for today. Nevertheless, by exploring Luther's understanding of vocation with particular attention to children, we find that a theological understanding of vocation that includes the child not only expands our view of vocation but also prompts further reflection on parenting, education, and the nature of children themselves. In addition, the above example from the Lutheran tradition can serve to challenge Christians of all denominations to reexamine their religious traditions and to articulate sound theological understandings of vocation that include children.

---

16. As Gerald Strauss concludes and as Strohl confirms: "Only in formal theology was a sharp and final distinction made between human effort and divine grace." In practice, Luther and his followers believed that mature faith and good citizenship are fostered in young people largely through religious education and the diligent work of adults. Strauss, *Luther's House of Learning*, 39.

Part 2: The Specific Calling of Children

If a Christian theological understanding of vocation can and should include children, then what does the specific calling of children look like? What are their specific duties, roles, and responsibilities that contribute to the life of the community? What is their "work" or "office"? What is their relationship to familial and social structures? By examining elements of the Bible and the Christian tradition, we find that the vocation of the child has at least eight dimensions, each dimension built on a rich theological understanding of who and what a child is, and each coupled with corresponding duties and responsibilities of parents and other caring adults.

1. Honor and Respect Your Parents

Throughout the Christian tradition, one of the most commonly cited duties of children is to honor and respect their parents. The fifth commandment is "Honor your father and mother so that your days may be long in the land that the LORD your God is giving you" (Exod. 20:12; Deut. 5:16), and several other biblical passages command children to honor and respect their parents (Lev. 19:3; Eph. 6:2-3; Heb. 12:9). The term for honor in Hebrew literally means "to make heavy," and the fifth commandment calls children to regard their parents as worthy of this weighty respect and dignity.

Corresponding to this first duty of children are also particular assumptions about the nature of children and the duties of parents. It assumes that children are dependent and vulnerable beings, and parents, in turn, are to love, serve, and protect them by providing them with food, clothing, and other basic needs. Children should honor their parents, in part, because parents must do so much for them to nourish them, protect them, and keep them alive.

Luther states, for example, that God commands children to honor their parents because parents have "nourished and nurtured" them, and they owe their parents "body and life" and "all honor."[17] Without parents a child would have, as Luther says so delicately, "perished a hundred times in his own filth."[18] He believes that even young children can honor their parents by being grateful for the love and protection of their parents or guardians. For him, children have a duty "to show gratitude for the kindness and for all the good things we have

17. Martin Luther, "The Large Catechism," in *The Book of Concord*, ed. and trans. Theodore G. Tappert (Philadelphia: Fortress, 1959), 383.

18. Luther, "The Large Catechism," 383.

received from our parents."[19] He believes that children should not grumble, and they should remember the many blessings they have already received.

However, the commandment to honor and respect parents does not stop with childhood, and the particular vocation of the "child" includes some duties that are lifelong. This particular duty of the "child" continues into adulthood, since as long as one's parents are alive, one still has an obligation to honor and respect them. Indeed, the Jewish scholar Elliot Dorff has stated that the rabbis understood the commandment to honor and respect parents as "primarily governing the interactions of adult children of elderly parents."[20] Thus, adult children of elderly parents have an obligation to provide food and clothing for them, and they honor their parents by caring for them as they grow older.[21]

2. Obey Your Parents

Another duty of children often cited in the Christian tradition is that children are to obey their parents. They are commanded: "Children, obey your parents in everything, for this is your acceptable duty in the Lord" (Col. 3:20). They are to obey their parents "in the Lord, for this is right" (Eph. 6:1). Several biblical passages call children to obey their parents, and their prosperity is often seen to be dependent on their obedience to parents (Deut. 4:40; 12:24, 28; Ps. 128:1-3). Obedience also includes recognizing the authority of parents over their children. The "younger must accept the authority of the elders" and "clothe" themselves with humility (1 Pet. 5:5-6). The New Testament also lists disobedience to parents as a particular vice (Rom. 1:30; 2 Tim. 3:2).

The duty to obey assumes that children are not yet able to discern fully right from wrong, and they need to learn from and follow the example of their parents and other adults in authority. They need to be told what is right and wrong and what God requires of them (Mic. 6:6). Parents, in turn, have an obligation to be good examples to their children and to be their moral and spiritual teachers. Given their authority and significance in a child's life, they should also understand that their example and actions can influence not only a child's relationship to other human beings but also his or her understanding of God.

Many Christian theologians have emphasized that children should honor and obey their parents to such a degree that they regard them as God's repre-

---

19. Luther, "The Large Catechism," 382.

20. Elliot N. Dorff, *Love Your Neighbor and Yourself: A Jewish Approach to Modern Personal Ethics* (Philadelphia: Jewish Publication Society, 2003), 128.

21. See the chapter by Vigen Guroian in this volume.

sentatives. Luther, for example, states children should honor and revere their parents "as God's representatives" and hold them in distinction and esteem above all things "as the most precious treasure on earth."[22] For Luther, "Honor includes not only love but also deference, humility, and modesty, directed (so to speak) toward a majesty hidden within them. It requires us not only to address them affectionately and reverently, but above all to show by our actions, both of heart and of body, that we respect them very highly and that next to God we give them the very highest place."[23] Luther claims that the greatest and noblest work of children is "obedience to father and mother, which God has appointed and commanded next to obedience to his own majesty."[24]

In the twentieth century, the Protestant theologian Karl Barth also spoke of parents as "God's representatives." "From the standpoint of children parents have a Godward aspect, and are for them God's primary and natural representatives."[25] For Barth, parents are really the "elders" in relation to their children, and they represent not only their own knowledge and experience to children "but that conveyed to them by their own predecessors." Thus, children are to heed and obey them. This does not mean, Barth clarifies, that children are the parents' "property, subjects, servants or even pupils." Rather, children are their parents' "apprentices, who are entrusted and subordinated to them in order that they might lead them into the way of life. The children must be content to accept this leading from their parents. In general outline, this is what the command of God requires of them."[26]

3. Disobey Your Parents and Other Adult Authorities

Although almost all theologians today and in the past would emphasize that children should honor and obey their parents, they often neglect a third and corresponding responsibility of children that is also part of the tradition: children have a responsibility and duty not to obey their parents if their parents or other adult authorities would cause them to sin or to carry out acts of injustice. Although children should honor and obey their parents, their ultimate loyalty is to God.

Several examples in the Bible illustrate that parents are sometimes unjust

22. Luther, "The Large Catechism," 379-80.
23. Luther, "The Large Catechism," 379.
24. Luther, "The Large Catechism," 381.
25. Karl Barth, *Church Dogmatics* II/4, ed. G. W. Bromiley and T. F. Torrance (Edinburgh: T. & T. Clark, 1961), 243.
26. Barth, *Church Dogmatics* II/4, 243.

and unfaithful or that children must follow God's law above the commands of parents when the two conflict. Ezekiel, for example, commands children, "Do not follow the statutes of your parents, nor observe their ordinances, nor defile yourselves with their idols. I the LORD am your God; follow my statutes, and be careful to observe my ordinances, and hallow my sabbaths" (Ezek. 20:18-19). In the New Testament, Jesus also points out potential conflicts between parents and children, when one is called to follow him.[27] Speaking to his disciples, he says, "You will be betrayed even by parents and brothers, by relatives and friends; and they will put some of you to death. You will be hated by all because of my name" (Luke 21:16-17).

Related to this responsibility is an understanding that children (whether young children or adults) are not subject to their parents absolutely. Rather, all children are made in the image of God (not primarily in the image of their parents), and even as young children, they are active moral agents with growing moral capacities and responsibilities of their own. Since they are made in God's image, they are to honor God above all things. They are also worthy of human dignity and respect from the start. The basis of this claim is Genesis 1:27, which proclaims that God made humankind, male and female, in God's image. It follows that children, like adults, possess the fullness of humanity. They are not "subhuman," "almost human," or "on their way to being human," as our treatment of them sometimes reflects.[28]

Since children are fully human moral agents who are made in God's image, and since their ultimate loyalty is to God and not to any adult authority, parents and other caring adults have a duty to recognize that they are certainly not gods on earth and that their authority over children is always limited. It is never absolute. Although the Bible emphasizes that children should obey their parents, it also warns parents not to provoke their children to anger (Col. 3:21; Eph. 6:4). Parents have a responsibility to examine critically their own actions and behaviors, to admit their mistakes, and to ask God and their children for forgiveness.

Although theologians esteem parents, they generally qualify absolute parental authority because they recognize parents are sometimes sinful, unjust, or just plain inept. They also recognize that as children grow and develop, their moral capacities and responsibilities also grow and develop, and children must be prepared to challenge the authority of their parents and even political and

27. For a fuller discussion of the tension between obedience to parents and following Jesus, see John T. Carroll, "'What, Then, Will This Child Become?' Perspectives on Children in the Gospel of John," in *Biblical Perspectives on Children and Childhood* (forthcoming).

28. The sense of the integrity of each person, including children, is also grounded in a view of God who intimately knows the number of "even the hairs of your head" (Matt. 10:30), forms your "inward parts," and "knit[s]" you together in the womb (Ps. 139:13).

ecclesiastical authorities if they lead to injustices. Thus, parents are given authority over their children, but this authority is limited, and it is never an excuse for treating children unjustly or unkindly or for failing to recognize that children are moral agents, too, who already as children can challenge and benefit the community.[29]

Although Luther, for example, compared the authority of parents to God's own authority, he gave examples of the abuse of parental authority. Building on Scripture, he believed that even though children should generally tolerate the injustices of their parents and obey them, they could under certain circumstances and in good conscience act contrary to the will of tyrannical or unjust parents.[30] He believed, for example, that parents should neither force nor hinder the marriage of their children and asserted:

> Parental authority is strictly limited; it does not extend to the point where it can wreak damage and destruction to the child, especially to its soul. If then a father forces his children into a marriage without love, he oversteps and exceeds his authority. He ceases to be a father and becomes a tyrant who uses his authority not for building up which is why God gave it to him but for destroying. He is taking authority into his own hands without God, indeed, against God. The same principle holds good when a father hinders his child's marriage, or lets the child go ahead on his own, without any intention of helping him in the matter.[31]

Barth, too, qualified absolute obedience to parents when he stated that "no human father, but God alone, is properly, truly and primarily Father. No human father is the creator of his child, the controller of its destiny, or its savior from sin, guilt and death."[32]

Another twentieth-century Lutheran theologian, Dietrich Bonhoeffer, helps explain the tension between a child's call to obedience and disobedience in his discussion of the intimate connection between obedience and responsibility. He recognizes that although not all human beings lead highly public professional lives with a range of duties and responsibilities, the lives of all human beings, even those who are most dependent and vulnerable, demand responsi-

---

29. Horace Bushnell, *Christian Nurture* (New York: Charles Scribner, 1861; reprint, Cleveland: Pilgrim Press, 1994), 63.

30. Martin Luther, "That Parents Should Neither Compel Nor Hinder the Marriage of Their Children, and That Children Should Not Become Engaged without Their Parents' Consent," in *Luther's Works*, 45:385-93.

31. Luther, "That Parents Should Neither," 386-87.

32. Barth, *Church Dogmatics* II/4, 245.

bility. This is because "even where free responsibility is more or less excluded from one's vocational and public life, one's relation to other human beings, from the family to one's co-worker, will always demand responsibility." As he states, "There will always be relationships based on obedience and dependence. The only thing that is important, though, is that they not eliminate responsibilities. . . . By no means does a relationship of dependence as such preclude free responsibility. Obedience without freedom is slavery, freedom without obedience is arbitrariness."[33]

Theologians have offered other ways of articulating the growing responsibility of children in connection with their understanding of child obedience, and we can all think of examples in our own day of the courage and competence of even very young children to face injustices and to challenge authority. Ruby Bridges, the first African American child in the United States to attend an all-white elementary school, for example, was just six years old when, escorted by federal marshals, she marched through an angry and jeering crowd of adults who demanded segregated schools. Even though the protests continued for months at the Frantz Elementary School in New Orleans, Ruby attended year after year and graduated from that school and went on to high school. She not only faced the protesters daily but also prayed twice a day, before and after school, asking God to forgive them. She had the love and support of her parents, and the courage to challenge unjust authorities in her community.

Recognizing the limits of parents and other adult authorities challenges a simplistic view of children as well as many popular Christian conceptions of discipline. Disciplining children, from a Christian perspective, should never be equated physically with punishing them. Parents are commanded to bring up their children "in the discipline and instruction of the Lord" (Eph. 6:4). True discipline is therefore Christ-centered and aims not to punish children but rather to help them become followers and disciples of Christ.

4. Fear and Love of God

Consonant with children's responsibility to evaluate adult demands and to disobey unjust authority is the call to fear the Lord.[34] Although parents are to be

33. Dietrich Bonhoeffer, *Ethics*, in *Dietrich Bonhoeffer Works*, vol. 6, ed. Clifford Green, trans. Reinhard Krauss, Charles C. West, and Douglas W. Stott (Minneapolis: Fortress, 2005), 286-87.

34. For rich discussions of the "fear of the Lord," see Patrick Miller, "That the Children May Know," and William Brown, "To Discipline without Destruction: The Multifaceted Profile of the Child in Proverbs," in *Biblical Perspectives on Children and Childhood*, ed. Marcia J. Bunge, Terence Fretheim, and Beverly Gaventa (Grand Rapids: Eerdmans, forthcoming).

honored and obeyed, God alone is to be feared and held in reverence. Again and again, the biblical texts emphasize that everyone, including children, is called to "fear the Lord" (Deut. 4:10; 6:1-2; 14:23; 17:19, 31:12-13). "The fear of the Lord is the beginning of knowledge; fools scorn wisdom and instruction" (Prov. 1:7; cf. 9:10). As the biblical scholar William Brown notes, in Proverbs the "fear of God is eminently edifying and life-enhancing" (10:27; 14:27; 19:23).

The duty of children to fear God is connected to the notion that both parents and children are to fear God. Here is where true security for both children and parents has its root: "In the fear of the Lord there is strong confidence, and one's children will have a refuge" (Prov. 14:26).

5. Learn About and Practice the Faith

A fifth part of a child's calling often emphasized in the Bible and the tradition is to learn about and to practice the faith. From an early age, children are to study the Scriptures and the law, to pray, and to praise and worship God.

Related to this fifth element of a child's calling is an understanding that children are developing beings in need of instruction and guidance and that their parents have a duty to nurture their faith. Several biblical passages speak about this parental responsibility. For example, parents are to "train children in the right way" (Prov. 22:6), teach them the love of God (Deut. 6:5), and bring them up "in the discipline and instruction of the Lord" (Eph. 6:4). They are to teach their children when they are at home and when they are away, when they lie down and when they rise (Deut. 11:18-19). Parents and caring adults are to tell children about God's faithfulness (Isa. 38:19) and "the glorious deeds of the Lord" (Ps. 78:4b). They are to teach children the words of the law (Deut. 11:18-19; 31:12-13), the love of God with the whole heart (Deut. 6:5), and doing what is right, just, and fair (Gen. 18:19; Prov. 2:9). Above all, parents should be examples to their children by living out their faith and their convictions. They should not only speak about the faith but also practice it in their everyday lives.

Certainly, for Christians, a major part of teaching children the faith and being an example is reading and discussing the Bible and interpretations of it. Augustine, Luther, John Calvin, Friedrich Schleiermacher, and many other theologians have emphasized the importance of this practice. Parents are to help their children know the biblical stories and to mine wisdom for life from them. Furthermore, they are also encouraged to carry out other practices of faith with their children in the home, such as praying, worshiping, singing, and serving those in need.

Some theologians in the past have emphasized the duty of parents to teach children the faith by speaking about the family as a "little church" or "sacred community." For example, John Chrysostom, an important figure in the fourth-century church and for Eastern Orthodox communities of faith today, and Horace Bushnell, a leading Congregationalist pastor and scholar of the nineteenth century, both speak of the family as a "little church." For them, this means that parents should read the Bible to their children, pray with them, and be good examples. Being a little church also means that the family itself, like the church, reaches out to the poor and needy in the community. Although both see the important role of the church in the faith development of children, they believe that the primary agent of grace is the family, not the church. Children need to be taught the faith not just at church by educators but at home by their parents. As Bushnell states, "Religion never thoroughly penetrates life until it becomes domestic."[35]

6. Teach Adults and Be Models of Faith

Although many theologians today and in the past have emphasized that parents are to teach children the faith and nurture them spiritually, they often neglect a sixth aspect of a child's vocation that is mentioned in several biblical passages: children are called, at times, to teach adults and to be models of faith for adults. This point is emphasized especially in the Gospels. Many Gospel passages turn upside down the common assumption held in Jesus' time and our own that children are to be seen but not heard and that the primary role of children is to learn from and to obey adults. In contrast, the New Testament depicts children

---

35. Bushnell, *Christian Nurture*, 63. This popular book envisions spiritual formation as a natural process that takes place not merely by reading the Bible and teaching children aspects of the faith but also through everyday practices and routines and the examples of adults and through play and a variety of fun activities. Throughout his work, he stresses the heroic importance of "small things" and claims that "it requires less piety . . . to be a martyr for Christ than it does to . . . maintain a perfect and guileless integrity in the common transactions of life." "Living to God in Small Things," in *Sermons for the New Life*, rev. ed. (New York: Charles Scribner's Sons, 1876), 291. As Bendroth explains, Bushnell, like Chrysostom, also has high expectations for parental influence. He believes that it would be almost impossible for a child who had been properly nurtured to reject the Christian faith. In the face of criticism by several of his contemporaries who claim that godly parents sometimes produce ungodly children for no apparent reason, Bushnell responds that there are so many ways to account for the failure of child rearing that doubts about his argument are unwarranted. He also claims that parents who neglect the spiritual well-being of their children will be judged by God. For a full discussion of Bushnell, see Margaret Bendroth, "Horace Bushnell's *Christian Nurture*," in *The Child in Christian Thought*, 350-64.

in striking and even radical ways as moral witnesses, models of faith for adults, sources or vehicles of revelation, representatives of Jesus, and even paradigms for entering the reign of God. Jesus identifies himself with children and equates welcoming a little child in his name to welcoming himself and the one who sent him. "Unless you change and become like children, you will never enter the kingdom of heaven," Jesus warns. "Whoever becomes humble like this child is the greatest in the kingdom of heaven. Whoever welcomes one such child in my name welcomes me" (Matt. 18:2-5).

Given this understanding of children as teachers and models of faith for adults, parents have a responsibility to listen to children and to learn from them. They should take their questions and concerns seriously. They are also to pay attention to the lessons that children can teach them. Viewing children as models for adults or vehicles of revelation does not mean that they are creatures who are "near angels," "closer to God," or "more spiritual" than adults. However, these passages and others do challenge parents and other caring adults to be receptive to the lessons and wisdom that children offer them, to honor children's questions and insights, and to recognize that children can positively influence the community and the moral and spiritual development of adults.

7. Go to School and Study Diligently for the Future

The tradition often emphasizes a seventh duty or responsibility of children: to go to school, to study diligently, and to cultivate their unique skills, gifts, and talents so that they can love and serve others and contribute to the common good in the future.

This duty is tied to the idea of vocation and built on the notion that children are uniquely created with diverse gifts and talents that enable them to serve others, thereby offering families and communities hope for the future. Indeed, many people today and in the past speak about children as our future or our hope. As Jürgen Moltmann and others have recognized, the child and childhood are powerful metaphors for hope, and children themselves give us hope and open up new possibilities for the future.[36]

Thus, a major responsibility of parents is to help children discern and name their gifts and to provide them with good schools and a solid education. By doing so, they prepare children to use their gifts in service to others, thereby strengthening the community and building for the future. In the Jewish tradi-

36. Jürgen Moltmann, "Child and Childhood as Metaphors of Hope," *Theology Today* 56, no. 4 (2000): 592-603.

tion, too, one of the major responsibilities of parents is to provide their children with an education that prepares them for a trade or a profession. Thus, many theologians and religious leaders in both the Jewish and Christian traditions have started or supported schools and colleges, fought for educational reform, and demanded that all children, including girls and the poor, be given an excellent education. What Luther stated in the sixteenth century can be affirmed still today: "We must spare no effort, time, and expense in teaching and educating our children" to serve God and the world.[37]

8. Play and Be in the Present

Finally, although children are to cultivate their gifts and talents to serve others in the future, at the same time, they have a role of strengthening and enlivening families and communities here and now simply through their openness, playfulness, and ability to laugh and be in the present. This aspect of their vocation or calling is another positive social role they serve as children right here and now.

This dimension of their specific calling is informed by the biblical conviction that children are gifts of God and sources of joy and that parents should cherish, enjoy, and be grateful for their children as they are now — not for what they will become in the future. Many passages in the Bible speak of children as gifts of God or signs of God's blessing and emphasize the joy that children bring to families and communities. For example, Sarah rejoiced at the birth of her son, Isaac (Gen. 21:6-7). An angel promises Zechariah and Elizabeth that their child will bring them "joy and gladness" (Luke 1:14). In the Gospel of John, Jesus says, "When a woman is in labor, she has pain, because her hour has come. But when her child is born, she no longer remembers the anguish because of the joy of having brought a human being into the world" (John 16:20-21).[38]

Furthermore, the notion of children at play is tied to visions of restoration and peace and to the notion of divine wisdom itself. For example, the prophet Zechariah included the image of children at play in his vision of a restored

37. Luther, "The Large Catechism," 388.

38. Furthermore, Leah, Jacob's first wife, speaks of her sixth son as a dowry, or wedding gift, presented by God (Gen. 30:20). Several biblical passages indicate that parents who receive these precious gifts are being "remembered" by God (Gen. 30:22; 1 Sam. 1:11, 19) and given "good fortune" (Gen. 30:11). To be "fruitful" — have many children — is to receive God's blessing. The psalmist says children are a "heritage" from the Lord and a "reward" (Ps. 127:3). Even in his terror and anguish, Jeremiah recalls the story that news of his own birth once made his father, Hilkiah, "very glad" (Jer. 20:15).

Zion. At a future time, when Jerusalem is restored as a faithful city, "the streets of the city shall be full of boys and girls playing in its streets" (Zech. 8:5). In Proverbs, divine wisdom, often portrayed solely as a woman, is also depicted as a child who is playing, delighting, and growing:[39]

> When [God] established the heavens, I [Wisdom] was there.
> When he circumscribed the surface of the deep,
> When he secured the skies above,
> When he stabilized the spring of the deep,
> When he assigned the sea its limit,
> Lest the waters transgress his command,
> When he carved out the foundations of the earth,
> I was beside him growing up.
> And I was his delight day by day,
> Playing before him always,
> Playing in his inhabited world,
> And delighting in the human race.
>
> (Prov. 8:27-31)

As Brown notes, such imagery highlights the "primacy of play when it comes to the sapiential way of life. The authority that wisdom embodies is not 'grave' but creative, and playfully so."[40]

We all recognize that children often have a sense of awe and wonder that delights and refreshes us. They are also often far more forgiving than adults and can often bring humor to difficult situations and help adults move forward. As some contemporary philosophers have recognized, children are also gifts in the sense that they offer us fresh and open perspectives. They often ask fundamental questions about life that open our eyes to new possibilities in our thinking. They are like the new employees in a company who can ask, "Why do you do things like this?" Their questions force us to reevaluate our priorities and to reexamine "business as usual." The biblical texts go further to suggest that play, too, is an aspect of true wisdom.

Implications

This list of eight elements is certainly not exhaustive, yet even these eight when held together and in tension can help articulate a meaningful Christian under-

39. Brown, "To Discipline without Destruction."
40. Brown, "To Discipline without Destruction."

standing of the vocation of the child. When Christians focus on only one or two of these elements, they narrowly restrict their view of and appreciation of children and thereby also limit their understanding of adult joys and responsibilities for children. A theological understanding of vocation that incorporates a complex view of the child and adult responsibilities to children has several positive implications for the church.

For example, a strong theological understanding of the vocation of the child can encourage the church to be a stronger national and international advocate for child well-being in areas such as health care and education. It stresses the need for parents and the community to provide for the needs of children. It also emphasizes that the common good of society requires educated citizens, that all children should receive a good education, and that the education of young people is a shared responsibility.

It also prompts the church to strengthen its religious education and faith formation programs and to support parents in their task of shaping the moral and spiritual lives of their children. Although the church certainly cares about children and young people and offers a number of programs to serve them, parents and other caring adults need to do more to nurture the faith of children and young people.

A strong concept of the child's vocation also prompts parents themselves to speak to children more intentionally about their beliefs and values, carrying out central religious practices that nurture faith in their homes, and listening to and learning from their children. In general, when we also consider that in our current consumer culture young people and now even very young children are the targets of intense and highly sophisticated marketing campaigns, vying for their money and brand loyalty and shaping their values and assumptions, the question we must ask is not, "Will our children have faith?" but rather, "What kind of faith will they have?" Our children and young people are and will be shaped by messages around them, and parents and churches must be more intentional about the messages they want their children to receive.

These are only a few implications, but they indicate that a view of the vocation of the child that is embedded in a solid theological understanding of children and child-adult relationships and responsibilities is bound to strengthen the church's concern for and care of children.

Conclusion

I have provided only a brief sketch of one theological view of the vocation of children, yet even this short sketch reminds all of us, regardless of our philosophical or religious backgrounds or convictions, that children, too, have vocations. Like people of all ages, races, genders, and social classes, children are meant to and already do participate in and contribute to the life of their families and communities. Furthermore, any strong view of the vocation of the child can be built only by cultivating, at the same time, a vibrant and complex understanding of children themselves that includes attention not only to their vulnerabilities and weaknesses but also to their gifts and strengths. Finally, reflection on the vocation of the child certainly challenges all of us to think more seriously about our own duties and responsibilities to children — whether or not we have children of our own.

2. In Search of Real Children: Innocence, Absence, and Becoming a Self in Christ

William Werpehowski

> *For in truth we are not called once only, but many times; all through our life Christ is calling us. He called us first in Baptism; but afterwards also; whether we obey His voice or not, He graciously calls us still. If we fall from our Baptism, He calls us to repent; if we are striving to fulfill our calling, He calls us on from grace to grace, and from holiness to holiness, while life is given us.*[1]

These words are taken from a sermon preached by John Henry Newman in the 1830s. They bear on scriptural instances of a divine call, as to Paul, to Peter, Andrew, James and John, and, significantly for my purposes here, to the child Samuel. "And the Lord came, and stood, and called as at other times, Samuel, Samuel. Then Samuel answered, speak, for Thy servant heareth" (1 Sam. 3:10). The sermon vividly depicts the "accidents and events" in which we may be called "all through our life," such as in circumstances of loss, or in the course of worldly temptation, or through the light of exemplars we may not fully appreciate or understand. We can imagine such accidents and events occurring in the lives of adults, like Paul, and of children, like Samuel; indeed, Newman's sermon may be understood to take up a version of the Kierkegaardian question of what it means for us to be contemporary with Jesus Christ.[2]

---

1. John Henry Newman, "Divine Calls," in *Callings: Twenty Centuries of Christian Wisdom on Vocation,* ed. William C. Placher (Grand Rapids: Eerdmans, 2005), 346.
2. But cf. Placher's remarks in *Callings,* 343.

I want to thank James M. Gustafson, Kevin Hughes, Gilbert Meilaender, Robert Orsi, Douglas Schuurman, Thomas Smith, Darlene Fozard Weaver, and my colleagues in The Vocation of the Child project for their encouragement and critical help with this chapter. — William Werpehowski

There is, however, a related issue about the nature not of "divine calls" such as these, but of "divine *callings*" or *vocations* that display a certain social texture and historical continuity, and that track, as it were, particular persons with respect to a specific activity or status or situated area of responsibility. With this issue and the parallels noted above, we may take pause. We can and should talk about and ponder "vocations" as they concern adults, be they young or old. But does it make sense to speak of the vocation of the *child?*

I believe that the idea of "the vocation of the child," as applied to young people up to, shall we say, their early adolescence, is dangerous because of the self-deception it can foster among those who care for children in societies like our own, and who may thus inflict damage in its name. Yet it is dangerous in a second, salutary sense; for the notion properly considered imperils that same partly willed, partial blindness through its challenge, through its *calling us out,* truthfully to see real children as they may be called by God. In this chapter I will try to explain both the problem and the promise, following a brief investigation of "vocation" as a Christian theological category.

1

Everyday Christian uses of "vocation" include, centrally, being called by God to love and serve him. A *people* may be so called *by name,* and called *out,* as is Israel and the Christian community. A Christian *individual's* calling can and should be taken to mean membership in such a community, with personal responsibilities appropriate to disciples of Jesus Christ. But "vocation" indicates not just "generic" responsibilities, as if they can and do apply to "anyone" of the people of God. Particular persons are called, and their specific callings reflect their particularity, including the limits and opportunities they discover in and around themselves under God's ruling grace. In the American Catholic environment I knew as a child, a significant case in point concerned "religious vocation," and firstborn sons like me inevitably faced the question whether *I myself* was called to the priesthood. Later, and analogously, there were other inquiries, about education, employment, state of life, parenthood, and more.

The "I myself," an engaged, individualizing discernment, seems to me to be a constitutive feature of the idea of Christian vocation. It is a complex and ramified conception, and there are at least three reasons for this complexity. First, the *self one is,* is a *creature.* He or she is finite and dependent, limited in space and time and by virtue of a host of relations that order and enable one's existence in the creative providence of God. This or that human creature's vocation must reflect this finitude, contingency, and sociality. Second, "one oneself" is, yet is finally no longer, a *sinner,* whose lingering tendencies to deny one's creatureliness may issue in following, not God's call, but a self-securing design of one's own making. Our awareness that we are sinners cautions us against reaching eagerly for a "calling" that "makes us happy" without testing its fidelity in service to the One in whom we live and move and have our being. Third, the self we are and are promised to be is an adopted child of God, reconciled to God in Jesus Christ; so our particular freedom in and for our vocation is not only finite, social, repentant, and vigilant, but also loyal in hope to God and the cause of universal community to which God is loyal.[3] Our particular callings to serve God and neighbor are limited but, as such, comprehensive, given God's will graciously to make a new heaven and a new earth under God's dominion.[4]

These descriptions of human identity conspire in the consideration of who "I myself" am summoned to be. We already have an example on hand. One's calling would concern one's given talents in some important way; nevertheless, one should be on guard about giving these, as supposed paths to one's self-designed self-fulfillment, an exclusively determining importance. A person's creaturely vocation in his or her specific time, place, and relationships should not be understood so narrowly as to exclude a more universal, reconciling loyalty; nor should that loyalty overwhelm our more "local" commitments. "Our vocation will call for our love to participate in both the universality and the particularity of the divine love, though not in the same way."[5]

Hence one's vocation involves oneself as summoned in one's own history before God. Now to what specific forms of existence does the summons refer? Christian theological traditions offer a number of answers.

V1. The human creature may be called to a sort of "public" work. The Reformation doctrine of vocation affirmed that our "worldly" employment and the good we do in it may be sanctified. "Forth in thy name, O Lord, I go, / My daily labor to pursue, / Thee, only thee resolved to know / In all I think or speak, or do."[6] Limited, "intraprofessional" norms that would govern customarily

3. This loyalty is also and especially a loyalty to the *church,* which is a "pioneer and representative" of such a community. See H. Richard Niebuhr, "The Responsibility of the Church for Society," chap. 5 in *The Gospel, the Church, and the World,* ed. K. S. Latourette (New York: Harper and Brothers, 1946), and William Werpehowski, *American Protestant Ethics and the Legacy of H. Richard Niebuhr* (Washington, D.C.: Georgetown University Press, 2002), 119-22, 203-21.

4. Douglas J. Schuurman, *Vocation: Discerning Our Callings in Life* (Grand Rapids: Eerdmans, 2004), 50-51.

5. Robert Merrihew Adams, *Finite and Infinite Goods: A Framework for Ethics* (New York: Oxford University Press, 1999), 302.

6. Charles Wesley, "Forth in Thy Name, O Lord, I Go," in *Working: Its Meaning and Limits,* ed. Gilbert C. Meilaender (Notre Dame, Ind.: University of Notre Dame Press, 2000), 116; see also 107-15.

creaturely service to the neighbor may be subject to reconsideration in terms of how a certain vocational sphere does or does not in fact serve the common good.[7]

V2. Vocation may also refer broadly to one's service within relational contexts of authority, mutuality, and need, and thus to human bonds that fall outside "employment." "God not only calls people into a given form of paid work; family relations, friendships, extracurricular commitments — indeed, all significant social relations are places into which God calls us to serve God and neighbor."[8] From this perspective the vocation of the child at least is intelligible in terms of the child's "place" in his or her family, but also, perhaps, with regard to "adults" in general, and/or to adults in their roles as teachers, pastors, etc.

Indeed, "vocation's tendency to insist upon larger moral contexts"[9] can alert us how a social practice of "childhood," constructed within and for some social body, may or may not advance a "common good" that well serves God, neighbor, and children themselves. When Martin Luther preached to parents to keep their children in school rather than removing them "and turning them to the making of a living and the caring for their bellies," he was alert to the importance of maintaining the office of ministry, as well as, we can imagine, to the excesses to which his own "doctrine of vocation" may have tended. He was also attacking a particular practice of childhood, an organization of children's spaces, time, relations, and aspirations that presupposes a certain view of who they are and what they ought to be in themselves and in and for the social body. A lesson he would teach in this regard to parents is that "your children are not so wholly yours that you need give nothing of them to God . . . and they are more his than yours!"[10] George Orwell's terrifying account of his school days in England also describes a social practice in which the education of children becomes a "commercial venture" directed toward filling slots in a stratified workplace, gaining prestige for his school, and enforcing wider social norms.

> That was the pattern of school life — a continuous pattern of the strong over the weak. Virtue consisted in winning: it consisted in being bigger, stronger, handsomer, richer, more popular, more elegant, more unscrupulous than other people — in dominating them, bullying them, making them suffer

---

7. William Werpehowski, "The Professions: Vocations to Justice and Love," in *Proceedings of the Theology Institute of Villanova University,* ed. Francis A. Eigo, O.S.A., vol. 18 (Villanova, Pa.: Villanova University Press, 1986); William F. May, *Beleaguered Rulers: The Public Obligation of the Professional* (Louisville: Westminster John Knox, 2001).

8. Schuurman, *Vocation,* xi.

9. Schuurman, *Vocation,* 11.

10. Martin Luther, "A Sermon on Keeping Children in School," in *Callings,* 222, 224.

pain, making them look foolish, getting the better of them in every way. *Life was hierarchical and whatever happened was right.*[11]

V3. There is also the "relational context" of the Christian community and the "varieties of gifts, services, and activities" employed to serve the needs of the body of Christ. "They are not the same as the call to be a Christian, but they do designate specific ways members of the church express their response to that call."[12] As such, they can be taken to be "offices" to which Christians are called, and these surely may be identified in overlap with the sorts of human bonds identified in V2. Consider, for example, Vigen Guroian's consideration of the office of being a good son or daughter, in parallel with other of his writings on the office of husband and wife who in their mutual fidelity give embodied testimony, in and for church and world, to the faithful love of God in Jesus Christ.[13] The more specifically ecclesial dimension of this notion of vocation, however, presents an opportunity to reflect on a Christian theological vision that evidently celebrates children in their paradigmatic fitness for the kingdom of God, as well as on the concrete implications of that vision for the life of the church. The kingdom of God *belongs* to children, and those who do not receive it "like a child" shall not enter it (Mark 10:14-15; cf. Matt. 18:2-4; 19:13-14). Receiving one such child in Jesus' name, moreover, receives Jesus, and equally weighty but opposite consequences attach to causing "one of those little ones who believe" in him to sin. Here children may become (and are even authorized to become) "privileged media for giving substance to religious meaning, for making the sacred present and material, not only *for* children but *through* them, too, for adults in relation to them."[14]

V4. Vocation may refer to the entirety of "the particularity, limitation and restriction in which every man meets the divine call and command."[15] It is what Karl Barth, following Dietrich Bonhoeffer, calls "the place of responsibility," "the *terminus a quo* of all recognition and fulfillment" of the divine sum-

11. George Orwell, "Such, Such Were the Joys . . . ," in *A Collection of Essays* (New York and London: Harcourt Brace and Co., 1946), 36, emphasis added. Cf. my discussion in "Reading Karl Barth on Children," in *The Child in Christian Thought*, ed. Marcia J. Bunge (Grand Rapids: Eerdmans, 2001), 389-90, 402.

12. Schuurman, *Vocation*, 30.

13. In addition to his chapter in this volume, see Vigen Guroian, "On the Office of Being a Good Son or Daughter," in *Rallying the Really Human Things* (Wilmington, Del.: ISI Books, 2005), 91-99, and "An Ethic of Marriage and Family," in *From Christ to the World*, ed. Wayne G. Boulton, Thomas D. Kennedy, and Allen Verhey (Grand Rapids: Eerdmans, 1994), 322-30.

14. Robert A. Orsi, *Between Heaven and Earth: The Religious Worlds People Make and the Scholars Who Study Them* (Princeton and Oxford: Princeton University Press, 2005), 77.

15. Karl Barth, *Church Dogmatics* III/4 (Edinburgh: T. & T. Clark, 1961), 599.

mons. The latter, in its turn, "will always mean something materially new for man, a broadening, lengthening, alteration or more precise definition of the frontiers within which he already has his being."[16] Calling as vocation is here distinct (but not separate) from calling as divine summons. The features of creaturely vocation in this sense include not only one's age, historical and social location, and personal aptitude, but also the "field of his ordinary everyday activity, the place in which he is in his own way an active member of human society."[17] So introducing personal volition into the account at this point (insofar as we choose our sphere of operation) also puts "vocation" and "summons," place and (new) movement, in close interrelation. We partly but really place ourselves in free obedience, ready for free obedience from that place. In fact, there is throughout this approach an appeal to human agency. It encompasses more or less fitting answers or responses within and toward one's situation in the world before God.

V5. While Barth reserves "vocation" to where one stands awaiting God's call, Robert Merrihew Adams applies the term to the self God calls us to become and be. We have "to distinguish clearly between the situation *in* which we are called and to which we must respond in our vocation, and the projects *to* which we are called."[18] Barth keeps this distinction, too, and places "vocation" on the other end of it, so to speak. He does so, I imagine, out of suspicion that the alternative risks giving some independent interpretation of "one's calling," a more or less fixed or frozen normative status that intrudes upon a divine freedom that beckons and a human freedom that hears and heeds. Adams, in contrast, wants to explore the "new" moral claims that can emerge with the "singular judgment" that there are some tasks in the universe that are "*mine* in a morally valid way."[19] Still, Adams understands that singular judgment in terms of a divine summons, command, or invitation. If you will, the self *to whom and to which* God calls, rather than the place *from which* one moves, is decisive.

Throughout the analysis of V1-V5, but perhaps in this last case especially, we must keep in sight a central christological qualification. Thomas Merton makes the point well: "Every man has a vocation to *be* someone: but he must understand clearly that in order to fulfill this vocation he can only be one person: himself. Yet . . . baptism gives us a sacramental character, defining our vocation in a very particular way since it tells us we must become ourselves in Christ."[20]

---

16. Barth, *Church Dogmatics* III/4, 598.
17. Barth, *Church Dogmatics* III/4, 630.
18. Adams, *Finite and Infinite Goods,* 309.
19. Adams, *Finite and Infinite Goods,* 294, 292.
20. Thomas Merton, *No Man Is an Island* (New York: Barnes and Noble Books, 2003), 133-34.

2

Considering a child's vocation, one ought not to disregard the "I myself." What I described as "an engaged, individualizing discernment" may appear to apply precisely to human persons who are *not* children; but such a reading too quickly passes by the sorts of agency and self-relation children may and do possess and develop.[21]

For the purposes of this chapter, however, I *will* disregard (or, better, "bracket") the relevance of V1 to children, while recognizing that there remain important and complicated questions to pose and answer.[22]

Again, V2 invites attention to children as members of a family: sons and daughters, brothers and sisters, and so forth. The fourth commandment's injunction to honor mother and father is especially germane, and I intend to focus on it.[23] V3 permits a variety of applications, especially given the overlap with V2. Hence the "office" of son or daughter may be a sign of trust or hope in and for the Christian community, as the "office" of spouse witnesses analogously to God's fidelity in Jesus Christ. But I am particularly interested in the formal or informal station that children keep as learners in and just so bearers of the faith that is taught to them. Barth's reflections, under V4, on the vocation of "youth" as a stage of life, and Adams's explicit observation that a version of V5, i.e., "becoming a self," constitutes the child's primary vocation[24] order the remainder of my critical and constructive analysis below.

21. Consider the contribution of John E. Coons to this volume.

22. For example, in personal correspondence that responds to a draft of this essay, Robert Orsi rightly notes that for early-twentieth-century immigrant families in America, "children's earnings were a key component not only of family survival but of how ethical responsibility was defined. . . . The Catholic Church even offered an odd defense of working children — or perhaps this was an argument against the progressive state — on the grounds of family expectations and authority." And in his own letter Douglas Schuurman admits that the claim that V1 was irrelevant to children "gave me pause. Though children may not be directly active in 'paid' or 'public' work, they may be preparing for it. My youngest daughter, for example, knew she wanted to be an elementary teacher since she was in the fourth grade. That sense of calling guided many of her decisions (e.g., the kinds of summer work, etc.) as she grew up. Perhaps we may see the child's V1 as a time of preparation for a 'public' work that may or may not be known to the child at earlier ages." Bonnie Miller-McLemore's contribution to this volume, finally, usefully raises the stakes with regard to the relation among children, vocation, and various forms of "work." I hope to take up these significant issues at another time.

23. One might relate this, as does Karl Barth, to more general attention to the roles of "students" and "respecters of elders." The key to the relation is a theological argument that grounds the fourth commandment, and the parental authority it presupposes, in the first.

24. "The call to become and to be oneself will plausibly be a part of each person's vocation, the self in each case being different. This is a peculiarly fundamental part of our vocation. It

Each of these applications is liable to corruption. The responsibilities of the good son or daughter can be construed and accordingly demanded as unquestioning obedience. They may also be articulated to enforce adherence to a familial "inner ring" that, as such, exists for the sake of exclusion,[25] or to an image of "one's self" that is dictated by parentally "given" readings of the "givens" of a child's existence, e.g., her abilities, social circumstances, and sex. In the first case, the "good son" keeps himself to the moral and insularly self-identifying terms set by his family, taking himself to be summoned by the magic of the surname x; in the second, the "good daughter" takes to heart and makes her heart into mother's or father's descriptions of her as "good at" this and "right for" that, given her background as the woman she is.[26] A child's vocation to learn and to bring forward the Christian faith may reflect not so much hope but rather the fear that "without such instruction children will be bereft and alienated on the deepest levels." Children, moreover, "represent among other things the future of the faith standing there in front of oneself"; and the apprehension of the vulnerability of that faith in vulnerable children can augment adults' attempt "to realize the meaningfulness of their religious worlds in their children."[27] Since the stakes are so high, adult expectations might presume upon the independence, and independent reality, of the young. Within this strategy of fear, a blurring of boundaries between adult and child by way of the religious meanings constitutive of adult lives is a consequence of kids' "knowing their place." In his analysis of the figure of the guardian angel in mid-twentieth-century American Catholic life, Robert Orsi points out that children were taught that their guardian accompanied them everywhere, and "*felt* children's behaviors in their own angelic beings." Poor behavior brought your angel sorrow, and kindness made your angel happy. "The angels thus contributed to the dissolution of children's boundaries," since everything about and inside of them was "under guard."

In this way . . . the angels guarded against children's autonomy: angel lore cast children as fundamentally in need of constant supervision, moral scru-

---

cannot be taken away from us by any misfortune that leaves us able to deliberate intelligently at all; in hard circumstances it may be virtually our whole vocation. It is probably the main vocation of children; and we never outgrow it, for we have never finished becoming ourselves. And this is not a merely personal project; it is to be our project, but it is also a responsibility." Adams, *Finite and Infinite Goods*, 312.

25. C. S. Lewis, "The Inner Ring," in *The Weight of Glory* (Grand Rapids: Eerdmans, 1965), 55-66.

26. The roles of "student" and "respectful subordinate" may breed, in their own right, unseemly uniformity and insidious passivity.

27. Orsi, *Between Heaven and Earth*, 77.

tiny, and accompaniment, a need endorsed by the fear of (or the threat of) harm and death. When children moved over to make room for their angels on the seat next to them in church or in school, they were moving themselves ever more securely into the moral and cosmic world that adults were making for and with them in the media of Catholic devotionalism.[28]

In addition, to focus on youth or childhood *itself* as a morally or religiously relevant — or even decisive — vocation may carry the temptation to require of children a kind of otherworldly "purity" or "spontaneity" they cannot and should not possess. A certain sentimentalization of children distorts our vision of them; they come to bear virtues and values serving, preferred, and protected by adults, and which are selective of only some young people after all. For example, visions of children's beauty, tied both to their "purity" or "innocence" and to their desirability as such, may give young people a "market niche" for adults who buy their clothes or enjoy their adorable cuteness in movies. Doing that, of course, commodifies them, renders them predicates of adult desire immunized from self-criticism, and generates questionable cultural understandings of "childhood" to which children are to conform. Those who do not and cannot conform (and there will be these, for these visions are particular and typically culturally dominant) are removed from view, or, in some cases (e.g., those where youngsters commit shocking acts of violence), are removed from the category of "children" altogether. That last self-protective move may further immunize grown-ups from considering the general social circumstances and conditions that do and do not support children's lives, and their responsibility for them.[29]

The appeal to the vocation to become and be a self, finally, can simply reiterate and then advance all the difficulties we have just surveyed, whereupon adults who make the appeal, as Natalia Ginzburg puts it, ironically

> cling to our children as a shipwrecked mariner clings to a tree trunk; we eagerly demand that they give us back everything we have given them, that they be absolutely and inescapably what we wish them to be, that they get out of life everything we have missed; *we end up asking them for all the things which*

---

28. Orsi, *Between Heaven and Earth*, 106. More generally on the theme of the surveillance of the child, see Chris Jenks, *Childhood* (London and New York: Routledge, 1996), 73-80.

29. James R. Kincaid, *Erotic Innocence: The Culture of Child Molesting* (Durham, N.C., and London: Duke University Press, 1998), 51-72, 111-64. I am indebted to Robert Orsi for alerting me to the importance of Kincaid's work. See also Henry A. Giroux, *Stealing Innocence: Youth, Corporate Power, and the Politics of Culture* (New York: St. Martin's Press, 2000), 1-64; Jenks, *Childhood*, 116-39.

can only be given us by our own vocation; we want them to be entirely our creation, as if having once created them we could continue to create them throughout their whole lives. We want them to be entirely our creation, *as if we were not dealing with human beings but with products of the spirit.*[30]

I realize that abuse of some moral or religious notion or practice does not bar proper use, and that Christian theological traditions contain resources that resist these corruptions. I rely on some of them, in fact, in part 3 of this chapter. Perhaps the greatest good of the very idea of the vocation of the child is to root out the very tendencies I have just described. Nevertheless, we should not rest in these comforts; for the imposters of vocation ought not to be authorized by the compliment of the title.

More importantly, there is the peril of self-deception in the way we conceive and employ the idea that our children are summoned to some behavior or responsibility. "Childhood" represents in manifold ways "the projections, aspirations, longings and altruism contained within the adult experience";[31] hence *our* relation to it and its "embodiments" inevitably prompt anxiety about our individual identities and the identity of our social world. We are in fact at risk of mistaking the embodiments of childhood we need and want (as parents, people of faith, teachers, citizens, and so on) for real children with their own needs and wants. To the extent that we are conscientious moral actors, meaning to do right by children, the danger of self-deception increases; we just must think of ourselves (vocationally!) as good parents and such, and to that degree may resist all the more "spelling out" our engagements with children. The persistent refusal fully to describe to ourselves what it is we are doing for the sake of preserving our particular identity is a hallmark of self-deception.[32]

A work of diagnosis and, following that, theological discrimination is therefore in order. My diagnosis begins with James Kincaid's proposal that a certain account of children's *innocence* opens a space, a "hollow" space, into which may speed a variety of adult desires, fantasies, imaginings, and evasions.[33] Consider, for example, the evasion in evidence in a poem by Billy Collins, "The History Teacher."

---

30. Natalia Ginzburg, *The Little Virtues* (New York: Arcade Publishing, 1989), 109-10, emphasis added.

31. Jenks, *Childhood,* 136.

32. Herbert Fingarette, *Self-Deception* (New York: Humanities Press, 1969); Stanley Hauerwas and David Burrell, C.S.C., "Self-Deception and Autobiography: Theological and Ethical Reflections on Speer's *Inside the Third Reich,*" *Journal of Religious Ethics* 2 (Spring 1974): 99-117.

33. Kincaid, *Erotic Innocence,* 15-16, 53-54.

Trying to protect his students' innocence
he told them the Ice Age was really just
the Chilly Age, a period of a million years
when everyone had to wear sweaters.
And the Stone Age became the Gravel Age,
named after the long driveways of the time.
The Spanish Inquisition was nothing more
than an outbreak of questions such as
"How far is it from here to Madrid?"
"What do you call the matador's hat?"
The War of the Roses took place in a garden,
and the Enola Gay dropped one tiny atom on Japan.
The children would leave his classroom
for the playground to torment the weak and the smart,
mussing up their hair and breaking their glasses,
while he gathered up his notes and walked home
past flower beds and white picket fences,
wondering if they would believe that soldiers
in the Boer War told long, rambling stories
designed to make the enemy nod off.[34]

Innocence "of the world" presents the child through vague ideals of generic goodness (not of the world?) that are unquestioned, closely guarded, and grossly mistaken. Crucially, the notion seems in great part simply to express what the child is *not* — not experienced, not corrupted, not able to fend for herself, not an adult. In any case, innocence in this sense tends to deny children any status other than their need to be protected as utterly vulnerable and malleable creatures. So it renders them, in their own reality, absent. "The discourse of innocence precludes children from having their own wants, needs, and desires, and their own understandings of things different from what adults propose for them. . . . Ironically, the discourse of innocence puts children at the greatest risk because the emptiness of innocence creates a space into which adult desire can be projected."[35] If and when that "hollow" category is filled with content specific to children, it may still, as I noted above, insidiously select and valorize features and characteristics without regard to how they reflect matters of social location and adult preference. Even a vision of children as naturally and ideally "open" to the divine can rob them of their agency; their

---

34. Billy Collins, *Sailing Alone around the Room* (New York: Random House, 2001), 38.

35. Robert A. Orsi, "A Crisis about the Theology of Children," *Harvard Divinity Bulletin,* http://www.hds.harvard.edu/news/bulletin/articles/orsi.html.

blessed privilege of being an instance of "childhood" is purchased at the cost of their real being in the world.[36]

If one rejects such a notion of innocence, one may still remain bound to its consequences, in a reflex flight to accounts of children's fearful otherness, their need, not now for consuming protection, but for adult control and order given their unruliness and threatening disorder. No longer present (and therefore absent) in their purity, children are made present (and therefore absent) in their depravity.

3

The task of theological discrimination has to do with critically describing the vocation of the child in a manner that responds to and attempts to remove these dangers. The description relies on comprehending, first, how it is that children are, after all, summoned by God; and second, how their reality, which includes their independence from the beings adults would make and take them to be, is recognized, protected, and advanced. The idea is to imagine relations in which caregivers may consent to a child's freedom for God, and in which the child may respond to the opportunities for it in ways that are fittingly and creatively one's own.

Corresponding to the four *going* senses of vocation I presented earlier — V2 through V5 — I want to work out theocentric and christocentric understandings of (a) the good son or daughter, who (b) calling upon God as an eager learner of the life of faith in Jesus Christ, (c) may step into freedom with a

---

36. Robert Orsi argues that the modern era in Roman Catholic culture can well be dubbed "the age of children," and that in that age "childhood — or 'childhood,' meaning the qualities presumed by adults to belong to children — became the model of adult faith." Orsi, *Between Heaven and Earth*, 79, 81. Although he clearly and wisely wants to avoid the consequence of substituting "childhood" for children, I sometimes think that some of what Hans Urs von Balthasar says about children moves toward it. He writes, for example, that "the ways of the child . . . open up an original dimension in which everything unfolds within the bounds of the right, the true, the good. . . . That zone or dimension in which the child lives . . . reveals itself as a sphere of original wholeness and health, and it may be even said to contain an element of holiness, since at first the child cannot yet distinguish between parental and divine love." Hans Urs von Balthasar, *Unless You Become Like This Child* (San Francisco: Ignatius, 1991), 12. Karl Rahner's identification of children's "infinite openness to the infinite" explicitly avoids appeals to "innocence" in "Ideas for a Theology of Childhood," in *Theological Investigations*, vol. 8 (New York: Herder and Herder, 1971), 33-51. For a fine study, see Mary Ann Hinsdale, "'Infinite Openness to the Infinite': Karl Rahner's Contribution to Modern Catholic Thought on the Child," in *The Child in Christian Thought*, 406-45.

"youthful objectivity." All of this serves the purpose (d) of becoming and being a *self* in Christ, i.e., becoming and being oneself as constituted by projects of committed self-giving.

a. A child is summoned to be a good son or daughter, who is to honor mother and father "in the Lord, for this is right." The child's vocation in this sense, however, is not entailed simply by an act of subordination to one's parents. Their authority is based on their being witnesses to a divine measure, and with that a moral law, to which they are subordinate as well. Consider Carlo Collodi's *Pinocchio*. The wooden puppet in this famous tale is a sort of scoffer, which the book of Proverbs defines as "the name of the proud, haughty man who acts with arrogant pride" (21:24). He does not heed advice, presumes to have far more self-control than he possesses in fact, and flies into rages when he does not get his way. But while a scoffer does not listen to rebuke, "a wise son hears his father's instruction" (Prov. 13:1), and Collodi's narrative tells of the manner in which Pinocchio does so.

It is important to see that, in contrast to the Disney feature, Pinocchio's transformation is not based on attaining a basically generic goodness, by being, shall we say, *simply* "brave and honest and true." He is brought to life by his good fairy mother as she says: "Children who love their parents and help them when they are sick and poor, are worthy of praise and love, even if they are not models of obedience and good behavior."[37] So he becomes a real boy by being a good son, who honors more general moral precepts regarding prudence, studiousness, hard work, and the golden rule within the context of honoring his father and mother. The precepts temper and orient his "good heart." More to the point, the puppet's transformation involves a double movement. It happens as a consequence of the moral precepts being ordered to and by filial piety, while, at the same time, the piety becomes identified with adherence to the precepts themselves. Pinocchio serves and honors his parents by doing what they taught him, now for them. He will, for instance, give up two shillings for his mother as this reminds him of his father's own sacrifice of his coat for him. Filial piety is directed toward authorities who teach a moral law that in a deep way authorizes them.[38] Conformity to it does go hand in hand with a proper ordering of the child — scoffer to the parent. The embodied act of subordination appears to en-

---

37. Carlo Collodi, *Pinocchio* (New York and London: Puffin Books, 1974), 229.

38. "The Book of Proverbs, which can be read as a large-scale commentary on the fifth commandment, is not in any sense an unspiritual book. In it we are not prescribed, ordered, or commanded, but persuaded and advised and invited to make a personal trial and well-considered decision, and this always with an appeal to the court ['Wisdom'] which stands above the fatherly teacher and adviser." Barth, *Church Dogmatics* III/4, 249.

able adherence to the law, while adherence to the moral law relativizes the subordination.[39]

Now surely there is a *special* responsibility to honor one's very own mother and father. But the fourth commandment may attain its fullness of purpose as a central moment in a history of learning to honor *every* human being, to sense the "sacredness of the person who is its object." Reverend John Ames, the protagonist and voice of Marilynne Robinson's novel *Gilead,* takes the Ten Commandments in their sequence to retell the story of creation. Their injunctions "set apart," for the sake of right understanding, the Lord God, God's Word, the seventh day, and (fourth) "the Universal Father and Mother, the Lord's dear Adam and His beloved Eve." The son and daughter begin and continue to perceive "essential humankind as it came from [God's] hand," "from this setting apart of mother and father, who usually labor and are heavy-laden, and may be cranky or stingy or ignorant or overbearing."[40] Freedom opens out to broader forms of faithfulness that clarify and also contain the claims parents may make on their children with reference to their rightful place.

b. A child is called to learn by asking, inquiring, calling upon God and upon those elders whose authority is grounded finally by their own vocation to bear witness to a gracious God for the child in the manifold ways they can. To be summoned to learn refers generally to the way that *children of God* are and always will be, even when they are no longer "children," needy beginners. A certain sort of *readiness* is what matters in part. That is itself a discipline in attention (which elders are duty bound to display and encourage) that would be free of self-preoccupation, which waits on its subject, and that, as Simone Weil has shown, is analogous to and preparatory for prayer in the love of God. Led by desire and accomplished, when it is, in joy, our learning happens in beholding rather than in controlling, through a patient readiness for the truth of the matter at hand, "setting our hearts upon it, yet not allowing ourselves to go out in search of it."[41] As the trajectory of honoring our mother and father may extend to heeding the beauty of every human being, so the faculty of attention may make possible seeing the neighbor in need rightly, "not only as a unit in a collection . . . but as a man, exactly like us. . . . This way of looking is first of all attentive. The soul empties itself of all its own contents in order to receive into itself the being it is looking at, just as he is, in

---

39. Cf. Guroian, "On the Office," 97-98. Guroian and I have had the occasion to discuss *Pinocchio* formally and informally over the years, and I have learned from him about the book. I think that my emphasis above may be distinct from his own general approach.

40. Marilynne Robinson, *Gilead* (New York: Farrar, Straus and Giroux, 2004), 138-39.

41. Simone Weil, "Reflections on the Right Use of School Studies with a View to the Love of God," in *Waiting for God* (New York: Harper Collins, 2001), 63.

all his truth."[42] Moreover, while attention, "directed toward God, is the very substance of prayer,"[43] it is also, when prayerfully directed toward one's life in relation with God, the substance of vocational discernment, which "is yielding, not fighting . . . yielding at every moment to the perfect freedom of single necessity."[44] Freedom in this instance and others (for truth, for God and neighbor) exists always in a *becoming* that waits and receives in the *beginning* that is kenosis, emptiness.

Children may readily learn the Christian faith in the manner and for the purpose of their calling upon God for new life and nourishment. They are therefore to comprehend, out of Scripture, tradition, ritual, and moral practice, the "Christian story," i.e., the identity of God in God's history of grace in Jesus Christ. As "beginners" in the faith, they may come to understand their place in that history as God's children, and in that sense, again, as never not beginners, never not in the deepest need for divine guidance and tutelage. But as bearers of this faith these "unproved pupils" may also be *called out* to *call upon* their Father over against the pretensions of their caregiving elders to play the role of "tested masters."[45] They may and should be welcomed to inquire about their faith and the way it is lived in their midst. They should be encouraged to pose challenging, truthful questions that could well stir up dust because they stir movements of repentance and conversion in the Holy Spirit. What distinguishes disciples is the ability to accept the radical new beginning that is made with men, apart from any enterprise of their own, in the gospel of the Father and the Son, in the Word of the cross. What distinguishes them is the willingness to begin at this new beginning. Note that it is not to the outside children of the world, to unbelieving Jews, proud Gentiles, idealists, materialists, and atheists, but to *Christians* that all these things are said and applied; it is they who obviously need to experience the call to begin again at this beginning and to take the place they precisely are assigned as the children of God.[46]

Without the revolutionary proviso that the place of children in the Christian community can and must include its overtly or covertly *calling to* that community to "start over" and anew in this or that dimension of the Christian life,

42. Weil, "Reflections," 64-65. Cf. Sara Ruddick, *Maternal Thinking: Toward a Politics of Peace* (Boston: Beacon Press, 1989), 120-23.

43. Weil, "Reflections," 58.

44. Annie Dillard, "Living Like Weasels," http://www.sheftman.com/ewrt1a/dillard/weasel.html. Cf. Weil on her own notion of vocation in *Waiting for God,* 23. There are fascinating convergences and contrasts between Weil and Dillard on "freedom" and "necessity," "searching" and "waiting," and the nature of human choice that I cannot consider here.

45. Karl Barth, *The Christian Life* (Grand Rapids: Eerdmans, 1981), 81.

46. Barth, *The Christian Life,* 82.

the proposal that "docility" or "obedience" or "vulnerability" or even "openness" marks children's fitness for the kingdom is dangerously misleading and faithless. Nevertheless, with this qualification, we may say that in the life of the church and other of their communities children may learn, and teach in their learning, that we may be companions in joy, reconciled to God, as the creatures we are, in Jesus Christ. It follows from our earlier discussion that this is a calling to see more thoroughly how one may live in one's interdependence as humbly, vigilantly, and hopefully loyal to God.

c. Calling upon God marks a human need that is never satisfied; resting in our need, we can make sense of the idea that the faithful may be "open" to divine grace.

> For the wholly new thing that has come in Jesus is open only to those people who are an adequate match, who are open to it, because they have nothing behind them, because they are not stopped or blocked up against it by any intellectual, moral, aesthetic, or religious a priori that they have brought with them, because they are empty pages.[47]

Young people have a special opportunity for movement into the reality of God's world without the encumbrances of custom, habit, and an established past. Barth refers to this as a "youthful objectivity" that in "fruitful astonishment" may hear God's call removed from any loaded representations that subjectively burden a human subject. One's relative lack of experience removes one from the dangers of being "traditionalistic, sophisticated, relativistic or skeptical. . . . He should have little cause to be seriously disillusioned, to be disappointed or even angry at far too many of his fellows. He should not be the victim of boredom because everything is so familiar. The thought of impotence in face of a blind fate should be far from him." There is a chance to step into freedom "with the serious aim of rivaling the objectivity of those who are older."[48]

---

47. Barth, *The Christian Life*, 81. Cf. Rahner on "openness," in "Ideas," especially 42. The parallels are instructive.

48. Barth, *Church Dogmatics* III/4, 612, 609. Darlene Fozard Weaver alerts us to a danger in approaching this account when she asks, in the face of all those "should's" in the passage above, what we are to say about children whose "youthful objectivity" is damaged? Gilbert Meilaender has raised a related concern with particular reference to the cruelty children can display. I do not at all deny that there is such wounding and such cruelty, and I agree that things need to be said about each that I cannot say in this limited space. I also note that, of course, the proposal here falls to pieces if this special call to youthful objectivity (which in principle applies to all) is made into a *law* that burdens or convicts, or that otherwise obscures or evades the fact that this may be good news, a *gracious* call and opportunity. It cannot be so, to take what is perhaps a

In Harper Lee's *To Kill a Mockingbird,* nine-year-old Dill breaks into tears over the prosecution's cross-examination of the accused Tom Robinson. It is a brutal and cruel line of questioning. Eight-year-old Scout, daughter of defending attorney Atticus Finch, takes Dill out of the courtroom.

> "It was just him I couldn't stand," Dill said.
>
> "Who, Tom?"
>
> "That old Mr. Gilmer doin' him thataway, talking so hateful to him — "
>
> "Dill, that's his job. . . ."
>
> Dill exhaled patiently. "I know all that, Scout. It was the way he said it made me sick, plain sick."
>
> "He's supposed to act that way, Dill, he was cross — "
>
> "He didn't act that way when — "
>
> "Dill, those were his own witnesses."
>
> "Well, Mr. Finch didn't act that way to Mayella and old man Ewell when he cross-examined them. The way that man called him 'boy' all the time and sneered at him, an' looked around at the jury every time he answered — "
>
> "Well, Dill, after all he's just a Negro."
>
> "I don't care one speck. It ain't right, somehow it ain't right to do 'em that way. Hasn't anybody got any business talkin' like that — it just makes me sick."[49]

Dill's response, in striking contrast to the "older and wiser" explanations of the *younger* counselor's child, displays a moral depth unencumbered by racist habits and the experience of customary prosecutorial practices. It clearly is not intrinsically "natural" to or automatic for children. Witness, again, Scout's replies, and add to that how that "evil man," town drunk, and general object of ridicule, Mr. Dolphus Raymond, concurs with Dill. This type of response is an *opportunity* that it makes sense to highlight, given simply the understanding of childhood as an early stage of living. Dill's insight and judgment hardly rule out the importance of an education in fairness and human decency; nevertheless, they get at a kind of freedom or "openness" that childhood may permit, and that persons, at any stage of life, ought never entirely to lose. Atticus Finch knows this, and his pointed remark about Tom's unjust conviction for the rape of Mayella Ewell brings this knowledge to a point: "They've done it before and

---

crude example, if we simply isolate a wounded youngster by telling and expecting him or her (in one way or another) to "just lighten up." It may be so, in contrast, in the case of Maime Trotter's (and, in time, Gilly Hopkins's) regard for the wounded William Ernest Teague. See the discussion of *The Great Gilly Hopkins,* below.

49. Harper Lee, *To Kill a Mockingbird* (New York: Popular Library, 1962), 201-2.

they did it tonight and they'll do it again and when they do it — seems that only children weep."[50]

d. This particular sort of openness is for the sake of becoming a self, and becoming a self calls for awareness that *who one is* may be rooted graciously in projects of fidelity and service that are one's own. "Projects are characterized by some level of ongoing personal commitment"; and as vocations, they are invitations to play a part in God's love that are received as "commissions with which one will be entrusted" and not just "an opportunity to do as one likes."[51] They are constitutive of who we are and ought to be by way of the goods we are called ourselves to love.

A child, then, needs to be aware of worthy projects that are not merely candidates for choice; they are gifts and tasks given to some and perhaps to "me, myself"; for we "learn to be a self by acquiring, and learning to value, the ongoing, self-referential projects of being a person of a certain kind and living a life of a certain kind. And we learn this by being *taught* to value and pursue such projects."[52] Thus a child ought to have teachers and exemplars of integrity who make present the blessings and challenges of a life so gifted and so bound. Atticus Finch is famously such an exemplar in the projects he assumes as attorney, father, neighbor, and citizen. His care for his children addresses them in intimacy and distance both, or with an intimate distance (Scout calls it "courteous detachment") that knows the importance of their reckoning, in their own time, with his own wholeness, in which "he's the same in the courtroom as he is on the public streets," and the same on the public streets as he is in his own home. Interestingly, a proof of Atticus's integrity and its parental power is in his appearing to relinquish it for the sake of Boo Radley; for it is vindicated by Scout's observation that disclosing the truth about his killing Tom Ewell in defense of the Finch children would be "like killing a mockingbird." With that remark and then later from Boo Radley's porch, she proves that she has learned well from her father the meaning of walking around in somebody else's shoes.[53]

Being a self who finally sees others with compassionate respect[54] includes the courage to stand with and for others in its name, even when prospects are dim, and children should learn that, too. They can learn it in surprising and unsuspected ways. In anticipation of his own legal stand with and for Tom Robinson, Atticus tries to teach it to his son Jem, but through the example of mean

---

50. Lee, *To Kill a Mockingbird,* 215.

51. Adams, *Finite and Infinite Goods,* 303-4.

52. Adams, *Finite and Infinite Goods,* 312.

53. Lee, *To Kill a Mockingbird,* 278-82.

54. See Margaret A. Farley, *Compassionate Respect: A Feminist Approach to Medical Ethics and Other Questions* (Mahwah, N.J.: Paulist, 2002).

and miserable Mrs. Dubose's struggle to overcome her morphine addiction. "I wanted you to see something about her — I wanted you to see what real courage is, instead of getting the idea that courage is a man with a gun in his hand. It's when you know you're licked before you begin but you begin anyway and you see it through no matter what. You rarely win, but sometimes you do. Mrs. DuBose won; all ninety-eight pounds of her."[55]

Katherine Paterson's *The Great Gilly Hopkins*, a novel for children, offers a good example of how a youngster's vocation to become a self can incorporate the kind of "engaged, individualizing discernment" that I named the "me, myself." Vulgar and manipulative, eleven-year-old Galadriel Hopkins has spent her life moving from one foster home to another. Having dared to trust the false promises of security that foster parents made when she was very young, she now prides herself on being tough and in control, in order, as it were, to beat her caretakers to the punch. She won't be "had" again, and so she will not be kept. Having been used and disposed of, she is content angrily and self-protectively to use and dispose of others. Gilly makes trouble wherever she goes, and has been in three homes in less than three years. She also harbors a hopeful reverence for her biological mother, who has written Gilly expressing timeless love and wishes for their reunion.

Paterson's novel tells of Gilly's last foster care stop, with the enormous, and enormously loving, Maime Trotter; her shy, sweet, and scarred first-grade foster son, William Ernest Teague; and their blind friend, neighbor, and standing dinner companion, Mr. Randolph. Gilly resists entering into this poor, eccentric, and thoroughly welcoming environment, but finds herself, in spite of herself, taken in by Trotter's fearless and cheerful nurturance of her and William Ernest. But no, the great Gilly Hopkins will *not* be taken in. While playing with William Ernest and cheering on his talent in throwing paper kites, she hears Trotter softly thank her. "For a moment Gilly looked at her, then quickly turned away as a person turns from bright sunlight." Then guiding Mr. Randolph home, she took "care not to look back over her shoulder because the look on Trotter's face was the one Gilly had, in some deep part of her, longed to see all her life, but not from someone like Trotter. That was not part of the plan."[56]

The plan is to leave Trotter in Thompson Park, Maryland, catch a bus, and travel to California to find her mother Courtney. Gilly tries to find her way to the fare by robbing Mr. Randolph, and her failure to get enough money from that source prompts her, enraged, to write a letter to Courtney with a plea to

55. Lee, *To Kill a Mockingbird*, 116.
56. Katherine Paterson, *The Great Gilly Hopkins* (New York: Thomas Y. Crowell Co., 1978), 52.

fetch her from her awful, desperate situation. Later, she is able to filch Trotter's welfare check and heads out, only to be detained by police as she tries to buy a ticket at the station. Trotter retrieves her from the police, and she and William Ernest make it clear to one and all (including the foster care agency) that they will not give her up.

Returning to Thompson Park, Gilly works off her debt with housework and tutoring William Ernest. Needed and wanted, she cares for her gang of three when they all fall ill. But Gilly's scurrilous letter brings her grandmother, at Courtney's request, to Thompson Park. Grandmother wants to take her to her home in Virginia, permanently, and Gilly is horrified. She "never meant to hurt them . . . what had she wanted? A home — but Trotter had tried to give her that. Permanence — Trotter had wanted to give her that as well. No, what she wanted was something Trotter had no power over. To stop being a 'foster child,' the quotation marks dragging the phrase down, almost drowning it. To be real without any quotation marks. To belong and to possess. To be herself, to be the swan, to be the ugly duckling no longer . . . Galadriel Hopkins, come into her own."[57]

Gilly moves to Virginia and, at first "for Trotter's sake," tries to take up life with her grandmother "Nonnie" with patience and compassion. The two of them eagerly await a visit from Courtney; but Gilly discovers within moments of their airport reunion that her mother's trip was exacted by Nonnie's cash, that she has no intention to take her with her, and that she "had thrown away her whole life for a stinking lie." Excusing herself, she calls Trotter. Trotter tells her that as far as the "dream of Courtney" is concerned, "you just fool yourself if you expect good things all the time." Gilly protests, "If life is so bad, how come you're so happy?"

> "Did I say bad? I said it was tough. Nothing to make you happy like doing good on a tough job, now is there?"
> "Trotter, stop preaching at me. I want to come home."
> "You're home, baby. Your grandma is home."
> "I want to be with you and William Ernest and Mr. Randolph."
> "And leave her all alone? Could you do that?"
> "Dammit, Trotter. Don't try to make a stinking Christian out of me."
> "I wouldn't try to make nothing out of you." There was a quiet at the other end of the line. "Me and William Ernest and Mr. Randolph kinda like you the way you are."

Gilly Hopkins returns to her family. "'Sorry to make you wait. . . . I'm ready to go home now.' No clouds of glory, perhaps, but Trotter would be proud."[58]

---

57. Paterson, *The Great Gilly Hopkins*, 124.
58. Paterson, *The Great Gilly Hopkins*, 148.

Gilly read aloud Wordsworth's "Intimations of Immortality from Recollections of Early Childhood" her first evening in Thompson Park, in unison with Mr. Randolph. "But trailing clouds of glory do we come from God, who is our home," and "the music of the words rolled up and burst upon Gilly like waves upon a beach." Later she wondered, "was that God with the huge lap smelling of baby powder? Or was that home?" However we or she might answer that question, it is clear that Maime Trotter's love for Gilly "without any quotation marks" helped give *her, herself,* leave to lose them (any of them — including "Gilly the Great") and go home now. Here a real child is really seen in the real world she inhabits. The child is thus empowered to discover herself her vocation to be herself, bravely and generously, in the "project" of membership in her family ("Trotter would be proud"). No longer disposable and as such trapped in this or that "unity of a collection" of "their" or her own choosing, Gilly Hopkins may come into her own.[59]

4

Being a good son or daughter in the Lord, learning as a needy beginner in attentive inquiry, and "being a child" in youthful objectivity are all ordered to becoming and being a self constituted by projects fit for disciples of Jesus Christ. Recalling the passage from Merton above, we should note that baptism is itself an individualizing act.[60] Caught up in their self-identifying relation with God, children may be themselves as they are summoned to their particular history in hope and reconciliation.

We could see this conclusion as one more instance of lack or absence. The child who is not (yet) a self is called to become one, and just so subject to all *our* ventures on *her* behalf.[61] Adults have to take this possibility with great seriousness. Yet must we view matters in this way? In the first place, if we adults have a vocation that we have lived and served, we may be better able "to keep all sense of ownership out of our love for our children." Then we "can let them develop quietly and away from us, surrounded by the shadows and space that the development of a vocation needs."[62] Second, we can and should apprehend a child's vocation, articulated in these ways, as being now what it always is: an engaged, individualizing discernment of who one is really, in belonging to God, and in

---

59. Cf. Katherine Paterson, "Are You There, God?" *Harvard Divinity Bulletin,* Spring 2005, 50-58.

60. Cf. Gilbert Meilaender, *Letters to Ellen* (Grand Rapids: Eerdmans, 1996), 32.

61. Cf. Adams, *Finite and Infinite Goods,* 312.

62. Ginzburg, *The Little Virtues,* 109-10.

ready movement to one's own selfhood from one's grateful and trusting readiness for it. This movement, we can finally say now if not sooner, marks the eternal dignity of the human creature, "who must become a child . . . who only becomes a sharer in God's interior life in that [one] becomes that child which [one] only begins to be in [one's] own childhood."[63]

63. Rahner, "Ideas," 50.

3. Luck, Obedience, and the Vocation of Childhood

John E. Coons

Only the devil has an answer for our moral difficulties, and he says: "Keep on posing problems, and you will escape the necessity of obedience."

Dietrich Bonhoeffer[1]

The first act of freedom is a moral act par excellence, and, at least implicitly, a religious act, since it can only be realized rightly if it is realized in divine charity. . . .

Jacques Maritain[2]

As a moralist, the late W. C. Fields occasionally lost focus. Still, one insight never failed him; Fields saw that children, even of tender years, could crave power over others and come to deserve moral judgment. He learned this the hard way from his nemesis, Baby Leroy — an urchin ever on the make at the great comedian's expense. In our own time such imperious brats have secured adult allies who would by law annul the natural vulnerability of children, ordaining their "rights" and even their "liberation"; they make Fields's pedophobia seem vaguely prophetic.

Later I suggest why any liberation of Baby Leroy and his tribe that might be executed by civil rights lawyers will remain largely a work of the imagination, typically displacing one adult sovereign with another. For this reason, and others, I incline to the Fields school of pediatric morality; currently it is the ideological underdog, and given my occasional and unregretted encour-

---

1. Deitrich Bonhoeffer, *The Cost of Discipleship* (New York: Macmillan, 1959), 63.

2. Jacques Maritain, *An Introduction to the Basic Problems of Moral Philosophy* (Albany, N.Y.: Magi Books, 1990), 141.

agement of children's rights, it is time that I acknowledge their corresponding responsibility and concede the blessings for family, society, and the child himself that depend upon it. Here I focus upon one prominent aspect of that responsibility, namely, obedience. I will ask what roles the child's free submission to authority plays in achieving the two distinct forms of human good. I conclude that obedience serves the realization of each, but in appropriately different ways.

The distinction I intend between the two goods entails assumptions about human nature that are shared by many but not all. Those who embrace them tend to stand in the tradition of either Aristotle or Judeo-Christianity, or both. I will assume specifically that:

1. an order of truth and correct conduct obtains and is authoritative apart from human will;
2. the human person is not reducible to its contingent material parts but, rather, includes an indestructible self with a specific responsibility respecting the order of truth and correct conduct.

For the steadfast relativist/materialist such premises, together with their moral and theological baggage, will appear to be nonsense, though, perhaps, nonsense with benign practical implications, even for the relativist. The specific significance of these ideas for children depends upon further considerations; and these will constitute the bulk of this chapter, once I have described the two types of human goods.

1. First and Second Good

First Good

Each good has its own form, which I will label respectively "first" and "second." First good is the unique perfection that every rational person either realizes or forgoes in his own self; I will use the conventional term "goodness" as its synonym. This perfectible (and corruptible) "self" I conceive to be an invulnerable and permanent capacity at the core of the person. Early in life the self — this capacity — becomes activated by consciousness of its responsibility toward the order of truth and correct conduct (hereafter called "second good"). This consciousness is the calling or "vocation" of authentic authority that invites the self's free allegiance; the self accepts by setting every *other* resource of the person in search of the specific content of second good. These other resources, intellectual and material, I will shortly label the "persona." First good (or "goodness") is the fruit of a free commitment of the self to seek truth and right practice.

It is, then, the consciousness of the option to obey or flout authority that renders the child fully capable of either goodness, or its opposite, thereby constituting the most consequential form of human freedom. So far as first good is concerned, Baby Leroy has the capacity for a plenary moral life. But, if this be correct, the manner in which this act of obedience to authority actually contributes to goodness is a question both fascinating and controversial; for the innocent child may misjudge the content of second good, or by trusting the wicked (or ignorant) adult, may cooperate in the promotion of error and bad behavior.

Second Good

Occupying the other box in my dichotomy are the endlessly varied examples of what I have just referred to as "second good." This set comprises all moral objects other than first good. It is literally *every human good other than goodness itself*. By a "human" good here, then, I mean any state of affairs that rational persons ought to seek and support because (if recognized and achieved) it would be what is right under the specific circumstances. The individual person might not grasp some specific answer, and therefore on occasion might act incorrectly out of ignorance. Nevertheless, whether he finds it or not, this right answer is the proper object of his free rational nature. Second goods are correct possibilities that the self is responsible to affirm and to seek.

Some instances of second good are realized in the actor himself, some in other individual persons, some in common. All represent outcomes worthy of our effort; by their nature, however, no matter how we try to identify and then realize them, none is guaranteed to occur, nor, if it occurs, to continue. So it is, for example, with our occasional achievements of knowledge, friendship, justice, and all other states and relations that in specific cases carry positive moral content and are the grist of our daily experience. We are obligated by nature (and, if one is a believer, by revelation) to seek to make such goods concrete in this world for ourselves and for others, even though they are elusive and contingent. Some of our contemporaries would sort them into subcategories that they label "basic human goods"[3] — and surely they are that — but I will call all of

---

3. See, e.g., John Finnis, *Natural Law and Natural Rights* (New York: Oxford University Press, 1980), 64-99.

them "second," in order to emphasize the primacy of simple goodness.[4] This distinction in dignity holds, even though the search for second goods is authoritatively commanded and even though, in some subtle manner, that search is implicated in the realization of self-perfection. The priority of first good still follows from (1) the sufficiency of our created capacity to fulfill its condition and (2) its invulnerability so long as one wills to serve truth and correctness. It is goodness alone that stands as a potentially permanent state or prize that can be ours independent of fortune; on both grounds it is prior in dignity.

"Second good" in its many forms is unequally accessible; whether by sheer luck or the effect of earlier choices, individuals acquire very different resources of intellect, wealth, and experience. We wield different sets of tools with which to discover what would be the correct outcome in a certain case and, then, to bring that outcome about; put in negative terms, we bear different burdens of ignorance and impotence. As noted, I label our unique and constantly changing individual packages of ways and means the "persona" (at this very moment you are dealing with mine). As I proceed, I will speak of the *self* and the *persona* as aspects of the whole *person*.[5] It is the self that determines whether or not the persona's activity is directed to the quest for second good.

It is my best judgment that, unlike second good — and from a very early age — access to first good, or the goodness of the self, is the same in kind and degree for every rational human, child or adult, who is capable of recognizing the calling to seek what is right. In this most crucial part of life, luck holds no sway. This is the most controversial part of the claim, depending, as I will show, upon a particular conception of the *manner* in which the self must cooperate in order to achieve its own perfection; in this conception the dramatic differences in the abilities of individual personas to discover correct conduct are irrelevant to the opportunity for personal goodness. It is our effort alone that secures or forfeits first good; this free effort bears the technical name "obtension."[6] I repeat: this claim that obtension suffices is contested. Historically, the competing and more typical interpretation of human access to goodness has emphasized

---

4. John E. Coons, "A Grammar of the Self," *First Things*, January 2003, 37.

5. Coons, "Grammar of the Self," 41-42. Regarding this usage, I risk one suggestive scriptural reference: "What will a man gain by winning the whole world, at the cost of his true self?" (Matt. 9:25, *The New English Bible* [1967]).

6. For the origin of this usage, see John E. Coons and Patrick McKinley Brennan, *By Nature Equal: The Anatomy of a Western Insight* (Princeton: Princeton University Press, 1999), 14. We claim that the sufficiency of obtension for salvation is necessary if human equality is to be taken as fact. I accept factual equality as true. Though it resists demonstration from nature or revelation, it consists with the Creator portrayed in the gospel and tradition; he invites each and all to full communion through the free commitment to seek second good.

these very differences in the acumen of our individual personas. Diverse gifts and experiences produce errors in our beliefs, moral insights, and judgments; and these errors, even when inadvertent, are thought to prevent achievement of *either* form of the good — self-perfection or a rightly ordered world and persona.[7] Because of their insistence upon correct knowledge and intending no disrespect, I call theories of this latter sort "gnostic." The gnostic criterion for goodness obviously bears upon my present inquiry; for children, though equipped to obtend — that is, to will second good — could vary markedly both from adults and from one another in their ability to understand moral rules and to apply them so as to get right answers in particular circumstances.

In the gnostic view it is also relevant that the range of each child's reason changes over time, making his or her ability to achieve either of the two forms of human good an unfolding story. At successive age levels moral theories of this sort have tended to stop the film and declare — with Aristotle and Aquinas[8] — that, here, or maybe there, begins the child's capacity to recognize correct answers and, thus by choice, to realize the good in both its forms. Taking snapshots of a young life at intervals in this manner has been a useful analytic device for moralists and theologians; but it has been most portentous — even ominous — when directed to the ultimate question: How are we to think about the child who dies or permanently loses rationality at some particular stage of his or her story? Is there a set of moral-theological terms that allows a nonsentimental assessment of a child's access to self-perfection? And is this opportunity of the child anything less than that enjoyed by adults?

This puzzle has long worried all but the most relentless materialists. Any mind that is open to hope of an afterlife is left uneasy by the thought that — whatever may be the dead child's state — the poor thing had so little to say about it. Unless we are John Calvin, this unease about responsibility sets us scrambling for a fallback position that can assure at least a minimally happy state for the lost child; and here, many Christians can take consolation from baptism.[9] Still, one cannot but feel anxious about those millions who die, not only unbaptized, but also too young for us to imagine even their "baptism by desire." We worry, too, about the fate of that older child who in life had seemed

---

7. Coons and Brennan, *By Nature Equal,* 78-84.

8. Christina L. H. Traina, "A Person in the Making: Thomas Aquinas on Children and Childhood," in *The Child in Christian Thought,* ed. Marcia J. Bunge (Grand Rapids: Eerdmans, 2001), 103. This is a very useful account of Thomas's recasting of the Aristotelian framework in Christian terms, including his taxonomy of the child's progressive stages of rationality (beginning roughly at age seven) and his equally well known speculation about Limbo.

9. On the interpretation of baptism I warmly recommend the chapter in this book by Fr. Anthony Kelly, C.Ss.R.

still uncommitted to responsibility and, perhaps, unconcerned for the good of others. I would never scoff at fears for dead children, and my own answer leaves room for anxiety.

C. S. Lewis was properly tortured by questions like these, addressing them in a romantic fashion in his novel *The Great Divorce*.[10] Lewis supposed that, after death, all of us pass through a sort of parentheses in which even those who were prerational (or postrational) at the moment of death are empowered freely to say yes or no to what is God's final invitation. Lewis's flight of fancy represents his — and, I fear, my own — deep concern to maintain the goodness of God by confirming the liberty of every man. Since it is not credible that God be arbitrary, theodicy must provide all of us — including children — the opportunity for real guilt and real goodness.

I will not here attempt such postmortem rescues; nor do I address the mystery of the status of the child prior to his consciousness of duty to seek the content of an authoritative order of truths and goods. However, like Lewis, I do suppose that human freedom is the critical element in the child's relation to that order. This raises the familiar "Pelagian" threat. Here, without argument, is my position on that issue: divine omnipotence can create beings who are free to say no or yes to God's invitation. To reject this as a possibility would constrain God's own liberty. The question about an efficacious human will thus is not whether its creation would be within the divine power; it is rather an issue of fact about how that power has been exercised. The evidence, including revelation, allows us to disagree without in any way challenging God. I would not stand with Pelagius,[11] but I do assert my belief in a real human agency that God fashions and maintains in each of us; he seems to prefer that we compose our own RSVPs to his eternal invitation. This is what he wants, and he gets it.

This problem about human freedom is certainly not confined to children. However, it becomes most strongly focused when posed for those young beings whose consciousness has only recently experienced responsibility. I take that experience to be prior in time to the grasp of the correctness of particular behaviors. The awakening child finds himself invited — ordered, if you prefer — to cooperate in an enterprise whose content he cannot possibly imagine but whose reality and authority are unmistakable. While still unable to grasp the

10. C. S. Lewis, *The Great Divorce* (New York: Macmillan, 1946). In principle, postmortem probation could extend to children snuffed at the embryonic moment. It is one of many solutions rejected by R. A. Webb, whose own answer is a Calvinist tour de force. God allows only elected children to die before the experience of responsibility; hence all are saved. R. A. Webb, *The Theology of Infant Salvation* (Richmond, Va.: Presbyterian Committee of Publication, 1907).

11. John Ferguson, *Pelagius: A Historical and Theological Study* (Cambridge: Heffer and Sons, 1956), gives the old heretic a rounded treatment.

terms of specific duty, the child is aware of the possibility of good and of a personal obligation toward it. Here is the opportunity for what I will call "primary obedience." The expression identifies the child's free choice to cooperate with this nonspecific "vocation"[12] — this consciousness of a general state of responsibility. The child's affirmation of authority coupled with his or her readiness for specification of duty, satisfies the condition of the self's highest possibility; at the same time, this commitment — this act of primary obedience — sets the child on the quest for second good in that other sphere of life that is affected by contingency. Later I will identify other and more mundane forms of obedience that function in that world of second good, forms that help the child to discover and realize the specific correct outcomes that he or she has already willed to seek.

2. The Pious Predator

All these species of obedience — primary and the rest — are illustrated in a cunning way by what I consider one of the finest short pieces in the moral theology of childhood. It is Phyllis McGinley's "The Giveaway."[13]

> Saint Bridget was
> A problem child.
> Although a lass
> Demure and mild,
> And one who strove
> To please her dad,
> Saint Bridget drove
> The family mad.
> For here's the fault in Bridget lay:
> She *would* give everything away.
> To any soul Whose luck was out
> She'd give her bowl
> Of stirabout;
> She'd give her shawl,

---

12. "Vocation" is variously used, as is deftly affirmed in William Werpehowski's contribution to this volume. I confine the term to the constant consciousness of obligation to seek the specification and actualization of second good. This sounds Kantian, but any serious pedigree would require more elaboration; my chief aim here is to be clear.

13. Phyllis McGinley, "The Giveaway," in *Love Letters of Phyllis McGinley* (New York: Viking Press, 1954), 50-52.

Divide her purse
With one or all.
And what was worse,
When she ran out of things to give
She'd borrow from a relative.
Her father's gold
Her grandsire's dinner,
She'd hand to cold
And hungry sinner;
Give wine, give meat,
No matter whose;
Take from her feet
The very shoes,
And when her shoes had gone to others,
Fetch forth her sister's and her mother's.
She could not quit.
She had to share;
Gave bit by bit
The silverware,
The barnyard geese,
The parlor rug,
Her little niece-
'S christening mug,
Even her bed to those in want,
And then the mattress of her aunt.
An easy touch
For poor and lowly,
She gave so much
And grew so holy
That when she died
Of years and fame,
The countryside
Put on her name,
And still the isles of Erin fidget
With generous girls named Bride or Bridget.
Well, one must love her.
Nonetheless,
In thinking of her Givingness,
There's no denial She must have been
A sort of trial

To her kin.
The moral, too, seems rather quaint
Who had the patience of a saint,
From evidence presented here?
Saint Bridget? Or her near and dear?

Saint Bridget seems the embodiment — or, better perhaps, the ensoulment — of my problem. To realize her own understanding of correct behavior, Bridget committed several apparent wrongs. These giveaways of others' property seem both a material mistake about the content of second good and a violation of two prominent commandments from the Decalogue. And what was the sequel of all this theft and disobedience? Bridget was canonized.

3. Gnostic Niceties

If that outcome seems to threaten contradiction, the worry may be credited in considerable part to the deep and continuing influence in Christian, certainly in Catholic, moral philosophy of what I have already called gnostic versions of natural law. Their relevant common themes often are traced to Aquinas and ultimately to Aristotle; their concept of the good bears on our assessment of Bridget's bungles. For convenience I will focus upon one of this school's distinguished contemporary representatives, John Finnis of Oxford and Notre Dame.[14]

Like their Greek and medieval predecessors, Finnis and company profess a version of first good, or personal goodness, which is strongly "intellectualist" — sufficiently so to justify my label "gnostic." Goodness is for them, first of all, an affair of right reason. In the gnostic's interpretation of Bridget's enterprises, there is no way that she could improve the state of her own self while ignorantly performing these well-intended acts of larceny.[15] True, a certain material form

14. Finnis's fellow travelers include Joseph Boyle, Germain Grisez, and Robert George, to all of whom I am indebted but wanting in space to do justice to their corporate treasury of scholarship.

15. Note well that in certain cases of ignorance the actor may be *excused* without *improving* his own moral state. See Coons and Brennan, *By Nature Equal,* 195-97. So could it be with children. Finnis does not focus upon the specific effect of being excused. Nor is this my subject, except to observe that the distinction I would draw between self and persona would probably entail separate interpretations of the function of excuse. That is, if perfection of the self depends only upon best effort, the concept of excuse is, for that purpose, redundant or even tautological. By contrast, in respect to the effect of mistake upon the persona, excuse might be understood to preserve some important innocence in the contingent elements of the blundering seeker of the good.

of *second* good would have been accomplished; for the poor, after all, did get fed.[16] But the circumstances — including her own noble ends — failed to justify the means; these things were not hers to give. Bridget has done what are unreasoned and incorrect deeds, and to that extent her goodness is compromised. If she, nonetheless, is good, this can be true only in spite of it all. In his later book, *Aquinas,* Finnis asserts that such acts of misconduct "are essentially self-determining — i.e. internal to and constitutive of an individual's character."[17] But if her acts are "self-determining," Bridget remains at best a paradox of good and evil. She is simultaneously a corruption and a very holy person.

The gnostic version of our moral nature clearly has strong implications concerning authority and obedience. The act of obedience *in itself* can never be effectual in advancing the goodness of a child or anyone else. If Bridget resolves from this day to follow the insights of her mother and father, she remains unsafe; not only may they be wrong in particular cases, but it is she whose reason must, in any case, be correct, and as yet she may have none of her own that she can trust. Finnis here allows Aquinas to speak for the gnostic tradition about children: "Before they reach the age of reason . . . children cannot make free choices . . . and when one does reach it, one is immediately confronted with the rational necessity of deliberating."[18]

In fairness, Finnis does as well with this moral conundrum as can anyone who is committed to these plausible and traditional premises. But here the gnostic settlement pinches and binds, and especially as it disposes of children. Cannot the dignity both of reason and of second good be honored without making correctness a condition of first good — of personal goodness? They can, and sometimes have. Specifically, that view can be found in, or at least teased from,

---

16. My assumption that her acts were unjustified is, of course, an interpretation of the poet's meaning, hence vulnerable but heuristic.

17. John Finnis, *Aquinas* (New York: Oxford University Press, 1998), 41. If the injury to the character of the blunderer is automatic, it is hard to grasp the benign aspect of being "excused." See McGinley, "The Giveaway." Note that, in effect, the gnostic view collapses the distinction between first and second good. Goodness ceases to be a separate and unique quality of the self; instead the self takes on the moral impress of whichever second goods happen to get accomplished or are left undone by the persona. I think we are allowed to hope that one day natural law theory will find coherence in its embrace of the two basic distinctions: that is, between self and persona and between first and second goods. At present it continues to merge these discrete elements of the moral person in ever more complex forms of gnosis. See, e.g., Darlene Fozard Weaver, "Taking Sin Seriously," *Journal of Religious Ethics* 31 (2003).

18. Finnis, *Aquinas,* 41 n. 68. For my part, on the role of free will I could leave it as summarized by Joseph Flanagan. "Our identity as choosers subsumes . . . our identity as knowers." *The Quest for Self Knowledge: An Essay in Lonergan's Philosophy* (Toronto: University of Toronto Press, 1997), 9-10.

other moral masters — some of them natural lawyers, some not. I think here of Maritain,[19] Barth,[20] Lonergan,[21] Liguori,[22] Balthasar,[23] and of course, Phyllis McGinley directly or indirectly — they and perhaps their churches[24] support the insight that earlier I adopted as my own, namely, that rational persons are so constituted by nature that they achieve each form of human good in its own distinctive way. The first form — goodness — comes to the person independently of correct works actually realized. It is the effect simply of commitment by the self to *the quest* for those same correct works; thus, it flourishes irrespective of all the errors that are made unavoidable by the feeble state of our personas. Bridget, in her ignorance, did bad deeds — acts that did not and could not make her a

19. See the introductory quote, which is from his *An Introduction to the Basic Problems of Moral Philosophy*. I thank Patrick Brennan for spotting this passage and add that he (Brennan) finds Maritain equivocal on the point.

20. Barth is extremely difficult to locate on the underlying question of freedom and election. But the forty-five pages of his essay "Parents and Children" are consistent with a responsibility for obedience by the child under the commandment, an obedience that seems disconnected from correct outcomes hence free of gnostic baggage. "[T]he nerve of the whole is always this willingness to learn. This is the honour which is required of children in relation to their parents." Barth, of course, stresses throughout that the primary obedience is to God alone. *Church Dogmatics* III/4 (Edinburgh: T. & T. Clark, 1961), 245.

21. The reference is to Bernard Lonergan, S.J.; Brennan and I do some of the necessary teasing of his work in our "Created Equal: Lonergan Explains Jefferson," in *Lonergan Workshop*, vol. 12, ed. Fred Lawrence (Chestnut Hill, Mass.: Boston College Press, 1996), 45-76.

22. For Saint Alphonsus Liguori (1698-1787), it is precisely in seeking the good that any person acts from reason and thereby "probably acquires merit" in spite of honest errors. He "ought to be meritorious on account of the good end by which he acts." *Theologia Moralis* 1.1.6, in *Liguori Opero*, vol. 5 (Turin: Marietti, 1846), 2.

23. Hans Urs von Balthasar, *Dare We Hope "That All Men Be Saved"?* (San Francisco: Ignatius, 1988).

24. See part III: "Could the Christians Believe in Human Equality?" in Coons and Brennan, *By Nature Equal*, 145-215. Summarizing roughly, we see many a difficulty among traditional Calvinist confessions in their official theology but — at the same time — probable acceptance among their lay adherents. Catholics seem comfortable with the antignostic view both in the pulpit and the pew. The Koran's strong focus on correct acts gives Islam a resolutely gnostic air, and there is no obvious clue to a different implication in the case of children; but here I would play the obedient child and accept correction. See John E. Coons, "Good Selves and Just Wars," *Notre Dame Journal of Law Ethics and Public Policy* 19 (2005): 71-90. Belief in many of its forms could invite analogy between (1) the relation of first to second good and (2) the relation of faith to works. Faith becomes salvific in its free acceptance, which entails a dedication to rectitude; goodness emerges in the self's free commitment to its calling to seek second good. The analogy could at first seem limited; not all are offered the gift of faith, while all receive the vocation to seek. But if full salvific effect attaches to a positive answer to either invitation, the practical difference would be narrowed; it would consist in the specifically religious duties incumbent upon the believer.

good person. What, nevertheless, did make her so was her earnest *pursuit* of good deeds, using whatever reason and experience were hers.

4. The "Obtending" Reasoner

Note well that, even in this nongnostic view, reason remains both relevant and necessary. Just as the gnostics insist, Bridget's salvific commitment cannot be a pure act of the will, for there is no such thing. Commitment is by its nature a response to the cognition of something, in this case of an insistent message of obligation with which we are all wired. Commitment is an act based upon knowledge. What Bridget knew — and all she needed to know — was that she had been invited to embark upon her personal search for second good. She had received a calling. She could have answered no, but in fact she answered yes and promptly began her benevolent campaign, which is where and when her behavioral blunders began. These errors made hash of the contingent order of "basic human goods," but the intelligent choice that preceded them had already made a saint of her.

Bridget's commitment honored a sufficient reason that was itself the experience of real obligation. It is this specific cognitive experience that moved Patrick Brennan and me occasionally to adopt the strange English word "obtension" to identify Bridget's choice to seek — her response to vocation. The *Oxford English Dictionary* defines the verb to obtend as "to act for a reason."[25] And so has it been for all of us adult humans, just as for Bridget. At the threshold of our rational life we encountered the insistent and permanent fact of responsibility. It was a form of knowledge, and we all faced the free necessity of giving it a conscious response.

Finnis might ask, "How can obligation arise from . . . just one more fact?" But, in this case of the awakened self, it happens to be the unique fact of an inescapable invitation (or command). This message is itself the content of the experience of obligation. Now, Finnis properly dreads the "naturalistic fallacy," but here, I think, he can safely drop his guard. In the case of human actors, the point is not to prove responsibility from some other fact — incautiously to infer an ought from an is. For the experience of responsibility is itself the fact. No inference of an ought is necessary, for, in this case, the is happens to be an ought.[26]

---

25. Coons and Brennan, *By Nature Equal*, 88-89. The *Oxford English Dictionary* seems to imply that the obtender acts for a reason he supposes to be justifying of the action. The most vivid example: "Origenes . . . did gelde hymselfe . . . for the obtente and will of chastity."

26. See Finnis, "The Illicit Inference from Facts to Norms," in *Natural Law and Natural Rights*, 33-48. So far as I know, psychology has never attempted empirical assessment of the

And the specific imperative that merges in the self is this: to seek the content of second good. *To seek it.* That is our vocation — and the whole of it. Which means that we have the opportunity to canonize not only infants and amnesiacs but also all those feeblest of minds who know only this most elementary of calls. I could not possibly be certain, but I do conclude — with some support from modern psychology — that children experience something like this vocation at a very early age.[27] In their otherwise indeterminate world of what must seem weird and shifting images, they grasp at least this: there is truth and there is correct conduct that one day I might be able to recognize and honor, and I am called right now to look for them. Shall I say yes or no to this vocation? As the child considers her choice, the better of these two possible responses is not self-evident (nor shall it ever be). For the vocation comes with the insight that there will be costs in either answer; to seek second good is to surrender so many other alluring possibilities. And so the self-perfecting yes, when and if it comes, does so as a responsible act, initiating the child's free dedication to the quest — a mission that in the ideal case remains uninterrupted for a lifetime.

5. Primary and Secondary Obedience

Now, back to my theme. If one believes all this, two distinct roles for childhood obedience become reasonably clear. The first is simply the child's embrace of this duty that is borne by every human of the most marginal rationality — the duty to commit to the search with whatever resources lodge in his or her persona. In this radical obtension or commitment — in this act of "primary obedience" — the child chooses to do the best he or she can for second good. This elemental and nonspecific vocation of the moral tenderfoot can be understood as natural, as religious, or, for my part, as both (though I confess that the idea of a purely natural calling is for me elusive for want of any caller with authority to

---

claim that moral consciousness originates in all children independently of environment. That inquiry would be challenging — but in theory possible — and far closer to authentic science than visions drawn post hoc from psychoanalysis of middle-age patients or the needs of radical evolutionary theory.

27. In any case, most children appear conscious of their condition of responsibility long before reaching traditional versions of the "age of reason." I note that the encyclical *Deus Caritas Est* refers to the human consciousness of vocation in terms (and in tone) that might encourage empirical inquiry into the initial appearance of consciousness of an obligation to seek as a phenomenon. For example, "the command of love of neighbor is inscribed by the Creator in man's very nature." Pope Benedict XVI, *Deus Caritas Est,* pt. 2, no. 31 (2005).

bind). Primary obedience, then, is the necessary and sufficient condition of the child's first good; it is, if you prefer, his or her first act of cooperation with grace.

But, if we accept this piece of very good news, it is not the end to the practical question about obedience, even in respect of first good. For, any child who offers primary obedience — who truly wills the quest for second good — must now proceed in practice to do his or her best to discover and realize it. And, if we return with this in mind to reassess young Bridget, we discover her in a rather awkward mode. Assuming that she has made the fateful act of primary obedience, this now drives her to seek correct conduct; but just how does an obtending child proceed in this world of which she knows so little?

Here — up to a point — we can join forces with the gnostic. The child, obviously, must seek the path of correctness by engaging her reason to consult whatever knowledge of human affairs is already available in her own persona. But, among the things she knows is the fact that she is only a beginner on this voyage of discovery and her resources are thin. Their weakness makes it her first practical task to seek the experience and information that might disclose the right answer to whatever moral question next faces her. Here reason itself insists that she look for the best older navigators available and follow their authority so long as her own ignorance persists. This submission to a specific adult or elder child is distinct in kind from her prior act of primary obedience to ultimate authority. It is obedience of an expedient and very practical form that addresses specific moral cases. For convenience I will call it "secondary" or "artless" obedience. It is the act of a pilgrim who puts confidence in a more experienced and discerning fellow human; one thinks of Dante and Virgil.

Finnis is reluctant to bless this prudential submission of one's judgment to that of another; for him any use of the minds of others is merely instrumental and, in the end, must issue in a reasoned and independent judgment by the actor himself. One must reach an autonomous conclusion that *this specific act* is the very one that is required or justified by reason.[28] I think that the case of young children really puts this idea to the test. For the beginner, this pure and pragmatic obedience to a particular adult may in specific cases be the *only* act of reason that is available. The child's intellectual resource consists in whatever experience justifies his or her trust in the other's mind. Given the vacuum of personal insight, the child's submission to the elder's view is an artless, but not a blind, obedience. It is an act founded upon the reasonable consideration that

---

28. On this aspect of Finnis's work I am indebted to James V. Schall, "On the Most Mysterious of the Virtues: The Political and Philosophical Meaning of Obedience in St. Thomas, Rousseau and Yves Simon," *Gregorianum* 79, no. 4 (1998): 755-56.

the judgment of this other is better in this particular matter than is my own. Just which substitute decider represents the ideal locus of authority for the individual child is a question that I will address in due course. To no one's surprise, except in extraordinary circumstances, it will turn out to be the parent.

Of course, roles can be reversed; even the younger child will sometimes see some specific correct answer that eludes the parent. I would not argue that the child's duty in such a case would be satisfied by a purely passive obedience that abandons reason. The child cannot in good conscience elude or shift responsibility by retreat to a comforting self-delusion of vicarious correctness (though this must be a sore temptation in cases of conflict). This problem of the child who faces an erring adult authority deserves more reflection than I can manage. For the moment I take practical refuge in an analogy to the way presumptions are used in the law. Acting as a reasonable person, the child should accord the parental judgment a rebuttable presumption of correctness. Its strength should correlate inversely with the child's age and experience (plus the parents' track record) and eventually shrink to an honorific deference; its basic justification correspondingly shifts over time from the child's relative intellectual imperfection to an ultimately symbolic role of the parents as "ambassadors" of the good.[29]

6. Holy Innocents?

To this point I have said only a little about the "Religions of the Book" and the various confessional views of the issue. The question of the goodness — and the salvation — of the child is, of course, a matter of historic theological conflict that I am competent to penetrate only so far. After several millennia, the main issues seem to remain unsettled. There is, however, for our edification, a contemporary religious literature about children that increasingly seeks its conceptual anchor in philosophy as well as revelation. Various fine essays in Marcia Bunge's collection, *The Child in Christian Thought,* are a good illustration;[30] and *Theology Today* has recently published a number of insightful articles displaying a range of interpretations of childhood.[31]

I find this literature elevating in spirit but analytically wanting on my specific question. Indeed, as a whole it seems almost to shy away from any serious

29. Karl Barth would have them "ambassadors of God." *Church Dogmatics* III/4, 256.

30. See generally Bunge, *The Child in Christian Thought.*

31. The January 2000 issue comprises a dozen essays, many quite useful. I especially recommend as an enthusiastic counter to my own conclusion here about the role of government schools, John Wall's "Animals and Innocents," *Theology Today* 59, no. 4 (2003).

apology for obedience. Few modern writers want to make company with what they take to be classic interpretations of childhood; some of these traditions have portrayed the child as a locus of evil who becomes only a bit less obnoxious when obedient. Michael Wigglesworth and even Augustine are definitely passé.[32] Today, instead, in terms drawn from Mark and Matthew, children are typically portrayed as exemplars of the kingdom of heaven. They have become not the absence of moral perfection but its one clear example. Perhaps we adults should be obeying them. It is easy to see how Christians tease this tender attitude out of the New Testament. And, of course, the apparent natural humility of most children is a thing well worth imitating; it suggests their uncorrupted intuition of an ineradicable human hope.

This contemporary vision of childhood innocence and excellence needs to make its analytic encounter with the more traditional constructions.[33] The infatuation with simplicity does not by itself rescue any child from the effect of moral errors arising either out of sheer ignorance or from mistakes of some authority whom the child artlessly obeys. If one happens to share the gnostic view that honest errors in belief and conduct stand in the way of the child's self-perfection, the mere rejection of Wigglesworth will be insufficient.

Happily, as I have argued, there is help available to spare us the gnostic conclusion. The alternative interpretation of goodness as the fruit of the act of primary obedience (obtension) could interest modern theologians of childhood. To be sure, this leaves a three-stage model of childhood consisting of (1) a prerational period followed now by (2) a stage of conscious responsibility to make the effort to think and choose and (3) a time of ripened "reason"; but at least the possibility of self-perfection comes much earlier in time. The barest awareness of responsibility empowers the child to commit to the search. At the same time, for the child, just as for any minimally rational adult, this responsibility to think and to seek implies freedom and thus the possibility that the child will reject the vocation. In short, responsibility al-

---

32. See virtually all the essays in Bunge, *The Child in Christian Thought;* see especially Mary Ann Hinsdale, "'Infinite Openness to the Infinite': Karl Rahner's Contribution to Modern Catholic Thought on the Child," 406. Rahner's own "Ideas for a Theology of Childhood," in *Theological Investigations,* vol. 8, trans. David Bourke (London: Darton, Longman and Todd, 1971), amounts to a celebration of the mystery of childhood that delicately (and typically) skirts the question here. My own take on Mark 10:14 would be this: Jesus made *these* children the type "of the kingdom of heaven" because they *chose* to come to him. Suffer them, he told the disciples; allow them to do what they willed to do. These children were answering a vocation. Were there others who turned away? We don't know.

33. Contributors Fr. William Harmless, S.J., and Fr. Anthony Kelly, C.Ss.R., give a rich account of the dense background of the soteriological questions referenced here.

ways introduces the possibility of tragedy. Children must be free to corrupt themselves in what is the primal act of *dis*obedience. One remembers Baby Leroy's despotic moments.

7. Rescue Declined

In the present climate of religious opinion, such a view of childhood responsibility may appear a bit upstream. This impression could be tempered by recalling that, in respect of his or her access to first good, the child who is invited does not differ in opportunity from the sophisticated adult. Each has plenary capacity for the gift of goodness. Each has been given the same commission: do your best with whatever tools you have been given. This capacity of the self to commit is unvarying in degree. Like an on/off switch, it is binary; one can say yes or no in the primary act of obedience that constitutes our calling and our access to goodness.

What could vary in degree is not the capacity to obtend, but individual effort. A person's commitment to seek the good may be carried out with varying degrees of devotion, hence of goodness. Among good people, some may be better than others, because they try harder. The diversity of our personas — our individual gifts and burdens — probably does make the exercise of "best effort" a thing different in many respects from person to person. But effort can properly be conceived as the activation by the self of some *proportion* of that sum of gifts, whatever that sum may be in the individual case. And so would I understand it. Now, just who is exercising which proportion of his or her gifts is a thing opaque to all but God. Constantly we are tempted to judge goodness, perhaps because we have to make practical decisions based upon our experience of individuals. But neither the reality nor the degree of anyone's goodness is transparent, and perhaps least of all in our observation of moral beginners. Baby Leroy himself must remain a mystery.

This obtensional view of childhood leaves the fate of the preresponsible child still unexplained. I see no reason to doubt that the child's first consciousness of the responsibility to seek the good is a postnatal event. But what, then, if anything, have we gained by taking the obtensional turn? At least this: the act of primary obedience becomes recognized as fully consequential for the achievement of first good. Though the child does not yet see the correct way, his obedience is the endorsement of the hope to find it. It is this act of cooperation with grace and nature that perfects the self; it constitutes the free human moment in the miracle of justification. And at some point very early in life the child shares this dignity in fullest measure.

8. Secondary Obedience

The focus now shifts from first to second good. This plenary capacity of the child for goodness may have implications, benign or otherwise, for that other world consisting of true ideas and right conduct. These implications deserve their separate accounting, and I turn now to consider the significance that the obtensional view of childhood and primary obedience might hold for the role of the child in society, the family, and civic life. At the start here I reemphasize that the very act of primary obedience wills the perfection of this contingent world (including the child's own persona); in the language of economics, we should "maximize" second good. Even though these trail in the order of dignity, the fundamental imperative for all of us is to seek them here and now. Thy will be done on earth.[34]

Primary obedience thus commits us to secondary obedience — i.e., to human authority — to the extent that (on the evidence available) this deference will enhance correct outcomes. Finnis is perfectly right; free submission to another's judgment is not a good in itself. It is merely an instrument. As I have already suggested, this is nowhere more obvious than in the artless submission of children to adult direction. As Yves Simon well observed, children are the archetype of that peculiar form of obedience in which authority is necessary as a *substitute* for the judgment of one whose own judgment is *deficient*.[35] Substitutional authority may be temporary or permanent, depending upon the nature of the deficiency in the subject person. In the case of the child, the deficiency ordinarily is temporary, and it is the role of the adult authority to hasten its disappearance; maturity ends the occasion for artless obedience (though not necessarily for obedience justified on other practical grounds).

If secondary obedience is directly instrumental for second good, it is reflexively so for the self-perfection (first good) of the child. It fulfills the terms of the invitation to seek. To be completely specific, the regime of substitutional adult authority and artless obedience by the child has three objects: (1) to reaffirm for the child the reality and authority of the order of second good that the child is invited to seek as a condition of goodness; (2) to reaffirm the child's fundamental responsibility or vocation to seek it; and (3) to identify the specific content of truth and correct conduct for the child when occasions of obedience arise in the practical order. The adult authority reinforces the general imperative of primary obedience while giving specific content to the immedi-

34. I read the Lord's Prayer as (1) a submission to the divine will, but also (2) our embrace of the vocation to cooperate by seeking an optimal moral state of contingent reality.

35. Yves R. Simon, *Philosophy of Democratic Government* (Chicago: University of Chicago Press, 1951), 7-19; *A General Theory of Authority* (Notre Dame, Ind.: University of Notre Dame Press, 1962), 133-34.

ate objects of artless or secondary obedience. What is common to the child and adult in this regime is the hope to serve both first and second good.

9. Practice: The Parent as Prevalent Authority

All these abstractions eventually take practical forms; in daily life one evident and consequential example is the framework of civil law as it recognizes and supports those adult authorities who substitute for the child's own judgment. The parent's general authority is conceded, but distinctive limited species of authority over the child are recognized in government. One of these provides legal guarantees of *minimums* such as education and medical care; the other forbids *abuse.* Taken together, these familiar regimes constitute a system of child welfare. Little Rodney shall be inoculated and sent to a licensed school for 180 days a year; he shall not be physically abused. This authority to intervene is narrow in principle and — with one exception — in practice. The de facto exception is the school system that conscripts children of ordinary and low-income families for education by the government. Otherwise, the legal norms of child welfare are few in number and modest in reach.

Indeed, apart from schools, all but last-ditch authority over children lies in their parents. For better or worse — outside the government's narrow authority to rescue — the parent makes the rules for the child and enforces his or her will in ways and for purposes about which the state is not entitled even to express an opinion. Thus, Bridget, you shall be in bed by nine; you shall not play with Marcia; and you shall attend this church service and say your prayers. Virtually every act of the child, from nutrition to worship, is subject in theory, and typically in fact, to the mandate or veto of the parent. Quite literally, the father and/ or mother will govern this young person. The power of the state itself may be enlisted as an instrument to support the authority of these millions of unique family dominions. Absent severe abuse, the sheriff will return the runaway to confront his brussels sprouts, to mow the lawn, and to attend his parents' church at their command.

Here, then, is the great practical domain of childhood obedience — the family. Yet, this fundamental authority to ordain the content of childhood could have been centered elsewhere, as Plato and Rousseau advised. This is a possibility that still lures at least a few of our contemporaries. Some of these would completely decommission parents;[36] children, they say, ought to be lib-

---

36. See, e.g., James Dwyer, "Parents' Religion and Children's Welfare: Debunking the Doctrine of Parents' Rights," *California Law Review* 82 (1994): 1371, 1375. Meira Levinson adopts

erated altogether from adult sovereignty and either left to their own devices or allowed to enjoy the parent as their indentured servant. Meanwhile, at an equally ambitious but opposite pole of reform, their opponents plausibly observe that the child will in any case be dominated by some adult, the only question being which one;[37] critics of this latter sort tend to be professionals who remind us that the law might wisely commission them to replace the parent. If some adult will in fact be running the show, it is best that it be someone competent. These professionals at least get the question right, namely, who is the best decider for this individual child? Would it be better for Rodney and Bridget to live under the dominion of their parents or under that of the Department of Children's Welfare?

Justifying the radical authority that historically and currently has been recognized to lie in the parents is no great task, at least for basic day-to-day choices.[38] Here the best interest of the child ordinarily is served by a comprehensive domestic dominion — and this for at least three reasons. First, it is the parent who *knows* the child (including the child's own view of things). A professional may have superior knowledge regarding some specific need or gift of Bridget's, but (as with lawyers or engineers) at decision time the expert should act as auxiliary to the clients. The ideal is to infuse the more intimate (if amateur) insight of the parent with the information of the professional. Second, it is parents who *care* for the child in a manner unique to the relation. Not always, but generally, this attachment helps assure that the decision will be made for the child's own sake and not to serve someone else's ideal of policy. Third, and most important, it is the parent who is *accountable* for errors in the use of authority; it is she who will suffer if the child turns out to be a disordered and dependent adult. Accountability makes for better decisions. I suppose I should add here a fourth reason; the parent is cheap labor, and no society could afford a comprehensive regime of child professionals.

Dwyer's replacement of right with "privilege" in her *The Demands of Liberal Education* (New York: Oxford University Press, 1999), 50, passim; see also 183 n. 35. I have no objection to the general idea of treating children instead of parents as the focus. But the ultimate gesture of respect for children is to recognize not merely their *rights* but also their *responsibility* — and then ask where authority over them is to be located. For some big person will inevitably have it.

37. Bruce Fuller and Richard Elmore, eds., *Who Chooses? Who Loses?* (New York: Teachers College Press, 1996). The book gives voice to a collection of educators generally devoted to keeping things in the hands of the professionals — at least for children from families too poor to escape by moving or paying tuition.

38. See John E. Coons, "Law and the Sovereigns of Childhood," *Phi Delta Kappan,* September 1976; John E. Coons and Stephen Sugarman, *Education by Choice* (Berkeley: University of California Press, 1978).

But if the presumptive parental authority well serves the child's own "best interest," it seems at first to be coupled only very loosely to the child's moral quest for second good and, even more importantly, for goodness. Assume that Bridget's original act of primary obedience has put her in search of the particular adult authority that will best teach her a specific set of authentic duties. Is her mother really up to this? Bridget is willing at her mother's direction to eat the spinach, but where in all this is the moral beef? How good is mother at leading me beyond mere health and security into the more challenging quest for truth and correct behavior that affects not only my selfish interest but my virtue and the common good? As Plato and the political sages of every age remind us, obedience is a question for the society as well as the child. In some manner, we — the collective — must seek a harmony between the terms of a real common good and those versions of it that gain acceptance in the minds of obtending individuals like Bridget and her mother.

10. Enter Luck

What are these versions of truth and correct behavior that are delivered to the individual child? They are legion. Children get born to adults who have rather different ideas about the good; and it is the ideas of particular parents that the child will hear. Call this providence; call it luck.

Nor are the differences among parents confined to the virtues of spinach. In diverse ways they identify for the child the roles that are correct for men and for women; the proper relation of humans to the natural aspects of their environment; the meaning and uses of our sexual powers; the significance of law; respect for life; assisted suicide; war and peace; contemplation versus striving; the duty to vote; attitudes and obligations toward the poor; lying for specific reasons; tax evasion; the authority of teachers; the value of book learning; the dignity of work; the idea and authority of God; claims about primary obedience; and the proper treatment of animals. On all these issues parents give explicit or implicit answers; among other things they say yes, no, maybe, I don't know, it doesn't matter, or ask your father.

Where does this jungle of contraries leave the rationale for parental sovereignty? Is there anything positive to be said for our historic regime of secondary obedience in a world where parents enforce the belief and practice of contradictory and often simply wrong ideas? The answer is a resounding yes. Even in an incoherent moral environment, obedience to parents is efficacious to both first and second good. But this takes a bit of seeing.

11. Luck and First Good Reconciled

With regard to first good — the child's own self-perfection or goodness — the principal justification for the historic parental authority is this: the spectacular diversity of parental worldviews paradoxically presupposes a universality that holds at the deepest level of moral conviction. That is, virtually all parents plainly share the imperative to pass these peculiar private convictions to their own children; whatever they believe they would transmit in ways effective or ineffective.[39] They acknowledge a real order of second goods that their child is obliged both to seek and attempt to realize. Few mothers indoctrinate their infants in theories of moral anarchy. And the father who plays the moral skeptic for his buddies at work rediscovers the rule of virtue whenever he enters the nursery. The office of parent reconfirms every child's experience of his or her own responsibility to the authority of a real order of correct behavior.[40] There is a good; here are its specific contents; believe it; do it. And, by contrast, outside the home this elemental ratification of the child's basic vocation to a real good is nowhere guaranteed.

Observe, however, that while the parents' affirmation of responsibility may encourage the child's own goodness, in respect to second good it is problematic and, again, paradoxical. For, by its very nature, this shared imperative of parents to indoctrinate their own children tends to preserve the overall riot of human opinion and belief. And this could be consequential for the common good. For, as my litany of differences was intended to show, parental convictions can conflict on matters of great moral and social significance.

12. Luck, Common Good, and Uncommon Curriculums

Plato warned us of the social threat posed by parental pluralism. He would have addressed it by relocating authority in professional guardians who would determine the specific beliefs and conduct for which children's obedience would be the important instrument. This policy retains its allure for certain confident Americans who discern those correct ideas we must all accept in order to be a true community. In our own time, techniques of per-

39. See John E. Coons, "The Religious Rights of Children," in *Religious Human Rights in Global Perspective: Religious Perspectives*, ed. John Witte, Jr., and Johan van der Vyver (The Hague: Martinus Nijhoff, 1996), 157.

40. Consider here Matt. 7:11: "You, evil as you are, know well enough how to give your children what is good for them." Trans. R. Knox (New York: Sheed and Ward, 1944). Among the possible constructions of this passage is that in my text.

suasion and organization that were unavailable to the Greeks have encouraged these intellectual descendants of Plato to hope for better luck at imposing uniformity.

To that end they have made the shared civics curriculum a central justification for a school system that is the Platonic exception to the rule of parents — at least for the lives of have-not families. In the face of parental discord, the common message of our public schools provides America its social glue. Obedience of lower-class children to the disparate values of their parents is the social problem; the constant message of the public schools is the solution.[41] Should we credit this broad challenge to the regime of parental authority?

First of all, I take this picture of intellectual accord among government teachers to be a claim of fact; and their curriculum is indeed common to the following extent: all government schools aim to teach the three Rs, math, science, computers, and obedience to positive law. Those students who actually master the ideas should wind up knowing roughly the same things about these specific subjects that consist mostly of uncontroversial skills taught also in every *non*government school.[42]

By contrast, the "civic" part of the curriculums of public schools is anything but common. It's rather a great patchwork of ideological retreats, each dominated by adults who are at least as fractious as the parents. They address children's minds in various ways as textbook writers, school board members, union leaders, administrators, or simply as teachers who rule within very private domains. The subject may be gay marriage, evolution, economics, abortion, marijuana, ethnic cultures, affirmative action, condoms, witchcraft, or vegetarianism; and the take on each issue will vary from teacher to teacher. Scholars as diverse as Rosemary Salomone,[43] Katherine Simon,[44] Christopher

---

41. See, e.g., Richard D. Kahlenberg, *All Together Now* (Washington, D.C.: Brookings Institution Press, 2001).

42. No doubt the Amish secondary system of education could be deemed an exception. See *Wisconsin v. Yoder*, 406 US 205 (1972); Michael S. Ariens and Robert A. Destro, *Religious Liberty in a Pluralist Society* (Durham, N.C.: Carolina Academic Press, 2002). Regarding legal "uniformity" of curriculum requirements, see 434-38.

43. Rosemary C. Salomone, *Visions of Schooling: Conscience, Community, and Common Education* (New Haven: Yale University Press, 2000). The current celebrations of "multicultural" pedagogy are earnest both of the fashion and the curricular fact.

44. "[T]eachers, like parents, regularly share with students what they see as indisputable wisdom and guidance with regard to moral and existential issues. And when sharing wisdom, they do not typically present 'the other side.'" Katherine G. Simon, *Moral Questions in the Classroom* (New Haven: Yale University Press, 2001), 192.

Barnes,[45] and Kenneth Karst[46] have confirmed the reality of this great smorgasbord. Among these moral pedagogies of our public schools the only one that might claim to be the mode is that of avoidance; many an educator ducks all civic questions. Who needs controversy?

Of course, the more primary and eternal question for the civics educator concerns the authoritative *source* (if any) of every human duty. Is a child in fact subject to any responsibility that precedes and transcends society and which itself makes citizenship an authentic calling? It is not clear under prevailing law that government schools are entitled to get serious about such a question.[47] In any case, on all these basic civic issues, by definition there can be no public answer, for that would require an American consensus, and there is none. There are only private answers that are delivered by teachers — whether these teachers hold forth in government or private schools.

13. Babel, Obedience, and the Suburbs

But if government teaching on civic subjects is such a Tower of Babel, is that so bad? I have not yet said so, and my answer is — not necessarily. So far, I have meant to be critical only of the public school masquerade of a common curriculum; for it is a thing that, in our present state, simply cannot be. Hence, I see nothing intrinsically wrong in the fact that diverse teachers do the best they can to transmit their own private versions of truth in the marketplace of ideas. Just as it is with parents, what else can these teachers give but what they think they know?

But recall that my subject is obedience and its place in the child's vocation. Now, it is not the children who choose these teachers; thus, what we seem to witness in government schools in America are very provincial regimes of authority in which adult strangers promote their parochial philosophies simply because the state has given them the opportunity to do so. Viewing the resulting hodgepodge, we are bound to ask — by what justification? One might defend a common curriculum democratically derived. But what argument could support this intellectual litter.

I can think of one, but it requires a premise: let us suppose that these petty

45. Christopher Barnes, "What Do Teachers Teach? A Survey of America's Fourth and Eighth Grade Teachers," *Civic Report* 28 (New York: Center for Civic Innovation, 2003).

46. Kenneth Karst, "Law, Cultural Conflict, and the Socialization of Children," *California Law Review* 91 (2003): 967.

47. There may somewhere be a public school course on the philosophy of Aristotle, but woe to the teacher who would "baptize" him with Scholastic refinements.

intellectual sovereignties were not in fact imposed by chance assignment but, rather, were freely chosen by parents; suppose, that is, that these variant educations were all on offer in a functioning market. Insofar as that were true, the regime of secondary obedience of the child to the parent would be intact. And in many cases in America this is the social reality: many parents are able to make choices of schools that tolerably reproduce their own regimes of obedience. These parents rule because they can afford to. They exercise their "freedom" (their authority over the child) by buying a home in Beverly Hills or by paying tuition at St. Mary's or College Prep. Their chosen school — public or private — is not merely, as lawyers say, *in loco parentis*. It is the very embodiment of the parental will concerning the moral regimen of the child. The school is their agent.

14. Eluding the Curriculum Lottery

The five-year-old of the middle class understands that this new thing they call school is just another expression of my parents' authority. It confirms the established order, teaching me the content of second good. I will attend to its voice as to the word of my father and mother.

The parent who decided for this same middle-class kindergartner has consciously exercised at least two distinct, if related, functions. The first, borrowing from Yves Simon, is the parental *substitution* for the *deficient* judgment and experience of the young person; the parent is the proxy for the child's untutored will, working toward an eventual state of autonomy that will include access to this parent's version of correct ideas.

This parent also carries out a second function of authority and obedience that is quite distinct. It is one that Simon identifies as a general justification for government itself, but which by analogy also explains the regime of the family. Simon specifies what he calls authority's "essential" function in establishing law and government.[48] Essential authority is that of the decision maker who is empowered to decide questions that competent and equal — but conflicted — people need to have settled. This same legitimating function must be served in that other lawlike system that is the family. When there is division among its members regarding alternative paths, decisions must nevertheless be made for the common good. Parents hold the authority to make them, and this continues even when the children have reached an age where they have their own distinctive and plausible views of what is the best course. On some issues this

48. Yves R. Simon, *General Theory of Authority*, 23-80.

group of people needs a corporate answer, or it ceases to be a family — which, for various reasons, it is important for it to be.

Both of these functions — the substitutional and the essential — are served when middle-class parents exercise authority to choose the school. They affirm their version of correct ideas, and, at the same time, preserve family integrity. It is not at all surprising that middle-class parents put such stock in their own authority and are willing to bear substantial burdens, both financial and personal, to exercise it effectively.

15. Losing the Curriculum Lottery

The very young child from the poor or working family also tends at first to see his or her parent as an authority figure — and much in the manner of the middle class. The parent is protector, teacher, and advocate, mediating every challenge and change in the child's environment. The child knows where the parent stands, and the parent governs.[49] Furthermore, this authority is the very glue of the family; in Simon's terms, it is the essential vehicle of decision for all those cases needing a decision for the collective good.

This application of Simon's insight to the family invites a second borrowing, this time from James Coleman, who compared the effects of Catholic, private, and public schools that enroll children from various social backgrounds.[50] My application of his conclusion will be a bit of an extension; his own focus was more upon the school and less upon the authority that selected the school. Coleman concluded that, for children from low-income families, the Catholic schools were the most successful, an outcome he attributed to a school's capacity to build "social capital." Later studies have confirmed this claim.[51] What I strongly suspect is that, while choice does generate a fair harvest of social capital in the school, an even greater bounty is experienced within the family itself; it is embodied in the child and in the parent who has managed to make the school an instrument of her authority. The critical mass of cooperating humans that became a particular Catholic school was assembled by specific acts of

---

49. The authority reserved to the family can be variously understood. It can, for example, be seen as an independent system of law in the sense of law that is common to American lawyers — it makes and enforces rules. It is a jurisprudential reality that lacks nothing but a literature. And that may come.

50. The relevant works of James S. Coleman and those scholars who later secured the ground he took are all cited and vetted in Joseph P. Viteritti, *Choosing Equality* (Washington, D.C.: Brookings Institution Press, 1999).

51. Viteritti, *Choosing Equality.*

parental responsibility — personal choices made among moral options. Such commitments do tend to make any school cohesive and effective, just as the champions of school choice claim. But in the final social calculus, that may be the lesser of their contributions.

In a freely chosen relationship, the family and the school obviously influence each other, and that is all to the good; but the real payoff here could consist in the confirmation of the family as the locus of childhood authority. It is precisely in this act of self-affirmation through choice that parents generate the derivative authority of the school, making it ready to serve them in the values to be taught — and to serve the child in his or her impulse to obey. Studies of the psychosocial effects of school assignment have to date neglected this relationship between these distinctive authorities, a relation that looms more ultimate — and, I fear, even more ominous — than the spectacle of the schools separately considered.[52] If our nation is at risk, the danger may lie less in the academic failure of particular schools than in the baneful effect of the system of assignment upon the ordinary family. How does the social capital of the family itself fare where the parent is unable to choose?[53]

Start with the perspective of the child within such a family. One September morning, she discovers herself at P.S. 27. She may at first mistake the school as mother's own choice; and mother may for a time encourage this impression. Inevitably, however, it dawns on the child that this was a decision made by no one at all. Worse, even if she would, the child's mother could do nothing about it; the child is here by the judgment of no human mind, and she will be so for the prime hours of the week for the next thirteen years.

The child soon grasps that her understanding of the idea of family was wrong; parents really are quite undependable as authorities and advocates. And the school has impeached not only their power but their judgment. Your mother, says the state, does not know best. What reason has our kindergartner now to credit the judgment of this adult whose ideas count for so little in the eyes of the world? I am not here suggesting that any child (or even any adult)

52. See my review of *The Education Gap*, by W. Howell and P. Peterson, *Education Next*, Fall 2002, 84.

53. That our systems of school assignment might corrupt the family that lacks choice is a rare theme among academics. Education writers have preferred to assume the opposite course of causation at least since Coleman reported that family and class greatly affect school performance. *Equality of Educational Opportunity* (Washington, D.C.: U.S. Government Printing Office, 1966). This intellectual habit may be traceable to the "Moynihan Report," *The Negro Family: The Case for National Action* (Washington, D.C.: U.S. Government Printing Office, 1965). Today even Bill Cosby seems unable to perceive that the school itself can be the efficient agent of the very social mischief by which it claims exoneration.

ever ceases to experience the responsibility to search for the right way — to give primary obedience and to keep on looking. This is a given in our nature. But she may well cease to check the content of second good with that specific adult who, until now, has been its only consistent cheerleader.

The child's teacher cannot become her substitute authority. Teachers are soon gone, and in any case, they must fail for all the reasons that prevent government schools — at least in this society — from delivering a coherent account of either first or second good. There can be no government version of either the practical content of the good life or even of a source of the responsibility to seek it. Nevertheless, with family now decommissioned, the child may well transfer her emotional allegiance to the school and its culture; in that event she may cease to know intelligible authority altogether. The American school can function morally as servant, but as master, it can be nothing but arbitrary.

But if the child is threatened with moral anomie, consider the plight of the parent. School people sometimes picture ordinary parents as feckless, uncaring nincompoops who will not stir themselves to help their child. Since it is the educator who has stripped parents of their authority, this comes as a nice piece of irony. Still, I cannot assert that ordinary parents are today in fact responsible. In respect of school, they cannot be; they have been rendered irresponsible by definition. They have nothing to say, and they are quite sensible to save their breath. Sadly, what they cannot save is their self-respect. They watch the middle class carefully planning every move for their children with the approval and collusion of the state and the free market; and they grasp all too well where have-not parents like themselves stand in this society. No message could be more poisonous. If mothers and fathers are passive to the point of pathology, it may be that we reap what the schools have sown.

The solution obviously is not to fix some one right answer to be imposed exclusively upon the poor — an answer that this society does not and could not possess. It is, rather, to respect and empower the ordinary parent as we have the parent of the middle class. And please notice. I have said nothing about raising test scores; nor shall I. The point here is not one of technical mastery. It is, rather, the soul of the child and, simultaneously, of the nation. America's practical support for the authority of ordinary parents and the obedience of their children would be a crucial affirmation of the dignity of families, and a positive and healing statement from this society, a bit of good news preached to the poor.

Would the poor respond with choices that intensify racial and religious hatred? Is that what empowerment does to people? My own experience is the opposite. People who are trusted tend to return that trust. A policy of parental choice would give parents and their distinctive schools every incentive to participate as equals in the unending social and moral debate. No longer forced to stand silent — compelled to be "tolerant" in the face of error — they would be invited authentically to tolerate the erring *person* and to offer him the compliment of a good argument. That is the constitutive meaning of a system of subsided parental authority — respect for persons and strong challenge among competing views of the world.

My friend the gnostic might have preferred a more uniform and compulsory school policy. For that, however, he would need a world in which more of us see the same correct answers. Meanwhile, perhaps, he can hope for the sort of transformed pluralism in which, for the first time, children of all social classes would experience the conventional rule of the parent, because that authority has finally been extended in a practical way over the school. This most truly civic response to pluralism would secure to every five-year-old the dignity of a free and saving obedience to the one coherent authority that a young child can know. It is the parent alone whose judgments can simultaneously affirm both our moral diversity and the universality of the child's responsibility to seek what is true and good.

Resketch

In common with adult actors, the child who is yet unable to discover what is specifically correct may nevertheless recognize the authoritative vocation to seek correctness. This choice (or "obtension") by the moral beginner to seek the right way is the very act of cooperation with grace and nature that issues in the self's own goodness; it merits the name "primary obedience." For believers primary obedience is owed to the Creator and fulfills the condition of his invitation to permanent loving union. The experience of vocation is thus consequential and may significantly precede the traditional "age of reason."

Goodness aims to achieve correctness in chosen action. For children the search for the right way entails a free subjection to some guiding human authority; ordinarily this "substitute" authority is the parent to whom is owed a respectful, if ultimately conditional, "secondary obedience." With rare exceptions for abuse this broad parental office is a universal principle of human ordering. Its salience becomes accentuated in a social context of moral pluralism; absent consensus, it is not merely wrong but incoherent to displace the authoritative teaching parent with functionaries of civil government.

4. The Office of Child in the Christian Faith: A Theology of Childhood

Vigen Guroian

Most of the chapters in this volume employ "vocation" in the traditional religious sense. "Vocation," thus understood, has to do with how God "calls" or "invites" even children to his work of salvation in this world, and includes them in the redeeming life of the church. Instead of speaking of the "vocation of the child," I prefer the "office of child." Omission of the article "the" emphasizes the objective character of an office. An office does not *belong* to someone. Rather it is a *station* into which a person is "placed" or "called." The office of child does not belong to any particular child, but all children hold that office because they are children.

William Werpehowski astutely observes that "'vocation' indicates not just 'generic' responsibilities, as if they can and do apply to 'anyone' of the People of God." Rather, "particular persons are called, and their specific callings reflect their particularity, including the limits and opportunities they discover in and around themselves under God's ruling grace."[1] This "subjective" and individualistic connotation of vocation is precisely what I wish to avoid. At the risk of overgeneralization, it may be said that the theological meaning of vocation is mainly a legacy of the Protestant Reformation, although Luther, who had one foot in the disappearing medieval world and another in the emergent modern world, was perfectly comfortable with the language of office as well as vocation.

Our meaning and use of "office" come from classical sources, such as Aristotle, Cicero, and Plutarch, as that passed through patristic and medieval Christian thought. This tradition still makes a claim upon us, for example, when we insist on distinguishing between the office of president and the person in that office. The Latin roots of "office" connote duty, work, and task. At base is the

---

1. William Werpehowski, "In Search of Real Children," in the present volume, 54.

word *officium.* It denotes performance of a task. *Officium* is the compound of *opus,* signifying "work," and *ficiere,* "to make" or "to do."

Historically, within both religious and secular realms, "office" also signifies a relationship with and responsibility toward others within a community. Because the child assumes his or her office by embracing the role of son or daughter, the office of child is presumptively related to the office of parent within the matrix of marriage and family. The essence of being a child is to act responsibly toward one's parents, family, and the larger community. In other words, the offices of child and of parent are reciprocal and inextricably related to one another. Each, however, has its own peculiar set of virtues. Trust, humility, and obedience belong especially to the office of child, whereas the virtues of the office of parent are presence, authority, and loving care.[2] Within the Christian faith, the life of Jesus Christ in his relationship to God the Father is the supreme example of the faithful performance of the office of child.

As one can surmise from the subtitle of this chapter, my interest and aim here reach well beyond the etymologies of "office" and "vocation." I want to explore the way "office" functions within a complete theology of childhood. Ironically, at this moment when churches lament the weakening of marriage and the family, they have very little of substance to say about the child, and the language of "office" has all but disappeared. Very often theologians, pastors, and religious educators simply adopt and adapt models of the child and childhood from the modern disciplines of psychology and sociology. But these models are insufficient or misleading. They do not penetrate the deep theological and even salvific significance that the Christian tradition has ascribed to childhood. They may even deny that significance.

The presence of children in the church doesn't just call out the responsibility of passing on the faith to them; children also are emblematic of what kind of a person a Christian needs to become to inherit the kingdom of heaven. Childhood is a harbinger of our eternal destiny; one might even go so far as to say a prophecy of it.

Having set down these preliminary observations, the remainder of this chapter breaks into three sections. The first is a short discussion of the theological meanings of childhood and the office of child. There follows a review and criticism of two contemporary views of childhood, the developmental (and

---

2. The virtues of the office of child are out of favor in our day. For instance, some feminists, like the philosopher Nietzsche, reject them as signs of weakness. They equate trust, humility, and obedience with servility or self-hatred. This is one important reason why it is so important for Christian theology to reclaim the office of child. While it is not the burden of this chapter to prove these critics wrong, I hope that the positive value of these virtues of the office of child will be evident.

stage) theory of childhood and the (postmodernist) social constructionist pro-posal. A serious Christian theology of childhood must, in my view, wrestle with these two competing models. In the last section of this chapter, I develop at some length the theological moorings of a Christian theology of childhood. I then turn, in particular, to the Christian sacrament of baptism as a source for that theology.

On the Meaning of Child

The meaning of child is not limited to the small or immature human individual, just as the tenure of the office of child does not terminate at puberty, or when a young man or woman leaves home and parents to live independently. Even at the age of sixty, I am the child, the son, of my father Armen Guroian and my mother Grace Guroian, and I strive to exercise responsible sonship in my relationship with them.

Of course, it goes without saying that it is in small children we find the essential elements of "childhood." Likewise, it is fair to say that the first office in the community that a human being holds is the office of child. Ancient strains of Christian spirituality make much of the fact that God in Christ stooped to be small, to be a child. Saint Ambrose of Milan wrote that the Divine Word, the Only Begotten Son of the Father, "was a baby and a child, so that you may be a perfect human."[3] John Saward recovers this theology of the birth and child-hood of Jesus in his book *The Way of the Lamb: The Spirit of Childhood and the End of the Age.* In the womb of his Mother Mary, he writes, "the Son took the way of childhood into the world, and thus united Himself to every child." He need not have done so. "He could have created for Himself, as He did for Adam, a human nature in adult form."[4] Saint John Chrysostom, writing in the fourth century, reminds us that it was "[t]o prevent you from thinking that his coming to earth was merely an accommodation, and to give you solid grounds for truly believing that his [Christ] was real flesh, [that] he was conceived, born and nurtured."[5]

Insofar as the second person of the Holy Trinity assumed our humanity completely and grew as we grow from embryo to adult, God has revealed some-

---

3. Saint Ambrose of Milan, *Luke, Ancient Christian Commentary on Scripture,* vol. 3, ed. Arthur A. Just, Jr. (Downers Grove, Ill.: InterVarsity, 2003), 38.

4. John Saward, *The Way of the Lamb: The Spirit of Childhood and the End of the Age* (San Francisco: Ignatius, 1999), 68-69.

5. Saint John Chrysostom, *Luke, Ancient Christian Commentary,* vol. 3, ed. Arthur A. Just, Jr. (Downers Grove, Ill.: InterVarsity, 2003), 39.

thing special about the economy of salvation. Ironically, in order that we "grow" into godlikeness we need to grow into what Saint Paul calls "perfect manhood," according to "the measure of the stature of the fullness of Christ,"[6] the virtues that are normally associated with the child: humility, simplicity, unaffected love, trust, and obedience. Christ exercised these virtues through the whole of his life. Unfortunately a consequence of the fall and the sin within our bodies is that we shed these gifts of natural childhood as we age.

Yet humankind is not bereft of hope; for through the sacrament of baptism God offers every human being the opportunity for a second birth into innocence and the grace to grow young again in his own image, Christ's image.[7] Saint Augustine says, "They went [into the baptismal font] as old men [and] they came out as infants."[8] Nerses Shnorhali, the great twelfth-century Armenian bishop and saint, articulates the paradox and the mystery of divine youth in his long poem *Jesus, the Son:* "Thou [Jesus] didst enter the temple to be presented; And thou, the Ancient of Days (Dan. 7:13), the aged man [Simeon] took thee up as a child in his saintly arms. I who was born in sin from vice, Thou didst create me anew at the font."[9] As I have mentioned above, we will return to this role of baptism later.

Developmental Child Psychology and the Postmodernist Critique

Today, two types of theories of the child contend for attention and acceptance. The first is developmental and stage theory of the child. The second is postmodernist social constructionist theory. The former issues principally from the field of psychology and the latter from sociology. These contending theories demand special consideration and discussion at the start. A Christian theology of childhood can embrace neither theory in its entirety, but it can accept something of each.

The writings of Jean Piaget and Lawrence Kohlberg, and their followers, are representative of the developmental model of the child. The reigning premise of developmental theory is that there are natural stages of moral development through which a normal and healthy human individual passes from infancy through adulthood. Kohlberg argued that individuals must progress through these stages one at a time: they cannot "jump" stages, though they can

6. Eph. 4:13 NKJV.
7. Col. 1:15 NKJV.
8. Saward, *Way of the Lamb,* 62.
9. Nerses Shnorhali, *Jesus, the Son,* trans. Mischa Kudian (London: Mashtots Press, 1986), 36-37.

regress. The model is, in this sense, "deterministic." It is based in a theory of a fixed human nature that develops according to a natural law. The goal is autonomous or independent moral conscience. The progression is not automatic, however. Progress through the various stages of moral development (six for Kohlberg) is not "inevitable." Human beings need social interaction to develop as moral beings. They require experience that is educative in the broadest sense, experience that challenges them to move ahead from one stage to the next. Children need to be challenged with dilemmas that prompt them to move on to the higher stages of moral development toward mature moral autonomy.

Against the developmental and stage model of childhood, postmodernist sociology advances a theory of childhood as social construct. This theory accuses developmental psychology of two baneful errors, a deterministic naturalism and philosophical essentialism. As we have seen in Kohlberg's case, developmental theory defines childhood as a natural and determinate stage (or series of stages) on the way to "becoming" a complete human being. Chris Jenks, a representative of the postmodernist school, argues that we should not think of childhood as a set of predetermined natural (or biological) stages of growth and maturation along a continuum from irrational premoral immaturity to adulthood reason and moral autonomy. "[P]hysical [or mental] morphology," Jenks maintains, "may constitute a form of difference between people in certain circumstances but it is not an adequately intelligible basis for the relationship between the adult and the child."[10] Indeed, this sort of naturalism and determinism diminishes the humanity of children. Rather, we must regard and treat children as "being" genuine human agents, not just becoming so.[11]

With respect to the essentialist error, the postmodernists argue that childhood "is neither a *natural* nor a *universal* feature of human groups but appears as a specific structural component of many societies."[12] "[T]he child is brought into being through the dominant modes of speech that exist [in a society] concerning age, dependency, development or the family."[13] Childhood is not "a single or universal phenomenon,"[14] but is, rather, diverse phenomena. "[T]here is no essential child [but many childhoods] . . . built up through constitutive practices, in either a strong or a weak sense."[15] There are no universally valid criteria for judging the moral status of the child. There is no "essential" child.

---

10. Chris Jenks, *Childhood* (London: Routledge, 2005), 6.

11. Jenks, *Childhood*, 8-9.

12. Jenks, *Childhood*, 50.

13. Allison James, Chris Jenks, and Alan Prout, *Theorizing Childhood* (New York: Teachers College Press, 1998), 213.

14. Jenks, *Childhood*, 51.

15. James, Jenks, and Prout, *Theorizing Childhood*, 212.

In sum, according to the postmodernists, childhood is "a social construct . . . [that] makes reference to a social status delineated by boundaries that vary through time and from society to society."[16] It is a linguistic-cultural invention that reflects the interests of the adult world and varies according to cultural setting. Developmental child psychology is merely one of these linguistic-cultural inventions.

The Christian Alternative to Developmental Theory

Christian theology must reject the social construct thesis of the postmodernist school. But it can agree with the postmodernists that developmental psychology devalues childhood. That is to say, when one views childhood principally as a stage (or stages) in a natural course of human maturation, the child is indeed reduced to an epiphenomenon on the way to becoming a morally autonomous adult.

The contemporary theologian Stanley Hauerwas criticizes moral development theory in just this way. "The problem [with which] . . . moral development" ultimately concerns itself, Hauerwas writes, "is how to reach the last stage of morality where moral growth ceases"[17] and moral autonomy is gained. By this view, childhood once left behind is of little significance as just "a pre- or non-moral stage of [human] development."[18] Much like the tadpole that metamorphoses into a frog, the importance of childhood is reduced solely to a function of the superior end toward which it invariably moves.

Growth Is Not Perfection

Instead of the tadpole and frog analogy, a better analogy for the child is the young oak sapling that grows into a mature tree and leaves lasting rings in the trunk. Jesus exhorts his listeners to emulate "childlikeness" and make the "childlike" virtues of trust, humility, and obedience their own — not to leave them behind; though he in no way suggests that every child possesses these virtues in exemplary fashion.

The great nineteenth-century English divine John Henry Newman drew

---

16. Jenks, *Childhood*, 6.

17. Stanley Hauerwas, *A Community of Character* (Notre Dame, Ind.: University of Notre Dame Press, 1981), 133.

18. Hauerwas, *A Community of Character*, 133.

from this gospel record to elaborate upon the eternal value of childhood. Newman held up for special attention the simplicity, innocence, artlessness in loving, and openness to mystery and spiritual reality that is found in children. But he added that children, nonetheless, lack "formed principle in [their heart(s)], . . . habits of obedience, . . . [and] true discrimination between the visible and the unseen, such as God promises to reward for Christ's sake, in those who come to years of discretion."[19] In other words, in children these virtues are not yet the perfections of the kingdom of God. "A child's innocence has no share in this higher blessedness. He is but a type of what is at length to be fulfilled in him. . . . What we were when children, is a blessed intimation, given for our comfort, of what God will make of us, if we surrender our hearts to the guidance of His Holy Spirit, — a prophecy of good to come, — a foretaste of what will be fulfilled in heaven,"[20] says Newman.

Despite the fact that children lack self-control and discipline, their status and station have inherent value, however. According to Newman, we may forgive children their lack of consistency in virtuous behavior precisely because they are young and inexperienced, while we remain open to what they can teach us about what we need to become in order to inherit the kingdom of God.

As with all figures of speech, even the oak sapling metaphor is limited. It does not suffice for a complete and accurate understanding of childhood. The oak sapling must *necessarily* become an oak tree with a *particular* shape and type of foliage. Personal life, however, is indeterminate and pluripotential, transcending mere biological growth.

Stage and developmental theory maintains that a determinate process of growth from infancy to youth and adulthood issues in freedom and autonomy when the individual reaches the age of reason. This theory does not, indeed it cannot, resolve this prima facie contradiction. How can a determinate process lead to freedom? Developmental psychology does not comprehend fully the self-transcendent (spiritual) nature of personal existence that even children possess.

Once again we are reminded of the limitations of the analogy of the oak tree. The metaphor of growth that we take from nature simply cannot comprehend the Christian doctrines of radical freedom, sin, and conversion. Sin is no mere failure in the system, such as when a disease shortens the height or distorts the shape of a tree. A sin is a creation that the self wills into being, although it contradicts the good to the agent and the will of God. "Conversion denotes the necessity of a turning that is so fundamental that the self is placed

19. John Henry Newman, "The Mind of Little Children," in *Parochial Sermons and Plain Sermons* (San Francisco: Ignatius, 1997), 267.
20. Newman, "Mind of Little Children," 268.

on a path of growth for which there is no end,"[21] Hauerwas writes. This "growth" is unlike any growing process known in nature, however; for this "growth" transcends necessity. Perfection is its end: the "growth" is self-directed. It is freedom enacted away from sin and toward God.

Freedom, so understood, explodes the determinacy of developmental theory. It certainly does not originate from a determinate process. That is why, says Hauerwas, the translation of the Christian language of perfection into the language of development is a great misfortune. It robs perfection of its religious and transcendent significance.[22] Christian perfection is sanctification (*theosis* or deification in the language of my own Eastern Christian tradition), a self-directed, self-enacted movement toward divine similitude. Holiness, not merely moral conscience, is the earmark of human maturity and perfection. What is more, there is no point along the way of perfection that is inferior to that which comes after it. There is no stage along the way that is mere necessity either.

The Lesson of Child Saints

Christian faith draws important lessons from those it names saints — for our purposes, especially, child saints and martyrs — as exemplars of the radical indeterminacy of human existence. The saints leap across psychological boundaries and growth-stage markers. Take for example Saint Peter Chrysologus's fifth-century sermon on Saint Matthew's account (Matt. 2:16) of Herod's slaughter of the children of Bethlehem. Chrysologus writes:

> He [Christ] gave to them [the children who were slaughtered] the gift of the crown even before their bodies had grown. It was Christ's will that they pass over vice for virtue, attain heaven before earth and share in the divine life immediately.[23]

The Christian church reckons these Holy Innocents as the first martyrs for Christ. Much theology and spirituality has been developed around this belief. We cannot review this here. But we can take a quick look at three main elements of this Christian theology of the child saint that Chrysologos deploys. First, the slaughtered children gained the crowns of holiness even before "their bodies had grown." Spirit transcends nature. Holiness does not follow nature; it

21. Hauerwas, *A Community of Character*, 131.
22. Hauerwas, *A Community of Character*, 130.
23. Saint Peter Chrysologus, *Matthew 1–13*, Ancient Christian Commentary, vol. 1a, ed. Manlio Simonetti (Downers Grove, Ill.: InterVarsity, 2001), 34.

is a "gift" of God. Second, "it was Christ's will that they pass over vice for virtue." Virtue, too, is a gift and not merely an achievement of human conscience or the fruit of biological maturation. Third, they "attain[ed] heaven before earth." The end or telos of human existence is not natural; it is spiritual. Spiritual "maturity" is something quite different from biological or psychological maturity. We may experience heaven on earth. Perfection and beatitude are not the result of living a full natural life, as the purple of the grape is the result of ripening a full season. Rather, human freedom is at play. Who we are and what we may become do not depend solely upon natural processes. Even human freedom does not wholly explain human perfection. For divine will and grace surpass and may even bypass nature and history.

The Shortcomings of Postmodernist Social Constructionism

Developmental psychology swings the pendulum much too far toward the pole of naturalism and determinism. Postmodernism points this out. The theory of social construction, however, swings the pendulum to the opposite pole of a radical historicism and cultural relativism. It affirms human freedom; but this is not a transcendental freedom. This is not freedom oriented to a spiritual end, such as the *imago Dei*.

Furthermore, social constructionism rejects the epistemological and ontological realism of the Christian tradition.[24] As I have suggested already, it rejects the notion of the "essential child." This would not be so troublesome if all that was meant by this denial is that, as an exercise in *thought*, we ought not to abstract the child from time and context. But social constructionism insists on more than that. Just as there is no essential child, so too there is no universal human nature.

At this juncture social constructionism and Christianity completely part company. The Christian faith affirms the existence of universal human nature, although it certainly does not, as postmodernists often claim, embrace this as a naked metaphysical proposition. Rather, Christianity grounds its doctrine of a universal human nature in the central Christian dogma of the incarnation. God in Jesus Christ assumed our "flesh," our whole humanity. The divine Word became a human child and his childhood is, if for no other reason than this, universally significant for humankind. The childhood of the incarnate Word predicates a universal human nature as well as a spiritual end for human existence. Following the logic of the postmodernist position, however, even if one were to

24. James, Jenks, and Prout, *Theorizing Childhood*, 17-19.

grant for argument's sake that God actually did become a human child in ancient Palestine, it is not possible that that event could have an ontological, let alone a salvific, bearing in all times and places.

Having set down these criticisms of the developmental and social constructionist models, we are now in position to discuss the distinctive features of a Christian theology of childhood, including the role of the office of child in a broad Christian vision of human nature and destiny.

A Christian Theology of Childhood

Childhood and Parenthood: What Has Sex Got to Do with It?

Sexuality does not belong to divine life, but it most certainly belongs to human existence. The Son is begotten of the Father in perfect freedom and spiritual love, whereas human procreation, parenthood, and childhood derive from both natural determinacy and sexual love. There is no such thing as pure instinct in the human being. Human eros is no mere sexual urge. It includes spirit, freedom, and choice. We cannot explain or account for human parental and filial love solely on the basis of animal sexual drive or a motherly or fatherly instinct to care for the child. We may say that human fathers sire their young and that mothers give birth to them. But being sired and being born do not alone make a child, or a son or daughter. Siring and giving birth alone do not make a father or mother, either.

That extraordinary Victorian writer George MacDonald asks in *Unspoken Sermons:* "Was Jesus ever less divine than God?" His answer is: "Never!"[25] But if this is so, adds MacDonald, then childhood must always have belonged to divine Being. The Word became flesh at a particular moment in time; he grew from an infant into a man over a span of years. Nevertheless, the Word is eternally begotten of the Father; the Word is eternally the Father's child. Even "before" his conception and birth by a woman, even "before" Christ assumed the office of human son, his divine hypostasis is related to the Father as Son and he "occupies" the office of divine Sonship. Childhood and sonship and daughterhood have a divine origin.

The seer of the book of Revelation states a related mystery. Jesus Christ is "the Lamb slain from the foundation of the world."[26] Our humanity is

---

25. George MacDonald, "The Child in the Midst," in *Unspoken Sermons* (Whitehorn, Calif.: Johannesen, 1997), 13.

26. Rev. 13:8 KJV.

preexistent within the life of God, through the Son, from all eternity. Childhood is itself an eternal attribute of God. "[H]e [Christ] was a child, whatever more he might be," says MacDonald. "Our Lord became flesh, but he did not *become* man. [Rather] He took on him the form of man: [but] he was man already. . . . He could never have been a child if he would ever have ceased to be a child, for in him the transient found nothing. Childhood belongs to the divine nature. . . . God is man, and infinitely more. . . . [H]e was, is, and ever shall be divinely childlike."[27]

Newman agrees. "What shall we say of the Eternal God," he writes, "but that He, *because* He is eternal, is ever *young,* without a beginning, and therefore without change, and, in the fulness [*sic*] and perfection of His incomprehensible attributes, now just what He was a million years ago? He is truly called in Scripture the 'Ancient of Days,' and is therefore infinitely venerable, yet he needs not old age to make Him venerable."[28] God has created humankind in his own image, and that image includes childhood.

Mary Ann Hinsdale has demonstrated that the twentieth-century Roman Catholic theologian Karl Rahner was similarly persuaded. Rahner believed that childhood is not restricted to "the first phase of our biological lives but is 'a basic condition' always appropriate to human existence lived rightly."[29] "The childhood which belongs to the child in the biological sense is only the beginning, the prelude, the foretaste and the promise of this other childhood, which is the childhood proved and tested and at the same time assailed, which is present in the mature man," says Rahner. "It is the childhood of the mature person [that] is 'the true and proper childhood.'"[30] Rahner concludes:

> In the last analysis, therefore, human childhood is not transferred by some dubious process of metaphorical or poetic transference to a quite different reality which we called childhood of God, but rather has its ultimate basis [in God's existence]. . . . Childhood is only truly understood, only realises the ultimate depths of its own nature, when it is seen as based upon the foundation of the childhood of God.[31]

---

27. MacDonald, "Child in the Midst," 13.

28. Saward, *Way of the Lamb,* 66-67 n. 26.

29. Mary Ann Hinsdale, "'Infinite Openness to the Infinite': Karl Rahner's Contribution to Modern Catholic Thought on the Child," in *The Child in Christian Thought,* ed. Marcia A. Bunge (Grand Rapids: Eerdmans, 2001), 427.

30. Hinsdale, "Infinite Openness," 427.

31. Hinsdale, "Infinite Openness," 427-28.

"Whoever Receives One of These Little Children"

Chapter 9 of the Gospel of Mark presents us with the scene wherein the disciples are arguing amongst themselves over which of them will hold the highest office in the kingdom. Jesus lifts up a child and says to his disciples: "Whoever receives one of these little children in My name receives Me; and whoever receives Me, receives not Me but Him who sent Me."[32] MacDonald writes that these verses "record a lesson our Lord gave his disciples against ambition, against emulation."[33] Jesus teaches the disciples a lesson concerning the true divine and redemptive nature of childhood.[34] The "lesson did lie, not in the humanity, but in the childhood of the child. . . . It was not, it could not be, in virtue of the humanity, it was in the virtue of his childhood that this child was thus presented as representing a subject of the kingdom."[35] And to this MacDonald also adds:

> It is the recognition of the *childhood as divine* that will show the disciple how vain the strife after relative place or honour in the great kingdom. . . . [W]hen he tells them to receive *such* a little child in his name, it must surely imply something in common between them all — something in which the child and Jesus meet — something in which the child and the disciples meet. What else can that be than the spiritual childhood?[36]

This is to say that when Jesus states, "Whoever receives these little children in My name receives Me," he means more than that he desires that the disciples receive the little child as himself. He also reveals two fundamental realities concerning God and the kingdom of heaven. First, the relation of children to their parents is an image of Jesus' own relationship to God the Father. Second, every baptized human being enters into a new relationship as adoptive son or daughter of God the Father and brother or sister of Jesus.

If we carefully attend to these two facts, then we stand to gain a deep and profound understanding of the triune God. God is in his very being the perfect communion of Father (parent) and Son (child) and the love that they share through the Spirit. Caryll Houselander writes in her modern classic of spirituality *The Passion of the Infant Christ*: "In our tenderness for those whom we love, above all our love for children, we know God in His image and likeness in

---

32. Mark 9:37 NKJV.
33. MacDonald, "Child in the Midst," 2.
34. MacDonald, "Child in the Midst," 7.
35. MacDonald, "Child in the Midst," 6.
36. MacDonald, "Child in the Midst," 7.

ourselves. We come to know God as Father and Mother and Lover. . . . [W]e learn the simplicity, the humility and trust of children, but only if we dare to love one another."[37]

MacDonald adds: "[T]o receive a child in the name of Jesus is to receive Jesus; to receive Jesus is to receive God; therefore to receive the child is to receive God himself."[38] God is not just Father of the divine Word, but stepfather to all who are baptized. God is not just a friend in Christ, but the stepbrother of all who are baptized. God is "altogether our friend, our father — our more than friend, father, and mother — our infinite love-perfect God."[39] Through the Spirit and in Christ, persons, children and adults alike, increase in God's own image, an image that illumines the full meaning and purpose of the offices of child and parent.

Bios and *Zoe*

Neither psychology nor sociology comprehends these transcendent, spiritual origins of childhood. Nor, by the very rules of inquiry that each follows, can either account for the offices of son and daughter and father and mother. Not mere nature nor instinct, nor even freedom, enables child or parent to fulfill his or her respective office. We must take into account the spiritual dimension of human existence and the role love plays.

Nevertheless, freedom and choice are powerful predicates of human parenthood and childhood, as well as evidence of spirit in nature. The Gospel narratives of the conception and birth of Jesus emphasize this, as do the great Christian feasts of the annunciation and nativity that explore the meaning of these narratives. Mary became a mother despite the fact that her motherhood did not issue from her sexual nature or from conjugal union. Mary freely accepted the call of God to assume the office of mother to God the Son. Joseph was not Jesus' biological father. Yet Joseph, of his own free willing, consented to be the stepfather of the incarnate Son of God, as God is stepfather to every baptized person. The Word eternally chose Mary and Joseph to be his earthly parents and accepted the office of human son through a supreme act of kenotic love, so that all humankind might inherit eternal life as his Father's children and his own brothers and sisters.

---

37. Caryll Houselander, *The Passion of the Infant Christ* (New York: Sheed and Ward, 1949), 79-80.

38. MacDonald, "Child in the Midst," 9.

39. MacDonald, "Child in the Midst," 14.

Thus do the Gospels attest that the parent-child nexus, though rooted in nature and human biology and reaching diverse forms in history, is transcendentally grounded in God's eternal triune Being. Human parenthood and childhood may be grounded in *Bios* (biological) existence, yet both originate and have their fulfillment in what C. S. Lewis calls *Zoe* (spiritual) existence.[40] *Bios* is the realm of necessity and *Zoe* the realm of transcendental freedom. Natural law defines and gives shape to *Bios*. The virtues constitute *Zoe;* for in the strictest and deepest sense all virtues are spiritual, since virtue is an attribute of personhood, and personhood is the divine image in humankind.

"God caused us to be loved by our parents for this reason, that we might have mentors in virtue," wrote Saint John Chrysostom. "You see," he adds, "[God] does not make fathers only for having children . . . nor . . . mothers [only] to give birth to children. . . . [I]t is not nature but virtue that makes parents."[41] Likewise, Saint Cyril of Jerusalem observes, "For like as Mary was called mother of John [the Apostle], because of her parental affection, not from having given him birth, so Joseph also was called father of Christ, not for having begotten Him (for *he knew her not,* as the Gospel says, *until she had brought forth her first-born Son*), but because of the care bestowed on His nurture."[42]

From this theological perspective, the holy family is not the exception to the rule, as some mistakenly characterize it, but rather the fullest human expression of the offices of parent and child and their relation. For in the end, to be a human parent or human son or daughter is an act of freedom, a willing to be so when love is present. Not even the fact that Jesus is the eternally begotten Son of God is the exception that might hinder our emulation of the holy family. God the Father is the author of the office of sonship/daughterhood just as he is the author of the office of fatherhood/motherhood. He revealed himself as such at Jesus' baptism in the waters of the Jordan and again also on Mount Tabor where Jesus was transfigured before the eyes of Peter, James, and John. "You are My beloved Son in whom I am well pleased"[43] and "This is my beloved Son. Hear Him!"[44] At Jesus' baptism and at his transfiguration God revealed the transcendent source of the human "family" as God's own trinitarian life.

Saint Cyril of Jerusalem states: "We came into holy sonship not of necessity

40. C. S. Lewis, *Mere Christianity* (San Francisco: HarperCollins, 2001), bk. 4, chap. 10.

41. Saint John Chrysostom, *Old Testament Homilies,* vol. 1, *Homilies on Hannah, David and Saul,* trans. Robert Charles Hill (Brookline, Mass.: Holy Cross Orthodox Press, 2003), 71.

42. Cyril of Jerusalem, "Catechetical Lectures," in *A Select Library of Nicene and Post-Nicene Fathers of the Christian Church,* 2nd ser., vol. 7 (Grand Rapids: Eerdmans, 1978), 46.

43. Mark 1:11 NKJV.

44. Mark 9:7 NKJV.

but by choice."[45] Every human child is a potential son or daughter of God. We cannot say the same about the lion cub or the canine puppy. Jesus is not only the pioneer of our salvation but also our model of human sonship and daughterhood and divine sonship and daughterhood that baptism confers upon us. Saint Cyril says of Christ, and as a reminder to all the baptized, that "He [Christ] obeys the Father, yielding, not a forced obedience, but a self-chosen accordance; for He is not a servant, that He should be subjected by force, but a Son, that He should comply of His free choice and natural love."[46] God the Father affords the same relationship and status to those who believe in Christ his Son. Thus, we come by this station not according to virtue alone or merely by reason of our human nature, but by our freely given obedience to the Father who loves each one of us as his own son or daughter.

Christian Anthropology and the Divine Character of Childhood

The primary speech of Christian anthropology is transformational: it is not the language of growth naturalistically conceived. To repeat what I have said, the Christian faith is perfectionist: not developmental or, for that matter, social constructionist. Hauerwas rightly maintains that the Christian idea of maturity (or perfection) suggests a much "more radical transformation and continued growth"[47] than child development theory imagines. In summary, from the standpoint of Christian belief, human "growth" transcends mere biological maturation. It is "growth" toward a spiritual perfection that transcends the natural course of life from conception to death. Because of sin and a corrupted will, human "maturation" into spiritual life requires penance and conversion enabled by God's freely offered grace.

Contrary to postmodernism's radical doctrine of historicity, the human person does not merely enact his or her own history, but may partake of and participate in a transcendent spiritual dimension of divine life, which God graciously offers to his creature that he has created in his very own image. Human existence transcends historicity. On the one hand, the spiritual dimension of human existence is indeterminate: it entails freedom. While, on the other hand, this freedom is not open-ended; it has an end (or telos) that is transnatural and transhistorical. God, not nature or history, gives human existence meaning, purpose, and direction. God accomplishes this through his

---

45. Cyril of Jerusalem, "Catechetical Lectures," 47.
46. Cyril of Jerusalem, "Catechetical Lectures," 113.
47. Hauerwas, *A Community of Character*, 131.

creative act, by making humankind free and self-transcendent. Our humanity is grounded in the eternal Spirit of God and God's perfect freedom. Saint Paul writes: "For the Lord is the Spirit and where the Spirit of the Lord is, there is freedom."[48]

According to Christian anthropology, childhood has a footing both in nature and its determinism and in historicity that is the outcome of immanent freedom. But God also has implanted in every human being a sort of force that impels and propels him or her into a spiritual dimension. The image of God is neither static nor merely a character trait or combination of human capacities. It is an inclination or movement toward a relationship in communion with God, toward a perfection of divine similitude, a participation in the love and life of God, the Father, the Son, and the Holy Spirit. Like the tree whose branches reach to the sky beyond the earth into which its roots grow, humankind, though made of dust, reaches toward spirit.

This capacity of transcendent participation in the life of the Spirit is no less present in children than in adults. If it were absent in children, the church could not justify infant and child baptism. Indeed, this inclination toward godmanhood and godwomanhood may be more pronounced, or at least more pristine, in children than in adults, because in children the original corruption (of sin) has not progressed as far as in adults, the habit of sin is still young (pun intended).

Childhood and Original Sin

In contrast to Western theologies, influenced by Saint Augustine, that attribute an "inherited" or "original guilt" to all human beings, no matter their age, my own Eastern Orthodox tradition believes that although all human beings are born into original sin, all at the start are also free from actual sin and do not carry the guilt of Adam. Infants, therefore, are innocents. Chrysostom writes: "We do baptize infants, although they are not guilty of any sins."[49] All human beings develop the habit of sin and may accumulate personal guilt as they experience life. Young children, however, are in a real sense more like what all Christians must become than are adults. Christians must become spiritual children.

---

48. 2 Cor. 3:17 RSV.

49. John Chrysostom, *The Later Christian Fathers*, ed. and trans. Henry Bettenson (Oxford: Oxford University Press, 1977), 169.

Spiritual Determinacy

The legal scholar Joseph Vining comments in his book *From Newton's Sleep* that the spiritual dimension of human existence is wholly different from both "[t]he biological (determinacy), which is a given," and "the malleable constrictions, called socially constructed," which connote that which is "wholly changeable and with no necessity whatever to it."[50] This spiritual dimension of human life has its own peculiar "determinacy." God destines us to be his adoptive sons and daughters — though paradoxically what God destines is also what we freely choose. When Saint Paul speaks of the Christian coming into the stature of the fullness of Christ, he is identifying this spiritual dimension of human existence.[51] He is pointing out a mystical (i.e., hidden) synergy of human will and divine energy, a movement of the human person toward holiness, wholeness, and perfection that God sets in motion by his act of creating man in his own image and perfecting humankind in Christ.

This perfection is not an end state, a mere stasis, however. Rather it is an everlasting participation in the divine life,[52] a transtemporal communion of the saints[53] that is perpetually transformation but not change, destiny but not necessity. And the offices of child and parent in their relation to one another are trajectories on this path to holiness, wholeness, and perfection. One way that God reveals these trajectories is through the Christian sacrament of baptism.

On Baptism and the Meaning of Childhood

> *"Know you what it is to be a child? It is to have a spirit yet streaming from the waters of Baptism."*
>
> Francis Thompson, from "Shelley"

By baptism we become sons and daughters of God; and by being made a son or daughter of God, adds early Christian writer Saint Clement of Alexandria, we are also "being made perfect . . . [and] immortal."[54] In other words, our biological, chronological childhood is both preparation for and symbol of the office of child of God, a spiritual, transtemporal childhood. Saint Clement argues that

---

50. Joseph Vining, *From Newton's Sleep* (Princeton: Princeton University Press, 1995), 12-13.

51. Eph. 4:13 NKJV.

52. 2 Pet. 1:3-4.

53. 1 Thess. 3:11-13.

54. Clement of Alexandria, "The Instructor," in *Ante-Nicene Fathers*, vol. 2 (Peabody, Mass.: Hendrickson, 2004), 215.

when Jesus speaks of children and childhood, "[w]e are the children"[55] he has in mind. Also, when God places children in our presence, God is instructing us in the virtues we need to fulfill the office of child of God that God bestows by baptism. Saint Clement writes:

> Discipline we declare to be right guiding from childhood to virtue. Accordingly, our Lord revealed more distinctly to us what is signified by the appellation of children. On the question arising among the apostles, "which of them should be the greater," Jesus placed a little child in the midst, saying, "Whosoever shall humble himself as this little child, the same shall be the greater in the kingdom of heaven" (Matt. 18:4). He does not then use the appellation of children on account of their very limited amount of understanding from their age, as some have thought.[56]

When Jesus says, "Except ye become as these children, ye shall not enter into the kingdom of God,"[57] Clement continues, our Lord commends to us the virtues of trust, humility, and obedience that belong to children. In this sense, children are our best guides to filling the office of sons and daughters of God. Clement's comments are neither naive nor romantic. If we presume that the Christian doctrine of original sin (or as Eastern theology prefers to call it, our ancestral sin) applies to children, then young children, let us say as young as one or two years of age, are most certainly not pure innocents. The resistance of even the very youngest child to these virtues bears a peculiar kind of witness, however, to the fact that they do belong quintessentially to childhood, since they are in utter contradiction to our intuitive sense of what children ought to be. These virtues are essential not only for "natural" childhood and the relationship of children with their parents but also for Christian men and women in their relationship to God as his adopted sons and daughters. Real human maturity is not the same thing as chronological adulthood, the end of which course is senility and death. Real human maturity is the rebirth of innocence (or, perhaps, in Paul Ricoeur's famous turn of phrase, "a second naïveté").

We arrive at a central paradox of the Christian life that John Henry Newman identified. As we have seen, Newman argues that childhood is "a type of the perfect Christian state." Christ said that we must become as little children to enter his kingdom; for "in them we are bound to see Christian perfection." But God does not ask us to perform what is impossible and return by our powers alone to our original innocence in the Garden of Eden or to become literally

---

55. Clement of Alexandria, "The Instructor," 212.
56. Clement of Alexandria, "The Instructor," 213.
57. Matt. 18:4 KJV.

children once again. "We are not, we cannot [literally] be children [again]; grown men have faculties, passions, aims, principles, views, duties, which children have not."[58]

Rightly do we desire that our children mature into responsible adults. Yet, ironically, in wishing this, we forget that the kingdom of heaven more nearly resembles our state of childhood with its innocence than spoiled adulthood. Children, of course, share in original sin. The "old Adam" in them is already corrupting their innocence. Yet they do not "know" original sin intimately, or at least they do not experience its consequences as their common base of knowledge. In some real and substantial way they have not yet eaten from the Tree of Knowledge. Only a child or an idiot will wonder how there might be evil people in the world.

Jesus understood these matters. That is why, according to Newman, Jesus did the unexpected and took a child in his arms as a specimen and example of what a disciple of his must become. "In aiming to be children again, we are aiming to be Adam on his creation,"[59] in the special sense that "children are saved, not by their purposes and habits of obedience, not by faith and works, but by the influence of baptismal grace [alone]; [as] into Adam God 'breathed the breath of life, and man became a living soul.'"[60] We, in our fallen and sin-smudged condition, in our adulterated adulthood, have but small traces of Eden left within us or that show on our faces, except for the few who are holy. We come to baptism not as children but rather to become children, having arrived at the truth not by instinct or intuition but by trial and error — mostly error — and by discipline and corrective. But we are in need of cleansing and refreshment just the same. As we are dead in sin, so we need to be revivified, made youthful, childlike, and innocent once again in the fount by water and Spirit. We need for God to breathe the breath of life into us once again.

Baptism and the Office of Child

Synchronically, the offices of parent and child may seem equally significant. Indeed, in our culture the latter is often emphasized at the expense of the former, an inversion of the wisdom of Christ and of the church fathers. Diachronically, and even more especially from the perspective of Christian soteriology and eschatology, the office of child and the virtues associated with it are more signifi-

---

58. Newman, "Mind of Little Children," 1024.
59. Newman, "Mind of Little Children," 1024.
60. Newman, "Mind of Little Children," 1027.

cant, however, than the office of parent with its virtues. Saint Paul writes that baptism sets free the Christian on a path of perfection, toward divine likeness "from glory to glory."[61] God assists his adoptive children on that path by the example of his only begotten Son. In the ancient baptismal hymn that Saint Paul incorporated into his letter to the Philippians, he predicates Christ's filial relationship to God the Father in trust, humility, and obedience. "He [Christ] humbled Himself and became obedient to the point of death, even the death of the cross."[62] According to Saint Paul, God calls every Christian to this very same office and the virtues that belong to it. Each person whom the church baptizes God adopts as his son or daughter. And he sends each one of them "the Spirit of His Son" so that they might cry out, "'Abba, Father!'"[63]

Our transformation and translation into *Zoe* life that baptism inaugurates, does not efface or negate nature. Baptismal grace builds upon human nature. The temporal human offices of child and parent have their own integrity (the integrity of creation), even as God also employs these offices in his redemptive work. I have said that the virtues of childhood are more significant in the scheme of redemption and sanctification than are the virtues of the office of parent. And I have hinted that the evidence for this is the incarnation itself, that Jesus through his life and death fulfilled all the requirements of the office of child and, thereby, showed us what perfection truly is.

This is a strong reason why Christian theology resists and rejects conceptions of childhood that conceive of it as either an ephemeral stage of human existence or deny its universal status. When we become adults and parents, we do not simply leave behind the office of child like the crab that sheds its first shell for a second and a third. Through the whole of our lives, we naturally continue to relate to our parents as their children. We also find it needful to "remember" and, in some real sense, recapitulate our childhood, so that we will be good and successful parents. Similarly, in our relationship with God, we never wholly cease to be children, nor do we completely "outgrow" the virtues of childhood, although they take on a different meaning and character. Newman writes: "As habits of holiness are matured, principle, reason, and self-discipline are unnecessary; a moral instinct takes their place in the breast, or rather, to speak more reverently, the Spirit is sovereign there. . . . We act from love."[64] When we come to the end of our earthly lives, we also leave behind the office of parent, even adulthood itself. We render up the office of parent to God alone. As spiritual

---

61. 2 Cor. 3:18 RSV.
62. Phil. 2:8 NKJV.
63. Gal. 4:5-6 NKJV.
64. Newman, "Mind of Little Children," 1028.

children we lovingly and trustingly give ourselves over completely to God's parental care. Ironically, we complete our course of natural existence by becoming children again. This, indeed, is "the measure of the stature of the fullness of Christ."[65] In this way, we fulfill perfectly the office of son or daughter, in relation no longer to human parents but wholly in relation to God, and, by this path, receive eternal blessing.

65. Eph. 4:13 NKJV.

II. Innocence, Depravity, and Hope for the Freedom of the Child

5. Christ the Pediatrician: Augustine on the Diagnosis and Treatment of the Injured Vocation of the Child

William Harmless, S.J.

Few have shaped Western thinking on the vocation of the child more profoundly than Augustine of Hippo (354-430).[1] Augustine saw the child's vocation as congenitally damaged, the catastrophic victim of Adam's primordial misdeed. To critics, both ancient and modern, Augustine's doctrine of original

---

1. In the notes throughout this chapter, I refer readers to the Latin texts of Augustine. Most of Augustine's works can be found in J.-P. Migne, Patrologia Latina, vols. 32-47 (hereafter cited as PL), which reproduces the excellent seventeenth-century edition by the Benedictines of St. Maur. The "Nuova Biblioteca Agostiniana" has provided a valuable service by posting this classic edition on the Internet. Nuova Biblioteca Agostina, http://www.augustinus.it/latino/index.htm. The PL edition is being steadily replaced by modern critical editions in the Corpus Scriptorum Ecclesiasticorum Latinorum (hereafter cited as CSEL) and the Corpus Christianorum, Series Latina (hereafter cited as CCL). Also valuable is the *Bibliothèque Augustinienne* (hereafter cited as BA) which has the Latin text with a French translation on facing pages. Certain sermons discovered after the Maurist edition are found in the *Miscellanea Agostiniana* (hereafter cited as MA) and the Patrologia Latina Supplementum (hereafter cited as PLS).

For English translations, I have generally drawn on the excellent but still incomplete Works of St. Augustine: A Translation for the 21st Century, ed. John E. Rotelle and Boniface Ramsey (Brooklyn/Hyde Park, N.Y.: New City Press, 1990-) (hereafter cited as WSA). Occasionally, I have tapped on translations from the Fathers of the Church series (Washington, D.C.: Catholic University of America Press) (hereafter cited as FC) and Ancient Christian Writers series (New York: Paulist Press) (hereafter cited as ACW). In several key instances, I have done my own translation. On the titles of Augustine's works and other information, see Allan Fitzgerald, ed., *Augustine through the Ages: An Encyclopedia* (Grand Rapids: Eerdmans, 1999); this has become the standard reference work on Augustine for the English-speaking world.

An earlier version of this chapter, "Christ the Pediatrician: Infant Baptism and Christological Imagery in the Pelagian Controversy," appeared in *Augustinian Studies* 28 (1997): 7-34. I am grateful to Allan Fitzgerald, O.S.A., for permission to reprint it here. This version is much revised in terms of the translations and bibliographic references, and includes additional material on the recently discovered Dolbeau sermons.

sin has seemed ruthlessly pessimistic, a flawed and fearsome theological inheritance. The great nemesis of Augustine's later years, Julian of Eclanum, used to rage with an almost modern vituperation against Augustine and his view:

> You ask me why I would not consent to the idea that there is a sin that is part of human nature? I answer: it is improbable, it is untrue; it is unjust and impious; it makes it seem as if the Devil were the maker of men. It violates and destroys the freedom of the will . . . by saying that men are so incapable of virtue, that in the very wombs of their mothers they are filled with bygone sins. You imagine so great a power in such a sin, that not only can it blot out the new-born innocence of nature, but forever afterwards, will force a man throughout his life into every form of viciousness. . . .
>
> Tell me then, tell me: who is this person who inflicts punishment on innocent creatures. You answer: God. God, you say! God! He Who commended his love to us, who has loved us, who has not spared his own Son for us. . . . He it is, you say, who judges in this way; he is the persecutor of new-born children; he it is who sends tiny babies to eternal flames. . . . It would be right and proper to treat you as beneath argument: you have come so far from religious feeling, from civilized thinking, so far, indeed, from mere common sense, in that you think that your Lord God is capable of committing a crime against justice such as is hardly conceivable even among the barbarians.[2]

"Persecutor of new-born children": a harsh epithet for Augustine's God, and by implication, for Augustine himself. There are some today who think it fits. Julian's polemic — and its modern counterparts — may have something to say, but it is essential here to give Augustine and his doctrine a fair hearing. Most have encountered his teaching only at second hand, whether through textbook summaries or, more obliquely, through its subtle recastings in the theologies of later thinkers. Rarely is Augustine heard in his own voice. And even more rarely is he heard in context, as a North African, as a pastor, and as a Christian deeply struggling to make sense of the biblical text.

In this chapter I would like to excavate Augustine's doctrine of original sin using two vantage points. The first will be theological. Too often presentations sever Augustine's teaching on original sin from his teaching on Christ. As we will see, Christology undergirds Augustine's whole doctrine. In his debate with the Pelagians, Augustine stressed that Christ, far from being a "persecutor of newborns," was rather the "Great Physician" *(magnus medicus)* whose potent medicine of baptism was the one best hope for rescuing infants from the infer-

---

2. *Opus imperfectum* 3.67-71, 1.48 (CSEL 85.1:402-3, 37-38; trans. Peter Brown, *Augustine of Hippo: A Biography*, 2nd ed. [Berkeley: University of California Press, 2000], 390, 394).

nal genetics of original sin. Augustine saw his Pelagian opponents as the real persecutors of newborns, for in their defense of infant sinlessness they undermined the gospel by removing Christ as the one mediator and risked leaving infants deprived of urgently needed medicine. The first two sections will explore the threads and nuances of this theological logic. The next two sections will explore a second vantage point. Here I will situate Augustine in his original social context: as a struggling North African pastor. We will see that the roots of Augustine's medical imagery lie in his pastoral experience of the church as "emergency room" and that the ancient debate over infant baptism needs to be set against the experience of North African women and the agonizingly high infant mortality rate of the ancient world.

Christus Medicus

In 430, an imperial messenger arrived in Carthage bearing an invitation for Augustine to attend what would become the Third Ecumenical Council, the Council of Ephesus. But Augustine had died a few weeks before. If he had survived, he would have faced the tumultuous showdown between Nestorius and Cyril of Alexandria and the debate over the unity of the person of Christ.[3] It was an issue Augustine had thought about — and thought about repeatedly. But it never received his sustained attention. Augustine wrote no full-scale treatise on Christology, nothing comparable to his *On the Trinity* or his sprawling controversial works. Yet as Brian Daley has noted, "it is strikingly clear to anyone who reads even a few pages of Augustine's writings that the mystery of Christ's person is never far from his mind. His theology of grace, his view of the Church and of the relation of time to eternity, his reflections on 'the Trinity which is God,' all find their center and anchor in a sophisticated, astonishingly balanced Christology — a Christology that is all the more striking for being developed, as it seems, in passing."[4] Despite this balance and this sophistication,

---

3. On the Council of Ephesus and the christological debate that took place in the Greek East during Augustine's later years, see John McGuckin, *St. Cyril of Alexandria: The Christological Controversy; Its History, Theology, and Texts* (Crestwood, N.Y.: St. Vladimir's Seminary Press, 2004); Thomas G. Weinandy and Daniel Keating, eds., *The Theology of St. Cyril of Alexandria: A Critical Appreciation* (Edinburgh: T. & T. Clark, 2003); Norman Russell, *Cyril of Alexandria, the Early Church Fathers* (New York: Routledge, 2000); Steven A. McKinion, *Words, Imagery, and the Mystery of Christ: A Reconstruction of Cyril of Alexandria's Christology,* Supplements to Vigiliae Christianae (Leiden: Brill, 2000), 55.

4. Brian E. Daley, "A Humble Mediator: The Distinctive Elements in St. Augustine's Christology," *Word and Spirit* 9 (1987): 101.

Augustine's Christology received relatively little attention from scholars in the twentieth century, though in recent years the pace has begun to quicken.[5] The difficulty in studying Augustine's Christology comes from the fact that his views are scattered about in a vast assemblage of treatises, letters, and sermons composed over more than thirty-five years. What emerges is what Joanne McWilliam has called an "episodic" or "mosaic" Christology and "is consequently harder to control than other aspects of his thought."[6]

The question is how best to approach this mosaic. One way has been to see how Augustine grappled with what his Greek contemporaries, like Cyril, were grappling with: the incarnation. There is no doubt Augustine thought it central. In the *Confessions,* he insisted that it was not John 1:1 but John 1:14 that distinguished Christianity from Platonism; that it was not the divinity of the Word but the taking-flesh of that Word that stood as the central revelation and mystery of Christianity.[7] When called on to express that mystery, Augustine often used terse antitheses: Christ was "the human God" *(homo deus);*[8] he was "the Word of God, the Word-made-flesh, . . . the Son of God, the Son of man, exalted that he might create us, humbled that he might re-create us."[9] Augustine

5. For a survey, see Joanne McWilliam, "The Study of Augustine's Christology in the Twentieth Century," in *Augustine: From Rhetor to Theologian* (Waterloo, Ontario: Wilfrid Laurier University Press, 1992), 183-205. The best overviews are by Brian E. Daley, "Christology," in *Augustine through the Ages,* 164-69, and by Goulven Madec, "Christus," in *Augustinus-Lexikon,* ed. Cornelius Mayer (Basel: Schwabe AG, Verlag Publishers, 1994), 1:845-908. The classic study is that of T. J. Van Bavel, *Recherches sur la christologie de saint Augustin, Paradosis* 10 (Fribourg: Éditions universitaires, 1954); see also Basil Studer, *Dominus Salvator: Studien zur Christologie und Exegese der Kirchenvater, Studia Anselmiana* 107 (Rome, 1992); Brian E. Daley, "The Giant's Twin Substances: Ambrose and the Christology of Augustine's *Contra sermonem Arianorum,*" in *Augustine: Presbyter Factum Sum,* ed. Joseph T. Lienhard, Earl C. Muller, and Roland J. Teske (New York: Peter Lang, 1993), 477-95; Joanne McWilliam Dewart, "The Christology of the Pelagian Controversy," *Studia Patristica* 17 (1993): 1221-44; H. R. Drobner, *Person-Exegese und Christologie bei Augustinus: zur Herkunft der Formel 'una persona'* (Leiden: Brill, 1986); Albert Verwilghen, *Christologie et spiritualité selon Saint Augustin: L'hymne aux philippiens, Theologie historique* 72 (Paris: Beauchesne, 1985); Lewis Ayres, "Augustine, Christology, and God as Love: An Introduction to the Homilies on 1 John," *Pro Ecclesia* 5 (1996): 470-84; and Michael Cameron, "The Christological Substructure of Augustine's Figurative Exegesis," in *Augustine and the Bible,* ed. Pamela Bright (Notre Dame, Ind.: University of Notre Dame Press, 1999), 74-103.

6. McWilliam, "Study of Augustine's Christology," 183.

7. *Confessiones* 7.9.13-14 (CCL 27:101-2). See *De civitate Dei* 10.29 (CCL 47:306-7), in which he recounts a story told him by Simplicianus: that a Platonist philosopher had once recommended that John 1:1 be set in letters of gold in every church; against this, Augustine insisted on John 1:14.

8. *In Johannis evangelium tractatus* 4.14 (CCL 36:38).

9. *In Johannis evangelium tractatus* 10.1 (CCL 36:100-101; my translation).

drew out the paradox of the incarnation masterfully in his Christmas sermons. In Sermon 188, for instance, he contrasted Christ the Word whose utterance made the universe with Christ the speechless infant in the manger:

> What praises, then, should we be singing to God's love, what thanks should we be expressing! I mean, he loved us so much that for our sake he came to be in time, though all times were made through him; and he was prepared to be younger in age than many of his servants in the world, though he is older in eternity than all the world. He loved us so much that he became man though he made man; that he was created from a mother whom he had created, carried in arms he had fashioned, sucked breasts which he himself filled; that he lay squalling in a manger wordless in infancy, though he is the Word without whom human eloquence would be at a loss for words.[10]

This passage illustrates Augustine's "rhetorical" Christology: a leaping back and forth between the divinity of Christ and his humanity, a reveling in antithesis and paradox. By such rhetoric, Augustine sought to awaken wonder.

One finds him, here and there, grappling with many of the technical issues that preoccupied his Greek contemporaries. Like Cyril of Alexandria, Augustine insisted on the unity of the person of Christ against any formulation that threatened to divide things: "there are not two Christs, two Sons of God, but one person, one Christ the Son of God and the same one Christ, not another, being the Son of Man."[11] Like Cyril, Augustine appealed to the union of body and soul in human beings as an analogy for the unity of the divine and human in Christ.[12] And like Cyril, Augustine stressed that the unity of Christ's person made possible the exchange of predicates *(communicatio idiomatum):* "if you pay attention to the distinction of the substances, the Son of God came down from heaven, the Son of Man was crucified; if you pay attention to the unity of the person, both the Son of Man came down from heaven and the Son of God was crucified."[13] On the other hand, Augustine, like John of Antioch and the *Formula of Reunion,* stressed that Christ must be "exactly the same nature as we ourselves are" and that "he had nothing less than we do as regards natures, but

---

10. *Sermo* 188.2 (PL 38:1004; trans. Edmund Hill, WSA III/6:32).

11. *Sermo* 294.9 (PL 38:1340-1341; trans. Hill, WSA III/8:186). Cf. *De peccatorum meritis* 1.31.60 (CSEL 60:60-61); *Enchiridion* 10.35 (CCL 46:69).

12. *In Johannis evangelium tractatus* 19.15 (CCL 36:199); 78.3 (CCL 36:524); *Epistula* 137.11 (CSEL 44:109).

13. *Contra Maximinum Arianorum Episcopum* 2.20.3 (PL 42:789-90; trans. Roland J. Teske, WSA I/18:302). See Joseph Torchia, "The Significance of the *Communicatio Idiomatum* in St. Augustine's Christology, with Special Reference to His Rebuttal of Later Arianism," *Studia Patristica* 38 (2001): 306-23.

also had nothing by way of fault."[14] One even finds passages that anticipate word-for-word the balanced sonorities of Pope Leo the Great's famous *Tome to Flavian:*

> We declare that Christ is true God, born of God the Father without any beginning in time, and that the same Christ is true man, born of a human mother at the determined fullness of time, and that the humanity, by which he is less than the Father, does not diminish in any way his divinity, by which he is equal to the Father. But both of these are Christ, who both as God most truly said, "I and the Father are one," and as man most truly said, "The Father is greater than I."[15]

To find Leo's *Tome* echoing passages such as these is, of course, no accident. One of Augustine's devoted disciples, Prosper of Aquitaine, would serve as Leo's secretary and seemed to have exercised important influence on Leo's formulation.[16]

While such technical formulations did matter to Augustine, they are not the best way to get a hold on him as a christological thinker. Augustine's favored way of setting forth the mystery of Christ was with images.[17] As one surveys his works, especially the sermons, one encounters a sort of christological portrait gallery. Augustine's Christ is the lion-hunter whose deadly quarry was Death itself;[18] he is the farmer who plants in us the seeds of faith and whose hand weeds us of the thorns and thistles of sin;[19] he is the cantor whose solo song of the Passion set the melody for the chorus of martyrs who followed his lead;[20] he is the liberator who released us from the bondage of slavery to Satan and the redeemer whose blood paid the ransom for those kidnapped by barbarians of the spirit;[21] he is the merchant from a faraway land who imported into our region an exotic

---

14. *Sermo* 174.2 (PL 38:941; trans. Hill, WSA III/5:258).

15. *De dono perseverantiae* 24.67 (*BA* 24:760-62; trans. John A. Mourant and William J. Collinge, FC 86:335-36). Cf. *Enchiridion* 10.35 (CCL 46:69).

16. See N. W. James, "Leo the Great and Prosper of Aquitaine," *Journal of Theological Studies*, n.s., 44 (1993): 554-84.

17. Two valuable studies of Augustine's poetic imagination are Suzanne Poque, *Le langage symbolique dans la prédication d'Augustin d'Hippone: Images héroïques* (Paris: Études augustiniennes, 1984), and Robert J. O'Connell, *Soundings in St. Augustine's Imagination* (New York: Fordham University Press, 1994).

18. *Sermo* 233.4 (PL 38:1114).

19. *Sermo* 229J.2 (*MA* I:583).

20. *Enarrationes in psalmos* 87.1-2 (CCL 39:1208).

21. *Sermo* 21.6-7 (CCL 41:281-83); *Sermo* 86.7 (PL 38:52); *Sermo* 344.4 (PL 39:1514-15). For a discussion of this imagery, see P. Eijkenboom, "*Christus Redemptor* in the Sermons of St. Augustine," in *Mélanges offerts à Mademoiselle Christina Mohrmann* (Utrecht-Anvers: Spectrum Editeurs, 1963), 233-39.

novelty, eternal life, and in a seemingly foolish business deal, exchanged this most valuable commodity for our death.[22] I should mention one other favorite image. Augustine repeatedly portrays Christ as "our expert lawyer" *(iurisperitus noster)*, the one whose carefully crafted legal brief known as the Our Father is guaranteed to win our lawsuit before God the divine emperor.[23]

In Augustine's christological portrait gallery, one image enjoys special prominence: *Christus medicus*, that is, Christ the Physician.[24] It is an image Augustine used frequently and in a variety of ways. He repeatedly contrasted Christ's healing powers with those of human physicians. Ordinary doctors make incorrect diagnoses or find diseases beyond their healing powers, but Christ the Physician found nothing incurable.[25] For Augustine, Christ is thus the "great physician" *(magnus medicus)*,[26] the "artful physician" *(medicus artifex)*,[27] the "best of physicians" *(optimus medicus)*,[28] the "complete healer of our wounds" *(totus medicus vulnerum nostrum)*.[29] Augustine sometimes compared the history of salvation to a history of medical cure. The human race, like a giant patient sprawled across the earth as though "in a kind of huge bed," suffered from a deadly "bloating," the result of pride. To keep down the swelling, Christ first sent the prophets ahead of his own coming, just as ancient physicians first sent nursing assistants ahead of them. Only at the moment of mortal crisis did Christ as "attending physician" arrive in person. This and other medical motifs appear prominently and repeatedly in the remarkable new sermons discovered by François Dolbeau and published through the 1990s.[30] In one ser-

---

22. *Sermo* 233.4 (PL 38:1114); see also *Sermones* 121.5 (PL 38:680) and 229H.1 (*MA* I:479-80). See Suzanne Poque, "Christus Mercator," *Recherches de Science Religieuse* 48 (1960): 564-77.

23. *In Johannis evangelium tractatus* 7.10-11 (CCL 36:72-73); *Sermo* 58.1 (PL 38:393); *Sermo* 213.6 (*MA* I:446).

24. The classic study is by Rudolph Arbesmann, "The Concept of '*Christus Medicus*' in St. Augustine," *Traditio* 10 (1954): 1-28. For a survey of its usage in the wider Christian tradition, see Regis Duffy, "The *Medicus* Image and Its Transformation from Its Patristic to Its Medieval and Tridentine Usages," in *Rule of Prayer, Rule of Faith: Essays in Honor of Aidan Kavanagh*, ed. Nathan Mitchell and John Baldovin (Collegeville, Minn.: Liturgical Press, 1996), 106-22; and Gervais Dumeige, "Medecin (le Christ)," *Dictionnaire de Spiritualité* 10 (1980): 891-901. See also Thomas F. Martin, "Paul the Patient: *Christus Medicus* and the '*Stimulus Carnis*' (2 Cor. 12:7); "A Consideration of Augustine's Medicinal Christology," *Augustinian Studies* 32 (2001): 219-56.

25. *Enarrationes in psalmos* 58.2.11 (CCL 39:752); 102.5 (CCL 40:1454-55); *Sermo* 97A.2 (PLS 2:533-34). Cf. *Sermo* 348A.4 (= Dolbeau 30).

26. *Enarrationes in psalmos* 45.11 (CCL 38:525); *Sermo* 346A.8 (PLS 2:440); *Sermo* 114B.15 (= Dolbeau 5).

27. *Sermo* 299O.1 (PLS 2:582).

28. *Sermo* 97A.2II, 114 (PLS 2:533).

29. *In Johannis evangelium tractatus* 3.3 (CCL 36:21).

30. *Sermo* 114B.15 (= Dolbeau 5); *Sermo* 374.16 (= Dolbeau 23). For the Latin text of these

mon, Augustine emphasized that just as experienced doctors do not simply treat symptoms, but get to the illness's root cause, so Christ "could see that pride was the root cause of all our disorders" and so "cured [us] with his own humility."[31] Augustine sometimes compared the incarnation to a doctor leaning over the sufferer, lowering himself to the level of a sick person's bed.[32] Christ comes thus as the *medicus humilis,* the "humble doctor."[33] His infusion of humility into the human condition reduces, by its opposite chemistry, the bloated swelling of pride:

> The doctor cures disease with its contrary: a cold condition with hot aids, a hot state with cold compresses, a dry state with moist dressing, a moist condition with dry ones. So if we see the art of medicine curing a patient with the application on contraries, it's not surprising if we who were sick with human pride are cured by the humility of God.[34]

Augustine often drew upon the *Christus medicus* image as a way of unraveling the meaning of pain and suffering. Sometimes Augustine compared such suffering to drinking a bitter cup of medicine, and stressed that Christ the Physician had first drunk from this cup before he asked us, his patients, to do so:

> If you're swollen, drink the potion so that the swelling of your insides may subside, and you can be restored to health. This potion has been mixed for you; drink the bitter cup, if you wish to be restored to health. This potion has been mixed for you by the doctor, for you to drink. The doctor himself has mixed a cup for you; drink the bitter cup, if you wish to be restored to health. Can't you see that you're swollen, can't you see that your insides are not

---

and the other newly discovered sermons of Augustine, see François Dolbeau, *Vingt-six sermons au peuple d'Afrique: Augustin d'Hippone retrouvé à Mayence* (Paris: Etudes augustiniennes, 1996) (hereafter cited as *Vingt-six*). For an overview of the Dolbeau sermons, see Henry Chadwick, "The New Sermons of St. Augustine," *Journal of Theological Studies*, n.s., 47 (1996): 69-91. Studies of individual sermons and themes are found in Goulvan Madec, ed., *Augustin Prédicateur (395-411): Actes du Colloque International de Chantilly (5-7 Sept, 1996),* Collection des Études augustiniennes, Série Antiquité 159 (Paris: Institut d'Études Augustiniennes, 1998); and William Harmless, "The Voice and the Word: Augustine's Catechumenate in Light of the Dolbeau Sermons," *Augustinian Studies* 35 (2004): 17-42. The theme of the human race as a giant patient appears also in *Sermo* 340A.5 (PLS 2:641), *Sermo* 345.7 (*MA* I:208), and *Sermo* 346A.6 (PLS 2:440-41).

31. *Sermo* 159B.11 (= Dolbeau 21) (*Vingt-six,* 281; trans. Hill, WSA III/11:157).

32. *Sermo* 87.13 (PL 38:538-39). Cf. *Sermones* 340A.5 (PLS 2:641); 345.7 (*MA* I:208).

33. *Sermo* 341A.1 (*MA* I:314-15).

34. *Sermo* 341.4 (= Dolbeau 22) (*Vingt-six,* 556-57; trans. Hill, WSA III/11:286). See also *Sermo* 77.11 (PL 38:488).

healthy? You think you're big, and you're really swollen. This isn't genuine bigness, but a disease. Do you want to be rid of the disease, do you want to be rid of the swelling? Drink the cup of humility; it has been mixed for you by the one who came to you in humility. And in case you should hesitate to drink, the doctor drinks it first, not because it was needed by the doctor, but to overcome the hesitation of the patient.[35]

Other times, Augustine described Christ as a surgeon who, upon finding us in dire condition, has been forced to wield a scalpel to excise the gangrene of sin and cauterize our badly infected wounds.[36] Augustine invoked this imagery as a way to explain prayers that seemed unanswered: that when we pray that our pain end and yet find that pain continuing, we should not presume God has turned a deaf ear; rather Christ the Physician hears our anguished cries, but like a surgeon, knows that pain is part of the healing process. And unlike that of a human physician, Christ's work is always life-giving and health-restoring — and what's more, it leaves no scars.[37] Sometimes Augustine noted Christ's diagnostic skills as a cardiologist: when Christ predicted Peter's triple denial, he did so as a doctor taking the pulse of Peter's heart.[38] As Augustine puts it in one of the Dolbeau sermons, Peter "didn't know what was going on in himself; he was utterly unaware of his inner infirmity. . . . [T]he doctor's judgment turned out to be truer than the patient's."[39]

Augustine invoked the *medicus* image especially when discussing the crucifixion. He compared those who scourged, mocked, and crucified Jesus to madmen, and then would point out that Christ the Doctor had not listened to them any more than doctors listened to ravings of lunatics.[40] Instead — and this is a good example of the unexpected in Augustine's poetic imagination — Christ the Physician administered an unusual pharmacology: he made his own blood the medicine for his killers' recovery; thus, "he himself is the doctor; he himself, the medication" *(ipse medicus, ipse medicamentum).*[41] When Christ appeared to

---

35. *Sermo* 159B.13 (= Dolbeau 21) (*Vingt-six,* 283; trans. Hill, WSA III/11:158-59). Cf. *Sermo* 299A.5 (= Dolbeau 4) (*Vingt-six,* 515-16); *Enarrationes in psalmos* 48.1.11 (CCL 38:560); 98.3 (CCL 39:1308).

36. *Sermo* 278.4-5 (PL 38:1270-71); cf. *Sermo* 113A.13 (*MA* I:153); *Enarrationes in psalmos* 93.7 (CCL 39:1308); *In Johannis evangelium tractatus* 7.12 (CCL 36:74); *In epistulam Joannis ad Parthos tractatus* 6.8 (PL 35:2023).

37. *In epistulam Joannis ad Parthos* 9.4 (PL 35:2048).

38. *Sermo* 229O.1 (PLS 2:582); *Sermo* 286.2 (PL 38:1298).

39. *Sermo* 299A.5 (= Dolbeau 4) (*Vingt-six,* 516; trans. Hill, WSA III/11:267-68).

40. *Sermo* 174.6 (PL 38:943); *Enarrationes in psalmos* 35.17 (CCL 38:335).

41. *Sermo* 374.23 (= Dolbeau 23) (*Vingt-Six,* 614-15; my translation). See also *Sermo* 175.3 (PL 38:946); *Sermo* 174.6 (PL 38:943); *Sermo* 229E.2 (PLS 2:559); *Sermo* 341A.1 (= Mai 22) (PLS 2:467).

the Eleven in the upper room, he bore the scars of his crucifixion to show that he was no ghost: "the doctor . . . approached, he applied a remedy, he saw the wounds in their minds, and what would cure their wounded minds, [and so] he brought along the scars in his body."[42]

Two comments at this juncture. First, the *Christus medicus* image is only one of many in Augustine's christological portrait gallery and is capable of many variations. I am reminded of the series of paintings that Monet once made of the cathedral in Rouen, each done at a different time of day and in different light. In a similar way, Augustine's *Christus medicus* appears in many variations, shifting according to the biblical texts or liturgical feasts it is set in conjunction with. As we will see, he would give it new and unexpected turns as the Pelagian controversy forced him to ponder the vocation of the child, its inabilities and vulnerabilities.

Second, Augustine's metaphorical imagination breaks down stock theological categories. It has been conventional since the Middle Ages to distinguish the person of Christ from the work of Christ, that is, to distinguish Christology from soteriology. Such categories give the impression that Augustine's contemporary, Cyril of Alexandria, was interested in Christology, in the person of Christ. But if one reads Cyril's writings, it is evident that he was deeply concerned about soteriology, especially deification and especially the deifying power of the Eucharist; and he believed that a duophysite Christology, at least as it appeared in the mouth of Nestorius, undermined the deifying power of Christ the incarnate Word. Augustine, by contrast, seems more interested in soteriology, in what the grace of Christ does for us. But Augustine too had christological interests, though he routinely exercised those interests in metaphorical language. Augustine's imagery breaks down or bypasses any easy distinction between the person and the work of Christ. Images of Christ the Physician (or Christ the Lawyer or Christ the Hunter) are at once christological *and* soteriological. Such images spell out both who Christ is and what he does. As we will see, Augustine, when he invoked the *Christus medicus* image against the Pelagians, was exploring both.

"So Great a Physician . . . Even for the Little Ones"

When one of Pelagius's disciples, Caelestius, applied to be ordained for the church of Carthage in 411, he faced a tribunal presided over by Aurelius, Augus-

---

42. *Sermo* 237.3 (PL 38:1124; trans. Hill, WSA III/7:53). See also *Sermo* 88.2 (PL 38:539); *Sermo* 242.3 (PL 38:1140); *In epistulam Joannis ad Parthos* 2.1 (PL 35:1989).

tine's friend and episcopal colleague in Carthage.[43] At this tribunal Paulinus of Milan, a deacon who would later serve as Augustine's biographer, accused Caelestius of several unorthodox positions. Two are relevant here: (1) that the sin of Adam injured no one but himself; and (2) that newborn infants are in that same state that Adam was in before the fall. Under stiff cross-examination, Caelestius was willing to grant the legitimacy of infant baptism as a practice. But he refused to accept that the transmission of original sin was integral to Christian teaching. He appealed to the views of a priest he had met in Rome, Rufinus the Syrian, and tried to claim that the whole matter was an open question about which Christians could legitimately disagree, "a matter for inquiry, not of heresy."[44] The tribunal did not agree and excommunicated Caelestius. Undaunted, he left town and moved to Ephesus, where he succeeded in getting himself ordained as a presbyter, much to the embarrassment of the North Africans.

Augustine at the time was a busy man. He was preoccupied with the aftermath of the great Council of Carthage that had forced the Donatists into unity. But in 412, after receiving a letter from Count Marcellinus about the affair of Caelestius, he composed the first of his anti-Pelagian treatises, *On the Punishment and Forgiveness of Sin and the Baptism of the Little Ones (De peccatorum meritis et remissione et de baptismo parvulorum)*. The debate, as it played itself out over the next eighteen years, would wend its way through a host of issues: original sin and infant baptism, grace and concupiscence, the origin of the soul, free will and predestination. Yet at the outset and at the often overlooked center of these was a central christological concern: that Jesus Christ, and he alone, is the source of salvation.[45] Augustine brought christological concerns center

43. For a basic survey of the Pelagian controversy, see Gerald Bonner, "Pelagianism and Augustine," *Augustinian Studies* 23 (1992): 33-51; and "Augustine and Pelagianism," *Augustinian Studies* 24 (1993): 27-47; reprinted in *Doctrinal Diversity: Varieties of Early Christianity,* ed. Everett Ferguson (New York: Garland, 1999), 191-232.

44. For the transcript of the trial, see *De gratia Christi et de peccato originali* 2.3.3 (CSEL 42:168-69); see also *De gestis Pelagii* 11.23 (CSEL 42:76) and *Epistula* 157.22 (*BA* 21:78-80); the list of charges is also given in a different order in Marius Mercator, *Commonitorium super nomine Coelestii* (PL 48:67-83).

45. J. Patout Burns, *The Development of Augustine's Doctrine of Operative Grace* (Paris: Études augustiniennes, 1980), 96, has mapped out this with terse precision. In particular, he has highlighted three "levels of assertion" within Augustine's doctrine of original sin: the first is christological, this fundamental claim that Christ alone is savior; the second level is the doctrinal theory of the transmission of original sin and death through the presence and operation of carnal concupiscence; the third was Augustine's studied indecision on the philosophic debates over the origin of the soul. As Burns insists, "Augustine pursued the doctrinal theories of the second level and the philosophical discussion of the third in order to explain the dogmatic affirmation of the first level" (96).

stage because, as he saw it, Caelestius and Pelagius dabbled with ideas that threatened to empty the cross of its meaning, and, in their defense of sinless-ness — whether of Old Testament notables or of newborn children — they charted a way of salvation that bypassed and thus undermined Christ's role as the one Mediator between God and humans.[46] It is here, at this early stage, that the *Christus medicus* figure appeared with special prominence, though it cer-tainly remained a regular image throughout the course of the controversy.

In the debate with the Pelagians, Augustine gave the *medicus* image a new twist: Christ the Physician became Christ the Pediatrician. As Augustine once put: "quaeritus etiam parvulis tantus medicus opitulator . . ." [so great a physi-cian is sought out to bring relief even for the little ones].[47] In the anti-Pelagian writings, there are, even by a conservative count, over forty references to Christ the Physician, and in at least eighteen of these, Augustine refers specifically to Christ as a physician of infants.[48] To begin exploring the role this image played in his argument, let us look at an extended example. The following is the first time he uses the figure in the very first of the anti-Pelagian treatises:

> Therefore, who would dare claim that without this rebirth [through bap-tism] infants are able to be saved — as though Christ had not died for them? For "Christ died for the ungodly" (Rom 5:6). But as for these infants — who, as is clear, have done nothing ungodly in their lives: If they are not held pris-oner by any chain of ungodliness from the outset, originally, then how did he who died for the ungodly die for them? If they are not wounded by any dis-ease of original sin, then why are they carried to Christ the Physician, that is, carried by those running in pious fear so that [these infants] might get to re-ceive the sacrament of eternal well-being . . . ? The Physician does indeed call

---

46. *De peccatorum meritis* 1.18.23 (CSEL 60:22-23); 3.4.7 (CSEL 60:133-34). This would be-come a stock objection, but its central place is articulated at a key moment in the controversy when Augustine (and Alypius) write a letter to the influential Paulinus of Nola noting Pelagius's *De natura* has convinced them that Pelagius "aims to set forth theories intended to destroy and remove from faithful hearts any belief in the grace of God bestowed on the human race through the one Mediator of God and men, Christ Jesus" (*Epistula* 186.1 [CSEL 57:45-46]); also *De natura et gratia* 6.6; 7.7; 19.21 [BA 21:252, 254, 275]).

47. *De natura et gratia* 21.23 (BA 21:282; my translation).

48. The clear references to Christ as physician for infants are: *De peccatorum meritis* 1.18.23–19.24; 1.23.33; 3.4.7; 3.13.23; *De natura et gratia* 5.5–6.6, 21.23; *De nuptiis et concupiscentia* 1.1; 2.3.9; 2.23.38; 2.33.56; *Contra Iulianum* 5.1.2; *Opus imperfectum* 3.144-46; 3.149; 3.153; 5.25; *Sermones* 115.4; 176.2-5; 293.11. Other explicit references to Christ the Physician in the anti-Pelagian writings include: *De peccatorum meritis* 1.27.54; *De perfectione iusticiae hominis* 3.5; 4.9; 21.44; *De natura et gratia* 1.1; 3.3; 19.21; 23.25; 26.29; 34.39; 39.46; 48.56; 49.57; 51.59; 54.63; 54.64; 55.65; 64.76; *De gratia Christi et de peccato originali* 1.50.55; 2.29.34; 2.29.35; *Contra Iulianum* 5.7.28; *Opus imperfectum* 6.20; *Epistula* 157.7; *Sermo* 299.6; 348A.2-4 (= Dolbeau 30).

them — the Physician who is not needed by the healthy, but by the sick, the One who came to call to repentance not the just, but sinners (Luke 5:31-32). And since infants are as yet held debt-bound by no sin from their own lives, then it must be the disease of original sin that is cured in them, cured by that grace of his which makes them healthy through the bath of rebirth.[49]

The logic here revolves around the two proof texts: Romans 5:6 and Luke 5:31-32 (Matt. 9:12). First, the citation from Romans. Here, as so often in Augustine's debate with the Pelagians, the argument centers on an interpretation of Paul, especially his letter to the Romans. The text he usually cites in tandem with the *Christus medicus* image is Romans 5:12 ("By one man sin entered into the world, and death by sin; and so it passed upon all men, in whom all have sinned").[50] But here his focus is not so much on the Adam/Christ polarity, but on the meaning of Christ's death on the cross. The argument is simple: to say infants are innocent would mean they are "godly." That would mean that Christ did not die for them, for Christ died *only* for the ungodly. However, if Christ died for all, Christ died for infants; if Christ died *only* for the ungodly, then infants must somehow be ungodly. But infants cannot be ungodly the way most of us are ungodly: by committing sins, that is, sinful acts. Since infants cannot act, they cannot sin; and yet they must be sinners for Christ to save them. Therefore, they must be original sinners, so to speak.[51] The logic Augustine

---

49. *De peccatorum meritis* 1.18.23–19.24 (PL 44:122-23; my translation): "Sine ista ergo regeneratione salvos in aeternum posse parvulos fieri, quis audeat affirmare, tanquam non pro eis mortuus sit Christus? Etenim 'Christ pro impiis mortuus est' (Rom 5:6). Isti autem qui, ut manifestum est, nihil in sua propria vita impie commiserunt, si nec originaliter ullo impietatis vinculo detinentur, quomodo pro eis mortuus est qui pro impiis mortuus est? si nulla originalis sunt peccati aegritudine sauciati sunt, quomodo ad medicum Christum, hoc est, ad percipiendum Sacramentum salutis aeternae, suorum currientium pio timore portantur. . . ? Vocat eos igitur medicus, qui non est opus sanis, sed aegrotantibus, nec venit vocare justos, sed peccatores in paenitentiam. Et ideo quia suae vitae propriae nullis adhuc tenentur obnoxii, originalis in eis aegritudo sanatur in ejus gratia qui salvos facit per lavacrum regenerationis." The CSEL edition gives a variant reading: ". . . suorum curantium *pio timore portantur*"; however, the Maurist text seems to be the right one: Augustine routinely speaks of mothers "running" with their infants to baptism. See the discussion of this below in note 83.

50. The conjunction of Rom. 5:12 and the *Christus medicus* image appears in *De peccatorum meritis* 3.4.8 (CSEL 60:134), 3.7.14 (CSEL 60:141); *De natura et gratia* 39.46 (*BA* 21:330); *Sermo* 115.4 (PL 38:657); *De gratia Christi et de peccato originali* 2.29.34 (CSEL 42:193); *De perfectione iusticiae hominis* 21.44 (*BA* 21:214-16). On developments in Augustine's understanding of Paul, see J. Patout Burns, "The Interpretation of Romans in the Pelagian Controversy," *Augustinian Studies* 10 (1979): 43-54.

51. The same argument is repeated elsewhere: *De nuptiis et concupiscentia* 2.33.56 (CSEL 42:314-15); *Contra Iulianum* 6.4.8 (PL 44:825-26).

uses here is deductive, deducing original sin from Christ's position as the one mediator of salvation.

With the other proof text, Luke 5:31-32, Augustine draws on a very different logic: not a logic of deduction, but what one might call a logic of image.[52] In citing this text ("It is not the healthy who need a physician, but the sick; for I came not to call the just, but sinners"), Augustine establishes the biblical warrant for calling Jesus a physician.[53] And this is a powerful warrant, for in Augustine's mind and that of his hearers, these are the words of Jesus himself, words in which Jesus himself describes who he is and what he does. In the anti-Pelagian writings, Augustine cites this proof text in conjunction with the *medicus* figure with almost monotonous frequency.[54] This repetition hammered home the link: Jesus = physician. This biblical text also established another link: sin = disease. With these links, the logic of image subtly comes into play. This medical imagery subtly taps into a whole cluster of experiences and expectations: doctors heal the sick; so who are the sick that Christ the Doctor heals? Doctors heal people from diseases; so what diseases does Christ the Doctor heal his patients from? Doctors use medicine; so what medicine does Christ the Doctor use? And it is exactly this chain of associations Augustine plays out in this passage: "If [infants] are not wounded by any disease of original sin, then why are they carried to Christ the Physician, that is, carried by those running in pious fear so that they might get to receive the sacrament of eternal well-being?"[55] Note Augustine's word choice here: original sin is a "disease" *(aegritudo);*[56] infants "are wounded" or "stricken" *(sauciati sunt).*[57]

Later, in book III of *De peccatorum meritis,* Augustine repeats and develops this medical vocabulary: "for no other reason are infants carried by pious hands to Jesus, that is, to Christ Savior and Physician, than that they may be healed of the plague of their sin by the medication of his sacraments."[58] In this case original sin is not simply a "disease" *(aegritudo),* but a "plague" *(pestis).* Calling original sin a "plague" evokes powerful associations: a devastation that

---

52. On the "associational logic" of "image-clusters," see O'Connell, *Soundings,* esp. 7-11.

53. Luke 5:31-32.

54. *De peccatorum meritis* 1.18.23; 1.19.24; 1.23.33; 3.13.23 (CSEL 60:22, 23, 33, 150); *De natura et gratia* 1.1; 19.21; 21.23 (*BA* 21:246, 280, 282); *De perfectione iusticiae hominis* 3.5, 21.44 (BA 21:132, 216); *De nuptiis et concupiscentia* 2.33.56 (CSEL 42:314); *Sermo* 293.11 (PL 38:1333); *Sermo* 176.2 (PL 38:950); *Epistula* 157.7 (*BA* 21:44). By contrast, the quoting of Luke 5:31-32 (or its parallel, Matt. 9:12-13) is not as common in texts before the Pelagian controversy; a few cases, however, are *Sermones* 88.7 (PL 38:542-43); 97A.3 (PLS 2:533-34); 278.5 (PL 38:1270-71).

55. *De peccatorum meritis* 1.18.23 (PL 44:122, my translation).

56. See also *De peccatorum meritis* 1.23.33 (CSEL 60:33).

57. See also *De nuptiis et concupiscentia* 2.33.56 (CSEL 42:315).

58. *De peccatorum meritis* 3.4.8 (CSEL 60:134; my translation).

is widespread and out-of-control; a disease that is highly contagious. And that is exactly the language that Augustine would later use in his *Against Julian:* original sin is a "contagion" *(contagio)*.[59] In Sermon 294, delivered in Carthage in June 413 and directed explicitly against the Pelagians, Augustine gave the pathology of original sin other variations: that in the fall, Adam had been snakebit, and so infants, however innocent in themselves, had inherited the deadly venom: "they have received the serpent's poison. . . . Don't deny it; admit the poison, in order to beg for the medicine."[60] Moreover, Christ alone possesses the precious antivenom of baptism. Again and again, Augustine speaks of baptism as "medication," as "treatment" *(medicina)*;[61] by it, an infant is "cured" *(sanatur)* and "made healthy" *(salvos facit)*,[62] and this medicine not only provides short-term relief, but is the "sacrament of eternal well-being" *(sacramentum salutis aeternae)*.[63] Even the very characterization of Christ as *medicus* leads Augustine to claim that just as those who go to doctors are sick, so those who go to Christ the Doctor — in this case, infants — are sick with sin. The logic of this seemed self-evident to Augustine, and to drive home its self-evidence he often phrased the matter with a string of rhetorical questions:

> What need did the infant have of Christ if it wasn't sick? If it's healthy, why through those who love it does it seek out the doctor? If infants are said to be entirely without any inherited sin, when are they brought along and come to Christ, why aren't those who bring them along told in the Church, "Take away these innocents; it is not the healthy who need the doctor, but the sick; Christ did not come to call the just but sinners"? . . . Those who come to Christ have something to be cured; if they haven't there's no point in presenting them to the doctor.[64]

What's important about Augustine's logic of image, of metaphor, is not simply the way it taps into our experiences and expectations. Rather it is the speed with which it moves. It jumps steps. It does not let us ask questions. Or better, it answers them before we ask them. After all, is sin really a disease? Is it a

---

59. *Contra Iulianum* 2.6.15; 3.5.11, 12; 3.6.13; 3.19.37 (PL 44:684, 708, 722). The term is also used by Cyprian, *Epistula* 64, cited in *Contra Iulianum* 1.3.6 (PL 44:644) and by Ambrose, *Apologia prophetae David* 11, cited in *Contra Iulianum* 1.3.10 (PL 44:646).

60. *Sermo* 294.12 (PL 38:1342; trans. Hill, WSA III/8:187).

61. *Sermo* 294.12 (PL 38:1342); *De peccatorum meritis* 3.4.8 (CSEL 60:134); *De natura et gratia* 52.60 (CSEL 60:277); *De nuptiis et concupiscentia* 1.1 (CSEL 42:211); *Opus imperfectum* 3.138 (CSEL 85:444).

62. *De peccatorum meritis* 1.18.23 (CSEL 60:24); 3.13.23 (CSEL 60:150).

63. *De peccatorum meritis* 1.18.23 (CSEL 60:23; my translation).

64. *Sermo* 176.2 (PL 38:950-51; trans. Hill, WSA III/5:273).

disease in the same way that smallpox is a disease or cancer is a disease? Not really. Sin is deliberate, conscious, a matter of decision, at least to some degree; but is disease deliberate, conscious, a matter of decision? Not really. And yet this is precisely what Augustine finds so attractive in the metaphor: original sin, like disease and unlike personal sin, works with an involuntary chemistry. This yoking together of sin and disease has other associations that Augustine plays on: namely, that diseases often pass from body to body. But do sins? Not really. But original sin, like disease and unlike sin, does pass from body to body — at least in Augustine's formulation of it. And it passes not only from body to body, but also from generation to generation. Original sin, in other words, has the chemistry of a congenital disease, not of a voluntary sin. Here, I am surfacing what Augustine leaves half buried. And that is precisely the power of his use of image: we tend to take in the image before we have time to question the logic or even realize that an argument has been posed. At the same time, this image cluster defines Christ, at once who he is and what he does. He is the great Physician whose medical expertise is not limited to adults, but extends to infant pathology. Christ the Physician alone has the antivenom for the genetics of snakebite; he alone has the potent waters that can halt the devastating worldwide plague, and thus stem the tide of this infant mortality of the spirit.

An Emergency Room Called Church

The image cluster I have charted — Christ as physician, original sin as disease, baptism as medicine — came not only from Augustine's meditation on biblical texts. It also came from his experience as a pastor. Note again the key sentence cited above: "If [infants] are not wounded by any disease of original sin, then why are they carried to Christ the Physician, that is, carried by those running in pious fear so that they might get to receive the sacrament of eternal well-being?"[65] Who were those piously fearful carriers of infants? Two parallel passages make this somewhat oblique reference clearer. In Sermon 293, Augustine noted that "the proof" that an infant needed Christ's healing "is its mother running to church with her baby to be baptized"; and in the exposition on Psalm 50, Augustine claimed that "if infants are completely innocent, why do mothers come running to church when their babies are ill?"[66] In

---

65. *De peccatorum meritis* 1.18.23 (CSEL 60:23; my translation).

66. *Sermo* 293.10 (PL 38:1333; trans. Hill, WSA III/8:155); *Enarrationes in psalmos* 50.10 (CCL 38:606; trans. Maria Boulding, WSA III/16:418). See also *Sermo* 176.2 (PL 38:950); *De nuptiis et concupiscentia* 2.2.4 (CSEL 42:256); *Contra Iulianum* 1.7.31 (PL 44:662).

other words, "those running in pious fear" to Christ the Physician were mothers carrying their sickly infants. Note Augustine's word choice here: each of these examples speaks of the women "running" *(currens)*. Did they really run? Or is this just pious hyperbole? It is true that sometimes Augustine spoke of catechumens who "are hurrying *(festinant)* toward the grace-giving bath."[67] But here the literal sense — of a mother running to bring an infant to baptism — is probably more accurate. The fear of dying before baptism got people running:

> This [dying in sin] is what every Christian ought to flee. For this reason, one runs to baptism. For this reason they who are in danger from sickness or any other thing desire to be helped. For this reason even a suckling child is brought by his mother to the Church with devout hands that he may not pass away without baptism and may not die in the sin with which he was born.[68]

Augustine once mentioned that seriously sick adults were hurriedly carried to church, given emergency baptism, and not infrequently died even before leaving the premises.[69] The situation of a "suckling child brought by his mother" could be far more heart-wrenching.

This was a pastoral experience that Augustine the bishop knew painfully well. In Sermons 323 and 324, Augustine tells the dramatic story that took place at Uzalis where his friend Evodius served as bishop. A woman had a young infant, still "at the breast," who had not been baptized, but according to the custom of the time had been made a catechumen. The boy fell suddenly ill, and died in his mother's arms. She rushed off with the dead child to the shrine of Saint Stephen, and demanded her son back:

> Holy martyr, you can see that I have been left without any consolation at all. I mean, I can say my son has gone ahead of me, since you know very well he has perished. You at least can see why I am so grief-stricken. Give my son back to me, so that I may have him in the presence of the one who crowned you.[70]

The child suddenly, miraculously, for a few precious minutes, revived. An emergency initiation was held: the child was "baptized, sanctified, anointed, hands were laid on him; when all the sacraments were completed, he was taken

---

67. *Enarrationes in psalmos* 41.1 (CCL 38:460; trans. Boulding, WSA III/16:239). Cf. *De fide et operibus* 6.9 (CSEL 41:44).

68. *In Johannis evangelium tractatus* 38.6 (CCL 36:341; trans. John Rettig, FC 88:109).

69. *Sermo* 393.1 (PL 38:1715).

70. *Sermo* 324 (PL 38:1446-47; trans. Hill, WSA III/9:166).

from her."[71] Augustine reports the mother's calm and relief at the funeral, that she "was laying him, not in the silence of the grave, but in the lap of the martyr Stephen."[72]

This incident vividly illustrates several matters. First, infant baptism was often emergency baptism. We should not presume that the *practice* of infant baptism was the pastoral norm, as it is today, just because Augustine and the Pelagians debated the *meaning* of infant baptism so frequently and so vigorously. In fact, fourth- and fifth-century Christians often delayed baptism until adulthood, and even then were very slow to turn in their names, despite regular and vigorous admonitions from their bishops.[73] Pious Christian parents, like this woman from Uzalis and like Augustine's own mother, did not have their children baptized; instead children, like this woman's infant son and like Augustine himself, were made catechumens: a cross was traced on their foreheads, a "tattoo" marking that they had been set apart and now belonged to Christ; hands were laid on them; they were given a taste of salt, a "sacrament" that in some way was seen to "preserve" and "season" them.[74] While such catechumens could rightly claim the name of "Christian," while they were counted as members of the "great household," they were still not "sons" or "daughters" and could claim no inheritance rights to the kingdom of heaven.[75]

Just because infant baptism was not the pastoral norm, that did not necessarily mean it was uncommon. Augustine's world endured a devastatingly high infant mortality rate. A recent study has ventured an estimate: the mortality rate was 300 per 1,000, compared with 10 per 1,000 in the First World today or

71. This passage implies something more clearly found in several other texts: that infants received not just baptism, but the whole rite of initiation. As he says here, they were "anointed," i.e., chrismation; "hands laid," i.e., consignation. They also received Eucharist, as is clear from *Sermo* 174.7 (PL 38:944) and *Epistula* 217.16 (CSEL 57:415); implied also in *De peccatorum meritis* 1.24.34 (CSEL 60:33-34).

72. *Sermo* 324 (PL 38:1446-47; trans. Hill, WSA III/9:166).

73. I treat these matters in considerable detail in my book *Augustine and the Catechumenate* (Collegeville, Minn.: Liturgical Press, 1995). For an analysis of the delay of baptism in the fourth and fifth centuries, see especially pp. 59-61, 170-72, 229-34; on the rites of entering the catechumenate, see pp. 150-51.

74. Augustine notes that he was made a catechumen while a child in *Confessiones* 1.11.17 (CCL 9:27); see also the mock dialogue in *Sermo* 294.14 (PL 38:1343). He discusses the sign of the cross on the forehead in *De catechizandis rudibus* 26.50 (CCL 46:173); *Sermo* 32.13 (CCL 41:405); *Sermo* 97A.3 (*MA* I:417); *Sermo* 301A.8 (*MA* I:88-89); *In Johannis evangelium tractatus* 3.2 (CCL 36:20). On the use of salt, see *De peccatorum meritis* 2.26.42 (CSEL 60:113); *De catechizandis rudibus* 26.50 (CCL 46:173).

75. *In Johannis evangelium tractatus* 11.4 (CCL 36:112); 44.2 (CCL 36:288); *Sermo* 46.31 (PL 38:288); *Sermo* 97A.3 (PLS 2:534); *Sermo* 301A.8 (PL 46:880).

between 50 and 200 per 1,000 in the Third World today.[76] Given this devastating rate, it is likely that infant baptism — as emergency baptism — was a frequent occurrence. As if public health conditions were not bad enough, there was also the widespread practice of infanticide. After a child was born, it was laid on the ground by the midwife; then its father would make the fateful choice: he could "take it up," thereby accepting it as his own and as a member of the family; or he could refuse it, in which case the infant was exposed in some public place, either to be rescued by a passerby or left to die.[77] Augustine reports that such exposed infants were sometimes rescued by consecrated virgins and brought in for baptism.[78] In fact, there is hardly any mention of baptizing healthy children.[79] It should be noted, however, that Augustine's outspoken opponent, Julian of Eclanum, had been baptized as an infant — at least that was the rumor Augustine had heard.[80]

What is perhaps most illuminating about the story of the woman at Uzalis is the glimpse it gives us into the emotional intensity surrounding infant baptism. It reveals something of the way an ordinary North African understood the theology of baptism. People like this woman had inherited not so much Augustine's theology as that of Cyprian of Carthage (d. 258). And the simple, stark claims that Cyprian had articulated 150 years earlier — that there is no salvation outside the church, that one cannot have God as Father if one does not first have the church as mother — could be felt by mothers with sick infants with wrenching intensity. It is little wonder that these women quite literally ran to church. This woman's story, however tragic, was less anguishing than others Augustine witnessed. Several times he discussed how parents with sick children rushed "in

76. Tim G. Parkin, *Demography and Roman Society* (Baltimore: Johns Hopkins University Press, 1992), 84. Parkin traces out the complex methodological problems of such study and offers a valuable survey of the literature. The often-cited study of Bruce W. Frier, "Roman Life Expectancy: Ulpian's Evidence," *Harvard Studies in Classical Philology* 86 (1982): 213-51, gives an even higher rate than Parkin's — 358.22 per 1,000 — but Parkin is critical of key assumptions governing Frier's study. Other important older studies include: M. K. Hopkins, "On the Probable Age Structure of the Roman Population," *Population Studies* 20 (1966): 245-64; and A. R. Burn, "*Hic Breve Vivitur:* A Study of the Expectation of Life in the Roman Empire," *Past and Present* 4 (1953): 1-31.

77. Paul Veyne, "The Roman Empire," in *History of Private Life*, vol. 1, *From Pagan Rome to Byzantium*, ed. Paul Veyne, trans. Arthur Goldhammer (Cambridge: Harvard University Press, 1987), 9-12.

78. *Epistula* 98.6 (CSEL 34:527-28).

79. A clear example of bringing healthy infants is in *Sermo* 115.4 (PL 38:657) where Augustine notes that while the children being presented that day for baptism might be healthy physically, they still suffer from the disease of original sin.

80. *Contra Iulianum* 1.4.14 (PL 44:649).

great desire and haste" and, even though the ministers were ready and waiting, the babies died before the medicine of baptism could be administered.[81]

The emotional force of Augustine's imagery comes into full view once one sees his pastoral context: that Augustine's Christ is Christ the Physician who has set up a clinic in a death-filled land; in this clinic called church, he inoculates infants with a precious vaccine called baptism. As Augustine saw it, these fearful mothers intuitively understood the meaning of Christ, of church, of sacrament in a way that neither Caelestius nor Pelagius, who went about promoting their natural health-craze of sinlessness, could ever grasp. J. Patout Burns has remarked that "Augustine overwhelmed [Pelagius] with issues he had never considered."[82] I think that is clearest here. Pelagius, the spiritual director, did not face mothers with dying children in their arms.

Augustine believed that these mothers running to church were "proof" of his interpretation of Christ and of original sin. They were, however, but one side of that proof. As he said in one sermon:

> Somebody asks: "Does an infant too need [Christ] the liberator?" Certainly it does; the proof is its mother faithfully running *(currens)* to church with her baby to be baptized. The proof is its mother the Church receiving the baby to be washed clean, and either to be let go in peace, now set free, or to be brought up in piety. Who would dare to take the stand against such a mother?[83]

A mother running with an infant; Mother Church receiving that infant: for Augustine, both were "proof" *(testis)*. And both spoke their testimony not with words, but with deeds. In saying, "Who would dare to take the stand against such a mother?" Augustine presumably means Mother Church. Yet it is ambiguous enough, as though the human mother and Mother Church were the same, or two sides of the same maternal care. Augustine did not oppose mothers easily.

Augustine took seriously this witness of Mother Church. He was convinced that the church's practice of infant baptism had been handed down from Jesus and the apostles.[84] He was equally convinced that baptism was always, in the

---

81. *Epistula* 217.6.17 (CSEL 57:417); *De dono perseverantiae* 12.31 (PL 39:1012). In one of the new Dolbeau sermons, Augustine grapples with the similarly anguishing instance of a teenage catechumen who died before baptism: for the text, see *Sermo* 142, Appendix (= Dolbeau 7) (*Vingt-six,* 289-95); for a study, see Harmless, "Voice and the Word," 20-24.

82. Burns, *Development,* 95.

83. *Sermo* 293.10 (PL 38:1333; trans. Hill, WSA III/8:155 — slightly altered). Hill renders *currens* as "hurrying"; that, I believe, is not precise enough. (Kelly also altered Hill's translation.)

84. *De peccatorum meritis* 1.26.39 (CSEL 60:38). See also *De Genesi ad litteram* 10.23.29 (*BA* 49:216); *Sermo* 174.9 (PL 38:945); *Sermo* 294.14 (PL 38:1343).

words of the church's creed, for "the remission of sin."[85] If infants were baptized, then they were baptized for the remission of some sin. But infants themselves were incapable of sin. Thus Augustine concluded that "the Catholic Church . . . truthfully baptizes little ones for the forgiveness of sins, not sins that they commit through imitation on account of the example of the first sinner, but sins which they contracted through birth on account of the defect of the origin."[86] This position was one Augustine had inherited from Cyprian.[87]

The witness of Mother Church was evident not only in the apostolic tradition of infant baptism, in the words of the creed, and in the venerable theological precedent of Cyprian; it was also evident in the rite of baptism itself. Augustine pointed out that infants, like adults, went through the *exsufflatio*, a rite of exorcism normally held during Lent, in which an exorcist breathed on the candidate and uttered a formal imprecation against Satan. This implied that infants, like adults, needed such an exorcism to release them from the devil's power.[88] In other words, Augustine's theology worked, in part, from the theological principle of *lex orandi, lex credendi* (that is, what the church prays is what the church believes). In fact, this famous theological dictum was first coined by Augustine's disciple Prosper of Aquitaine, precisely in reference to the baptismal *exsufflatio* to defend Augustine's position on original sin against those who claimed it to be a novelty.[89] In his *Unfinished Work against Julian,* Augustine would chide his op-

---

85. *De gratia Christi et de peccato originali* 1.32.35 (PL 44:377); *Sermo* 293.11 (PL 38:1334). The creed as Augustine knew it can be reconstructed from the sermons he gave during Lent to *competentes* (*Sermones* 212-15). For a discussion of the North African creed and its function in baptism, see Harmless, *Augustine,* 274-86; see also Lewis Ayres, "Augustine on the Rule of Faith: Rhetoric, Christology, and the Foundation of Christian Thinking," *Augustinian Studies* 36 (2005): 33-49.

86. *De gratia Christi et de peccato originali* 2.15.17 (CSEL 42:178; trans. Roland Teske, WSA I/23:442).

87. Cyprian, *Epistula* 64.5 (CSEL 3:720; trans. G. W. Clarke, ACW 46:112): "No one is denied access to baptism and grace. How much less reason is there then for denying it to an infant who, being newly born, can have committed no sins. The only thing that [the infant] has done is that, being born after the flesh as a descendant of Adam, he has contracted from that first birth the ancient contagion of death. And he is admitted to receive remission of his sins all the more readily [than an adult] in that what are being remitted to him are not his own sins but another's." Augustine cited this passage repeatedly: *De peccatorum meritis* 3.5.10 (CSEL 60:136-37), *Sermo* 294.19 (PL 38:1347-48), *Contra duas epistula Pelagianorum* 4.8.23 (PL 44:625), *Contra Iulianum* 1.3.6 (PL 44:644), and *Epistula* 166.23 (CSEL 44:579).

88. *De peccatorum meritis* 1.34.63 (CSEL 60:63-64); *De symbolo ad catechumenos* 1.2 (CCL 46:186); *De nuptiis et concupiscentia* 1.20.22; 2.29.50 (CSEL 42:235-36, 306); *Epistula* 194.46 (CSEL 57:212); *Contra Iulianum* 3.5.11 (PL 44:708); 6.5.11 (PL 44:829); *Opus imperfectum* 3.144 (CSEL 85:450).

89. Prosper of Aquitaine, *Auctoritates* 8-9 (PL 51:209-10). See Rebecca Harden Weaver, *Di-*

ponent for "declaring open warfare against the most ancient and worldwide church" by ignoring the manifest import of this rite.[90] Augustine saw the rite as medicinal: "infants are under the devil's power — for those to be baptized are exorcised *(exsufflatur)* in order to be freed from that power — and yet you deny them Christ who is the necessary doctor."[91] Augustine had once attacked the Donatists for failing to grasp that sacraments were actions not of human ministers, but of Christ. Here, in the same way, Augustine insisted that infant baptism was not just the expression of the loving care of Mother Church, but also of the healing care of Christ the Physician. The church was Christ's emergency room where the potent medicine of baptism was distributed pro bono.

The Pathology of Congenital Sin

The fears of mothers and the traditions of Mother Church shaped Augustine's assessment. So did crying infants:

> The baby itself bears witness to its wretchedness by crying. As best it can, feeble nature, understanding practically nothing, gives its testimony. . . . We should speak for the babies all the more mercifully, the less they can do it for themselves.[92]

Sometimes, as here for example, Augustine interpreted the infant's tears as a wordless, though eloquent, request for baptism. But just as often, he saw the tears infants shed while receiving the sacrament as a wordless resistance to it:

> And yet, we see them resist it with much weeping, and we pay no attention to their ignorance at that age so that we perform for them, even as they resist, the sacraments which we know are of benefit to them.[93]

This resistance posed for him a real problem. Baptism is, of course, the sacrament of faith, and the early church did not baptize the unwilling. For that very reason, in *Adulterous Marriages* he discussed the emergency baptism of

---

vine Grace and Human Agency: A Study of the Semi-Pelagian Controversy, Patristic Monograph Series 15 (Macon, Ga.: Mercer University Press, 1996); and Conrad Leyser, "Semi-Pelagianism," in *Augustine through the Ages,* 761-66.

90. *Opus imperfectum* 3.144 (CSEL 85:450; my translation).

91. *Opus imperfectum* 3.146 (CSEL 85:452; my translation).

92. *Sermo* 293.10 (PL 38:1333; trans. Hill, WSA III/8:155-56). Cf. *Sermo* 294.12 (PL 38:1342; *Contra Iulianum* 6.7.21 (PL 44:909).

93. *De peccatorum meritis* 1.25.36 (CSEL 60:35; trans. Teske, WSA I/23:54). Cf. *De gratia et libero arbitrio* 22.44 (PL 44:909).

adults and raised the thorny issue of baptizing someone who was not fully conscious and perhaps unwilling; he thought it better to err on the side of baptizing the unwilling than that of withholding baptism.[94] In a similar way, here Augustine did not interpret the resistance of infants as a sign leading him to deny them the sacrament and its healing power. He saw the faith that the sacrament called for voiced by those who had brought the infant and who spoke for the infant twice during the rite: first, when one renounced Satan, and second, when one formally professed one's faith in Father, Son, and Spirit. Augustine refers to these people, whether parents or godparents, as "faith-speakers," *fidedictores.*[95] As in the case of the *exsufflatio,* Augustine was convinced that this ritual action held a hidden wisdom about the power of Christ the Physician: "Here, you see, the answer is given by those who are carrying the babies. They are healed at someone else's words, because they're wounded at someone else's deed. For infants who can't speak, who remain silent, who cry, and by crying are somehow or other praying to be helped, the answer is given, and is effective."[96]

Augustine was a shrewd watcher of babies. In book I of the *Confessions,* he notes how they sleep, how they nurse, and how eventually they acquire language. At one point, he even seems to dabble with the idea that infants were capable of sin. He tells the story of two infants, presumably twins, one of whom was jealous of the other:

> I have personally watched and studied a jealous baby. He could not speak and, pale with jealousy and bitterness, glared at his brother sharing his mother's milk. Who is unaware of this fact of existence? Mothers and nurses claim to charm it away by their own private remedies. But it can hardly be innocence, when the source of milk is flowing richly and abundantly, not to endure a share going to one's blood-brother, who is in profound need, dependent for life exclusively on that one food. But people smilingly tolerate this behavior, not because it is nothing or only a trivial matter, but because with coming of age it will pass away. You can prove this to be the case from the fact that the same behavior cannot be borne without irritation when encountered in someone of more mature years.[97]

At this juncture in his career, it sounds as if Augustine was arguing that the infant was, in some sense, a sinner, that "the feebleness of infant limbs is inno-

---

94. *De coniugiis adulterinis* 1.26.33 (PL 40:460-70). In *Confessiones* 4.4.7-8 (CCL 27:43-44), he records the transformation of a teenage friend of his who was baptized while unconscious.

95. *Epistula* 98.7 (CSEL 34:528).

96. *Sermo* 294.12 (PL 38:1342; trans. Hill, WSA III/8:187).

97. *Confessiones* 1.7.11 (CCL 27:6; trans. Chadwick, 9).

cent, not the infant's mind."[98] Given these ruminations in the late 390s, one would have predicted that once the Pelagian controversy began, Augustine would have held out for the view that infants were genuinely capable of sin. But that is not the conclusion he adopted. Instead, he insisted repeatedly and forcefully that "infants, whom everyone calls innocents . . . , have committed nothing evil by means of their own will — without which there can be no sin belonging to one's own life."[99] Thus he could ask:

> Look at their great weakness of mind and body, their ignorance of everything, their complete inability to obey a command, their inability to understand or observe any law, whether natural or written, and their lack of the use of reason for either side of a question. Does not all this proclaim and demonstrate their freedom from personal sin with a silence that bears stronger witness than any language of ours?[100]

What struck Augustine was the expressiveness of that silent witness. He contrasted the children of animals with human children: that young animals can spot their mothers, discover their mother's breast, even when hidden, whereas human infants have feet unfit for walking, hands unable to scratch, and even when hungry are "better able to cry of hunger than to suck"; "this weakness of body corresponds perfectly to the weakness of the mind."[101] He went on to trace out the horrible afflictions that plagued certain infants: birth defects, blindness and deafness, feeble-mindedness and demonic possession.[102] In Augustine's mind, these anguishing phenomena were symptoms of that primeval contagion of original sin: "If it did not exist, little ones would not be subject to any evil and would not, under the mighty power of the just God, suffer any evil either in their body or in their soul."[103] In other words, the horrors infants suffered were Adam's doings, not God's; "after all, God who is the creator of souls, is also the creator of bodies, and in creating human nature he certainly did not inflict defects upon a nature that did not deserve them."[104] Augustine stared hard at the devastation on the far side of the fall. Any theology that ig-

---

98. *Confessiones* 1.7.11 (CCL 27:6; trans. Chadwick, 9).

99. *De peccatorum meritis* 1.35.65 (CSEL 60:65; trans. Teske, WSA I/23:73). Other examples: *De peccatorum meritis* 1.19.24 (CSEL 60:24); 3.4.7 (CSEL 60:133-34); *De nuptiis et concupiscentia* 2.11.24 (CSEL 42:276); *Enchiridion* 13.42-43 (CCL 46:73).

100. *De peccatorum meritis* 1.35.65 (CSEL 60:65; trans. Teske, WSA I/23:73).

101. *De peccatorum meritis* 1.38.69 (CSEL 60:69-70; trans. Teske, WSA I/23:75-76).

102. *De peccatorum meritis* 3.10.18 (PL 44:196); *Contra Iulianum* 3.4.10 (PL 44:707).

103. *Contra Iulianum* 3.5.11 (PL 44:707-8; trans. Teske, WSA I/24:345); cf. *Opus imperfectum* 3.236 (CSEL 85.1:349).

104. *Contra Iulianum* 3.6.13 (PL 44:709; trans. Teske, WSA I/24:346).

nored that devastation, that watered it down, that turned a deaf ear to the anxieties of mothers and the afflictions of infants was not Christian theology.

Precisely on this point Augustine exploited the *Christus medicus* image. He accused the Pelagians of hard-heartedness: "You pass over entirely and fail to see the evil of little ones . . . those which all of us see they suffer. You stroll about as a man of eloquence, and you exercise your talent and tongue on the praise of nature. This nature that has fallen into such great and obvious miseries needs Christ to save it, to set it free, to purify it, and to redeem it; it does not need Julian, Caelestius, or Pelagius to praise it."[105] As Augustine saw it, the Pelagian defense of infant sinlessness was a backhanded way of slashing Medicare for needy children: "This man [Julian] is, then, an enemy of this salvation of little ones, because he maintains their innocence to the point that he denies them the medicine necessary for their injuries and wounds."[106] Augustine spoke of the Pelagian view of the innocence of babies not only as "useless praise" but — paradoxically — as a "cruel defense."[107] A refrain running through Augustine's *On Nature and Grace (De natura et gratia)* is that Pelagius, in his zealous defense of Christ's role as creator, denied Christ's role as Physician:

> [T]hough [Pelagius] thinks that he is pleading God's case in defending nature, he fails to notice that, in declaring this same nature healthy, he rejects the mercy of the Physician.
>
> Let [Pelagius] not weaken the grace of such a great Physician by refusing to admit that human nature was corrupted!
>
> Nature has been injured . . . it begs the Physician; it cries out, "Save me, Lord" (Ps. 12:2); it cries out, "Heal my soul" (Ps. 41:5). Why does [Pelagius] cut off these cries so that, in defending the alleged present ability, he prevents future good health?[108]

In *On Nature and Grace,* the *Christus medicus* image appears with remarkable frequency, some fourteen times.[109] The reason — apparently — is that Pelagius himself had used the metaphor. Taking the same proof texts that Au-

---

105. *Contra Iulianum* 3.3.9 (PL 44:706; trans. Teske, WSA I/24:343).

106. *De nuptiis et concupiscentia* 2.33.56 (CSEL 42:314-15; trans. Teske, WSA I/24:90); see also *Opus imperfectum* 3.151 (CSEL 85:456).

107. *De nuptiis et concupiscentia* 2.35.60 (CSEL 42:318). See also *Contra Iulianum* 5.1.2 (PL 44:783); *De nuptiis et concupiscentia* 2.3.9 (CSEL 42:260).

108. *De natura et gratia* 34.39; 39.46; 49.57 (BA 21:316, 330, 352; trans. Teske, WSA I/23:244, 248, 254).

109. *De natura et gratia* 1.1; 3.3; 6.6; 19.21; 21.23; 23.25; 26.29; 34.39; 39.46; 49.57; 54.63; 54.64; 55.65; 64.76; not all of these focus on infants, but many focus on the more general plight of the human condition.

gustine had appealed to — Luke 5:31-32, Matthew 9:12-13 — Pelagius claimed: "those for whom you seek a physician are in good health" and that "it is the duty of a physician to be ready to heal a man who is now wounded; however, he ought not to wish that a man who is sound should be wounded."[110] Against such usage, Augustine chided the Pelagians: "Why do you call this child healthy, if not simply to contradict the doctor?"[111] For Augustine, the Pelagian tendency to pronounce that children had a clean bill of health was alarming, and in alarmist tones he proclaimed that Pelagian propaganda would undermine the practice of infant baptism. People would become so convinced of the health of infants that they would see no need for Christ's medicine and no longer bring infants for baptism.[112] He even said such neglect was a spiritual equivalent of infanticide.[113] The Pelagians saw themselves as defenders of infant innocence against the purveyors of the doctrine of original sin, against people like Augustine whom they considered "persecutors of newborns." But using the *Christus medicus* image, Augustine turned the tables on them and tried to show them "not as helpers of babies, but as oppressors of the wretched."[114]

Conclusion

At one level the clash between Augustine and the Pelagians was a clash of anthropologies, a conflicting diagnosis over what in the human condition and who in the human race needed healing. What has been overlooked and underestimated is the underlying Christology, one shaped not by technical formulations of "person," "nature," "union," but rather by a cluster of images: Christ as physician, original sin as disease, baptism as medicine. This was not just a fight over biblical texts; it was a war of metaphors. But it was more than an argument. Augustine the rhetor was also Augustine the pastor. And as a pastor Augustine faced stark realities: dying children and frightened mothers. He exegeted these realities with the same intensity that he exegeted the biblical text. He believed that when the Word of God had entered into human speech as words in the Bible, that Word came with a density and dynamism of meaning that was masked beneath a simple surface. In a similar way, Augustine used to

---

110. Pelagius, in *De natura et gratia* 21.23 (*BA* 21:284) and 26.29 (*BA* 21:296). Augustine mocks the Pelagian use of this text in *De nuptiis et concupiscentia* 2.3.9 (CSEL 42:260); *Sermo* 293.11 (PL 38:1335); *Sermo* 176.2 (PL 38:950-51).

111. *Sermo* 293.11 (PL 38:1335; trans. Hill, WSA III/8:157).

112. *De nuptiis et concupiscentia* 2.3.9 (CSEL 42:260).

113. *Sermo* 176.2 (PL 38:951).

114. *Sermo* 294.5 (PL 38:1338).

read beneath the surface of the world around him to decode its silences and decipher its subtleties. He read the "silent testimony" of infants who wailed during baptism. He read the veiled meanings in the rites of a church that exorcised seemingly innocent infants and let godparents speak for those who were speechless. Most of all, he read the panicked faces of mothers who came running to his church. All these "texts" spoke to him of Christ, a Christ ignored, or at least perilously underestimated, by the Pelagians. At the end of his life, Augustine would point to this as the crux: "But what separates you from us is this: you deny that God the savior is necessary for infants, asserting their nature to be good, that there is nothing evil in them, you say, that would require Christ the Physician."[115]

---

115. *Opus imperfectum* 3.144 (CSEL 85:450; my translation).

6. Thomas Aquinas and the Paradigms of Childhood

Philip L. Reynolds

I propose in this chapter to establish what was Thomas Aquinas's *paradigm* of the child. Readers familiar with Thomas's work may wonder whether he provides enough material for such an inquiry, for childhood was not a topic that preoccupied him. With one major exception, he referred to children only in passing, applying to their case commonplace assumptions that he accepted uncritically. Yet we may still discover a paradigm of childhood in Aquinas if his references to children have a consistent, clearly understood basis; which, in fact, they do. Moreover, there is the exception: Thomas's treatment of disputed questions about the infants of Eden was unusually extensive and involved a detailed account of the mental and physical condition of the very young.[1]

Because Thomas's idea of childhood was largely an inherited one, I shall devote more space to his background than to Thomas himself. To set a scholastic theologian in context, we normally focus on a few especially pertinent texts by other authors in an effort both to identify the author's sources and to establish a *status quaestionis* in the schools. This method has some application here, but I shall view Thomas's background more broadly, partly because most of his assumptions about childhood were commonplace, and partly because of the influence of medical scholarship. Like most scholastic theologians, Thomas adopted medical ideas readily but usually without engaging closely with the literature or citing authorities. Encyclopedias such as those by Bartholomaeus Anglicus, O.F.M. (d. ca. 1250), and Vincent of Beauvais, O.P. (d. ca. 1264), are a good source of background on childhood because encyclopedists summarized rather than contributed to knowledge, holding up a mirror to the culture of the day.[2]

---

1. See Philip L. Reynolds, "The Infants of Eden: Scholastic Theologians on Early Childhood and Cognitive Development," *Mediaeval Studies* 68 (2006): 89-132.

2. Bartholomaeus Anglicus, *De rerum proprietatibus* (Frankfurt, 1601; reprint, Frankfurt am

I should mention three methodological decisions at the outset. First, I have for the most part ignored the chronology and particular settings of Thomas's works, for his thinking about childhood remained essentially the same throughout his career.

Second, in reporting what medieval scholars say about children, I have tried to replicate rather than mitigate their male-centered attitude. There is some distinction in scholastic usage between *puer* meaning "child" and *puer* meaning "boy," just as there is a distinction between *homo* ("man" in the sense of "human being") and *vir* (denoting man rather than woman). Yet when medieval scholars thought of human beings as such or contrasted one age with another, they were thinking of males, not in view of their masculinity but because they considered humanness (the formal cause of human beings and the final cause of human generation) to be most fully represented in them.[3] Even when they spoke of *pueri* in an apparently gender-neutral manner, they easily slipped into including male-specific attributes (e.g., the onset of facial hair). References to girls and women entailed a different distinction: not that between species or between ages, but that between the sexes. The girl was therefore a special topic, distinct from that of the child. Bartholomaeus's chapter on the *puer* is on children in general but is chiefly about boys; the next chapter is on the girl *(puella)*.[4] We no longer see things in that way. But to impose gender inclusivity upon Thomas Aquinas, in my view, is as pointless as correcting his physiology of the brain.

Third, by "childhood," I refer to the entire period of life before puberty (conventionally set at twelve for girls and fourteen for boys), which was the age at which medieval persons became capable of marrying. Thomas says little specifically about adolescents in the third *septennium* (fourteen to twenty-one). Moreover, the adolescent, as we now understand the term, is a modern construct. Medieval *adolescentia* extended into midlife (roughly to age twenty-five or thirty), and medieval people had no concept of "teenage" (a hybrid of childhood and adulthood). I shall disregard Thomas's treatment of the responsibilities and obligations of offspring toward their parents,[5] for these continued into adulthood and were not age-specific.

Main, 1964) (hereafter cited as *DRP*); Vincent de Beauvais, *Speculum quadruplex sive Speculum maius*, 4 vols. (Douai, 1624; reprint, Graz, 1964), vol. 1, *Speculum naturale* (hereafter cited as *SN*).

3. Cf. Thomas Aquinas, *Summa theologiae* I, q.92, a.1, ad1[m], 5 vols. (Ottawa, 1941-45), p. 569a (hereafter cited as *ST*). I discuss the scholastic view of women, passim, in "Bonaventure on Gender and Godlikeness," *Downside Review* 106 (1988): 171-94, and in "Scholastic Theology and the Case against Women's Ordination," *Heythrop Journal* 36 (1995): 249-85.

4. Bartholomaeus, *DRP* 6.5-6 (238-41). Bartholomaeus's depiction of the girl is roughly that of the nursery rhyme: "sugar and spice and everything nice."

5. E.g., *ST* II-II, q.101, a.2 (1954).

The Background to Aquinas

Aging and the Life Cycle

To understand how the schoolmen regarded childhood, one must begin with their idea of the life cycle.[6] They inherited two compatible but distinct schemata for dividing the human life span into ages, respectively, Isidorean and medical.

The Isidorean schema of six human ages had a complex history. It began in Augustine as a hermeneutical key linking human ages both to the days of creation and to world ages.[7] Isidore modified it and added definitions in years, assuming that the life span should be divided into seven-year periods *(septennia).*[8] It underwent some minor modifications again in the high Middle Ages, partly as a result of medical influence. There were some significant changes in the course of this history, especially regarding the naming and characterizing of the last two ages. Suffice it to say that as received by both Bonaventure, O.F.M., and Thomas Aquinas, the schema involved the following ages: *infantia,* to the age of seven; *pueritia* (childhood proper), to fourteen; *adolescentia* ("growth"), to twenty-five or twenty-eight; *iuventus,* to fifty; *senectus* or *gravitas,* a period of decline that went to about seventy; and finally *senium,* also known as the *aetas decrepita,* until the end of life. The corresponding world ages are Adam to Noah, Noah to Abraham, Abraham to David, David to the Babylonian captivity, the captivity to Christ, and Christ to the world's end.[9]

According to this schema, *iuventus* is the prime of life: a central plateau of vigor and independence.[10] Both Augustine and Isidore characterize *iuventus* as

6. See Michael E. Goodich, *From Birth to Old Age: The Human Life Cycle in Medieval Thought, 1250-1350* (Lanham, Md.: University Press of America, 1989), and Shulamith Shahar, *Childhood in the Middle Ages* (London: Routledge, 1990), 21-31.

7. Augustine, *De Genesi contra Manichaeos* 1.23/35-41, ed. D. Weber, Corpus Scriptorum Ecclesiasticorum Latinorum 91 (1998), pp. 104-11 (hereafter cited as CSEL); *De diversis quaestionibus* 83, q.58, no. 2, ed. A. Mutzenbecher, Corpus Christianorum Series Latinorum 44A (1975), p. 106 (hereafter cited as CCL).

8. Isidore, *Etymologies* 11.2 and 5.38-39, ed. W. M. Lindsay (Oxford, 1911).

9. Bonaventure, IV *Sent.,* d.40, dub.3, *Opera omnia,* 10 vols. (Ad Claras Aquas, Quaracchi, 1882-1902), vol. 4, p. 854; Bonaventure, *Breviloquium,* prol. 2 (ibid., 5:204). Thomas Aquinas, IV *Sent.,* d.40, q.1, expositio textus, *Opera omnia,* vol. 7 (Parma, 1858), p. 1035b. For Thomas's *Scriptum super libros Sententiarum,* I have used the unfinished edition by P. Mandonnet and M. F. Moos (Paris, 1929-47) up to IV, d. 22, and thereafter the Parma edition (Parma, 1852-73; reprint, New York, 1948-50), vol. 7.

10. Thus Bartholomaeus, *DRP* 6.1 (232): "Huic adolescentiae succedit iuventus, & haec inter omnes aetates est media, et ideo fortissima."

the "firm" age.[11] Isidore derives the word *iuvenis* from *iuvare* ("to help"), whereas both young and old *need* help, the *iuvenis* is in a position to give it. As we shall see, theologians (mainly for christological reasons) attributed the qualities of *iuventus* to the thirtieth year in particular. Isidore says that just as oxen and other draft animals are strongest in their third year, so the thirtieth year is the perfect age of human beings.[12]

The central age of *iuventus* is preceded by growth and maturation and followed by decline. Isidore correctly explains that *infans* is from *fari* and means "unable to speak," an incapacity that he associates with the absence of teeth.[13] He derives the terms *puer* and *pueritia* from *purus* ("pure"), explaining that the child is beardless and unable to procreate.[14] At the other extreme of life, the *senes* ("the elderly") are so called because they lack *sensus* (i.e., reason). Life proceeds in a cycle: children are foolish because their blood has not yet warmed up, while the elderly are foolish because their blood has cooled down, for heat is conducive to wisdom and prudence.[15]

The correspondences envisaged between human ages and world ages shed some incidental light on the former. According to Augustine, for example, just as the flood obliterated the ancient world, so we forget what happened in infancy; just as Abraham (initiator of the third world age) was the patriarch of God's people (Gen. 17:5-8), so procreation begins in *adolescentia;* and just as Christ illumines the last age of the world, so the inner man is renewed from day to day even as the outer man decays.[16] Bonaventure adds some details that are only implicit in Augustine, comparing the acquisition of language in *pueritia* to the "distinction of tongues" (i.e., Babel), and the flourishing of a human life in *iuventus* to the flourishing of the synagogue. Strength and beauty begin to decline in the penultimate age *(senectus).* The last human age, according to Bona-

11. Augustine, *De Gen. c. Manich.* 1.23/38 (106): "inter omnes aetates regnat iuventus et ipsa est firma ornamentum aetatum omnium." Isidore, *Etym.* 11.2.5: "Quarta [aetas est] iuventus firmissima aetatum omnium."

12. *Etym.* 11.2.16.

13. *Etym.* 11.2.9. The deponent verb *fari* ("to speak") was already archaic in classical Latin, where it was reserved for oracular and prophetic utterance. (Our word "fate" is from the past participle.) Augustine too regards the ability to speak as what distinguishes the *infans* from the *puer:* see *Confessions* 1.8/13, ed. L. Verheijen, CCL 27 (1981), 7: "Nonne ab infantia huc pergens ueni in pueritiam? . . . Non enim eram infans, qui non farer, sed iam puer loquens eram."

14. *Etym.* 11.2.2 (etymology of *pueritia*) and 11.2.10 (etymology of *puer*). Isidore derives *puella* ("girl") from *pulla* ("chick") in 11.2.12.

15. *Etym.* 1.2.27. High-medieval scholars, on the contrary, considered the child's constitution to be hot.

16. See Augustine, *De Gen. c. Manich.* 1.23/35-36 (104-5), on infant amnesia; 23/37 (105-6), on procreation and Abraham; and *De div. quaest.* 58.2 (106), on spiritual renewal in the final age.

venture, like the last world age, is "joined with death" but contains "a great light of wisdom."[17]

The Isidorean schema implies a curve of value as well as of vigor, which rises from infancy to the plateau of *iuventus* and then declines again. The Visigothic code plots much the same curve: the value of a life as measured by *wergeld* (blood money) was at its maximum between the ages of twenty and fifty, when the *wergeld* was five times what it had been at birth. After fifty it declined, and by age sixty-five it had fallen to what it had been at ten.[18] This sense of life's value was not peculiar to barbarians or to the early Middle Ages: Thomas Aquinas argues that Christ died in the *aetas iuvenilis* to manifest his love for us, for he gave up his life when it was most precious, in the perfect condition.[19]

It seems odd that the Isidorean schema regards the inability to speak as the chief characteristic of infancy yet extends that age until the seventh year. William of Conches (ca. 1080-1154) explains that infancy lasts "from birth as far as the seventh year . . . because during a certain part of that period, he is unable to speak [*fari*], but in the other, if he speaks, he speaks imperfectly."[20] William's precision may be a result of medical influence, for medical scholars generally distinguished between an early stage of infancy (ranging from six months to two years) and the remainder of the first *septennium*.[21] According to Bartholomaeus, the early period lasts until the seventh month.[22]

Although the Isidorean schema was a familiar and influential guide to the life cycle, the schoolmen did not apply its divisions rigidly or attempt to make their vocabulary conform to it. The ends of the first two *septennia* (seven and fourteen) had some legal and customary significance and could be decisive turning points in a person's status (as to a lesser extent did the end of the third *septennium*, at twenty-one), but the other boundaries were merely descriptive approximations. The schoolmen refer to children by using terms such as *puer* ("child," "boy"), *parvulus/a* ("little child," sometimes "baby"), *proles* ("offspring"), and *filius/a* ("son/daughter") rather freely, relying on the context to

17. *Breviloquium*, prol. 2 (5:204).

18. See David Herlihy, "Medieval Children," in *The Walker Prescott Webb Memorial Lectures: Essays on Medieval Civilization*, ed. Bede Karl Lackner and Kenneth Roy Philp (Austin: University of Texas Press, 1978), 115.

19. *ST* III, q.46, a.9, ad4^m (2724a).

20. William of Conches, *De philosophia mundi* 4.15/23, ed. Gregor Maurach as *Philosophia* (Pretoria: University of South Africa Press, 1980), 100.

21. See Luke Demaitre, "The Idea of Childhood and Child Care in Medical Writings of the Middle Ages," *Journal of Psychohistory* 4 (1976-77): 461-65.

22. Bartholomaeus, *DRP* 6.1 (231).

establish what age in years they had in mind. Thomas in one place speaks of *pueri* still in the mother's womb.[23]

The terms *iuventus* and *iuvenis* are troublesome because they had (at least) two senses.[24] In the Isidorean schema, *iuventus* occurs in midlife, but *iuventus* and *iuvenis* often have a sense nearer to that of "youth" in modern English, such that the age of *iuventus* is roughly equivalent to *adolescentia* in the Isidorean schema. The latter sense is usually associated with a dichotomy between young men and their elders, while the Isidorean sense is associated with a division of the entire life span into several ages. Georges Duby argues that in the aristocratic society of northern France during the twelfth century, the *iuvenis* was a young knight, usually still unmarried, who had not yet come into his inheritance (at which point he became a *vir*).[25] Similarly, the *iuvenes* of Aristotle's *Nicomachean Ethics* (as translated by William of Moerbeke) are young men, not men in midlife. They are vigorous and lusty but depend on the counsel and restraint of older men (the *senes*). Partly through inexperience and partly because of their changing and turbulent physiology (for they are still growing), these *iuvenes* are imprudent, they are clever yet limited in intellectual scope, they make friends easily but just as easily lose them, they live only for the present moment, they are hedonists, and they are deficient in virtue.[26] While the Isidorean schema was associated with hermeneutical correspondences, the medical schema was based on empirical observations and presupposed a physiology of aging. (Ancient medicine was not empirical in the modern sense, but it was the result of interpreting empirical observations in the light of preconceived theory.) Among the variants with which the schoolmen were familiar were those to be found in Constantinus Africanus's *Pantegni* and Avicenna's *Canon* (the latter in the twelfth-century Latin translation by Gerard of Cremona).[27]

23. II *Sent.*, d.11, q.1, a.3, ad3^m (ed. Mandonnet, 276).

24. On the variations of usage, see Joseph De Ghellinck, "Iuventus, gravitas, senectus," in *Studia mediaevalia in honorem admodum Reverendi Patris Raymundi Josephi Martin* (Bruges, 1948), 39-59.

25. Georges Duby, "Dans la France du Nord-Ouest au XIIe siècle: Les 'jeunes' dans la société aristocratique," *Annales E.S.C.* 19 (1964): 835-46; = "Youth in Aristocratic Society: Northwestern France in the Twelfth Century," in Duby, *The Chivalrous Society*, trans. Cynthia Postan (London, 1977), 112-22.

26. Aristotle, *Nicomachean Ethics* 1.1095a2-4; 4.1128b16-19; 6.1142a11-15; 7.1154b9-15; 8.1156a31-1156b6, 1158a1-10.

27. Bartholomaeus combines the Isidorean schema with Constantine's (*DRP* 6.1, 231-32), placing the end of adolescence at the third *septennium* (i.e., age twenty-one) but adding that according to Isidore it extends through the fourth *septennium* (age twenty-eight), and according to the medical scholars to thirty or thirty-five. Vincent (*SN* 31.75, 2348-49), in his usual manner,

Constantine divides the life span into four periods: *pueritia, iuventus, senectus,* and *senium.* The first age is the period of growth and continues until about thirty. It may be divided into two fifteen-year periods, in which case the first is called *infantia* and the second *pueritia* or *adolescentia.* Growth is completed during *iuventus,* which lasts until about thirty-five or forty. In *senectus,* which continues until about sixty, the body is already in decline, but there is no obvious loss of power. Finally, in *senium,* the body's powers *(virtutes, vires)* decline as well.[28] There seems to be no plateau in Constantine's division: life is in a state either of growth or of decline.

Avicenna (Ibn Sina, d. 1037) likewise divides the life span into four ages: a period of growth *(aetas adolescentiae),* which lasts until about thirty; a period of strength and beauty *(aetas pulchritudinis),* until about thirty-five or forty; and then two phases of decline. In the *aetas senectutis,* which lasts until about sixty, there is no obvious loss of power, while in the last stage *(aetas senum),* loss of strength is severe and evident. Avicenna subdivides the growth period into five stages: first, infancy proper, in which the limbs are not ready for movement and the teeth have not yet formed; second, the period in which the child can walk but the limbs are still weak, and in which the teeth are growing but not complete; third, the period after the limbs are strong and there is a full set of teeth but before emission of semen; fourth, the period between puberty and the growth of facial hair (obviously, Avicenna is thinking mainly of boys); and fifth, the age of strength *(aetas fortitudinis),* which continues until growing stops (at around thirty).[29] Repeating this account, Vincent of Beauvais adds the gloss, "that is, of *iuventus,*" where Avicenna speaks of the *aetas fortitudinis.*[30]

Medical scholars interpreted empirical observations about aging in terms of the theory of complexion: the mixture and relative proportions of the various qualities and humors of the body, especially the hot, the cold, the wet, and the dry. Different species of animal have different complexions, as do different

---

quotes first Isidore (*Etym.* 11.2.1-8) and then Avicenna (*Canon,* lib. I, fen1, doct. 3, c.3) without trying to combine them.

28. Constantinus Africanus, *Pantegni,* pt. 1, lib. I, c. 21, printed in Isaac Israeli, *Opera omnia* (Lyons, 1515), vol. 2, fols. 1r-144r, at fol. 4va. See also Marco T. Malato and Umberto de Martini, eds., Constantino l'Africano, *L'arte universale della medicina (Pantegni) Parte I — Libro I* (Rome, 1961), 66-67. Constantine (d. before 1098/99) was a Tunisian monk at Monte Cassino. His *Pantegni* is divided into two parts, on theoretical and practical medicine respectively. He borrowed the content of part 1 (the *Theorica*) and the plan of the entire work from a treatise by the Persian physician Haly Abbas (Ali ibn Abbas al-Majusi, d. 994).

29. Avicenna, *Liber canonis* (Venice, 1507; reprint, Hildesheim, 1964), lib. 1, fen1, doct. 3, c. 3 (fol. 3v).

30. Vincent, *SN* 31.75 (2349).

parts of the same animal and different sexes.[31] The male's complexion is relatively dry and hot, while the female's is relatively cold and wet.[32] Ages, too, have their proper complexions.[33] In the beginning, the body is hot and moist, since these are salient qualities of semen and menstrual blood (the two ingredients of conception), and the womb is itself a warm and moist environment. (According to William of Conches, it is because of the shock of coming suddenly into a relatively dry and cool environment — and not, as some supposed, as a result of philosophical reflection on the human condition — that babies cry at birth.)[34] At the second age, the body is drier but still hot (and in comparison with old age, still relatively moist). In old age, the body is cold and dry, partly because of internal, self-destructive processes, and partly because of the drying effect of the surrounding atmosphere.[35] There was some debate about the relative heat of the first and second phases. According to one theory, the heat of childhood is quantitatively the same as that of *iuventus* but qualitatively less intense, because moisture quenches and moderates it.[36] But everyone agreed that moistness was the salient feature of childhood, and that the body became cooler and drier as it aged. According to a popular florilegium of Aristotelian doctrines, "the complexion of the young [*iuvenum*] is hot and moist, but that of the old [*senum*] is cold and dry."[37]

There were really only three complexion phases in the medical theory, respectively, hot-moist, hot-dry, and cold-dry. Yet at the very end of life, the decay of the body's members, the decline of vital heat, and an inability fully to digest food all result in the production of phlegmatic humors such as sputum, mucus, and tears, so that the body appears to be moist.[38] Clerics predisposed to symmetry and correspondences could therefore achieve a fourfold division by characterizing extreme old age as cold and moist. According to John Balbi, O.P.,

31. On complexion, see Constantine, *Pantegni* 1, 1.6-23, fols. 2r-4r (or Malato and Martini, 50-70); and William of Conches, *De philosophia mundi* 4.18 (ed. Maurach, 103-4). For a summary of the theory, see Nancy G. Siraisi, *Medieval and Early Renaissance Medicine: An Introduction to Knowledge and Practice* (Chicago: University of Chicago Press, 1990), 101-4.

32. *Pantegni* 1, 1.22, fol. 4rb (or Malato and Martini, 69).

33. *Pantegni* 1, 1.21, fol. 4r (or 66-69).

34. *De philosophia mundi* 4.14/22 (99).

35. *Canon*, lib. I, fen1, doct. 3, c. 3 (4ra).

36. See Constantine, *Pantegni* 1, 1.21, fol. 4ra (or Malato and Martini, 67); Avicenna, *Canon*, lib. 1, fen1, doct. 3, c. 3 (3vb).

37. Jacqueline Hamesse, ed., *Les auctoritates Aristotelis* (Louvain and Paris, 1974), p. 205, no. 118. The statement is taken from Averroes's commentary on Aristotle's *De longitudine et brevitate vitae*. This collection is in fact the *Parvi Flores* by Joannes de Fonte, O.F.M., composed at some time between 1267 and 1325.

38. Constantine, *Pantegni* 1, 1.21, fol. 4rb (or Malato and Martini, 69).

for example, *pueritia* is hot and moist, like spring; *iuventus* is hot and dry, like summer; *senectus* is cold and dry, like autumn; and *senium* is cold and moist, like winter.[39]

The Augustinian Child

The schoolmen were familiar with two contrasting views of childhood. On the one hand, there was Augustine's theological depiction of the child, which presupposed the fall and emphasized perversion of the will (although there was a corporeal, embodied dimension to Augustine's idea of original sin). On the other hand, there was the biological view of the child, which treated the mental and behavioral peculiarities of children as results of immature physiology and regarded childhood as natural. During the high Middle Ages, medicine was the dominant influence on the biological paradigm. The difference between the two ideas of the child is striking in Vincent de Beauvais, for he represents both views separately by assembling texts from Augustine and from medical authorities respectively, making no attempt to combine or conciliate them.[40]

I shall first sketch the Augustinian child as received in the Middle Ages, relying mainly on the texts from which Vincent collected his material. This is a partial view, overlooking the context, development, and complexity of Augustine's thought about childhood (for which I refer readers to Fr. Harmless's chapter).

Reviewing the passages from Augustine on which Vincent drew, one might wonder whether they really articulate a concept of the child as such. Augustine does not focus here on children for their own sake but for the light that they shed on the human condition. We find him rejecting the notion that infants were innocent, seeing instead clear signs of original sin in their behavior; and we find him emphasizing the misery and wretchedness of childhood. Yet his chief intention was arguably to show that *even* children were sinful, or that they were sinful *already*, and not to show that there was anything unusually or distinctively bad

39. John (Giovanni) Balbi, *Catholicon*, cited by Goodich, *From Birth*, 61. Balbi died ca. 1298. His *Catholicon* was a lexicon for interpretation of Scripture.

40. See Vincent, *SN* 31.75-91 (2348-65); c. 75, on the division of ages, is from Isidore and Avicenna; c. 76, "De infantia, et eius miseria," is mainly from Augustine (*De civ. Dei* 21.14-15 and 22.22, *Conf.* 1.7/11-12); c. 79, "De regimine infantium in dieta et moribus," is mainly from Razi (another Persian physician) and Avicenna; c. 80, "De pueritia, et eius miseria," is again mainly from Augustine (*De civ. Dei* 21.14 and 22.22); c. 81, "De regimine puerorum in dieta et moribus," is from Avicenna and Razi; c. 91, "De varietate complexionis secundum gradus aetatis," is from Avicenna and Constantine.

about the child. And to some extent the wretchedness that Augustine described was the result of harsh treatment by adults, a harshness that he seemed to regret.[41] Yet he sometimes implied that there was something egregiously sinful or miserable about the very features that distinguished the child from the adult.

Reflecting on the "sin of my infancy" in the *Confessions,* Augustine sees in the greedy, selfish, and spiteful behavior of infants, evidence that no one, not even a day-old child, is free from sin. Yet Augustine judges the infant here by adult standards, for he notes that if he himself cried for food now as he must have done for the breast as a baby, he would be justly rebuked. By such standards, infantile behavior must be worse, or at least look worse, than adult behavior. Augustine observes that we regard infantile misdeeds leniently not because they are not faults or are minor faults, but only because we expect them to pass away with age. If there is any innocence in the infant, it consists in the weakness (*imbellicitas*) of its limbs, and not in its *animus* (its mind or will or intention).[42]

Augustine was horrified by the ignorance and mental ineptitude of children. In *De civitate Dei,* reflecting on the wretchedness of the human condition, Augustine argues that boys are subject to harsh schooling only because their "folly or inexperience" (*insipientia vel imperitia*) would be an even worse punishment. He observes that anyone would recoil with horror and choose to die if offered a choice between death and a return to infancy (a statement that Vincent omits), and here he seems to be thinking of infancy per se rather than of its treatment by adults. Yet his chief contention in this passage is that children already share the misery of the human condition. When he explains why infants cry when they are born (a topos of literature on birth and infancy), he seems to mean that their plaint is about the human condition, not about infancy.[43] And when he speaks of the "dreadful depth of ignorance" besetting the "sons of Adam," he is referring to all human beings. In the same context he speaks of a great "ignorance of the truth, which is already apparent in infants," and of the "abundance of empty desire" that begins to appear in childhood.[44] Here too, it seems, children manifest common failings of mankind.

Nevertheless, in at least two places Augustine explicitly abhors the very ignorance that *distinguishes* the infant from the adult. In *De Trinitate,* inquiring whether the infant knows itself, he says that the infant is "submerged in such great ignorance of things that a human mind that knows something is horrified by the darkness of its mind." The infant knows itself in some existential man-

41. See especially *Confessions* 1.9/14-15 (CCL 27:8-9).

42. *Confessions* 1.7/11 (6). Fr. Harmless shows that Augustine did not always maintain, and perhaps moved away from, this estimation of the infant's actual sinfulness.

43. *De civ. Dei* 21.14 (CCL 48:780-81).

44. *De civ. Dei* 22.22 (842).

ner, Augustine argues, but it is too sensual to think about itself. All its attention is pulled outwards. Infants suffer vehement detestation and desire, and they become easily fixated on a sensible object, such as a nightlight.[45]

The other passage (which, unlike all the above, is not among those on which Vincent drew for his portraits of *infantia* and *pueritia*) was the root of the disputed questions about the infants of Eden in the medieval schools. In *De peccatorum meritis et remissione*, Augustine assumes that infancy itself is a penalty for original sin, a penalty that Christ shared only to show solidarity with us. It is not so much the size or the weakness of infants that is penal as their "appalling ignorance [*horrenda ignorantia*], a weakness that is not of the flesh but of the mind."[46] Augustine therefore wonders whether the children who would have lived in the earthly Paradise if there had been no sin would have been begun life as infants, or rather would have miraculously grown up at once, as soon as they were born. He is not sure, but he suggests that like the young of many animals even now, they would at least have been able to move about, to recognize their mothers, and to find their mother's breast. The helplessness that we observe now in babies, on the contrary, is a punishment for sin, for the weakness of their bodies befits the weakness of their minds.[47] Without entirely rejecting Augustine's depiction of paradisal infancy, the schoolmen rejected the assumptions underlying it, arguing instead (with some qualifications) that even fallen infants are not ignorant but merely nescient, that their debility is not punitive but natural, and they are as incapable of sin as of virtue.

The Biological Child

The idea of fluidity is conspicuous in the medieval vocabulary of childhood. Children have soft, malleable bodies; their humors are changeable and flowing; and their bodies are moist. The fluidity of children extends to their minds, which are changeable and unsettled. While largely medical in origin, these ideas were not peculiar to medicine. Anselm of Canterbury is said to have likened education (especially moral education) to impressing a seal on wax. Being "tender

---

45. Augustine, *De Trinitate* 14.5/5, ed. W. J. Mountain, CCL 50A (1968), 429: "Quid itaque dicendum est de infantis mente ita adhuc parvuli et in tam magna demersi rerum ignorantia ut illius mentis tenebras mens hominis quae aliquid nouit exhorreat?"

46. Augustine, *De peccatorum meritis et remissione et de baptismo parvulorum ad Marcellinum libri tres* 1.37/68, ed. C. F. Urba and J. Zycha, CSEL 60 (1913), 69: "propter horrendam ignorantiam atque infirmitatem non carnis, sed mentis."

47. Augustine, *De peccatorum meritis et remissione et de baptismo parvulorum ad Marcellinum libri tres* 1.37/68–38/69 (pp. 69-70).

in age and in knowledge," children are unable to distinguish between good and evil. Because their mental wax is "soft and virtually liquid [*mollis . . . et quasi liquens*]," no permanent impression can be made on it. At the other extreme, old persons are too set in their ways to change, for their mental wax is too hard to receive an impression. But *adolescentes* (youths) and *iuvenes* (men in the prime of life) are capable of instruction, for their mental wax is "fittingly tempered from softness [*teneritudo*] and hardness."[48]

Medical scholars assumed that the peculiarities of children were chiefly the result of their moist complexion. The context of this view of childhood was literally therapeutic. (I say "literally," because Augustine's account was therapeutic too, as Fr. Harmless shows in this volume, but only in a transferred, metaphorical sense, whereby sin was the disease and Christ the physician.)[49] The aim of medicine in the Galenic tradition was to correct imbalances and to maintain harmony. When the complexion was distempered, the physician applied correctives of a contrary nature. For example, because fever indicated the presence of a hot and dry disease, the physician would apply moist remedies. But "in childhood," Galen says, "which is not a disease but in accordance with nature, that which is most similar is most advantageous."[50] Since infants are naturally moist, one should maintain a moist regime, giving them only liquid food and bathing them frequently.[51] Galen's harmonious regime for the infant includes frequent bathing, massage with sweet oil, and regular meals of appropriately soft, moist food. As he grows older, the infant should be allowed to play whenever he pleases.[52] The regime is only gradually adapted over the first fourteen years, as the constitution begins to dry out while retaining its heat. Exercise during this period should not be excessive or violent. From around the seventh year, parents should begin to prepare the child for his future vocation, cultivating the mind or the body in appropriate ways.[53]

Avicenna likewise prescribes a gentle, calm, and indulgent regime for the infant, with bathing, massage, and lullabies. Because the infant's body is soft and fluid, it should be swaddled, and for the same reason it can be manipulated

---

48. R. W. Southern, ed., *The Life of St. Anselm Archbishop of Canterbury* (London: Thomas Nelson & Sons, 1962), c. 11, 20-21.

49. On the *Christus medicus* metaphor and on theologians' appropriation of medicine in the Middle Ages, see Philip L. Reynolds, *Food and the Body: Some Peculiar Questions in High Medieval Theology* (Leiden: Brill, 1998), 120-46.

50. Robert Montraville Green, *A Translation of Galen's Hygiene (De sanitate tuenda)* (Springfield, Ill.: Charles C. Thomas, 1951), c. 7, p. 23.

51. Green, *Translation of Galen's Hygiene*, 23-24.

52. Green, *Translation of Galen's Hygiene*, c. 10, pp. 31-32.

53. Green, *Translation of Galen's Hygiene*, c. 12, pp. 37-38.

into better shape.[54] As the child begins to walk and approaches childhood proper *(pueritia)*, one must take great care not to upset him, for intense emotions not only unsettle the mind and generate vices but also distemper the complexion: anger heats up the constitution, sorrow dries it out, and sloth generates phlegmatic humors. Therefore one should give the child whatever he wants and avoid whatever displeases him.[55] (Vincent omits the last statement.) Nurses should bathe the young child as soon as he awakes, let him play for an hour, and then feed him in moderation before letting him play as much as he likes. At the age of six, he is ready to be assigned to a teacher, but his education should be gradual and moderate, and he should not be forced to remain at his lessons if he is unwilling.[56]

Qualities of moisture, softness, and fluidity are conspicuous in Bartholomaeus's account of childhood as well. The body of the newborn infant is extremely soft *(mollis)*, tender *(tener)*, and malleable *(fluidus)*, and it should therefore be swaddled and cosseted.[57] Children's limbs are still soft and flexible in *pueritia*, because the complexion is still hot and moist.[58] Bartholomaeus moves easily from physiology to behavior, presenting a charming depiction of innocence: children are free from care; they love games and jokes; they fear no danger greater than a blow from a stick; being unaware of the true value of things, they prefer an apple to gold and grieve more over the loss of a pear than of an inheritance; they value the opinions of other children more than those of their elders. Because of the changeability *(mobilitas)* of their bodies and humors, they are easily angered but easily placated. They are always active and always hungry. They are always shouting, laughing, and chattering, and are quiet only when they go to sleep.[59] Bartholomaeus's depiction of the child does not support the theory that childhood is socially constructed, for it suggests that medieval children behaved in much the same way as modern children do. What was different was how adults interpreted and explained that behavior.

The treatment of age and infancy by William of Conches anticipates, apparently without any direct influence, some features of the infants-of-Eden debate in the thirteenth-century schools. He combines a biological theory of ag-

---

54. Avicenna, *Canon*, lib. 1, fen3, doct. 1, c. 1 (53va-b), on the regime of the infant from birth until it begins to walk. Cf. Vincent, *SN* 31.79 (2352).

55. Avicenna, *Canon*, lib. 1, fen3, doct. 3, c. 4 (56r): "Et istud fit considerando semper ut ei adhibeatur quod desiderat et appetit, et non permittatur esse coram eo aliquid quod ipse adhorreat."

56. Avicenna, *Canon*, lib. 1, fen3, doct. 3, c. 4 (56r). Cf. Vincent, *SN* 21.81 (2354).

57. Bartholomaeus, *DRP* 6.1 (231); 6.4 (237).

58. Bartholomaeus, *DRP* 6.5 (239).

59. Bartholomaeus, *DRP* 6.5 (239-40).

ing derived from the *Pantegni* with a homegrown, north European Platonism, and he emphasizes the influence of complexion on cognition. The soul by its very nature, William maintains, receives from its Creator universal understanding. Such was the condition of Adam in the beginning. But now, because of the corruption and the weight *(gravitas)* of the flesh,[60] infants come into the world without knowledge and remain so until they are ready to acquire it through practical experience *(usus experientia)* and instruction *(doctrina)*.[61] The infant is like someone with good eyesight incarcerated in a dark prison, who cannot see until his eyes become accustomed to the gloom or until he is given a lamp.[62]

In the first phase of life, William continues, the infant is not ready for practical experience or instruction. He eats frequently because of his hot, moist complexion, and therefore dense fumes, a by-product of digestion, collect in his head and impede understanding. (In a previous passage, William says that infants have sensation but neither reason nor understanding.)[63] Because the next age, *iuventus,* is drier, the fumes are less dense and the brain is less disturbed. This is when discernment begins, "especially if the lamp of diligent instruction is lit." Next follows *senectus,* when the complexion is cold and dry. Although natural heat wanes and the body gets weaker, the constringent power of the cold, dry complexion causes memory to thrive. Finally, because of the loss of vital heat, cold phlegmatic humors accumulate. This causes memory to fail, and the elderly become like children again *(pueriles)*.[64]

The Infants of Eden

The question about the hypothetical infants of Eden that Augustine had raised in *De peccatorum meritis et remissione* resurfaced in the twelfth century: Would they have grown up at once or developed gradually? In his *De sacramentis christianiae fidei* (1130/31-37), Hugh of St. Victor argues that the infants of Eden would probably have matured gradually, much as they do now, because such development is natural. All living things develop in the same manner, and it stands to reason that a species would be perfect only at the very beginning, when God created it, and would achieve perfection gradually thereafter, for such is its natural mode of coming into being. The imperfection of infants in

60. Cf. Wisd. 9:15: "corpus enim quod corrumpitur aggravat animam."

61. The coupling of *doctrina* and *usus experientia,* which occurs twice in this passage, appears as well in 1.2/9 (ed. Maurach, 21).

62. *De philosophia mundi* 4.29/53 (113).

63. 4.15/23 (100).

64. 4.29/54 (113-14).

Eden would not have been a fault *(vitium)*. Hugh considers a counterargument: immaturity entails ignorance, which is a penalty for original sin. He replies by distinguishing between *ignorance* and *nescience*. Ignorance is more than the absence of knowledge; it is not knowing what one *ought* to know. (Hugh is thinking chiefly of the knowledge required for salvation.) Even in this fallen world, children are not ignorant, Hugh says, until they reach the age of discernment. Similarly, there is nothing sinful in their sensuality.[65] Hugh does not mention Augustine, but his discussion turns on the putative ignorance of infants, and Augustine had emphasized their "appalling ignorance."

The author of the *Summa sententiarum* (1138-41), who was probably Odo of Lucca, recast the question (perhaps unfairly) as a pair of contrary alternatives. On one side is Augustine (in *De peccatorum meritis et remissione*), whom Odo quotes. On the other side are certain theologians *(quidam)* who maintain that the infants of Eden would have developed gradually. Odo clearly prefers the latter view, which is essentially Hugh's, although Odo emphasizes the behavioral and corporeal rather than cognitive aspects of infantile debility.[66] Peter Lombard, in his *Sentences* (1154-57), compiled a comprehensive account from Hugh's and Odo's,[67] and Lombard's treatment became the basis of the discussion in the thirteenth-century schools.

By the mid–twelfth century, then, a standard position had become established. First, the infants of Eden would have been not only small but mentally and physically weak, and they would have developed gradually. Second, infantile imperfection is natural, and therefore consistent with a condition of perfect nature. Not every imperfection is a fault. Third, infants are nescient but not ignorant, since ignorance is a privation of *due* knowledge, that is, of knowledge that one *ought* to have.[68]

Thirteenth-century theologians accepted and elaborated these essential points.[69] That infants lack actual reason and understanding and depend instead entirely on the senses was a commonplace of medieval thought.[70] But in that

---

65. Hugh of St. Victor, *De sacramentis Christianae fidei* 1.6.26, PL 176:278D-280B.

66. *Summa sententiarum* 3.4, PL 176:95A-C.

67. Peter Lombard, *Sententiae in IV libris distinctae*, 2.20.4-5, vol. 1.2 (Grottaferrata, 1971), 429-32.

68. As well as the above sources, see Rolandus, *Sentences,* in *Die Sentenzen Rolands nachmals Papstes Alexander III,* ed. Ambrosius M. Gietl (Freiburg im Breisgau, 1891; reprint, Amsterdam, 1969), 122-23; and Bandinus, *Sent.* 2.20, PL 192:1047D-48B.

69. See my article, cited n. 1 above.

70. Cf. Vincent, *SN* 31.78 (2351): "Et homo quidem huius aetatis scilicet infantiae quae natiuitate coniuncta est, usque septimum annum sensum habet. Videt, enim & audit, & olfacit, & gustat, & tangit, sed ratione, & intellectu scilicet quantum ad usum caret."

case, one cannot justly accuse them of ignorance. To illustrate the distinction between nescience and ignorance, some thirteenth-century theologians cited the example of puppies, who cannot see at birth but are not called blind before they are nine days old, for until then they are not *supposed* to see.[71]

The first major thirteenth-century master to treat the question was Thomas's mentor, Albertus Magnus, O.P., in his sentential commentary (composed in the 1240s).[72] Albert was an eclectic thinker, and he was fascinated by the natural world. He therefore readily introduced medical ideas into the standard account (for which he was dependent on Peter Lombard). He reasons that unlike the young of some other animals, the infants of Eden would not have been able to feed themselves or to walk, because what precludes movement in the human infant is the natural softness *(mollities)* of its body. It is true that our upright posture befits the dignity of human nature, but although infants must crawl around on their hands and knees, this debility results from the special complexion of human beings, which is nobler than that of any other animal. Contrariwise, animals that are fully mobile at birth have ignoble features resulting from their earthy complexion, such as a hairy skin and hard, rigid limbs.[73] Much the same idea appears in Vincent of Beauvais, as one possible explanation for the helplessness of human infants. Only human beings are rational, and reason requires temperate, soft, fleshy members. Other animals are mobile at birth because they lack reason and have rigid limbs, befitting the work that they need to do.[74]

Albert argues that because complexion influences cognition as well as bodily powers, the debility of the infant's mind is natural.[75] Replying to the objection that ignorance is a penalty for sin, Albert explains that because the in-

71. Albertus Magnus, *Summa theologiae* II, tr. 14, q.85, ad2[m] (Borgnet edition, 33:137a). *Summa Fratris Alexandri* 2.1, no. 502, ad1[m] contra, in Alexander of Hales, *Summa theologica*, vol. 2 [Ad Claras Aquas, Quaracchi, 1928], 718b. (The SFA is in reality the work of the Franciscan school in Paris, and not of Alexander himself. The passage cited here is from an appendix that was probably added in the 1260s.)

72. Albertus Magnus, II *Sent.*, d.20, a.7, in *Opera omnia,* ed. Auguste Borgnet, 38 vols. (Paris 1890-99), vol. 27, 349.

73. Ibid., ad1[m] (349b). William of Conches says that human infants, unlike those of other animals, cannot walk at birth because the human fetus is nourished on menstrual blood: see *De philosophia mundi* 6.11/19 (ed. Maurach, 97).

74. *SN* 31.78 (2351).

75. On Albert's theory of sensory cognition in relation to the brain, see Nicholas H. Steneck, "Albert the Great on the Classification and Localization of the Internal Senses," *Isis* 65 (1974): 193-211; and Steneck, "Albert on the Psychology of Sense Perception," in *Albertus Magnus and the Sciences: Commemorative Essays, 1980,* ed. James A. Weisheipl (Toronto: Pontifical Institute of Medieval Studies, 1980), 263-90.

fant's constitution is still soft *(mollis),* the complexion of the infant's brain is too humid and changeable for clear thought.[76] Here Albert quotes a dictum derived from Aristotle's *Physics:* "It is in settling down and becoming quiet that the soul becomes knowing and prudent."[77] (In the passage to which Albert refers, Aristotle compares the turbulence of the child's mind to drunkenness.) It would be unnatural if the infant were capable "of the strong impression of species and of strong conversion upon them." (Albert is referring here to the intentional forms in the knower by which the knower knows the known.)[78] The infant's moist complexion prevents it from focusing on one thing at a time, and thus from actually considering whatever it knows habitually.[79]

There is a similar treatment of the question in the earlier of Bonaventure's two commentaries on the *Sentences,* the *Dubia circa litteram Magistri.*[80] Bonaventure argues that the infants' stature in Eden and the use of their limbs would probably have developed gradually, because their development "would have been not miraculous but natural, even in the time of instituted nature." The tenderness *(teneritudo)* of human limbs is a result of the excellence and harmoniousness of human nature.[81] Unlike Adam, the infants of Eden would not have come into existence with perfect actual cognition (although they would have had perfect habitual knowledge). Sensory and intellective cognition would have developed gradually, for although the soul per se does not undergo alteration over time, it "imitates the complexion of the body." To illustrate how the soft and fluid complexion of the brain precludes what he too calls the "strong impression of species and strong conversion upon them," Bonaventure draws an analogy: "just as a face is not reflected in moving water, so young children [*parvuli*] are not suited at once to the use of cognition." When Aristotle refers to the intellect's settling down and becoming quiet with maturity, therefore, he is thinking of the "movement and fluidity [*fluxibilitas*]" of the young child's complexion. But Bonaventure reasons that paradisal children, unlike children now, would have acquired knowledge quickly and effortlessly.[82]

---

76. Albert, II *Sent.,* d.20, a.7, ad2[m] (349b).

77. Albert, II *Sent.,* d.20, a.7, ad2[m] (349b): "Sedendo et quiescendo fit anima sciens et prudens." Cf. Aristotle, *Physics* 7.3, 247b9-11.

78. II *Sent.,* d.20, a.7, ad2[m] (349b). On the function of intentional species in cognition, see Leen Spruit, *Species Intelligibilis: From Perception to Knowledge,* vol. 1, *Classical Roots and Medieval Discussions* (Leiden: Brill, 1994).

79. II *Sent.,* d.23, a.1, ad2[m] (391b). Unlike Thomas, Albert believed that the infants of Eden, as well as Adam, would probably have begun life with infused universal knowledge.

80. Bonaventure, II *Sent.,* d.20, dub. 5-6 (Quaracchi edition, 2:488-89).

81. Bonaventure, II *Sent.,* d.20, dub. 5, resp. (488b).

82. Bonaventure, II *Sent.,* d.20, dub. 6, resp. (489a-b).

The Innocent Child

The innocent child of Christian tradition is not only an image or a characterization of childhood: it is also (and often chiefly) a rhetorical topos or a hermeneutical key. Part of the idea is that children are not yet capable of certain adult vices, but this theme is often linked to biblical passages presenting the child as a model of the Christian life, such as Matthew 19:4 ("Suffer the little children and forbid them not to come unto me, for the kingdom of heaven is such") and Matthew 18:2-6, where Jesus takes a little child *(parvulus)* to teach the disciples a lesson in humility, explaining that unless they too become like little children, they will not enter the kingdom of heaven.

Commenting on Matthew 18:2-6, Jerome explains that Jesus did not want the disciples to have the age of little children but only their innocence. Adults should achieve through effort what children have by their age. They should be childlike as regards malice, and not as regards wisdom (1 Cor. 14:20). Jerome goes on to explain that the little child is a good example because he does not persevere in anger or remember an injury, because he experiences no pleasure on seeing a beautiful woman, and because he does not think one thing and say another.[83] (These are perennial topoi of the innocence theme.) Commenting on Mark's version of the text (Mark 9:35-37), Hugh of St. Cher, O.P. (d. 1263), lists eighteen qualities that "assimilate" good children to Christ. For example, they do not experience motions of the flesh, they obey their parents, they have confidence in others rather than in themselves, they are content with little, and they are carefree, easily placated, and truthful.[84]

Do such passages imply or presuppose a positive evaluation or "sentiment" of childhood? It is hard to know, and one should be cautious. Children provide a lesson in humility not because they themselves are humble but because they are powerless and abject, attributes that might or might not be perfections in the child. The little child's example teaches a lesson of forgiveness, chastity, and honesty, but the child does not possess these virtues. Rather, his mind and body are not yet sufficiently developed for the corresponding vices. The foundation of the child's innocence is his lack of reason and his volatility: as Isidore puts it, children do not know what they do because of unruliness *(lascivia)* and lack of age, just as the elderly become silly through excessive age.[85] Innocence, therefore, is a result of imperfection or deficiency.

---

83. Jerome, *Commentariorum in Mathaeum Libri IV*, ed. D. Hurst and M. Adriaen, CCL 77 (1969), pp. 156-57.

84. Hugh of Saint Cher, *Opera omnia in universum vetus & novum testamentum*, vol. 6 (Venice, 1732), 105v. I am grateful to Mary Dzon for bringing this text to my attention.

85. Isidore, *Etym.* 11.2.27: "pueri per lasciviam et infantiam ignorant quid agant." Cf.

Thomas Aquinas

Aging and the Life Cycle

Thomas considered the life span to be a cycle *(circulatio)* that begins in the deficiency *(defectus)* of childhood, achieves "the state of due perfection" *(status debitae perfectionis)* in midlife, and eventually returns to deficiency in old age *(senectus)*.[86] The perfect age is called *iuventus* or the *aetas iuvenilis*. Just as a human life approaches perfection in *iuventus* and then declines from it, therefore, so also those who were nearest in time to Christ, such as John the Baptist and the apostles, had the most explicit faith.[87] The notion of *iuventus* as the central age is dependent on the Isidorean schema, which Thomas sets out in its traditional form (complete with correspondences between human ages and world ages).[88] When he comments on the parable of the vineyard (Matt. 20:1-16), Thomas adapts the Isidorean schema to the stages of the day mentioned in the parable, likening *adolescentia* to the third hour and *iuventus* to the sixth. Here too, *iuventus* is the perfect age. Just as the sun begins to be hot in the third hour, Thomas comments, so the light of understanding begins to shine in *adolescentia,* and "just as the sun is in its perfection in the middle of the day, so is a man in *iuventus.*"[89]

According to the Isidorean schema, *iuventus* is a plateau lasting for some twenty-five years (i.e., roughly from age twenty-five to age fifty), but Thomas sometimes assumes that the perfect age occurs at around thirty. The relevant passages always have some connection with the life of Christ. It was fitting that Jesus was baptized at the "perfect age" of thirty, Thomas argues, partly because that is the ideal time for anyone to begin a career of teaching and preaching (as also of ruling and prophesying), and partly to symbolize how baptism generates "perfect men," for all will rise again "unto a perfect man, unto the measure

---

Bartholomaeus, *DRP* 6.1 (232): "pueri propter lasciviam et levitatem quid agant, ignorant, ut dicit Isidorus." On the senses of the difficult words *lascivus* and *lascivia* (and of their medieval English equivalents, "wanton" and "wantonness"), see Mary Dzon, "The Image of the Wanton Christ Child in the Apocryphal Infancy Legends of Late Medieval England" (Ph.D. diss., Toronto, 2004), 23-32. As applied to children, *lascivia* implies something uncontrolled, irrational, wild, or playful, but has no libidinal connotations.

86. II *Sent.,* d.22, q.2, a.1, resp. (ed. Mandonnet, 510). Here Thomas argues that the initial deficiency, and not the latter, would have existed in Eden. He makes the same argument in *ST* I, q.99, a.1, arg. 4 & ad4[m] (604b-5a, 605b).

87. *ST* II-II, q.1, a.7, ad4[m] (1408b).

88. IV *Sent.,* d.40, q.1, expositio textus (Parma edition, 7:1035).

89. *Lectura super Mathaeum,* c.20, lect. 1 (Turin, 1951). I have consulted this text (in a digitized version prepared by R. Busa) via Enrique Alarcón's *Corpus Thomisticum* Web site.

of the fullness of Christ" (Eph. 4:13). Even the number thirty itself implies spiritual perfection, since it is the product of three and ten: three to symbolize faith in the Trinity, and ten to symbolize obedience to the commandments.[90]

The idea of a cycle of perfection is manifest when Thomas explains why all human beings will have the same age, the *aetas iuvenilis,* at the general resurrection.[91] Here he construes the perfection of midlife as a final cause. Just as God created human nature in the beginning without deficiency *(defectus),* so also will God restore human nature to this condition in the end. Now human nature may be deficient in two ways: first, when it has not yet reached final perfection *(perfectio ultima),* as in children *(pueri);* and second, when it has receded from final perfection, as in the elderly *(senes).* Therefore all will rise in the state of perfection, namely, the *aetas iuvenilis.* The traditional, christological support for this doctrine appears here in an argument *sed contra:* according to Ephesians 4:13, all will rise "unto a perfect man, unto the measure of the fullness of Christ." Now "Christ arose in the *aetas iuvenilis,* which begins around the thirtieth year, as Augustine says." Just as it is fitting that all will rise in *iuventus,* therefore, so it was fitting that Christ died in *iuventus.*[92] Thomas makes the same point when commenting on Ephesians 4:13: "The body of Christ had been brought to the full age of manhood [*plena aetas virilis*], namely, 33 years, when he died. Therefore the age of the blessed who rise again will be conformed to the fullness of age of this kind, in which there is no imperfection [of childhood], nor the deficiency of old age."[93]

Thomas concedes that both childhood and old age have certain perfections, but he argues that these are insufficient as criteria for the age of the bodily resurrection. According to an Aristotelian theory of mortality that Thomas defends, the digestion of food gradually adulterates the body (by assimilating the body to food), corrupting its "species" (its humanness) and resulting eventually in death. From this point of view, human nature is truest and most perfect in the beginning. But such perfection, Thomas replies, consists precisely in the power to assimilate nutriment. (As this power deteriorates, the body wanes and dies.) The

90. *ST* III, q.39, a.3, resp. (2668b-69a).

91. IV *Sent.,* d.44, q.1, a.3, q³1, resp. (Parma edition, 7:1082). Compare the Victorian children's hymns "Around the throne of God in heaven / Thousands of children stand" (by Anne Shepherd), and "There's a friend for little children / Above the bright blue sky" (by Albert Mildane).

92. IV *Sent.,* d.44, q.1, a.3, q³1, s.c. (1081a).

93. *Super Epistolam B. Pauli ad Ephesios lectura,* c.4, lect. 4, no. 216. (Uncorrected *reportatio.*) Thomas uses the same constellation of arguments in *Summa contra gentiles* IV, c. 88, no. 4231 (ed. C. Pera, P. Marc, and P. Caramello [Turin, 1961-67]), and *ST* III, q.46, a.9, ad4ᵐ (2724a).

vigor of the species is "more perfect as regards the terminus of completion" (its finality or teleology) in the *aetas iuvenilis*.[94] Again, the elderly are venerable, but reverence is due to them "not because of the condition of the body, which is deficient, but because of the soul's wisdom, which one presumes to be present because of their advanced age." In any case (the elect at the bodily resurrection) will be wise and venerable through a gift of God.[95]

Thomas often refers to *iuventus* of the other kind, presupposing a dichotomy between young men *(iuvenes)* and old men *(senes)*. Many of these passages are in his commentary on the *Nicomachean Ethics*. Because this is a literal commentary, one cannot be sure, even when he goes beyond mere paraphrase, whether Thomas means to express his own opinions or only to explicate Aristotle. Perhaps he was not aware of a distinction. Be that as it may, I can see no reason to doubt that Thomas accepts what Aristotle himself says here both about boys *(pueri)* and about young men *(iuvenes)*. Thomas comments that young men are not good students of ethics or politics because judgment about such matters requires experience, which they have not yet had time to acquire.[96] Having vivid imaginations, they are good at mathematics, but they are too inexperienced for the branches of philosophy that surpass sense and imagination.[97] Because of the "fervor" of the *aetas iuvenilis* as well as inexperience, young men live by the passions and are often kept under control only by shame.[98]

The *iuvenes* as young men are not limited to Thomas's commentaries on Aristotle. He is referring to them when he argues in his sentential commentary that *iuvenes* experience carnal pleasure more readily than *senes*, just as sulfur can be set alight by a small flame while wood requires a greater one. (Here Thomas construes the human subject as the material cause of pleasure, and the pleasurable object as the formal cause.) Thomas adds that *senes* are just as easily, and indeed more easily, moved to spiritual pleasure.[99] And he is referring to young men when he compares the hopefulness of *iuvenes* to that of drunkards

---

94. IV *Sent.*, d.44, q.1, a.3, q^a1, arg. 3 and ad3^m (1081a, 1082a). The argument involves the "truth of human nature": on this topic, see Reynolds, *Food and the Body*, especially 50-66 (on the *veritas humanae naturae*), 67-104 (on the origins of the Aristotelian theory of mortality), and 360-95 (on Aquinas).

95. IV *Sent.*, d.44, q.1, a.3, q^a1, arg. 1 & ad1^m (1081a, 1082a).

96. *Sententia libri Ethicorum* 1.3, in *Opera omnia*, Leonine edition, vol. 47, p. 12 [no. 38, 1095a2-4]. I have retained the familiar section numbers of the earlier Leonine and Marietti editions.

97. *Sententia libri Ethicorum* 6.7 (358-59) [nos. 1210-11, 1142a15-20].

98. *Sententia libri Ethicorum* 4.17 (260) [no. 872, 1128b16-19].

99. IV *Sent.*, d.49, q.3, a.2, ad5^m (Parma edition, 1218a).

in the *Summa theologiae,* for here he argues that *iuvenes* are hopeful because they have little of the past behind them and most of their future ahead of them.[100] Commenting on Jesus' words to Peter in John 21:18 ("when you were younger . . . but when you shall have grown old"), Thomas cites not only Aristotle's *Rhetoric* but also Ecclesiastes 11:9: "Rejoice, therefore, O young man [*iuvenis*], in thy youth [*adolescentia*], and let thy heart be in that which is good in the days of thy youth [*iuventus*]."[101]

Commenting on Psalm 36:25 ("I was younger [*junior*], and now I have grown old [*senui*]"), Thomas combines the *iuvenis-senex* dichotomy with a fourfold division of life similar to that of the *medici.* He explains that one may interpret the passage in two ways. On the one hand, it may be understood as referring to corporeal age, for someone flourishes in *iuventus* and then becomes a *senex.* But the psalmist has picked out the two extremes of a fourfold division: *pueritia, iuventus, senectus,* and *senecta.* Following Galatians 4:3-4, one may interpret these allegorically as periods of the church's history, namely, the ages of Abel, the patriarchs, the apostles, and the end of the world. On the other hand, the text may be understood as referring to spiritual age, for as Saint Paul explains (1 Cor. 13:11), someone who delights in childish, vain things is mentally a child *(puer),* and he may leave behind such pleasures to take delight in mature things, like an older man *(senex).*[102]

The Imperfection of the Child

Thomas consistently characterizes childhood in terms of deficiency and imperfection. Explicating 1 Corinthians 13:11, Thomas says that whereas imperfection belongs accidentally to the human being *(homo),* it belongs essentially or by definition to the child *(puer).*[103] This notion of perfection is flexible. Sometimes the perfection is explicitly that of the adult.[104] At other times, it is an indefinite way of referring to whatever age the child must reach to acquire the fac-

---

100. *ST* I-II, q.40, a.6, resp. (931a).

101. *Super Evangelium s. Ioannis lectura,* c.21, lect. 4, no. 2629, ed. R. Cai (Turin, 1952), 484.

102. *Lectura super Psalmos* 36, no. 18, Parma edition (1863), consulted via the *Corpus Thomisticum* Web site.

103. *Super primam Epistolam ad Corinthios lectura,* c. 13, lect. 3, no. 795, in *Super Epistolas s. Pauli Lectura,* ed. R. Cai, vol. 1 (Turin, 1953). (Uncorrected *reportatio.*)

104. *ST* I-II, q.96, a.2, resp. (1237a): comparison of *puer* to *vir perfectus. ST* I-II, q.88, a.6, ad1[m] (1199a): *puer* is to *vir* as imperfect is to perfect. Cf. I *Sent.,* d.44, q.1, a.1, s.c.2 (ed. Mandonnet, 1016), on whether God can cause what he made to become better, where the progression from *pueritia* to *iuventus* is given as an example of natural improvement.

ulty in question. (For example, children "are incapable of instruction before the perfect age.")[105] The sacrament of confirmation marks a certain "perfect age" in spiritual development, even if this occurs during the corporeal age of childhood.[106] But whatever its connotations, the term "perfect" (from the past participle of *perficere:* "to make thoroughly," "to bring to completion," "to finish") always denotes completeness in the sense of actuality (the full realization of potency), and such actuality in our sublunary world of generation and corruption is usually the result of a process of generation.[107]

In what respects is the child imperfect? Chiefly, according to Thomas, as regards understanding and the use of reason. Thomas emphasizes the cognitive immaturity of children (and cognition, in his view, is essentially conceptual). With the power to speak comes some use of reason, but it is impeded and deficient until puberty.[108] To the extent that children lack reason, they also lack free choice *(liberum arbitrium),* which presupposes rational discernment. Like irrational animals, children can be said to act voluntarily inasmuch as their actions are done freely *(sponte)* rather than under compulsion, yet they act by the sensitive and not by the intellective appetite.[109] Where Aristotle says that the child *(puer)* cannot be happy because he lacks virtue, Thomas explains that because of the "deficiency of age," the child does not have sufficient use of reason for virtuous deeds.[110] Contrariwise, lacking rational discernment, children focus on the senses and sensitive appetites. When Aristotle compares intemperance to childhood to illustrate the need for discipline and restraint, Thomas comments: "this analogy is reasonable, because children live above all according to desire [*concupiscentia*], because they seek pleasure very much, which pertains to the nature of desire."[111] Hence children, to the extent that they are immature, cannot merit or have virtues and vices.[112] Indeed, they are permitted to do

---

105. II *Sent.,* d.11, q.1, a.3, arg. 4 (275). That this is an "objection" has no bearing on my use of it here.

106. *ST* III, q.72, a.1, resp. (2909a), and a.8, resp. (2917a).

107. Cf. *ST* I, q.4, a.1, ad1^m (24a), where Thomas explains how one must perforce extend the term "perfect" to God, even though his supreme actuality is not the result of the bringing of a potency into act.

108. *ST* II-II, q.24, a.9, resp. (1536-37).

109. *Sent. lib. Eth.* 3.4 (130) (no. 427, 1111a25-26).

110. *Sent. lib. Eth.* 1.14 (52) (no. 176, 1100a1-5). Aristotle adds (and Thomas too, in his gloss) that a child may be called happy by anticipation, in the sense that he shows promise of future happiness.

111. *Sent. lib. Eth.* 3.22 (192) (no. 645, 1119b3-10). Thomas elaborates this comparison in *ST* II-II, q.142, a.2 (2119-20), where Aristotle's text appears as the *sed contra*.

112. Cf. III *Sent.,* d.18, q.un., a.3, arg.5 (ed. Moos, 561-62): infants "because of the weakness of their corporeal organs do not have perfect imagination or use of free will," and therefore can-

things for which adults are punished by law or at least contemned.[113] Thomas therefore excuses the young child from mortal sin,[114] although he will not define a precise boundary: children develop differently, and some may be ready for mortal sin even before the age of seven.[115]

The mental deficiency of children limits their spiritual life. The virtues that little children receive in baptism remain unactualized habits until they grow up.[116] Contrariwise, Eucharist and extreme unction are not given to (young) children because they have no "actual devotion."[117] Nevertheless, because it is the soul that receives grace, and not the body, someone may achieve a spiritual perfection even in childhood as a special gift of the Holy Spirit. For example, some children have given up their lives fighting for Christ.[118] But in that case, they miraculously behave like adults.

It is because of deficiency in reason and in free will that children cannot take solemn religious vows before puberty.[119] A private religious vow, which is between the individual and God, may well be binding at an earlier age, if reason is sufficiently developed. But because rules about the solemn vows of religious profession are based on general, not individual, considerations, the church decrees that the minimum age is puberty, that is, twelve for girls and fourteen for boys.[120]

Likewise, it is because they lack discernment and prudence that children are

---

not merit. The article concerns whether Christ merited from the moment of conception. In the reply (ad5[m], 563-64), Thomas refuses to apply the argument to Christ but does not question the premise about children in general.

113. *ST* I-II, q.96. a.2, resp. (1237a).

114. II *Sent.*, d.42, q.1, a.5, ad7[m] (1065).

115. Cf. IV *Sent.*, d.27, q.2, a.2, ad2[m] (Parma edition, 7:932b), regarding the young boy in Gregory's *Dialogues* (4.18, PL 77:349) who was taken off to hell by the devil because he blasphemed. Thomas does not specify his age, but in the original story he was about five years old.

116. *ST* II-II, q.47, a.14, ad3[m] (1676a); *ST* III, q.69, a.6, resp. & ad1[m] (2894b).

117. IV *Sent.*, d.23, q.2, a.2, q[a]4, resp. (Parma ed., 7:881a). See also *ST* III, q.80, a.9, ad3[m] (3003b), on children and Eucharist. In the first passage, Thomas refers simply to *pueri*, but in the second passage he refers to *pueri recenter nati*. On children and the sacraments in canon law, see René Metz, "L'enfant dans le droit canonique médiéval: Orientations de recherche," *Recueils de la Société Jean Bodin* 36 (1976): 58-67; reprint, Metz, *La femme et l'enfant dans le droit canonique médiéval* (London: Variorum Reprints, 1985).

118. *ST* III, q.72, a.8, ad2[m] (2917a).

119. IV *Sent.*, d.38, q.1, a.1, q[a]3, resp. (Parma ed., 1005b); *ST* II-II, q.88, a.9 (1883-84). On children and the religious life in medieval canon law, see René Metz, "L'entrée des mineurs dans la vie religieuse et l'autorité des parents d'après le droit classique: Le réaction contre l'ancien rigorisme en faveur de la liberté des enfants," *Studia Gratiana* 20 = *Mélanges G. Fransen,* vol. 2 (Rome, 1976), 187-200; reprint, Metz, *La femme et l'enfant.*

120. *ST* II-II, q.189, a.5, resp. (2404).

incapable of marriage vows, or indeed of any sacrament presupposing use of reason, such as penance.[121] To explain why children can become betrothed at seven but cannot marry until puberty, Thomas adapts from Aristotle a threefold division of the capacity to understand:[122] some cannot understand at all, some can understand with the help of others, and some can understand for themselves. Before the age of seven, children cannot understand at all and therefore cannot enter into any contracts. Toward the end of the first *septennium,* when boys are sent to school, children can understand with the help of others and can therefore enter into certain contracts, including betrothals. (If their parents have betrothed them before that age, the contract is conditional on their own consent when they reach it.) Yet lacking "firm will," they are not yet ready to commit themselves in the present to a permanent bond. They reach that level toward the end of the second *septennium,* when they can understand for themselves and can enter into binding obligations as regards their own persons, such as marriage. Yet they are not ready for agreements that affect others until the end of the third *septennium* (age twenty-one), when they become able to alienate property.[123] Thomas concedes that "because the use of reason develops more quickly in some than in others," some children are ready for betrothals even before seven. Certain authorities allow for a margin of six months, but Thomas argues that it is better to consider individual cases on their own merits.[124] The same goes for marriage: in most cases, puberty arrives at age fourteen in boys and twelve in girls, but if "the vigor of nature [i.e., sexual maturity] and of reason supplies the defect of age," an underage marriage need not be dissolved.[125] Thomas does not explain why girls attain sufficient discernment for marriage before boys: he merely observes that marriageable age differs in boys and girls because it is a function not only of use of reason but also of the capacity to procreate.[126] Perhaps he unconsciously assumes that the girl's consent is less critical, but he seems to assume too that sexual and rational maturity coincide.

The causes of the child's rational deficiency, according to Thomas, are physiological. Here he draws on medicine as well as on Aristotle. One source of impedance is growth itself and the humoral turbulence that accompanies it. Discussing whether the infants of Eden would have been cognitively deficient, Thomas cites the maxim derived from Aristotle's *Physics,* which Albert and Bonaventure cite in the same context: "It is in becoming quiet that the soul be-

---

121. IV *Sent.,* d.36, q.1, a.5, resp. (Parma ed., 997); ibid., d.25, q.2, a.1, q^{a}2, resp. (908).
122. *Nicomachean Ethics* 1.1095b4-13.
123. IV *Sent.,* d.27, q.2, a.2, resp. (Parma ed., 7:932).
124. Ibid., ad7^m.
125. IV *Sent.,* d.36, q.un., a.5, resp. (997b).
126. IV *Sent.,* d.27, q.2, a.2, ad3^m (932).

comes knowing and prudent."[127] He continues: "But the body cannot be perfectly quiet in childhood because of many motions and above all because of growth."[128] This is only an argument *sed contra,* but Thomas makes the same point affirmatively when he explains why young children are incapable of marriage vows: reason becomes strong "to the extent that the motions and the changeability [*fluxibilitas*] of humors become quiet."[129] And in a quite different context (a critique of Averroes's supposed theory of a universal possible intellect), Thomas observes that the child *(puer)* is potentially rather than actually intelligent not because he lacks an intellect but because his understanding is impeded, "for he is impeded from understanding because of motions of many sorts existing in him, as [Aristotle] says in *Physics* VII." Therefore "once the impediment is removed, he understands at once."[130]

Because the impediment of humoral "flexibility" continues throughout the growing period, it affects young men too. Commenting on the *Nicomachean Ethics,* Thomas explains that young men seek pleasure because "there are many motions of spirits and humors in [them] . . . because of growth, as also happens in drunks."[131] He makes the same comparison in the *prima secundae pars:* because of their hot temperament, young men have many spirits and their heart is enlarged. Heat and the "multiplication of spirits" make them hopeful and ready to overcome obstacles, as it does in drunks.[132] In the same work, Thomas observes that young men "pursue pleasures above all, because of the many changes [*transmutationes*] taking place in them while they are in the stage of growth."[133] Both children and young men, therefore, are limited by humoral fluxibility. But in discussing the infants of Eden, Thomas develops a different (but compatible) theory that applies only to the very young.

The Infants of Eden

Thomas's treatment of questions about the infants of Eden was unusually extensive. He first discussed the topic in his commentary on Peter Lombard's *Sentences;* he discussed the cognitive dimensions of the topic again in the

127. Cf. Aristotle, *Physics* 7.3, 247b9-11.

128. II *Sent.,* d.20, q.2, a.2, s.c. (513).

129. IV *Sent.,* d.27, q.2, a.2, resp. (932a)

130. *Summa contra Gentiles* II, c. 60, no. 1380.

131. *Sent. lib. Eth.* 7.14 (438) (no. 1531, 1154b9-11).

132. *ST* I-II, q.40, a.6, resp. (931a). As an irascible passion, hope includes a readiness to pursue "arduous" ends.

133. *ST* I-II, q.32, a.7, ad2^m (893a).

Quaestiones disputatae de veritate; and he reviewed the whole topic again in the *Summa theologiae.*[134] His position is generally the same as Albert's. He agrees that the infants of Eden would probably have acquired mental and physical strength gradually (although with God, anything is possible). He agrees that gradual maturation is natural,[135] and that infants are not ignorant but merely nescient.[136] He argues that the cause of the physical debility of infants is their moist complexion. This not only makes the limbs soft but reduces the efficiency of the motor nervous system, which originates in the rear part of the brain, for the brain is an especially moist region of the body. Yet the infant's incapacity is a by-product of the noble complexion of human beings.[137] Contrariwise, animals that are more capable at birth have a drier complexion and require a narrower repertoire of actions.[138] In agreement with Augustine, though, Thomas argues that the infants of Eden (unlike children now) would have been able to achieve all their immediate ends as infants: to move around and find their mothers, to latch onto the breast, and so on.[139] Likewise, they would have had sufficient prudence, based on rules close to the principles of the natural law, to make whatever practical decisions were necessary for them.[140]

Thomas's original contribution to the topic was in his more precise and detailed account of the natural cognitive deficiency of infants. Because he was committed to Aristotle's premise that the intellect is by nature a blank slate,[141] he assumed that each human being begins life with no knowledge at all.[142] One acquires knowledge of the essences of things through the senses. The internal media of cognition are intentional forms known as species. First, there are the sensible species with which an object informs the external sense organs. (For

---

134. II *Sent.,* d.20, q.2, aa.1-2, (ed. Mandonnet, 509-15); *Quaestiones disputatae de veritate,* q.18, aa.7-8, Leonine edition, vol. 22.2, pp. 554-59; *ST* I, q.99, a.1 (604-5); q.101, in two articles (608-10). For detailed references, see my article "The Infants of Eden." Thomas was still editing his *Scriptum* when he became a Regent Master in Paris in 1256; the questions *De veritate* date from this regency (1256-59); and the *prima pars* of *ST* is from the Roman period (1265-68).

135. II *Sent.,* d.20, q.2, a.1, ad3^m (511).

136. *De ver.,* q.18, a.7, ad3^m (556); *ST* I, q.101, a.1, ad2^m (609a).

137. II *Sent.,* d.20, q.2, a.1, ad5^m (512); *ST* I, q.99, a.1, resp. (605a).

138. *De ver.,* q.18, a.8, ad6^m (559b); *ST* I, q.99, a.1, ad2^m (605b).

139. *ST* I, q.99, a.1, resp. & ad1^m (605).

140. II *Sent.,* d.23, q.2, a.2, resp. (576-77); *De ver.,* q.18, a.7, resp. & ad2^m (556b); *ST* I, q.101, a.1, ad3^m (609a).

141. See II *Sent.,* d.23, q.2, a.2, arg.3 (575); *De ver.,* q.18, a.7, resp. (556a); and *ST* I, q.101, a.1, s.c. & resp. (608-9). The source of the *tabula rasa* simile is Aristotle, *De anima* 3.429b30-440a2.

142. Except in the special sense that the ability to grasp the truth of a first principle immediately (i.e., nonsyllogistically, without a middle term) as soon as its terms are understood can be construed as an innate habit.

example, one sees colors through sensible species of these colors in the eye.) Then the agent intellect abstracts from this data the immaterial, intelligible species by means of which one knows universal intelligibilia. Intelligible species are retained in the possible intellect as habits of knowledge.[143] Since the intellect is immaterial (i.e., it does not have an organ), it is not affected per se by complexion. And the external sense organs of the infants of Eden would probably have been perfectly functional. Nevertheless, the exceptionally moist complexion of the infant's brain naturally impedes cognition.

Thomas maintains that the intellect cannot obtain sensory data directly from the external sense organs but only via the internal senses: the common sense, the cogitative-estimative sense, sense memory, and imagination.[144] These are organic faculties: common sense and imagination are in the anterior ventricle of the brain, the cogitative or estimative sense is in the middle ventricle, and sense memory is in the posterior ventricle.[145] More precisely, the intellect depends on phantasms, which simulate sensory experience in the absence of the corresponding objects. Phantasms are generated by the internal senses and are therefore organic and embodied.[146] Now the intellect depends on phantasms in two ways: not only as sources of information (Thomas is fond of quoting Aristotle's maxim that phantasms are to the intellect what colors are to vision),[147] but also as instruments of actual thought. For Thomas maintains that even when an intelligible is habitually known, the intellect cannot actually understand it or think about it without using phantasms, in which it regards universals as if instantiated in material particulars.[148] In discussing the cognition of the infants of Eden, therefore, Thomas divides what had been a single

143. On cognition in Aquinas, see Edward P. Mahoney, "Sense, Intellect, and Imagination in Albert, Thomas, and Siger," in *Cambridge History of Later Medieval Philosophy,* ed. Norman Kretzmann, A. Kenny, and J. Pinborg (Cambridge: Cambridge University Press, 1982), 602-22; Robert Pasnau, *Thomas Aquinas on Human Nature* (Cambridge: Cambridge University Press, 2002), 267-324; Georges Van Riet, "Le théorie thomiste de la sensation externe," *Revue philosophique de Louvain* 51 (1953): 374-408; Van Riet, "La théorie thomiste de l'abstraction," *Revue philosophique de Louvain* 50 (1952): 353-93; and Spruit, *Species intelligibilis,* 156-74.

144. On the internal senses, see *Quaestiones disputatae de anima,* q.13, resp. (Leonine edition, vol. 24.1, 115-20); and *ST* I, q.78, a.4 (477-79). Unlike Albert and most others, Thomas did not regard *imaginatio* and *phantasia* as separate faculties (respectively retentive and creative).

145. On the medieval localization of faculties in the brain, see Simon Kemp, *Cognitive Psychology in the Middle Ages* (Westport, Conn.: Greenwood Press, 1996).

146. Or more precisely by the innermost senses, excluding the common sense.

147. E.g., II *Sent.,* d.20, q.2, a.2, resp. (513-14); *De ver.,* q.18, a.8, ad4ᵐ (559). Cf. Aristotle, *De anima* 3.7, 431a14.

148. II *Sent.,* d.20, q.2, a.2, ad3ᵐ (514-15). On the need for the intellect to "turn itself" toward phantasms to understand what it already knows habitually, see *ST* I, q.84, a.7 (521-22).

question into two, pertaining respectively to the *acquisition* of knowledge and to the actual *use* of such knowledge. (The term "use" always implies actuality.) Use of reason, therefore, as well as the acquisition of knowledge, is naturally limited by the moist complexion of the infant's brain, which causes phantasms to be blurred, confused, and unstable.[149] Exactly the same thing occurs in drunks because of vapors rising into the head.[150] The infants of Eden, therefore, would have been cognitively inept, for their blurry phantasms would have impeded their intellects. Even if, like Adam, they had begun life with infused universal knowledge (although Thomas considers that improbable), they would not have enjoyed actual use of such knowledge. But here Thomas introduces a qualification: understanding may be impeded in a merely negative manner, through the absence of an instrument; or the body may impede understanding by working against it and "weighing down" the soul (Wisd. 9:15). The infants of Eden would have been cognitively impeded only in the first sense, whereas fallen infants are impeded in both senses.[151]

The Innocent Child

Thomas, it seems to me, construes childish innocence as deficiency or imperfection. Interpreting Matthew 18:2, Thomas uses 1 Corinthians 14:20 as a key: "Do not become children in sense [i.e., in reason], but in malice." But children, in Thomas's view, lack malice because they lack reason and rational consistency. Again, he explains that Jesus used the little child not only as an example of humility but also in view of certain traits of childhood that adults might emulate: children are immune to lust, the "adultery of the heart" (Matt. 5:28), and they do not desire great things (Rom. 12:16).[152] But children lack lust not through the virtue of temperance but through immaturity and deficiency. Contrariwise, the childlike absence of sexual desire in an adult is not a virtue but a vice (known as "insensibility"), because every virtue is a medium between extremes: temperance is the moderation, not the absence, of desire.[153] Again, it is because boys "lack understanding and virtue" that they "regard certain childish things on which they spend time as precious and best, which however are not of

149. II *Sent.*, d.20, q.2, a.2, ad4^m (515); *De ver.*, q.18, a.8, ad5^m & resp. (559b, 558); *ST* I, q.101, a.2, resp. (609b).

150. II *Sent.*, d.20, q.2, a.2, resp. (513-14).

151. *De ver.*, q.18, a.8, ad1^m & ad7^m (558-559); *ST* I, q.101, a.2, ad1^m (609b).

152. *Lectura super Matthaeum*, c.18, lect. 1 (Turin, 1951, but consulted via the *Corpus Thomisticum* Web site).

153. *ST* II-II, q.142, a.1, resp. (2118).

great value, and are not counted as anything by grown men."[154] What appears as childish innocence in one context appears as imperfection in another. Expounding 1 Corinthians 13:11, where Paul explains how he left behind childish things to become a man, Thomas says that children speak by babbling *(balbutiendo)* and that their judgments are foolish; they despise valuable things and prefer vile things (Prov. 1:22); lacking reason, they think only about empty things *(vana);* therefore people who prefer earthly things to spiritual ones, Thomas concludes, are thinking like children.[155]

Conclusions

Thomas's paradigm of the child was as follows: First, the child is essentially an imperfect (i.e., not fully realized) human being. The imperfection of childhood is a function of incompleteness, and not (as in the elderly) of corruption. It consists in physical and, above all, rational debility: the child cannot think clearly or consistently. Second, the cause of the child's imperfection is the body's humoral constitution, which impedes corporeal powers directly, and mental powers indirectly. For although the mechanisms and capabilities involved (both organic and inorganic) are already fully formed in the beginning, they are impeded by the infant's excessively moist complexion, and throughout the growing period by humoral fluxibility. The brain is especially susceptible to these conditions. Third, the impediments are for the most part natural concomitants of growth and immaturity and need not be construed as punishments for original sin. Children share the corruption that affects all of Adam's descendants, but one should not regard the very features that *distinguish* children from adults as penal. Although Thomas retained aspects of the Augustinian paradigm, therefore, the biological child prevailed.

The first feature of this paradigm is familiar in the literature on childhood in the Middle Ages. Thomas's child is consistent with the "deficiency paradigm" that James A. Schultz finds in Middle High German texts. Schultz shows that this literature regarded children as different from adults, but that the differences were deficiencies. Contrariwise, when children received special approbation, it was because they had acted like adults.[156] Schultz suggests that such was the

---

154. *Sent. lib. Eth.* 10.9 (581) (no. 2074, 1176b17-28).

155. *Super primam epistolam ad Corinthios lectura,* c. 13, lect. 3, no. 797 (ed. Cai).

156. James A. Schultz, *The Knowledge of Childhood in the German Middle Ages, 1100-1350* (Philadelphia: University of Pennsylvania Press, 1995), 246-49. Schultz affirms at the outset that childhood per se is mainly socially constructed (see 9-13), but this assumption has no role in his study, which focuses on the adult's idea of childhood.

prevalent view of children until the eighteenth century, when people (or at least, poets and intellectuals) began to think of children as pristine and admirable.[157] Gareth Matthews suggests that even today, many people still have what he characterizes as a "broadly Aristotelian" conception of childhood, such that "a human child is an immature specimen of the organism type, human, which, by nature, has the potentiality to develop into a mature specimen with the structure, form, and function of a normal or standard adult." In Aristotelian terms, Matthews explains, the final cause of an organism is "the function that organism normally performs when it reaches maturity," while the formal cause is "the form or structure it normally has in maturity."[158] This statement might serve rather well as a summary of Aquinas, who would surely construe humanness as the formal cause of human beings, and who explicitly construes *iuventus* as "final perfection" *(perfectio ultima)*, the term of a process of generation.

It is worth emphasizing that according to any version of the deficiency or imperfection paradigm, children are markedly different from adults. I mention this because the aim of much of the literature on medieval childhood has been to show that people regarded and treated children differently from adults.[159] While this accumulation of evidence has been richly informative, the general conclusion is perhaps too obvious. The question is: What manner of difference? The stimulus for this effort in differentiation was Philippe Ariès's notorious theory of a postmedieval "discovery of childhood."[160] Ariès maintained that in the Middle Ages there was no *sentiment* of childhood (a term that regrettably became "idea" in the English translation of this work). He defined *sentiment* as an awareness of the "particularity" of childhood and distinguished it from love or affection, although it seems to have an affective dimension.[161] While Ariès's

---

157. Schultz, *The Knowledge of Childhood*, 249-10. Note that the Romantic child (as in Wordsworth's *Prelude*) was conceived as much through introspection and autobiographical reflection as through observation of children.

158. Gareth Matthews, "The Philosophy of Childhood," in *The Stanford Encyclopedia of Philosophy* (Winter 2005), ed. Edward N. Zalta, URL = http://plato.stanford.edu/archives/win2005/entries/childhood/.

159. See, for example, Shahar, *Childhood in the Middle Ages;* Danièle Alexandre-Bidon and Didier Lett, *Les enfants au Moyen Age, Vᵉ-XVᵉ siècles* (Paris: Hachette, 1997), translated by Jody Gladding as *Children in the Middle Ages: Fifth–Fifteenth Centuries* (Notre Dame, Ind.: University of Notre Dame Press, 1999); and Nicholas Orme, *Medieval Children* (New Haven: Yale University Press, 2001).

160. On the historiography of childhood and Ariès's legacy, see Hugh Cunningham, "Histories of Childhood," *American Historical Review* 103 (1998): 1195-1207.

161. Philippe Ariès, *L'enfant et la vie familiale sous l'Ancien Régime* (Paris: Librairie Plon, 1960), 134. Cf. Robert Baldick's English translation, *Centuries of Childhood: A Social History of Family Life* (New York: Knopf, 1962), 128.

methods were seriously faulty and his general conclusions suspect,[162] his thesis about the absence of a *sentiment* of childhood in the Middle Ages is interesting and (at least on some interpretations) probably correct for the most part. Nevertheless, the term "particularity" is too vague. One needs to distinguish between positive particularities (perfections) and negative ones (defects or imperfections), and again between vicious and value-neutral imperfections.

Another scholarly legacy of Ariès was the merging of childhood itself (as lived by children) with the adult's idea of childhood (explicit or implied), the regulation of children, the de facto treatment of children, and so forth. These topics are all interrelated, but their conflation begs many difficult questions. In this study, I have limited my attention to adult ideas about the nature of childhood, ideas that are explicitly stated (in words). At the other extreme, it is possible to study the actual situation of children in the past without positing *ideas* of childhood at all.[163]

The second aspect of Thomas's paradigm is less familiar, but I suggest that it was rooted in the same notion of deficiency. Lacking any account or measure of children's peculiarities other than their deficiency in relation to adults, people could only assume that they had exactly the same cognitive capabilities, mechanisms, and apparatus as adults but that these were impeded. The result was a superficial account of development. Indeed, what Thomas posits is not so much cognitive as physiological or humoral development. Contrariwise, a deeper account of cognitive development, whereby the child's mode of cognition is different in some positive sense rather than merely muddled or inept, opens up the possibility that the distinctive features of the child's mentality are perfections, at least in relation to that phase of life. When Thomas observes that young children babble and know nothing, he seems not to have noticed their prodigious ability to acquire language. He saw what we see, but he interpreted it differently.

I suspect (but obviously cannot prove) that Thomas's paradigm of childhood was a version of the prevailing view during his era. His emphasis on conceptual cognition (the abstraction of and reflection on intelligibilia) was a scholastic trait, but the underlying assumptions were probably common prejudices. If there was a competing paradigm in the high Middle Ages, one might look for it in a new "sentiment" of childhood among churchmen, beginning in the twelfth century, a sentiment associated with the cult of the infant Jesus.[164]

---

162. See Adrian Wilson, "The Infancy and the History of Childhood: An Appraisal of Philippe Ariès," *History and Theory* 19 (1980): 132-53.

163. Cunningham, "Histories of Childhood," 1202-7.

164. Herlihy, "Medieval Children," 127-30; Dzon, "Image," 244-49.

Partly because of an increasing emphasis on imagination in devotion, and partly through a kind of domestication of the objects of veneration and worship, people during this period began to think of Mary and Jesus as typical mother and child rather than as iconic, regal figures. Some liked to imagine themselves in the role of the baby Jesus' parents. (Ritual devotion to the crèche begins in this era.) But it is far from clear that such attitudes always implied or presupposed a more positive evaluation of childhood per se, and it is too easy for us to see Romantic sentiments in the mirror of medieval sources. I take one example here to illustrate this point.

David Herlihy argues that during the twelfth century, the cult of the Christ child "implies an idealization of childhood itself." For evidence, Herlihy quotes a passage from a Christmas sermon by a Cistercian, Guerric of Igny (d. 1157): "O sweet and sacred childhood, which brought back man's true innocence, by which men of every age can return to blessed childhood and be conformed to you, not in physical weakness but in humility of heart and holiness of life."[165] But the "sweet and sacred childhood" that Guerric apostrophizes is *Christ's* childhood, not childhood in general, and the infant Christ (in medieval theology) was unlike any other child. Beginning with the idea that God emptied himself in the incarnation (Phil. 2:7), Guerric skillfully weaves the usual topoi of childish innocence into a perennial theme of atonement rhetoric: in the Christmas mystery, God overthrew evil not through might, as human wisdom would predict, but through meekness, taking on not only a mortal body but even "the weak and tiny age of infants." What Guerric idealizes is not childhood per se but the paradoxical childhood of God. Whether this idealization implies, inversely, an idealization of childhood per se is not clear.

Yet there are interesting cases that seem, in retrospect, to anticipate the Romantic view of childhood. The vita of Hugh of Lincoln (ca. 1140–ca. 1200) records that the bishop loved young children and admired their purity, simplicity, and innocence, and that they loved him in return. His biographer comments that Hugh exemplified Mark 10:14 ("Suffer the little children . . ."), and that both he and his little admirers exemplified Matthew 5:8 ("Blessed are the pure in heart . . .").[166] Around the middle of the thirteenth century, Walter of Wimborne dedicated a poem to the boys whom he taught as a secular canon of Wimborne Minster, in Dorset. He even wishes, with the help of their prayers, to

165. Herlihy, "Medieval Children," 129, quoting Guerric of Igny, *Liturgical Sermons,* vol. 1 (Spencer, Mass.: Cistercian Publications, 1970), sermon 6, p. 38. For the Latin text, see Guerric d'Igny, *Sermons,* vol. 1, ed. J. Morson and H. Costello, Sources chrétiennes 166 (Paris, 1970), 166-68.

166. Decima L. Douie and Hugh Farmer, eds., *The Life of St. Hugh of Lincoln,* 2 vols. (London: Thomas Nelson, 1961), 1:129-30.

become a child again *(repuerascere),* to recover not their levity or inexperience but their innocence.[167] These examples are embedded in complex rhetorical conventions (hagiographical in one case, poetic in the other), but they do seem to express a real sentiment of childhood, a sentiment of which I can detect no trace in Thomas.

Different paradigms imply different concepts of the vocation of childhood, whether one construes that vocation as a contribution in the present (as Marcia Bunge does in this volume) or as a future-oriented summons, an orientation of personal growth. Schultz shows that the people in medieval German literature looked fatalistically for signs of the future adult in the child but did not suppose that they could shape the adult by influencing the child. The Romantics may have discovered the principle that the child (as Wordsworth put it) is father of the man. Thomas's paradigm implies only a weak notion of vocation: there is little for adults to do but wait until the child becomes sober enough to acquire knowledge and virtue; meanwhile, the child can enrich the life of adults only as a recipient of care. But if the child goes through distinctive learning periods, such as the cognitive "revolutions" that Philippe Rochat has studied (whereby the child becomes progressively aware of self, then of the immediate context, and then of the wider world),[168] then each phase is a formative experience, a foundation for later life — and potentially (in cases of deprivation) a lost opportunity. (Compare the rings of the oak tree to which Vigen Guroian refers in this volume.) According to the Romantic paradigm of childhood, which has left its mark on us, the child has precious gifts that are distinctively childlike but should somehow be preserved in adult life.[169] Gareth Matthews finds not only that children are capable of philosophy, but that their distinctive manner of inquiry is intrinsically philosophical, as if professional philosophers are those who have retained a childish sense of wonder.[170] Stronger accounts of childhood development imply stronger accounts of what the child can contribute in the present to parents, family, and communities.

But how should we decide which view is best? Should we defer to scientific findings? (In which case, to what extent are children independent from how adults regard them? To what extent is childhood itself socially constructed?) Or

---

167. A. G. Rigg, ed., *The Poems of Walter of Wimborne,* Studies and Texts 42 (Toronto: Pontifical Institute of Medieval Studies, 1978), p. 64, stanza 161. I am grateful to Mary Dzon for bringing this text to my attention.

168. Philippe Rochat, *The Infant's World* (Cambridge: Harvard University Press, 2001).

169. See Judith Plotz, *Romanticism and the Vocation of Childhood* (New York: Palgrave, 2001).

170. Gareth B. Matthews, *The Philosophy of Childhood* (Cambridge: Harvard University Press, 1994).

are we free to imagine childhood according to our own ideological, autobiographical, or even theological preferences, allowing our preconceptions or sentiments to be mirrored in our conception of the child? Thomas's child had many sources, including hermeneutical keys; very general philosophical (even metaphysical) assumptions; an ideology of order, discipline, and rationality; a general naturalism; and specific medical doctrines based on empirical observations (as interpreted in the light of theory).

Thomas's view of childhood is salutary in two ways. On the one hand, it is a refreshing corrective to Romantic or sentimental excess. We should not impose a burden of nostalgia on children that they are not equipped to bear. Heightened expectation is the source of much unnecessary anxiety in the modern world. On the other hand, it reminds us that although all people at all times are familiar with children (at least inasmuch as they were once children themselves), people of the past held ideas about childhood that were radically different from our own. It is facile to conclude that childhood per se is largely socially constructed, and it is almost a truism to affirm that *paradigms* of childhood are socially constructed. But we do well to remember that our own paradigm of childhood is not inevitable, that it is relatively recent (even when we see it in Scripture), and that it has a history. And those considerations should make us wonder about the causes and the rationale of our view of childhood, and about the firmness of its supports.

7. Children Play with God: A Contemporary Thomistic Understanding of the Child

Patrick McKinley Brennan

Jacques Maritain stands out among recent Catholic thinkers for the breadth of his interests. God and angels, nature and art, liturgy and contemplation, sign and signified, individual and person, man and the state, and, yes, the child were the subjects of Maritain's penetrating philosophical gaze. Maritain identified himself as a Thomist, explaining that "[o]ne is a Thomist because one has repudiated every attempt to find philosophical truth in any system fabricated by an individual . . . and because one wants to seek out what is true — for oneself, indeed, and by one's own reason — by allowing oneself to be taught by the whole range of human thought, in order not to neglect anything of that which is."[1] As one commentator has observed, Jacques Maritain is "the philosopher of *all that is*."[2] That Maritain constitutes an exception to the general neglect on the part of Catholic and other thinkers in considering what the child is, then, is not an accident.[3]

---

1. Jacques Maritain, *The Degrees of Knowledge* (Notre Dame, Ind.: University of Notre Dame Press, 1995), xiii.

2. "Maritain ever remains a philosopher of all that is, of God and nature, of logic and metaphysics, of mathematics and art, and, yes, of man and the state." James V. Schall, *Jacques Maritain: The Philosopher in Society* (Lanham, Md.: Rowman and Littlefield, 1998), 225. See also Jean-Luc Barre, *Jacques and Raïssa Maritain: Beggars for Heaven,* trans. B. Doering (Notre Dame, Ind.: University of Notre Dame Press, 2005).

3. Maritain thus constitutes a partial exception to the appearance that "Catholicism does not have a developed teaching on what children are." Todd David Whitmore with Tobias Winright, "Children: An Undeveloped Theme in Catholic Teaching," in Maura A. Ryan and Todd David Whitmore, *The Challenge of Global Stewardship: Roman Catholic Responses* (Notre Dame, Ind.: University of Notre Dame Press, 1997), 161. The exception is only partial, because Maritain's developed teaching has to be pieced together from dozens of disparate sources, mostly his many writings on the ends of education.

I gratefully acknowledge the research assistance of Erin Galbally. — Patrick McKinley Brennan.

Considering the child, Maritain discovers a person, a person who, like all others, must become in actuality what he or she is in potency. "According to a commonplace expression, which is a very profound one, man must become what he is. In the moral order, he must win, by himself, his freedom and his personality."[4] What Maritain says of the human person in general is writ large of the small child: "As to the human person, he is but a person in embryo."[5] The winning of personality and freedom begins, if it does, in the "first act of freedom," an act of which the child is capable as soon as he realizes, perhaps unconsciously, the difference between what is good and what is bad. In the "first act of freedom," the child chooses the good *because* it is good. This first act of freedom is not only chronologically prior to, but exemplary of any subsequent acts of freedom, that is, of winning personality and freedom. Although childhood is surely a period of development, already children play with God.[6]

Before laying out Maritain's rich account of the child, a word about the choice of Maritain as guide to the child may be advisable. In some circles, "pre–Vatican II Thomism" is passé, or worse. Scholastic categories, definitions, and distinctions make unusual demands on contemporary readers, and Maritain's "unnecessarily difficult" style does not make the going any easier.[7] Maritain is not a parrot of inherited scholastic formulae, however; his is a thoroughly up-to-date mind, fully engaged in the contemporary problematics and urgent problems of modern man. The perennial questions framed and transmitted by some of the great historical figures studied elsewhere in this volume, and Thomas Aquinas above all, find contemporary expression, development, application, amendment, and emendation in the writings of Maritain.

There is value in exploring how a more or less contemporary Thomist understands the child. There is additional value in seeing how the philosopher who more than any other influenced the social doctrine of the Second Vatican Council (1962-65) thinks about the child. Beyond or before these archaeological reasons, though, I would submit this other reason, on Maritain's behalf: who and what "the child of man is" matters. It matters who she is called to be, and how she, with help both natural and supernatural, is to realize that potential.

---

4. Jacques Maritain, *Scholasticism and Politics*, 3rd ed. (London: Geoffrey Bles, 1954), 52.

5. Maritain, *Scholasticism and Politics*, 107.

6. This was the theme of the homily delivered by Joachim Cardinal Meisner at World Youth Day 2005 in Cologne: "Each one of us has one life. There is no 'trial' period that is exempt from responsibility. Consequently, there is no life, love, faith or death that can be tested. We are always at a state of emergency. We always have full responsibility." Available at www.vatican.va/gmg/documents/gmg_2005_20050816_opening-card-meisner_en.html.

7. Valentine Rice, "A Critical Exposition of the Educational Philosophy of Jacques Maritain" (Ph.D. diss., Harvard University, 1965), xx.

Not wanting anyone to take his word for anything, Maritain would ask exactly the following of the reader: "Is what I say true?"

The pages ahead fall into four parts and a conclusion. In part I, we begin where Maritain begins, with the act of existence. In Maritain's judgment, everything that is, is part of a going forth from Being Itself, which is God, and it falls to every person, including the child, to use his created freedom to decide whether to be a part of that great wave of being or to block the divine generosity through sin. Part II articulates the "first act of freedom," which is at once the child's and the man's. Part III considers the education the child needs if she is to begin to win her personality and freedom; it is, above all else, an education into her own essentially good tendencies or, in other words, the natural law. Part IV recognizes the place of the child, first, in the family and, second, in the economy of divine grace. By nature, the child is part of family society. By supernature, like it or not, the child plays with God. The very act by which an adult includes himself in or excludes himself from God's will that all be saved, is performed first, and exemplarily, by the child.

Part I: "The Gushing Forth of the Act of Existence"

"Existentialism" is Maritain's preferred shorthand for the Thomist philosophy, and he uses it as something of a corrective of a failure by some to appreciate "the dynamic aspect of the thought of St. Thomas."[8] Maritain acknowledged that the term brings to the modern mind the ideas of Martin Heidegger and Jean-Paul Sartre and Albert Camus, which amount, in Maritain's judgment, to a "transcendental embezzlement."[9] The word needed recapturing and "reclaiming"[10] by Thomists because, according to Maritain, they have a "prior right"[11] to it. For, as Maritain says in language that bears no trace of the brittle Latin of the textbook Thomist tradition with which Maritain is sometimes wrongly associated:

> At this point appears an aspect of Thomism which is in my opinion of first importance. By the very fact that the metaphysics of St. Thomas is centered, not upon essences but upon existence — upon the mysterious gushing forth of the act of existing in which, according to the analogical variety of the degrees of being, qualities and natures are actualized and formed, which quali-

8. Maritain, *Scholasticism and Politics*, 106.

9. Jacques Maritain, *Existence and the Existent*, trans. Lewis Galantiere and Gerald B. Phelan (New York: Pantheon Books, 1948), 6.

10. Maritain, *Existence and the Existent*, 1.

11. Maritain, *Existence and the Existent*, 1.

ties and natures refract and multiply the transcendent unity of subsistent Being itself in its created participations — this metaphysics lays hold, at its very starting point, of being as superabundant. Being superabounds, everywhere; it scatters its gifts and fruits in profusion. This is the action in which all beings here below communicate with one another and in which, thanks to the divine influx that traverses them, they are at every instant — in this world of contingent existence and of unforeseeable future contingents — either better or worse than themselves and than the mere fact of their existence at a given moment. By this action they exchange their secrets, influence one another for good or ill, and contribute to or betray in one another the fecundity of being, the while they are carried along despite themselves in the torrent of divine governance from which nothing can escape.

Above time, in the primary and transcendent Source, it is the superabundance of the divine act of existing, superabundance in pure act, which manifests itself in God Himself (as revelation teaches us) by the plurality of the divine Persons, and (as reason is of itself qualified to know) by the fact that the very existence of God is Intelligence and is Love, and by the fact that this existence is freely creative. Moreover this divine plenitude does not merely give, it gives itself. And it was, in the last analysis, in order to give itself to spiritual beings apt to receive it that, specifically, it created the world.[12]

Good Aristotelians that they are, Thomists affirm that every natural kind is what it is because of its essence, its specific organizing principle. There will be much to say about the human essence and how it is known, but first, following Maritain's lead, we linger over the act of existence. To jump too quickly to essences can obscure the *ne plus ultra* point that whether an essence exists, or fails to exist, *makes all the difference.* Not satisfied with a mere "philosophy of essences," a "thumbing through a picture-book," Maritain presses for a "philosophy of existence and existential realism."[13]

That philosophy affirms that all the things of creation "are permeated by the activating influx of the Prime Cause." Because of this, things "ceaselessly pass beyond themselves, and give more than they have."[14] Maritain's embrace of existence is nothing short of lyrical, and in this lies a clue to the direction of the entire philosophy. The philosophy that recognizes and celebrates the primacy of *the act of existence* is at the same time a philosophy of the *good.* As Maritain says in language resonant with the whole Thomist tradition: "Every

12. Maritain, *Existence and the Existent*, 42-43.

13. Maritain, *Existence and the Existent*, 2.

14. Jacques Maritain, *Creative Intuition in Art and Poetry* (Princeton: Princeton University Press, 1953), 127.

thing is good to the extent that it is, that it has *esse* [being]. Being and the good are convertible notions."[15] That which exists, is good. This existing world of creation is the going forth of being from Subsistent Being, the person of God, and it abounds and superabounds according to God's universal governance, the Eternal Law, and this is all very *good*. And, except where angels and persons are concerned, this is the simple and glorious end of the story.

Where persons — and angels, though they are not our current focus — are concerned, the story depends on the right exercise of freedom. The human person can block being's going forth from God and increase! Maritain explains that the going forth from the First Cause of being and goodness could have been an "unshatterable impulse," an overflowing that is "infallibly efficacious" in its increase of being. In actual fact, however, the First Cause has allowed the possibility that this impulse be shattered and rendered inefficacious. The human person, like the angelic person, can stop the increase of being, and thereby goodness, by acting not in conformity with his essence. When the person acts thus, he acts alone. "He puts an absence at the head of its acting, [thus] introduc[ing] the condition which will cause the texture of being to give way; that is why there will be faultiness now that it acts with that voluntary non-consideration; such an act will bear in itself the teeth-marks of nothingness." Maritain continues:

> Were we to put that into picturesque present-day language, we should say, in trying to express this initiative of nonbeing, this initiative of absence on which I have placed so much emphasis — we should say that the will *nihilates,* that it *noughts;* it has an initiative, yet we can only translate that initiative by words that express action. But it is an initiative of nonaction: we must therefore necessarily have recourse to a paradoxical language and say that created will then "does nothingness," "makes nonbeing"; and this is all it can do by itself. It "makes" nonbeing, that is to say that in all freedom it undoes, or it nondoes, or it noughts; the creature slinks, not by an action but by a free nonaction or dis-action, from the influx of the First Cause — which influx is loaded with being and goodness — it slinks from it insofar as this influx reaches the free region as such, it renders this influx sterile, it *nihilates* it.[16]

Conversely, when the free agent does not nihilate, but instead acts in conformity with his or her essence, and thus leaves the divine impulse unshattered, it is the First Cause who is at work through and in human freedom:

15. Jacques Maritain, *An Introduction to the Basic Problems of Moral Philosophy,* trans. Cornelia N. Borgerhoff (Albany, N.Y.: Magi Books, 1990), 32-33.

16. Jacques Maritain, *Saint Thomas and the Problem of Evil* (Milwaukee: Marquette University Press, 1942), 33-34.

[W]hat it is important to set forth here with unmistakable clarity is that the created existent contributes nothing of its own, does nothing, adds nothing, gives nothing — not the shadow of an action or of a determination coming from it — which would make of the shatterable impulse an unshatterable impetus or an impetus that comes to grips with existence. Not to nihilate under the divine activation, not to sterilise that impetus, not to have the initiative of making the thing we call nothing, does not mean taking the initiative, or the demi-initiative, or the smallest fraction of the initiative of an act; it does not mean acting on one's own to complete, in any way whatever, the divine activation. It means not stirring under its touch, but allowing it free passage, allowing it to bear its fruit (the unshatterable activation) by virtue of which the will (which did not nihilate in the first instance) will act (will look at the rule efficaciously) in the very exercise of its domination over its motives, and will burst forth freely in a good option and a good act.

To allow the shatterable impetus free passage is to let it fructify of itself and disappear into the unshatterable impetus by virtue of which the good act is produced, namely the rule efficaciously regarded in the very act of option.[17]

In sum, according to Maritain, the First Cause is the sole generative cause of the increase of being and goodness, and, if we can say that being and goodness come from the human creature as a *second* cause, the only condition on the side of the creature is its "having done nothing by its first initiative as nihilating first cause."[18] The person's freely non-nihilating satisfies a condition of the shatterable impulse's reaching its fructification.[19] This is the existential metaphysics according to which the person would become in actuality what he or she already is in potency or — in that memorable phrase — "in embryo."

Before going into more detail, it might be helpful to observe that, with this metaphysics, Maritain anticipatorily exorcises every ghost of Pelagius, every specter of Molina. From the theological perspective, which we shall explore in part IV, Maritain explains that while "God does not refuse His grace to one who acts to the best of his ability," a proposition that flirts with heresy, "it is under the action of grace that man prepares to receive grace,"[20] an affirmation that assures orthodoxy. Maritain's philosophy and his Catholic theology to which it is always "subalternated" assure that, whatever the vocation or office of the child, or of the man, it is not in any way to be the cause of one's own or anything's

---

17. Maritain, *Existence and the Existent,* 99-100, 100 n. 10.
18. Maritain, *Existence and the Existent,* 101 n. 10.
19. Maritain, *Existence and the Existent,* 99 n. 9.
20. Jacques Maritain, *The Range of Reason* (New York: Charles Scribner's Sons, 1952), 74.

goodness. Occasionally, when speaking in passing, or in describing the rigors of the moral life (a topic of part III), Maritain might give the impression that man is somehow a co-cause of being and goodness, but his considered and foundational view is that all being and goodness go forth from Subsistent Being as cause, with the created, rational agent's part being only, but freely, not to block that going forth. Man can nihilate, only God can create being and goodness.

Part II: To Win Personality and Freedom of Independence

From the essence of the human person comes the potential freely to win the full stature of personhood or personality. *Personality* or *personhood,* what it is to be a *person,* is among the most important concepts in Maritain's philosophy, and by it he means something quite precise and distinctive (and only approximately related to the notions of personhood developed by the philosophies of "personalism" that came later). Maritain distinguishes between two metaphysical aspects of the unified reality that is the human being or, simply, "the person." Under one aspect, a person is an "individual," by which Maritain means "a simple power of receptivity and of substantial mutability, an avidity for being."[21] It is the material aspect of the person, but "the word matter designates here, not a concept used in physics, but in philosophy: that of the *materia prima,* pure potentiality, able neither to *be* nor to *be thought* by itself, and from which all corporeal beings are made."[22] Under the second aspect, the same person is properly a person, that is, by virtue of what he receives not from matter but "from spirit."[23] Personality "is a great metaphysical mystery."[24]

> What do we mean precisely when we speak of the human person? When we say that a man is a person, we do not mean merely that he is an individual, in the sense that an atom, a blade of grass, a fly, or an elephant is an individual. Man is an individual who holds himself in hand by his intelligence and his will; he exists not merely in a physical fashion. He has spiritual super-existence through knowledge and love, so that he is, in a way, a universe in himself, a microcosmos, in which the great universe in its entirety can be encompassed through knowledge. By love he can give himself completely to beings who are to him, as it were, other selves. . . . Spirit is the root of personal-

21. Maritain, *Scholasticism and Politics,* 48.
22. Maritain, *Scholasticism and Politics,* 48.
23. Maritain, *Scholasticism and Politics,* 52.
24. Jacques Maritain, *The Education of Man* (Notre Dame, Ind.: University of Notre Dame Press, 1967), 164.

ity. . . . To say that a man is a person is to say that in the depths of his being he is more a whole than a part and more independent than servile. It is to say that he is a minute fragment of matter that is at the same time a universe, a beggar who participates in the absolute being, mortal flesh whose value is eternal, and a bit of straw into which heaven enters.[25]

Here, we are at the heart of the matter: "[M]an must complete, through his own will, what is sketched," but only sketched, "in his nature" as a person.[26] Unconstrained all the way down in our metaphysical root, we must win our freedom and personality. On the other hand, "[e]vil arises when, in our action, we give preponderance to the individual aspect of our being. For although each of our acts is simultaneously the act of ourselves as an individual and as a person, yet, by the very fact that it is free and involves our whole being, each act is linked in a movement towards the supreme center to which personality tends, or in a movement towards that dispersion into which, if left to itself, material individuality is inclined to fall."[27] We win our personality, we win our "freedom of independence" by becoming masters of our own actions, by freely choosing to become the persons we can be:

> In each of us personality and freedom of independence increase together. For man is a being in movement. If he does not augment, he has nothing, and he loses what he had; he must fight for his being. The entire history of his fortunes and misfortunes is the history of his effort to win, together with his own personality, freedom of independence. He is called to the conquest of freedom.[28]

The human person is a person only in embryo — and he is "called" to win his freedom of independence and the personality that are rightly his.

And it all begins, if it does begin, in childhood, at the instant when, at some probably unspectacular and perhaps even unmemorable moment, the child for the first time decides about the direction of his life by choosing to do what is good *because* it is good, that is, to do what is necessary to win his personality. This act, "the first act of freedom," is, "in a moral sense, an absolute beginning."[29] It is, moreover, "a moral act par excellence."[30]

25. Maritain, *The Education of Man*, 163-64.

26. Maritain, *Scholasticism and Politics*, 52.

27. Jacques Maritain, *The Person and the Common Good*, trans. John J. Fitzgerald (Notre Dame, Ind.: University of Notre Dame Press), 43-44.

28. Maritain, *The Education of Man*, 165.

29. Maritain, *The Range of Reason*, 66.

30. Maritain, *Problems of Moral Philosophy*, 141.

The child, Maritain explains, has from his earliest days engaged in many acts "in which freedom was not lacking," but prior to the decisive "first act of freedom," "the part played by freedom was inchoate and superficial." In the "*primal* free act," the child, having reached the age at which he can reason about himself,

> takes himself in hand; he frees or delivers his own self from the deterministic crust under which he had lived until that moment; he ushers himself into the universe of moral life by freely deciding about the direction of his life. At the root of such an act there is a reflection upon oneself that takes place in the intellect and answers the question: "What do you live for?" Yet this reflection is not explicitly signified to the mind, and the question it answers is not formulated in clear concepts. This question, on the contrary, is altogether engaged and involved in a choice whose immediate object may be a bit of straw, a trifle, but which is pregnant with a spiritual vitality, a decisive earnestness, a commitment, a gift of oneself the plenitude of which will not be experienced by adult age except in rare and miraculous occasions. *Puerile decus.* Children are told not to play with fire; they play with God.[31]

What Maritain has in mind — and revels in — is the "root-act" by which the person, first and exemplarily as child, commits himself to that for which his freedom of choice has been given him, that is, to win personality, the freedom of independence that consists in doing and pursuing what is *good* for human persons.[32]

There is more to say about this, but one must immediately add, as Maritain does, that a given act of commitment to seek the good qua good by no means ensures a bright future. The child "has decided about the direction of his life insofar as an act of the human will, exercised in time, can bind the future: that is to say in a fragile way. He is not forever confirmed in his decision; throughout his life he will be able to change his decision concerning his last end and the direction of his life, but by just as deep an act of freedom and of deliberation about himself."[33] In that first act of freedom, whenever and however often it occurs, the person "goes down to the sources of [his] moral life,"[34] and this because he recognizes, however dimly, that his freedom is to be ordered according to the personhood that is his only in embryo.

But from this implication of the first act of freedom, Maritain draws an-

---

31. Maritain, *The Range of Reason*, 66-67.
32. Maritain, *The Range of Reason*, 66.
33. Maritain, *The Range of Reason*, 67; see also 83.
34. Maritain, *The Range of Reason*, 66.

other, and it is decisive. The first act of freedom, which is a *"moral act par excellence,"* is moreover, "at least implicitly, a religious act, since it can only be realized rightly if it is realized in divine charity, whether the subject knows it or not."[35] Maritain elaborates that, by freely committing himself to the good and pursuit of its specific instances, the child commits himself, though he need not know it, to what the philosopher calls "Goodness itself," which is what the theologian knows to be God.

> The initial act that determines the direction of life and that — when it is good — chooses the good for the sake of the good, proceeds from a natural élan that is also, undividedly, an élan by which this very same act tends all at once, beyond its immediate object, toward God as the Separate Good in which the human person in the process of acting, whether he is aware of it or not, places his happiness and his end.[36]

This is radical doctrine, especially as one turns the page and discovers that Maritain goes on to clarify that in this act personal salvation is won, the person's redemption made effective. Yes, according to Maritain, there is no salvation without faith, and no faith without grace; but, in the person exercising the primal act of freedom for the good, Maritain finds the grace of faith at work.[37] We return to the workings of grace below, in part IV, recalling the while that the first act of freedom is necessarily, "at least implicitly, a religious act" because it is realized in divine charity. For Maritain, there is no winning of freedom and personality without grace and charity, and yet the conquest is an act of which every rational person — with a possible exception to be noted at the end — is capable.

What the child does, is the *type* of what a person, of whatever age, does if she is winning her freedom and personality: "Every time a man pulls himself together in order to think out his last end and to decide his destiny, he is in some sense back again at the absolute beginnings that mark the child."[38] Indeed, according to Maritain, a person's adult ability to grow in freedom may be in part a function of how he or she as a child responded to that first question about whether to do the good because of its goodness: "Adults are usually inclined to make light of childhood. They forget that their world of reason, civi-

---

35. Maritain, *Problems of Moral Philosophy*, 141.
36. Maritain, *The Range of Reason*, 69.
37. See Maritain, *The Range of Reason*, 75-85.
38. Jacques Maritain, "The Philosophy of Freedom," chap. 1 in *Integral Humanism, Freedom in the Modern World, and a Letter on Independence* (Notre Dame, Ind.: University of Notre Dame Press, 1996), 11.

lized and corrupt, depends in awful measure on the intuitive and tempestuous life of childhood and that the most important decisions which control their existence, and which they may have forgotten, have most often been taken in the course of their life as children."[39] Maritain's child is, in a strong sense, father to the man.

Part III. Education and "the Internal Principle"

A pervasive theme in Maritain's work is the *difficulty* of the moral task set before the human person. Over and over, if with different emphases and diverse tones, Maritain laments that the process of winning one's personality and freedom involves "a sorrowful cost and . . . formidable risks."[40] It is only "through constant effort and struggle" that a person can win his personality and freedom of independence.[41] One commentator, with an especially keen insight into the texture of the moral universe as understood by Maritain, notes that "What is said to be 'natural' seems uncommonly difficult to attain by ordinary means"[42] — even, one might add, with the help of supernatural grace.

The difficulty of the task, combined with the fact that nothing less than the point of man's existence is ineluctably at stake, leads Maritain to discern a stunning importance in education. One can hardly read Maritain without being impressed, if not frightened, by the importance he attaches to a child's having the right kind of education. Maritain of course acknowledges that the child will need to learn how to add, subtract, multiply, and divide, and so forth, and in his many writings on education he enters into surprisingly much detail about curricula and the like. Maritain is fond of touting the virtues of liberal education, but he is admittedly "much more fond of featuring the child who is being liberated through education."[43]

What leaps off the page is Maritain's judgment that the young person needs to be educated into how to be a person, into how to win his personality and freedom of independence. It is instructive that Maritain raises the topic and exigence of education, among other places, immediately after delving into the difficulty of the person's following the "slope of personality" rather than the destructive

39. Maritain, "The Philosophy of Freedom," 11.

40. Maritain, *The Person*, 44.

41. Jacques Maritain, *Education at the Crossroads* (New Haven: Yale University Press, 1971), 11.

42. Schall, *Jacques Maritain*, 146.

43. Joseph W. Evans, *Jacques Maritain: The Man and His Achievement* (New York: Sheed and Ward, 1963), 201.

"slope of individuality."[44] Education is a "crucial problem,"[45] according to Maritain, because without it the child will have no chance of mastering the means by which alone personality can be won. Every child is needful of a pedagogy into freedom; therefore, education itself "needs primarily to know what man is."[46] The program is clear: "The prime goal of education is the conquest of internal and spiritual freedom to be achieved by the individual person."[47]

A more concrete way of describing the goal of education is this: to develop the person's essentially good tendencies.[48] To be sure, the task of the moral life is arduous, because we are the heirs to the consequences of Adam's fall. It is Maritain's view, however, that, *pace* Luther and Calvin, our human nature is wounded, but it is not thoroughly corrupted: "our nature, certainly not corrupted in its essence, but weakened (by) those profound impairments which are called wounds."[49] Or again: "Man is not born free *save in the basic potencies of his being:* he becomes free, by warring upon himself and thanks to many sorrows."[50] Paradoxically, postlapsarian man *is* born free in his basic potencies; however, the inherited consequences of the fall, as well as any personal sin with which a person may encrust himself, ensure a severe labor as the price of the freedom of independence, and make an education into the person that he already is in embryo exigent. "The basic principle underlying Maritain's educational thought is that a person is to be liberated by fostering the most basic human dispositions. Rooting out dispositions which enslave people is important also; but Maritain is confident that the best means for achieving that is by fostering the good dispositions."[51] As Maritain sees it, the worthy education of which the child is in need will be an education into who by the integral dynamism of nature and supernature she is called to become.

We can begin to unpack what Maritain would have the educator do for the child by recovering and developing the concept of "essence" or "nature" that we introduced at the outset but have yet fully to explore. As we saw, Maritain understands the point of creation to be the going forth and increase of being and goodness. Thomist existentialism emphatically is not, however, "a philosophy of pure

---

44. Maritain, *Scholasticism and Politics*, 52. See also Maritain, *The Person*, 44-45.

45. Maritain, *Scholasticism and Politics*, 53.

46. Maritain, *Education at the Crossroads*, 5.

47. Maritain, *Education at the Crossroads*, 11.

48. See Edith Weaver Schell, "Some Educational Implications of Jacques Maritain's Theory of the Nature of Man and of the Knowledge Process" (master's thesis, Loyola College, 1958).

49. Translation of Maritain taken from Schell, "Some Educational Implications," 154.

50. Maritain, *The Education of Man*, 168, emphasis added.

51. James E. Hug, "Moral Judgment: The Theory and the Practice in the Thought of Jacques Maritain" (Ph.D. diss., University of Chicago, 1980), 100.

becoming";[52] being is differentiated according to the range of natural kinds. As is obvious, different kinds of things exist. A thing's nature or essence specifies what is and what it is to become; it specifies, in other words, what is *good* for it to be or to do. This "normality of functioning," as Maritain calls it, is at the same time this specific natural kind's "natural law." Moreover, "[a]ny kind of thing existing in nature, a plant, a dog, a horse, has its own natural law, that is, the normality of its functioning, the proper way in which, by reason of its specific structure and specific ends, it 'should' achieve fullness of being either in its growth or in its behavior."[53] Man, like every other thing in the natural order, has an essence or nature.

> [P]ossessed of a nature, being constituted in a given, determinate fashion, man obviously possesses ends which correspond to his natural constitution and which are the same for all — as all pianos, for instance, whatever their particular type and in whatever spot they may be, have as their end the production of certain attuned sounds. If they don't produce those sounds they must be tuned, or discarded as worthless. But since man is endowed with intelligence and determines his own ends, it is up to him to put himself in tune with the ends necessarily demanded by his nature. This means that there is by virtue of human nature, *an order or a disposition which human reason can discover and according to which the human will must act in order to attune itself to the necessary ends of the human being. The unwritten law, or natural law, is nothing more than that.*[54]

In the case of man, his ends include life at the biological level, for without satisfying the conditions of nutrition and growth, he cannot meet the conditions of his higher end, which is to reduce his individuality so that his personality might expand.

The specific ends or goods that the person *ought* to seek constitute, in Maritain's idiom, the natural law in its *ontological element.* Maritain introduces this locution to help distinguish the natural law in its *gnoseological element,* that is, the natural law in the mode by which it is known. Human persons know some things by way of reason and concepts; for example, the meaning of a statute or the content of the law of nations. But some knowledge enters by way of what Maritain refers to as connaturality. Connatural knowledge — by which, for example, the musician knows the musical, the poet the poetical, and the mystic the mystical — is "implicit and preconscious and . . . advances, not by mode of rea-

---

52. Maritain, *The Education of Man,* 162.

53. Jacques Maritain, *Man and the State* (Chicago: University of Chicago Press, 1951), 87.

54. Jacques Maritain, *The Rights of Man and Natural Law,* trans. Doris C. Anson (New York: Gordian Press, 1971), 60-61.

son or concepts, but by the mode of inclination."[55] Not of just any inclination, however. Maritain distinguishes inclinations that come from instincts rooted in humankind's animal nature from those that "issu[e] from reason or from the rational nature of man."[56] The latter inclinations, Maritain explains,

> *presuppose* the instinctive inclinations — for example, the animal instinct to procreate for the survival of the species — let us say more generally that they presuppose the tendencies impressed in the ontological structure of the human being. But they also presuppose that these tendencies and instinctive inclinations have been grasped and transferred into the dynamism of the intellect's field of apprehension and the sphere of human nature where it is most typically itself, that is, as endowed and imbued with reason. They are a specifically new recasting, a transmutation or recreation of these tendencies and instinctive inclinations which originates in the intellect or reason as the "form" of man's interior universe. . . . Here are inclinations which are properly *human,* even if they concern the animal realm. Nature has passed through the lake of Intellect (functioning unconsciously). The element which fixes these inclinations is not an ontological or instinctive structure, a "building code," but rather the object of an (unformulated) view of the intellect, let us say certain essential ends perceived or anticipated in a non-conceptual or preconscious way.[57]

This knowledge is by "intuition." Intuitive knowledge, which, for Maritain, is a category broader than and inclusive of "connatural knowledge," is direct and immediate.[58] If the reader will forgive the uncouth mouthful made necessary by Maritain's neologizing, one can say that a person's intuitive knowing of the natural law in its ontological element through the connatural mode of inclination is the natural law in its gnoseological element. The knowledge most necessary for a person to become in reality what he or she is in potency is reached connaturally through inclination:

> The genuine concept of Natural Law is the concept of a law which is natural not only insofar as it expresses the normality of functioning of human nature, but also insofar as it is *naturally known,* that is, known through inclination or through connaturality, not through conceptual knowledge and by way of reasoning.

55. Maritain, *Problems of Moral Philosophy,* 53.
56. Maritain, *Problems of Moral Philosophy,* 54.
57. Maritain, *Problems of Moral Philosophy,* 54.
58. See Maritain, *The Range of Reason,* 22-27. See also Jacques Maritain, *A Preface to Metaphysics* (New York: Sheed and Ward, 1948), 50-51.

My contention is that the judgments in which Natural Law is made manifest to practical Reason do not proceed from any conceptual, discursive, rational exercise of Reason; they proceed from that *connaturality or congeniality* through which what is consonant with the essential inclinations of human nature is grasped by the intellect as good; what is dissonant, as bad.[59]

Some readers have criticized in general Maritain's theory of intuitive knowledge; others have focused their objection on his theory of connatural knowledge, especially as it concerns the natural law. Still others have embraced Maritain's connatural theory of the natural law, appreciating it especially for liberating from the bonds of rationalism the means by which a human being comes to know his or her own ends.

That knowledge of who are to become enters, if at all, connaturally has decisive consequences for education, especially education of the child. Because the primary end of education is to equip the child to win his personality, and because the knowledge necessary for that battle is preconceptual, connatural, and by way of inclination, the teacher's art will be to encourage the conditions in which the child can, in an age-appropriate way, put himself in tune with his essential inclinations and, then, again in an age-appropriate way, begin to turn this prerational knowledge into developing intellectual, moral knowledge. The teacher's "function is supplementary and ministerial."[60] The educator's role is not merely to make the child free to trust himself, of course. It is the far more demanding one of possessing such sensitivity and discernment of the workings of the child's mind that he can penetrate those and then present the experiences and tools that will allow the child to progress in attuning himself to his essential inclinations.[61] This is an art in which the teacher can hardly be trained, yet without this sensitivity the teacher will fail to meet the child at the place where growth toward freedom can occur:

[I]f the teacher keeps in view above all the inner center of vitality at work in the preconscious depths of the life of the intelligence, he may center the acquisition of knowledge and solid formation of the mind on the freeing of the child's and the youth's intuitive power.[62]

59. Maritain, *The Range of Reason*, 26-27.
60. Rice, "A Critical Exposition," 326.
61. Schell, "Some Educational Implications," 161.
62. Maritain, *Education at the Crossroads*, 43 (discussed in Schell, "Some Educational Implications," at 162).

It is a paradox of this primary education of which the young person is needful that what is most essential — the intuition by which he knows connaturally — cannot be inculcated. The paradox is not a cul-de-sac. The teacher can encourage five basic human dispositions, which include (1) love of truth, (2) love of good and justice, (3) a free contemplative openness to reality, (4) a sense of responsible engagement with it, and (5) a sense of cooperation.[63]

The process by which this occurs is a complex one, of which one element merits singling out here. One way — indeed, though we mentioned it only in passing in quoting Maritain's description of the metaphysical mystery of personality,[64] the privileged way — of describing the person who is winning her personality and freedom, is that she is becoming a lover. In this regard, "[m]an's perfection consists of the perfection of love, and so is less the perfection of his 'self' than the perfection of his love, where the very self is in some measure lost sight of."[65] To love what is worthy, is the mark of the person possessed of his freedom, and in aid of this, what is of most importance in educators themselves is a respect for the soul as well as for the body of the child, the sense of his innermost essence and his internal resources, and a sort of sacred and loving attention to his mysterious identity, which is a hidden thing that no techniques can reach. And what matters most in the educational enterprise is a perpetual appeal to intelligence and free will in the young.[66]

Those who know and care about the particular child are best able to impart the loving attention he or she wants. In this manner, "[l]ove does not regard ideas or abstractions or possibilities, love regards existing persons,"[67] and ordinarily it is in the family that the child will learn love and, consequently, how to become a lover, of God and of neighbor.

Whether in the family, or in school or church, with both of which responsibility to educate the child is shared,[68] the educator faces a freedom that is only incipiently developed because the child's reason has only begun to be developed.[69] In adolescence, "judgment and intellectual strength are developing,"[70]

---

63. Maritain, *Education at the Crossroads*, 36-38. See also Hug, "Moral Judgment," 100.

64. See supra at 195-96.

65. Maritain, *Education at the Crossroads*, 36.

66. Maritain, *Education at the Crossroads*, 9-10.

67. Maritain, *Education at the Crossroads*, 96.

68. The sharing of this responsibility with the school is contingent, for sometimes schools will not be established or parents will not elect to use them. The church, by contrast, exists now necessarily, and has a mandate to teach the child the secrets of the faith and to introduce the child into the sacramental economy; the church has a claim on the child, though the church will not exercise this claim against the will of the parents.

69. Maritain, *Education at the Crossroads*, 33.

70. Maritain, *Education at the Crossroads*, 61.

but, according to Maritain, "[t]he universe of a child is the universe of imagination."[71] Maritain advises that "[in] his task of civilizing the child's mind," the educator

> must progressively tame the imagination to the rule of reason, while ever remembering that the proportionally tremendous work of the child's intellect, endeavoring to grasp the external world, is accomplished under the vital and perfectly normal rule of imagination.
>
> I should like to add that beauty is the mental atmosphere and the inspiring power fitted to a child's education, and should be, so to speak, the continuous quickening and spiritualizing contrapuntal base of that education. Beauty makes intelligibility pass unawares through sense awareness. It is by virtue of the allure of beautiful things and deeds and ideas that the child is to be led and awakened to intellectual and moral life.[72]

Maritain adds that occasionally "the vitality and intuitiveness" of the spirit at work in the child pierce the world of imagination with flashes of intelligence that enjoys "lucid freedom," while on other occasions the "immature workings of instinct and the violence of nature make him capable of intense resentment, wickedness, and manifold perversion."[73] Play is part of childhood, and it contributes to children's learning the difference between the real and the imagined: "When children play by building sand castles, these castles are truly castles for them. If you trample them, the children will cry with rage and indignation. But once their play is at an end, what were castles are only sand."[74]

In sum, Maritain understands education to be an art, the art whereby the person is helped to become in actuality what he is in potency. The teacher is an artist, a co-operator with nature: "the principal agent in education, the primary dynamic factor or propelling force, is the internal vital principle in the one to be educated; the educator or teacher is only the secondary — though a genuinely effective — dynamic factor and a ministerial agent."[75] Maritain elaborates:

> In reality, what is especially important for the education and the progress of the human being, in the moral and spiritual order (as well as in the order of organic growth), is the interior principle, that is to say, nature and grace. The right educational means are but auxiliaries; the art, a co-operating art, at the

71. Maritain, *Education at the Crossroads*, 60.
72. Maritain, *Education at the Crossroads*, 60-61.
73. Maritain, *Education at the Crossroads*, 61.
74. Maritain, *The Range of Reason*, 207.
75. Maritain, *The Range of Reason*, 31.

service of this interior principle. And the entire art consists in cutting off and in pruning — both in the case of the person, and of the individual — so that, in the intimacy of our being, the weight of individuality should diminish, and that of real personality and of its generosity, should increase. And this, indeed, is far from easy.[76]

The education that Maritain judges necessary has as an aim the increase of the learner's knowledge, but it also includes as a coordinate aim the strengthening of the will. Maritain's understanding of the fundamental purposes of education even lead him to affirm the priority of shaping the learner's will: without an effective and affective will for the good, what knowledge we acquire will be for naught.[77]

Withal, what matters above all is the moment of that first act, when the child takes himself in hand and freely chooses the good for what it is, and thus begins to win his personality.

IV. The Graced Life of the Child (in the Family)

The picture of the child painted so far is incomplete in two ways. Filling up the detail will reveal more of the child's place in the family, the family's (and thus the child's) place in the world, grace's operation in nature, and the destiny of children who with God's grace have chosen the good in the first act of freedom. Mention must also be made of Limbo.

Maritain does not assign parents the role of primary educator of the child merely on the supposed, contingent ground that children are infallibly loved in the family. Maritain is a realist: "The history of the family, all through the centuries, is no prettier than any human history."[78] Sometimes orphanages and boarding schools do better, and Maritain anticipates that, in the extreme case, either the state or nonfamily societies (including the church) that coordinate with the family will by right and duty take over the responsibility in which the family has failed. In the first instance, however, it is *by nature* that the child belongs in the family. The emergent view today is that "the law creates the family, and things could not be otherwise."[79] Maritain is so old-fashioned as to think

---

76. Maritain, *Scholasticism and Politics,* 53-54.

77. "[T]he shaping of the will is throughout more important to man than the shaping of the intellect." Maritain, *Education at the Crossroads,* 22.

78. Maritain, *The Education of Man,* 119.

79. James G. Dwyer, "Spiritual Treatment Exemptions to Child Medical Neglect Law: What We Outsiders Should Think," *Notre Dame Law Review* 76 (2000): 147, 167.

that the family is not the contingent legal creation of the state, but rather *the creation of nature,* in a "rough-hewn" way that awaits development.[80] "What I maintain," Maritain records,

> is that nature exists and nothing can get rid of nature. There are freaks in nature; then exceptional measures must be taken. But let us speak of what happens as a rule. Even at the most mediocre average level, nature at play in family life has its own spontaneous ways of compensating after a fashion for its own failures, its own spontaneous processes of self-regulation, which nothing can replace, and provides the child with a moral formation and an experience of mutual love, however deficient it may be, which nothing can replace. Many birds fall from the nest. It would be nonsense to undertake to destroy all the nests fairly well prepared by mother-birds, and to furnish the forests of the world with better-conditioned artificial nests, and improved cages.[81]

Love ever remains the goal, and it enters, not in utopian purity, but in the "daily love which pushes forward in the midst of slaps and kisses . . . the normal fabric where the feelings and the will . . . of the child are naturally shaped. The society made by his parents, his brothers and sisters, is the primary human society and human environment in which . . . he becomes acquainted with love."[82]

By nature, as a rule, the family ensures the child's best hope of experiencing and thus learning love, thereby beginning to win personality and freedom. Over and over again Maritain affirms that family is the creation of nature. "[I]t is an essential law of the nature of things . . . that the vitality and virtues of love develop first in the family."[83] Again: "No matter what deficiencies the family group may present in certain particular cases . . . , the nature [of the family] cannot be changed."[84] The examples could be multiplied, and individually and cumulatively they attest Maritain's judgment that not only individual substances (such as persons or peaches) have their respective essential natures, but also some societies, of which the family is exemplary. Merely "rough-hewn" by nature, family society awaits development through reason and will.

Maritain's frequent, unqualified invocations of "nature" and the "natural" can be misleading. Whenever the human person is implicated, Maritain's references to "nature" and "the natural" presuppose the presence of grace. We come

---

80. Maritain, *Man and the State,* 4.
81. Maritain, *The Education of Man,* 119.
82. Maritain, *The Education of Man,* 118-19.
83. Maritain, *The Education of Man,* 118.
84. Maritain, *The Education of Man,* 118.

to the tasks that are naturally ours in an elevated way. *Human nature has always already been graced.* The relationship between nature and grace, and what it means for moral philosophy (as distinguished from moral theology), is a vast and complex topic in Maritain's corpus, to the details of which he returned time and time again. For purposes of the present analysis, the main points are both clear and encouraging, in ways that anticipate, in some particulars at least, the theology of hope developed in Anthony Kelly's contribution to this volume.

A helpful angle on Maritain's understanding of how grace has transformed the world of pure nature is his reaction to Greek ethics, and Aristotle's in particular. Maritain took a conspicuously compassionate interest in the sad fate that befell most people in the ethical universe as comprehended by Aristotle. According to Aristotle, self-perfection required the right friends, therefore the right city, therefore the right laws, and so forth. Maritain even remarks critically on Aristotle's excluding children from the possibility of virtue or moral self-perfection by limiting it, as Maritain says, to what is achievable "at the end of a long term, after long exercise, at a ripe age, when the hair is beginning to turn silver."[85] Even prescinding from the striking Athenian elitism that marks Aristotle's prognosis for people's moral chances, Maritain is impressed (or depressed?) by how the consequences of an unmitigated or unameliorated ethical naturalism are, predictably, a lot of moral failures and mediocrities. Maritain himself is clear on the inevitable consequences of man's having a nature that he may fail, either voluntarily or involuntarily, to live up to: "Men know [the natural law] with greater or less difficulty, and in different degrees, running the risk of error here as elsewhere."[86]

That, however, is not the last word. There is Good News. "The great novelty introduced by Christianity," Maritain trumpets, "is this appeal to all, to free men and slaves, to the ignorant and the cultivated, adolescents and old men, a call to perfection which no effort of nature can attain but which is given by grace and consists in love, and from which therefore no one is excluded except by his own refusal."[87] And through this love, made possible by grace, a person is saved.

No one is excluded; not adolescents or old men, and certainly not the child — unless by one's own refusal, in the first act of freedom. A failure at the natural level — because of ignorance, involuntary lack of opportunity, etc. — is no longer, as it was for Aristotle, the last word. According to Maritain, the human perfection that is love is offered to all people, through grace that, unless the person should opt out by nihilating, leads to salvation.

85. Jacques Maritain, *Moral Philosophy* (New York: Charles Scribner's Sons, 1964), 33.

86. Maritain, *Rights of Man*, 62.

87. Maritain, *Moral Philosophy*, 85.

The *universalism* of God's salvation is a strong current in Maritain's thinking. The universalist *locus classicus,* 1 Timothy 2:4, where Saint Paul assures his readers that "God wishes all men to be saved, and to come to knowledge of the truth," is quoted and discussed by Maritain remarkably many times, and from his early writings through his very late ones. In his 1942 book *The Living Thoughts of St. Paul,* for example, Maritain offers this commentary on 1 Timothy 2:4:

> There is therefore no predestination to perdition. But there is a predestination to glory, since it is by virtue of his eternal love, which precedes all merit on the creature's part, that God saves all those who do not of themselves cut themselves off from his love, and whom he knows from all eternity, and whom the proveniences of his grace have abundantly filled.[88]

In *Existence and the Existent,* for another example, published in 1948, Maritain parses 1 Timothy 2:4 in the very context of explaining how God allows man to nihilate without man's becoming capable of causing being and goodness.[89] Most instructive is what Maritain said in a seminar late in his life to the Little Brothers of Jesus, later published in *Notebooks.* There Maritain argued vehemently against the proposition, which many in the church inherited from Augustine, that the damned are many, the saved few.[90] The error, Maritain avers, is to assimilate salvation to natural perfection. Natural perfection is indeed elusive, but "salvation is not . . . a summit of *natural perfection* which goes beyond the common state of nature, it is something entirely supernatural and which belongs to an order entirely different from that of nature. And the law of nature is not abolished by grace, but there is *another law,* proper to the supernatural order. . . ."[91] Without for a moment denying that humans can use their free will to frustrate God's antecedent will that all be saved, Maritain registers a reason for concluding that theological opinion is, and should be, changing with respect to the number of the saved:

> [T]he wounds of Original Sin have less efficacy to impair our nature than the wounds of Christ to elevate us by grace to friendship with the God who pardons. I am persuaded that the idea of the *greater number of the chosen* imposes itself and will impose itself more and more on the Christian con-

88. Jacques Maritain, *The Living Thoughts of Saint Paul* (New York: Longmans, Green and Co., 1942), 142.

89. Maritain, *Existence and the Existent,* 100-103 nn. 10-12.

90. See Fr. Harmless's chapter in this volume.

91. Jacques Maritain, *Notebooks,* trans. Joseph W. Evans (Albany, N.Y.: Magi Books, 1984), 270-71.

science. . . . On the one hand, there is God who "wills that all men be saved" and who sends His Son to redeem them by the death on the Cross. On the other hand, there is man who through the nihilations of which he is the first cause evades the love of God. Who can be persuaded that man through his evasions is *stronger* than God through His love? This does not exclude there being perhaps a great multitude in Hell, but it does mean that there is surely a much greater multitude in Paradise.[92]

The christological triumph that forms the heart of the movement chronicled in Kelly's chapter herein was anticipated and affirmed by Jacques Maritain.

Maritain's unwavering affirmation that no one, except by his own choice, is excluded from salvation requires *either* that salvation be in some sense a natural occurrence, and thus common to all persons in virtue of their human nature, or that supernatural grace sufficient for salvation is offered to all who enjoy human nature. As the material quoted above reveals, Maritain follows the tradition in affirming that the order of nature is *toto caelo* different from the order of grace, but, as we have noted, his own theological opinion is that every human person is in fact graced. No one lives in pure nature, and in fact, according to Maritain, there is but one internal principle in every human, not two. Over and over Maritain refers, in the singular, to "the interior principle, namely, nature and grace."[93] Again, it is this *single* principle, Maritain insists, "which matters most in the education,"[94] a fact to which we shall turn by way of noticing an apparent anomaly in Maritain's theology of a universally graced human nature.

So convinced was he of the power of God's universal salvific will, Maritain speculated that Christ might save even the devil from the fires of hell. "No one leaves Hell," and certainly not the devil.[95] But the topography of hell is not uniform. In its nether reaches, the damned experience flames of wrath. In "the higher places of Hades"[96] there is Limbo. "The fire cannot touch it. . . . There is no desolation there, but well-ordered nature. . . . This is the land of Limbo, the land of natural happiness, where the soul does not see God face to face, and which, because of that, is still a kind of hell compared to Glory."[97] The

---

92. Maritain, *Notebooks,* 271. On the "virtual distinction" between God's antecedent and consequent will as concerns who gets saved, see Maritain, *Existence and the Existent,* 101-2 nn. 10 and 11. See also Maritain, *Problems of Moral Philosophy,* 196.

93. Maritain, *The Person,* 46. See also, e.g., Maritain, *Existence and the Existent,* 41.

94. Maritain, *The Person,* 46.

95. Jacques Maritain, "Eschatological Ideas," chap. 1 in *The Collected Works of Jacques Maritain,* vol. 20 (Notre Dame, Ind.: University of Notre Dame Press, 1997), 21.

96. Maritain, "Eschatological Ideas," 21.

97. Maritain, "Eschatological Ideas," 6.

devil does not get saved, but perhaps by a loving "miracle"[98] Christ delivers him to Limbo.

Maritain advanced this arresting idea in an essay, "Eschatological Ideas," that he wrote and circulated in mimeographed form in 1939, recirculated again in 1961 in the same form, and published, with corrections and additions, in 1972, the year before his death. The essay offers Maritain's most systematic treatment of Limbo, one of his favorite ideas. Maritain's commitment to Limbo, which he faithfully submits "to the judgment of the Church, a judgment to which I adhere in advance,"[99] introduces a lacuna into the universality of God's saving will, and any account of Maritain's measure of the child must acknowledge it.

Maritain speculates — and his insistence upon the *speculative* nature of his inquiry is unequivocal — that "the souls of little children who died long ago," before Christ, "without the sacraments of the ancient Economy of Salvation," "or now," after Christ, "without the sacrament of baptism,"[100] will sleep (and dream, perhaps "the sweetest of dreams")[101] forever, never called to glory. At the general resurrection, their bodies will be restored to them, but they will forever inhabit the highest reaches of hell — not punished, but aware that they were not called to the beatific vision. Theirs will be the state of pure nature raised to its highest degree. Maritain found himself conspicuously "attached to the notion of Limbo,"[102] because it respects the reality of a pure nature not raised by the grace of the sacraments. What he has to say about their destiny is really quite remarkable:

> Oh, little children who have died without baptism, rejected though you have never done evil, you are not an accident in the divine economy, a peculiar case from which the theologians, pressed on all sides, extricate themselves as they can, an insignificant parenthesis. Your role is great, and your destiny well determined and very significant. You are the first fruits of natural felicity, of nature divinely restored.[103]

Maritain's text is full of admissions that people may think his views odd or foolish, but the final text, which includes much more speculative detail than concerns us here, was the product of more than a third of a century's reflection.

98. Maritain, "Eschatological Ideas," 21.
99. Maritain, "Eschatological Ideas," 4.
100. Maritain, "Eschatological Ideas," 13 n. 14 (translation corrected based on Jaques Maritain, "Idées Eschatologiques," in *Jacques et Raïssa Maritain Oeuvres Complètes*, vol. XIII [Suisse: Universitaires Fribourg, 1992], 458 n. 13).
101. Maritain, "Eschatological Ideas," 13 n. 14.
102. Maritain, "Eschatological Ideas," 16.
103. Maritain, "Eschatological Ideas," 17.

The single most striking element of the text is what it fails to say as it dispatches unbaptized babies to Limbo, for sweet dreams but with no experience of the beatific vision. Maritain utterly neglects to consider to reconcile the eternal *rejection,* as Maritain calls it, for which unbaptized children are not responsible, on the one hand, with God's *otherwise* universal salvific will, on the other, according to which, in Maritain's judgment the rest of the time, no one is excluded except by personal choice.[104]

Ordinarily, Maritain allows God to be much freer with the grace that is necessary for salvation, not restricting its operations to visible sacraments. Especially in view of the message of hope Anthony Kelly discerns in current theology, the church's pastoral practice, and the prayer of the church, the following passage of Maritain's is worth quoting at length. It is taken from the essay in which he offers his most extensive analysis of the "first act of freedom":

> God does not leave man to the weakness of his fallen nature . . . ; grace, before healing and vivifying man anew, is still present to envelop and attract him, to call him and incite him in anticipation. Our fallen nature is exposed to grace as our tired bodies are to the rays of the sun. In the years before his first act of freedom, the child had his own span of history, during the course of which his moral life was being prepared as in a morning twilight — nor was he left to the sole influence of his fallen nature; even if he was not baptized he was spurred by actual grace on various occasions and guises as diverse as the contingencies of human life and the by-ways of divine generosity; in his first motions within that incipient freedom that could be his, he was able to accept or refuse these incitations of grace; thus he has been more or less well prepared to meet the test, a test out of all proportion to the preparation for it and which occurs when, for the first time, he is called upon to decide on the direction of his life. In any case, at that decisive moment when he enters upon his life as a person (and later at the other crucial moments that may occur until his last day) grace will still call to him, while being entangled with more or less strength amidst the more or less good tendencies

104. "The infant who dies without baptism loves God above all with a love of the natural order"; the love arises from "freedom"; "springs forth under the infallible action of an (unshatterable) operating grace of the natural order as soon as the soul of the infant begins its separated life. The possibility of turning toward God as his freely chosen ultimate end when he reaches the age of reason has been taken away from the infant by a premature death, and the separation of his soul has placed him in *statu termini.*" Jacques Maritain, *The Sin of the Angel,* trans. William L. Rossner (Westminster, Md.: Newman Press, 1959), 34-35 n. 31. But how then explain how baptized infants are called to glory? They do not choose God as their ultimate end upon reaching the age of reason. But if the church "supplies" that act, then why not also for those who are not baptized? See Kelly's chapter within this volume, at 230, 236-37.

and the more or less great obstacles which derive from nature, heredity and environment. As a result, if he does not decide upon the good, it means that he has slipped away from the help which would have given fallen nature in him the power to choose good for the sake of good and to direct itself toward man's true end, by "healing" that nature and raising it to participation in the divine life.[105]

Conclusion

With the exception of his curious but tenacious hold on Limbo for unbaptized babies, Maritain anticipated the sense of the universalism of God's salvific will that is more and more pronounced in Catholic theology today. (Catholic theologians are by no means unanimous in downplaying the likelihood that some souls will in fact be finally lost.)[106] Through his doctrine of the first act of freedom that is, at least implicitly, a religious act, Maritain invests the child with, at the risk of sounding Pelagian, plenary moral potency. His understanding of the first act of freedom has won him the attention of those contemporary moral philosophers and theologians who identify a "fundamental option" in the person's moral life.[107] Not only would it be anachronistic to align Maritain with this theory, however, it would also be unprofitable and misleading; the diversity of meanings of "fundamental option" in contemporary theory rules out any clear alignment.[108] Still, Maritain does affirm, in conspicuously strong terms, that "[i]n a human life many births, deaths and resurrections may occur" through the "radical decision" that is "the first act of freedom," and it is the child's that is "the most obvious example of such an act of freedom."

As Maritain sees it, childhood is on a continuum with the rest of human existence. The human must always be developing by winning his personality and freedom, but he does so by imitating the child, who takes himself in hand and "ushers himself into the moral universe of life." "Vocation" is not a term of art in Maritain's writings, nor is "calling," but both words, and many like them, occur frequently.[109] Prior to professional or religious calling, there is a calling

105. Maritain, *The Range of Reason,* 73.

106. See Richard Schenk, O.P., "The *Epoche* of Factical Damnation? On the Costs of Bracketing Out the Likelihood of Final Loss," *Logos* 1 (1997): 122.

107. John Mahoney, *The Making of Moral Theology: A Study of the Roman Catholic Tradition* (Oxford: Clarendon, 1989), 32.

108. Maritain discerns natural moral significance in a person's doing in fact what the moral norm requires; the person who mistakes the moral law is merely excused, not perfected. See 208.

109. For extended discussion of the "call" all people receive to holiness, see Jacques

that is common to all, including the child. Working through rational human instincts connaturally known, and elevated through grace, and perhaps through the preaching of the Word and the celebration of the sacraments, God calls everyone, including the (baptized?) child, to win his personality and freedom of independence, that is, to achieve the perfection of love. As love grows, the self recedes from view. The selfish child must learn his better instincts, and obey them, for they are God's will for his creature.

The education of which Maritain judges the child needful is laughably or lamentably far from what the current American apparatus is prepared to provide, except perhaps to the rich who can choose their own schools. From Maritain's angle, schools that "on principle" would prescind from the nature of the human person in favor of "moral neutrality" would spell almost certain human ruin. What emerges especially clearly from reading Maritain on the child is "how one thing leads to everything else."[110] We might want to talk about only this or that topic, and carve the world up into more manageable or even neutral chunks. But, at least for a Thomist such as Maritain, there is a unity that precedes and will survive difference and distinction, a divine economy in which we are caught up in virtue of our creation, from childhood up. "In casting a good action into the universe, a free agent increases the being of the universe; the universe then increases the being of that free agent so that the balance between them will remain stable."[111] If, by contrast, he nihilates, "he will escape the order of the 'expansion of being' as well as the order of divine intentions and regulations. . . . The deficiency and privation which man has freely produced in himself will produce in the universe a direct fructification of evil."[112] The child who can choose for or against the good plays with fire and with God, whether she likes it or not. Tucked within the liberating rough-and-tumble love of family, the child may have a fighting chance.

Maritain, "Preface to Layman's Call, by William R. O'Connor," in *Jacques et Raïssa Maritain Oeuvres Complètes*, vol. VII (Suisse: Universitaires Fribourg, 1988), 1320-29. For vocation as a professional calling, see, e.g., Maritain, *The Education of Man*, 69.

110. Schall, *Jacques Maritain*, 223.

111. Maritain, *Problems of Moral Philosophy*, 80.

112. Maritain, *Problems of Moral Philosophy*, 80.

8. Hope for Unbaptized Infants: Holy Innocents after All?

Anthony J. Kelly, C.Ss.R.

Erasmus's famous anti-Scholastic jibe about how many angels can dance on the head of a pin may have been well deserved in Renaissance times. Theology must always keep a keen sense of the ridiculous. In dealing with the infinities of God's wisdom, love, and freedom, there is much we can never comprehend nor are meant to understand, especially when it comes to the ultimate salvation of the human race and transformation of all creation. A sense of proportion — and even a sense of humor — is necessary, lest one trivialize big questions with overconfident answers. Still, the church, when all is said and done, is simply that part of the world that has come alive to the mystery of love and mercy in which every human life is wrapped. It must witness as best it can, given the opacity of the human condition, to the clouded apprehensions of faith, and the tentative, halting quality of human intelligence.[1]

---

1. I have attempted a theological account of hope and its main themes in a recent book, Anthony J. Kelly, C.Ss.R., *Hope and Eschatology* (Maryknoll, N.Y.: Orbis, 2006).

The International Theological Commission is preparing, through one of its subcommittees presided over by Professor Dominic Veliath, S.D.B., a statement on the topic I address in this essay. As a member of the ITC, I have had access to the preparatory documents and contributed to the discussion, though I am not a member of the subcommittee concerned. In what follows, I gratefully acknowledge the work of this subcommittee, for it has influenced my presentation of the topic it addresses; on the other hand, neither the ITC nor this particular working group must be held responsible for my own elaboration of the matter. For a fuller elaboration of the history of church teaching and theology, I refer the reader to the ITC document due to appear in the future. — Anthony J. Kelly, C.Ss.R. [Ed. On April 19, 2007, the International Theological Commission, with the approval of Pope Benedict XVI, published "The Hope of Salvation for Infants Who Die without Baptism."]

I. Introduction and Conclusion

The present question as to the fate of unbaptized infants dying without baptism must seem to many as marginal, to say the least, given the enormity of the evils and oppression facing the human race. If Christian faith has painted itself into a corner by demanding sacramental baptism as the precondition for the entry into fullness of life, that is a problem of its own making, which seems even to contradict the love and mercy it speaks of so fulsomely. Does it mean that theology has been distracted into an outer limit of irrelevance, or that serious questions were in fact being faced? On the other hand, in a perspective from within the Christian, and particularly the Catholic tradition, the issue is not so simple. Despite the extremes that will become evident, basic issues were involved, reaching deeply into one's philosophical, theological, and pastoral assumptions.[2] Though the question of the salvation of the unbaptized child may seem marginal, the character of God, the reality of redemption, the impact of original sin, the mission of the church, to say nothing of hope for the unbaptized, are all implied, and all impinge on "the vocation of the child," the focus of this present collection.

In expressing hope for the salvation of unbaptized infants, theologians are aware that simplified media reports will speak of "abolishing Limbo" and so forth, without any sense of the history of this particular doctrine or the context in which it has been discussed. At the moment, it is also a matter of wearing the charge of indulging in useless speculation when, pastorally, catechetically, and liturgically, a positive hope in the saving will of God has replaced the ostensibly more restricted approach associated with the doctrine of Limbo in the past.

Nonetheless, given that a new sense of things has emerged, a more extensive reflection will have its own value. Saint Peter encourages Christians to give "an account of the hope that is within you" (1 Pet. 3:15 NRSV). Yet it would be incomplete if such an "account" did not indicate how such hope develops, and has developed in recent decades, in contrast to the more restrictive positions that were common in the past. Any such account will considerably affect many other questions not specifically treated here, but which are the subject matter of interfaith dialogue, and of the hope that, in the end, all will be saved. Christian hope in all its aspects is of critical importance in a world vulnerable to despair on many fronts.

---

2. John E. Coons, "Luck, Obedience, and the Vocation of Childhood," in this volume, wittily explores many of these related questions. Patrick Brennan, "Children Play with God: A Contemporary Thomistic Understanding of the Child," deftly refers to the profound philosophy of Maritain in outlining the ultimate issues involved in the developing freedom of the child.

A good place to start is to draw attention to the illuminating chapter of Professor William Harmless, an eminent Augustinian scholar, in this volume, "Christ the Pediatrician: Augustine on the Diagnosis and Treatment of the Injured Vocation of the Child." Julian of Eclanum taunts Augustine for presenting God "as the persecutor of new-born infants . . . sending tiny babes into eternal flames."[3] As Harmless points out, the greatest of the Latin fathers of the church came to a keen sense of urgency of infant baptism because of the virulence of original sin, and the absolute necessity of Christ's healing grace. Augustine asks,

> What need did the infant have of Christ if it wasn't sick? If it's healthy, why through those who love it does it seek out the doctor? If infants are said to be entirely without any inherited sin, when they are brought along and come to Christ, why aren't those who bring them along told in the Church, "Take away these innocents; it is not the healthy who need the doctor, but the sick; Christ did not come to call the just but sinners." . . . Those who come to Christ have something about them to be cured; if they haven't there's no point in presenting them to the doctor.[4]

Original sin has to be cured; and there is only one physician. Augustine poses a question:

> Somebody asks: "Does an infant too need [Christ] the liberator?" Certainly it does; the proof is its mother faithfully running *(currens)* to church with her baby to be baptized. The proof is its mother the Church receiving the baby to be washed clean, and either to be let go in peace, now set free, or to be brought up in piety. Who would dare to take the stand against such a mother?[5]

Sixteen hundred years have passed, and the church has come to offer hope to the distressed mother in another way. The authoritative *Catechism of the Catholic Church* (1994) observed,

> As regards children who have died without baptism, the Church can only entrust them to the mercy of God, as she does in her funeral rites for them. In-

---

3. William Harmless, "Christ the Pediatrician: Augustine on the Diagnosis and Treatment of the Injured Vocation of the Child," 128.

4. *The Works of St. Augustine: A Translation for the 21st Century,* pt. 3, vol. 5, *Sermons,* ed. John E. Rotelle, trans. Edmund Hill (New Rochelle, N.Y.: New City Press, 1992), 273. See also Augustine, Patrologiae cursus completus . . . series Latina, ed. J.-P. Migne, vol. 38, *Sermo* 176 (Paris, 1841), 950-51 (hereafter cited as PL).

5. *The Works of St. Augustine,* pt. 3, vol. 8, *Sermons* 155 (slightly altered). See also PL, *Sermo* 293, 38:1333.

deed the great mercy of God who desires that all men be saved, and Jesus' tenderness toward children which caused him to say, "Let the children come to me, do not hinder them" (Mk. 10:14) allow us to hope that there is a way of salvation for children who have died without baptism.[6]

Earlier in 1980, the Congregation for the Doctrine of the Faith stated:

Regarding children who die without baptism, the Church can do nothing but entrust them to the mercy of God, as is the case in the funeral rite that has been introduced for them.[7]

In the Funeral Rite for an Unbaptised Child referred to, the church prays:

Father of all consolation, from whom nothing is hidden, you know the faith of these parents who mourn the death of their child. May they find comfort in knowing that s/he is entrusted to your loving care. We ask this through our Lord Jesus Christ. . . .[8]

True, this prayer is a prayer, addressed to God and leaving everything to God. But clearly a great change has occurred, sufficient to cause Augustine to be regarded as a "dissident theologian" were he alive today! Theology seems to have moved, in this regard, out of its classic Anselmian character of "faith seeking understanding," to that of "hope seeking its most inclusive expression." Something has been going on. Not only has there been a development of doctrine, but an expansion of hope. Faced with the child, in the presence of the child, all thinking is affected, be it philosophically or theologically. I will write in the two sections following, first on what I term, "the phenomenon of the child," and then on the more piercing phenomenon of the dead child. I will then pass on to explicitly theological considerations.

II. The Phenomenon of the Child

Grave concerns are today expressed at the power of the consumer society to so colonize the imagination of the child that in effect the child is robbed of childhood and parents of parenthood. When the cultural imagination is pos-

6. *Catechism of the Catholic Church* (Homebush, N.S.W., Australia: St. Pauls, 1994), par. 1261, p. 321.

7. Vatican City. "Instructio de Baptismo parvulorum," *Acta Apostolicae Sedis* 72 (1980): 1144.

8. National Conference of Catholic Bishops, *Order of Christian Funerals* (Collegeville, Minn.: Liturgical Press, 1988), 261.

sessed by the forces of exploitation, the child embodies a vocation to something else.[9]

In this regard, to use a distinction given currency by Jean-Luc Marion, the child is not to be figured as an "idol," reflecting back to us our own needs and responsibilities, but an "icon" through which the light of another world shines through, in its original otherness.[10] A genuine phenomenological method seeks to escape the self-referential and projective mechanisms of dominating ideologies, and counteracts generalizations that focus on abstract principles rather than on the wonder or tragedy of what is actually given into experience in its particularity.[11] Neither philosophical nor theological thinking is dealing with abstract ideas in a theoretical world, nor with "data" in a neutral sense, but with the reality of unique human beings — however unnamed — in the actual world that, to the Christian vision, is created and redeemed by an original and ultimate love.

Marion in his later writings appeals to "saturated phenomena" of different kinds, as they are found in such experiences named as revelation, the event, the flesh, the work of art, and the face.[12] Though some have reproached him for transgressing the limits of philosophy by appealing to theological considerations, that is not our problem here. What is our concern is the phenomenon, the particularly "saturated" phenomenon, of the child. Inspired by his approach, I will focus on the phenomenon of the child, as it "saturates" our capacities to think about our shared world and the deeper reaches of its meaning: "Unto us a son is given," as Handel's *Messiah*[13] has it (cf. Isa. 9:6). In the birth of a child, life is taken to a new frontier: the limit to present experience, and a further limit of what is coming to be.

First of all, the child comes in the form of a unique revelation. It breaks into the experience as the occurrence of the new, at once a gift and a promise given into the heart of life, the focus of wonder at the generativity of the uni-

9. For an illuminating discussion of current cultural and political issues in relation to Christian tradition, see, in this volume, Robert K. Vischer, "The Best Interests of the Child: Modern Lessons from the Christian Traditions."

10. See Jean-Luc Marion, *God without Being: Hors-Texte,* trans. Thomas A. Carlson (Chicago: University of Chicago Press, 1991), 12-16, 29-30, 69.

11. Jean-Luc Marion, "Phenomenology of Givenness and First Philosophy," in *In Excess: Studies of Saturated Phenomena,* trans. Robyn Horner and Vincent Berraud (New York: Fordham University Press, 2002), 1-29.

12. See especially Marion, *In Excess,* 30-103, and *Being Given: Toward a Phenomenology of Givenness,* trans. Jeffrey L. Kosky (Stanford: Stanford University Press, 2002), 235-36. For a discerning theological commentary see Robyn Horner, *Jean-Luc Marion: A Theo-logical Introduction* (Burlington, Vt.: Ashgate Publishing, 2005), 103-50.

13. 1742.

verse manifest in this way, and a call to responsibility for the human family, if it is to receive this gift of a new beginning in reverence and care. It embodies a question: What new thing is being given, being revealed? What creative source, what ultimate giver, what guiding providence is involved as revealed in this gift?

Secondly, the child is an event that, despite the vulnerability of both the child and its mother, has the power to affect all it touches, with a new sense of both immemorial past and undetermined future. It is an open-ended, transformative event. It is no fait accompli in terms of assignable causes and predictable effects, but an event overflowing into the constitution of family, society, and even world history. It is an event that resists prediction, and insists on waiting, fidelity, and hope, if it is to be received in its incalculable significance. The child as event also poses a question: What generative happening has taken place? How will it overflow into the existence of parents, family, society, the world? How will this gift be played out in the all-encompassing event of creation itself?

Thirdly, it is a gift and event, "incarnate" — in the flesh of human life. This embodiment can, of course, be analyzed in terms of genetics and biology; but, more than being an instance of natural animal offspring, the child is enfleshed, incarnate, in a world of human, embodied persons. Born out of intimate union of its parents who have come together in the flesh, the child is conceived as an irreducible "other," handed over to their care. Despite the possibilities of violence and exploitation in a purely sexual objectification of relationships, the child is a witness, within the intimacy, ecstasy, and generativity of our incarnate existence, to the distinctively personal. It demands to be received as something more than a biological product of two sex agents, and so provokes a larger sense of life. As an incarnate gift, event, and revelation, the child poses further questions: What is this larger sense of life? What mystery of life does it point to? How, in the Christian phenomenology of life centered in the incarnation, is the child related to the Word made flesh, given into the world from the eternal generativity of God himself? Parents are more than agents of biological procreation, and their child is more than either a designed product or unwanted by-product of their union.

Fourthly, the phenomenon of the child occurs with something of the impact of a work of art. Great art resists any one-dimensional approach. In the case of great painting, for example, the beholder or succession of beholders is never confined to one point of view. What is depicted resists containment; it overflows any one perception. Such a work may be an object in the art market, and even reduced to a feature of interior design or decoration. But, of its nature, it never fits into a predesigned space: its power is to command its own space and change the place in which it is given. The phenomenon of art can be analogically related to the phenomenon of the child, even if it is not "artistically" produced by human agency. First, without indulging in sentimentality, the child is "given" as embodying a revelation of the wonder and luminous tenderness of being. As Francis Webb in the well-known poem, "Five Days Old," writes,

> The tiny, not the immense,
> Will teach our groping eyes.
> So the absorbed skies
> Bleed stars of innocence.
> . . . .
> Now wonderingly engrossed
> In your fearless delicacies,
> I am launched upon sacred seas,
> Humbly and utterly lost
> In the mystery of creation. . . .[14]

There is a further point to the poet's words. Despite its vulnerability, like the impact of the beautiful, the child is a disruption. It is not given to "fit in," as a technical product might be. It calls for a new vision and reconciliation among those whose murderous demands have foreclosed on new possibilities and made the world a dangerous place for children. The Gospels present the Christ child lying in the manger as both hymned by the angels and discovered by the lowly shepherds, while the imperial world was engaged in a census. Webb concludes his poem:

> If this is man, then the danger
> And fear are as lights of the inn,
> Faint and remote as sin
> Out here by the manger.
> In the sleeping, weeping weather
> We shall all kneel down together.[15]

Lastly, the presence of the child can be viewed in terms of the saturated phenomenon of the face. The face of the other is not a projection on one's part of the other as an object, useful, exploitable, or ignored, as the case might be. It stands for the totality of the reality of the other as given, calling me to responsibility. To allow oneself to be "faced" by the other in this way, is to be called out of oneself, to make room for this other, however unsettling this might be. In the child, society and culture are faced with fresh responsibility and care. The tears

---

14. Francis Webb, "Five Days Old," in *The Oxford Book of Australian Religious Verse,* ed. Kevin Hart (Melbourne: Oxford University Press, 1994), 225.

15. Webb, "Five Days Old," 225.

of a child demand an assurance that all is well — ultimately — and in as much making all to be well depends on our responsibility. Once more the question: In the name of what do we respond to the child and assure it of hope, and promise a peace that will not betray it?

These five aspects of the phenomenon of the child as "saturating" our perceptions of self, the world, and its ultimate mysteries will hardly coincide with the strange notions of the "right-to-be-wanted-child" of today. Past anxieties of another mouth to feed are reissued in the cultural version of the "wanted" child of today. These aspects as I have presented them bear not so much on the vocation of the child in a passive sense, but on the more active meaning of what the child calls us to, and what is demanded of the various communities that affect it. Each of these aspects occupies a limit, either negatively, of a limit beyond which the culture will not go; or, more positively, the limit of a region of love and care in which this vulnerable other will be safe. The more one moves into this realm of responsibility, the more deeply philosophical and religious considerations stir.[16] Does the child call us to a sense in which we are all "children of the universe" — and more ultimately, "children of God"? Is the child simply there in an extreme of vulnerability, or the incarnate symbol of our common contingency in the universe, and of the hopes that a generative, healing love is at its heart?[17] Does the phenomenon of the child approached in these ways call the church itself into a new kind of thinking?

III. The Child in Scripture

As regards our particular question, it is more a matter of considering this issue in the larger biblical context, rather than the impossible task of searching for texts that treat of the fate of the unbaptized child. Jesus' own teaching must be located in his own Jewish world and its rejection of the violence of the Gentile world against children, as with child sacrifice, exposure, abortion, etc.[18] Furthermore, in that Jewish tradition, "The surprising, apparently arbitrary pri-

16. It would be intriguing to relate this phenomenological approach with Philip L. Reynolds's informative study, "Thomas Aquinas and the Paradigms of Childhood" — but that would take another volume!

17. For a profound meditation on these points, see Karl Rahner, "Ideas for a Theology of Childhood," in *Theological Investigations,* trans. David Bourke (New York: Herder and Herder, 1971), 8:33-50; also Christophe Potworowski, "The Attitude of the Child in the Theology of Hans Urs von Balthasar," *Communio* 22 (Spring 1995): 44-55.

18. See, in this volume, Charles J. Reid, "The Rights of Children in Medieval Canon Law," 245-56, for valuable references.

macy of the youngest child is a constant theme"[19] in the sacred writings of Israel, as in the case of Abel, Isaac, Jacob, Joseph, Ephraim, David, and Solomon. It points to a divine reversal of values, and God's absolute freedom, as Paul came to experience: "My grace is sufficient for you, for my power is made perfect in weakness" (2 Cor. 12:9). There is always the unlikely choice of the "little one," the weakest and most vulnerable.

The "lost" or "inner child" of modern pop-psychology is never the issue. Rather, the challenge resides in the vocation common to all, of allowing oneself to be born anew into the realm of eternal life — by the gift of One who is the source of life, and united to Christ who is at once the eternal Son of the Father and "the first-born of all creation" (Col. 1:15). Becoming a child from this perspective is the goal, not just a stage that is to be left behind.

The Gospel's account of the child Jesus being brought to the temple communicates a sense of both promise and crisis: he will be a sign of contradiction and judgment (Luke 2:34-38). Just as Pharaoh's infanticide, perpetrated to control the Jewish slave population in Egypt, led to the deliverance of the exodus, so Herod's slaughter of the innocents promised something new.[20]

The novelty of what Jesus promises can be described from a number of converging perspectives.[21] Children are at once the recipients, models, and the measure of the kingdom of God. They are special recipients of the kingdom (cf. Mark 10:13-16; Matt. 19:13-15; Luke 18:15-17). Jesus blesses little children brought to him and teaches that the reign of God belongs to them. They evoke the spirit of the Beatitudes (Matt. 5:3-12; Luke 6:20-23), for in contrast to proud self-assertiveness of adults against God, they are not full of themselves, but anticipate the character of the kingdom as a "kingdom of nobodies," receiving all from God: "Whoever does not receive the reign of God as a child will not enter it" (Mark 10:15). Such a statement was subversive to Jewish — and Hellenistic — sensibilities: prized attainments of wisdom and fidelity to the law were being demeaned; everything had to be received as a pure gift. And so the challenge: "unless you change and become like children, you will never enter the kingdom of heaven" (Matt. 18:1-5). It is children who recognize Christ, and in their humble receptivity, come to know what has been revealed (Matt. 21:14-16; Luke 10:21-22).[22]

Children, and "little ones" generally, are the object of God's special care: "so

19. Robin Maas, "Christ as the Logos of Childhood: Reflections on the Meaning and Mission of the Child," *Theology Today*, 1999, 459.

20. Maas, "Christ as the Logos," 460.

21. Cf. Judith Gundry-Volf, "'To Such as These Belong the Reign of God': Jesus and Children," *Theology Today*, 1999, 469-480.

22. For further reference here, see, in this present volume, Elmer J. Thiessen, "The Vocation of the Child as a Learner," 381-82.

it is not the will of your Father in heaven that one of these little ones be lost" (Matt. 18:10-14). Authority is to be realized in service of those who are powerless: "Whoever welcomes one such child in my name, welcomes me, and whoever welcomes me welcomes not me but the one who sent me" (Mark 9:33-37 and parallels). In its dependence, trust, and powerlessness, the child has been described as the "real presence of Christ — a living sacrament of the kingdom of heaven."[23] The vulnerability of Jesus himself is evoked ("in my name"), as well as his origin in the one who sent him — the generative mystery of the Father.

In short, the reign of God is a world of children, children of the Father, children united in the Son and breathing his Spirit, living from him who is the firstborn from the dead.

This is a brief indication of the field of meaning in which the child is presented in the New Testament. There is no mention, of course, of the fate of children dying without baptism, but theology cannot ignore what is suggested, leaving it to wonder whether it has been too "adult" in its understanding of the ways of God.

Even Friedrich Nietzsche anticipated a stage in culture when a self-vaunting freedom would be the originating value of the New Man. As a stage in this self-realization, the great soul needs to undergo three metamorphoses — from camel to lion, and then from lion to child.[24] The camel, staggering under the responsibilities of a new freedom, wanders into the desert. There, a metamorphosis occurs: by disencumbering freedom from its burdens, the camel becomes a lion, the lord of the desert, asserting its power and will over all. But, before that willful domination can occur, it must become a child, in "innocence, forgetfulness, a new beginning . . . a sacred Yes" to the new world in which it is born.[25] The burdens of the past — above all, the Judeo-Christian past — must be cast into oblivion, so that an untrammeled, wide-eyed innocence in a new phase of history can begin.

Over a century after Nietzsche wrote those words, we are aware of the miseries resulting from the growth of the child he envisaged. The egophanic sovereign freedom that Nietzsche promised so failed to bring about a new world that serious thinkers become more camel-like than ever, wandering in a desert, overloaded with responsibilities, as hope for the new and the more humane dwindles. And yet the figure of the child, the call of the child, along with the vocation of the individual child, still promise a new beginning. But what of our problem?

23. Maas, "Christ as the Logos," 458.

24. See Friedrich Nietzsche, *Thus Spoke Zarathustra: A Book for Everyone*, trans. R. J. Hollingdale (London: Penguin Books, 1969), 54-55.

25. Nietzsche, *Thus Spoke Zarathustra*, 55.

IV. The Unbaptized Child

After this rather long digression, we can now return to our main theme: the fate of the unbaptized child. The child is always a liminal phenomenon, a revelatory event, irrupting into the mediations of adult culture. Yet it is *infans,* literally, a nonspeaker, unable to speak, let alone speak for itself. It depends on the carers and thinkers who can speak for it, and speak to it, out of sense of life's promise and value. Yet the dead child reduces us all to speechlessness, to the state of *infantes.* If Virgil spoke of the "tears at the heart of things, and all dying affects our thinking" *(Sunt lacrimae rerum et mentem mortalia tangunt),*[26] the death of a child means a grief beyond tears and a heart left to its own silence. There is nothing and no one to appeal to. There is no joy of accomplishment; and the promise of a new life can never be kept.

Unless through baptism. The earliest Christian tradition — which Augustine vigorously represents — believed that the child, having died after receiving baptism, was newly born to eternal life. Whatever the worldly judgments on the value of the dead child, it was conformed to Christ, and made a citizen of heaven.

Yet, the child dying without baptism? For many in the church, Augustine preeminently, there was no hope, because faith in Christ required what could not be given in any other way. The grace-less existence of original sin had its tragic result. The dead child was doubly dead: to this life, and to the life of the world to come, an eternal failure in God's redemptive design for the human race. The defeat of parents to have the child baptized was necessarily a defeat for the church, and even a defeat for God — since "God our savior wishes everyone to be saved and to come to the knowledge of the truth" (1 Tim. 2:4). The teaching of the Gospel was clear: "no one can enter the kingdom of God without being born of water and Spirit" (John 3:5). Without baptism, eternal damnation and loss of God were inevitable. There was no way out. Later theologians, Aquinas among them, tried to mitigate this judgment in various ways with the hypothesis of Limbo in which the child would enjoy natural happiness. But Limbo was not another way to heaven: it was the end point, not one of suffering the pains of hell, but still never a state of enjoying ultimate union with God in the beatific vision. Faith seeking further understanding came up against three obstacles: first, the limits of human intelligence in speaking of the ultimate; second, the utter gratuity of God's gift of salvation to the sin-infected world; third, the necessity of human cooperation in receiving it. The doctrine of Limbo was at least a way of admitting the limits to our understanding of the

---

26. Virgil, *Aeneid* 1.462.

ways of God, and the need to take with the utmost seriousness what had been revealed, while at the same time respecting human freedom and its history.

So there are three limited questions. First, how is the child representing the positive limit of new life, and promise, intimating deeper, wider, and ultimate questions of human destiny? The second is the limit of grief: How is the dead child the limit of all that was promised, now seemingly brought to nothing? The third limit is the child dying without baptism: Is it forever condemned to be deprived of eternal life? Though the hypothesis of Limbo was in fact the common teaching of the church and the common teaching of theology right into the middle of the last century, the appalling problem it posed never quite went away. Faith might reach the limit of what it can determine, but hope and love kept reaching further, prompting the present settled position of the church, which amounts to entrusting the fate of the unbaptized child to God's merciful love — with the implication that God, more than anyone else, loves everyone and everything a divine creative love has called into existence. How might we express, then, the new context in which this issue has been discussed, and in a sense, prayerfully resolved?

V. Some Historical Considerations

George J. Dyer, in his historical survey of theological opinion concerning the fate of unbaptized infants,[27] gave a noteworthy mid-twentieth-century exposition of what was for him still classifiable as an "unsettled question." He saw the problem clearly: at least three volatile ideas were in play, namely, the existence and effects of original sin, the necessity of the church and its mission to baptize, and the salvific will of God. He crisply summarizes:

> If we say that such a child is somehow saved, we have to reappraise the doctrine that the Church is necessary for salvation. If we defend the existence of limbo, we must be prepared to answer those who doubt the sincerity of God's salvific will. A dozen peripheral questions confront us, whatever direction our questioning may take, proving that theology is an organic thing with a remarkable interrelation among all its members.[28]

In making such a remark, Dyer proves quite prescient, because it is precisely in the reconfiguring of the "organic" interrelationship of theological themes that hope eventually found its prayerful resolution. He ends his work

27. George J. Dyer, *Limbo: Unsettled Question* (New York: Sheed and Ward, 1964).
28. Dyer, *Limbo*, 4.

with keen pastoral sympathy for those who are most likely to be troubled by this "unsettled question," namely, the parents, even if he feels the weight of the complex and confused tradition that he has so deftly outlined:

> Is there any possibility, they will ask, that the child is in heaven? In my opinion, the evidence to the contrary is not so clear or compelling that it should force us to deny them all hope of the infant's salvation.[29]

A small step forward perhaps, but he had noted that from the 1930s, "seldom has there been evidenced so much dissatisfaction with any of the tenets of theology."[30] Let us then backtrack a little, using Dyer as a valuable resource in documenting a long and often painful history, as both theology and church doctrine struggled to keep different biblical texts in tension, above all, 1 Timothy 2:4 and John 3:5.[31]

Harmless has already amply documented the extreme pressure under which the great Augustine worked when confronted by Pelagius and his followers.[32] Certainly, there was a huge problem. Mass conversions in the Constantinian era had created a situation in which the pastoral resources of the church could not provide adequate instruction for these new "converts." Baptism was being understood in many cases as of little more than talismanic significance, leaving the old way of life untouched. Pelagius had tried to restore some sense of human dignity in the midst of all this, even if he ended up endorsing a kind of exaggerated humanism that had no need of God's grace. For him, all the resources were to be found in human freedom, largely unaffected by original sin. But what if there were no possibility of human freedom, as with the dead child? What if the child died without baptism? These questions forced Pelagius to make his famous distinction between the possibility of entering into eternal life without being baptized and entering the kingdom of God as only possible through baptism — in accord with John 3:5.

Augustine had insisted on the devastating effect of original sin. He left no room for a halfway station between eternal life and the kingdom of God.[33] Everyone was either on the left or on the right hand of the divine judge: there was

---

29. Dyer, *Limbo*, 182.

30. Dyer, *Limbo*, 6.

31. Note the differences in the entry under "Limbo" between the first and second editions of the *New Catholic Encyclopedia;* cf. *New Catholic Encyclopedia,* ed. P. J. Hill (New York: McGraw-Hill, 1967) and *New Catholic Encyclopedia,* ed. P. J. Hill and K. Stasiak, 2nd ed. (New York: Thomson Gale, 2003).

32. Harmless, "Christ the Pediatrician."

33. Dyer, *Limbo*, 13.

no middle ground. Without baptism into Christ, the condemnation to eternal death was the only outcome for the child — even if it would suffer only minimal sufferings. Besides, this was "preferable to annihilation."[34] There was no injustice on God's part. Salvation is a pure gift; it is owed to no one.

Though the sixteenth Council of Carthage (418) condemned Pelagius's view that these infants occupied a middle place, thus enjoying eternal life without being able to enter the kingdom of God (John 3:5), it did not endorse Augustine's extreme view, though it was certainly shared by such formative figures as Jerome and Gregory the Great.

The result of Augustine's passionate teaching as it resonated through the later ages of theology was that Limbo — a word not used until the Middle Ages, probably coined by Albert the Great (from the Latin, *limbus,* meaning "frontier") — would always look like a "Pelagian fabulation." Still, while the early Council of Carthage supported Augustine against Pelagius, it did not go all the way with him.

The Greek Fathers seldom treated the question, due in large part to their characteristic apophatic reserve expressed in a reluctance "to probe the judgments of God."[35] For the Greek theological tradition, the crucial issue was the realism of the incarnation, and the transformation of humanity and all creation that this implied. To this degree, the Greeks maintained a more ontologically objective focus on a transformed creation in a way that contrasted with the intense subjectivity of Western disputations. Gregory of Nyssa was something of an exception.[36] The fate of the unbaptized child, he admits, is something greater than the human mind can grasp, and escapes all notions of virtue and reward. The blessedness of eternal life, *zoe,* is so meant for human life that it is a "reward" only in a transferred sense. Certainly, in these infants there is no basis for condemnation or merit, though "the One who has done everything well in wisdom" (Ps. 104:24) is able to bring good out of evil. He allowed for a certain development in all children who die, baptized or not.[37] Gregory of Nazianzus was more concerned with getting people to be baptized when they were tempted to defer it until late in life. A universalist outlook was a major influence, stemming from the teaching of Origen on the final restoration of all in Christ, even the importance of a distinction between a theological af-

34. Dyer, *Limbo,* 15, and 187 n. 13.

35. Anastasius of Sinai in *Quaestiones et Responsiones,* in Patrologia cursus completus. Series Graeca, ed. J. P. Migne. Vol. 89, Quaestio LXXXI (Paris 1857-66), 709.

36. See Gregory of Nyssa, "De Infantibus Premature Abreptis," in *Gregorii Nysseni Opera Dogmatica Minora,* ed. Hadwiga Hörner with the assistance of Hilda Polack and others (Leiden: Brill, 1987), 65-97.

37. See Dyer, *Limbo,* 27-31.

firmation of such a restoration and a prayerful hope for it was not yet explicitly made.[38]

The two lungs, the Western and the Eastern, of the church were not yet breathing in unison. Later ages would try to bring these two authentic traditions together, and with fruitful results.

Compared to the strictness of the original Augustinian position, the high Scholastic period tended in a milder direction. Augustine's view had continued right through to the medieval *magistri*, in Anselm of Canterbury and Hugh of St. Victor. Still, a more positive view did emerge. The "mildest punishment" that Augustine allowed was interpreted as the privation of the beatific vision to which human beings are destined though redeeming grace. Apart from this deprivation, unbaptized infants would enjoy a natural happiness and knowledge of God (Abelard, Aquinas, Duns Scotus).[39] This opinion continued right through to the Council of Trent and beyond, to become the common church teaching.

In short, the state of the unbaptized child, even though lacking the beatific vision, implied no distress. The natural happiness and advanced understanding of creation that these children enjoy included a resurrection of the body appropriate to their destiny, and even a reunion with their parents — even when these latter were enjoying the beatific vision.[40] On this point, theology had traveled a long way from Augustine. In fact, one could be forgiven for thinking that the developing notion of Limbo was beginning to look like a popular version of heaven itself, at least for anyone unable to appreciate the profound theological import of the beatific vision.[41]

But the theological situation was more complex in its past and in its future than can be so easily represented. For example, discussions were shadowed by the Second Council of Lyons in 1274 and the Council of Florence in 1439. This latter council had declared that, without the grace of redemption, those dying in mortal or original sin would end immediately in hell, but with different punishments.[42] The force of the conciliar statements seems directed to the immediate resolution of human fate after death for those who in fact are guilty of mortal sin or who were in fact infected with original sin.

The whole issue was further complicated by the Reformation and its aftermath. As reformers looked back past what they considered the unwieldy scho-

---

38. See Kelly, *Hope and Eschatology,* 131, 157.

39. Dyer, *Limbo,* 54.

40. Dyer, *Limbo,* 4 — noting the opinion of Leeming in 1954; and Aquinas's approach, 52-54.

41. Dyer, *Limbo,* 62-67, for the remarkable views of Politi and Suarez.

42. Dyer, *Limbo,* 59.

lastic systems of abstract thought, Augustine beckoned as the theologian of experience and Scripture, shorn of the oppressive superstructure of scholastic systems.

Limbo became the flash point as Augustine's teaching on grace was retrieved in the seventeenth and eighteenth centuries — but in a three-way standoff: Jansenists rejected the scholastic inheritance for the sake of pure grace doctrine in Augustine, and thus rejected Limbo as a "Pelagian fable" in the Synod of Pistoia in 1786.[43] For their part, the Jesuits and Dominicans, who wanted to hold on to scholastic developments toward a more positive view of Limbo, had to criticize Augustine on this point. On the other hand, the influential Augustinian Order was keen to defend its eponymous inheritance even if it meant rejecting Limbo.[44]

Church teaching responded by treading a fine line. Pius VI's *Auctorem Fidei* (1794) defended those holding to the common teaching of Limbo from any implication of heresy, Pelagian or otherwise. In effect, however, it signaled the beginning of the end of the extreme Augustinian view. A century later the denial of Limbo became no longer a matter of despairing of salvation for unbaptized children, and more a growing conviction of the possibility — however explained — of more gracious eschatological possibilities.

The early modern period was deeply influenced by the discovery of the New World. Theology had to envisage a world where the law of the gospel had not been promulgated, and the possibility of grace being offered in ways beyond the general theological imagination — perhaps in sacraments of nature or religious rituals with parallels in the Old Testament. God, after all, is greater than the laws of nature, but also greater then than previous understandings of the laws of grace. All are reborn into a world made new. The eminent Cardinal Cajetan at Trent provoked intense discussion on the substitutionary or supplementary role of the parents' faith for that of the child — a position taken up later and extended by Heris, so as to include the faith of the church.[45]

Both the preparatory statements of Vatican I (1870) and Vatican II, over ninety years later, witness to the topicality of this question; indeed, so common was the agreement on Limbo, that considerable energy went into commending it as worthy of becoming defined doctrine. Vatican I concluded without addressing this issue; while, in the preparation of Vatican II, any insistence on defining the matter once and for all was countered by the equally strong insistence that such a definition would be too precipitate, because of the lack of a scrip-

---

43. Dyer, *Limbo*, 80.
44. Dyer, *Limbo*, 86, on the influence of Berti.
45. Dyer, *Limbo*, 102-7.

tural basis and the clearly more flexible notions of baptism deriving from the notions of baptism "of desire" and "in blood" (the Holy Innocents), to say nothing of the maternal mediation of the church itself. God did not give the supreme gift of salvation automatically, but that did not mean that God's freedom was limited.

In the following centuries, practically every possibility for the salvation of the unbaptized child (and adult) was canvassed.[46] For example, some appealed to a kind of unconscious desire made possible by the very fact of the redemption of all in Christ. Others argued that the desire of the church, aligning itself with God's intention to save all, would be sufficient. Other opinions focused on a decision in death or after death as the situation in which the desire for salvation could be realized, so that death assumed a kind of sacramental reality. The power of Christ's resurrection would overflow to all, as long as serious personal sin and its rejection of God was not involved.

In the meantime, as theology reflected further on such scriptural texts as 1 Timothy 2:4, Vatican II opened the door for the development of hope.[47]

VI. Theological Perspectives

We have already mentioned the aporias that face theology and church teaching: original sin encloses all humanity in a situation of common defeat and alienation. It can be remedied only by Christ. The clear command of Christ to the church can never lessen her responsibility to baptize. These positions coalesce at a point beyond which hope could not go: the hypothesis of Limbo for unbaptized infants was the best theology could do, without interfering with basic teachings of faith.

a. "Hierarchy" of Truths

But today the question can be posed in a different form. What it presupposes is a principle employed by Vatican II, stating that "in Catholic doctrine there ex-

---

46. Dyer, *Limbo*, 109-34.

47. See Vatican Council II, *The Conciliar and Post Conciliar Documents of Vatican II*, ed. Austin P. Flannery, rev. ed. (Grand Rapids: Eerdmans, 1984), for key texts in the "Dogmatic Constitution on the Church" *(Lumen Gentium)*, n. 16 (pp. 367-68), the "Declaration on the Relation of the Church to Non-Christian Religions" *(Nostra Aetate)*, n. 1 (p. 738), the "Pastoral Constitution on the Church in the Modern World" *(Gaudium et Spes)*, n. 19 (pp. 918-19), n. 22 (pp. 922-24).

ists an order or 'hierarchy' of truths, since they vary in their relation to the foundation of the Christian faith."[48] Beyond the metaphor of hierarchy, there is that of nexus or interconnection of the doctrines of faith among themselves as they cohere within the overall revealed mystery of Christ.[49] Admittedly, there have been innumerable ways in which this "hierarchy" of truths and their interconnections have been configured in the history of theology and church teaching. It would seem that we are going through a reconfiguration in recent decades, motivated more by a praying hope than the clear determinations of faith.

b. Christ and Adam

In the complexity of seemingly conflicting truths and values characterizing previous discussion, the centrality of Christ is now more clearly the focus. This is hardly surprising, yet it does emerge as something of a breakthrough when any consideration of the relationship of the unbaptized infant to Christ had been notably missing. In effect, the child's situation was more determined by Adam than by Christ, so that the first parent's original sin far outweighed the influence of God's redemptive mercy. Note the following Pauline texts:

> For the free gift is not like the trespass. For if the many died through the one man's trespass, much more surely have the grace of God and the free gift in the grace of the one man, Jesus Christ, abounded for the many. (Rom. 5:15; cf. vv. 18-20)

> Since death came through a human being, the resurrection of the dead has come through a human being; for as all die in Adam, so all will be made alive in Christ. (1 Cor. 15:21-22)

Paul often rings the changes on the Christ-Adam parallel. There is no doubting that he, along with the Christian tradition he received and shaped, found in the disobedience of Adam an "original" sin of wanting to usurp God's power. This initial rebellion worked its way into human history through Cain's murder of his brother Abel, and the hubris of the Tower of Babel: alienation from God, violence, and a disrupted world resulted, affecting everyone born into it. Death, instead of being a peaceful transition into the fullness of life in the presence of the "God of the living" (cf. Mark 12:18-27; Matt. 22:23-33; Luke

---

48. See *Documents of Vatican II,* "Decree on Ecumenism" *(Unitatis Redintegratio),* n. 11 (pp. 462-63).

49. See *Catechism of the Catholic Church,* n. 90, p. 28.

20:27-38), received a dreadful power over self-enclosed existence, exerting its influence as the focus of fear, threat, mendacity, and failure. A deathbound horizon of existence projected onto God himself, the idolatrous character of the threatening other, the great rival who had to be appeased and where possible manipulated. Where death ruled, the idols of greed, security, and domination of others — the powers of this world — held sway. For those who are "full of themselves," "god" can exist only to maintain the world in which they are the center and the measure.

In contrast, Christ in giving himself to the will of God even unto the end, unmasked the lethal power of death and became the exemplar and source of a new godly and God-ward life. He is the gift, the Son sent by the Father to human history at the point where the problem of evil is most intense: "the free gift is not like the trespass" — so that "surely, the gift of God and grace of the one man, Jesus Christ, abounded for many." By raising him from the dead, God has vindicated Christ as the true image of humanity, and caused the power of this resurrection to overflow into the lives — and deaths — of those who would follow him: "so all will be made alive in Christ."

In such a perspective, the image of God is changed. In Paul's letter to the Philippians, in his effort to recall them to a more other-directed way of life, he quotes almost in passing one of the earliest Christian hymns (Phil. 2:6-10): "Though he was in the form of God, he did not count equality with God as something to be exploited," but humbled himself to take on the form of enslaved human existence, right to the limit of death. In this extreme of self-giving love, Jesus is exalted by the Father, and given the holiest of names, so that all may find in him the image of God and of humanity made in the divine image. In this status, he is to be adored by all creation, confessed as Lord to the glory of the Father.

We can, then, already begin to ask, how original and all determining is the original sin of Adam? Is there not an original gift of God's self-giving love that conditions every aspect of creation and brings it to fulfillment? True, it is not about the fate of the unbaptized child, but if this "original gift" is moved further up the order or "hierarchy" of truths, and the fact of original sin proportionately demoted, things appear differently. Regarding the primordial salvific intention of God, we can read the following two texts with the question, does the unbaptized state of the dead child weigh so much more strongly against God's intent, that it can frustrate it?

> He [God] has made known to us the mystery of his will, according to his good
> pleasure that he set forth in Christ, as a plan for the fullness of time, to gather
> up all things in him, things in heaven and things on earth. (Eph. 1:9-10)

As we turn to a second text (Col. 1:15-20), we note, first of all, that God's saving intention is not, first of all, to reveal original sin, but to manifest the original divine intention to gather up, or "recapitulate," the whole of creation under Christ. The "fullness of time" in which the divine will is disclosed runs counter to that dismal history of contagious human defeat and alienation so aptly symbolized by our solidarity in original sin.

Paul points to another and more original vision of creation, mediated to faith by Christ as both the icon of God and the firstborn of creation: "He [Christ] is the image of the invisible God, the firstborn of all creation" (Col. 1:15). Christ is the focus and center of God's creation: "for in him all things in heaven and on earth were created, things visible and invisible . . . all things have been created through him and for him" (Col. 1:16). Because he is the first in the divine intention, everything imaginable in heaven and earth finds its coherence in him: "He himself is before all things, and in him all things hold together" (Col. 1:17). In this regard, he is the head of the body of the new and God-intended humanity, here identified with the community of the church: "He is the head of the body, the church" (Col. 1:18a). As the God-given inauguration of this new humanity no longer under the thrall of death, "he is the beginning, the first born from the dead, so that he might come to have first place in everything" (Col. 1:18b). Such a primacy demands that it be the prime consideration in the understanding of every aspect of Christian life and hope, for he is the accomplishment and enactment of everything God is and wills to be for the created world: "For in him all the fullness of God was pleased to dwell" (Col. 1:19). The self-giving death of Christ has reversed the power of sin and death, to make creation appear in its pacific and ultimate form: "and through him God was pleased to reconcile to himself all things, whether on earth or in heaven, by making peace through the blood of his cross" (Col. 1:20).

The grandeur of this vision and the range of this expression of Christian assurance, if reappropriated in the context of a world immeasurably more vast than what Paul could have experienced, cannot but overflow into the consideration of the question we have been considering. Is the fate of the unbaptized child to be located somewhere outside the "recapitulation" and originality, the coherence of all things and their finality in Christ? A prayerful hope would necessarily tend to put no limit on God's saving action.[50]

---

50. The unprecedented canonizing/beatifying activity of John Paul II, especially in regard to martyrs, tends to create a mood of such eschatological assurance that it overflows into any consideration of innocent unbaptized children.

c. Original Sin

A nagging aspect of the question is the meaning of original sin and the manner of its transmission throughout history. In general, theology thought of original sin as a lack of an originally intended ordination to God. This distortion permeated the whole of human history so that human existence was driven more by idolatry than by surrender to the one, true God. Through union with Christ, this perverted order is reversed: Christ is the new Adam, restoring creation to its original God-wardness. The question is sharpened when we consider the manner of its transmission. Is it a natural condition communicated by what is most natural to human generation, and most a prey to disordered intentions, namely, sexual procreation? If that is the case — a more Augustinian approach — then the infant comes into existence marked or stained with a congenital disorder. On the other hand, is original sin better interpreted in cultural terms, as the overwhelming bias to selfishness and violence conditioning all human life in its beginnings? If that is the case, the child is born into a state of original sin, and in the language it will learn to speak, in the models of authority conditioning its freedom, in the enormous and God-less influences forming its identity, it cannot but conform to a world in which the meaning of God, love, forgiveness are unrealities in the "real world" of its particular history.

It seems, then, that the more we conceive of original sin, not in physical or naturally genetic terms, but as a mimetic contagion infecting human culture, the more removed the dead child is from the disorder embedded in culture. In terms of a cultural analysis of violence, the work of René Girard has affected theology. James Alison's *The Joy of Being Wrong: Original Sin through Easter Eyes* is a notable example.[51] Alison and others make one of those deeply obvious points that theology so easily forgets. It is only because the crucified Jesus is risen from the dead that the church — and theology — came to realize the character and power of original sin. It is not as though everyone knew what it was, and then turned to Christ to be saved from it. The opposite is the case: only when the true form of our humanity and the true character of God was disclosed in Christ, only when we touch on the novelty of what humanity is meant to be, can we come to realize the destructiveness of our previous existence. In other words, Christ is not to be interpreted in relation to original sin, but the desperate situation manifest in original sin is interpreted in terms of new humanity embodied in Christ. The consequences of this shift in the configuration

---

51. James Alison, *The Joy of Being Wrong: Original Sin through Easter Eyes* (New York: Crossroad, 1998) and the very insightful *Raising Abel: The Recovery of the Eschatological Imagination* (New York: Crossroad, 1996).

of Christian doctrine are clear: Is the manner in which we might nourish hope for the unbaptized child to be overwhelmed by the doctrine of original sin — or to be inspired by the Christian faith's focus, Christ's resurrection from the dead? A rearrangement in the "hierarchy of truths" can thus take place.[52]

d. The Mission of the Church

Finally, there are the always delicate questions relating to the mission of the church. No expression of hope, no theology, can undercut the mission of the church to evangelize nations and baptize all into Christian faith. But in the case of the child dying without baptism, hope enters a zone beyond the world of the church's usual scope of action. It must look beyond its determined responsibilities to their source — to God, to Christ, to the Spirit who can operate beyond the institutional practice of the church itself. Tradition is long familiar with exceptions to the ordinary sacramental means of conferring baptism. Faith, looking beyond the ordinary means of salvation to their goal and source, recognizes the "substitutions" for sacramental baptism, namely, baptism by desire and that of blood or martyrdom. The saving love of God, though celebrated in the sacraments, is not constricted by them. Hope enters a territory where only God can act where all other human means fail.

How this might be best expressed is the question. In the horizon of hope, the church can refresh its imagination by recalling that Mary, the mother of Jesus, was preserved free from original sin by the divine prevision of the redemptive power of her Son. The Gospel recounts how John the Baptist was sanctified in the womb of his mother, Elizabeth. The apostle Paul attests to God-given vocation in the womb of his mother, long before he realized it (Gal. 1:15-16). Furthermore, if the child dies after receiving baptism, it can enter into eternal life and enjoy the beatific vision: obviously, an empirical act of freedom on its part is not presupposed. Can it be that for all infants, baptized or not, that the original solidarity of all human beings "in Christ" is the ultimately deciding factor when it comes to expressing hope and addressing the grief of their parents?

Another dimension inherent in the church's expression of hope for the

---

52. Related to this, a more gracious hermeneutics of biblical texts is in evidence: passages expressing judgment and condemnation tend to be seen more as appeals to present liberty, to underline the critical situation of human freedom, and its tendencies to presumption and despair (Matt. 13:13, 24-30, 36-43, 47-50; 18:23-25; 22:1-4; 25:1-13, 31-46; Luke 16:19-31; Rom. 2:2-11; 1 Cor. 3:11-15; 2 Cor. 5:10; 1 Thess. 1:5-10). Other passages invite the reader to place no limits on hope, e.g., 1 Cor. 13:7; Rom. 11:32; Eph. 1:10; 2:14-18; 1 Tim. 2:4; 4:10; 2 Pet. 3:9. See Kelly, *Hope and Eschatology*, especially 138-59.

unbaptized might be best expressed in terms of a fresh awareness of her maternal role. It is rather more than the ancient principle of *ecclesia supplet* — the church "supplies" when there is any defect in the matter or form of the sacraments, especially in regard to baptism. Related to the accepted possibilities of baptism by desire *(in voto)*, there is the more encompassing activity of the intercessory prayer of the whole church for each and all. The spirit of this is caught in Paul's injunction to Timothy:

> First of all, I urge that supplications, prayers and intercessions, and thanksgivings, be made for everyone. . . . This is right and acceptable to God our Savior, who desires everyone to be saved, and to come to the knowledge of the truth. For there is one God; there is also one mediator between God and human kind, Christ Jesus, himself human, who gave himself a ransom for all. (1 Tim. 2:1-6)

The compassion and hope of the church must try to be worthy of the clearly inclusive extent of God's universal salvific will. The solidarity of all in Christ is thus matched with the inclusive range of the church's outreach in prayer in the maternal extent of her hope. The ancient symbolism of "Mother Church" is modeled on the maternity of Mary, the mother of Christ and the mother of the new family of Christ represented in the Beloved Disciple at the foot of the cross (John 19:26). Through faith in Christ, the Marian and maternal church conceives Christ and his members within her. This pregnancy is both a presence and a concealment. The true face of Christ, head and members, will appear only when the child of hope is born. In the meantime, the faith and prayer of the church is the womb in which Christ, head and members, is coming to term. The prayer of the church is the mode of its waiting for the time of the child to be born, hidden within her. It hopes for Christ, to be fully born as the embodiment of the "one new humanity" (Eph. 2:15; 4:12-14). A hitherto fragmented human family will in this birth find the joy of its final peace and reconciliation (cf. Eph. 2:15-22).

To speak of the efficacy of the intercessory prayer of the church is not to imply that it somehow changes the mind of God. Rather than changing God's mind, the prayers that the Spirit inspires on behalf of all are an indication of that mind. The prayer of the church is a manifestation of the saving will of God, involving all in the salvation of each one. All are included in the compassion of the saints, to such a degree that no limit need be placed on God's love and mercy: "my hopes touch upon the infinite" (Thérèse of Lisieux).[53] Here, Saint

53. Her words: "mes espérances qui touchent à l'infini," in Lettre A, Soeur Marie du Sacré Coeur, Manuscrit (B 2v, 28) in *Sainte Thérèse de l'Enfant-Jésus et de la Sainte-Face: Oeuvres*

Thérèse is accompanied by many of her sisters in the past — who, in fact, left little mark on the theological tradition until quite recently. From the Middle Ages on, we mention Mechtilde of Hackenborn, Mechtilde of Magdeburg, Angela of Foligno, Lady Julian of Norwich, and Catherine of Siena — note, too, that the Dominican Catherine of Siena and the Carmelite Thérèse have been recently proclaimed Doctors of the Church by Pope John Paul II. The hope-filled witness of these holy women is preceded by a more hopeful patristic tradition, many centuries before them. It is represented by such figures as Clement of Alexandria, Origen, Gregory Nazianzen, Gregory of Nyssa, Didymus the Blind, Evagrius Ponticus, Diodorus of Tarsus, Theodore of Mopsuestia, Maximus Confessor, and John Scotus Erigena. To hope for the ultimate reconciliation of all with God is to find oneself in good company, an illustration of the axiom *lex orandi, lex credendi* — the way faith prays is the way it believes. A parent's prayer for a child dying before it could be baptized is a manifestation of the prayer of the whole church, the *lex orandi* in action.

An ecclesiology of institutional limits, marking the divide between those who are "in" and those who are "out," is being expanded into an ecclesiology of communion and mission — to be served by the institutional forms that the church must inevitably assume. All in some way belong to the church, because all belong in Christ, the revelation of God's saving will.[54] In regard to the salvation of all in Christ, Vatican II states:

> All this holds true not only for Christians, but for all people of good will in whose hearts grace is active invisibly. For since Christ died for all (cf. Rom 8:32), and since all are in fact called to one and the same destiny which is divine, we must hold that the Holy Spirit offers to all the possibility of being made partners, in a way known to God, in the paschal mystery.[55]

"In a way known to God" is no doubt the best way to summarize the conclusion of this prolonged reflection on the fate of the child dying without baptism. What faith knows about God invites us in its every lineament to leave to

---

Complètes (Paris: Cerf-Desclée de Brouwer, 1992), 224.ILL. See also *The Story of a Soul: An Autobiography of Saint Thérèse of Lisieux,* trans. John Clarke, 3rd ed. (Washington, D.C.: ICS Publications, 1996), 192: "my desires and longings which reach even unto infinity."

54. An accessible account of this hope-filled outlook is found in Hans Urs von Balthasar (hardly an irresponsible theologian!), in his last book, *Dare We Hope "That All Men Be Saved"?* trans. Dr. David Kipp and Rev. Lothar Krauth (San Francisco: Ignatius, 1988). His conclusion: not only may we hope for all, but also we have a duty to do so! For a treatment of all related issues, see Kelly, *Hope and Eschatology.*

55. See *Documents of Vatican II, Gaudium et Spes,* n. 22 (pp. 922-34); *Lumen Gentium,* nn. 8-9 (pp. 357-60).

God what is necessarily beyond human determination. A grieving parent can find no other consolation. Any expression of a prayerful hope and renewed theology have value only in inviting to a deeper surrender to the Love (1 John 4:8, 16) that gives what is most intimate to itself into pain and darkness of our human existence. When all theories or human judgments are silenced, the ultimately determining realities are found only in depths of divine wisdom and in the extent of mercy that has no end.

In the second book of Samuel, the wise woman of Tekoa pleads for the life of Absalom. Hope can only be enlarged by such age-old wisdom:

> We must all die; we are like water spilled on the ground, which cannot be gathered up. But God will not take away a life; he will devise plans so as not to keep an outcast banished forever from his presence. (2 Sam. 14:14)

III. The Rights, Duties, and Work of the Child

9. The Rights of Children in Medieval Canon Law

Charles J. Reid, Jr.

In 1991, in his book on the history of the "children's rights movement," Joseph Hawes wished to take issue with those who believed that children's rights were something new on the American political and legal landscape. In fact, the cause of children's rights, Hawes wrote, is much older than most modern advocates or policy analysts might suspect. Writing specifically of the American context, Hawes declared:

> [There is] actually . . . a long history of efforts to use public power and pressure to improve the lives of American children and thereby to reform or improve American society generally. . . . Contrary to the teachings of some historians, Americans have a long tradition of being sensitive to the needs and rights of children.[1]

Despite its title, however, Hawes's book is not precisely about the history of the *rights* of children. He is not concerned with determining when the expression "rights of children" came to be coined or its exact scope or meaning. Rather, he uses the term "rights" as a means of indicating a general societal solicitude for the well-being of the young that he traces as far back in American history as colonial-era New England. Looking to sources like the common-law doctrine of *parens patriae* — the principle that the state stood in the position of a parent to see to the welfare of children in cases of last resort — Hawes built the argument that from colonial days onward, there was an enforceable public interest to see to the care and nurturance of children.[2] Statutes from the colonial era and the early republic addressing child abuse and cruelty, the establish-

---

1. Joseph M. Hawes, *The Children's Rights Movement: A History of Advocacy and Protection* (Boston: Twayne Publishers, 1991), ix.

2. Hawes, *The Children's Rights Movement,* 1-10.

ment of state-managed schools, the creation of societies for the prevention of abuse against children, and the judicial supervision of the placement of orphans into acceptable homes, all figure in Hawes's story.[3] Only in the final chapter, entitled "The Children's Rights Movement Comes of Age: 1960-1990," does Hawes consider the language of rights as it influenced the shape of public debate concerning child welfare.[4]

None of these remarks is intended as a criticism of Hawes's fine book. Hawes has drawn deeply from a disparate body of sources to create a powerful synthetic whole. His work remains an important contribution to the history of public concern for the welfare of children in the United States. My opening observations are instead intended to illustrate the difficulty of writing on a topic like the welfare of children: How do we define our terms? This problem is especially vexing, it seems, the further back one wishes to push the analysis. When we address children's rights in the Middle Ages, do we mean by that term the broad concern that every society has for the well-being and the comfort and the education of the younger generation? Or do we mean something narrower? Something that fits well under the rubric of rights as something claimable by the child and enforceable through social or legal mechanisms? As something correlative with a duty that might compel others to act on behalf of the child?

My intention in this chapter is to pursue the narrower, not the broader agenda. I am concerned in particular with how the conceptual apparatus and terminology of rights came to shape European thought about children in the pre-Reformation Christian world. Even narrowed in this way, the undertaking is formidable. Rights were understood in the medieval world — as they are understood in our own time — as collections of claims, freedoms, powers, privileges, and immunities.[5] They carried with them the clear implication of enforceability. They correlated tightly with duties. Medieval writers, as much as their modern counterparts, grew weary at the possibility that there might be rights that lacked corresponding remedies for their breach.

In this chapter, furthermore, I shall not only concentrate on the narrower, legal conception of rights as it pertained to the welfare of children, but I have also narrowed the set of sources that I wish to consider. I intend to focus on the canon law of the Catholic Church, as it developed from patristic and early me-

---

3. Hawes, *The Children's Rights Movement*, 2-8 (protection from abuse); 13-15 (establishment of public schools); 17-24 (the creation of the Children's Aid Society and the Society for the Prevention of Cruelty to Children); and 7-9 (care for orphans).

4. Hawes, *The Children's Rights Movement*, 96-121.

5. For an analysis of these aspects of medieval rights, with respect particularly to canon law, see Charles J. Reid, Jr., "The Canonistic Contribution to the Western Rights Tradition: An Historical Inquiry," *Boston College Law Review* 33 (1991): 59-72.

dieval sources into a rich and diverse and highly complex system in the high Middle Ages of the twelfth through the fifteenth centuries. At points, I shall consider the writings of Catholic theologians and philosophers, and I shall also steal a glance toward medieval secular legal systems, but these moves will chiefly be made by way of contrast and comparison. It is hoped that my narrow focus does justice to the richness of the sources at hand. A broader examination of children's welfare in the first millennium and a half of the Christian era would be a large and daunting undertaking and lies well outside the scope of this project.

The Right to Life and to Support

I shall concern myself first not with the continued vitality of a particular right, but rather with its discrediting and disappearance. The right of which I speak is the freedom and authority of the father in the ancient Roman world to dominate his household. The ancient world of the first three centuries of the Christian era — before Christianity had had the opportunity to shape and form Roman sensibilities or social expectations — put great premium on the father's power to govern hearth and home.[6] This power was called *patria potestas,* and it embraced the broad range of the father's commanding authority over children and slaves, estates and retainers. With respect specifically to children, this power additionally embraced the "right and power of life and death" *(ius et vitae necisque potestas).*[7] This rightful power was exercised only rarely where adult sons were concerned,[8] and its application to grown children was explicitly condemned by Emperor Hadrian in the early second century of the Christian era.[9]

It was a different story, however, where infants were concerned. Infanticide was an acceptable practice throughout pagan antiquity.[10] Indeed, so notable a

6. In the *Institutes,* Justinian declares that "the right of power, which we have over our children, is proper to Roman citizens; for nearly no other have the sort of power over their children that we have over ours." *Institutes* 1.9.2 (my translation).

7. Charles J. Reid, Jr., *Power over the Body, Equality in the Family: Rights and Domestic Relations in Medieval Canon Law* (Grand Rapids: Eerdmans, 2004), 69-70. The emperor Augustus reiterated this right in his reform of the marriage laws, the *Lex Iulia de Adulteriis,* which reasserted the right of fathers to put to death their daughters caught in illicit liaisons (70).

8. An important study of the application of this power to adult children is William V. Harris, "The Roman Father's Power of Life and Death," in *Studies in Roman Law in Memory of A. Arthur Schiller,* ed. Roger S. Bagnall and William V. Harris (Leiden: Brill, 1986), 81-95.

9. *Digesta Iustiniani Augusti,* ed. Mommsen (Berlin, 1870), 48.9.5 (hereafter cited as *Digest*).

10. See generally W. V. Harris, "Child-Exposure in the Roman Empire," *Journal of Roman Studies* 84 (1994): 1-22.

philosopher as Seneca the Younger admonished those contemplating the exposure of the young to undertake the task with equanimity. Some children, Seneca wrote, such as those who are sick or those born defective in some way, really ought to be culled from the family: just as we kill rabid dogs or wild oxen or sickly sheep, so also we must "extinguish" *(exstinguimus)* unnatural offspring and drown sickly children. In so acting, Seneca assured his readers, we behave properly because we thereby remove the "useless" *(inutilia)* from the world of the healthy and sound.[11] Such thinking, furthermore, was not restricted to children suffering from some mental or physical handicap; the right and power over life and death extended to all newborns, whether healthy or ill.[12]

Where a child was admitted to the household and permitted to survive, the support the child might expect to receive from parents or caregivers was conditioned substantially on the child's status. The law itself distinguished among a variety of classes of children, depending upon the condition of their birth and the relationship and legal status of their parents. Children born of *iustae nuptiae*, that is, children born of legitimate marriage between a male and female enjoying *conubium,* were considered *liberi iusti* — i.e., legitimate in the eyes of the law.[13] These children came under the paternal power of their father and enjoyed full inheritance rights. They thus enjoyed what Justinian would call the *legitimum ius* — "the right of legitimacy."[14]

Marriage, however, was not the only permissible sexual outlet, especially for upper-class Roman males. Men of a certain class might also enter long-term, stable relationships with women who were themselves unable, for reasons of class or birth, to enter into legitimate marriage. The Romans called this sort of relationship *concubinatus* — "concubinage."[15] Concubinage was distinguished from legitimate marriage by the absence of *maritalis affectio* ("marital affection") that was expected to prevail between the parties.[16] Concubinage,

---

11. Seneca, *De Ira* 1.15.2. I have analyzed this text further in a paper that remains unpublished at the time of writing. See Charles J. Reid, "Perspectives on Institutional Change" (paper presented, McGill University conference on marriage and the family, Banff, Alberta, May 2005), 10-11.

12. Max Radin, "The Exposure of Infants in Roman Law and Practice," *Classical Journal* 20 (1925): 337-43.

13. W. W. Buckland, *A Textbook of Roman Law from Augustus to Justinian,* ed. Peter Stein, 3rd ed. (Cambridge: Cambridge University Press, 1963), 105-6.

14. See Reid, *Power over the Body,* 199.

15. Adolph Berger, *Encyclopedic Dictionary of Roman Law* (Philadelphia: American Philosophical Society, 1953), s.v. "Concubinatus."

16. Berger, *Dictionary of Roman Law,* s.vv. "maritalis," "affectio." On the emergence of "marital affection" as a term of art in Roman and canon law, see John T. Noonan, Jr., "Marital Affection in the Canonists," *Studia Gratiana* 12 *(Collectanea Stephen Kuttner)* (1967): 481-89.

however, was more than a casual sexual liaison. In the late Roman Republic, for instance, entry into concubinage might be marked by a special ceremony acknowledging the creation of enduring rights and duties.[17]

Children born of such relationships, however, were deemed by the law to be of uncertain paternity. They did not fall under the paternal power of their fathers and lacked the capacity to inherit through the paternal line. On the other hand, they might look to their mothers for support while also enjoying inheritance rights through the maternal line.[18] These rules, of course, did not mean that fathers were barred from providing for such children. They were free to look after the children of their concubines and to provide for them in estate planning.[19] Children, however, lacked reciprocal rights against their fathers.

The classical Roman legal system recognized two additional categories of children. The first were children classified variously as *spurii* or *volgo concepti*.[20] These were children born of illicit sexual liaisons, such as adulterous or incestuous unions (but not concubinage). Like the children of concubines, however, such children lacked the right to claim support or inheritance from their fathers, although they retained the right to claim support from their mothers.[21]

Finally, there were the children of slaves. Roman slavery differed in some respects from the chattel slavery that prevailed in the American South prior to 1865. Roman slaves filled a wide variety of occupations in the Roman Empire — from highly skilled accountants and teachers, to laborers on large plantations, to toilers in the salt and silver mines — some of the grimmest imaginable environments in which to work.[22] The children of slaves, furthermore, frequently received vocational education of some sort. The poet Martial writes of the offspring of slaves receiving training as *calculatores* (accountants) and *notarii* (secretaries or bookkeepers).[23] A well-educated slave was usually a financial asset of great worth to his or her master.[24]

Legally, however, the children of slaves, like their parents, ranked at the

---

17. Alan Watson, *The Law of Persons in the Later Roman Republic* (Oxford: Clarendon, 1967), 10. As Watson puts it: "a *concubina* is a lady with whom one has openly set up house" (9).

18. Reid, *Power over the Body,* 196-97.

19. Reid, *Power over the Body,* 196-97.

20. Buckland, *Textbook,* 105 n. 2.

21. Buckland, *Textbook,* 105 n. 2.

22. Keith Hopkins has identified some of the diverse occupations slaves held in the Roman Empire: slaves might be "doctors, teachers, writers, accountants, agents, bailiffs, overseers, secretaries, and sea-captains." Keith Hopkins, *Conquerors and Slaves,* Sociological Studies in Roman History, vol. 1 (Cambridge: Cambridge University Press, 1978), 123.

23. Beryl Rawson, *Children and Childhood in Roman Italy* (Oxford: Oxford University Press, 2003), 187.

24. Rawson, *Children and Childhood,* 187.

bottom of the social order and enjoyed no rights of their own. Slave parents were prohibited from marrying one another. In virtue of their status, slaves lacked the *conubium* that was a requirement for legitimate marriage among the free.[25] Slaves were not prohibited from maintaining sexual relationships, but their relationships bore instead the label of *contubernium* — a status that "was not protected by law and [that] created no juridical relationship between the parties."[26] The slave father's paternity went legally unnoticed, although social practice — but not the law — made some accommodation for the slave mother's role in the rearing of the child.[27] Legally, of course, the slave child became the chattel of the master.

Christians, of course, challenged these arrangements radically. Early Christians regularly denounced in ringing terms the related Roman practices of infanticide and exposure. Justin Martyr in the latter half of the second century, and Minucius Felix and Tertullian in the third century, denounced exposure as a most cruel form of murder.[28] And when Christians gained control of the imperial levers of power, emperors proceeded legislatively to condemn the ancient paternal power of life and death over children. In official legislation, the emperor Constantine referred to the *vitae necisque potestas* in the past tense, implying that it been abrogated in his own day.[29] The emperors Valens, Valentinian, and Gratian, writing in the year 374, outlawed exposure and declared infanticide a "capital evil" *(capitale . . . malum).*[30] In this way an ancient paternal right was systematically discredited by the new Christian lawgivers for the realm.

Having destroyed the ancient paternal right to dispose of unwanted offspring, Christians felt obliged to build a set of social structures that would give safe haven and comfort to such unfortunate children. One example was the development by pastors and churchmen of various ranks and orders of a network of laws and practices designed to rescue and shelter children otherwise at risk.

25. On the legal concept of *conubium,* see Susan Treggiari, *Roman Marriage: Iusti Coniuges from the Time of Cicero to the Time of Ulpian* (Oxford: Clarendon, 1991), 43-49.

26. James A. Brundage, *Law, Sex, and Christian Society in Medieval Europe* (Chicago: University of Chicago Press, 1987), 36.

27. Keith Hopkins has observed that slave mothers were conceded this role "because it was in the slave owners' interest that slave children should be nurtured." *Conquerors and Slaves,* 165.

28. Reid, *Power over the Body,* 73-74 (collecting and analyzing the texts of these authors).

29. In a decree preserved in Justinian's *Codex,* Constantine addressed "fathers to whom the right and power of life and death over their children was once permitted." *Codex* 8.47.10 ("ut patribus quibus ius vitae in liberos necisque potestas olim erat permissa . . ."). In a decree preserved in the Theodosian Code, Constantine declares that those who expose children immediately lose all paternal rights over them. *Codex Theodosianus* 5.9.1.

30. *Codex Theodosianus* 9.14.1.

For these purposes, one might consider the legislation of the Council of Vaisons, promulgated around the year 490.[31] The preamble of the decree condemned the evil of exposure, stressing that children should be the objects of love and should therefore not be left alone in the wind and the cold to die of the elements or be torn apart by wild dogs. The decree went on to create a system of informal adoption designed to ensure that children whom a mother might be unable to raise might be placed with another family.[32] Other early medieval sources tell us of arrangements that were similarly made to protect abandoned children from harm and to see to their rearing.[33]

Child oblation — the presentation of sons and daughters to monasteries or convents as a kind of offering to God — also took hold in the sixth and seventh century and gained legal acceptance in the great monastic rules published during this time. The Rule of Saint Benedict, in particular, featured child oblation as a crucial aspect of the community's existence, "firmly situating it in the sacrificial context of a mass."[34] John Boswell has described "[o]blation [as] in many ways the most humane form of abandonment ever devised in the West."[35] Par-

---

31. "Concilium Vasense Primum," in Patrologia Latina, vol. 84, ed. J.-P. Migne (Paris: 1850), 261-62. I previously analyzed this decree in Daniel Pollack and others, "Classical Religious Perspectives of Adoption Law," *Notre Dame Law Review* 79 (2004): 716. This article is a broadly ecumenical study of adoption in the great religious traditions of the Book — Judaism, Christianity, and Islam. I authored the portion on Christian adoption.

32. I previously wrote, describing the details of this legislation:

> [T]he Council enacted the following rules:
> (1) finders of [abandoned] children are encouraged to take them and raise them;
> (2) finders should furthermore notify their pastors of their discoveries;
> (3) pastors are to announce such discoveries at Sunday Mass;
> (4) should the children then be claimed by those responsible for the abandonment, compensation should be made to the finders;
> (5) if no one came forward to make such a claim, the finders were presumably free to raise the children as their own.

Pollack, "Perspectives on Adoption Law," 716-17. John Boswell has observed that the purpose of this decree was to "encourag[e] people to pick up and rear abandoned children without fear of unpleasant consequences or of losing the child in whom they invest time and money." John Boswell, *The Kindness of Strangers: The Abandonment of Children in Western Europe from Late Antiquity to the Renaissance* (New York: Pantheon Books, 1988), 173.

33. See, for instance, the discussion of the method of placing a child for adoption in early medieval Trier, as recorded in the hagiographical life of Saint Goar, discussed in Pollack, "Perspectives on Adoption Law," 717. This text is also discussed in Boswell, *The Kindness of Strangers*, 218-19.

34. Mayke de Jong, *In Samuel's Image: Child Oblation in the Early Medieval West* (Leiden: Brill, 1996), 24.

35. Boswell, *The Kindness of Strangers*, 238-39.

ents compelled by economic or social circumstance to pledge their children as oblates gained the reasonable assurance that their children would be well provided for and would grow up in a stable, predictable way of life.[36] In an early medieval Europe still wracked by famine, war, invasion, and pestilence, these assurances no doubt counted a great deal for parents already living at the margins.

In the high Middle Ages of the twelfth through fifteenth centuries one sees a continuation of efforts to provide shelter and sustenance to children otherwise facing abandonment. The greater political and economic stability of this time meant that some practices, like oblation, would gradually fade into the background. Orphanages and foundling homes eventually succeeded to the role filled by monasteries, providing shelter for abandoned and needy children, especially in the new urban centers of Europe.[37] The canonists also worked up a flexible system of adoption law that employed a greater or lesser degree of formality based on the needs of children and the status of parents.[38] Jack Goody once surmised, on the basis of what can be described as a selective if not distorted reading of the sources, that adoption was disapproved of theologically and became a practical impossibility in medieval Europe.[39] This interpretation of the sources, however, would seem unable to survive the scholarship of the last two decades, which points to the existence of substantial evidence demonstrating the use and acceptability of adoption in widely varying regions and periods of the medieval West.[40]

Christians not only abolished the ancient father's right of life and death over his offspring in favor of solicitude for the life and welfare of vulnerable infants and children; they also made the case that all children enjoyed a funda-

---

36. Boswell, *The Kindness of Strangers,* 239-40.

37. Innocent III set an example for Europe when he established a foundling home in Rome, the Hospital of the Holy Spirit. See Constance M. Rousseau, "Innocent III, Defender of the Innocents and the Law: Children and Papal Policy (1198-1216)," *Archivum Historiae Pontificiae* 32 (1994): 31-42.

38. I have previously reviewed medieval canonistic adoption law in two venues. See Pollack, "Perspectives on Adoption Law," 714-21, and Reid, *Power over the Body,* 182-93. Essentially, the canonists developed two sets of rules governing adoption: one set of rules, which I have termed "informal adoption," governed the situation of an abandoned child taken into a new home. This body of rules developed in the early Middle Ages but continued to be repeated in high medieval documents like Gratian's *Decretum.* A second, more formal adoption process, modeled on classical Roman examples, emerged in the twelfth and thirteenth centuries and existed to the end of the Middle Ages as a parallel system to the older less formal means of adoption.

39. Jack Goody, *The Development of the Family and Marriage in Europe* (Cambridge: Cambridge University Press, 1983), 99-101, 158-59.

40. I have reviewed recent scholarly developments in *Power over the Body,* 193-95.

mental right to be provided for. To be sure, even some pre-Christian Roman authors appreciated that this should be the case. The early-third-century jurist Paulus thus wrote that those who denied nourishment to their offspring were held to "kill" *(necare)* them.[41]

But to appreciate the radical nature of the change worked by Christian lawyers, we need to skip forward a millennium, from the second and third centuries, to the twelfth and thirteenth. The Roman Empire no longer held sway over the Mediterranean. Indeed, the political center of gravity, for our purposes, had shifted west and north toward the new sovereignties and powers of western Europe. Indeed, this portion of the world now conceived of itself as "Christendom." Its legal and political orders were dominated by a shared Christian worldview that expressed itself in a common language, Latin, and that looked for guidance to a received body of writings comprising not only the Bible but also the teachings of the doctors of the church and the legislation and letters of popes, bishops, and ecclesiastical councils.

The twelfth and thirteenth centuries were a time of legal revival for Christendom. For our purposes, we shall concentrate on two branches of this revival — the renewed interest in the Roman law of Justinian[42] and the development of a systematic body of canon law.[43] Medieval Roman law had been the first of these two great systems to revitalize itself. Centered first in the universities of northern Italy, in schools like the University of Bologna, the sustained and systematic study of the corpus of Justinian's works spread outward throughout western Europe over the course of the twelfth through fifteenth centuries.

Our concern is with the teaching of the jurists with respect to the legal and moral requirement that parents support their children. On this point, one discerns a strong differentiation between the medieval Romanists and the canonists. The medieval commentators on Roman law tended to retain the old restrictions on support found in their sources. Thus they were inclined to assert

---

41. *Digest* 25.3.4. Paulus condemned exposure, starvation, and suffocation as forms of killing. He did not, however, identify the precise crime parents who committed such acts were guilty of, nor did he prescribe a penalty for these acts. Paulus's voice appears to have been a lonely one in his own time — exposure remained a consistent social practice long after Paulus's time.

42. The revival of Roman law has been the subject of innumerable studies. One classic work, recently reprinted and worth consulting, is Paul Vinogradoff, *Roman Law in Mediaeval Europe* (Union, N.J.: Lawbook Exchange, 2001).

43. A good summary of the main lines of this revival and systematization of canon law can be found in James A. Brundage, *Medieval Canon Law* (London: Longman, 1995). Brundage's work also provides helpful summaries of the lives of leading canonists, and an outline of the canonistic citation system. This chapter generally follows the citation system Brundage sets out at pp. 190-205.

that children born outside of regular marriage lacked the juridical capacity to make any claims on their fathers for support. The canonists, on the other hand, took a more humane approach allowing for broad legal recognition of all children's rights to receive the necessities of survival from both fathers and mothers regardless of condition of birth or relationship of parents.

Let us consider the Romanists first. Manlio Bellomo has seen the twelfth-century jurist Azo of Bologna and the thirteenth-century jurist Odofredus as examples of divergent ways of approaching the ancient documents. Azo, who served as the model for the thirteenth-century Accursius, was more abstract, conceptual, and removed from the events of the day; while the methodology of Odofredus and his school embraced a concern for the ebb and flow of current events.[44]

What is significant for our purposes, however, is that even though Azo and Odofredus employed different methodologies, they reached similar results in denying that children born outside of regular marriage had any rights that they might assert against their fathers. Children born outside of "just intercourse," Azo asserted, lacked all right to support from their fathers.[45] Odofredus employed even harsher Latin in condemning claims raised by children born outside of wedlock: such children were offspring conceived in criminal intercourse *(filii concepti ex nefario coitu)* and were not really sons or daughters of their father at all.[46] They were thus lacking all capacity to seek support from him.[47]

While the civilian jurists of medieval Europe relied upon and sustained the teachings of their classical sources, the canonists were just as vigorous in defending the rights of children — even children born outside of wedlock — to paternal support and nurturance. Indeed, the canonists explicitly repudiated the analysis of the Romanists, taking them to task for their barbarous disregard of the needs of innocent children.

The roots of the medieval canonistic synthesis in favor of the rights of even illegitimate children to paternal support can be traced back to an early stage of Christian development. The fourth-century Council of Gangra denounced parents who pretended to hide behind "piety and religion" in order to neglect the needs of their children.[48] The wording of the conciliar decree

44. Manlio Bellomo, *The Common Legal Past of Europe, 1000-1800,* trans. Lydia G. Cochrane, 2nd ed. (Washington, D.C.: Catholic University of America Press, 1995), 170-74.

45. Azo, *Summa Aurea Super Codice,* bk. V, sec. "De Alendis Liberis a Parentibus," p. 133va.

46. Odofredus, *Summa super Codice* (Bologna: Forni, 1968), vol. I, p. 268ra.

47. Odofredus, *Summa super Codice,* 1:268ra. I review this controversy in *Power over the Body,* 84.

48. Council of Gangra, c. 15, in Mansi, *Sacrorum conciliorum nova, et amplissima collectio* (Florence, 1759), vol. II, col. 1103.

was sufficiently broad to cover not only legitimate children but also children of irregular birth.[49]

The thirteenth-century canonists looked to this Christian past, harshly criticizing the Romanist analysis. Bernard of Parma (ca. 1200-1266) stressed that parents were obliged to see to their children's needs and cited as support not the Roman law but the natural law.[50] Bernard took note of the rigor of the civil law, which he explained was an effort to stamp out illicit sexual intercourse.[51] Canon law, however, chose to pursue a kinder *(de benignitate)* route. The "education" of children — by which Bernard meant not vocational training alone but spiritual and bodily sustenance — took priority on the basis of a natural, human instinct *(instinctu naturae precedit).*[52] Hence the right of all children — legitimate or illegitimate — to support and education took priority over the teaching of the civil law *(unde ius istud praefertur civili).*[53]

Bernard's contemporary, Henry of Susa (ca. 1190-1270), popularly known as Hostiensis, also repudiated the Romanist teaching. Hostiensis was in many respects the most notable of the thirteenth-century canonists. His summa on canon law was nicknamed "the Golden" *(Aurea)*;[54] he wrote a second, larger work on canon law entitled the *Lectura*, which was completed shortly before his death. Had he not taken ill, he very possibly would have been elected pope at the conclave of 1270. Indeed, Hostiensis was so well known in his day that Dante gave him a role in the *Divine Comedy.*[55] Trained in Roman as well as canon law, Hostiensis's canonistic writings are replete with sophisticated, often quite showy, displays of Romanist virtuosity.

Despite his familiarity with the Romanist sources, however, Hostiensis was prepared to reject its teaching on the matter of child support. He began his

---

49. Reid, *Power over the Body,* 84.

50. Bernard of Parma, *Glossa Ordinaria* 10.4.7.5, v. *facultates.* On Bernard of Parma, see James A. Brundage, *Medieval Canon Law* (London: Longman, 1995), 210. Cf. Reid, *Power over the Body,* 84 (reviewing Bernard's arguments).

51. Reid, *Power over the Body,* 84.

52. Bernard of Parma, *Glossa Ordinaria* 10.4.7.5, v. *facultates.*

53. Bernard of Parma, *Glossa Ordinaria* 10.4.7.5, v. *facultates.* Although the canonists never made the following point, a modern reader might nevertheless ask: What was the more effective means of fighting "criminal" intercourse: holding a father responsible — financially and otherwise — for children he has sired outside of marriage or excusing him from all ongoing responsibility? The Romanist solution excused him in the name of opposing criminal intercourse; the canonistic situation imposed liability in the name of the rights of the child. But might the canonistic approach also have served to discourage illicit intercourse more effectively than the means the civilians adopted?

54. Hostiensis, *Summa Aurea* (Venice, 1574).

55. Brundage, *Medieval Canon Law,* 214.

analysis of the civilian teaching with a case that civil lawyers found easy: the case of a child born in an incestuous liaison.[56] In Odofredus's language, this was a child born of a "criminal" liaison, unworthy even of the name or dignity of "child." Hostiensis, however, condemned this treatment as a harsh example of the sophistry and rigor of the "world's law" *(legum secularium)*.[57] Canon law, on the other hand, reflected the kindness and sweetness of natural law and equity. In accord with the strictures of canon law, which reflect the commands of natural justice, children "are always to receive sustenance."[58] And, Hostiensis concluded, the natural law that is embodied in the canon law ought always and everywhere to prevail since it is "first in time and dignity among all the laws" *(inter omnia iura primatum tenet et tempore et dignitate)*.[59]

This teaching, furthermore, was not confined to abstract and arid classroom disquisitions. Richard Helmholz, in his study of English ecclesiastical records, has demonstrated that at least in England canonists took an active role in enforcing child support orders against fathers, even fathers of children born in irregular unions.[60] To understand the operation of the English canonists, one must appreciate that jurisdiction in medieval England was not unitary: the church and state divided their competence over different areas of life. The English secular courts claimed jurisdiction over issues involving transfers of land and the commission of felonies. But the ecclesiastical courts exercised real coercive jurisdiction over matters such as marriage, domestic relations, and child support.

The *filius nullius* in English common law was, quite literally, the "child of no one." Modern Anglo-American common lawyers, lacking a sense of the lively interaction between ecclesiastical and common-law courts that was a prominent feature of medieval law, have maintained, wrongly, that English law had no regard for children born out of wedlock. These modern English and American lawyers and judges expressed their regrets and were most sorry, but they simply felt compelled by the common law tradition itself to deny to children born out of wedlock the rights that medieval English ecclesiastical judges and tribunals regularly accorded them.[61]

---

56. Hostiensis, *In Primum [-Sextum] Decretalium Librum Commentaria (Lectura)* (Venice: Apud Iuntas, 1581), 10.4.7.5, v. *secundum facultates.*

57. Hostiensis, *In Primum [-Sextum] Decretalium Librum Commentaria (Lectura)* 10.4.7.5.

58. Hostiensis, *In Primum [-Sextum] Decretalium Librum Commentaria (Lectura)* 10.4.7.5.

59. Hostiensis, *In Primum [-Sextum] Decretalium Librum Commentaria (Lectura)* 10.4.7.5.

60. R. H. Helmholz, "Support Orders, Church Courts, and the Rule of *Filius Nullius:* A Reassessment of the Common Law," *Virginia Law Review* 63 (1977).

61. Helmholz, "Support Orders," 431. A classic expression of regret can be found in *Mercer v. Mercer's Administrator*, 87 Ky. 30, 7 S.W. 401 (1888), where the court declared "a just sympathy

In making these assertions, of course, contemporary common lawyers revealed their own ignorance of the history of English law. In fact, the common law did not make provisions for children born out of wedlock precisely because this matter belonged to the competence of the ecclesiastical courts.[62] A one-eyed focus on what the courts of common law did simply misses the true picture of the way English courts of different competences interacted with each other and shared responsibility for the good governance of English society.

Helmholz provides a wealth of detail demonstrating the truth of this proposition. English ecclesiastical courts of the fourteenth and fifteenth centuries regularly entertained two types of cases seeking to impute the obligations of paternity to the fathers of illegitimate children: ex officio prosecutions, brought by ecclesiastical officials, and private complaints, brought by the mothers or relatives of the affected children.[63] Regarding proof of paternity, the canonists "adopted a two-step procedure weighted slightly in favor of the child."[64] Helmholz notes that child support typically was ordered for significant lengths of time, described in the sources as "until [the child] should come to legitimate age."[65] The purpose, it is clear, was to see to the welfare of the affected children during their vulnerable years.

Why were the canonists willing to make this large move in the direction of children born out of wedlock? Clearly, they were operating in a "thought world" very different from the secular legal systems that preceded them and, in fact, surrounded them. The Roman law was not nearly so generous. Perhaps the best answer to this question comes from the canonists' understanding of the demands of Christian charity. Conditioned by their reading of the Bible and the interpretation of the sacred texts by generations of scholastic philosophers and theologians, the canonists moved in an intellectual universe very

---

for the innocent and helpless," but ultimately chose not to act in light of the weight of the common-law tradition. *Mercer*, 87 Ky. 32, 7 S.W. 402.

62. Helmholz, "Support Orders," 432-33.

63. Helmholz, "Support Orders," 437-39.

64. Helmholz, "Support Orders," 439. Helmholz identifies the two steps in the process: "The first step was to be handled summarily. If access was established [i.e., if it was demonstrated that the putative father had access to the woman], and the woman named the man as the father, he was required to support the child until full hearing and determination of the claim of paternity. . . . In the second hearing, the medieval commentators called for further proof. But even at that hearing, in the nature of things, proof of paternity could never reach a high level of accuracy. As a result the jurists were prepared to sanction 'proof by presumption and conjectures.'" Helmholz, "Support Orders," 439-40.

65. Helmholz, "Support Orders," 443 (quoting a child-support decree of the ecclesiastical court of Lichfield, dated to 1528).

different from Roman law. And they were quite willing to allow this background to influence their analysis of the demands of the law. Indeed, they were even open to the breaking down of whole categories of legal thought in the name of Christian principle. We saw this in the abolition of the Roman father's right of life and death. And we see this again in the case of the provision of child support even for children born out of conventional wedlock.

The Freedom to Contract Marriage and to Enter Religious Life

The children I have discussed so far were the most vulnerable: young children, typically not yet adolescents; indeed, the most likely to be affected by support issues of the sort we have discussed would have been children under the age of six or seven. But eventually, children reached their adolescence, at which time they were faced with an array of choices: two of the most basic involved the choice of marriage or a religious vocation. And each of these choices required that parents respect the freedom and autonomy of their children — who, in the context of the Middle Ages, were most typically adolescents, often, indeed, in their early teens.

I should like to begin with one of the most remarkable developments of twelfth-century law — the reversal of over a thousand years of legal tradition and the almost universal lived social experience to that time. I am speaking about the emergence of a set of rules that permitted young people to choose a marriage partner and that, in fact, invalidated marriages brought into being through the coercive influence of the parents.

Almost the entire legal tradition of the West stood against this freedom. Roman law, to be sure, made the consent of the parties the constitutive element of marriage.[66] Consent to hold another with marital affection was virtually a truism of Roman marital formation, enshrined deeply in law and social expectations.[67] Classical Roman lawyers, however, did not see these attributes as inconsistent with arranged marriages, or marriages in which parents took the lead in bringing them about. A son who did not oppose his father's choice of bride would not be heard to object afterward: his silence was deemed to constitute consent.[68] The rules governing a daughter's consent were even more

66. "Not sleeping together but consent makes marriages," Ulpian is recorded as declaring (*nuptiae enim concubitus, sed consensus facit*). *Digest* 35.1.15.

67. Noonan, "Marital Affection," 482-89. Noonan notes that among the attributes of marital affection in Roman law were: monogamy, openness to procreation, emotional affection, and a commitment to an enduring if not permanent union (486-89).

68. An excerpt from Celsus, found in the *Digest*, declared: "If at a father's compulsion, one

one-sidedly in favor of giving effect to paternal arrangements. Where a daughter did not "fight" *(repugnat)* her father's choice, she was deemed to consent. And, furthermore, she might only legitimately resist her father's selection where the young man he had selected for her was "unworthy in his conduct or foul."[69]

Christian teaching in the early Middle Ages was entirely consistent with the proposition that marriages of young people should ordinarily be arranged. Hincmar of Rheims, in the ninth century, wrote that "among equals, legitimate marriages occur when the girl is sought from and legally betrothed and endowed by her parents, who have an interest. . . ."[70] Hincmar looked to the example of Mary and Joseph. Projecting his own society's expectations onto this biblical paradigm, he asserted that the Old and the New Law, by which he meant the Old and the New Testaments, and the willing submission of Mary to the choice of her parents, all pointed in one direction: that a prospective husband should seek the hand of his bride from those who had authority over her and that it belonged to the girl's parents or guardians to grant or withhold permission.[71]

In the twelfth century, however, Gratian, the founder of the systematic study of canon law, saw fit to challenge this long and imposing tradition. In a remarkably one-sided commentary, with necessarily slender authority, Gratian concluded "that coupling with another is not possible unless by free will."[72] In a most remarkable development, Gratian's insight carried the day virtually unchallenged. Within a few years, one finds his teaching on marriage repeated in the standard canonistic and theological textbooks of the time.[73] Gratian, clearly, spoke to an audience that was ready to receive what must have seemed like a radical message of Christian freedom.

---

takes a wife whom one would not have taken if left to one's own devices, he has contracted marriage, since marriage is not contracted among the unwilling; but he appears to have preferred it." *Digest* 23.2.22.

69. *Digest* 23.1.12. One might observe that the extent to which children's consent was valued — and some legal significance was attributed to it — it counted as a limitation on the otherwise vast authority the Roman father wielded over his household.

70. Hincmar of Rheims, "De Divortio Lotharii Regis et Theutbergae," in *Monumenta Germaniae Historica, Concilia,* ed. Letha Böhringer (Hannover: Hahnsche Buchhandlung, 1992), vol. 4, supp. 1, 133; Patrologia Latina 125: 648.

71. I am here summarizing Reid, *Power over the Body,* 36-37.

72. C. 31, q. 2., d.p.c. 4. Gratian's treatment of the freedom to select one's marriage partner is reviewed in John T. Noonan, Jr., "Power to Choose," *Viator* 4 (1973): 419-34.

73. On the quick and nearly universal acceptance of the freedom to choose one's marriage partner, see Reid, *Power over the Body,* 42-44. So great a theologian as Peter Lombard simply repeated Gratian's analysis with only slight embellishment (44).

I should like to consider two aspects of the chief legal doctrine the canonists developed in order to give strength to Gratian's new marital ideal. The doctrine the canonists developed came to be known under the general rubric of "force and fear" *(vi et metu)*. A marriage that was brought about by an external force sufficient to elicit great fear in the person on the receiving end invalidated the union.[74] The invalidating effects of force and fear were frequently invoked to protect women, most especially young girls still in their teens, from entering into unwanted marriages.

One can consider a decree of Pope Alexander III, dating to the later twelfth century, as typical of the solicitude the popes showed in such circumstances. Two men from Pavia each sought the hand of a young girl *(puella)* in marriage.[75] Pope Alexander's choice of verbs in describing the actions of the men suggests that they must have been vigorous if not overbearing in their pursuit.[76] Echoing Gratian and what had become the received wisdom of the time, Pope Alexander wrote that it was necessary that consent have a place in marriage; indeed, he made it clear that the "assent of each [party]" was required.[77] To ensure that the girl had her freedom of choice preserved, the pope ordered that she should be removed to a safe house where she was to be permitted to make her choice freely.[78]

Related to the development of the doctrine of force and fear, the canonists established a standard of proof by which to measure the degree of force sufficient to invalidate consent. This standard came to be known as the "steady man" *(constans vir)* test and was explicitly declared by Pope Honorius to extend to women.[79] The pope was concerned that women might make false allegations that they were compelled into marriage, but where they were able to prove that they "never truly consented but that they were compelled by fear brought to bear to express words of consent even while dissenting internally," they de-

---

74. Tancred, an early-thirteenth-century canonist, described the implications of this doctrine pithily and well: "For where force and coercion intercede, consent has no place. . . . Thus, if consent has no place, neither is there any marriage, since it is contracted by consent alone." See Tancred, *Summa de Matrimonio,* ed. Agathon Wunderlich (Göttingen: Vandenhoeck and Ruprecht, 1841), 46, my translation.

75. *Glossa Ordinaria* 10.4.1.14.

76. The verb Alexander used to describe the men's insistent pursuit was the impersonal *ventilatur.* This verb has its origin in agriculture, where it was used to describe the tossing of grain in the air. In the context in which the pope used this term, it carried the clear connotation of unwanted or disturbing behavior. 10.4.1.14. Cf. Charlton T. Lewis and Charles Short, *A Latin Dictionary* (Oxford: Clarendon, 1975 imprint), s.v. "Ventilo."

77. *Glossa Ordinaria* 10.4.1.14.

78. *Glossa Ordinaria* 10.4.1.14.

79. *Glossa Ordinaria* 10.4.1.29.

served to be heard.[80] And the standard by which the allegations should be judged, the pope continued, was the "constant man" standard already in general use.[81]

Perceptive commentators on the canon law like Hostiensis established a carefully drawn set of guidelines to use when assessing the differential impact of force and fear on young women — often, really, teenage girls — as opposed to men. Marriage, Hostiensis wrote, "required free consent."[82] Compulsion accompanied by fear sufficient to shake a steady man, he continued, served to vitiate consent because it deprived the party of the requisite freedom.[83]

The argument to this point was nothing more than a recitation of what had become generally accepted doctrine. Hostiensis's argument took a more interesting turn, however, when he came to advise his audience on how they were to apply these principles to women coerced into marriage. He commenced his analysis by reviewing Roman law, which actually made it more difficult for women than for men to allege the invalidity of their marriage on the basis of force and fear.[84] Hostiensis, however, dismissed these texts as immaterial to his analysis. He wished to show how it was that parents or someone close to the family *(familiarius)* might come to exert coercion and how it might fall differently on men than on women. A "lesser fear," Hostiensis wrote, will invalidate a woman's consent because women "are the more fragile sex and more easily terrified."[85] The word "woman" *(mulier)*, he noted in a mistaken attempt at etymology, is derived from the Latin *mollicie cordis* — "softness of heart."[86]

To a modern reader this discussion might appear misogynistic, but it seems that Hostiensis appreciated that in the context of his day women might be subject to a different range of threats than men. Women are less likely to be subjected to

---

80. *Glossa Ordinaria* 10.4.1.29 ("se nunquam in illos veraciter consensisse, sed metu illato compulsas verba protulisse consensus, licet animo dissentiret . . .").

81. *Glossa Ordinaria* 10.4.1.29.

82. Hostiensis, *Summa*, bk. IV, "De Matrimoniis," sec. 26.

83. Hostiensis, *Summa*, bk. IV, "De Matrimoniis," sec. 26.

84. Hostiensis, *Summa*, bk. IV, "De Matrimoniis," sec. 27. Hostiensis cited two provisions of Roman law. The first text, found at *Digest* 23.2.22, declared that a son who did not object to an arranged marriage prior to the union was not to be heard to complain afterward of compulsion. The implication was that the son might be heard to complain prior to the union. The second text, pertaining to daughters and found at *Digest* 23.1.12, forbade women still in the power of their fathers from protesting their fathers' selection of marriage partners unless the prospective partner was "unworthy in his conduct or foul" *(indignum moribus vel turpem)*. This test narrowed the possible grounds for a woman to complain — she might allege coercion but she will only be heard where it is clear that the prospective husband is himself an unworthy match.

85. Hostiensis, *Summa*, "De Matrimoniis," sec. 27.

86. Hostiensis, *Summa*, "De Matrimoniis," sec. 27.

paternal threats of bodily harm, Hostiensis believed, but they might be subject to other forms of coercion. And so, he concluded, "the good judge" *(bonus iudex)* will consider the sort of person before him *(qualitate personarum)* and will examine and consider the force exerted and the submissiveness or ability of the party to resist that pressure. Did the party alleging force and fear expressly or silently dissent from the arranged marriage, or did the party ratify the consent afterward? These are the sorts of questions the sensitive judge would need to answer satisfactorily in determining a marriage's legal validity or invalidity.[87]

That young women sometimes exercised this freedom is attested by court records[88] and by literary evidence.[89] Indeed, the later Middle Ages witnessed some notorious cases of clandestine marriage in which women from the upper classes defied the wishes of their fathers and married men from lesser origins for reasons of love.[90] This whole belief system and the practice of clandestine marriage that it encouraged were challenged at the time of the Protestant Reformation. The Lutherans and others wished to return to the system that prevailed prior to the twelfth century, in which parents had the decisive say in determining whom their unemancipated children might marry. Thus Martin Bucer denounced the canonistic system of free consent as something opposed to "[t]he Roman law, the law of nature, the law of God, and the law of all nations."[91] At the Council of Trent, in the mid–sixteenth century, Catholic re-

87. Hostiensis, *Summa*, "De Matrimoniis," sec. 27.

88. After surveying the caseload of English ecclesiastical courts, R. H. Helmholz concluded: "Matrimonial litigation in later medieval England was, above all else, litigation over the interpretation and enforcement of marriage contracts. The principal business of the Church courts was not determining whether an existing marriage could be dissolved: their main task was the settling of disputes about the initiation of the marriage relationship." See R. H. Helmholz, *Marriage Litigation in Medieval England* (Cambridge: Cambridge University Press, 1974), 72. Many of the cases Professor Helmholz investigated were clandestine unions — some of them, at least, entered into by young persons without the consent of their parents (25-33).

89. I have reviewed two leading late medieval cases in my book, *Power over the Body, Equality in the Family*. These were the cases of Joan Plantagenet, the "Fair Maid of Kent," discussed on 61-63; and Margery Paston, discussed on 58-61.

90. Thus Joan Plantagenet, granddaughter of the king of England, married a knight of lesser origin but of considerable military talent against the desires of her family. Reid, *Power over the Body*, 62. Similarly, Margery Paston, born to the wealthiest man in England in the mid–fifteenth century, married the family bailiff in the face of substantial familial opposition (58-59).

91. Reid, *Power over the Body*, 64. See also John Witte, Jr., *From Sacrament to Contract: Marriage, Religion, and Law in the Western Tradition* (Louisville: Westminster John Knox, 1997), 56-61. Witte notes, regarding the swift and widespread acceptance the Lutheran reforms received: "The requirement of parental consent to marriages, particularly for children who had not yet reached the age of majority, won virtually unanimous acceptance in sixteenth-century Germany among jurists and legislators alike" (59).

formers modified the system that prevailed throughout the high Middle Ages by requiring for validity that all marriages take place *in facie Ecclesiae* — "before the Church" — in the presence of a priest and two official witnesses. Thus the Catholic Church compromised between the absolute freedom of the high and later Middle Ages and the Protestant movement to return to an older system of parental consent.

This expanded legal understanding of freedom was not confined to the marital relationship. Young persons were increasingly recognized as possessing the freedom to determine for themselves whether to pursue a religious vocation. It is, of course, true that no one has a right to a religious vocation, at least if that term is understood as a claim right assertable against competent religious authority for the purpose of obtaining admission to Holy Orders or to a monastery or a convent.

To illustrate this point, one might compare the way hagiographers presented the call to religious vocation in the early Middle Ages with the treatment found in the twelfth and thirteenth centuries. Saint Boniface, the great archbishop and missionary to the German people, was born around the year 672 in modern Devonshire, in England. From an early age, we are told, he was deeply drawn to spiritual matters and craved, in his heart, to spread the word of God and Christ to those who had never heard the good news.[92] He was opposed in these ambitions by his father, who, "[e]mploying all the subtle craft of human wisdom, . . . endeavoured by long discussions to dissuade the boy from carrying out his purpose."[93] Saint Boniface, however, remained fixed on a career in the service of the church, which stirred his father to increase his opposition. "The more his father attempted to hold him back," Boniface's hagiographer recorded, "the more stoutly and doggedly he determined to pursue the heavenly ideal and to devote himself to the study of sacred letters."[94] Eventually, God himself intervened, striking Boniface's father dead and thereby freeing the young man for service in the mission fields of pagan Germany.[95]

Such drastic and direct divine intervention was largely unneeded in the twelfth and thirteenth centuries as the freedom of children to pursue their callings came to gain legal recognition and at least a modicum of social acceptance. This is not to say that parents never put up stiff resistance to their children's vocations. One can take any number of hagiographical accounts as examples of the new attitude. Thus the twelfth-century Abbess Christina of Markyate, from

92. See Willibald, "Life of St. Boniface," in *The Anglo-Saxon Missionaries in Germany*, trans and ed. C. H. Talbot (New York: Sheed and Ward, 1954), 25-62, here 27.

93. Willibald, "Life of St. Boniface," 27.

94. Willibald, "Life of St. Boniface," 27.

95. Willibald, "Life of St. Boniface," 27.

Anglo-Saxon stock like Boniface before her, was faced with parents who insisted that she ignore her religious vocation, marry, and live in the world.[96] Although Christina had to struggle mightily to realize her vocation, it was not necessary that God strike her father dead. Christina, by this time, had legal sources to fall back on that she could use to good effect in resisting her parents' wishes.

The same was even truer for Thomas Aquinas in the thirteenth century. His father, Landulf, was count of Aquino, a relative of several of the royal families of Europe, and a man willing and eager to make use of his progeny in the furtherance of his own dynastic ambitions. Thomas, a younger son who showed considerable intelligence and promise at a very tender age, was thus placed with the Benedictines at Monte Cassino for schooling in the hope that he would join that order, profess a monastic vocation, and perhaps one day even become an abbot.[97] Thomas, however, had other plans, preferring to join one of the new mendicant orders, the Dominicans, with whom he might be free to teach in a university and pursue the life of the mind. Thomas's family, especially his mother, strenuously objected. Indeed, Thomas's mother arranged to have him kidnapped and confined in what a biographer has called a *carcer* — a "jail."[98]

If Bernardo Gui is to be believed, Thomas's escape from confinement was not without excitement; according to Bernardo, Thomas managed his flight by means of a rope conveniently placed in a castle window.[99] A modern biographer doubts the authenticity of this story, seeing in it parallels to Saint Paul's own escape from Damascus — parallels that medieval readers would have noticed instantly.[100] Jean-Pierre Torrell would rather credit the more

96. C. H. Talbot, ed. and trans., *The Life of Christina of Markyate: A Twelfth-Century Recluse* (Oxford: Clarendon, 1959; Toronto: University of Toronto Press, 1998), 36-41. Citations are to the Toronto edition.

97. On this background, see Jean-Pierre Torrell, *Saint Thomas Aquinas*, vol. 1, *The Person and His Work*, trans. Robert Royal (Washington, D.C.: Catholic University of America Press, 1996), 1-4.

98. Guillelmo de Tocco, "Vita Sancti Thomae Aquinatis," in *Fontes Vitae Sancti Thomae Aquinatis*, vol. 2, ed. Dominicus Prümmer (Toulouse: Privat, 1912), 74. Torrell tries to soften the impression left by the hagiographer: "It was more a kind of house arrest than imprisonment." Torrell, *Saint Thomas Aquinas*, 10. Bernardo Gui, however, in his account of Thomas's life, uses language similar to Tocco's concerning the conditions of Thomas's confinement. See Bernardus Guidonis, "Vita Sancti Thomae Aquinitatis," in *Fontes Vitae Sancti Thomae Aquinatis*, vol. 3, ed. Dominicus Prümmer (Toulouse: Privat, 1912), 173-76.

99. Bernardo Guidonis, "Vita Sancti Thomae Aquinitatis," in *Fontes Vitae Sancti Thomae Aquinatis*, 2:175-76. By this time, Bernardo states, some time had elapsed and Thomas's mother, repenting of her harsh treatment, had arranged in advance for the guard to be relaxed on the evening of the escape.

100. Torrell, *Saint Thomas Aquinas*, 1:11.

mundane workings of the political and legal orders with obtaining Thomas's eventual release.[101]

The larger point, however, is that the legal climate had changed from the days of Saint Boniface. God no longer had to intervene so directly to ensure that one of his zealous advocates could pursue his proper calling. Nor might one's parents any longer simply deposit a child at a monastery with the intent of making him an oblate and expect that the child would be without recourse if he did not wish to pursue a monastic vocation. Children were now recognized as possessing a degree of autonomy in determining their own vocations. Again, Torrell makes the point well: an oblate, who would have been placed in a monastery by his parents, consented only vicariously to such a placement. "Since it was not a personal decision, it required later ratification by the person himself at the proper age; he remained free to accept the commitment established by his parents or to embrace another form of life."[102]

The Natural Right to Inherit from One's Parents

The Anglo-American legal tradition, which can be found alive and well in forty-nine of our fifty states (Louisiana represents the exception), has always celebrated the freedom of the testator to do anything he pleases with his property, subject to little in the way of legal restraint. A few states have developed the legal doctrine of the "unnatural will" that at least allows for the close scrutiny of testamentary arrangements that have as their effect the disinheritance of natural objects of the testator's bounty, that is, the testator's children. But only Louisiana has what is ominously known — at least to ears of common lawyers — as "forced heirship." This is the legal requirement that testators must set aside a certain portion of their estate to be distributed among their children, prior to making any other bequests.

This system of forced heirship — still with us in Louisiana even though its continued vitality has been challenged from time to time as an anachronism and a violation of testamentary freedom — has roots in the Roman law of Justinian and the medieval canon law. Roman law had long required parents to make provision in their estate planning for their children. Justinian codified these expectations in language that came close to invoking a robust doctrine of natural rights. In the *Codex*, he spoke of the amount of an estate "naturally owed" *(debito naturali)* to heirs entitled to receive a share.[103] And in *Novella* 115,

---

101. Torrell, *Saint Thomas Aquinas,* 1:11-12.
102. Torrell, *Saint Thomas Aquinas,* 1:5.
103. *Codex* 3.28.36.2.

he wrote of the *legitima portio* — "the legitimate portion" owed to children upon the death of their parents.[104]

At the hands of the medieval canonists, this vocabulary would be transformed into the language of natural rights. Particularly important to this transformation is a decretal issued by Pope Innocent III and known by the name of the testator — *Raynutius*.[105] The factual details of the decretal are as complicated as any wills and trusts problem can be and are best skipped over in the interests of brevity. What matters for us is the language Innocent III used in describing the *legitima portio*. The legitimate share, as reinterpreted by Pope Innocent, became "the claim owing by reason of nature" *(iure natura debita)*.[106]

As a matter of natural law, parents were obligated to set aside a certain minimum portion of their estate to satisfy the natural right of children to inherit. What we see, in short, is a natural duty correlating tightly with a natural right. Children might be disinherited only for grave and specified reasons. And where a parent was arbitrary and capricious in his estate planning, the canonists were willing to give effect to a cause of action to vindicate the children's natural rights.[107]

Hostiensis, the thirteenth-century canonist, was especially bold in the case he set forth on behalf of children's rights to inherit. They might avail themselves of the remedy known as the "inofficious will" *(inofficiosi testamenti)*.[108] The Latin *inofficiosi* — with its etymological root in the word *officium*, "duty" — meant nothing less than the breach of one's natural obligations. Both parents and children, Hostiensis asserted, owed one another duties, which he classified under the broad rubric of *pietas*, a word that is misleadingly translated as piety.[109] For a medieval readership the term would have embraced deeply held values of respect, reverence, even a sense of mutual awe. Children were to be deferential toward their parents' wishes and respectful of the commanding position they filled in the hierarchically structured medieval family. In return, however, parents were to be respectful of the needs and desires, even, indeed, the autonomy of their children. *Pietas*, in short, described a reciprocal relationship. The relationship was hierarchical, to be sure, but like so many medieval hierarchies, those filling the lesser rungs were never without recourse where the superior abused the relationship. And where parents violated the expectations

---

104. See Reid, *Power over the Body,* 169.

105. *Glossa Ordinaria* 10.3.26.16.

106. *Glossa Ordinaria* 10.3.26.16.

107. Reid, *Power over the Body,* 170-74.

108. See Hostiensis, *Summa,* bk. III, "De Testamentis et Ultimis Voluntatibus," secs. 11-12.

109. On Hostiensis's use of *pietas* and the deep resonance this word would have for medieval readers, see Reid, *Power over the Body,* 172 and 284 n. 177.

and obligations defined and determined by this exquisitely layered Latin term of art, their estates might be taxed in an amount to satisfy their children's claims.

Conclusion

The vocabulary of children's rights is not new to the late twentieth century. Indeed, it has a medieval pedigree, stretching back to the twelfth and thirteenth century and with even deeper roots in the Roman law of Justinian. The introduction and development of this vocabulary in the high Middle Ages, furthermore, were not without social consequences. Long-established patterns of organizing human affairs were thereby challenged. Canonists insisted that the natural rights of children born out of wedlock should be enforced. Litigation records prove that this legal doctrine was something more than academic speculation. Children, as they entered their adolescence, were also to be respected in the choices they made. Parents might still arrange the marriages of their offspring, but if the child challenged the arrangements, and was sufficiently persistent, the ecclesiastical courts were equipped and inclined to side with the principle of marital freedom. The freedom of children to make choices regarding religious vocation was given a similar respect. And the exquisite language of natural duty and familial devotion that characterized Roman testamentary practice was also given a natural-rights gloss in the twelfth and thirteenth centuries. Children were now held to have a natural right to receive a portion of their parental estates — a right that might be prosecuted through defined actions in the courts of canon law. This is not the place to draw comparisons between the medieval and the modern worlds. It suffices to observe, in closing, that the language of natural rights, when applied to children, has a very respected and deep history.

10. The Duties of Love: The Vocation of the Child in the Household Manual Tradition

John Witte, Jr., and Heather M. Good

In his *Commentaries on the Laws of England* (1765), William Blackstone wrote: "The duties of children to their parents arise from a principle of natural justice and retribution. For to those who gave us existence, we naturally owe subjection and obedience during our minority, and honour and reverence ever after; they, who protected the weakness of our infancy, are entitled to our protection in the infirmity of their age; they who by sustenance and education have enabled their offspring to prosper, ought in return to be supported by that offspring, in case they stand in need of assistance. Upon this principle proceed all the duties of children to their parents, which are enjoined by positive laws."[1] The contemporaneous *Book of Common Prayer* (American Version, 1789) described the child's vocation thus: "To love, honour, and succour my father and mother: To honour and obey the civil authority: To submit myself to all my governors, teachers, spiritual pastors and masters: To order myself lowly and reverently to all my betters."[2] Hundreds of comparable sentiments can be found in standard textbooks of law and theology in early modern times — both Catholic and Protestant, European and American.

The common source for many of these traditional legal and theological sentiments was the Bible, particularly the commandment "Honor your father and your mother, that your days may be long in the land which the Lord your God gives you" (Exod. 20:12; Lev. 19:5; Deut. 5:16) and its various New Testament echoes (Matt. 15:4; Mark 7:10; Eph. 6:1-2). Also important were the Bible's

---

1. William Blackstone, *Commentaries on the Laws of England* (London, 1765), bk. 1, ch. 16.
2. The Protestant Episcopal Church, *The Book of Common Prayer* (New York, 1789), x.

We wish to thank Mr. Timothy Rybacki for his excellent research assistance, and Mr. Will Haines and Ms. Kelly Parker for their fine library services.

repeated admonitions to believers to "be subject to the governing authorities" (Rom. 13:1-7; Titus 3:1; 1 Pet. 2:13). But what precisely did it mean for a Christian child at various stages of development to "love, honor, and obey" or to "serve, succor, and sustain" parents, guardians, teachers, and other authorities? And what did "natural justice" (as Blackstone put it) add to these obligations of "biblical righteousness"? The answers to these questions came in sundry texts — in sermons, catechisms, and confessional manuals as well as in a growing early modern industry of legal texts on domestic relations.

In this chapter, we sample an interesting, but largely neglected, historical medium for teaching the duties and vocation of the child — the household manuals. These manuals were something of the spiritual "Dr. Spock's" of their day — pious "how to" manuals, usually written in the vernacular (unlike the Latin confessional manuals), sometimes highly illustrated (for the young child's benefit), and used regularly by priests and teachers, parents and guardians, tutors and catechists to instruct children at various stages of their development as budding communicants in the church and budding citizens of the state. These household manuals sometimes grew out of or merged into catechisms and religious teaching manuals, on the one hand, and books of etiquette, manners, and deportment, on the other. By the later sixteenth and seventeenth centuries, household manuals were increasingly recognized as their own distinct genre of literature, with the duties of love by and to children broken out in separate sections.

The earliest household manuals in English that we have found are from the fourteenth century. The most famous was penned by the early English reformer John Wycliffe, *Of Weddid Men and Wifis and of Here Children Also* (1390). With the advent of the printing press in the fifteenth century, these manuals became more common, finding their way into myriad church, school, city, and home libraries, Catholic and Protestant alike. They also became more complex and comprehensive, reaching their apex in the massive 800-page tome of Anglo-Puritan divine William Gouge published in 1622. Scores of these household manuals have come down to us. They provide an illuminating window on what a late medieval or early modern child was taught to be his or her vocation in life, what rights and freedoms the child must enjoy in exercise of these duties, and what rights and duties the child's parents, guardians, teachers, and tutors had in helping the child achieve his or her vocation. These manuals helped to bridge law and theology, practice and theory, belief and action in Catholic and Protestant Europe and North America.

This chapter provides a brief tour of the high points of these household manuals. We sample nearly 100 manuals from the fourteenth to the nineteenth century that have survived in English.[3] We focus especially on the common and enduring Western formulations of the vocation of the child set out in these manuals — a rich latticework of virtues, values, and vocations that boys and girls respectively should consider at various stages in life.

The vocation of the child as revealed in these manuals consists of two main types of duties: (1) the duty of the child to love God, neighbor, and self and thereby to become beloved to others; and (2) the duty of the child to *be* loved by parents, guardians, and others. This latter duty was sometimes also cast as the child's right to be loved — though talk of a child's rights remained controversial in the manuals. While the child's basic duties to love did not change much over the five centuries of manuals that we have sampled, the child's duties and rights to be loved and to be beloved did change significantly in substance and form, as we note in the final section of this chapter.

The Child's Duty to Love

Love of God

The household manuals make clear that the first and most essential duty of the child is to love, revere, and worship God. The German Reformer Martin Luther put it thus in 1531: "[Y]ou must continually have God's Word in your heart, upon your lips and in your ears. Where the heart is unoccupied and the Word does not sound, Satan breaks in and has done the damage before we are aware."[4] For the first commandment of the Decalogue is "that we are to trust, fear and love [God] with our whole hearts all the days of our lives."[5] An influential Catholic pamphlet, *L'Instruction des Enfans* (1543), stated that the primary command for every child is to "love the lord God with all your heart" and that the first responsibility of parents and siblings alike is to teach the child to obey that primal command.[6] Richard Baxter's *Rules & Directions for Family Duties* (1681) encouraged parents to "[w]isely break [children] of their own wills, and let them know that they must obey and like God's will" first and foremost.[7] Eleazer Moody's comprehensive manual *The School of Good*

3. See appendix for a list of the household manuals we studied.

4. Martin Luther, "Large Catechism" (1529), in *Luther on Education, Including a Historical Introduction and a Translation of the Reformer's Two Most Important Educational Treatises*, ed. and trans. F. V. N. Painter (St. Louis, 1928), 64.

5. Luther, "Large Catechism," 65.

6. Anonymous, *L'Instruction des Enfans* (London, 1543), folios 1-2.

7. Richardt Baxter, *Rules & Directions for Family Duties* (London, 1681), 1.

Manners (1775) listed as the first duty of a child the duty to "fear and reverence God."[8] The duty to face God daily with fearful and loving reverence, the vast majority of the manuals made clear, is the foundation of the Christian child's life.

The manuals often invoked the duty to love God to compel the child to fulfill his or her other duties, especially the duty to love parents, who are regularly described as God's "priests," "bishops," "kings," and "queens" to their children.[9] Of the duty to love parents, the Catholic *Christian Instructions for Youth* (1821) stated: "You cannot manifest your gratitude towards your parents by any other means but by loving them; this love must not be a natural affection only; it must be a rational love, and according to God; that is to say you must love them, because such is God's will, and you must give proofs of this love."[10] Thomas Becon, the sixteenth-century Anglican divine and confessor to Thomas Cranmer, wrote similarly that children must see their parents as gifts "by the singular providence and good-will of God," and they must love their parents "not feignedly, but from the very bottom of the heart and in wishing unto them all good things from God."[11] It is the child's duty "to honorably esteem them, godly to think of them, heartily to love them, humbly to obey them, [and] diligently to pray for them."[12]

While love of God and love of parents are conjoined, love of God is the primary commandment. Many of the household manuals make clear that when a parental command and a biblical command conflict, the child must follow the Bible. The manuals limited examples of such "wicked" commands of parents to obvious rejections of God or God's laws, such as a parental command that a child "forsake the true living God and his pure religion and to follow strange gods" or where parents, seeing a lucrative and evil opportunity, encourage their daughter "to play the whore."[13] God commands children to obey parents, and the corollary is that in obeying parents a child obeys God. However, "in a matter clearly contrary to the law of God, and to your conscience . . . you do not

---

8. Eleazer Moody, *The School of Good Manners* (Boston, 1775); see also William Smith, *Universal Love* (1668), 41-56.

9. See examples in John Witte, Jr., *From Sacrament to Contract: Marriage, Religion, and Law in the Western Tradition* (Louisville, 1997).

10. Anonymous, *Christian Instructions for Youth*, 2d rev. ed., trans. from French (London, 1821), 34; see also Richard Whitford, *The Werke for Householders* (1537), folios Ei-Fiii; Thomas Cobbett, *A Fruitful and Useful Discourse Touching the Honor Due from Children to Parents* (1656), 9-68.

11. *The Catechism of Thomas Becon* [ca. 1560] (Cambridge, 1844), 358.

12. *Catechism of Thomas Becon*, 85.

13. *Catechism of Thomas Becon*, 87.

owe [parents] obedience; but be cautious on such occasions; and when in doubt of the justness of their commands, take the advice of prudent and discreet persons."[14] Later American Protestants like Samuel Phillips commented in his manual *The Christian Home* (1860) that "the authority of God supersedes that of the parent. Obey God rather than man," but obey parents in "all things lawful and Christian."[15]

Honor and Obey Parents

Except in these cases of absolute conflict with divine law and conscience, the manuals stress the child's duty to show "unhesitating obedience"[16] to her parents, often invoking the commandment to "Honor your father and mother" and its elaborations in later biblical passages. The manuals required children to "obey your parents . . . do what they command, and do it cheerfully. For your own hearts will tell you that this is a most natural extension of honor and love."[17] One manual went so far as to say that children "should have no other will" than the will of their parents, and thus, even those things that are good and righteous should not be undertaken without the consent of the parents.[18] Luther explained the duty of love to parents thus: "God has exalted fatherhood and motherhood above all other relations under his scepter. This appears from the fact that he does not command merely to love the parents, but to honor them. As to our brothers, sisters, and neighbors, God generally commands nothing higher than that we love them. He thus distinguishes father and mother above all other persons upon earth and places them next to himself. It is a much greater thing to honor than to love."[19] Thomas Becon nicely summed up the parameters of the duty of obedience: "Not only to give them outward reverence, to rise up unto them, to give them place, to put off our caps, to kneel unto them, to ask them blessing . . . but also . . . charitably to conceal and hide their faults, in all honest things to gratify them, in their need

---

14. *Christian Instruction for Youth*, 34.

15. Samuel Phillips, *The Christian Home as it is in the Sphere of Nature and the Church* (New York, 1860), 218.

16. Francis Wayland, "Early Training of Children," in *The Fireside Miscellany; and Young People's Encyclopedia* (February, 1864), 60-61.

17. W. E. Channing, *The Duties of Children* (Boston, 1807), 5; see also Cobbett, *Fruitful and Useful Discourse*, 69-127; W.C., *A School of Nurture for Children: The Duty of Children in Honoring their Parents* (1656), 1-62.

18. William Fleetwood, *The Relative Duties of Parents and Children* (London, 1716), 2-3.

19. Luther, "Large Catechism," 66.

to help and succor them, and . . . at all times to do all good things for them, whatsoever lieth in our power."[20]

For most manualists, the one-sentence commandment to "honor your father and mother" was the foundation for a whole range of forbidden activities from the obvious to the tenuously related: striking or kicking parents; desiring a parent's death; hating, mocking, or deriding parents; angering parents; failing to help parents who are in poverty or to pay offerings to the church or to keep fasting days; nonconformity with the divine rights of rulers; fostering unrest or treason against their own rulers or against their city; and depriving someone of an honor or a favor and keeping him from something he is entitled to out of "brotherly love."[21] As this list of proscriptions makes clear, the manuals extended the duty to honor and obey parents to all other earthly authority figures. As the German Catholic Dietrich Kolde put it in *A Fruitful Mirror* (1470), this commandment "requires and teaches us to assist and serve our parents with a loving heart, a polite mouth, and a respectful body. This applies not only to our natural parents, but also to spiritual and earthly authorities."[22]

Obedience to parents requires submission to Christian correction. Children have a duty to submit to punishment when it is deserved and must not resent their parents for punishing them.[23] One manual warned: "Forget not, young people, that your parents and masters have a right to correct you. They are bound to correct you, when you deserve it; should a slight correction in this case be not sufficient, it is their duty to use more severity." Children are expected to love parents for correcting them because "they correct you solely for your good, and to make you discreet and virtuous."[24] Some manuals took this duty further: "Should you not perchance have deserved that correction, suffer it patiently, remembering that it is less than your sins deserve; and that Jesus Christ, though innocent, suffered without complaint the torment of the cross, and death itself."[25] As we shall note further below, this duty of obedience even in the face of abuse was dangerous instruction in a world where children were abused and tortured, and sometimes fell to "death itself" at the hands of

20. *Catechism of Thomas Becon*, 85.

21. Kolde, *A Fruitful Mirror* (1470), in *Three Reformation Catechisms: Catholic, Anabaptist, Lutheran,* ed. and trans. Denis Janz (New York, 1982), 55-56.

22. Kolde, *A Fruitful Mirror,* 55-56.

23. Henry Dixon, *The English Instructor* (Boston, 1746), 55; see also Richard Baxter, *Rules & Directions for Family Duties* (1681); Anonymous, *True and Faithful Discharge of Relative Duties* (1683); John Gother, *Instructions for Children* (1698); Benjamin Wadsworth, *The Well-Ordered Family* (1712), 90-102; *Christian Instructions for Youth* (1821), 51-55.

24. *Christian Instructions for Youth,* 36.

25. *Christian Instructions for Youth,* 37.

their parents. The danger of children thinking that their Christian duty required them to suffer at the hands of tyrannical parents is further complicated by instructions throughout the manuals "charitably to conceal and hide" their parents' "faults."[26]

Obedience also requires that a child attend school and aim constantly for excellence in both spiritual and secular education. The manuals frequently admonished children, for their parents' sake, to work at school and aim at high standards of intellectual power and attainment. In the early manuals, this duty was simply one derived from obedience and the obligation to learn about God. Later manuals, however, tied the need for good education to the child's duty to fulfill her social responsibility as well as her duty to find a calling that should help her recompense her parents should they fall into poverty or need aid in old age.

The duty to obey requires a child to seek the consent of his or her parents to court and marry another. Marriages without parental consent violate the law of God, both Catholic and Protestant manuals insisted repeatedly.[27] The ultimate authority for choosing at least a minor child's spouse rests with the parents. The child's wishes must be considered, Anglican preacher William Fleetwood advised in *The Relative Duties of Parents and Children* (1716), for children must have a say "with whom they are to live and die" and "with whom they are to venture being happy or unhappy all their days."[28] But, while parents are encouraged to respect their child's wishes, the parents' decision is absolute, and an obedient Christian child is ultimately bound by their decision.

Respect

The heart of the duty to honor and obey is to have respect for one's parents and other superiors — to develop what the popular American manualist William Ellery Channing called a "submissive deportment."[29] Channing explained in *The Duties of Children* (1807) that "[y]our tender, inexperienced age requires that you think of yourselves with humility . . . that you respect the superior age and wisdom and improvements of your parents" and "express your respect for [parents] in your manner and conversation. Do not neglect those outward signs of dependence and inferiority which suit your age." Such outward signs

---

26. *Catechism of Thomas Becon*, 85.
27. Fleetwood, *Relative Duties*, 32-33.
28. Fleetwood, *Relative Duties*, 35.
29. Channing, *The Duties of Children*, 3.

include a requirement to "ask instead of demand what you desire," and because children "have much to learn" they should "hear instead of seeking to be heard." Channing was not arguing for a "slavish fear" of parents: "Love them and love them ardently; but mingle a sense of their superiority with your love. Feel a confidence in their kindness; but let not this confidence make you rude and presumptuous, and lead to indecent familiarity. Talk to them with openness and freedom; but never contradict with violence; never answer with passion or contempt."[30]

Learning parental respect is a foundational duty of the child, because respecting parents eventually translates into learning the good manners, restraint, and decorum that are essential for later success in church, state, and society. To cultivate this respect, the manuals sometimes went to great lengths to dictate every aspect of the child's manners and accompanying emotions preparing the child for the norms and habits of adult life. In many of these manuals, the litany of duties is almost overwhelming: be pious, work in school with all your heart, beware of being beaten and corrected, do not offend the schoolmaster or schoolmates in word or deed, read continually, be eloquent in speech and writing, go hastily home from school each day without tarrying, learn the catechisms, pray often, honor the Sabbath, do household chores, set the table for dinner, keep yourself upright and proper at the table, walk modestly, avoid "unchaste women," dress neither too sumptuously nor too poorly, study diligently, avoid evil persons — and the list goes on.

Eleazer Moody's wildly popular *The School of Good Manners,* first published in the United States in 1715, outlines 163 rules for children's behavior — 14 rules for behavior at home, 43 for the table, 10 for at church, 41 for company or in public, 28 for speaking to superiors, and 13 for school. The directives range from the impossible ("approach near thy parents at no time without a bow"), to the practical dinner table instruction ("take no salt with a greasy knife"), to the amusing ("throw not anything under the table"), to the improbable ("be not hasty to run out" of church "when worship is ended, as if weary of being there").[31] *Christian Instructions for Youth* (1821) devoted 258 pages to the duties of young persons ranging from how they should honor their parents, to how they should take correction, to the means of preserving their chastity, to choosing and maintaining friendships. Good manners also included a range of simple rules of etiquette: taking care to clean one's body, covering with clean and modest apparel, keeping elbows off the table at dinner, not drinking wine and ale excessively and preferably not at all, purity of speech in all encounters (not

---

30. Channing, *The Duties of Children,* 3-4.
31. Moody, *School of Good Manners,* 7-8, 11-12.

to swear, interrupt, or speak of vile things), not contending with another, humility, keeping to one's own affairs, and ignoring information one should not have overheard.[32]

According to many household manuals, humble and limited speech is a critical characteristic of a good and respectful Christian child. Evil speech and swearing are telltale signs of inner impurities and utter disrespect. But early manuals also warned children to limit their chatter (whether pure or not), speaking to their parents and other adults only when absolutely necessary. Out of the duty of obedience and good manners, children were also required to listen attentively to parents and never to speak to them with derision or mocking tones. Luther remarked that honoring parents requires "that they be esteemed and prized above everything else as the most precious treasure we have on earth. That, in conversation with them, we measure our words, lest our language be discourteous, domineering, quarrelsome, yielding to them in silence, even if they do go too far."[33]

Some of the early household manuals called for a child to have complete control over his or her emotions in order to demonstrate this requisite respect. In his *Little Book of Good Manners* (1554), the great Dutch humanist Desiderius Erasmus called children to be "merry and joyful" at the dinner table, and never "heavy-hearted." In *The Civility of Childhood* (1560), Erasmus admonished children not to be "angry" when corrected or to "rejoice" when praised, for such habits were not becoming of a "courteous Christian child."[34] The child's duties to honor, love, obey, and respect parents, Erasmus insisted, require a child to exert and exercise full control over his emotional state, requiring tenderness in place of torment, happiness in place of heartache, and delight in place of despair.

Respect and Recompense

This calling of the child to respect parents continued into adulthood, even after the duty to obey parents in daily life had expired. American writer Timothy Shay Arthur made this point in his *Advice to Young Men on Their Duties and Conduct in Life* (1848), a highly popular manual, and often reprinted on both sides of the Atlantic: "Although the attainment of mature age takes away the

---

32. See, e.g., Desiderius Erasmus, *A Little Book of Good Manners* (London, 1554); see also Desiderius Erasmus, *The Civility of Childhood* (1560); Robert Crowley, *The School of Virtue . . . Teaching Children and Youths Their Duties* (London, 1621); Robert Abbott, *A Christian Family Builded by God* (London, 1653).

33. Luther, "Large Catechism," 66.

34. Erasmus, *The Civility of Childhood.*

obligation of obedience to parents, as well as the right of dependence upon them, it should lessen in no way a young man's deference, respect, or affection."[35] William Blackstone wrote similarly in his *Commentaries on the Laws of England* (1765), that as children we owe our parents "subjection and obedience during our minority, and honor and reverence ever after."[36]

One of the most important expressions of ongoing respect is the child's duty to "recompense his parents" for rearing him, especially if his parents fall ill or become poor. For younger children, the manuals insisted, the duty to recompense is bound up with the duty to obey. William Channing, for example, instructed children: "Do not expect that your parents are to give up every thing to your wishes; but study to give up every thing to theirs. Do not wait for them to threaten; but when a look tells you what they want, fly to perform it. This is the way in which you can best reward them for all their pains and labors."[37] The child's duty of recompense also requires "concealing, hiding, covering and interpreting all their parents' faults and vices." Further, it requires "never objecting nor upbraiding them by any thing done amiss; but quietly and patiently to bear all things at their hands, considering that in thus doing [children] greatly please God, and offer unto him an acceptable sacrifice. . . . It becometh a good and godly child not to display, but to conceal the faults of his father, even as he wishes that God should cover his own offenses."[38]

For mature and emancipated children, the duty to recompense also requires them to give their parents aid, comfort, and relief in accordance with their own means and their parents' needs. The Catholic manualist Barthelemy Batt put it thus in *The Christian Man's Closet* (1581): "To honor parents is to relieve and nourish their parents in case they fall into poverty and decay. And when they are old, to guide, lead, and bear them on their shoulders if need be." If the parents "shall fall into any grievous sickness, poverty or extreme old age, it shall be the children's duty willingly to relieve and comfort them by all possible means."[39] Luther taught similarly that honor is due to parents by our actions, "both in our bearing and the extension of aid, serving, helping, and caring for them when they are old or sick, frail or poor; and that we not only do it cheerfully, but with humility and reverence, as if unto God. For he who is rightly disposed to his parents will never let them suffer want and hunger, but will place them above and beside himself, and share with them all he has to the

---

35. T. S. Arthur, *Advice to Young Men on Their Duties and Conduct in Life* (Boston, 1848), 100.

36. Blackstone, *Commentaries*, 1.16.

37. Channing, *The Duties of Children*, 7.

38. *Catechism of Thomas Becon*, 358.

39. Barthelemy Batt, *The Christian Man's Closet* (London, 1581), 60-101, esp. 61, 71, 74.

best of his ability."[40] Becon called for children "to requite their parents for . . . [the] great benefits as they have received of God by them and their labors." And "if their parents be aged and fallen by their own industry and labor, then ought the children, if they will truly honor their parents, to labor for them, to see unto their necessity, to provide necessaries for them, and by no means, so much as in them is, to suffer them . . . to lack for any good thing" because parents care and provide for children when they are unable to provide for themselves.[41]

A child must discharge this duty of recompense even if the parent does not deserve or appreciate it. Recompense is due to parents "in their old age" even when they were "hard and cruel" earlier in life, or if they now betray "unwieldy crookedness," wrote Heinrich Bullinger, the sixteenth-century Swiss Protestant.[42] Luther counseled similarly that "even though [parents] may be lowly, poor, frail, and peculiar, they are still father and mother, given by God. Their way of living and their failings cannot rob them of their honor."[43] Benjamin Wadsworth, American clergyman and later Harvard president, insisted in his *Well-Ordered Family* (1712) that it was "a natural duty" for a child to take care of his parents, when they revert to the feeble and fragile state brought on by age and sickness, as a way of recompensing them for their earlier care of the child who was once just as feeble and fragile. You are "bound in duty and conscience" to "provide for them, nourish, support and comfort them."[44] "[T]he time is coming when your parents will need as much attention from you as you have received from them, and you should endeavor to form such industrious, obliging habits that you may render their last years as happy as they have rendered the first years of your existence."[45]

The Duty (and the Right) to Be Loved

The child's duty to love, honor, obey, respect, and recompense his or her parents and other guardians and loved ones was only one-half of the domestic ethic envisioned by the household manuals. The manuals also spoke of a child's "duty to be loved" by his or her parents and others. The child was regarded as both an agent of love and an object of love — one who discharged

40. Luther, "Large Catechism," 66.

41. *Catechism of Thomas Becon*, 358.

42. Heinrich Bullinger, *The Christen State of Matrimony Moost Necessary and Profitable for All*, trans. Miles Coverdale (n.p., 1546).

43. Luther, "Large Catechism," 66.

44. Benjamin Wadsworth, *The Well-Ordered Family*, 98-99.

45. Channing, *The Duties of Children*, 9.

the duties of love and one who induced parents and others to discharge their reciprocal duties of love to that child. These twin duties of love *by* and *of* a child were interdependent. The child had to discharge his duties of love in part in order to make himself beloved and thus to become the object of the love of his parents. But these twin duties of love were not mutually conditional. The child had to discharge her duty of love to parents even if the parents did not or could not reciprocate. The parents, in turn, had to discharge their duty of love to the child even if the child was incapacitated, recalcitrant, or unruly.

The later manuals sometimes put these duties of parental love for their children in sweeping emotional terms. T. S. Arthur's *Advice to Young Men on Their Duties and Conduct in Life* (1848), for example, described a mother's love thus: "She watched over you, loved you, protected and defended you; and all was from love — deep, pure, fervent love — the first love, and the most unselfish love that has or ever will bless you in this life, for it asked for and expected no return. *A mother's love!* — it is the most perfect reflection of the love of God ever thrown back from the mirror of the human heart."[46] Such talk of emotional love was largely absent from the earlier Catholic and Protestant household manuals. More typically, the duty of the child to be loved was expressed as the duty Christian parents, guardians, and other members of the community had to rear and raise the child properly so that he could prepare properly for his Christian vocation.

The later manuals also sometimes translated the child's duty to be loved into the child's right to receive love, support, education, and nurture. As Charles Reid shows in his chapter herein, some medieval canonists and moralists spoke of the rights of the child in these terms.[47] None of the early household manuals that we have sampled, either Catholic or Protestant, spoke of "children's rights." In fact, this language was sometimes explicitly rejected. Anglican bishop Jeremy Taylor, author of *Bishop Taylor's Judgment Concerning the Power of Parents Over Their Children* (1696), for example, put it thus: "So long as the son is within the civil power of his Father, so long as he lives in his house, is subject to his command, is nourished by his father's charge, [he] hath no distinct rights of his own, he is in his father's possession, and to be reckoned by his measures."[48] This was doubly true for daughters, whom the

---

46. Arthur, *Advice to Young Men,* 101, emphasis in original.

47. See the chapter by Charles J. Reid herein, and further exposition in Charles J. Reid, Jr., *Power over the Body, Equality in the Family: Rights and Domestic Relations in Medieval Canon Law* (Grand Rapids, 2004), 213ff.

48. Jeremy Taylor, *Judgment Concerning the Power of Parents Over Their Children* (London, 1696).

manualists and common lawyers alike readily treated as the property of their fathers and families.

Explicit talk of a child's rights to the love and support of his or her parents entered the manual tradition only at the turn of the eighteenth century, and it remained controversial. An early example was the 300-page English manual *The Infant's Lawyer* (1697), which gave a detailed guide to the status of children at common law and contended that "the law protects children in their persons, preserves their rights and estates, executes their laches and assists them in their pleadings."[49] This manual, which was largely a set of instructions to litigators, showed how children may not be convicted of felonies until "the age of discretion," and how even minor children can be protected in their "estates and rights."[50] Such language became more popular with the rise of Enlightenment thought, particularly through the influence of John Locke and Jean-Jacques Rousseau, though, as we shall see, children's rights language was sometimes staunchly resisted, especially by Protestant writers.

The manuals' dominant genre was a discourse of parental duty to children. On the one hand, the manuals encouraged active parental involvement and attentiveness to children, and chastised parents for neglecting their children's temporal and spiritual needs. On the other hand, the manuals increasingly sought to prohibit abusive parenting.

Parental Duties of Love

The manuals rooted parents' duty to love and care for their child in the commandment that children must honor their fathers and mothers. The parent's duty to the child was the correlative and complement to the duty that the child owed parents — per this commandment and many later biblical instructions for children.[51] Luther put it thus: "Although the duty of superiors is not explicitly stated in the Ten Commandments, it is frequently dwelt upon in many other passages of Scripture, and *God intends it to be included even in this commandment, where he mentions father and mother.* . . . God does not purpose to bestow the parental office and government upon rogues and tyrants; therefore, he does not give them that honor, namely, the power and authority to govern, merely to receive homage. Parents should consider that they are under obliga-

---

49. Anonymous, *The Infant's Lawyer* (London, 1697), A2.

50. Anonymous, *The Infant's Lawyer*, 15-16.

51. See the detailed biblical analysis in the chapter by Marcia Bunge herein, and in Marcia Bunge, ed., *The Child in Christian Thought* (Grand Rapids, 2000).

tions to obey God and that, first of all, they are conscientiously and faithfully to discharge all the duties of their office; not only to feed and provide for the temporal wants of their children . . . but especially to train them to the honor and praise of God."[52] This was a typical sentiment of the household manuals, both Protestant and Catholic.

The manuals presented this parental duty to love their child as a duty owed first and foremost to God. A child is made in the image of God, and as one of God's own, is to be embraced and loved as such. But the child is also made in the image of the parent, and thus to love and embrace that child is, in a real sense, to love oneself. The duty to love one's child, therefore, is one of the most sublime gifts by which a parent can live out the primal command to love God, neighbor, and self at once.[53]

Right rearing of children involves constant attentiveness, the manualists insisted. Parents must not be lulled into a sense that "the parental office is a matter of your pleasure and whim, but remember that God has strictly commanded it and entrusted it to you, and that for the right discharge of its duties you must give an account." Parents are not blessed with children as merely "objects of mirth and pleasure" or "servants to use, like the ox or the horse." Nor are parents to raise children "according to [their] own whims — to ignore them, in unconcern about what they learn or how they live."[54] Children must not be neglected, but should be "objects of conscientious solicitude." They must be cared for but not coddled. "If we wish to have worthy, capable persons for both temporal and spiritual leadership, we must indeed spare no diligence, time or cost in teaching and educating our children to serve God and mankind." Parents must know that, under the threat of "loss of divine grace," their "chief duty is to rear . . . children in the fear and knowledge of God; and, if they are gifted, to let them learn and study, that they may be of service wherever needed. . . . The children . . . we have are the children . . . we [must] rear." And, if we are negligent in this duty, not only will the child be harmed, but social discipline and peace will suffer.[55]

The manuals focused on four main duties of love and attentiveness that parents must discharge for their children. First, parents must instruct their children about God and God's commands — by baptizing them, taking them to

52. Luther, "Large Catechism," 77, emphasis added.

53. Kolde, *Fruitful Mirror*, 53ff.; see also Richard Baxter, *Rules & Directions for Family Duties* (1681).

54. Luther, "Large Catechism," 77. See further such sentiments and other early Protestants in John Witte, Jr., *Law and Protestantism: The Legal Teachings of the Lutheran Reformation* (Cambridge, 2002), 262-77.

55. Luther, "Large Catechism," 78.

church, and teaching them about sacramental and virtuous living, and guiding them through catechism to confirmation.[56] This duty, the manualists emphasized, begins as soon as the child is able to speak. In *Of Weddid Men and Wifis and of Here Children Also,* Wycliffe opined that the greatest downfall of parents is in tending more to the temporal than the spiritual welfare of their children.[57] Kolde's *Fruitful Mirror* emphasized that parents must discharge this first duty both by good instruction and by setting a good example of doing virtuous works. Parents must not curse, nag, or scold a child or do anything else to set a bad example for their children. Nor should they "constantly torment or beat or kick their children," thereby "inducing them to have evil thoughts." Kolde emphasized that "carelessness and neglect by parents who do not instruct their children well when they are young . . . is the main reason why people are so evil in the world and why so many evil afflictions and plagues come over the world. When children grow up doing and being as they please, they are without fear and anxiety and shame. And so they remain hard-headed, horrible, obstinate and disobedient." When these children are grown, "they ruin their parents and themselves as well," becoming poor and criminal, and "often die in their sins and are damned. Thus they make themselves a whip and a rod to be beaten with."[58]

This points to the second main parental duty, viz., of subjecting children to proper Christian discipline and correction. A few of the early manuals, both Catholic and Protestant, countenanced severe discipline and violence against children. John Bradford's *Letter Sent to Master A.B. from the Most Godly and Learned Preacher I.B.* (1548), for example, advocated violent beatings of children, and called parents to be "deaf" to their cries and moans of pain even while whipping and scourging "not only until the blood runs down, but even until we have left wounds in the flesh." Bradford believed that severe discipline is the only way to save a rebellious child from eternal damnation. He adduced the Bible in support of his views. Deuteronomy 21:18-21,[59] he argued, gives par-

---

56. John Wycliffe, *Of Weddid Men and Wifis and of Here Children Also* (1390), reprinted in *Selected English Works of John Wyclif,* ed. Thomas Arnold (Oxford, 1871), 195-97.

57. Anonymous, *A Glass for Householders* (London, 1542), n.p.

58. Kolde, *Fruitful Mirror,* 114-15.

59. Deuteronomy 21:18-21 (NRSV) reads: "If someone has a stubborn and rebellious son who will not obey his father and mother, who does not heed them when they discipline him, then his father and his mother shall take hold of him and bring him out to the elders of his town at the gate of that place. They shall say to the elders of his town, 'This son of ours is stubborn and rebellious. He will not obey us. He is a glutton and a drunkard.' Then all the men of the town shall stone him to death. So you shall purge the evil from your midst; and all Israel will hear, and be afraid."

ents the right to take their rebellious children of any age before the town's people, who may stone them to death.[60] While stoning may no longer be expedient, Bradford argued, this passage underscores that parents have absolute control over their children, including the power to "scourge" them severely as needed.

But even Reverend Bradford insisted that such harsh treatment be reserved only for the most rebellious child who was "more than twenty years old" and should by now know better. He further qualified his remarks by chastising the parents to whom he addressed his letter for failing to punish this particular son at a younger age, which would have spared all of them this later and greater severity of treatment: "If you had brought up your son with care and diligence, to rejoice in obedience toward his parents; and on the other side to be afraid to do evil and shun disobedience, and to fear the smart of correction, you would then have felt those comforts which happy parents receive from their good and honest children."[61] Because these lax parents had allowed their child to "run the course of his own will" in his early years, and had "foolishly foregone to spend the sharp rods of correction on the naked flesh of his loins," they were now required to save him from hell by making "his blood run[] down in streams, scourged loins, and forty days of pain." Any further indulgence or forbearance would put their son "in hazards of bitter confusion" and most assuredly put them in judgment before the Lord for "carelessly and negligently bringing up their children."

Most manualists, particularly by the sixteenth century, called for more "reasonable" forms of discipline and correction. A good early example was Alberti's *Della Famiglia* (ca. 1570). "Children must always be corrected in a reasonable manner, at times with severity, but always without anger or passion. We must never rage as some furious or impetuous [*sic*] fathers do, but must . . . not punish anyone without first putting anger aside." While "[i]t is a father's duty . . . to punish his children and make them wise and virtuous," punishment must be "reasonable and just." Similarly, William Gouge's *Of Domestical Duties* (1622) taught that parental authority should evoke fear in children, but parental love should evoke affection in children. "Love, like sugar, sweetens fear, and fear like salt seasons love."[62]

The call for moderate and reasonable correction was even more pronounced in later manuals. In *The Christian Home* (1860), for example, Samuel

---

60. John Bradford, *A Letter Sent to Master A.B. from the Most Godly and Learned Preacher I.B.* (London, 1548), A-Cii (modernized spelling).

61. Bradford, *A letter Sent,* A-Cii.

62. Leon Batista Alberti, *The Albertis of Florence: Leon Batista Alberti's Della Famiglia,* trans. Guido A. Guarino (Lewisburg, Pa., 1971), 74-77; William Gouge, *Of Domestical Duties* (London: John Haviland, 1622), 428.

Phillips called parents to find a moderate middle between "over-indulgence" and "the iron rod of tyranny." Parents must take steps to rule their households and execute their commands, or children will "end up ruling them." But no household should feature "parental despotism," "making slaves of children, acting the unfeeling and heartless tyrant over them . . . and making them obey from motives of trembling fear and dread." That is not only "un-Christian" but ineffective, said Phillips. Parental despotism engenders in children "the spirit of a slave" rooting out "all confidence and love," and making their obedience "involuntary and mechanical." A proper Christian home must find a middle way between these extremes: "It is mild, yet decisive," and it is "not lawless, yet not despotic." It "combines in proper order and harmony, the true elements of parental authority and filial subordination." In the Christian home, "[l]ove and fear harmonize; the child fears because he loves; and is prompted to obedience by both."

Phillips condemned those who favored severe corporal punishment in reliance on the adage from Proverbs that "he that spareth the rod, spoileth the child." The term "rod," in this passage, he argued, does not necessarily mean "the iron rod of the unfeeling and unloving despot" but instead could be interpreted as the "rod of a compassionate father" who "does not always inflict corporal punishment," and when he does, he does so out of love. Phillips argued that corporal punishment does more harm than good, resulting in "depravity" of character, resentment, and ultimately criminal acts against and by the children. "Christian correction is the interposition of love acting according to law in restraining the child." We should "correct but not punish" our children in a manner where "true severity and true sympathy . . . unite and temper each other."[63]

Third, beyond the parental duties of divine instruction and Christian discipline, the manuals emphasized that parents must teach a child a "trade" or "occupation" — or what the Protestant manualists frequently called a "divine calling" or "Christian vocation."[64] Heinrich Bullinger's instruction was quite typical. He emphasized that teaching a child a proper Christian vocation was a matter of "mutual discovery" for the parent and the child. Parents must observe and assess the child's talents and inclinations, and prepare and place the child in the occupation for which the child is best suited. This vocation should be one that is not only most conducive to the child's abilities and interests but also the "most profitable and necessary" for the church and commonwealth. One of the chief parental responsibilities is to "place his children with expert and cunning

---

63. Phillips, *The Christian Home*, 218-31.
64. Batt, *The Christian Man's Closet*, 65; Bullinger, *Christen State*, lxix-lxxii.

workmen" who will "teach them some handicraft" and livelihood — or, as later manualists emphasized, to place them in a school to train them for their proper vocation. Placement in a job or a school should be determined by the "children's wit" and aptitude, and by mutual determination of where children would find the "most delight."[65]

Consideration of what vocation would bring the child the "most delight" became more explicit in later manuals — but principally for males. Most of the manuals restricted young women only to the vocation of being a wife and mother — or a nun or religious servant in a few of the late medieval Catholic manuals. Rather than seeking a vocation "most profitable and necessary for the commonwealth," the manuals encouraged that parents place daughters in a vocation "profitable for the family."

Fourth, the manuals emphasized parents' duty to find a suitable mate for their children, the reciprocal of the child's duty to procure parental consent before marriage. Bullinger insisted that while children "must" not marry without parental consent, "[s]o *should* not the parents without any pity compel their children to marry before their time, nor wickedly neglect them, nor leave them unprovided for in due season."[66] This was a common sentiment in early modern Protestant and post-Tridentine Catholic circles that insisted on parental consent for valid marital formation.[67] While the children "must" obey parents in this matter, at least when they are minors, the parents "should" act reasonably. Children objecting to their parents' choice of a mate should do so "comely and with good manner," and recognize that the parental word is final in the matter.[68] Similarly, Nathaniel Cotton's *Visions for the Entertainment and Instruction of Young Minds* warned young women "impatient of a parent's rule" not to rush into marriage without parental permission. Such foolish "rebels," Cotton warned, will only suffer a "joyless" life and, to add insult to injury, will become "barren."[69]

---

65. Bullinger, *Christen State,* lxix-lxxii; Henry Bullinger, "The Fifth Precept of the Ten Commandments" [ca. 1542], in *Decades of Henry Bullinger, Second Decade* (Cambridge, 1849), 267-98.

66. Bullinger, *Christen State,* xv-xviii, emphasis added.

67. See examples in Witte, *From Sacrament to Contract;* John Witte, Jr., and Robert M. Kingdon, *Sex, Marriage, and Family in John Calvin's Geneva I: Courtship, Engagement, and Marriage* (Grand Rapids, 2005), 165-201.

68. Bullinger, *Christen State,* xv-xvii.

69. Nathaniel Cotton, *Visions for the Entertainment and Instruction of Young Minds* (Exeter, N.H., 1794), 76.

Evolving Ideals

Gender Roles

Not surprisingly, the manuals revealed the common double standards for men and women that prevailed in late medieval and early modern society. While much of the language in the household manuals was gender neutral and addressed to "children" or "youths," the manuals were directed principally at young men — as is clear from the prevalent warnings against "whoremongering" with women and proper habits of courting women. When the manuals did distinguish between gender roles, they generally called boys to learn to be bold and courageous and girls to be fearful and gentle. A 1542 manual made the father primarily responsible for rearing courageous and God-fearing young men and the mother responsible to raise gentle and virtuous females: "So in women . . . there is nothing more laudable than fearfulness and gentleness of manner. To the mother, your wife, give charge to do her duty in bringing up your women children virtuously and in the law and fear of God, as you do the men children."[70]

The Christian Man's Closet (1581) set out a typical list of duties that were "especially applicable to daughters." These include: (1) speaking and understanding (that is, learning) only about the fear of God; (2) not using filthy words; (3) being modest in appearance (meaning limited makeup and natural hair color); (4) avoiding wine and overindulgence in food; (5) learning to make woolen and linen cloth; (6) donning appropriate apparel without focus on silks; and (7) avoiding unvirtuous ("light") maidens.[71] Typically, in the early manuals, the duties of young women also included "shamefastness," meekness, chastity, modesty, "sadness," and sobriety. The most important thing for a daughter to learn and to be taught, the manuals emphasized, is "how to please her husband through gentle behavior, discreet conversation, prudence, wisdom, and virtue." As to education, "[d]aughters should be instructed in prayer and Christian knowledge, but should not be too busy in teaching and reasoning openly."[72]

A few of the manualists had other vocations in mind for young women beyond demure marriage and dutiful motherhood. Juan Luis Vives' *Instruction of a Christian Woman* (1523), which appeared in some forty editions, was a good early example. Vives, a Spanish humanist and philosopher, recognized that

---

70. Anonymous, *A Glass for Householders* (1542), n.p. (modernized spelling).
71. Batt, *The Christian Man's Closet*, 75-76.
72. Bullinger, *Christen State*, p. xv (modernized spelling).

many young women would pursue marriage, and their mothers had to teach them the proper ways and means of "keeping and ordering . . . a house." But other women "are born unto [learning], or at least not unfit for it." They were "not to be discouraged, and those that are apt should be heartened and encouraged." Vives acknowledged that "learned women are suspect to many." Thus "young women shall only study that which leads to good manners, informs her living and teaches the ways of a holy and good life." Eloquence and learnedness, while not necessary among women, are shameful only when they lead to indiscretion or deceit. Above all, women need goodness and wisdom. However, a woman is never to teach, because she is a "fragile thing," and, "like Eve," may be deceived by a weak argument.[73] These were only dim foreshadowings of the more ambitious vocations and aspirations for girls and young women projected by nineteenth- and twentieth-century feminist writers.

Enlightenment Influences

John Locke's *Some Thoughts Concerning Education* (1693) challenged many of the traditional notions of childhood, child rearing, and education. Locke advocated much more intimacy between parents and children. He rejected the idea that the child is marred by original sin, and instead saw the child as a free form ready to be shaped by experience and education. The parent's role was to guide and mediate those experiences for the benefit of the child. Education of children, Locke argued, is not simply for acquiring knowledge, but especially for building a virtuous and useful character. "Virtue is harder to be got than knowledge of the world; and, if lost in a young man, is seldom recovered." The aim of education is not simply knowledge, but to teach a child how to live life, and to live it well. Locke urged parents to teach their children self-discipline so that corporal punishment would be unnecessary. "I told you before that children love *liberty* and therefore they should be brought to do the things that are fit for them without feeling any restraint laid upon them. I now tell you they love something more: and that is *dominion*." He urged parents to restrain a child's cravings and desires by not giving in to the child's every whim.[74]

While Locke's treatise on education made a splash, Jean-Jacques Rousseau's *Emile* (1762) changed the tide of childhood education. Rousseau wrote: "Everything is good coming from the Creator, everything degenerates at the hands of men." Thus a child ought to be free to experience life in every respect irrespec-

---

73. Juan Luis Vives, *Instruction of a Christian Woman* (London, 1585), 8, 18, 25-30, 322.
74. John Locke, *Some Thoughts Concerning Education* (London, 1693), secs. 54-69.

tive of potential harm, for a child's "joy of freedom compensates for many injuries." Rousseau criticized the heavily duty-bound ethic of earlier household manuals, catechisms, and educational texts; parents and others, he insisted, should "[n]ever tell the child what he cannot understand."[75] He minimized the importance of book learning, and promoted instead the idea of educating a child's emotions and affections. Rousseau urged parents and teachers to focus on the passionate side of the child's human nature, something that earlier teachings had neglected, in his view. Like Locke, he specially recognized the virtue of a child's learning through experience — by trial and error, experiment and failure.

Rousseau's Enlightenment ideas of children and their education were highly controversial in their day, but they slowly found their way into the household manual tradition. Enos Weed's *Educational Directory* (1803), for example, echoed Rousseau in arguing for a less rigid educational structure. Children should be exposed to a variety of experiences, and they must be allowed to question parents, teachers, and other authorities, especially as they grow older. Furthermore, while parents have a duty to correct children in all manner of wrongs, Weed warned against strict punishment. Good parenting requires taming an unruly will without breaking a child's spirit. Children's "trifling playish temper and disposition," which had been stifled by the strict traditional requirements, "should be encouraged, as being beneficial to them."

Weed, like Rousseau, criticized the heavily duty-bound ethic of the earlier manual tradition, calling for "very few" rules, lest the child's "natural development" be impaired and impeded. He had little sympathy for traditional instruction in decorum, etiquette, and manners, for this endless "heaping on [children] a large number of rules about their putting off their hats or making legs or courtesies" are mere "outward gestures to the neglect of their minds." Weed also railed against the earlier manualists' calls for emotional control of children, advising instead that children "should always . . . speak and act according to the true sentiments of their hearts." He despised compulsory use of courteous addresses made "for show and not from affection." Children should be free to express themselves to parents and other superiors according to the "true sentiments of their heart."[76]

Weed did not fully dispense with tradition. He thought that moderate corporal punishment to correct a child when necessary was best. He counseled that children should not be indulged in all their desires, and they should be taught

---

75. Jean-Jacques Rousseau, *Emile* (Paris, 1769), 292ff.

76. Enos Weed, *The Educational Directory Designed for the Use of Schools and Private Families* (New York, 1803), 21-22.

to dress modestly, eat moderately, and avoid wicked speech and actions. Parents should likewise provide a good example for their children, a common theme of the earlier manuals.

Tennessee Celeste Cook went further in her chapter on children in *Constitutional Equality a Right of Woman* (1871). Cook was a feminist writer and reformer, most popular because her sister was the first woman to run for president of the United States. Cook wrote: "The teachings of Christianity are well; they have been taught persistently. But we have now arrived at that practical age of the world which demands adequate results as proofs of the validity of assumed positions." Among other things, practice has proved that while parental education and proper rearing of children are essential, "society is responsible for the character of the children which it rears." Heretofore, the household manuals had stressed the personal responsibility of the parent in rearing children, and the personal responsibility of the child to be well taught. Cook, following Rousseau and Locke, made this a paramount social duty as well, particularly through widespread schooling for young men and women.

Traditional schools, Cook argued, had failed to educate children in their duties as citizens of humanity: "We are arguing . . . [for] the rights of children . . . which shall make every child, male and female, honorable and useful members of society. . . . Scarcely any of the [traditional] practices of education . . . in regard to children are worthy of anything but the severest condemnation." Ignoring the child's "inherent rights," traditional schools cultivate virtues and "affections to the exclusion of all reason and common sense. They forget that the human is more than an affectional being; that he has other than family duties to fulfill, and that he belongs to humanity." Especially with respect to young women, Cook insisted, "[v]ery much of the fashionable external nonsense, which forms so great a part of young ladies' education might well be dispensed with, and they, instead, be instructed in their mission as the artists of humanity; artists not merely in form and feature, but in that diviner sense of intellectual soul." Cook viewed all children, male and female, as having both the ability and the responsibility to contribute to the common good. Indeed, she went so far as to urge the state to take children from parents not best suited to raise them in a vocation good for the commonwealth. "To make the best citizens of children, then, is the object of education, and in whatever way this can be best attained, that is the one which should be pursued, even if it be to the complete abrogation of the present supposed rights of parents to control them."[77]

77. Tennessee Celeste Cook, *Constitutional Equality a Right of Woman* (New York, 1871), 130-47.

While Weed and Cook were more radical than most, a number of more traditional manualists did absorb some of the Enlightenment concern for greater gender equality and greater respect for children's rights. A good example was *The Christian Home as it is in the Sphere of Nature and the Church* (1860), authored by American minister Samuel Phillips. Phillips called the Christian home "a little commonwealth jointly governed by the parents," rather than principally governed by the paterfamilias. It is "the right of the parents to command; and the duty of the child to obey," he insisted. But "parental authority" must be limited, and parents must not "enact arbitrary laws." While they should not be "despotic" to their children, they must also not be "indifferent" or "permit children to do as they please, and to bring them up under the influence of domestic libertinism." While children must obey their parents, "obedience of the child is not that of the servile, trembling subject." This "is not unnatural" and results in *"no infringement upon the rights and liberties of the child"* because "[h]is subordination to the parent is the law of his liberty." Indeed, "he is not free without it."[78] According to Phillips, a home "destitute of reciprocated affection" between parent and child is lacking Christian family values.

Some Christian manualists were more critical of these new Enlightenment views. For example, John Wesley, the father of Methodism, derided Rousseau's *Emile* as "the most empty, silly, injudicious thing that ever a self-conceited infidel wrote." Upon reading Rousseau on matters of education, Wesley harshly commented, surely "a more consummate coxcomb never saw the sun!"[79] Joseph Benson's *Hymns for Children,* collected from the works of John Wesley, included this hymn entitled "Obedience to Parents," to be sung in services and Sunday schools: "Children your parents' will obey, the Lord commands it to be done; and Those that from the precept stray, To misery and ruin run. . . . The disobedient children meet the vengeance of the Lord Most High; His curse pursues their wand'ring feet, And ere they reach their prime, — they die!"[80]

New Protestant Emphases

While early manuals did speak of obedience to the political authorities as an extension of the duty of obedience owed to parents, eighteenth- and nineteenth-century American Protestant household manuals placed increasing stress on

78. Phillips, *The Christian Home,* 213-17, emphases added.

79. John Wesley, "Entry of February 3, 1770," in John Wesley, *Journal and Diaries,* ed. W. Reginald Ward and Richard P. Heitzenrater, in *The Bicentennial Edition of the Works of John Wesley* (Nashville: Abingdon, 1975), 5:214.

80. Joseph Benson, *Hymns for Children* (London: Geo. Story, 1806), 32.

patriotism as a duty of children, especially young men.[81] Samuel Deane's *Four Sermons to Young Men* (1774), for example, instructed young men thus: "It is glorious to love your country. It is fashionable to profess this love. It is necessary that you abound in it, in the present distressed and alarming state of our public affairs. You can in no way so much befriend your country, I am sure, as by your being truly religious."[82] Similarly, Arminus Calvinus's *First Principles of our Religious and Social Duties* (1795) urged young men to esteem and emulate the virtues of love of country, exemplified by President George Washington, so that "future ages know his worth and venerate his memory."[83]

Likewise, while earlier manuals stressed good manners, affections, and recompense toward parents, eighteenth- and nineteenth-century manuals laid increasing stress on a child's charitable duties to others. John Barnard's *Discourses on the Great Concern of Parents and the Important Duty of Children* (1737) urged children to "cultivate and improve their natural disposition to pity and compassion." Charity was to be exercised in "inward affection" by showing love for God and all humanity, but especially to the "church family."[84] Charity also requires outward affection in the form of counseling and relieving the poor. Focusing more on the financial aspects of charity, Henry Dixon's *The English Instructor* (1746) required children to give to the poor as they are able.[85]

Summary and Conclusions

"We must not forget one very important admonition, which should be frequently inculcated to young students; that is, to pray often and fervently to God for his grace to know their vocation."[86] Amidst a litany of instructions, copious "how to's" and multitudes of good-manners books, this simple counsel is the most timeless teaching of the household manuals.

The foundation of a child's Christian vocation is the love of God, most manuals insisted. The child truly loves God by living a life in profound, awe-filled reverence to God. This love for God involves a tenderness of feeling and a deep personal attachment to God that flows from God's power and majesty as

---

81. See, e.g., Arminius Calvinus, *A Catechism Containing the First Principles of Religious and Social Duties* (Boston, 1795), 16.

82. Samuel Deane, *Four Sermons to Young Men* (Salem, 1774), 30.

83. Calvinus, *Catechism*, 18.

84. John Barnard, *Discourses on the Great Concern of Parents and the Natural Duty of Children* (Boston, 1737), 57-58.

85. Henry Dixon, *The English Instructor* (Boston, 1746), 11.

86. *Christian Instructions for Youth*, 252.

the giver and sustainer of life. Love of God, in accordance with the first commandment of the first table of the Decalogue, leads a child to honor of parents, in accordance with the first commandment of the second table. Children are called to obey and respect their parents as a gift of God, to accept their correction and direction in life and learning, to cultivate the habits and manners of Christian living, to offer them recompense and support in their time of need, to accept their counsel in choosing a mate and in preparing for their own vocation in church, state, family, and society.

The child's duty to honor and obey his or her parents also defines the parents' duty to nurture and educate their child. Parents are called to cherish their children as divine gifts who are images both of God and of themselves. They are to protect and support their children in their infancy, to teach them by word and example the norms and habits of the Christian life, to offer them correction and discipline, to prepare them for independence, and to direct them in their marriages and in their Christian vocations as adults.

Though sometimes quaint and idealistic, and occasionally offensive to modern ears, some of the lessons of these historical household manuals still ring true for young men and women struggling to find their direction and vocation in a world of conflicting loyalties and duties. On a practical level, the requirement that children be modestly dressed and primped says much to a culture numbed by the latest designer fashions for children. Cautions about moderation in food and drink provide an important message for a society with nearly half of its children suffering from obesity. The repeated instruction for children to work hard in school and to prepare for a vocation that serves the common good is good counsel for children who neglect or despise their education or parents who treat the school as a convenient child warehouse and daycare center. For the older child, the duty to recompense, care, and honor parents in old age is a valuable lesson as aged parents struggle on social security or live their twilight years lonely and isolated in nursing homes. On a social level, the requirement of parental attentiveness and attention to children alerts parents of the dangers of placing other vocational duties before their principal vocation as a parent.

There is also a hard, but enduring, lesson in the traditional teaching that the duties of love by and for a child are mutually dependent, but not mutually conditional. The manuals make clear that the failure of the parent does not alter the duties of the child to that parent. Indeed, a parent's failure increases, rather than diminishes, the child's duties to irresponsible parents. Children reared by wicked, abusive or drunkard parents, the manuals emphasize, must cover up the faults of their parents and "meekly" admonish them to return to their duties. A Christian child must fulfill her duties to God, including the duty to honor and love her father and mother, even if the parents are undeserving. This traditional teaching goes entirely against modern views that children are less culpable for their personal failures when they suffer from poor parenting. The household manuals call children to rise above poor parenting, to set aside excuses, and to fulfill their duties of love, even when they are hated and despised. Their duty of love to God demands no less. Overcoming child adversity and taking responsibility can be a source of great empowerment. When the child understands that she belongs to God, she also realizes that her vocation belongs to her. Outside forces do not absolve the child of her duty, but they also cannot deprive the child of her vocation.

The rich history in the household manual tradition reminds us of something else that we might be apt to forget in a modern Western world voracious in its appetites for the latest technological innovations. Reading these manuals allows our minds to drift to a historical place where father, mother, son, and daughter taught and learned the Christian traditions together by the soft glow of candlelight at the common dinner table. There is a great benefit to be derived from the familial bonds created by dinner conversations rather than by TV dinners, as several recent social science studies again underscore.[87] The unspoken, unwritten, and invaluable lesson of the household manual tradition lies in how those lessons were transmitted — a direct and loving line of communication between parents and children that requires the sacrifice and commitment of all parties.

---

87. See the summary of recent research on the importance of family table talk by Robyn Fivush, "The Family Narratives Project: Building Strength through Stories" (March 23, 2005). (www.law.emory.edu/cslr/Fivushtext.pdf).

Appendix: List of Sampled Manuals in Order of Publication

John Wyclif, *Of Weddid Men and Wifis and of Here Children Also* (1390)

Kolde, *A Fruitful Mirror* (1470)

Jacque LeGrand, *A Little Book of Good Manners* (1498)

Martin Luther, *The Law, Faith, and Prayer* (1517)

William Harrison, *Condemnations of Matrimony* (1528)

Martin Luther, *Small Catechism* (1529)

Martin Luther, *Large Catechism* (1529)

Richard Whitford, *The Werke for Householders* (1537)

Anonymous, *A Glass for Householders* (1542)

Anonymous, *L'Instruction des Enfans* (1543)

Heinrich Bullinger, *The Christen State of Matrimony* (1546)

John Bradford, *A Letter Sent to Master A.B.* (1548)

Erasmus of Rotterdam, *A Little Book of Good Manners* (1554)

Erasmus of Rotterdam, *The Civility of Childhood* (1560)

Leon Batista Alberti of Florence, *Della Famiglia* (?)

Barthelemy Batt, *The Christian Man's Closet* (1581)

Richard Greenham, *A Godly Exhortation & Fruitful Admonition to Virtuous Parents and Modest Matrons* (1584)

Juan Luis Vives, *Instruction of a Christian Woman* (1585)

Pierre Viret, *The School of Beasts (The Good Householder)* (1585)

Henry Smith, *A Preparative to Marriage* (1591)

Dudley Fenner, *The Order of Household Government* (1592)

Robert Cleaver, *A Godly Form of Household Government* (1598)

Stefano Guazzo, *The Court of Good Counsel* (1607)

William Perkins, *Christian Oeconomie* (1609)

William Phiston, *School of Good Manner* (1609)

Edward Topsell, *The Householder* (1610)

William Martyn, *Youth's Instruction* (1612)

Leonard Wright, *A Display of Duty* (1614)

Robert Crowley, *The School of Virtue . . . Teaching Children and Youths their Duties* (1621)

William Gouge, *Of Domestical Duties* (1622)

Thomas Carter, *Carter's Christian Commonwealth* (1627)

William Lily, *The Fairest Faring for a School-Bred Son* (1630)

Matthew Griffeth, *Bethel: A Form for Families* (1633)

Henry Peacham, *The Complete Gentleman* (1634)

Thomas Ridley, *A View of the Civil and Ecclesiastical Law* (1634)

Baron William Burghley, *Directions for the Well-Ordering and Carriage of a Man's Life* (1636)

Robert Abbott, *A Christian Family Builded by God* (1653)

Thomas Cobbett, *A Fruitful and Useful Discourse Touching the Honor Due from Children to Parents* (1656)

John Horn, *Brief Instructions for Children* (1656)

W.C., *A School of Nurture for Children: The Duty of Children in Honoring their Parents* (1656)

William Smith, *Universal Love* (1668)

Joseph Church, *The Christian's Daily Monitor* (1669)

Owen Stockton, *A Treatise of Family Instruction* (1672)

Peter Du Moulin, *Directions for the Education of a Young Prince till Seven Years of Age* (1673)

R. Mayhew, *The Young Man's Guide to Blessedness* (1677)

Samuel Crossman, *The Whole Duty of Youth* (1678)

Richard Baxter, *Rules & Directions for Family Duties* (1681)

Edward Lawrence, *Parents' Groans over their Wicked Children* (1681)

George Fox, *The State of the Birth, Temporal and Spiritual* (1683)

Anonymous, *True and Faithful Discharge of Relative Duties* (1683)

Henry Swinburne, *A Treatise of Spousals* (1686)

William Smythies, *Advice to Aprprentices and Other Young Persons* (1687)

John Hart, *The School of Grace* (1688)

Bishop Jeremy Taylor, *Judgment Concerning the Power of Parents over their Children* (1690)

John Locke, *Inculcating Self-Discipline* (1690)

Lancelot Addison, *The Christian's Manual in Three Parts* (1691)

John Hawkins, *The English School-master Completed* (1692)

Oliver Heywood, *Advice to an Only Child* (1693)

John Locke, *Some Thoughts Concerning Education* (1693)

James Kirkwood, *A New Family Book (Advice to Parents)* (1693)

James Kirkwood, *Advice to Children* (1693)

Anonymous, *The Infant's Lawyer* (1697)

John Gother, *Instructions for Children* (1698)

Church of England Catechism from Book of Common Prayer (1698)

Cotton Mather, *A Family Well-Ordered* (1699)

Benjamin Wadsworth, *The Well-Ordered Family* (1712)

William Fleetwood, *The Relative Duties of Parents & Children* (1716)

Benjamin Bass, *Parents and Children Advised and Exhorted to their Duty* (1729)

William Cooper, *Serious Exhortations Addressed to Young Men* (1732)

The New England Primer Enlarged (1735)

John Barnard, *Discourses on . . . the Important Duty of Children* (1737)

Henry Dixon, *The English Instructor* (1746)

Jean-Jacques Rousseau, *Emile* (1769)

Samuel Deane, *Four Sermons to Young Men* (1774)

Eleazar Moody, *The School of Good Manners* (1775)

Shippie Townsend, *Practical Essay: Part III — An Inquiry into the case of Children* (1783)

Nathaniel Cotton, *Visions for the Entertainment and Instruction of Young Minds* (1794)

Arminius Calvinus, *A Catechism containing the First Prinsiples of Religious and Social Duties* (1795)

John Willison, *The Mother's Catechism* (1795)

Enos Hitchcock, *The Parents Assistant* (1796)

Enos Weed, *The Educational Directory* (1803)

Joseph Benson, *Hymns for Children* (1806)

W. E. Channing, *Sermon Delivered on Lord's Day* (1812)

Christian Instructions for Youth (1821)

Francis West, *The Responsibilities and Duties of Children of Religious Parents* (1837)

Lydia H. Sigourney, *Do Your Duty to Your Brothers and Sisters in Youth's Magazine* (1837)

Thomas Becon, *The Catechism* (1844)

Mark Trafton, *The Duties and Responsibilities of Young Men* (1845)

Thomas Becon, *The Principles of Christian Religion*

T. S. Arthur, *Advice to Young Men on their Duties and Conduct in Life* (1848)

Henry Bullinger, *The Fifth Precept of the Ten Commandments in Decades of Henry Bullinger, Second Decade* (1849)

Horace Bushnell, *A Milder and Warmer Family Government in Christian Nurture* (1849)

Sara Willis Payton, *Children's Rights in Fern Leaves from Fanny's Portfolio* (1853)

Francis Wayland, *Early Training of Children in The Fireside Miscellany* (1854)

Alfred Beach, *A Sermon Addressed to Parents* (1858)

Samuel Phillips, *The Christian Home* (1860)

Rev. Daniel Wis — , *The Young Man's Counselor* (1865)

Lady Tennessee Celeste Cook, *Constitutional Equality a Right of Woman* (1871)

Robert Speer, *A Young Man's Questions* (1903)

For an overview of this and other English literature, see Chilton Latham Powell, *English Domestic Relations, 148-1653: A Study of Matrimony and Family Life in Theory and Practice as Revealed by the Literature, Law, and History of the Period* (New York: Columbia University Press, 1917).

11. Children, Chores, and Vocation: A Social and Theological Lacuna

Bonnie J. Miller-McLemore

Several years ago on a field trip to a 4-H agricultural center with one of my sons, I listened as a volunteer explained dairy production on a farm years ago to two classrooms of third-grade children. She had an old butter-churn and other tools used to process the milk. Who, she asked, did they think churned the butter? Everyone just stared at her. So she hinted, "Do you have chores?" There was a resounding chorus of "No-o-o" from about fifty eight- and nine-year-olds. No, they did not have chores.

I have recounted this disquieting story before.[1] But until the invitation to explore children's vocation from the editor of this volume, I had not delved deeply into its theological implications. When I heard about the project on the vocation of children, my immediate reaction was surprise. Do children *have* a vocation? I wondered. Shaped powerfully by adult-centric Christian theology, I thought of vocation in strictly adult terms. To what are kids called, without jobs and children of their own?

Such was the narrowness of my initial view of vocation and the depth of my subtle devaluation of children, despite my own efforts to revalue them[2] and to redefine more justly the vocation of women and men.[3] I have argued that the church and Christian theology must include children as knowing agents in more active ways and that women and men must share housework more equally. But I have yet to consider what these claims mean for children's

1. Bonnie J. Miller-McLemore, *Let the Children Come: Reimagining Childhood from a Christian Perspective* (San Francisco: Jossey-Bass, 2003), 2, and *In the Midst of Chaos: Care of Children as Spiritual Practice* (San Francisco: Jossey-Bass, 2006), 60. My historical analysis relies on this previous research.

2. Miller-McLemore, *Let the Children Come* and *In the Midst of Chaos*.

3. Miller-McLemore, *Also a Mother: Work and Family as Theological Dilemma* (Nashville: Abingdon, 1994).

vocation, particularly in the place where they spend lots of time — the home.[4]

I am not alone in this oversight. Few people in either the social sciences or religion have paid much attention to children's domestic role. Although psychologists have a longer history of studying children and have looked at the consequences of work for their development, sociological interest has arisen more slowly. Neither field has consistently included children's work as a factor in family interaction and organization.[5] Coming even later to the table, theologians have not thought much about children in general in the last century, and they have thought even less about children, vocation, and domestic work. Although children's place in the family has changed dramatically in the last century, scholars in Christian theology have not seen this as noteworthy.

That the children on the field trip said no — that they no longer saw themselves as directly responsible for the welfare of their families — may seem like a small matter. But in actuality it exemplifies a sea change of major proportions. In the distribution of farm labor not all that long ago, as the 4-H speaker went on to say, children close to their age churned the butter as one among many chores. They knew their place in the household economy. Most children today no longer do.

What *do* today's children owe their families? Does a child's vocation include assuming a share of the housework or the unpaid labor of maintaining a home and family?[6] This chapter explores the question of children's chores as one dimension of their responsibility within the family and argues that this is not just a psychological or economic concern but also an important matter

---

4. Although children's paid employment also deserves further study, it is beyond the scope of this chapter and worthy of a chapter of its own, distinct from my focus on the dynamics of family life.

5. Lynn K. White and David B. Brinkerhoff, "Children's Work in the Family: Its Significance and Meaning," *Journal of Marriage and the Family* 43 (November 1981): 789, and Jacqueline J. Goodnow and Jeanette A. Lawrence, "Work Contributions to the Family: Developing a Conceptual and Research Framework," *New Directions for Child and Adolescent Development* 94 (Winter 2001): 5. Goodnow and Lawrence observe that children and adult work in the home are seldom seen as interconnected. There are, of course, exceptions to this generalization, such as a study by Frances L. Cogle and Grace E. Tasker, "Children and Housework," *Family Relations* 31 (July 1982): 395-99. Cogle and Tasker conclude, "children are being overlooked as a source of household help" (395-98).

6. For the purposes of this chapter I rely upon a "fairly consistent" definition used in household studies identified by B. A. Shelton and D. John, "The Division of Household Labor," *Annual Review of Sociology* 22 (1996): 300, cited by Scott Coltrane, "Research on Household Labor: Modeling and Measuring the Social Embeddedness of Routine Family Work," *Journal of Marriage and the Family* 62 (November 2000): 1210.

for theology, even if heretofore a huge lacuna. Indeed, theology has something unique to offer. There is a crisis in the domestic place of children that is not just a question of social and economic dislocation but of moral and spiritual displacement. I examine the monumental change in children's domestic status from contributing member to expensive proposition and then reconsider the Christian concept of vocation and its implications. The U.S. middle class in particular has seriously underestimated children's responsibility in the family, just as they have also overindulged in their own individual children. A reinvigorated understanding of vocation that sees children as "useful," not in market terms but in the eyes of God and God's people, offers one possible antidote.

Certainly vocation as a theological term means a great deal more than housework. But when Reformation theologian Martin Luther reclaimed all walks of life as a realm for faith several centuries ago, it did include at least this much. For Luther himself, vocation involved all forms of "bitterness and drudgery" arising from his domestic duty as husband and father.[7] Would the same not be true for baptized children? This is, as it turns out, a tough question. But as costs of having children rise, economic benefits dwindle, and confusion about children's role abounds, it is also a pressing issue.

From Useful to Sheltered Childhood: Changing Historical Constructions

Childhood and adolescence have distinct biological markers. But they are also shaped by social, political, economic, and religious ideals that have changed dramatically from premodern to modern and postmodern times. Among the most striking transformations across these historical periods is children's place in the home. At a young age, premodern children entered into what we would call adult work today. In modernity, such work was gradually redefined as beyond children's capacity. A compelling ideal of an extended childhood free from adult responsibility replaced that of a working childhood. This ideal has begun to fall apart in postmodernity. Young people today are more exposed to adult realities and have more independence and discretionary income than a few decades ago. But they also seem to have "fewer socially valued ways to contribute to their family's well-being" than in previous eras, as historian Steve Mintz observes, even though adults overwhelmed by work and family demands

7. Martin Luther, "The Estate of Marriage," in *Luther's Works*, vol. 45, ed. Walther I. Brandt and Helmut T. Lehmann (Philadelphia: Muhlenberg, 1962), 39.

could use their help.[8] No longer stranded as binary opposites of adults, kids have yet to be welcomed fully back into the fold.

Histories of family and children recount much the same story when it comes to domestic work.[9] Although in premodern and early modern times children remained subordinates in a highly structured, patriarchal family, they had essential roles. As soon as they were old enough, they took their place in family industries, weeding and hoeing gardens, herding domestic animals, carding and spinning wool, making clothing, and caring for younger brothers and sisters. The seventeenth-century American family in general existed as a more cohesive whole, bringing together under one roof the labors of economic production, domestic life, social interaction, and political participation. As family historian John Demos puts it, "[E]ach could appreciate — could *see* — the contributions of the others; and all could feel the underlying framework of reciprocity."[10] Although children may have had to subordinate their interests to family and community needs and submit to the arbitrary authority of harsh fathers or weary mothers, they knew where they stood in relationship to the family's economic welfare.

A similar pattern of work existed elsewhere. In northwestern Europe "as late as the nineteenth century, seventy-five per cent of boys and fifty per cent of girls . . . were in service," reports Joan Acocella in her review of a recent three-volume history of the European family. Boys between the ages of ten and fifteen

---

8. Steven Mintz, *Huck's Raft: A History of American Childhood* (Cambridge: Harvard University Press, 2004), x.

9. See, for example, Mary Cable, *The Little Darlings: A History of Child Rearing in America* (New York: Charles Scribner's Sons, 1972); Carl N. Degler, *At Odds: Women and the Family in America from the Revolution to the Present* (New York: Oxford University Press, 1980); John Demos, *Past, Present, and Personal: The Family and the Life Course in American History* (New York: Oxford University Press, 1985); N. Ray Hiner and Joseph M. Hawes, eds., *Growing Up in America: Children in Historical Perspective* (Urbana and Chicago: University of Illinois Press, 1985); Steven Mintz and Susan Kellogg, *Domestic Revolutions: A Social History of American Family Life* (New York: Free Press, 1988); Stephanie Coontz, *The Social Origin of Private Life: A History of American Families, 1600-1900* (New York: Verso, 1988); Louise A. Tilly and Joan W. Scott, *Women, Work, and Family* (New York: Routledge, 1989); Karin Calvert, *Children in the House: The Material Culture of Early Childhood, 1600-1900* (Boston: Northeastern University Press, 1992); Anne Higonnet, *Pictures of Innocence: The History and Crisis of Ideal Childhood* (New York: Thames and Hudson, 1998); Peter N. Stearns, *Anxious Parents: A History of Modern Childrearing in America* (New York: New York University Press, 2003); and Mintz, *Huck's Raft*. See also Donald Hernandez, with David E. Myers, "Revolutions in Children's Lives," in *Family in Transition*, ed. Arlene S. Skolnick and Jerome H. Skolnick, 10th ed. (New York: Addison-Wesley, 1997), 236-46.

10. Demos, *Past, Present, and Personal*, 10, emphasis in the text. See also his *A Little Commonwealth: Family Life in Plymouth Colony* (New York: Oxford University Press, 1970).

worked as apprentices or farmhands whereas girls served as domestic servants. Even upper-class youths went into service as well, often to "perfect their manners and extend their patronage networks."[11] Domestic work began even earlier. By age seven children on farms tended sheep and gathered firewood, or carded wool and spun cotton if part of a home industry.

With industrialization, children steadily lost their place as contributing members of household economies. This shift occurred more slowly for girls and for working-class and slave children whose labor in textile mills and coal mines or as field and domestic workers initially made it possible for white middle-class mothers and children to retreat to the private realm of the home. But by the middle of the twentieth century, emancipation, mandatory education, and child labor laws had altered domestic life for almost all U.S. children. By and large, as Mintz observes, a "useful childhood" where children helped sustain families and repay "their parents' sacrifices" gave way to a "sheltered childhood, free from labor and devoted to play and education."[12] Instead of workers, children were seen as vulnerable, even delicate, and in need of vigilant care.

Over time, this perceived dependency became more acute in length and nature. Puritan childhood in the 1600s was relatively brief, ending around the age of seven, followed by an extended period of transitional dependency during which young people assumed a variety of responsibilities. Contemporary childhood has doubled or even tripled from seven to fourteen to twenty-one years. At the same time, puberty arrives earlier and creates an odd period of physical maturity in the midst of emotional and social dependence. People express concern about the sexual jeopardy in which this gap between maturity and marriage places young people. But they often overlook the trials of a second gap between physical maturity and finding a place in the world of work.

From Sheltered to Useless Childhood: The Underside of Progress

There is real value in protecting children from inappropriate and inhumane work. Horrendous reports of children's exploitation internationally in factories

---

11. Joan Acocella, "Little People: When Did We Start Treating Children Like Children?" *New Yorker*, August 18-25, 2003, posted at: http://www.newyorker.com/critics/books. She reviews the first two of the three volumes of *The History of the European Family*, ed. David I. Kertzer and Marzio Barbagli: *Family Life in Early Modern Times, 1500-1789* (New Haven: Yale University Press, 2001) and *Family Life in the Nineteenth Century, 1789-1913* (New Haven: Yale University Press, 2002). The final volume appeared after the review, *Family Life in the Twentieth Century* (New Haven: Yale University Press, 2003).

12. Mintz, *Huck's Raft*, viii.

or prostitution, for example, reinforce the positive advances behind child labor laws, compulsory education, and children's rights. Strides have been made in recognizing the humanity of children and securing their safety and advancement.

This should not prevent notice, however, of several disturbing consequences of the revolution in children's economic role: the trivialization of children as "priceless," the expansion of women's domestic work, the ensuing confusion about children's work in the family, the bifurcation of adult work and child play, the view of children as a burden, and ultimately the obsession with one's own child to the exclusion of other children.

Ironically enough, the more productively useless children became in the "real" world, the more emotionally priceless they became in the home, as sociologist Viviana Zelizer documents.[13] Almost as if overcompensating for expelling children from the adult world, debates about the nature and amount of attention adults should lavish on them have raged in the years since industrialization. New social science experts on the intricacies of child rearing, aided by theologians who depicted a mother's love as the epitome of Christian sacrifice, happily offered variations on an answer. Precious children or the "little darlings" (as one child-rearing history is titled) were to be inordinately and unconditionally loved in the private sphere — that is, loved without any limit on parental excess or expectation of return on the child's part.[14]

As this implies, the decrease in children's work ultimately meant an increase in mother's. Exultation of the child "went hand in hand," says historian Carl Degler, "with exalting the domestic role of woman."[15] Or as scholar of American studies Nancy Pottishman Weiss remarks, the "shearing of moral obligations from the child's role accompanies an expansion of maternal moral re-

---

13. Viviana A. Zelizer, *Pricing the Priceless Child: The Changing Social Value of Children* (Princeton: Princeton University Press, 1994). Zelizer sees the development of an emotional pricelessness or sacralization of children as a powerful counterargument to the imperialism of rational choice theorists who essentially contend that the economy rules culture, shaping all its values according to the maximization of utilitarian material value. Instead, she argues that social, moral, and sacred values powerfully shape market views of the child. I use her work but am struck more by the eventual shallowness of children's pricelessness and its subtle transformation into worthlessness. Even though her book is now more than twenty years old, it is still relevant in its grasp of the confusion surrounding children's domestic value and role.

14. Cable, *The Little Darlings,* see especially chapter 5, "Christian Nurture." See also Margaret Lamberts Bendroth, *Growing Up Protestant: Parents, Children, and Mainline Churches* (New Brunswick, N.J.: Rutgers University Press, 2002); Ann Taves, "Mothers and Children and the Legacy of Mid-19th Century American Christianity," *Journal of Religion* 67, no. 2 (April 1987); and Horace Bushnell, *Christian Nurture* (New York: Charles Scribner, 1861; reprint, Eugene, Oreg.: Wipf and Stock, 2000).

15. Degler, *At Odds,* 74.

sponsibility."[16] The less a child owed the family, the greater a mother's obligation. On a pragmatic level, this inverse relationship began innocently enough but over time led to a disproportionate division of labor at the heart of family life. So one study of 1,300 white, two-parent families in 1976 revealed that while mothers on average put in fifty hours of housework a week, children between six and eleven spent three and a half hours.[17] Today these three and a half hours might even be considered a lot by some children.

Resistance to the idea of children as workers has led to the assumption that sharing domestic labor goes inherently against the grain of genuine childhood. Consequently, parents struggle with how to fit children into the household economy. Although a family allowance offers a solution to children's exclusion from the cash economy, even here common child-rearing advice argues against letting it function as a direct payment for chores. That comes too close to giving a child an earned wage.[18] When most U.S. parents assign chores, therefore, they do so for strikingly different reasons than in preindustrial times or developing countries. Household tasks are considered good for children because they cultivate valuable character traits of altruism and reliability or teach skills needed when children grow up. They are something supposedly done out of love or duty and not because families need children's material or financial support. Sometimes, when parents weigh the poorer job, the extra time, and the nagging needed to get "help," they just do the job themselves. The only thing children owe parents is devotion and loyalty, and today even this is sometimes in short supply.

Adults are perplexed not only about children's work but also about children's play. Modern models of play romanticize children's activity and foster a problematic bifurcation between playing children and working adults. This is evident in the avid, often guilt-ridden response provoked by the modern guru of the "hurried" child, psychologist David Elkind, and his widely read book by that name. Now in its second edition, the book warns that parents, schools, and the media have exposed children today to age-inappropriate pressures, forcing them to grow up too fast and robbing them of a natural time of innocence and "pure play." Elkind contends that today children "work much more than they play and this is the reason that they are so stressed."[19]

16. Nancy Pottishman Weiss, "Mother, the Invention of Necessity: Dr. Benjamin Spock's *Baby and Child Care*," in *Growing Up in America*, 292.

17. Kathryn E. Walker and Margaret Woods, *Time Use: A Measure of Household Production of Family Goods and Services* (Washington, D.C.: Center for the Family of the American Home Economics Association, 1976), 38, cited by Zelizer, *Pricing the Priceless Child*, 3.

18. Stearns, *Anxious Parents*, 138; see also Zelizer, *Pricing the Priceless Child*, 103-12.

19. David Elkind, *The Hurried Child: Growing Up Too Fast Too Soon*, rev. ed. (Reading, Mass.: Addison-Wesley, 1988), 198. See also 10-41 and 150-51.

Although it may be true that adults overprogram children's lives and ruin their play with adult-organized activity and aspirations, do children today really "work much more than they play"? How hard do they really work these days? Here Elkind, like many other people, accepts without question the modern construction of childhood as a time of unbridled innocence, carefree play, and sheltered security. Adults not only associate childhood more and more with enjoyment. As historian Peter Stearns argues, they increasingly see themselves as "responsible for providing it."[20] By the mid–twentieth century play had essentially become children's "work," but this pertains most fully to young children, changes as children grow, and includes aspects of work, such as bringing in the groceries or picking up toys. He invites children to consider the nature of work and its odd mixture of toil and enjoyment. Play is an important practice of faith, as I have argued elsewhere, but one best shared generously, even justly, across generations.[21] The nostalgia for a time when "unhurried" children "played" perpetuates a truncated portrait of work, play, childhood, and adulthood. It also reveals a limited understanding of the history of childhood.

One need not look too far to find historical and contemporary exceptions. As Mintz notes in *Huck's Raft: A History of American Childhood,* before author Samuel Clemens left home at age seventeen, he had "worked as a printer's apprentice; clerked in a grocery store, a bookshop, and a drug store; tried his hand at blacksmithing; and delivered newspapers."[22] Herman Melville, author of *Moby Dick,* "worked in his uncle's bank, as a clerk in a hat store, as a teacher, a farm laborer, and a cabin boy on a whaling ship — all before the age of twenty."[23] Mintz does not just cite famous authors. He documents numerous cases of nineteenth-century "laboring children" who went to work in textile mills at age eleven, pulled weeds and protected crops on family farms at age five, separated coal from slate and rocks in mines at age nine, braided leaves into hats in home industries, drove wagons across the western prairie, and taught in frontier schoolhouses at age fifteen. Indeed, the "frontier could not have been settled without children's labor." One Kansas father brags about his two-year-old son who could "fetch up cows out of the stock fields, or oxen, carry in stove wood and climb in the corn crib and feed the hogs and go on errands."[24]

Although industrialization displaced middle-class children from household

20. Stearns, *Anxious Parents,* 191.

21. Miller-McLemore, *Midst of Chaos,* chap. 7.

22. Mintz, *Huck's Raft,* 2.

23. Mintz, *Huck's Raft,* 75. See also chapter 7, "Rich Children, Poor Children," in Cable's *The Little Darlings* for other examples.

24. Mintz, *Huck's Raft,* 150. For detailed depiction of the other examples, see chapter 7, "Laboring Children."

economies, it actually heightened the work of children in laboring classes. Family survival depended on them. It was not until the mid–twentieth century that the ideal of a protected childhood was universalized beyond the middle-class context.[25] Contrary to common assumptions, a long, carefree, idyllic childhood is largely a post–World War II invention that has never applied to all children equally. As author and psychoanalyst Robert Coles reports from his conversations with children from all walks of life, children of migrant workers "take care of one another, pick crops fast, go fetch water and food at the age of two or three and know what size coins or how many dollar bills must be brought home."[26] These are children about whom it might truly be said they work more than they play, more than the middle-class children about whom Elkind and others worry.

In the end, the obsession with childhood as a sanctioned time and space has had a covert and inverse relationship with disinterest in the often-dire situation of less favored children. Less privileged classes and nationalities, especially children in underdeveloped countries, have not lived by this modern construction and at times indirectly suffer the consequences of those who try to uphold it. It might even be argued that the protected, safe, and unproductive play of middle-class children has been largely subsidized by less fortunate children both in the United States and around the world. The heightened pace of middle-class children's extracurricular activities and the billions of dollars in discretionary income available to them contrasts sharply with the lack of opportunities and resources for the large number of children living in poverty.

In this confusion over children's work and play, the view of children as a liability has become increasingly harder to resist. No longer participants in home industries, or farmed out as servants and apprentices and eventually banned from factories, children no longer increase a family's chances of survival but instead drain limited resources. Their position in the family has changed dramatically from asset to burden.

Consequently, calculations of the cost of raising a child have become incredibly common. According to the U.S. Department of Agriculture (USDA), a child born in 2005 and supported until seventeen (that is, not including college) will cost middle-income parents about $190,980 ($250,530 when adjusted for inflation) compared to $25,230 in 1960.[27] Although the USDA began esti-

25. Mintz, *Huck's Raft*, 135.

26. Robert Coles, *Migrants, Sharecroppers, Mountaineers*, vol. 2 of *Children of the Crisis* (Boston: Little, Brown, 1971), 63, cited by Zelizer, *Pricing the Priceless Child*, 214.

27. See "Expenditures on Children by Families," available on the Web at: http://www.cnpp.usda.gov/ExpendituresonChildrenbyFamilies.htm. Costs for 2005 vary according to income with low-income families projected to spend $139,110 (with inflation $182,920) and upper-income families $279,450 ($366,020).

mating costs in 1960 to aid policy decisions about child support and foster care, the figures have inadvertently slipped into common parlance and hyperbole about what it really takes to have kids. Once when I presented some of this material, a colleague waved that day's local paper. An editorial cartoon showed two parents holding a newspaper with the headline: "Cost of Children $233,850." Turning to look at their slouching teenager with headphones and baseball cap on backwards, they remark, "Seems our investment's taken a downturn."

The heightened burden of children also affects those in developing countries. People often presume that in poor countries families need children to contribute to income, and the more the merrier. However, contrary to common understanding, even though children often work hard to support families, their contribution "is not large enough to prevent them [from] becoming an economic burden," as economists Thomas Espenshade and Eva Mueller demonstrate.[28] "Consumption far outweighs production," Mueller says, and the more children the "greater the cost."[29] Even among farm families, children under fifteen cost more to raise than they bring in. This public pricing of children as a major family liability, something foreign less than a century ago, epitomizes the revolution that has occurred in daily life.

From Useless to Useful Childhood: Household Studies

If children are investments and this investment has taken a downturn worldwide, are they ultimately of no worth, particularly children with the least of means? This is a loaded moral and religious question. Surprisingly, in the past two decades social scientists have been more eager to answer it than theologians. Not only history but social science research has begun to call into question the whole idea of childhood as sheltered. It is time, many say, to redeem the useful child.

On first blush, the acceptance of children as "useless" is nowhere more evident than in research on the division of labor in households. Time-use studies almost always focus on adults. One analysis, *Men, Women, and Household Work*, is typical, as the title itself makes clear.[30] The only sustained mention of chil-

28. T. J. Espenshade, "The Value and Cost of Children," *Population Bulletin* 32, no. 1 (1977), cited by "Children Cost More to Raise Than They Contribute through Their Work, Even in Developing Countries," *International Family Planning Digest* 3 (September 1977): 8. Espenshade relies on research conducted by Eva Mueller, an economist at the University of Michigan.

29. "Children Cost More," 8.

30. Jacqueline J. Goodnow and Jennifer M. Bowes, *Men, Women, and Household Work* (Oxford: Oxford University Press, 1994).

dren appears in a brief discussion of how childhood shapes adult domestic arrangements and in brief reference to demands of child care. Children themselves drop out of the picture, except as extra work for parents. They are not seen as contributing members of the household. (It is also interesting to note that from the 1950s through the 1970s most household studies did not pay any explicit attention to the influence of moral and religious factors either and have only recently thought about an expanded consideration of moral discourse — a problem I will come back to in a moment.)[31]

In the past few decades, however, household labor studies have begun to take children more seriously.[32] This research throws fresh light on children and chores, even though social scientists falter when they step into the muddier moral and theological waters of assessing children's responsibility and worth. Canadian sociologist William N. Stephens is a great example. He does not try to hide the agenda that drives his conversations with two hundred children and young people in his 1979 book, *Our Children Should Be Working*. Nonetheless, a review of his "case studies" confirms historical findings about why children's housework has diminished. Fewer live on farms and rural settings. Families work less as a team than they once did. As adults travel to workplaces farther removed from the home, there is less opportunity for the natural "learning-to-work sequence," in which children as young as three years imitate the work of parents and older siblings, adding new tasks as they grow older.[33] New labor-saving devices, such as plumbing, hot and running water, electricity, and central heating, eliminate previous tasks. Children's help may really be less necessary. At the same time, instead of the "low-skill, low-strength, low-responsibility" work that children did in the past, today's jobs are often more complex, demanding, and dangerous.[34] Household standards, even for lawn care, have risen.[35] Meanwhile, children themselves are busier, preoccupied with school projects, extracurricular activities, and other responsibilities.

Stephens's empirical research is driven, however, by a not-so-subtle partiality. Repeatedly he dubs nonworking children "lazy" or "spoiled" and then lavishly praises those he labels "enterprisers" who model discipline and seek out experience, projects, and achievements. Relying on anthropological studies,

31. Coltrane, "Research on Household Labor," 1215.

32. Coltrane, "Research on Household Labor," 1225. See 1225-26 for a more exhaustive overview of the recent literature than I attempt in this section. See also the bibliography in Goodnow and Lawrence, "Work Contributions," 20-22.

33. William N. Stephens, *Our Children Should Be Working* (Springfield, Ill.: Charles C. Thomas, 1979), 77.

34. Stephens, *Our Children*, 37.

35. This final change actually appears in Stearns, *Anxious Parents*, 136.

such as Margaret Mead's *Coming of Age in Samoa* and Beatrice and John Whiting's *Children of Six Cultures,* he speculates that work shapes character. More than this, chores just make kids "all-around nicer": "I think that working at home tends to make children and teenagers easier to live with . . . less demanding, . . . more appreciative. . . . This is merely my impression, and it is a biased impression at that."[36] Behavioral modification is a good means to reinforce helpfulness through praise. Moreover, it is women who need to stay home to modify, reinforce, and train, even if this isolates them. On this problem, he has "no revolutionary proposal."[37] In fact, girls in particular must learn "to step aside or to let others' needs take precedence," a feature "correlated with femaleness," he says, and learned from mothers.[38]

As this example discloses, research that begins with an intriguing premise revaluing children's place in the home can slide down a slippery slope to a moralistic remolding of children along gender-stratified lines to meet adult needs and to supply able laborers for an industrious market economy. A deep ambivalence surrounds children and work in general, running from nostalgia for bygone times when they supported household economies, evident in Stephens, to grave concern about the domestic burden placed on them by women's large-scale return to paid employment or single parenting. Some scholars in the heyday of women's return to work in the 1960s and 1970s even argue that making children do chores is a "sign of rejection."[39] A topic that begins to draw such fundamental and sometimes questionable judgments about human nature and action practically begs for richer moral and theological analysis.

Some studies attempt a more balanced approach. Sociologists Lynn White and David Brinkerhoff, for example, decry the extent to which study of children's work has focused narrowly on its impact on psychological development or its consequences for working women. In a 1982 study, they used telephone interviews with 790 Nebraska parents to learn about not only the extent and kinds of tasks assigned children but also the meaning of this work for the family. Another study done in the early 1980s by an interdisciplinary team of social scientists (Elliot A. Medrich, Judith Roizen, Victor Rubin, and Stuart Buckley) gave children an unusually active voice, inviting them rather than adults to talk about how they used their time outside school, the factors that shaped this use,

---

36. Stephens, *Our Children,* 28-29.

37. Stephens, *Our Children,* 30.

38. Stephens, *Our Children,* 24, 29-30.

39. Prodipto Roy, "Maternal Employment and Adolescent Roles: Rural-Urban Differences," *Marriage and Family Living* 23 (November 1961): 340-49, and D. C. McClelland, *The Achieving Society* (New York: Free Press, 1961), cited by White and Brinkerhoff, "Children's Work," 789.

and its meanings. Chores were one of five time domains, even though on average the 764 children in five neighborhoods of Oakland, California, spent the least amount of time on them.

Both studies state forthrightly that their research is exploratory. Little holistic exploration has been done, and much more needs doing. Contrary to most historical analysis, they contend that children's chores are "ubiquitous," "not so very different" from other historical periods.[40] But they temper such claims. So Medrich et al. admit that "most frequently performed chores took relatively little time," "required little creativity or initiative," and "were not central to the organization of the household."[41] Tellingly, children are "rarely regarded as bona fide workers" in today's economy.[42] They are more often "products, not producers, of domestic work."[43] Children's chores, White and Brinkerhoff offhandedly comment, "probably represent more, rather than less, work for the parent," who must ask questions, supervise, and help.[44] They certainly create a wealth of conflict comparable to the tension between husbands and wives.

Because chores play such a reduced and conflicted role, Medrich et al. confirm that parents are "uncertain as to the significance of these activities."[45] They even wonder how children will acquire a positive understanding of work as a worthy part of adult life.[46] White and Brinkerhoff are more suggestive. They actually design their study to uncover how parents see work as part of life. They characterize four different kinds of rationales or meanings parents assign chores. A *developmental* rationale is the most common: approximately 75 percent of parents interviewed assume "chores are assigned to children for the benefit of the child."[47] Housework "makes them grow into responsible adults," reports a parent of an eight-year-old daughter. In other words, it builds character, as Stephens says.

Three other rationales — what they call *reciprocal obligations, extrinsic learning,* and *task learning* — are less frequently voiced, although they became

---

40. Elliot A. Medrich, Judith Roizen, Victor Rubin, and Stuart Buckley, *The Serious Business of Growing Up: A Study of Children's Lives Outside of School* (Berkeley: University of California Press, 1982), 134, and White and Brinkerhoff, "Children's Work," 797.

41. Medrich, *Serious Business,* 140.

42. Medrich, *Serious Business,* 133.

43. Medrich, *Serious Business,* 144.

44. White and Brinkerhoff, "Children's Work," 792. See also Stearns, *Anxious Parents,* 156-57.

45. Medrich, *Serious Business,* 149.

46. Medrich, *Serious Business,* 157.

47. White and Brinkerhoff, "Children's Work," 796.

more common as children grow older. One parent states flatly and simply that her twelve-year-old son works "because he's a member of the family." Another parent expands this: chores make children "a part of the family." They are "living at home"; they must "share in making it a home." Yet one other parent claims, "A family becomes a family when we all take part and they have to learn that."[48] Finally, children work, parents simply state, because "I need the help" and because children need to learn to do certain tasks — rationales White and Brinkerhoff call *extrinsic* and *task learning.*

Again, as becomes evident on closer inspection, this topic is alive with moral and religious dimensions. As White and Brinkerhoff themselves recognize, adults need help in articulating more clearly the moral and philosophical reasons they expect children to work, especially when parents push beyond the socially acceptable answer that it is good for children to less common answers of duty, obligation, solidarity, and pragmatic value. Society is living, one might say, with outdated ideologies that create confusion and ambivalence about children and housework. Even though the structural realities of domestic organization have changed, public images have been slow to catch up. There is a need to find fresh understandings to replace ideas about children that have become dysfunctional and destructive.

Social scientists are not afraid to forge ahead, even though they tread rather unknowingly on delicate moral and religious ground. The idea of "useful children" is making a "comeback," Zelizer says, despite those like Elkind bent on retrieving a privileged period of unencumbered childhood. At the grass roots and among a pool of psychologists, sociologists, anthropologists, educators, and lawyers, there is a "growing interest in finding innovative ways to include children in the productive life of the community."[49] Indeed, popular magazines, like *Working Mother,* run ahead of scholarship in testing new domestic ground rules about how to share housework. Zelizer herself reports more than advocates, not so much because she does not consider the return of useful childhood a good move but more because of insufficient knowledge about children and what they can do.

Others, like economists David Stern, Sandra Smith, and Fred Doolittle, go a step further. Their research on the changing economic role of children calls into question the "whole idea of childhood as a period of involuntary dependency."[50] This has rendered children "useless, compared to the past." Without the

48. White and Brinkerhoff, "Children's Work," 793.

49. Zelizer, *Pricing the Priceless Child,* 209.

50. David Stern, Sandra Smith, and Fred Doolittle, "How Children Used to Work," *Law and Contemporary Problems* 39 (1975): 115-17.

"chance to be economically useful," they "doubt their own worth." Like Stephens, they conclude their essay with a moral mandate, loaded with assumptions about the nature of children, selfishness, and responsibility: "Why accept the unnatural dichotomy between the role of productive but self-denying adult and the role of self-indulgent but dependent child?" Society needs new institutions, such as schools, in which children can "learn to work in a new way."[51]

As these studies reveal, much more goes on with household chores than meets the eye. White and Brinkerhoff recognize that parents themselves, perhaps inadvertently, slide into and sometimes flounder about in their search for a moral language or a family "ethos" of values and obligations among members. More than 25 percent of the parents "spontaneously used the word 're-sponsibility.'"[52] Even more interesting, the term "responsibility" itself gets used in both a teleological sense as something a child will gain from doing chores ("work gives them a sense of responsibility") and a deontological sense as something a child owes to others ("their responsibility is to help the family").

On closer investigation, the four rationales actually correspond to central ethical categories. The dominant response, that chores benefit and shape the individual child in the long run, resembles both ethical egoist thinking, in which the good is equated with the pursuit of one's own good, and a virtue ethic that supports character-shaping practices or the development of moral character over time through right habits. If pushed to articulate a reason why children should work, most parents and scholars seems to agree: it is good for them. However, other approaches may have equal or even greater importance, even if used less frequently. Parents justify chores as good or right in themselves, a duty or obligation, regardless of consequence, outcome, or some other end goal. They also justify them pragmatically or through a pragmatic ethic that believes value or good will be proven in practice and gained in the very doing of chores.

A deontological rationale powerfully redefines the family away from the narrow role cast by the last few centuries as merely a child-rearing agency back toward a former role as a working unit, deserving greater endorsement today. The view of the family as a working unit has a distant relationship to former theological categories for the family's place in the world as a "little church," as Protestants used to say, or a "domestic church" as Catholics are reconsidering today. The family was seen as a covenant community or an instantiation of God's grace at work in the world. When the family is seen as a working unit or a

---

51. Stern, Smith, and Doolittle, "How Children," 117. See also Arlene Skolnick, *The Intimate Environment* (Boston: Little, Brown, 1978), 331, cited by Zelizer, *Pricing the Priceless Child*, 219.

52. White and Brinkerhoff, "Children's Work," 792.

domestic church, chores in childhood are understood as contributing to family justice and solidarity as well as the common social good. They are, in other words, one piece of a greater whole that includes work, love, and play in fluctuating balance among its members. As Vigen Guroian notes in his chapter in this volume, parents and children exist in a relationship of significant responsibility to one another.[53] In this context, chores gain vocational meaning. Domestic justice and love are vocation worthy of all, a vocation all can embrace. They contribute to communal welfare and they are what each member owes the other.

Likewise, pragmatic rationales of extrinsic need and task learning have their own place of importance. The need for domestic help is genuine and valid, perhaps even more so today as parents struggle to earn a living and care for a home and as the market economy undermines the role and value of children. Children create more domestic work and women more than men still assume responsibility for it. "Women are doing less housework and men are doing slightly more, but the redistribution of household labor has been slower and less profound than anticipated," reports sociologist Scott Coltrane.[54] In fact, the transition to parenthood heightens women's sense of obligation to the home, increases their work, decreases mutual sharing of chores, and increases men's hours on the job. On this score, children imitate fathers more than mothers. As Zelizer observes, they "follow their father's reluctant footsteps . . . increasing only slightly or not at all their participation in household chores."[55] Some studies even indicate that children do less when mothers work outside the home[56] and in single-father families.[57] So the expectation that men and children should assume greater domestic responsibility makes practical and moral sense in the immediate and in the long run. Indeed, as White and Brinkerhoff observe, "working mothers or single parents are more likely to say

53. See Vigen Guroian, "The Office of the Child in the Christian Faith," in this volume, 113-14, 122-24.

54. Coltrane, "Research on Household Labor," 1208. By the late 1980s women's "second shift" had been well documented and publicized by sociologist Arlie Hochschild's landmark 1989 book, *The Second Shift: Working Parents and the Revolution at Home* (New York: Viking Penguin), describing the "extra month of twenty-four hour days a year" women work in the home above and beyond their husbands, regardless of demographic circumstances.

55. William H. Gauger and Kathryn E. Walker, "The Dollar Value of Household Work," *Information Bulletin* 60 (Ithaca: New York State College of Human Ecology, Cornell University, 1977), cited by Zelizer, *Pricing the Priceless Child*, 225.

56. Cogle and Tasker, "Children and Housework," 397. They also cite B. O'Neil, "Children Sharing Household Work," *Human Ecology* 10 (1979): 10, 18-21.

57. Geoffrey L. Greif, "Children and Housework in the Single Father Family," *Family Relations* 34 (1985): 353, 356.

that they ask their children to work because the work needs to be done and they need the help." Medrich et al.'s study also confirms that children of working mothers have a greater range of responsibilities and spend more time doing them.[58] Children whose work is justified only as developmentally beneficial or good for individual children themselves "work the fewest hours."[59] Moreover, according to other research, children's experience in childhood affects the amount and kind of work they assume as adults and how they later divide chores in families.[60]

In short, deontological statements ("you have an obligation") and pragmatic statements ("we need help" and "you need to learn") do not have the current popularity of the more utilitarian rationale ("it's good for you"). But they have greater importance than ever today. These other rationales enrich the standard response in household time-use studies that see children's domestic work as geared toward preparation for entry into the workforce and as beneficial to the child alone. Such emphasis on what is good for individual children and on children's needs and rights often overshadows equally important discussion of children's obligations to the family and domestic need for children's help. Clarifying alternative rationales for household chores is precisely the place where theological argument might confirm children's inherent worth in a life of faith and bolster parental confidence in expecting their fuller participation. In fact, one reason why the idea of vocation has significant potential to enrich our understanding of household labor is precisely because it suggests a richer ethical stance that weaves together teleological, virtue, deontological, and pragmatic rationales for domestic responsibilities as an important aspect of children's lives.

From Useful to Called Childhood: Home and Vocation Reexamined

What *do* today's children owe their families? This topic has been a major lacuna among theologians in the last century. They have not deemed mundane matters like children and housework worthy of much notice. Even in a recent, otherwise outstanding collection, *The Child in Christian Thought*, terms like "chore,"

---

58. Medrich, *Serious Business*, 142.

59. White and Brinkerhoff, "Children's Work," 797.

60. C. A. Thrall, "Who Does What? Role Stereotyping, Children's Work, and Continuity between Generations in the Household Division of Labor," *Human Relations* 31 (March 1978): 249-65, and M. A. Strauss, "Work Roles and Financial Responsibility in the Socialization of Farm, Fringe, and Town Boys," *Rural Sociology* 27 (September 1962): 257-74, cited by White and Brinkerhoff, "Children's Work," 791. See also Goodnow and Bowes, *Men, Women*, 162-64.

"housework," and "work" itself do not appear in the fairly extensive index, even though "play," "instruction," and "vocation" do. When the vocation of children is discussed, it means something rather intangible, like a child's discernment of gifts or a child's witness to God. It does not refer to a child's duties in family life.[61]

Does the Christian idea of vocation have anything to do with children and chores? Does it at least have something to say to a middle class that has seriously underestimated children's responsibility in the family? As important, how might it reframe the work of a growing pool of social scientists ready to reimpose children's usefulness?

Useful Children and the Problem of Market Logic

In the end, social science as empirical descriptive research alone does not have the tools to comprehend the moral and religious consequences of resurrecting a useful childhood. More specifically, it often overlooks a fundamental a priori assumption that colors today's economic climate — the bottom-line assumption that children are investments. All too often, the reclamation of a useful childhood presumes a market definition of "use" as instrumental utility and profit. This threatens to collapse the moral and religious value of children into commercial terms, where they are assessed according to their benefits and achievements.

Market logic has a fundamental problem when it comes to work and children: it tends to reduce everything to cash value. In this schema, as Catholic theologian Todd Whitmore lays out well, one is either a *commodity*, a product of economic exchange, in which one gives oneself to get something else; a *consumer* whose values rests on how much one can purchase; or a *burden*. Children are especially vulnerable because their ability to function as either a commodity or a consumer is limited by their general position outside the economy.

A two-tier division arises between "those who have the wherewithal to produce and consume and those who do not." Children almost unavoidably fall into the camp of those who can do neither and whose worth, in market terms, is negated. When one can neither produce nor consume, one is ultimately a burden. "If persons' only worth derives from their being commodities or consumers,

---

61. Marcia J. Bunge, "Education and the Child in Eighteenth-Century German Pietism: Perspectives from the Work of A. H. Francke," in *The Child in Christian Thought*, ed. Bunge (Grand Rapids: Eerdmans, 2001), 268-70; William Werpehowski, "Reading Karl Barth on Children," in *The Child in Christian Thought*, 393.

then if they are neither of these things," Whitmore argues, "they have no worth at all: they have no intrinsic dignity."[62] Protestant pastoral theologian Joyce Mercer's work on children is driven by a similar concern.[63] But it is not just the global market she decries. Consumption creeps into daily patterns and practices, shaping a way of living, or *habitus,* completely at odds with the Christian life. Indeed, she is less worried about children as burden than children as consumers.

It is at this point that Christian theology serves a distinctive role. A "countervailing understanding" or "alternative narrative" is needed, both Whitmore and Mercer insist. For Whitmore, this means a stronger articulation of religious claims about children as gift, future promise, and obligation, even if there is no developed theology of children comparable to that on subjects such as war:

> Faith implies that children are gifts of creation (as opposed to being commodities), hope suggests that they are the signs of future that extends beyond adult desires (as opposed to being present consumer for the profit of adults), and love illuminates the fact that children are our present responsibility in stewardship (as opposed to burdens).[64]

Mercer also argues for a Christian counternarrative that prizes children not as consumers but as amazingly wonderful creations of God. An "emancipatory theology of childhood" means recognizing them as fully human, whole-yet-broken gifts, and participants in God's realm. Children have the capacity to make God known and to embody a rich nonmaterial divine abundance. Religious traditions and communities, in other words, march to a different economy, an economy of grace, justice, and love that welcomes children regardless of cost, burden, contribution, or achievement.

Useful Children as Called Children

This is good as far as it goes. It just does not go far enough. It ultimately fails to resituate children in the actual institutional economy of family life. There really

---

62. Todd David Whitmore, with Tobias Winright, "Children: An Undeveloped Theme in Catholic Teaching," in *The Challenge of Global Stewardship: Roman Catholic Response,* ed. Maura A. Ryan and Todd David Whitmore (Notre Dame, Ind.: University of Notre Dame Press, 1997), 170.

63. See Joyce Ann Mercer, "The Child as Consumer: A North American Problem of Ambivalence concerning the Spirituality of Childhood in Late Capitalist Consumer Culture," *Sewanee Theological Review* 48 (Christmas 2004): 65-84, and *Welcoming Children: A Practical Theology of Childhood* (St. Louis: Chalice, 2005), especially chapter 3.

64. Whitmore, "Children," 176.

is domestic work to be done. Granted, children have intrinsic worth; so do adults. So who is going to do this work?

Efforts to reclaim children's inherent worth and theological discussions of vocation consistently fail to acknowledge and explore children's role as contributors to family well-being. We certainly must acknowledge the serious problem of mistaking children as a means to another end. But there is still some value hidden in the desire to embrace the idea of useful children and in the impulse to redeem housework, including recognizing and rewarding its contribution to the economy.

Paradoxically, one consequence of children's emotional pricelessness is their economic pricing. Inversely paradoxical, one consequence of the return of economically useful children is their devaluation. In place of both of these social constructions — *children as useless* and *children as useful* — children should once again be considered useful, but not in market terms. They should be seen as useful through a richer articulation of Christian vocation of children as called.

No matter how you look at it, there is something wrong with the picture in my own household, where my husband and I run ragged, washing piles of laundry, sweeping out the garage, stacking groceries, and cleaning the toilet, while our kids play video games. The older my children have grown, the more difficult it has become to determine what they should contribute and how to orchestrate that involvement. Years ago after I asked one of my sons to do some chore, he remarked, "You're the adult. You're supposed to do that; I'm not." It seems that his developing conception of childhood and adulthood, likely shared with many peers, ran something like "you work, I don't." As we have seen, this was not just his personal opinion. It reflects a fairly standard view shared by many today. Adults work. Children play. Once again we hear the theme in yet another key: Shouldn't children work?

One big problem with domestic work that eludes both economic and theological inquiry: it receives no monetary reward and therefore seems without value or use. In a recent *Foxtrot* cartoon the kid says to his mom, "You'd better be paying us for this. If I'm going to waste this week cleaning, I want fair compensation. Just because we're your kids doesn't make us your personal slave labor." "Fine," responds the mom. "I'll pay you what I get paid." Surprised, the kid pauses to think, "She buckled too easily. There must be a catch."

There certainly is a catch, and women have long borne its brunt and reaped its hidden benefits. "What all women have in common," asserts political scientist Hilda Scott, "is that they share most of the unpaid work of the world."[65]

---

65. Hilda Scott, *Working Your Way to the Bottom: The Feminization of Poverty* (London: Pandora, 1984), x.

This unpaid work "underpins the world's economy, yet it is peripheral to the world's economy as men define it, and therefore has no value."[66] This renders women a "category of persons who are economically invisible, whose work is non-work" — and, I would add, whose work is deemed useless.[67] "Why bother to clean out the garage?" asked my son in another interchange. Why change the sheets, dust, vacuum, paint, mow, weed, mulch, or any other sordid task? What is the use of housework? What is the use of children doing it? Housework *is* useful, I find myself insisting. There is usefulness in children doing it.

Children and work must be redefined both economically and theologically. Reframing the relationship between children and chores as part of children's vocation may be one way to do so. Instead of reducing all life to its cost value and rational utility, the concept of vocation distinguishes between the dehumanizing effects of economic price (e.g., in dollars) and sanctity of human worth. But it does so without undermining the usefulness of domestic work as an obligation, a crucial part of formation, and a contribution to the common good to be shared by all. Ultimately work has both economic and spiritual value, and children are useful precisely because they have a vocation as full members of the household of the family and the household of faith.

Onerous Housework as a Christian Calling

"Every person surely has a calling," exclaims Luther in his lecture on Genesis.[68] This includes kings who govern, mothers who tend babies, fathers who earn a livelihood, pupils who apply themselves to studies, and children who honor parents.[69] With these words, he dramatically redefines vocation as part and parcel of a broader theological vision in the sixteenth-century Reformation of the availability of God's grace directly to all and not dependent on the mediation of church authority and its corrupted practices. No longer should Christians distinguish between temporal and spiritual realms because all Christians — priests and laypersons, bishops and farmers, monks and parents — are "truly of the spiritual estate, and there is no difference among them except that of of-

---

66. Scott, *Working Your Way,* x.

67. Scott, *Working Your Way,* x.

68. Martin Luther, "Lectures on Genesis 17:9," in *Luther's Works,* 3:128, cited by Leonard Schulze, "Vocation: The Crux of the Matter," *Journal of Lutheran Ethics* 4 (July 2004), available at: www.elca.org/scriptlib/dcs/jle/article.asp?aid=332. See also D. Michael Bennethum, *Listen! God Is Calling! Luther Speaks of Vocation, Faith, and Work* (Minneapolis: Augsburg Fortress, 2003).

69. Luther, "Lectures on Genesis 17:9," 3:128.

fice."[70] Each person lives out a primary vocation to love God and neighbor within a variety of offices as parent, worker, citizen, friend, student, or spouse. Christian baptism itself reflects this reality, for "we are all consecrated priests through baptism."[71]

In a short essay on children, baptism, and vocation, historian of Christianity Timothy Wengert makes the connection among the three clear. Through baptism, a sacrament whose "chief blessing" is for children, Luther declares children "initiated and sanctified" in the Christian faith.[72] Baptism welcomes everyone to the vocation of priesthood, vanquishing all barriers, including those of age.

Luther's claims about baptism and doctrine of vocation in daily life, including the vocation of children, arose out of his criticism of monasticism. *Vocatio* was a technical term used in the late Middle Ages primarily for the call to the monastic life. But in Luther's hands it became "a word for the day-to-day world in which Christians found themselves." In essence vocation means life in Christ. "See to it first of all that you believe in Christ and are baptized," he said. "Afterward, see to your vocation."[73] Baptism, in short, makes children equal inheritors of Christian vocation. They are no longer spectators of adults or second-class citizens in an adult household or the household of God. "In one stroke," Wengert says, "childhood had become a holy order!"[74]

Most people recognize that Luther challenged celibate life as the primary religious avenue for Christian faith and embraced marriage as an "estate of faith." Fewer notice that he included children and housework in this estate in new ways. The running of a household, he says, is a holy work, capable of becoming an "expression and exercise" of faith.[75] Luther himself said he found God in stinky diapers, adorned as if with jewels! Each tool, broom, rag, mop, iron has God's Word inscribed on it:

> Everywhere you look, it stares at you. Nothing that you handle every day is so tiny that it does not continually tell you this, if you will only listen. Indeed, there is no shortage of preaching. You have so many preachers as you have

70. Luther, "To the Christian Nobility of the German Nation," in *Luther's Works*, 44:127, cited by Schulze, "Vocation."

71. Luther, "To the Christian Nobility," 44:127.

72. Luther, *Luther's Works*, 36:57, cited by Timothy J. Wengert, "Luther on Children: Baptism and the Fourth Commandment," *Dialogue* 37 (Summer 1998): 186.

73. Luther, "Sermon from 1534," in *D. Martin Luthers Werke. Kritische Gesamtausgabe* (Weimar, 1883-), 37:480, cited by Schulze, "Vocation."

74. Wengert, "Luther on Children," 187.

75. Luther, *Luther's Works*, 44:86-87, cited by Wengert, "Luther on Children," 188.

transactions, goods, tools, and other equipment in your home and house. All this is continually crying out to you: "Friend, use me in your relations with your neighbor just as you would want your neighbor to use his property in his relations with you."[76]

Although children's office concerns life as a student and schoolwork, they also have a vocation as family members. In his *Large Catechism,* reworked for publication in 1529, Luther addresses the question of "what a child owes to father and mother" under the general rubric of the fourth commandment, to honor parents. "Is it not a wonderful thing," Luther exclaims, "to be able to boast to yourself, 'If I do my housework faithfully, that is better than the holiness and austere life of all the monks'?"[77] Although in this case he refers to the utterance of a servant girl, it is clear that for all those in the household it is faith alone that "makes a person holy," even or especially faith made evident in domestic labor.[78] In contrast to the devaluation of domestic work in the market economy, Christian vocation embraces it. All work, even the most mundane, has a place in a Christian economy of grace and therefore ultimate economic and spiritual value.

Vocation Reexamined

With the dramatic changes in work, love, and gender in the last few decades, the idea of Christian vocation has come under question once again, provoking a re-examination perhaps as ground shaking as Luther's departure from the cloister several centuries ago. New family structures and egalitarian ideology have created dilemmas of paid work and family responsibility, particularly for women, but not only for them. Many now ask, in Presbyterian theologian Cynthia Rigby's words, just how they can be "called *both* to the vocation of raising children and to other vocations."[79] How can adults pursue their own talents and gifts and not compromise what they owe their children? How can they care for all the details of the household without compromising themselves? Does any of this nonstop work glorify God, the real purpose of Christian vocation?

Given the significant changes in gender roles, it is sometimes easier to spec-

76. Luther, *Luther's Works,* 21:237, cited by Schulze, "Vocation."

77. Luther, "Large Catechism, Ten Commandments," par. 145-47, cited by Wengert, "Luther on Children," 189.

78. Luther, "Large Catechism, Ten Commandments," par. 145-47.

79. Cynthia L. Rigby, "Exploring Our Hesitation: Feminist Theologies and the Nurture of Children," *Theology Today* 56 (January 2000): 540, emphasis added.

ify what vocation is *not* rather than what it is. Theologian Nancy Duff concludes her exploration of vocation by arguing that there are *no* precise definitions of "masculine" and "feminine," *no* set rules for gender roles, and *no* set pattern for the relationship between men and women.[80] Women, as both Duff and Rigby insist, should no longer be forced to choose one vocation to the exclusion of others. Motherhood, Rigby argues, is a vocation that is "equally important to, but not more important than, other vocations to which women are called."[81] Nor, I would add, are men called solely to paid employment. In place of previous stereotypes that *men work* and *women love*, new conceptualizations call for a "future where parenthood and other callings not only co-exist, but mutually enhance one another."[82] In this understanding, *men and women work and love.*

What about children, however? Again, as with household studies, the primary focus has been women, men, and changes in understandings of gender and work. Although theologians subject stereotypes of gender and race to fierce debate, they seldom examine commonly accepted age stereotypes. If previous understandings of the division of household labor were a product of assumptions about the nature of women and men, new assumptions about the nature of children as full members of the household demand fresh understandings of vocation. Christian vocation calls *all people* — men, women, and children — to *work, love, and play.*

Some of what has been said about women and men's vocation can be extended to children. Previous vocational patterns dictating that men work and women love have been based on a "shallow understanding of the relation between work and life," in the words of poet, essayist, and conservationist Wendell Berry.[83] The supposed "choice" between work and family is in fact a falsehood. There is no real choice when distorted ideals and structures of work and family go unquestioned.

A similar kind of claim might be made about the dichotomy between adults and children in domestic responsibility. Just as the vocational polarization of men and women has been destructive to their relationship, so also has the polarization of adults and children worked havoc. Just as men and women's vocation should not be limited and determined by gender, neither should that

---

80. Nancy J. Duff, "Vocation, Motherhood, and Marriage," in *Women, Gender, and Christian Community,* ed. Jane Dempsey Douglass and James F. Kay (Louisville: Westminister John Knox, 1997), 79-80.

81. Rigby, "Exploring Our Hesitation," 553.

82. Rigby, "Exploring Our Hesitation," 553.

83. Wendell Berry, "The Specialization of Poetry," in *Standing by Words* (San Francisco: North Point Press, 1983), 21-22.

of children, even though social science tells us that we assign girls and boys different sorts of chores. If the doctrine of vocation has the capacity to help resolve domestic tensions between men and women, as Duff asserts, perhaps it also has the power to reorient adult-child relationships.

Rather than common assumptions about hierarchy of men over women or equality between men and women, Duff suggests that we understand the vocational division of domestic labor in terms of "reciprocal responsibility." Reciprocal responsibility recognizes differences of "power, needs, gifts, and limitations" and yet "does not assign power to only one person in the relationship." It also suggests that an individual must have "both a centered sense of self as well as the capacity for self-giving."[84] God's call to men and women, fathers and mothers, husbands and wives to reciprocal responsibility has, it seems to me, equally powerful implications for children and adults.[85]

Children's Domestic Work Today

Of course, I am not about to assign a chore and then tell my kids that God calls them to take out the recycling or empty the dishwasher. That would be ludicrous and hypocritical. That said, in the larger scheme of a genuine faith life, caring for the home together is part of a Christian call for everyone in the family, including children.

"What can adults ask of children?" moral theologian Julie Rubio inquires in her retrieval of a Catholic theology of the family.[86] "What would it mean to take them seriously as disciples in their own right?"[87] She asks a fairly radical question here as a broad theoretical matter of faith but also as a pragmatic query about household labor. As Stearns concludes, there is now "little clear definition of what work obligations might remain reasonable" — a situation that has the capacity to breed both conflict and resentment.[88] However, history

---

84. Duff, "Vocation, Motherhood, and Marriage," 78-79.

85. For more on the evolving development of mutuality between adults and children, see "Sloppy Mutuality: Just Love for Children and Adults," in *Mutuality Matters: Faith, Family, and Just Love,* ed. Herbert Anderson, Edward Foley, Bonnie Miller-McLemore, and Robert Schreiter (New York: Sheed and Ward, 2004), 121-35; Miller-McLemore, *Midst of Chaos,* chapters 5 and 6; and Don S. Browning, Bonnie J. Miller-McLemore, Pamela D. Couture, K. Brynolf Lyon, and Robert M. Franklin, *From Culture Wars to Common Ground: Religion and the American Family Debate* (Louisville: Westminster John Knox, 1997), 288-89.

86. Julie Hanlon Rubio, *A Christian Theology of Marriage and Family* (New York: Paulist, 2003), 147.

87. Rubio, *A Christian Theology,* 147.

88. Stearns, *Anxious Parents,* 126. See also 135, 156-57.

does verify that young people are far more "adaptable, resilient, and capable" than contemporary society assumes, as Mintz argues.[89]

That children have family duties and responsibilities is "perhaps the most important insight" gained from the recent claims that children are knowing subjects.[90] Even if children's work begins in a lopsided fashion, with parents giving and children mostly taking, children need family duties, Rubio concludes, "not just because they will learn discipline by doing so, but because through this work they will understand that no one in the home exists just to serve them."[91] They will also see that they are deeply connected to others; that "we are all in this together."[92] Even though her children are still young, she tries to tell them that "we work because we feel called to, not because we need the money, that they have to help because we are a team, not because we cannot do it alone, that we expect a lot of them because they have an obligation to engage in loving service, not because it will teach them to be tough."[93]

Contemporary theological discussion of radical mutuality or just love or shared responsibility in families also inevitably and necessarily demands more of children. "It is within the family," political scientist Susan Moller Okin argues, "that we first come to have that sense of ourselves and our relations with others that is at the root of moral development."[94] The family must be just, she asserts, if we are to have a just society.[95] This cultural redefinition of families not only as a place for love but also as a site of "interpersonal justice" does not rule out genuine acts of sacrifice, affection, and passion but, as philosopher Pauline Kleingeld says, invites the intentional pursuit of "fairness and reciprocity in the recognition of each other's interests" and a "just distribution of benefits and burdens."[96]

Failure to include children in this redefinition is common. But not to include them as fully as possible, with careful consideration for their developmental immaturities and vulnerabilities, underestimates their role in just love and household economics. As Rigby suggests, "Perhaps if we all make sacrifices, mothers will not be forced to choose between perpetually sacrificing or not sac-

---

89. Mintz, *Huck's Raft*, 4.

90. Rubio, *A Christian Theology*, 162-63. She cites my own work in both *From Culture Wars*, 297, and *Also a Mother*, 166:

91. Rubio, *A Christian Theology*, 162-63.

92. Rubio, *A Christian Theology*, 163.

93. Rubio, *A Christian Theology*, 163.

94. Susan Moller Okin, *Justice, Gender, and the Family* (New York: Basic Books, 1989), 14.

95. Okin, *Justice, Gender*, 22.

96. Pauline Kleingeld, "Just Love? Marriage and the Question of Justice," in *Mutuality Matters*, 31.

rificing" at all.[97] Children's participation must be grounded in a dual tension — respect for their agency and awareness of their particular limits.

Years ago I talked about this in terms of a new kind of "pitch-in family," borrowing this phrase from a friend who has expected more of her children in the daily round of family maintenance. For just love to flourish, everyone has to pitch in. "Is not the narrative of the 'pitch-in' family more wholesome than the 'cookies and milk' narrative," I ask, "even if it conjures up images of overt conflicts rather than temporary tranquility? Embodied in this pithy phrase is the idea that given love, children also need daily exercise of the practice of loving others as they love themselves, and this means a family system in which their pitching in is also essential to the family's functioning." This used to mean that "cookies are store-bought, baked at odd hours, or more likely, our kids drag their own stools over to the stove and 'pitch in' . . . to make them, or even the main course."[98] Today, it means asking our kids to take up less appealing chores. Grocery shopping and weeding are not half as much fun as making cookies. But the principle still stands even though it is harder to implement: children need an incremental transfer of power and responsibility for family welfare as appropriate to age and situation.

Rubio makes clear that domestic vocation is not the be-all and end-all. "Families are about more than themselves," she argues.[99] Although she mostly addresses conservative Christians and women caught between home and paid work, this claim should also be extended to children. Christians are disciples of Jesus first and then parents or children. The family is not the "haven in a heartless world" whose demise public intellectuals like Christopher Lasch mourn. For Christians, it is a "community of disciples" whose members are called to "serve one another and the world."[100] Hence no one is called to serve the family as a private concern alone. Everyone has a broader public vocation or calling to contribute to the wider society. This calls into question any definition of vocation that limits the terrain to the home alone. Children are called, like parents, "to be Christians at home *and in the world*."[101]

Sometimes I let my children off easy when it comes to chores and even when it comes to getting a paid job. But when assessed from this perspective, I have valid reason. I find myself saying something like, "If you work hard in school, participate actively in church, and do other significant activities like music, sports, Model UN, then that's your job right now." As Medrich et al. ob-

---

97. Rigby, "Exploring Our Hesitation," 551.
98. Miller-McLemore, *Also a Mother*, 126.
99. Rubio, *A Christian Theology*, 107.
100. Rubio, *A Christian Theology*, 184, 189.
101. Rubio, *A Christian Theology*, 92, emphasis added.

serve, the "exclusion from the world of work came with the arrival of a more re-fined, more prolonged preparation for it" — education.[102] So children are not really "insulated from the world of work," as many people suppose.[103] They simply do not recognize the important work to which children are called. Doing well in school, participating actively in church, and contributing to the wider community — all this is "every bit as tied to the economy" as children's work of the past and, I would add, every bit as important to children's calling as public work is for adults. Children have work. The challenge is to draw the con-nection more clearly.

When I began this chapter, I knew I would be writing my own indictment at various points. Although I have tried not to pamper or indulge my kid, I have not escaped the quandary. If anyone needs theological, spiritual, and moral support to ask more of her children, *c'est moi*. But I suspect I am not alone here in muddling through the hard question of how much to expect of children these days. The sentimental valuation of modern children as "priceless" turned out to be a shallow attempt to compensate for the disconcerting loss of their economic value. Efforts to reinstitute children as useful are an improvement. History and social science remind us that children are not as weak, innocent, or incompetent as the images we inherited. But what does children's new social and religious visibility mean for their domestic role and responsibility? The re-turn of "useful" children raises complicated moral and theological questions about parental exploitation, moralism, and misuse of children.

The notion that children are called does not necessarily avoid such dan-gers. Yet when viewed from the perspective of Christian vocation, children are not an investment or achievement from which one expects a return. They are not slaves to adult bidding. They are a gift that one hopes will flourish. Part of that flourishing involves work, but work of a different sort, done in the best of circumstances for the good of creation and its redemption. Christian theology encourages us to consider children's call to contribute to the common good around them. In the most immediate sense the family constitutes the first expo-sure to a lifelong practice of meeting communal obligations and caring for the common good.

As is true in social science, reflection on chores, children, and vocation is just in its nascent form. There is need for more understanding of work, value, and children. Questions Zelizer raised over two decades ago about what chil-dren can do at different ages in settings that vary by ethnicity, class, or occupa-tion of the parent need more discussion. The jury is also still out on whether a

---

102. Medrich, *Serious Business*, 135.
103. Medrich, *Serious Business*, 135.

reinvigorated understanding of vocation can perform the triple agenda of valuing the intrinsic worth of children and work, while also recognizing the usefulness of children's domestic work. To be successful, a Christian doctrine of vocation must recognize that children are valuable in themselves and not as a means to another end. It must redefine the intrinsic worth of domestic work when understood as part of one's vocation. But finally it must find a solid place to understand work's economic value as a means to an end and to advocate for justice in the fair distribution of this labor among family members. Rather than the divisive segregation of work, love, and play among men, women, and children that taints our history, a Christian conception of vocation invites people to embrace all three as a matter of good faith.

IV. Deciding Who the Child Will Become

12. Who Should Decide What the Child Will Become?

Charles L. Glenn

Each child who grows to adulthood will ultimately determine through countless choices what sort of person he or she will become. Contrary, however, to certain progressive educators who — in the tradition of Jean-Jacques Rousseau — overemphasize the child's autonomy in making such choices, Elmer John Thiessen reminds us that "children learn to be rational by imitation and identification, and these processes are non-rational. Such non-rational initiation should not therefore be condemned as indoctrinatory."[1] And again, "Christian parents are often accused of indoctrinating, but this accusation is misguided because initiation is a necessary part of forming a self. Liberal parents, too, of necessity, initiate their children into a liberal tradition."[2]

To put it bluntly, *someone* will initiate the child into a way of understanding and engaging with the world. I began this inquiry with a reading of a poem by William Butler Yeats ("A Prayer for My Daughter") in which the poet expresses both his fears and his hopes for his infant child, born in a time of civil war in Ireland. In the sixth stanza he prays:

> May she become a flourishing hidden tree
> That all her thoughts may like the linnet be,
> And have no business but dispensing round
> Their magnanimities of sound,
> Nor but in merriment begin a chase,
> Nor but in merriment a quarrel.
> O may she live like some green laurel
> Rooted in one dear perpetual place.

1. Elmer John Thiessen, *Teaching for Commitment: Liberal Education, Indoctrination, and Christian Nurture* (Montreal: McGill-Queen's University Press, 1993), 115.
2. Thiessen, *Teaching for Commitment*, 128.

And he goes on to explain,

> My mind, because the minds that I have loved,
> The sort of beauty that I have approved,
> Prosper but little, has dried up of late,
> Yet knows that to be choked with hate
> May well be of all evil chances chief.
> If there's no hatred in a mind
> Assault and battery of the wind
> Can never tear the linnet from the leaf.
> An intellectual hatred is the worst,
> So let her think opinions are accursed.

Oppressed by the clashing opinions and animosity all around, Yeats asks, for his daughter, that she grow into a woman without such hatred, so that,

> She can, though every face should scowl
> And every windy quarter howl
> Or every bellows burst, be happy still.

Like countless other parents before and since, the poet would have agreed with Jack Coons's celebrated observation that "the opportunity over a span of fifteen or twenty years to attempt the transmission of one's own deepest values to a beloved child provides a unique arena for the creative impulse."[3] For Yeats, those values were intimately bound up with an Anglo-Irish culture that he was determined should be an equal partner with the Celtic-Irish culture of the majority of his fellow citizens of what would become Eire.

But the new nation that was being born through this time of "troubles" would, like its contemporaries around the world, seek to use schooling as a means for transmitting a single basis for national identity and citizenship, in this case the use of the Irish language, which was spoken by a rapidly declining minority of the population. To those who had fought for independence from Britain, "it was held that the schools ought to be the prime agents in the revival of the Irish language and native tradition which it was held were the hallmarks of nationhood and the basis for independent statehood."[4] Proficiency in the Irish language became the primary goal of schooling, even if that required sacrifice of other aspects of the curriculum. The minister of education announced,

---

3. John E. Coons, "Intellectual Liberty and the Schools," *Notre Dame Journal of Law, Ethics and Public Policy* 1 (1985): 495, 511.

4. John Coolahan, *Irish Education: History and Structure* (Dublin: Institute of Public Administration, 1981), 38.

in 1925, that "the chief function of Irish education policy is to conserve and develop Irish nationality."[5] The goal was to make Irish the dominant instructional medium in all schools, beginning with the youngest pupils.

The case of compulsory Irish in schools is a relatively innocent one; after all, at the same period schools in Germany and Italy and the Soviet Union were engaged in the most naked indoctrination. Nevertheless, it is a useful example, since it illustrates the role that is often assigned to formal schooling in societies that are in most respects committed to personal freedoms and are respectful of the rights of parents. Even though Article 42 of the Irish Constitution of 1937 (heavily influenced by Roman Catholic social teaching) "acknowledges that the primary and natural educator of the child is the Family and guarantees to respect the inalienable right and duty of parents to provide . . . for the religious and moral, intellectual, physical and social education of their children," the Irish government could not resist seeking to use formal schooling as an instrument to shape the worldviews and the loyalties of their citizens in ways that many parents — especially the Protestant minority — came to resist.

Famously, the United States Supreme Court declared, in 1925, that "The child is not the mere creature of the state; those who nurture him and direct his destiny have the right, coupled with the high duty, to recognize and prepare him for additional obligations."[6] Those who cite this ringing declaration, however, do not generally pause over the significance of the word "additional." The Court went on, in fact, to stress "the power of the state reasonably to regulate all schools, to inspect, supervise, and examine them, their teachers and pupils; to require that all children of proper age attend some school, that teachers shall be of good moral character and patriotic disposition, that certain studies plainly essential to good citizenship must be taught, and that nothing be taught which is manifestly inimical to the public welfare."

Even in this affirmation of parental rights, then, the responsibility and authority of the state toward children were asserted. The policy challenge in every country that claims to value individual liberty is to find the right balance between educational freedom on the part of parents acting on behalf of their children, and the role of the state in ensuring that every child subject to its authority receives an adequate education, however defined.[7]

This challenge is by no means a new one, although it was not until the nineteenth century that some nation-states developed sufficiently effective ad-

---

5. Sean Farren, *The Politics of Irish Education, 1920-65* (Belfast: Institute of Irish Studies, The Queen's University, 1995), 107.

6. *Pierce v. Society of Sisters*, 268 US 510, 535 (1925).

7. Charles L. Glenn and Jan De Groof, *Balancing Freedom, Autonomy, and Accountability in Education, I-III* (Tilburg, the Netherlands: Wolf Legal Publishing, 2004).

ministration to extend a measure of control over schooling. Thousands of years earlier, however, the authority of the state over education of its people had been asserted by Plato and others. Indeed, Plato's *Republic* has this issue at its heart. The fundamental characteristics of a just society, Plato argued, would be social and political unity and stability, both achieved by eliminating the causes of division. To provide a clean slate on which the legislator could write in the light of the knowledge of the Good alone, and not of any prevailing customs or loyalties,[8] Socrates insists in book 7 that "all those in the city who happen to be older than ten they will send out to the country; and taking over their children, they will rear them — far away from those dispositions they now have from their parents — in their own manners and laws."[9]

Though it would not be until the nineteenth century that any country achieved an approximation of universal elementary schooling, based upon free provision and compulsory attendance, Plato prophetically insisted that, in his ideal city-state, "[c]hildren must not be allowed to attend or not attend school at the whim of their father; as far as possible, education must be compulsory for 'one and all' (as the saying is), because they belong to the state first and their parents second."[10]

Although resolutely anti-utopian, Aristotle also attributed an important role to the state over against families in the education of children. In the *Politics* he urged that "of all the things which I have mentioned that which most contributes to the permanence of constitutions is the adaptation of education to the form of government, and yet in our own day this principle is universally neglected. The best laws, though sanctioned by every citizen of the state, will be of no avail unless the young are trained by habit and education in the spirit of the constitution."[11]

> And since the whole city has one end, it is manifest that education should be one and the same for all, and that it should be public, and not private — not as at present, when every one looks after his own children separately, and gives them separate instruction of the sort which he thinks best; the training in things which are of common interest should be the same for all.[12]

Here Aristotle anticipates the theme, given so much stress by Horace Mann and others, of the "common school" through which — they proposed — the nation

---

8. Plato, *The Republic,* trans. Allan Bloom (New York: Basic Books, 1968), 501a-b.

9. Plato, *Republic* 540e-541a.

10. Plato, *The Laws,* trans. Trevor J. Saunders (New York: Penguin Books, 1970), 293.

11. Aristotle, *Politics,* bk. 5, ch. 9, trans. Benjamin Jowett (New York: Random House, 1943), 1310a.

12. Aristotle, *Politics,* bk. 8, ch. 2, 1337a.

would be bound together and all children come to share a common set of loyalties and dispositions. Aristotle also anticipates the idea that there is a necessary conflict between parental decision-making about education and the paternal role of the state in deciding what is best for them and for the common good.

> Neither must we suppose that any one of the citizens belongs to himself, for they all belong to the state, and are each of them a part of the state, and the care of each part is inseparable from the care of the whole. In this particular as in some others the Lacedaemonians [Spartans] are to be praised, for they take the greatest pains about their children, and make education the business of the state.[13]

This theme reappeared in French political thought in the late eighteenth century, and has been a recurrent refrain in education policy discussions ever since, to such an extent that, as we have seen, the United States Supreme Court felt constrained to point out that "the child is not the mere creature of the State."

Aristotle was enough of a realist, however, to point out that while education should be regulated by law and be an affair of state,[14] there were fundamental disagreements about "what should be the character of this public education. . . . The existing practice is perplexing; no one knows on what principle we should proceed — should the useful in life, or should virtue, or should the higher knowledge be the aim of our training; all three opinions have been entertained. Again, about the means there is no agreement; for different persons, starting with different ideas about the nature of virtue, naturally disagree about the practice of it."[15] Aristotle's prescriptions, like those of Plato, would have to wait for two thousand years before they were realized in public policy. The lack of agreement on both the goals and the means of education, however, defines the scope of education policy debates today.

Education under Christian Auspices

In general, distinctively and self-consciously Christian schooling did not emerge during the centuries when, and in countries where, the Roman Empire survived. Not that teaching was neglected in the churches, even during difficult times. In one of the epistles of Clement, the third or fourth bishop of Rome, written in about A.D. 90, the Christians in Corinth are urged:

13. Aristotle, *Politics*, bk. 8, ch. 2, 1337a.
14. Aristotle, *Politics*, bk. 8, ch. 2, 1337a.
15. Aristotle, *Politics*, bk. 8, ch. 2, 1337a-b.

Let us instruct the young in the fear of God, let us lead our wives to that which is good. . . . Let our children share in the instruction which is in Christ.[16]

The Greek word translated in each case by "instruct" is a form of *paideia*, the evocative word that, as Werner Jaeger has shown, means far more than simple instruction and is a central concept in Hellenic thought. "Education in Christ," while it posited a fundamentally different goal than, for example, that of the Athenian gentleman five centuries earlier, had at least this much in common with the Hellenistic understanding of education, that it was not the same thing as instruction "to perform certain definite external duties" but rather was concerned with the shaping of a life. And it had this in common, as well, that it was not primarily something that was expected to occur in school. "Education in Christ" would occur through the whole life of the local Christian community, including its worship, its charitable activities, its fellowship, as well as its baptismal instruction, since "the early generations of Christians had not worked out any specifically Christian form of education, any more than they had worked out a Christian system of politics."[17]

The "catechesis" provided to new Christians, whether adults or children, was supplemental to the instruction Christian children received (as their families' means allowed) in ordinary schools of the sort that their non-Christian peers attended. "Augustine . . . never proclaimed the need for separate parochial schools. To him and to others, the Roman schools remained sufficient, *if* supplemented by catechizing in the faith."[18] In this respect, "Christians did not follow the example of the Jews who organized their own schools around the study of the Bible, the Mishna, and the Talmud."[19]

On the other hand, we find frequent exhortations to Christian parents to see to the education — in the broader sense of the word — of their children. John Chrysostom (d. 430) advised the faithful to raise their children to care for virtue more than for wealth and honors, and to be more concerned for wisdom than for eloquence, though he was himself famously eloquent.

During the entire period up to the Reformation, there were only scattered examples of what could be called "educational policy," that is, an effort on the

16. Clement of Rome, "First Epistle to the Corinthians," in *The Apostolic Fathers,* vol. 1, trans. Kirsopp Lake (Cambridge: Harvard University Press, 1952), 21:6, 8.

17. Henri-Irénée Marrou, *A History of Education in Antiquity* (New York: Sheed and Ward, 1956), 319.

18. Harvey J. Graff, *The Legacies of Literacy* (Bloomington: Indiana University Press, 1991), 36.

19. John L. Elias, *A History of Christian Education* (Malabar, Fla.: Krieger, 2002), 24.

part of government to promote its goals through the use of schooling. There are, it is true, a few glimmers of such a policy. Charlemagne and other rulers occasionally sought to ensure themselves a supply of trained civil servants through encouraging educational institutions for a tiny elite.

The Reformation of the sixteenth century brought a change in northwestern Europe, though this change did not work itself out fully for three centuries. One of its effects was to make popular schooling a central instrument of religious competition; it was, for example, in those areas of France with a strong Protestant presence that Catholic schooling was most extensively developed.

In Protestant territories, the Lutheran, Anglican, or Reformed church was in effect the handmaiden or domestic chaplain of the government authorities, while in those that remained under Catholic control the position of that church was more clearly autonomous. One of the results, over time, was that the alliance of state and church in Protestant areas, together with a strong emphasis on individual literacy, led to the development of fairly complete systems of popular instruction. There were significant variations, of course: for example, near-universal literacy was achieved in Sweden as an expanded function of local Lutheran parishes.[20]

> Urbanization, commercialization, and industrialization had nothing to do with the process of making the Swedish people perhaps the most literate in the West before the eighteenth century . . . regular personal examination by parish clergy, the church stood above a system rooted in home education . . . piety, civility, orderliness, and military preparedness were the major goals.[21]

In Denmark and Norway (then a single kingdom), by contrast, much the same result was achieved through a network of elementary schools, while in Iceland literacy was nearly universal without schools.[22]

In the Protestant areas of Germany, however, it was a priority of the Reformers to convince governmental authorities to take responsibility for the schooling of all children. Luther argued that parents were generally not competent and could not be expected to educate their children themselves, and that, if the younger generation was sinking ever further into ignorance and uselessness, it was the fault of the municipal authorities, "who have left the young peo-

---

20. Knut Tveit, *Schulische Erziehung in Nordeuropa 1750-1825: Dänemark, Finnland, Island, Norwegen und Schweden, in Revolution des Wissens? Europa und seine Schulen im Zeitalter der Aufklärung (1750-1825)*, ed. Wolfgang Schmale and Nan L. Dodde (Bochum, Germany: Verlag Dr. Dieter Winkler, 1991), 57.

21. Graff, *The Legacies of Literacy*, 13.

22. Tveit, *Schulische Erziehung*, 89, 75.

ple to grow up like saplings in the forest, and have given no thought to their instruction and training."[23] His summons did not pass unheeded; more than a hundred school ordinances were adopted in Protestant cities and territories in Germany during the sixteenth century.

Schooling became a priority in Protestant areas, since each person was expected to read the Bible for himself . . . or herself. Luther advocated for and took steps to establish schools for girls, and, in his sermon "Keeping Children in School" (1530), used especially strong language, even for him: "I maintain that the civil authorities are under obligation to compel the people to send their children to school, especially such as are promising."[24]

The Synod of Dordt in 1618, a sort of Constitutional Convention of the Dutch Reformed Church, stressed that the responsibility for religious instruction of youth was shared among the family, the school, and the church. "Schools, in which the young shall be properly instructed in the principles of Christian doctrine, shall be instituted, not only in cities but also in towns and country places where heretofore none have existed."[25] Magistrates were urged to ensure that "the children of the poor may be gratuitously instructed, and not be excluded from the benefits of the schools."[26]

While it did not cause a system of universal schooling to spring up overnight in the Netherlands or elsewhere, there is ample evidence that the Reformation led to a greater stress upon literacy in place of the limited oral instruction that had previously been the norm in schools serving the children of common people. A study of rural schooling in Utrecht province found that, after the Reformation, the little schools sponsored by local churches began to emphasize reading; previously, the emphasis had been largely upon oral instruction, including liturgical responses and memorization of the catechism. Thus the significant change had to do with the goals of schooling rather than with its availability. While the impetus continued to be from the local church and the ultimate goal continued to be to raise children to be good Christians, the Reformation led to an emphasis upon making the Bible available to everyone through literacy.[27]

23. Martin Luther, "To the Councilmen of All Cities in Germany That They Establish and Maintain Christian Schools," in *Luther's Works*, vol. 45, trans. Albert T. W. Steinhaeuser (Philadelphia: Muhlenberg, 1962), 357.

24. Sol Cohen, *Education in the United States: A Documentary History*, vol. 1 (New York: Random House, 1974), 45.

25. Cohen, *Education*, 59.

26. Cohen, *Education*, 59.

27. Engelina Petronella De Booy, *De Weldaet der Scholen: Het Plattelandsonderwijs in de Provincie Utrecht van 1580 tot het begin der 19de eeuw* (Bilthoven, Germany: Stichtse Historische Reeks, 1977), 37.

Similar activities occurred in those areas under Catholic control that were threatened by Protestantism, though (significantly) not in areas far from the Protestant infection.

> It was the Protestant heresy which democratized writing among the masses
> . . . after the end of the 16th century, Catholics after [the Council of] Trent
> were in agreement with their Protestant rivals: literacy is a universal voca-
> tion. This was the great revolution, separating two epochs. . . . The history of
> mass literacy, like that of the school, has its origins in the conflictual but nev-
> ertheless complicit confrontation of the Reformation and Counter-
> Reformation.[28]

Nor were the initiatives only on the Protestant side. The Catholic Counter-Reformation was in important ways itself an educational movement. The difference was that the Catholic Church itself in most cases was not willing to entrust the oversight, much less the provision, of schooling to government. Although many schools were provided by private initiative, diocesan officials insisted upon supervising them and called upon government only for enforcement of its sanctions. Catholic leaders stressed, at the Fifth Lateran Council (1514), that schools should teach prayers, the creed, hymns, and stories about the saints, suggesting to us that this was not already common practice. Bishops directed their parish priests to instruct parents to send their children to school, and to ensure that schoolteachers "teach their pupils the rudiments of our faith, the understanding of which is absolutely essential for all." After a few Protestant teachers were discovered in Italy, Pope Pius IV issued the bull *In sacrosancta beati Petri* (1564) ordering that all teachers profess their adherence to Catholic doctrine before the local bishop or his representative.

This emphasis on popular schooling on the part of Catholic authorities was a direct response to the new situation created by the Reformation.

> Medieval Christianity had associated without discomfort the theological
> elaboration of the clergy and the nature religion of a peasantry with an oral
> tradition. The very small ecclesiastical and urban elite which had a monop-
> oly on written culture coexisted with a multitude attached to images, rituals,
> and spells. . . . But the Reformation raised for everyone, even the ignorant,
> the problem of doctrine.[29]

---

28. François Furet and Jacques Ozouf, *Lire et écrire: L'alphabétisation des français de Calvin à Jules Ferry* (Paris: Les Éditions de Minuit, 1977), 355, 70.

29. Furet and Ozouf, *Lire et écrire*, 70.

The celebrated archbishop of Milan, Cardinal Carlo Borromeo (1538-84), threw his support behind a lay confraternity that, since 1536, had been mobilizing volunteers to provide part-time "Schools of Christian Doctrine" to teach poor children on Sundays and feast days when they were not working. These programs were an anticipation of the Sunday schools that would be so significant in England and the United States during the nineteenth century. By 1564, about 200 adults were teaching more than 2,000 children in twenty-eight "schools," and in Bologna there were nearly 4,900 children enrolled; there was instruction for girls as well as for boys, although always separately and with women teachers.[30]

The Catholic "internal missionaries" of the Counter-Reformation, like Vincent de Paul, discovered that the peasantry, after more than a thousand years of Christianity, were in fact massively ignorant of even the fundamentals of Christian doctrine; they seemed to know as little as the Hurons and Iroquois of the forests of New France to whom other missionaries were going at the same time.[31]

Several religious congregations were developed specifically to provide education to girls, especially in regions where the competition between Catholics and Protestants was most lively. In contrast with cloistered nuns, who could teach only in convent schools, the new "secular" congregations were organized to provide instruction and social services through parishes. The Ursulines, an order of teaching sisters, was founded in Italy in 1535 and then in France in 1592; in a few years it had schools in Paris (1608) and many smaller cities. The Congregation of Notre-Dame was founded in Lorraine in 1598; Pierre Fourier, the priest who drafted its statutes, pointed out the value of a group of women teaching together, so that the different capacities and levels of pupils could be accommodated in an orderly and efficient way. In addition, he pointed out, such a school could serve to train young women who, though not joining the order, would offer primary instruction in nearby villages. By teaching sewing and other practical skills, the schools operated by the order could attract pupils from poor families for whom more academic instruction was not appealing and thus give these girls training in religion as well as the ability subsequently to earn an honest living.

The Brothers of the Christian Schools, which became the leading order providing elementary instruction without charge to boys, was founded in 1680

---

30. Paul F. Grendler, *Schooling in Renaissance Italy: Literacy and Learning, 1300-1600* (Baltimore: Johns Hopkins University Press, 1989), 333-62.

31. Jean Quéniart, *L'éducation par l'école (1660-1789)*, in François Lebrun, Marc Venard, and Jean Quéniart, *Histoire de l'enseignement et de l'éducation II. De Gutenberg aux Lumières (1480-1789)* (Paris: Perrin, 2003), 395.

by Jean-Baptiste de La Salle (1651-1719). Unlike the earlier orders, this was made up of laymen, though under vows of obedience, stability, and association (later, at the insistence of Rome, changed to poverty, chastity, and obedience). The order established and staffed many schools including, in the nineteenth century, hundreds of French public schools. The founder ordered the Brothers to refuse "money or presents, however small, on any occasion whatsoever."[32] Their emphasis upon simultaneous instruction of classes that could number up to a hundred was an important departure from the prevailing practice of individual teaching of classes of mixed ages and proficiency. Teacher training was a major element in the success of these schools; arguably, the "normal schools" established in France and in the United States in the 1830s and afterward were inspired by the example of the teacher-training institutions of the Brothers of the Christian Schools, as also by the Protestant "teacher seminaries" in Germany.

The effort to compete with Protestantism on — so to speak — its own ground led to what seems to be the earliest mandatory school attendance law, when Louis XIV required Protestant parents to send their children to Catholic schools. Coming to the French throne after a number of decades of intermittent civil war, some of it with religious pretexts, the king's "concern for indivisibility extended to the domain of conscience, disallowing even the division between the interior conviction and exterior conformity."[33]

As he sought to achieve religious unity, Louis XIV turned to compulsory education, legislating for the first time in a field that the monarchy had always before left to the exclusive initiative of the Catholic Church. His officials reported that the Catholic clergy were incapable of converting Protestants, lacking the talent to preach, the arguments to convince, the morality to inspire respect. When, in 1685, the king repealed the Edict of Nantes, which had granted toleration to Protestants, he devoted articles 6 and 7 of the Edict of Fontainebleau to ensuring that "private schools for their instruction" could not continue and that Protestant parents, on pain of a very large fine, would raise their children "in the Catholic, Apostolic, and Roman religion." A royal decree provided for the appointment of Catholic guardians for Protestant children.[34] "It was thus with the intention of stamping out heresy and not that of raising the cultural level of the nation that the State intervened through law, in a com-

32. Richard Arnandez, *Primary Education in France in the Time of Jean Baptist de La Salle,* in *So Favored by Grace: Education in the Time of John Baptist de La Salle,* ed. Lawrence J. Colhocker (Romeoville, Ill.: Lasallian Publications, 1991), 141.

33. Dale K. Van Kley, *The Religious Origins of the French Revolution: From Calvin to the Civil Constitution, 1560-1791* (New Haven: Yale University Press, 1996), 39.

34. Janine Garrisson, *L'Édit de Nantes et sa révocation* (Paris: Éditions du Seuil, 1985), 12, 195.

pletely unprecedented fashion, in the organization and expansion of primary schools, while moreover leaving all the financial burden upon communities."[35]

It is significant that what was probably the first effective measure of compulsory school attendance was specifically aimed at turning children against the religious beliefs of their parents.

The State as Educator

While in most Protestant territories through the nineteenth century schooling was provided through cooperation between government and the churches, in Catholic Europe the development of a state role in education was a direct challenge to the previous authority of the Catholic Church and was so perceived by both its advocates and its opponents.

The Enlightenment of the eighteenth century was a time of intense discussion about the potential of education to reshape humanity. To European intellectuals influenced by Locke and Condillac, "it was self-evident that man was the product of his environment — of nature and the institutions under which he lived — and that by reshaping his environment in accord with the invariable and determinable laws of nature, his material and spiritual regeneration might be speedily accomplished."[36] Education, Helvétius contended in *A Treatise on Man,* can accomplish anything, both good and evil, if we think of it in the broadest possible terms: "'everyone, if I may say so, has for teachers both the form of government under which he lives, and his friends and mistresses, and the people about him, and the books he reads, and, finally, chance. . . .' The legislator is therefore a pedagogue, a moralist; morality and legislation are 'one and the same science.'"[37] With the right education it would be possible "to produce at will men of genius, or, at least, men of talent."[38] Unlimited possibilities for remaking humanity are created by the recognition that "education makes us what we are. . . . The philosopher therefore perceives, at a greater or less distance, the time when power will adopt the plan of instruction presented by wisdom; and let him, animated by this hope, endeavour in the meantime to under-

35. Bernard Grosperrin, *Les petites écoles sous l'Ancien Régime* (Rennes: Ouest France, 1984), 18.

36. Carl L. Becker, *The Heavenly City of the Eighteenth-Century Philosophers* (New Haven: Yale University Press, 1932), 138.

37. Elie Halévy, *The Growth of Philosophic Radicalism,* trans. Mary Morris (Boston: Beacon Press, 1955), 20.

38. Gabriel Compayré, *The History of Pedagogy,* trans. W. H. Payne (Boston: D. C. Heath, 1901), 328.

mine those prejudices that oppose the execution of his plan."[39] Similarly, Helvétius's ally Holbach insisted that those who guided human affairs, including educators, are like "gardeners who can by varying systems of cultivation alter the character of men as they would alter the form of trees."[40]

The English utilitarian Jeremy Bentham (1748-1832), reflecting the influence of Helvétius, claimed that

> if one could find a method of becoming master of everything which might happen to a certain number of men, to arrange everything around them so as to produce on them the impression that one wishes to produce, to make sure of their actions, of their connections, and of all the circumstances of their lives, so that nothing could escape, nor could oppose the desired effect, it cannot be doubted that a method of this kind would be a very powerful and a very useful instrument which governments might apply to various objects of the utmost importance.

"The passage is so rich," Professor Eric Voegelin notes, "that it could serve as the text for a sermon of book length."[41]

A century after Locke, Immanuel Kant would observe, as an obvious truth requiring no justification, that "Man can only become man by education. He is merely what education makes of him."[42] Here we are near the origins (though it had been anticipated by Plato) of the idea of the "make-ability" of human beings and of society that we will see come to its full expression in totalitarian schemes of indoctrination in the twentieth century; at its heart is a denial that there is any such thing as an essential or "normal" human nature that should not be violated, and a conviction that a totally fresh start can be made by stripping away all the "prejudices" (of which traditional religious faith was considered the most harmful) acquired from parents and from the prevailing culture.

Inspired by this confidence, Morelly urged, in his *Code of Nature* (1755), that "at the age of five children shall be taken from their parents and educated communally at government expense and on uniform lines."[43] Du Pont de

39. Louis I. Bredvold, *The Brave New World of the Enlightenment* (Ann Arbor: University of Michigan Press, 1961), 107-8.

40. Bredvold, *The Brave New World,* 112.

41. Eric Voegelin, *From Enlightenment to Revolution,* ed. John H. Hallowell (Durham, N.C.: Duke University Press, 1975), 60.

42. Immanuel Kant, *Education,* trans. Annette Churton (Ann Arbor: University of Michigan Press, 1960), 6.

43. Alexis de Tocqueville, *The Old Regime and the French Revolution,* trans. Stuart Gilbert (Garden City, N.Y.: Doubleday, 1955), 164.

Nemours promised the king that the educational reforms he was proposing would totally transform the nation, make it "unrecognizable" in ten years.[44]

In the same spirit, Breton parliamentarian Louis-René de La Chalotais, having helped to engineer the suppression of Jesuit education in France, wrote (in 1763), "I make bold to demand for the Nation an education that will depend upon the State alone; because it belongs essentially to it, because every nation has an inalienable and undeniable right to instruct its members, and finally because the children of the State should be educated by members of the State."[45]

Of more lasting influence was Jean-Jacques Rousseau. In his *Discourse on Political Economy* (1755), Rousseau insisted that education had a major part to play in the maintenance of political authority, since

> that government which confines itself to mere obedience will find difficulty in getting itself obeyed. If it is good to know how to deal with men as they are, it is much better to make them what there is need that they should be. The most absolute authority is that which penetrates a man's inmost being, and concerns itself no less with his will than with his actions. It is certain that all peoples become in the long run what the government makes them. . . . Make men, therefore, if you would command men. . . . If you would have the general will accomplished, bring all the particular wills into conformity with it; . . . establish the reign of virtue.[46]

Rousseau's phrase "the reign of virtue" came to have a sinister connotation during the radical phase of the French Revolution, when his name was frequently invoked as the authority for purging society of all those considered to have a corrupting influence and as the model of Republican virtue and the prophet of a society in which there would be no classes or divisions but only the most perfect unity in obedience to the General Will.

In his 1755 discourse, written as an article for the *Encyclopédie*, Rousseau placed great stress on education under state direction as essential to a sound political system.

> To form citizens is not the work of a day; and in order to have men it is necessary to educate them when they are children. . . . government ought the less indiscriminately to abandon to the intelligence and patriotism and preju-

44. Grosperrin, *Les petites écoles,* 24.

45. Bernard Lehembre, *Naissance de l'école moderne: Les textes fondamentaux 1791-1804* (Paris: Nathan, 1989) 12-13.

46. Jean-Jacques Rousseau, *The Social Contract and The Discourses,* trans. G. D. H. Cole (New York: Everyman's Library, 1993), 139-40.

dices of fathers the education of their children, as that education is of still greater importance to the State than to the fathers. . . . public education . . . under regulations prescribed by the government, and under magistrates established by the Sovereign, is one of the fundamental rules of popular or legitimate government.[47]

Through such a system of education, Rousseau argued, the future citizen could be taught "to will nothing contrary to the will of society."[48] So important was this instrument of government, subordinated to "the Magistrates destined to preside over such an education," that it should be considered "certainly the most important business of the State."[49]

The same emphasis upon education as an instrument of government marks Rousseau's most influential political writing, *The Social Contract:*

He who dares to undertake the making of a people's institutions ought to feel himself capable, so to speak, of changing human nature, of transforming each individual, who is by himself a complete and solitary whole, into part of a greater whole from which he in a manner receives his life and being; of altering man's constitution for the purpose of strengthening it. . . . He must, in a word, take away from man his own resources and give him instead new ones alien to him, and incapable of being made use of without the help of other men. . . . each citizen is nothing and can do nothing without the rest.[50]

The French Revolution gave an impetus to the implementation of such ideas . . . at least on paper, in an outpouring of essays and reports. As the Revolution took a radical turn, extreme claims were made for the authority of the state over the formation of children. Jacques-Nicolas Billaud-Varenne, an ally of Robespierre, wrote in his *Elements of Republicanism* (1793), a publication consisting "largely of paraphrases of the *Contrat social* and elaborations of Rousseau's arguments": "You will lose the younger generation by abandoning it to parents with prejudices and ignorance who give it the defective tint which they have themselves. Therefore, let the fatherland take hold of children who are born for it alone and let it begin by plunging them into the Styx, like Achilles."[51] No doubt he had in mind the image used by Rousseau as a frontispiece for *Emile.*

47. Rousseau, *The Social Contract*, 147-49.
48. Rousseau, *The Social Contract*, 149.
49. Rousseau, *The Social Contract*, 149.
50. Rousseau, *The Social Contract*, 213.
51. Carol Blum, *Rousseau and the Republic of Virtue: The Language of Politics in the French Revolution* (Ithaca, N.Y.: Cornell University Press, 1986), 183.

Robespierre himself told the National Convention, the same year, "I confess that what has been said up until now does not correspond to the idea I have formed for myself of a complete plan for education. . . . I am convinced of the necessity of operating a total regeneration, and, if I may express myself in this way, of creating a new people."[52] Blum comments that "Robespierre was invoking a state that would create the citizens it desired, not one that would accommodate those it had."[53] Similarly, radical leader Danton told the National Convention that

> It is time to reestablish the grand principle, which seems too much misunderstood, that children belong to the Republic more than they do to their parents. . . . We must say to parents: We are not snatching them away from you, your children, but you may not withhold them from the influence of the nation. And what can the interests of an individual matter to us beside national interests? It is in national schools that children must suck republican milk. The Republic is one and indivisible; public instruction must also be related to this center of unity.[54]

The logic of this explicitly political use of schooling on behalf of the state, inspired in part by Plutarch's famous account of ancient Sparta as well as by Rousseau, was worked out in detail by Michel Lepelletier de Saint-Fargeau. "Never," he wrote, "in elementary schools will we be able to find other than imperfect instruction. Their radical fault is that they take hold of only a few hours and abandon all the others. . . . In the public institution [which he proposed], by contrast, the entire existence of the child belongs to us; the material, if I may put it this way, never comes out of the mold . . . between the ages of five and twelve."[55]

Lepelletier's proposal was presented to the National Convention by Robespierre in July 1793. The plan would have removed all children from their families between the ages of five and twelve (eleven for girls), placing them in common schools where they would receive "an education truly national, truly republican," under close supervision "every day, every moment" to ensure that they would form the correct attitudes and habits.[56] They would all, whatever the social class of their parents, wear the same clothing, eat the same food, receive the same instruction and care.

---

52. Blum, *Rousseau*, 193.

53. Blum, *Rousseau*, 242.

54. Victor Pierre, *L'école sous la Révolution française* (Paris: Librairie de la Societé Bibliographique, 1881), 70f.

55. Dominique Julia, *Les trois couleurs du tableau noir: La Révolution* (Paris: Belin, 1981).

56. Lehembre, *Naissance de l'école moderne*, 65-72.

Thus, Lepelletier and Robespierre claimed, "will be formed a new race, laborious, regulated, disciplined, one which an impenetrable barrier will separate from the impure contact with our obsolete species."[57] Similarly, Robespierre's ally Saint-Just proposed, in his notes for a book on "republican institutions," that boys be educated from age five to sixteen by the State, and that "they will not return to their parents' home until age 21." "Children belong to their mother," he wrote, "until age five, if she has nursed them, and to the Republic subsequently as long as they live."[58] Municipal authorities in Paris proclaimed, in 1798, that "our children will be republicans . . . they will be orators," and reported proudly that "already the young pupils are no longer taken to mass or to other religious ceremonies, already (finally) elementary books have entirely chased away the books of superstition in most schools."[59]

Constant recourse to legislation can be an indication of serious problems with implementation. Those who sought to implement the radical program of popular education were continually frustrated both by teachers and by parents. Those teachers who were "patriots" were too often incompetent, while the more experienced teachers tended to be former members of the abolished religious orders and could not be trusted to teach pure republican morality. Parents seemed to prefer the old instruction of Catholic catechism and Bible stories, often refusing to send their children to the republican schools. They had little interest in the sort of neo-Spartan education recommended by Lepelletier, Robespierre, and Saint-Just.[60] There is considerable evidence that the condition of popular education actually worsened after the adoption of the educational program of the Revolution. Alternative private schools flourished, often with teachers who had taught in church-sponsored schools before they were abolished. In the Seine, in 1798, there were an estimated two thousand private schools but only fifty-six public primary schools.[61] In many other communities, only those schools that did not use the prescribed books had fee-paying students, so we hear again complaints that the "culpable prosperity" of private schools "seems to grow as a result of the perversity of the principles which youth receive there."[62]

---

57. Blum, *Rousseau*, 186.

58. Saint-Just, *Théorie politique*, ed. Alain Liénard (Paris: Éditions du Seuil, 1976), 265-66.

59. A. Aulard, ed., *Paris pendant la Réaction Thermidorienne et sous le Directoire: Receuil de documents*, vol. 5 (Paris: Maison Quantin, 1903), 168f., 273f.

60. Furet and Ozouf, *Lire et écrire*, 99.

61. A. Aulard, ed., *Paris pendant la Réaction*, vol. 4, 348. See also Maurice Gontard, *L'enseignement primaire en France de la Révolution à la Loi Guizot (1789-1833)* (Paris: Société d'édition Les Belles Lettres, 1959), 163.

62. E. Allain, *L'oeuvre scolaire de la Révolution, 1789-1802* (New York: Burt Franklin, 1969), 101.

The revolutionary program was a failure, but its underlying premise, that the child belongs to the state rather than to his or her family, would continue to be an element of radical and utopian proposals down to the present day. Nor was it long before the idea was introduced into the United States. In the Workingmen's Associations that flourished in the 1820s and 1830s, some leaders urged that children should be taken away from their parents at age two and educated by the state in order to eliminate inherited class distinctions. In a set of *Essays on Public Education* first published in 1830, the authors "proposed a national system of boarding schools for all children aged two to sixteen, designed to eliminate the unequal influence of family wealth and culture."[63] Under this proposed system, "parents interested in maintaining contact with their children would be allowed occasional visits, but were to have neither control nor supervision over their nurture."[64]

While American voters, in general, were not impressed with the claim that state-run schools could eliminate social class distinctions, they were more responsive to the warning that only a public school monopoly could respond adequately to the threat posed by the massive immigration of German and Irish Catholics in the 1840s and beyond. The intellectual climate that placed such confidence in the redeeming capacity of public schools had been created, over the previous decade, by James Carter, Horace Mann, and others, who had asked (adapting evangelical vocabulary to their purposes):

> How shall the rising generation be brought under purer moral influences [so that] when they become men, they will surpass their predecessors, both in the soundness of their speculations and in the rectitude of their practice? . . . The same nature by which the parents sank into error and sin, preadapts the children to follow in the course of ancestral degeneracy. Still, are there not moral means for the renovation of mankind, which have never yet been applied?[65]

The question had already been answered in his previous annual report. "How many are there of those, who swarm in our cities, and who are scattered throughout our hundreds of towns," he had asked rhetorically, "who, save in the public schools, receive no religious instruction? They hear it not from the

---

63. Carl E. Kaestle, *Pillars of the Republic: Common Schools and American Society, 1780-1860* (New York: Hill and Wang, 1983), 144.

64. Edward J. Power, *Religion and the Public Schools in Nineteenth Century America: The Contribution of Orestes A. Brownson* (New York: Paulist, 1996), 70.

65. Horace Mann, *Ninth Annual Report of the Secretary of the Board* (Boston: Dutton and Wentworth, 1846), 64-65.

lips of an ignorant and a vicious parent. They receive it not at the sabbath-school, or from the pulpit. And if in the Common School, the impulses of their souls are not awakened and directed by judicious religious instruction, they will grow up, active in error, and fertile in crime."[66]

In his first annual report as secretary of the Massachusetts Board of Education, Mann wrote that

> Amongst any people, sufficiently advanced in intelligence to perceive that hereditary opinions on religious subjects [that is, the beliefs of parents] are not always coincident with truth, it cannot be overlooked, that the tendency of the private school system is to assimilate our modes of education to those of England, where churchmen and dissenters . . . maintain separate schools, in which children are taught, from their tenderest years, to wield the sword of polemics with fatal dexterity; and where the gospel, instead of being a temple of peace, is converted into an armory of deadly weapons, for social, interminable warfare. Of such disastrous consequences, there is but one remedy and one preventive. It is the elevation of the common schools.[67]

Of course, he was wrong about England, where the maintenance, to this day, of publicly funded schools of various denominations has been accompanied by a high degree of secularization rather than by religious conflict.

Commenting on Horace Mann's initiatives to extend the state role, Catholic convert Orestes Brownson argued that "the more exclusively the whole matter of the school is brought under the control of the families specially interested in it, the more efficient will the school be. . . . Government is not in this country, and cannot be, the educator of the people. In education, as in religion, we must rely mainly on the voluntary system. . . . Government here must be restricted to material interests and forbidden to concern itself with what belongs to the spiritual culture of the community. It has of right no control over our opinions, literary, moral, political, philosophical, or religious. Its province is to reflect, not to lead, nor to create the general will. It, therefore, must not be installed the educator of the people."[68]

From this perspective, the issue was not one of free thought against orthodoxy but of resistance to the imposition of a new sort of orthodoxy, which de-

---

66. Horace Mann, *Eighth Annual Report of the Secretary of the Board* (Boston: Dutton and Wentworth, 1845), 16-17.

67. Horace Mann, *First Annual Report of the Secretary of the Board* (Boston: Dutton and Wentworth, 1838), 56.

68. R. Freeman Butts, *Public Education in the United States: From Revolution to Reform* (New York: Holt, Rinehart and Winston, 1978), 86-87.

nied a right to provide schooling based upon religious views — whether Protestant or Catholic — differing from those promoted by a liberal elite. Thus Frederick Packard, in one of a series of attacks upon Horace Mann and the Massachusetts Board of Education for its refusal to approve the books of the American Sunday School Union for use in the common schools, wrote, "we protest against the interference of the government with the matter and manner of instruction, and especially against annexing any condition to its grants, that shall affect in the slightest degree the independence of the whole district or of the teacher whom they employ — and least of all on the subject of religious instruction."[69] Hodge, Packard, and others were not calling for a state-imposed orthodoxy in public schools but for local freedom to provide orthodox religious instruction in those areas where that reflected the desires of parents. Ironically, this was a central aspect of the Prussian system that its American admirers chose to overlook; Prussian schools were explicitly Protestant or Catholic depending upon the local population.

The efforts of Mann and other promoters of the state role in education were greatly assisted by a sort of panic over the effects of Catholic immigration. A group of educators in Ohio expressed, in 1836, their concern with the "vast tide of immigration, yearly flowing in upon us, from all nations."[70] The only answer was "to take their children . . . and educate them in the same schools with our own, and thus *amalgamate them* with our community."[71] In 1851, an editorial in the *Massachusetts Teacher* complained that

> Our chief difficulty is with the Irish. The Germans, who are next in numbers, will give us no trouble. . . . But the poor Irish, the down-trodden, priest-ridden of centuries, come to us in another shape. . . . In too many instances the parents are unfit guardians of their own children. If left to their direction the young will be brought up in idle, dissolute, vagrant habits, which will make them worse members of society than their parents are. . . . the children must be gathered up and forced into school, and those who resist or impede this plan, whether parents or priests, must be held accountable and punished.[72]

It was in large part in response to the apparent threat posed by so many Catholic immigrants that, in Boston, New York, Philadelphia, and other cities,

69. Frederick Packard, "Religious Instruction in Common Schools," *Princeton Review* 13 (July 1841): 367.

70. Sol Cohen, *Education in the United States: A Documentary History*, vol. 2 (New York: Random House, 1974), 991.

71. Cohen, *Education*, 991.

72. Cohen, *Education*, 996-97.

systems of public schooling were put in place intended to forestall the creation, by immigrants, of Catholic schools. This had not been the original impetus for "charity schools," nor were denominational initiatives to create schools seen as dangerous, so long as the denominations were Protestant. In New York, for example, when the Free School Society was founded, in 1805, its concern was to supplement the educational work of churches through "extending the means of education to such poor children as do not belong to, or are not provided for by, any religious society."

At first the Free School Society by no means had a monopoly on education of poor children, or on the state funds for that purpose. Funds appropriated by New York State for the schooling of poor children, under laws enacted in 1795 and 1813, were granted directly to private and church-run charity schools in New York City. But then Bethel Baptist Church opened a school for poor children of all faiths and, having obtained a portion of the common school fund, was able to open others, and other churches followed the example and established nondenominational charity schools. Stung by this competition, the Free School Society, renamed the Public School Society in 1826, took the position that it should have a monopoly on state funding.

Far from reducing "sectarian" tensions, the enhanced role of the renamed Public School Society would lead to bitter conflict with the growing Catholic population of New York City. Catholic parents complained that the Society's schools had a bad effect on their children, "that they become intractable, disobedient, and even contemptuous toward their parents — unwilling to learn anything of religion — as if they had become illuminated, and could receive all the knowledge of religion necessary for them by instinct or inspiration."[73] The "controlling influence" on these schools, the parents charged, was that of Quakers.[74]

Supporting the concerns of Catholics, New York Secretary of State John Spencer argued, in 1841, that "in a country where the great body of our fellow-citizens recognize the fundamental truths of Christianity, public sentiment would be shocked by the attempt to exclude all instruction of a religious nature from the public schools; and that any plan or schema of education, in which no reference whatever was had to moral principle founded on these truths, would be abandoned by all." Citing the First Amendment, Spencer argued that government had wisely abstained "from all legislation whatever on those subjects . . . connected with religious faith, profession, or instruction" by leaving it up to

73. Daniel Calhoun, *The Educating of Americans: A Documentary History* (Boston: Houghton Mifflin, 1969), 162.
74. Calhoun, *The Educating of Americans,* 162.

local communities to decide how religion would be treated in their schools. Thus "each district suits itself, by having such religious instruction in its school as is congenial to the opinions of its inhabitants." As a result, "the records of this department have been searched in vain for an instance of a complaint of any abuse of this authority, in any of the schools" outside New York City. In a religiously diverse city like New York, however, finding a form of religious instruction that would satisfy all the different groups was impossible, and

> even the moderate degree of religious instruction which the Public School Society imparts must, therefore, be sectarian; that is, it must favor one set of opinions in opposition to another, or others; and it is believed that this always will be the result in any course of education that the wit of man can devise. . . . If that Society had charge of the children of one denomination only, there would be no difficulty. It is because it embraces children of all denominations, and seeks to supply to them all a species of instruction which is adapted only to a part, and which, from its nature, cannot be molded to suit the views of all, that it fails, and ever must fail, to give satisfaction on a subject of all others the most vital and the most exciting.[75]

The position of the Public School Society, Spencer charged, also "calls for no action or cooperation on the part of those parents, other than the entire submission of their children to the government and guidance of others, probably strangers, and who are in no way accountable to these parents."[76] The only solution was to leave "the degree and kind" of religious instruction to the choice of parents in small homogeneous communities, in the city as in small towns. According to Spencer, "If it was the will of the people to have religious training in the public schools, then so be it."[77] Consistent with this prescription, the state legislature enacted, in 1842, a system of ward schools in New York City, managed by locally elected school boards as in smaller communities across the state, under the financial supervision of a city-wide elected Board of Education. Under this arrangement, local ward committees were responsible for overseeing schools in their districts and could adjust their program to local and parental sensibilities. Spencer predicted that competition among the new school districts in New York City would improve school quality, since the funds would be allocated on the basis of enrollment.[78] "The Public School Society

75. Calhoun, *The Educating of Americans,* 166-67.

76. Diane Ravitch, *The Great School Wars: New York City, 1805-1973* (New York: Basic Books, 1974), 63.

77. Ravitch, *The Great School Wars,* 63.

78. Ravitch, *The Great School Wars,* 64.

continued to receive public money for its existing schools" but, in 1853, turned over its remaining schools to the Board.[79]

As in New York, where the Public School Society recommended that poor parents who failed to send their children to its schools be denied public assistance, those who saw schooling as the primary instrument for turning the children of immigrants into Americans often called for making that schooling compulsory. The example of Prussia was frequently used to illustrate what could be accomplished by a state-run system of compulsory schooling. American voters, however, generally rejected such measures as extreme, and Massachusetts was the only state to adopt a compulsory schooling law — not effectively enforced — until after the Civil War. In the Pennsylvania Constitutional Convention of 1873, for example, former state superintendent Charles A. Black opposed an amendment giving the legislature authority to make schooling compulsory: "I can think of no measure," he said, "that could be presented to the people of the State which would be more unpopular. . . . The people claim the right, and they have the right, to regulate this matter for themselves, and we have no right to interfere with their prerogative. They claim the right to send their children to school or not, and the case of monarchical Prussia is no example for them."[80] As late as 1881 Pennsylvania Superintendent of Public Instruction E. E. Higbee expressed his "very serious misgivings as to the propriety of any strictly compulsory law."[81]

This insistence upon parental and local rights lies behind the resistance Horace Mann experienced (though he and generations of historians have chosen to interpret it as the last gasps of religious obscurantism), and explains why, despite his efforts and those of his allies, American education continued to be largely a local affair well into the twentieth century. Protestant theologian Charles Hodge, in 1846, saw clearly that the issue of the content of religious instruction in schools was tied to a structural issue.

> What right has the State, a majority of the people, or a mere clique, which in fact commonly control such matters, to say what shall be taught in schools which the people sustain? What more right have they to say that no religion shall be taught, than they have to say that popery shall be taught? Or what right have the people in one part, to control the wishes and convictions of those of another part of a state as to the education of their own children? If the people of a particular district choose to have a school in which the West-

79. Calhoun, *The Educating of Americans,* 143.

80. *Debates of the Convention to Amend the Constitution of Pennsylvania,* vol. 7 (Harrisburg: Benjamin Singerly, State Printer, 1873), 691.

81. Forest Chester Ensign, *Compulsory School Attendance and Child Labor* (1921; reprint, New York: Arno Press and The New York Times, 1969), 177.

minster or the Heidelberg catechism is taught, we cannot see on what principle of religious liberty, the state has a right to interfere and say it shall not be done; if you teach your religion, you shall not draw your own money from the public fund? This appears to us a strange doctrine in a free country . . . unjust and tyrannical, as well as infidel in its whole tendency.[82]

In most European countries (Prussia being the most notable exception) the resistance to state control of popular schooling continued throughout the nineteenth century. This was most evident in countries and provinces where the Catholic Church was strong, but it was also true in England, the Netherlands, and other predominantly Protestant countries. Even the totalitarian regimes of the twentieth century did not in every case establish a state monopoly of schooling: while that was the case in Germany and the Soviet Union, in Mussolini's Italy, Franco's Spain, and Vichy France the regimes did not choose to seek to extend effective control over the Catholic schools, which educated a significant proportion of children.

Replacing Parents

In my historical study *The Myth of the Common School* (1988), I traced the debates over whether the state should use popular schooling as a means of achieving, in Guizot's phrase, "a certain government of minds." Continuing investigation of this issue, however, has convinced me that I was missing a crucial element in the process by which parents more and more lost control over the education of their children. It was not a naked seizure of control by government — along the lines of what occurred in Bolshevik Russia or Nazi Germany — but a subtle and gradual imposition of a set of ideas that undermined parental authority in education.

To understand this process, it is fundamental to make a distinction, clear in the Romance languages but not so clear in English, between "instruction" (teaching knowledge and skills) and "education" (formation of character and worldview). Perhaps this can best be done by contrasting two representatives of the eighteenth-century French Enlightenment, Condorcet and Rousseau.

"Public instruction," Condorcet wrote in his *Cinq mémoires sur l'instruction publique* (1790), "is a duty of society toward citizens."[83] His use of the word

---

82. Charles Hodge, "The General Assembly, Parochial Schools," *Princeton Review* 18 (July, 1846): 439.

83. Condorcet, *Cinq mémoires sur l'instruction publique,* ed. Charles Coutel and Catherine Kintzler (Paris: Flammarion, 1994), 61-68.

"instruction" was deliberate, since he was convinced that *education* was the responsibility of families and not of the state; that government should be restricted to ensuring that adequate instruction was provided to everyone, to girls as well as to boys. As a matter of fundamental justice, "it will be important to have a form of public instruction which does not allow any talent to escape from notice, and which offers it all the help now reserved to the children of the rich."[84] After all, "the laws may declare equality of rights, but only institutions for public instruction can make that equality real."[85] So government's role in relation to schooling was to ensure justice and equal opportunity, not to use schools to impose particular loyalties and perspectives.

Rousseau, by contrast, insisted in his fictional account of how he would educate Emile from infancy to adulthood, that he would demand that the boy's parents surrender all authority to him; Emile "ought to honor his parents, but he ought to obey only me. That is my first or, rather, my sole condition."[86] And the parents are never mentioned again. Emile is not to be instructed — indeed, he is not even taught to read — but *educated,* shaped into a personality type chosen by his tutor on philosophical grounds. He will learn science to some limited extent by unsystematic observation, history, literature, revealed (as contrasted with "natural") religion not at all; "I hate books," Rousseau, the prolific author, tells us.

Rousseau, Allan Bloom points out, "is at the source of the tradition which replaces virtue and vice as the causes of a man's being good or bad, happy or miserable, with such pairs of opposites as sincere/insincere, authentic/inauthentic, inner-directed/other-directed, real self/alienated self."[87] Emile may not know anything as he approaches adulthood, but he will be sincere and indifferent to the opinions of others; only thus will he be authentic.

While the educational method described by Rousseau in *Emile* is intended to create a "man" rather than a "citizen," it anticipates in at least one important way the education for and by the state proposed by the radical legislators during the Revolution: the denial of authority or influence to parents. Influenced by Rousseau, Kant would express his concern that, in current practice, "the child is called upon to obey the teacher's rule, and at the same time to follow his parents' whims. The only way out of this difficulty is for the parents to surrender the whole of their authority to the tutor."[88] From this it was only a step to

84. Condorcet, *Cinq mémoires sur l'instruction publique,* 78.
85. Condorcet, *Cinq mémoires sur l'instruction publique,* 96-104.
86. Jean-Jacques Rousseau, *Emile; or, On Education,* trans. Allan Bloom (New York: Basic Books, 1979), 53.
87. Allan Bloom, introduction to *Emile; or, On Education,* 4.
88. Kant, *Education,* 25.

positing a necessary conflict between educators, concerned to teach the shared values of the Republic — or of humanity — and the narrow perspectives and loyalties of the family. This idea would have a long and significant history, down to the American John Dewey (like Rousseau and Horace Mann, a Calvinist who lost his faith in God and replaced it with Education) and beyond.

The Common School Crusade of the antebellum period was in a sense the first stage in the development of a self-conscious education profession with its own goals and ways of understanding society and human nature, a profession often out of step with parents and indeed with elected officials and many rank-and-file teachers but never lacking confidence that it held the key to a brighter future. "The history of education bills in the state legislatures indicates that even though the idea of public education commanded support and won some victories . . . that support was always limited and qualified so that the overall results were inconsistent and piecemeal. . . . no legislature adopted the idea that children belonged to the state rather than their parents."[89]

The source of the idea that the state — and thus its schools — had ultimate authority over the shaping of children, in fact, emerged from this nascent profession of "educators" rather than from political leadership or popular demand. It was consistent with this view that it was the Wisconsin Teachers' Association, and not elected officials, who declared in 1865 that "children are the property of the state."[90]

This view gained force with the continued emergence of education as a profession. Unlike in other professions, teachers did not gain status individually, but there was a compensating exaltation of the dignity and almost transcendent significance of the mission of education. According to William Heard Kilpatrick, John Dewey, and other education progressives, by the early twentieth century the decline of rural life, the family, and the local community left it up to the school to "provide for the child what the family is not providing."[91]

You will mostly look in vain, in the indices of the many books by Dewey, for references to "family" or "parent" or "mother" or "father," but it seems very likely that families as well as churches and other traditional sources of meaning and authority are among the "social habits and institutions" that are to be "reconstructed" in order to create a "democratic society" to Dewey's taste. Thus in his article "Impressions of Soviet Russia, IV: What Are the Russian Schools Doing?" (1928), Dewey wrote that, in Russia, "the great task of the school is to

89. Richard D. Brown, *The Strength of a People: The Idea of an Informed Citizenry in America, 1650-1870* (Chapel Hill: University of North Carolina Press, 1996), 98.

90. Kaestle, *Pillars of the Republic,* 158.

91. John A. Beineke, *And There Were Giants in the Land: The Life of William Heard Kilpatrick* (New York: Peter Lang, 1998), 107, 140.

counteract and transform those domestic and neighborhood tendencies that are still so strong, even in a nominally collectivistic regime."[92] After all, he told his American readers, "to anyone who looks at the matter cold-bloodedly, free from sentimental associations clustering about the historic family institution, a most interesting sociological experimentation is taking place, the effect of which should do something to determine how far the bonds that hold the traditional family together are intrinsic and how far due to extraneous causes; and how far the family in its accustomed form is a truly socializing agency and how far a breeder of non-social interests."[93] Implicitly accepting the latter assumption, Dewey noted how the Soviet authorities had promoted "the role of the schools in building up forces and factors whose natural effect is to undermine the importance and uniqueness of family life,"[94] and observed with apparent approval that "we have here a striking exemplification of the conscious and systematic utilization of the school in behalf of a definite social policy."[95]

Dewey and other influential educational theorists concluded that the crisis had called into question all the institutions of the economy, society (including families and churches), and the political order, and that schools — if appropriately guided by "social engineers" — could play a decisive role in shaping their replacement. In the article "Can Education Share in Social Reconstruction?" (1934), Dewey insisted that

> the schools will surely, as a matter of fact and not of ideal, share in the building of the social order of the future according as they ally themselves with this or that movement of existing social forces. This fact is inevitable . . . according as teachers and administrators align themselves with the older so-called "individualistic" ideals — which in fact are fatal to individuality for the many — or with the newer forces making for social control of economic forces . . . the teacher will . . . not be content with generalities about the desired future order. The task is to translate the desired ideal over into the conduct of the detail of the school in administration, instruction, and subject-matter.[96]

If it were simply a matter of making the instructional process more interesting and engaging, of course, there would have been few opponents; the real

92. John Dewey, *Impressions of Soviet Russia, IV: What Are the Russian Schools Doing?* in *The Later Works, Volume 3: 1927-1928*, ed. Jo Ann Boydston (Carbondale: Southern Illinois University Press, 1984), 228.
93. Dewey, *Impressions of Soviet Russia*, 230.
94. Dewey, *Impressions of Soviet Russia*, 230.
95. Dewey, *Impressions of Soviet Russia*, 231.
96. John Dewey, *Can Education Share in Social Reconstruction?* in *The Later Works, Volume 9: 1933-1934*, ed. Jo Ann Boydston (Carbondale: Southern Illinois University Press, 1986), 207-8.

difficulty was that "Kilpatrickism is *not* a method for making traditional learning more enjoyable; it is a substitution of new educational aims for those which are understood by many parents as the usual aims of a school."[97] These aims were nothing less than a profound transformation of society through developing, in its children, a fundamentally different way of understanding and interacting with the world.

Progressive educators in the 1920s and 1930s "never doubted that they — not parents, not local school boards, not teachers — should decide what should be taught in the nation's public schools, and to which group of children."[98] Above all, "the progressive education movement wanted to make education into a profession. It wanted to curb the influence of laymen, especially in poor and immigrant neighborhoods, in decision making about the schools."[99] Increasingly, parents were pushed to the margins and often persuaded that they had no competence to guide the education of their children. "Today our schoolman," Mortimer Smith wrote just after World War II, "with his determination to educate 'the whole child' finds the home and parents simply embarrassments to the accomplishment of his purpose."[100]

This was recently illustrated by a survey of "teachers of teachers," professors in teacher-training institutions. Seventy-nine percent of the 900 professors surveyed agreed that "the general public has outmoded and mistaken beliefs about what good teaching means," and communication with parents was considered important, not to learn what parents wanted for the education of their children, but so they could be "educated or reeducated about how learning ought to happen in today's classroom."[101]

The professors of education surveyed were convinced, for example, that "the intellectual process of searching and struggling to learn is far more important . . . than whether or not students ultimately master a particular set of facts."[102] Sixty percent of them called for less memorization in classrooms, with one professor in Boston insisting that it was "politically dangerous . . . when students have to memorize and spout back."[103] By contrast, according to another study by the same public-interest organization, "eighty-six percent of the

97. Albert Lynd, *Quackery in the Public Schools* (Boston: Little, Brown, 1953), 246.

98. Diane Ravitch, *Left Back: A Century of Failed School Reforms* (New York: Simon and Schuster, 2000), 163.

99. Ravitch, *Left Back*, 54.

100. Mortimer Smith, *And Madly Teach* (Chicago: Henry Regnery, 1949), 36.

101. Steve Farkas and Jean Johnson, *Different Drummers: How Teachers of Teachers View Public Education* (New York: Public Agenda, 1997), 15-16.

102. Farkas and Johnson, *Different Drummers*, 10.

103. Farkas and Johnson, *Different Drummers*, 13.

public, and 73% of teachers, want students to memorize the multiplication tables and do math by hand before using calculators."[104]

Arguably, the greatest challenge today for educational policy is to find a
way to rebuild the confidence that should exist between parents and the schools
to which they entrust their children. It is difficult to see how this can be accomplished so long as the prevailing orthodoxy among educators is that parents
and what parents want for their children are a large part of the problem they
face.

Sociologists of education have frequently pointed out that teachers often
feel very vulnerable to the criticisms of parents, and expect school administrators to back them against parents on all occasions. It is certainly true that parents may have a distorted sense of what has actually occurred in the classroom,
or of their own children's effort and behavior. In conferences about problems
that have arisen, they may be as defensive as are the teachers they are supposedly collaborating with. Sometimes one wishes that there were a recognized
profession, parallel to that of marriage counselors, of school/home mediators.
These tensions can arise even when teachers and parents share the same religious views, the same convictions about right and wrong, the same concept of
what is required for human flourishing.

But the problems are much deeper when parents are compelled, by law or
by economic necessity, to send their children to schools whose mission they
cannot in conscience support, schools that operate on the basis of an understanding of the nature of a life well-lived that differs in important ways from
that held by the parents. When such differences "go all the way down," it is understandable that parents would be reluctant to entrust their children to
schools that threaten to undermine what they have spent years of anxious effort
to achieve in the lives and character of those children.

And there is another sort of harm done under those circumstances: schools
that cannot count on the wholehearted support of parents are unlikely to possess the sort of focus that allows them to be effective. Teachers engage in "defensive teaching," what has been called "the bland leading the bland." The curriculum is emptied of any material that might cause controversy so that many
history textbooks neglect almost entirely the role of religion in American life.

American schools have become unfocused and too often unable to engage
their students; Laurence Steinberg's *Beyond the Classroom* is a good brief account of the realities, though insufficiently penetrating about their causes. In a
free society whose government is not able — at least in most respects — to seek
to indoctrinate its young citizens, it is difficult to see how lowest-common-

104. Farkas and Johnson, *Different Drummers,* 19.

denominator public schools can in fact be coherent, can stand for something. The same issue has arisen in the Netherlands, where two-thirds of the pupils attend nonpublic schools that are free to have a distinctive *richting,* or focus, while public schools struggle to find a basis for a comparable distinctiveness.

In fact, both the effectiveness of schools and respect for the central role of parents in the education of their children would be served by a consistent implementation of educational freedom, within the context of public policies designed to ensure equal access to a diverse spectrum of good schools. This is not the place to spell out how that can best be done; the forty national educational systems discussed in our book *Balancing Freedom, Autonomy, and Accountability in Education* (2004), soon to be supplemented with a fourth volume adding twelve to fifteen countries, give a sense of how many different ways there are to address this challenge. Each has its strengths and weaknesses. The fundamental conclusion of that study, however, is that almost all Western democracies have concluded that only a system permitting choice of schools at no or little expense to parents is consistent with freedom and with justice.

Much as I and many others believe in the virtues of well-designed parental choice, however, we should not delude ourselves into believing that this will automatically overcome the gulf created by the prevalent attitude among many educators. Of course teachers have competencies that many parents lack, of course teachers often see a side of their pupils, even gifts their pupils possess, that parents may fail to perceive. These are reasons why the role of teachers is deserving of high respect, and why it would be well to help many of them be less defensive in relation to parents, and vice versa.

But the deeper issue is to challenge the assumption on the part of the teaching profession qua profession, by no means shared by every individual teacher, that attributes to educators the role of transforming society through their influence on children, and resents fiercely any challenge to that influence. No true partnership with parents can develop without modesty about the teacher's role and its limits. That role is a noble calling, but it should be exercised without illusions and without pretensions.

13. Soul for Soul — the Vocation of the Child in Lasallian Pedagogy

George Van Grieken, F.S.C.

"The end of the Institute is to give a Christian education to children."[1] Since its foundation, the Brothers of the Christian Schools[2] have aimed their educational ministry toward children. The educational principles and practices that emerged from this tradition are ones that have stood the test of time through 325 years of daily experience in the classroom.

To speak today of the "vocation" of the child is to immediately endow childhood with a dignity and an incipient but substantial decision-making potential that would be readily recognized by anyone associated with the educational tradition of John Baptist De La Salle and the educational movement he created. From the time the movement began in 1680 with a small tuition-free parish school for poor boys in Reims, France, up to this very day when there are some thousand schools in eighty-two countries teaching over 900,000 students, the consistent thread and the unfailing motivation of the teaching encounter have revolved around the daily recognition of the dignity of each student along with the conviction that each student grows by exercising his or her ability to make and act on choices small and large. In other words, children by definition

---

1. The entire paragraph from the 1705 Rule of the Brothers of the Christian Schools reads: "The purpose of this Institute is to give a Christian education to children, and it is for this purpose the Brothers conduct schools, that having the children under their guidance from morning until evening, these teachers may be able to teach them to live a good life by instructing them in the mysteries of our religion and inspiring them with Christian maxims, and so give them a suitable education." John Baptist De La Salle, *Rule and Foundational Documents* (Landover, Md.: Christian Brothers Conference, 2002), 14. Note that the word "Christian" on a practical level meant "Catholic" in seventeenth-century France.

2. The congregation is also known more popularly as Christian Brothers, or De La Salle Brothers, or De La Salle Christian Brothers (the last to distinguish them from the Congregation of Christian Brothers, formerly known as the Irish Christian Brothers).

are growing into their vocation for living, and the school is one privileged and formative context for doing so.

Although the notion of a child's vocation has been part of the lifeblood of our particular educational heritage for over three centuries, this tradition — called a "Lasallian" tradition in honor of its founder — has consistently remained somewhat under the radar when it comes to the larger educational world. Few seem to be aware of the foundational perspectives and influential writings of De La Salle, or the role that his writings and heritage played in the formation of the various teaching congregations that others founded in the eighteenth and nineteenth centuries. The Roman Catholic Church highlighted his role in education when, in 1950 on the fiftieth anniversary of his canonization, he was declared the patron saint of all teachers of youth,[3] and his statue — posed in company with a student — stands in the main nave of St. Peter's in Rome. Judging from the experience of the last twenty years, once educators of all stripes are exposed to the writings of De La Salle and the practices these writings shaped, they are uniformly captured by the same genuine, caring, and professional spirit that continues to inspire more teachers today than ever before.[4]

De La Salle and His Context

De La Salle grew up in the second half of the seventeenth century. This was the age of King Louis XIV, the "Sun King," who ruled France with an iron, if clever, fist. It was an age when social standing, good manners, benefices, political intrigue, and grand living were the rule. And that was just in the church. The state had all of this, plus it was engaged in one war after another, taxed the populace as much as it could tolerate, followed a system of governance and justice that had as many exceptions as it had applications, and for a time built up France's status to that of a "superpower."

France had a well-established school system geared mostly for the nonpoor, consisting of schools, colleges, and universities run by religious orders, secular priests, and lay professors. Education in France was under church control, essentially religious in content, inspiration, and direction. The bishop

---

3. Pius XII declared him the special patron of all teachers of youth on May 15, 1950. Br. Athanase Emile, F.S.C., *Circular No. 331* (Rome: Teachers of the Christian Schools, 1950), 13-16.

4. One testament to the enduring character of De La Salle's educational movement consists in the variety of formational programs that continue to flourish. Among these in the United States are the three-year Buttimer Institute of Lasallian Studies that studies his life, pedagogy, and spirituality, and the Lasallian Leadership Institute geared toward developing educational leaders in the schools.

was the local superintendent of public instruction, acting through an appointed superintendent of schools who saw mainly to the financial concerns of the individual teachers under his patronage.[5]

By the time De La Salle became involved in primary education in 1680, primary schools were plentiful, although widely divergent in style and quality.[6] Without intending to, nor actually really wanting to, De La Salle, as a newly ordained priest with a Ph.D. in theology and a very bright future in the church ahead of him, gradually became involved with a dedicated layman from Rouen who was determined to start schools for poor boys in Reims. De La Salle helped him become established in a local parish, and then gave some advice and help with the first teachers that were recruited. Retreats followed, regular school visits, meals at his home, and finally an invitation to have the teachers come and live with him. What had started out as pure charity turned into a life's vocation.[7] As he wrote later in his life:

5. The Council of Trent (1545-63) had mandated free parish schools (on the primary level) for the poor, establishing the parish priest as the new authority overseeing the religious instruction and schooling of the poor. In response to the Council of Trent's mandate of free parish schools for the poor, numerous "charity schools" were established with mixed success. Parish priests could now open their own schools, but anyone else had to have the superintendent's permission to open or teach in a primary school. Qualifications among teachers varied widely. Often they were tradesmen (cobblers, tailors, ropemakers, and so on) who gave some daily time to instructing children. Most parish schools continued to suffer from a lack of adequately trained full-time teachers, sufficient money, and appropriate school buildings.

6. Among the choices of the time were the following: (1) *Being tutored at home.* This was the preferred option of the wealthy. It was also the way De La Salle himself was educated. (2) *Attending a grammar school.* These were primary schools connected with some university. It was presumed that education would be continued there. (3) *Attending choir school.* Those singing in the cathedral choir attended their own school on the cathedral grounds. (4) *Attending a "Little School."* These were taught by schoolmasters who belonged to the Guild of Schoolmasters. They were paid a modest fee by the parents and were supervised by the diocesan superintendent of schools. (5) *Attending a convent school.* These were boarding and day schools taught by nuns. Such schools were almost always the exclusive domain for girls. (6) *Attending a writing school.* These schools were taught by the Guild of Writing Masters, officially protected by the civil authorities. Along with other writing and reading, such schools also taught bookkeeping. (7) *Attending a charity school.* These schools, operated by the poorhouse or by a parish, were for the destitute, that is, those listed on the parish list of the poor. Today we would consider these people paupers or welfare cases. The poor in the towns and cities would rarely attend any of these schools. A nonworking child represented a lack of income to the family, and there was little relationship between the subjects studied in most schools and the daily concerns of working people.

7. A very good description of this personal journey over a period of five critical years is given in Michel Sauvage, "The Gospel Journey of John Baptist de La Salle," in *John Baptist de La Salle Today,* ed. William Mann (Manila, The Philippines: De La Salle University Press, 1992), 24-57.

I had imagined that the care which I assumed of the schools and the masters would amount only to a marginal involvement committing me to no more than providing for the subsistence of the masters and assuring that they acquitted themselves of their tasks with piety and devotedness. . . . Indeed, if I had ever thought that the care I was taking of the schoolmasters out of pure charity would ever have made it my duty to live with them, I would have dropped the whole project. For since, as naturally I set below my manservant those I was obliged, especially in the beginning, to employ in the schools, the mere thought that I might have to live with them would have been unbearable. . . . It was apparently for this reason that God, who guides all things with wisdom and gentleness, and is not in the habit of forcing the inclinations of men, wishing to encourage me to take full responsibility for the schools, did so in a most imperceptible manner and over a period of time; so that one involvement led me into another, without my having foreseen it in the beginning.[8]

Br. Luke Salm, F.S.C., provides a summary of De La Salle's educational contributions that succinctly completes the story.

The Christian Schools might not have been established at all if De La Salle had not been willing to put his own spiritual formation and advanced education at the service of those in need. In the process, he created a new type of school system for the elementary education of the poor, a new set of standards that would transform teaching school into a profession and a vocation, and a new community of consecrated lay teachers as a new form of religious life in the Church.

To achieve all of this, to enter into the world of the poor with creativity and authenticity, Father De La Salle had to sacrifice all of his personal ambition, his family fortune, his ecclesiastical honors, his comfortable lifestyle, and even his personal reputation. People thought that he was crazy. His own family disowned him. The educational authorities of the time had him hauled into court, condemned, and fined because the educational policies he introduced threatened to break down the established social barriers. In his determination to give rich and poor the same education in the same classroom, and all for free, he had to act against the law.

Then there were the Church authorities. Pastors, bishops, and even the Cardinal Archbishop of Paris, hounded De La Salle relentlessly. They could

---

8. Jean-Baptiste Blain, *The Life of John Baptist de La Salle, Founder of the Teachers of the Christian Schools,* vol. 1, bk. 1, trans. Richard Arnandez (Romeoville, Ill.: Christian Brothers Conference, 1983) 1, 60-61.

neither understand nor control this persistent innovator who didn't want his Brothers to be priests, who had his own ideas about how to run a school, and how to make the Christian message appealing to those who rarely heard good news of any kind.

De La Salle did not limit his educational vision to gratuitous elementary schools for the poor. He realized that there were other needs. Well trained teachers were high on his list of priorities. On three distinct occasions he was able to establish experimental training schools for lay teachers. Aware that there was no provision at the time for working teenagers to continue their education, De La Salle founded a Sunday program of advanced courses in practical subjects just for them. He opened a boarding school with offerings in advanced technical and pre-professional courses, unavailable, unheard of, and unthinkable in colleges and universities. He pioneered in what we now call programs of special education to backward students. He opened one of the first institutions in France to specialize in the care and education of young delinquents.[9]

When De La Salle died in 1719, after forty years of labor, there were only 100 Brothers in twenty-three communities who operated some thirty-four schools in various parts of France — very small, compared for example with Saint Francis of Assisi, who in twenty-two years gathered some ten thousand disciples. Yet the influence of De La Salle's convictions, as evidenced both in his writings and in the practices they led to, came to be the inspiration for generations of educators and other religious teaching orders. De La Salle succeeded where so many had failed because, in the words of the French historian Georges Compayré, he launched an educational "movement," and it is one that is more alive today than at any other time in its history.

The Lasallian Perception of Children

John Baptist De La Salle was first and foremost concerned about the education of children. That became his passion and his life's work. He knew children, related to children, spoke about children, and prayed for children as individuals who reflected God's presence and were growing and learning persons with a dignity of their own. He realized that they were struggling with real-life issues both inside and outside of the classroom, and the best thing their teachers could do for them was to take them seriously, both professionally and personally, and to care for them as older brothers would.

9. Luke Salm, "Who Is Saint John Baptist de La Salle?" (unpublished article), 2.

First, it should be said that he came to have a very honest assessment of the state of affairs that the poor of his day found themselves in. He writes:

Consider that it is a practice only too common for the working class and the poor to allow their children to live on their own, roaming all over like vaga-bonds as long as they are not able to be put to some work; these parents have no concern to send their children to school because their poverty does not allow them to pay teachers, or else, obliged to look for work outside their homes, they have to abandon their children to themselves.

The results of this condition are regrettable, for these poor children, ac-customed to lead an idle life for many years, have great difficulty adjusting when it comes time for them to go to work. In addition, through association with bad companions they learn to commit many sins which later on are very difficult to stop, because of the persistent bad habits having been con-tracted over such long time.

God has had the goodness to remedy so great a misfortune by the estab-lishment of the Christian Schools, where the teaching is offered free of charge and entirely for the glory of God, where the children are kept all day, learn to read, to write, and their religion, and are always kept busy, so that when their parents want them to go to work, they are prepared for employ-ment. (*M* 194.1)[10]

The school's focus was on the salvation of these students on two levels, both on the spiritual level (which was not insignificant at the time) and on the practical level (which was probably much more to the interest of parents, how-ever, even then). From this viewpoint the vocation of children would seem to be rather objective, uniform, and indiscriminating as to personal interests, tal-ents, and the like. But as we shall see, the lived experience of De La Salle's schools supports a notion of the child's vocation that has much warmer, com-passionate, and personally sensitive overtones.

The Identity of Children

Throughout his meditations, De La Salle rarely uses the term "students" (*élèves*) for the children that came to the schools, but he most often uses the term "dis-

10. John Baptist De La Salle, *Meditations by St. John Baptist de La Salle*, ed. Augustine Loes, F.S.C., and Francis Huether, F.S.C. (Landover, Md.: Christian Brothers Conference, 1994), 434-35. Hereafter cited in text as *M*. All references from De La Salle will follow the numbering stan-dardized in this text. This reference is to meditation number 194, section 1. Subsequent refer-ences in the chapter will give only the number of the meditation along with its relevant section.

ciple."[11] While this referred directly to the mission or vocation of the teacher to make these children disciples of Jesus Christ, it also informed the relationship between teacher and pupil. Popular education in the seventeenth century being what it was, the relationship between teacher and pupil was, in most cases, hardly ever more than a commercial one at best. Teachers largely worked to earn a living, dispensing their knowledge for a fee. Young students, especially poor ones, were often looked upon as undisciplined, ignorant, and wholly un-cultured necessities for the teacher's livelihood. By describing them as disciples, De La Salle not only established a fundamentally religious component in the re-lationship between teacher and pupil but also introduced an element of re-sponsibility that gave students a central place in the educational enterprise.

De La Salle highlights the value that children in the schools have by articu-lating the nature of their religious identity. "[L]ook upon the children God has entrusted to you as the children of God himself" (*M* 133.2). For De La Salle, all students were a proximate incarnation of Jesus Christ. "Recognize Jesus be-neath the poor rags of the children whom you have to instruct. Adore him in them" (*M* 96.3). Yet they are also described as "weary and exhausted travelers" (37.1), "abandoned orphans" (37.3) on the road of life seeking direction, sup-port, and guidance in a confusing world. Children, for De La Salle, carry a dig-nity that belies their practical circumstances and reaches beyond the popular perception of childhood. Although De La Salle does not use the word "voca-tion" in reference to children, clearly his perspective on childhood combines a unique, essentially religious identity with very practical experience. Their "vo-cation" is to grow into the mature fulfillment of who they are, and they do so in concert with their educational progress and with the guidance of "older broth-ers," their teachers.

Children are the most innocent part of the church and are usually best dis-posed to receive the impressions of grace (*M* 205.3). But the "innocence" of which he speaks is not the sentimental and distorting kind of innocence re-ferred to by William Werpehowski, whereby "they come to bear virtues and val-ues serving, preferred, and protected by adults."[12] It is a notion of innocence rooted firmly in a deeper, longer faith perspective that looks beyond and be-hind the challenging and often disturbing realities prevalent outside, and some-times inside, the classrooms of the time. De La Salle was all too conscious of the

---

11. The word "disciple" is used 230 times in all his writings — 133 times in his meditations, and not once in the *Conduct of Schools* school handbook. The term *enfant* (child) is used 324 times — 177 times in his meditations, and not once in the *Conduct of Schools*. For an analysis of these terms and their contexts, see Alfredo Morales, "Child — Scholar — Disciple," *Lasallian Themes* 1, no. 66 (Rome: Brothers of the Christian Schools, 1992).

12. William Werpehowski, "In Search of Real Children," in this volume, 61.

fact that teachers in schools had to deal with a wide variety of children. He knew firsthand the kinds of characteristics and behaviors that children of the poor were likely to have. This was simply the way things were, and this was the substance of one's prayer (and work). "You have two sorts of children to instruct: some are disorderly and inclined to evil; the others are good, or at least inclined to good. Pray continually for both" (*M* 186.3).

The teachers in De La Salle's schools, through their lifestyle, association, and religious commitment, participated in an endeavor whereby one looked solidly both at and through the realities of children's lives. Rather than viewing children with a sentimental or distorted perspective, these "older brothers" were likely to be the first adults who considered them with more serious attention than they had previously encountered in either their families or society, a care and attention from teachers who saw themselves as fully and finally responsible. "Consider that the account you will have to give to God will not be inconsequential, because it concerns the salvation of the souls of children whom God has entrusted to your care, for on the day of judgment, you will answer for them as much as for yourself."[13]

"Best Practices" for Children

Identifying children in this way has clear implications in how they should be treated. The respect and sense of discipleship that emerge from De La Salle's meditations are backed up by specific practices that may be found in the "handbook" for the schools, *Conduite des Ecoles (The Conduct of Schools;* hereafter *The Conduct).*[14] This practical reference work came to be produced through years of experimentation and practice, and it systematized the "best practices" that had become most successful in the many schools and situations that the Brothers had encountered.[15]

Among *The Conduct's* practices were the following: large groups of stu-

---

13. De La Salle, *Meditations,* 205.2. "You must be convinced of this, that God will begin by making you give an account of their souls before making you give an account of your own. For when you took responsibility for them, you committed yourself at the same time to procure their salvation with as much diligence as your own, for you engaged yourself to work entirely for the salvation of their souls."

14. John Baptist De La Salle, *Conduct of Christian Schools,* ed. Richard Arnandez and William Mann (Landover, Md.: Lasallian Publications, 1996). These references indicate the specific chapter and subsection of *Conduct of Christian Schools.* Hereafter cited in the text as *CS.*

15. The first copy dates from 1706, with the first printed edition appearing in 1720, the year after De La Salle's death.

dents divided into sections based on ability and level, a highly structured method of questions and subquestions, and communication beyond teacher questions and student answers through an elaborate set of "signals" with a pointer/clicker designed for the purpose.[16] A significant portion of the text is devoted to the means for maintaining order. Looking beyond the common notions of punishment that were popular at the time, even as part of the upbringing of Louis XIV, De La Salle's innovation lay in how these means for maintaining order were seen as part of the overall educational picture.

De La Salle knew that neither piety nor learning would be fostered by punishment. The overall atmosphere of the school created by its organized methodology, the seriousness of its teachers, the religious character of all its operations, the standard, pervasive silence of its buildings, all contributed to a situation where the use of punishment was a clear exception to common practice.[17]

He also knew, however, that on the practical level punishment was a reality in elementary education. A class full of young boys, no matter how silent or how well organized, would need correcting. Experience had shown him that teachers must act in a manner both gentle and firm, and they must never let a passion or anger have a part in the correction (*CS* 2.5). A detailed section in *The Conduct* deals with the kinds of children who should and should not be punished. Discrimination in this case is essential, since everyone is not alike.

It is important to see that such discrimination is not a faceless categorization simply based on external behavior. It is a discrimination that respects the child's character while addressing his behavior. William Werpehowski ad-

16. Each classroom consisted of a number of levels and grades together, with each group of students following its own program of activities. Each group would be addressed in turn by the teacher, with the other groups quietly working on their own material. In reading, for example, one student reads while all are reading the same material to themselves, the teacher calling on students out of turn in order to make sure they are following the same section. In arithmetic, individual pupils do examples of particular lessons for the class, being questioned by the teacher to make sure that each concept and term is fully understood. Everything explained to the pupil should be repeated by the pupil before moving on. If the one doing the example failed in any respect, another student doing the same lesson was called on to make the correction, or failing that, a student doing a more advanced lesson was called on. After each correction, the original student repeated the correct answer. Every single student was to do an example on the board of the lesson being covered, with the teacher paying close attention to what the student both does and says. Integral to De La Salle's method was the policy of personally involving each student every day.

17. "To avoid frequent correction, which is a source of great disorder in a school, it is necessary to note well that it is silence, restraint, and watchfulness on the part of the teacher that establish and maintain good order in a class. It is not harshness and blows that establish and maintain good order. A constant effort must be made to act with skill and ingenuity to keep students in order while making almost no use of correction" (*CS* 2.5.2).

dresses the dangers inherent in categorizing children based simply on their behavior, activities that "immunize grown-ups from considering the general social circumstances and conditions that do and do not support children's lives,
and their responsibility for them."[18] This kind of categorization limits both
what children can do and how we subsequently see ourselves related to them.
These dynamics become especially critical in the area of correction, as most of
us are able to attest from early educational experience; e.g., one of the more serious "sins" that teachers can make is to misjudge a situation and make a false
judgment about a student. De La Salle takes steps to prevent such mistakes by
emphasizing the critical importance of discerning the individual character of
students.

> Jesus Christ compares those who have charge of souls to a good shepherd
> who has great care for the sheep. One quality he must possess, according to
> our Savior, is to know each one of them individually. This should also be one
> of the main concerns of those who instruct others: to be able to understand
> their pupils and to discern the right way to guide them.
>
> They must show more mildness toward some, more firmness toward
> others. There are those who call for much patience, those who need to be
> stimulated and spurred on, some who need to be reproved and punished to
> correct them of their faults, others who must be constantly watched over to
> prevent them from being lost or going astray.
>
> This guidance requires understanding and discernment of spirits, quali-
> ties you should frequently and earnestly ask of God, for they are most neces-
> sary for you in the guidance of those placed in your care. (*M* 33.1)

De La Salle shows a keen eye for the emotional dynamics that children are
subject to. He wants to make sure that corrections indeed accomplish what they
should; i.e., that they help students recognize and correct wrong behavior.
Children are never to be publicly humiliated, and punishments are given only
when students recognize and accept the reason for them. Correction also included the immediate opportunity to make the appropriate correct response.
The focus was on the child's capacity to change his behavior for the better.[19]

18. Werpehowski, "In Search," 61.

19. One example: "By their modesty and restraint, teachers will give an example of the
manner in which the students should walk. In order that the teachers may easily see the students
and observe how they behave themselves on the way to holy Mass, teachers will walk on the opposite side of the street from them, ahead of the line, with their faces sufficiently turned toward
their students to be able to see them all. While on the street, teachers will not admonish students
for any faults of which they may be guilty, but will wait until the next day, just before going to
holy Mass, to correct them" (*CS* 8.1).

Nothing was left to chance in the administration of school discipline. *The Conduct* is filled with sound advice in this respect. In fact, some of the advice he gives is extremely unusual for the historical time period, revealing an educational wisdom that deeply respects the integrity of both teachers and students. A striking example of this is the list of six ways in which the teacher can be unbearable to the students. Some examples: "[W]hen the *teacher* is too insistent in urging upon a child some performance which the child is not disposed to do, and the teacher does not permit the child the leisure or the time to reflect. . . . [W]hen the teacher exacts little things and big things alike with the same ardor. . . . [W]hen the teacher immediately rejects the reasons and excuses of children and is not willing to listen to them at all."[20] Instead of putting the burden on the children, it is the teachers who must look at how they make themselves or their actions unbearable to those entrusted to their care.

The Experience of Children

De La Salle was deeply aware of the experience of children among the poor and the working class of the cities of seventeenth-century France. He knew that they were subject to difficult challenges on a daily basis. "It often happens that students do not have enough strength of body or of mind to bear the burdens which many times overwhelm them" (*CS* 2.5). The children of the poor were largely neglected or ignored, allowed to amuse themselves in whatever way they wished until they were able to begin working at some trade or craft. De La Salle came to see that children were being educated into forms of thinking and behaving that would remain with them throughout their lives. That was why it was so important to shape their character in a Christian fashion at an early age.

Two meditations are particularly revelatory of De La Salle's viewpoint re-

---

20. First, the teacher's penances are too rigorous and the yoke the teacher imposes upon the students is too heavy. This state of affairs is frequently due to lack of discretion and judgment on the part of the teacher. It often happens that students do not have enough strength of body or of mind to bear the burdens that many times overwhelm them. Second, when the teacher enjoins, commands, or exacts something of the children with words too harsh and in a manner too domineering. Above all, the teacher's conduct is unbearable when it arises from unrestrained impatience or anger. Sixth, when the teacher is not mindful enough of personal faults that he does not know how to sympathize with the weaknesses of children and so exaggerates their faults too much. This is the situation when the teacher reprimands them or punishes them and acts as though dealing with an insensible instrument rather than with a creature capable of reason (*CS* 2.5).

garding the situation within which students found themselves. In one of them, he notes the ease with which children can be taken captive by a habit of doing wrong.

> People are naturally so inclined to sin that they seem to find no other pleasure than committing it. This is seen especially in children, because their minds have not developed yet and they are not capable of much serious reflection. They seem to have no other inclination than to please their passions and their senses, and to satisfy their nature. . . . [I]f they are abandoned to their own will, they will run the risk of ruining themselves and causing much sorrow to their parents. The reason for this is because the faults turn into a habit which will be very difficult to correct. The good and bad habits contracted in childhood and maintained over a period of time ordinarily become part of nature. . . . [I]t can be said with reason that a child who has acquired a habit of sin has in some sense lost his freedom and has made himself a miserable captive. (*M* 203.2)[21]

This observation about the captivity of sin and the loss of freedom echoes modern observations regarding compulsive or addictive behaviors and their tenacious hold over individual lives, limiting one's interests, options, and horizons. The freedom of which De La Salle speaks is based on what he had seen in his own schools, places where structure, vigilance, and good example allowed children to relax enough, as children, to benefit from all the child-centered instruction, cognitive and behavioral, that the school provided. It's the kind of relaxed freedom that any teacher would immediately recognize in a well-run class. And while he undoubtedly was subject to the influences of Jansenism and its negative perceptions of human behavior vis-à-vis salvation, De La Salle came to know children well and has an empathy for the kinds of troubles children can bring onto themselves, describing with perfect candor and keen insight the process by which they proceed to make themselves captive.[22]

It would be accurate to say that he did not have any romantic or idealistic ideas about children. Forty years with the poor would quickly erode the best of intentions in that regard. Instead, De La Salle gave children their due, recognizing both their limitations and their strengths, and setting their vocation firmly

---

21. This meditation retains greater relevance today in terms of its insights into the formative status of habits than it does in terms of its theology. It reflects the seventeenth century's pessimistic outlook on human nature.

22. De La Salle knew that there was many a boy in the Christian school who "has walked the way of sin, seeking to satisfy his passions in the world, and finding there nothing but vice and vanity, misery and disappointment" (*M* 37.1).

in the midst of their experience. Children have a vocation to see themselves as part of the world around them, and they have a God-given right to be treated with a respect that reaches beyond their years, drawing them forward to live into the deeper version of their vocation as a child of God.

In this connection, De La Salle's notion of childhood bears strong resemblance to Vigen Guroian's description of the "office of child" — including both the responsibilities and graces associated with that office.[23] The essentially spiritual identity of children and childhood highlighted by Guroian's references from Saint Peter Chrysologos, John Henry Newman, George MacDonald, and Karl Rahner is something with which De La Salle would resonate. His deep familiarity with the fathers of the church, found throughout his meditations, and his lengthy exposure to the realities of urban education among the poor, led De La Salle to develop a profoundly spiritual, yet practical, appreciation of children. While there was a fundamentally spiritual identity at their core, children still needed to be taught reading, writing, math, and manners. The content, context, and method of that teaching, personalized in no small measure in the teacher, identified that spiritual identity and brought it to the fore. If De La Salle had not viewed children in this light, he clearly would not have dedicated his life to their welfare.

The anthropological foundation for De La Salle's educational perspective, on the other hand, may appear to be somewhat condescending or paternalistic and is seen in another one of his meditations. However, given the popular movements of seventeenth-century France (Jansenism, Quietism, Gallicanism, etc.) and De La Salle's own wide-ranging educational experience, it should still be also seen as remarkably insightful and direct.

> It can be said that children at birth are like a mass of flesh. Their minds do not emerge from the matter in them except with time and become refined only little by little. As an unavoidable consequence, those who are ordinarily instructed in the schools are not yet able by themselves to understand easily the Christian truths and maxims. Christian truths are hidden from the human mind. If this is true of all men, it is incomparably more true of children, whose minds are more dull because they are less free of their senses and of matter. Children, then, need someone to develop the Christian truths for them in a more concrete fashion, one that is harmonious with the limitations of their minds, for these truths are hidden from the human mind. If this help is not given, they often remain all their lives insensitive and opposed to thoughts of God and incapable of knowing and appreciating them [1 Cor.

23. Vigen Guroian, "The Office of the Child in the Christian Faith," in this volume, 104-6.

2:14]. For this purpose the goodness of God has provided children with teachers who will instruct them in all these things. (*M* 197.1)[24]

The limitations that poor children carry become the occasion for the teacher's ministry. De La Salle highlights the distinctions between children and adults. They are neither "little adults" nor fully developed persons of any particular kind. They are children, individuals subject to their senses and to concrete, immediate things who only gradually "emerge" and "become refined." Therefore their instruction must be appropriate to their nature. Their vocation as children includes the development of reason, judgment, and moral behavior — things that De La Salle's schools, through their structure, teachers, and environment, were established to provide. And while De La Salle's emphasis on reason and critical stance toward most things dealing with passion, feeling, or emotional attachments might seem uncaring or stunted, it's clear from everything he writes that he grew to develop a great love for children and their needs, and he became as empathetic and as practically responsive to the real needs of poor children as anyone of his time could have been.[25]

Two of the practical ways that the experience of children were addressed inside and outside the classroom were through a communal sense of school ownership, in today's terms, that was cultivated by having a plethora of student responsibilities, and through the individual care demonstrated by the keeping of individual student records.

It seems that most, if not all, students had some responsibility or job in the classroom, from the student who would open the doors to the school — *before* the teacher arrived — to prayer leaders, bell ringers, and street supervisors. It seems that if there was a job to be done in school, there was a student to do it.[26]

---

24. De La Salle observed that many children of the time "are little accustomed to use their reason, and because nature is, consequently more lively in them, are strongly inclined to enjoy the pleasures of the senses" (*M* 56.2).

25. There are sections of De La Salle's writings, especially those dealing with the religious life of his followers, that place an emphasis on obedience, mortification, sacrifice, and humility that sounds overblown to our contemporary ears. And some of that seventeenth-century religious sensibility was certainly an aspect of his educational outlook. This makes it all the more remarkable that the educational practices in *The Conduct* and the educational perspectives from his meditations can stand on their own even today.

26. Such duties with their qualifications and terms of office were carefully described, rotated among the pupils either as a reward or as an incentive toward developing responsibility. Some examples: Leaders of prayers did so throughout the day, distinctly and without distraction. Holy water bearers made holy water available when entering or leaving church. The rosary keeper and his assistants gave rosaries out in class and in church, distributing them and counting them when returned. The bell ringer had to be vigilant, exact, and punctual, ringing the bell

And these jobs were given with a full understanding of the ways that children might behave, if left totally unsupervised. For example, a "class inspector" over-saw the arrival of students prior to the arrival of the teacher, reporting anything observed and never interfering with anything that happened. But there were two further monitors, unknown to the class inspector or to one another, who would validate the reports of that inspector. "Trust but verify" has a long history.

An attention to, and respect for, individual student experience is also demonstrated by the fact that each teacher drew up a record for each student in class. This record began with an interview when the pupil was admitted, recording his family, background, home life, particular traits, and other significant data. During the year the teacher would enter pertinent information about the student, passing it on to the next teacher at the end of the year. When the student left, the record would be filed for future reference. The value of such acquired insights into an individual student, despite the risk of acquiring a skewed viewpoint based on a single teacher's experience, makes personal attention a realistic possibility. One example:

> Francis Delevieux: 8½, two years at school, in 3rd section of Writing since July 1st. Somewhat turbulent; little piety at church or prayers unless supervised. Lacks reserve. Conduct satisfactory; needs encouragement to effort; punishment of no avail; light-headed. Rarely absent except when with bad companions; often late. Application moderate but he learns with ease. Twice nearly dismissed for negligence. Submissive to a strong hand. Not a difficult character. Must be won over. Spoiled at home. Parents resent his being punished.[27]

If any one of us received such an overview of a student, we would quickly have a good basis upon which to proceed both inside and outside the classroom. Such a summary also indicates the kinds of traits that teachers found significant in developing the child's individual character.

The Guidance of Children

Recognizing both the challenging situations within which many students dwell and the eminent value that they have in the sight of God, De La Salle specifies

---

each half hour and at the beginning and end of the school day. Papers were given out and returned by students, who followed a set routine. The sweeper kept the classroom clean, and the doorkeeper saw to it that only Brothers, pupils, and the parish priest were admitted.

27. Jean-Baptiste De La Salle, *Oeuvres Complètes* (Rome: Frères des Ecoles Chrétiennes, 1993), 657.

particular dimensions for approaching their Christian formation and practical education.

In summary fashion, De La Salle points out the need to teach the young both spiritual and practical realities with a view toward cultivating piety.[28]

> You will procure the good of the Church by making them true Christians and docile to the truths of faith and the maxims of the holy Gospel. You will procure the good of the state by teaching them how to read and write and everything else that pertains to your ministry with regard to exterior things. But piety should be joined to exterior things, otherwise your work would be of little use. (*M* 160.3)

He insists that the teacher's first care should be "to make sure they grasp fully the doctrine of the holy apostles, to give them the spirit of religion, and to make them practice what Jesus Christ has left us in the holy Gospel" (*M* 116.2). This is done by interpreting Christian truths in more concrete ways, ones that resonate with their ways of thinking.[29]

At the same time, the practical goals of education are never far behind; i.e., a knowledge of all the practical truths and skills that will enable the students to become responsible members of society — reading, writing, calculating, good manners, and pious example.

Success will have been reached if "they often think of Jesus, their good and only Lord, that they often speak of Jesus, that they long only for Jesus, and desire only for Jesus" (*M* 102.2). All their actions will be united with Jesus Christ. They "practice what Jesus Christ has left us in the holy Gospel" (*M* 116.2) and grasp the doctrine of the apostles.

Emphasis is placed on docility to the truths of faith and the maxims of the

---

28. *Piété* (n.): piety. For De La Salle the word *piété* had a much broader and key meaning than the word "piety" in English today, which at times can carry a connotation of childish or superficial devotion. De La Salle uses the word 149 times in the meditations to signify a range of meaning. It can refer to conversation on religious or spiritual topics, to the practice of prayer, to acts of devotion, to a solid spirit of religion, or to the practice of one's religion.

29. "It is not enough to procure for children the Christian spirit and teach them the mysteries and doctrines of our religion. You must also teach them the practical maxims found throughout the holy Gospel. But since their minds are not yet sufficiently able to understand and practice these maxims by themselves, you must serve as visible angels for them in two things: (1) you must help them understand the maxims as they are set forth in the holy Gospel, (2) you must guide their steps along the way that leads them to put these maxims into practice. You must win them to practice the maxims of the holy Gospel, and to this end you must give them means that are easy and accommodate their age. Gradually accustomed to this practice in their childhood, they will be able when older to have acquired them as a kind of habit and practice them without great difficulty" (*M* 197.2).

gospel, along with piety and the spirit of religion. Piety "is the principal object and the purpose of your work. . . . The trouble you take to do this will in the end make your students docile and solidly submissive to their parents . . . , self-controlled and well-behaved in public, pious in church, and in all that refers to God, to holy things, and to everything that relates to religion" (*M* 186.1). While on the one hand it may seem that such an emphasis would confirm the suspicion that the only real goal in this entire enterprise is to render children docile to the prevalent social structure of the day — and there would be evidence to support at least a partial validation of this — it is far more true to recognize the authentic context and import of this result as representing a genuine appreciation and desire to see children deepen their identity as children of God.

The role of personal example in the attainment of these educational goals is key. It speaks to both the nature of the child's vocation and the nature of the teacher's role as mentor, guide, and "older brother." De La Salle observed at numerous times that the "tendencies of the young are easily guided, so that they accept without great difficulty the impressions we seek to give them" (*M* 186.1).[30] This is why it is so important that teachers "act so wisely in their regard that nothing in themselves or in their conduct is able to give these youths any dislike for the service of God, or cause them to deviate even slightly from their duties" (*M* 115.1). Their approach to students must be one of constant example, since this addresses their recognized learning patterns and confirms the content of one's teaching.

> Example makes a much greater impression on the mind and heart than words, especially for children, since they do not yet have minds sufficiently able to reflect, and they ordinarily model themselves on the example of their teachers. They are led more readily to do what they see done for them than what they hear told to them, above all when the teachers' words they hear are not in harmony with their actions. (*M* 202.3)

> Do you wish your disciples to do what is right? Do it yourself. You will persuade them much more readily through your example of wise and prudent behavior than through all the words you could speak to them. Do you want them to keep silence? Keep it yourself. You will make them prudent and self-controlled only in so far as you act that way yourself. (*M* 33.2)

---

30. These sentiments seem to contrast with his earlier remarks regarding the difficulty children have of forming good habits and the ease with which they fall into sin. His overall understanding seems to be that children are readily formed by whatever influences surround them. If these are bad influences, the child will develop bad habits. If these are good influences, the child will develop good habits. The teacher must insure that the child is surrounded by good influences so that good habits, and piety, may be developed.

Instruction supported by example is one of the chief characteristics of the teacher's zeal. Without it, one's zeal "would not go very far and would not have much result or success." Zeal must be realized within one's behavior as a model to the students. This is the only way "the instructions you give to those whom you have to instruct" will become "effective in drawing them to the practice of good" (*M* 193.3). "Is it enough for them to see you in order to be well behaved? Is your behavior sufficient to encourage them to practice virtue? This is the main benefit which you should impart to them, the best gift you can give them when they leave you" (*M* 98.3). One contemporary Lasallian scholar has noted: "In light of this, it is very obvious that De La Salle believed in the moral redemption of the child, and he placed his confidence in Christian education as an effective means for obtaining it."[31]

Coons gives contemporary substance to this impression when he asks, "how does an obtending child proceed in this world of which she knows so little?" and then answers that she must "look for the most reliable (or more experienced) older navigator who is available and follow such authority so long as her own ignorance persists. . . . it is an act of a pilgrim who puts confidence in a more experienced and discerning fellow human."[32] In the life of virtue, as encountered by the child, De La Salle would have us realize both the grave responsibility given to teachers vis-à-vis those who may only recently have made forays into the world of obedience and the pivotal effect teachers have in influencing the present and future direction of a child's life by virtue of their example.[33]

For De La Salle, there was another means by which the importance of example, the practice of virtue, and effective communication of values came about, and that was through a genuine interest in, and practice of, Christian decorum and politeness. Social graces were more than an optional component in the stratified and socially conscious society of seventeenth-century France. Good manners were seen as both a component of acceptable integration in society and a dimension of one's faith life. As such, proper manners were a com-

---

31. Morales, "Child — Scholar — Disciple," 69.

32. John Coons, "Luck, Obedience, and the Vocation of Childhood," in this volume, 88.

33. It was striking to read in the chapter by John Coons that Karl Barth referred to "an ultimate state of the parents as 'ambassadors' of the good." De La Salle, in a key section of his meditations, refers to his teachers in a similar way, although focused specifically within the Christian context: "Since you are *ambassadors and ministers of Jesus Christ* in the work that you do, you must act as representing Jesus Christ himself. He wants your disciples to see him in you and receive your instructions as if he were giving them to them. They must be convinced that your instructions are the truth of Jesus Christ who speaks with your mouth, that it is only in his name that you teach, that it is he who has given you authority over them" (*M* 195.2).

ponent in the way that children were approached by teachers, and by such example such manners should become part of how they might, in turn, treat others both now and in the future.

For De La Salle, civility was the practical manifestation of a person's faith life, the way in which Christianity became part of one's everyday existence. He defines civility, or Christian politeness, as "a sensible and regulated mode of behaviour that one exhibits in one's speech and outward actions through an attitude of due moderation, or of respect, or of union and charity toward one's neighbour, paying attention to the times, places and persons with whom one is dealing."[34] De La Salle recognized and respected the traditional relationships that existed between the various social classes, classes that also extended to children, but he also gives these relationships wider application by extending the scope of politeness to include all those within one's social sphere.[35] It wasn't enough to be polite only to those who were members of one's own social class. Christian sensibilities demanded that one also was polite to those of other social classes. The popularity of De La Salle's contribution to politeness education is attested by the fact that over 150 editions of his book have been published since 1703.[36]

Since it was one of the "textbooks" for teaching reading, *The Rules of Christian Decorum and Politeness* was published in an elaborate script form, so that when students were ready to read it, they would not only learn societal conventions of behavior but would be further challenged by a formal writing style that they would encounter as adults.

But besides being a resource text for teaching reading, the contents of the book highlight the essentially religious outlook that governed all of De La Salle's perspective about children and their relationship to the world around them. He writes:

> It is surprising that most Christians look upon decorum and politeness as merely human and worldly qualities and do not think of raising their minds

---

34. Alfred Calcutt, *De La Salle: A City Saint and the Liberation of the Poor through Education* (Oxford: De La Salle Publications, 1993), 435.

35. For example, where other texts will specify the proper way to disagree with someone of a higher social standing, or the proper way to knock on the door of a lord, De La Salle extends those same standards universally. These are proper ways of disagreeing with anyone, or the proper way to knock when visiting anyone. See Calcutt, *De La Salle,* 436.

36. According to Alfred Calcutt, with this text De La Salle "provided the most important contribution to this form of social education in the schools of France for the next two centuries" (Calcutt, *De La Salle,* 433). The latest edition, a translation of the original edition of 1703, was published in 1990. For an overview of the work, see the preface of the English edition. Also see Gregory Wright, "Why Read the Rules of Christian Decorum and Politeness," *Lasalliana* 24 (May 1992): 3-4.

to any higher views by considering them as virtues that have reference to God, to their neighbor, and to themselves.[37]

These social graces were not merely conventional practices of social propriety, they were manifestations of an awareness of God's presence in the world, of respect for oneself and for others. It was a means of growing into one's faith, to "live like true Christians." Through them, a child's vocation was once more invited to mature along authentic lines and in real life. Such development could not be a passive acceptance of society's rules. This was not a nominal faith. It was also a form of discipleship, a practicing of one's faith, and seeing social graces and politeness from the viewpoint of one's faith was something that De La Salle also recommended to parents.[38]

In fact, through these teachings on politeness, as well as through other activities at the school, parents came to be instructed by way of their children. Writing classes used Christian maxims as models, and these writings were brought home each day. They portrayed in great measure a humanitarian and cultural ideal, and moral and social values that the parents, even the illiterate ones, enjoyed hearing their children read aloud to them. Similarly, children at home would have prepared the reading they would do in class the next day, or a short speech on a topic in the catechism or the politeness book, and in doing so they shared their religious and social formation with their parents.

Specific instructions in the book on politeness would have a positive influence on both children and parents. Some examples: "It is impolite to wipe one's nose with the fingers and then clean them on one's clothes . . . which should always be clean no matter how poor they are since they are the adornments of a servant of God." "Good behavior demands that before a meal one should wash one's hands and bless the food. . . . When there is a child present, it often happens that such a person is given this task." "Children especially should make it a rule to be the last to start and first to finish a meal. . . . Children should always leave the table first, excusing themselves appropriately."

The breadth of practices and activities covered by the politeness book is ev-

37. John Baptist De La Salle, *The Rules of Christian Decorum and Politeness,* trans. Richard Arnandez (Romeoville, Ill.: Lasallian Publications, 1990), 3. For a modern reflection on this work, see Wright, "Why Read the Rules," 3-4.

38. "Fathers and mothers . . . far from telling the children for whom they are responsible that if they do such-and-such a thing, they will be blamed, and no one will like them, people will laugh at them . . . when they want them to adopt exterior practices regarding bodily welfare . . . will take care to motivate them through the presence of God. . . . If they teach them and get them to practice politeness to their neighbor, they will teach them always to treat people with politeness and respect as the members of Jesus Christ." De La Salle, *Politeness,* preface.

ident in the chapter headings, all of which represent topics relevant to the present and future social life of young, untrained, inner-city boys. Three further examples from the text illustrate the variety of situations that the book addresses:

- It is against decorum to spit in front of yourself while with others, or to spit too far, so that you have to go looking for the spittle in order to step on it. In places that are usually kept clean, turn aside slightly and spit into your handkerchief, then fold it immediately without looking at it, and replace it in your pocket.
- You should remove your hat: (1) in a place where there are important people; (2) when you greet someone; (3) when you give or receive anything; (4) when you are being seated at table; (5) when you hear the names of Jesus or Mary; (6) when you are in the presence of persons to whom you owe great respect.
- It is entirely contrary to decorum to grow overexcited when you play. Still, you should not play in a careless manner nor lose deliberately as a way of flattering your opponent. This would make the person with whom you are playing think that you care little about contributing to his enjoyment in a well-played match.

What a child does has consequences that are immediate and long-term. In the situation itself, the child's behavior is a vehicle for the expression of one's religious convictions — one's faith — and deepens that faith life through the thoughtful practices involved. But more importantly, by behaving in a specific way — according to the convictions of faith — children are building their relationship with God through their relationship with others. Common interactions become a "school of Christian life" and children deepen their vocation as human individuals outside the classroom as they had been doing, hopefully, inside the classroom, where their teacher, their classroom protocols, their interactions with other students, and their exposure to a highly structured environment geared toward their growth has established the basis upon which their other experiences might be judged.[39]

---

39. An especially compelling illustration of this was recently demonstrated to me through a French film documentary entitled *Être et Avoir* that covers a year in the life of a small French country school. Numerous scenes echoed sections from De La Salle's writings or practices and attitudes illustrated in both *The Conduct* and the *Meditations*. Many, of course, are now commonly appreciated in all sorts of schools. Still, it was gratifying to once again note how the best teaching has universal appeal.

Conclusion

A child's vocation may be seen, through De La Salle's educational vision and practice, as a sort of apprenticeship to life. The primary components of this apprenticeship are the child and the teacher and their relationship to one another. Not only is the teacher a "Brother" in title, he is also to be an older brother to the child, demonstrating a care and concern that allows the child to be both at ease and to confidently move forward in academic studies, the life of faith, and individual identity.[40] The teachers' solicitude for the students' welfare and the care with which they attended to their duties resembled those of a serious older brother more than those of a schoolmaster.

As much as the teachers came to know their students in a variety of daily situations, the students also came to know their teachers. Such a relationship as De La Salle advocated became established over a long period of time through a wide variety of activities, ranging from direct teaching experiences during class to supervision at school meals, at recreation, and at church. A certain kind of relationship along with the particular teaching drew students to the practice of their faith. The combination of firmness and gentleness,[41] teaching and example, applied to all the subjects taught in the school and pervading all aspects of school life, was the vehicle for Christian instruction and the means for developing the child's vocation, a vocation that was based on, was aimed at, and was centered on God.

The teacher, in a curious and rather dramatic twist, has offered himself to God in place of the children that he educates. Similar to Jesus Christ himself and echoing the religious experience of other traditions, the "master" takes on full responsibility for his "disciples."[42] De La Salle writes: "You have committed

---

40. It is at least parenthetically significant that the Brothers were, and are, identified by their first names — as in Brother James or Brother Charles — by the students and parents, and not by their last names — as in Brother Kennedy or Brother McMann — which is the case in most other religious orders involved in education. This aspect of "formal familiarity" reveals an educational relationship similar to that which is so well described in William Werpehowski's chapter in this volume when he speaks about the relationship between Scout and Atticus Finch in *To Kill a Mockingbird*.

41. "Do you have these sentiments of charity and tenderness toward the poor children whom you have to educate? Do you take advantage of their affection for you to lead them to God? If you have for them the firmness of a father to restrain and withdraw them from misbehavior, you must also have for them the tenderness of a mother to draw them to you, and to do for them all the good that depends on you" (*M* 101.3).

42. The idea of discipleship that defines the relationship between teacher and student is one that is informed by Jesus Christ's own example. De La Salle recommends the model of Jesus in the Gospels as the perfect example of the kind of teacher appropriate in a Christian school. By

yourselves to God in the place of those whom you instruct. By taking upon yourselves the responsibility for their souls, you have, so to speak, offered to him soul for soul [Ex. 21:23]" (*M* 137.3). It is as if the vocation of the child is subsumed into the vocation of the teacher. One proceeds in concert with the other. There can hardly be a more religiously intimate responsibility than the one taken up under this conviction.[43]

Finally, the task of fostering the vocation of children is a divine work, according to De La Salle. "You carry out a work that requires you to touch hearts, but this you cannot do except by the Spirit of God" (*M* 43.3). "You must . . . imitate God to some extent, for he . . . loved the souls he created" (*M* 201.3). That imitation of God becomes incarnated in the teacher's daily relationship with students. "Every day you have poor children to instruct. Love them tenderly . . . following in this the example of Jesus Christ" (*M* 166.2). Through such fraternal devotion and deep attachment to the good of their students, teachers are able to draw down God's graces upon those entrusted to their care. The child's vocation flourishes by way of the graces that the teacher makes possible through his prayer and his daily efforts on the child's behalf.

De La Salle's favorite image for the activity of teaching, or of forming a child's vocation, is the winning and this touching of hearts (*M* 43.3). "Do you have faith that it is able to touch the hearts of your students and to inspire them with the Christian spirit? This is the greatest miracle you could perform, and the one that God asks of you, for this is the purpose of your work" (*M* 139.3). Such an image captures the essentially interior nature of forming a child's vocation. Facts and figures neither have the formative power nor constitute the major component of the activity of teaching. True personal formation involves dynamics of the heart, as salvation itself does. The salvation of souls is a matter of touching hearts (*M* 57.2), of leading children to live in a Christian manner through winning their hearts. Failing to do this will not fail to draw them to God but will instead drive them away (*M* 115.3). Therefore, teachers have the duty "of learning how to touch hearts" (*M* 129.2) through earnest application to interior prayer and the conscientious performance of their teaching responsibilities.

---

looking at the ways that Jesus led his disciples to understand and practice the Gospel's truths, teachers will discover how they might similarly lead their own disciples toward the same goal. For that, the teachers' example for their students is again key, as Jesus' example is key to the teachers.

43. For teachers, the students will be their glory; "the glory that you have procured for them will reflect on you" (*M* 208.1). In heaven, the students will then fully appreciate the work that has been done on their behalf and will beseech God to bestow upon their teachers the fullness of heaven's rewards. In this way, the vocation of both the teacher and the student will have been brought to maturity.

Children "themselves are a letter which Jesus Christ dictates to you, which you write each day in their hearts, not with ink, but by the Spirit of the living God" (*M* 195.2). Children have an openness, a capacity for learning and for inspiration, and an identity all their own. They are like a letter waiting to be written, ready for the kind of personal encounter from God that the teacher provides. The light that is enkindled in the hearts of students through the inspiration of the teacher brings about the warmth of soul and the intimacy that a letter often brings. Such teachers may be the first instance that children experience of God's loving concern for them. In a very real way, along with learning how to write, students come to know the foundation out of which writing receives its power. By touching their hearts, writing Christ's gospel with the Spirit of the living God, teachers awaken and enkindle in the hearts of students their capacity to participate in their heritage as children of God; i.e., they fulfill their vocation as children.

14. The Vocation of the Child as a Learner

Elmer John Thiessen

"Please let the child be a child." This is my silent response when, all too often, I see children not being allowed to experience the joys inherent in the unique calling of childhood. Yes, I believe it is very appropriate to talk about the calling and the vocation of the child, and in our day there is a need to understand what this might mean. I want to focus on the vocation of the child as a learner. But first, some comments on the notion of calling or vocation.

As various authors in this volume point out, the Christian understanding of vocation refers centrally to being called by God to be and do something. There are, of course, a variety of vocations. This is perhaps seen most clearly in the writings of the apostle Paul. In a passage that is not easy to interpret, Paul addresses the issue of marriage, and three times in this context he refers to the notion of calling or vocation. "[E]ach one should retain the place in life (or 'station in life') that the Lord assigned to him and to which God has called him" (1 Cor. 7:17, 20, 24 NIV). This is not the place to sort out the hermeneutical complexities of Paul's application of this principle to slavery. Instead I want to apply this passage to the calling and vocation of children, and I believe that such an application is justified because Paul himself does so elsewhere. We see this in what scholars have come to refer to as the *Haustafeln,* household tablets, which summarize the ethical teaching of the early church. In three different passages, Paul and Peter address the ethical principles that apply to a variety of vocations — wife, husband, slave, master, citizen (Col. 3:18–4:1; Eph. 5:21–6:9; 1 Pet. 2:13–3:7).

In two of these *Haustafeln* children are addressed separately. "Children, obey your parents in the Lord, for this is right. 'Honor your father and mother' — which is the first commandment with a promise — 'that it may go well with you and that you may enjoy long life on the earth'" (Eph. 6:1-3). Here it should be noted, first of all, that children are addressed in their own right. They themselves are being asked to respond to their calling. They are told to obey and honor their parents — that is their calling. Fathers are addressed next in this same passage, and they are told not to exasperate their children, but instead "bring them up in the training and instruction of the Lord" (Eph. 6:4). Although this admonition is directed at fathers, there is here an implication concerning another aspect of the calling of children. If fathers are called to train and instruct their children, then it follows that children are called to learn. Even the call to honor parents contains in it an implicit call to learn. To honor parents surely includes honoring what they believe, and thus again learning from them. It is this description of the call to learn that is the focus of my chapter.

There are other passages of Scripture that suggest that learning is an essential part of the vocation of the child. Moses, after reviewing the Decalogue and the celebrated Hebrew Shema, called on the people of Israel to "impress" these commandments on their children. "Talk about them when you sit at home and when you walk along the road, when you lie down and when you get up" (Deut. 6:7). In other words, teach your children, and give them a thorough initiation into the will of God for his people. In the New Testament we discover that Joseph and Mary and the religious community within which Jesus grew up had obviously taught him well as a child. And it becomes very apparent that Jesus must have been an avid learner, causing even the Jewish teachers of the law in the temple courts to be "amazed at his understanding and answers" (Luke 2:41-50). Jesus' response to his parents' "gentle" admonition when he failed to join them on their return journey from Jerusalem comes in the form of a question: "Didn't you know I had to be in my Father's house?" (Luke 2:49). His parents didn't understand Jesus and his implicit reference to his unique vocation that he needed to be about his Father's business. After this episode we read that Jesus returned to Nazareth and was obedient to his parents, and that he "grew in wisdom and stature, and in favor with God and men" (Luke 2:51-52). He continued to respond to a normal child's vocation of obedience and growth in knowledge and wisdom.

Status of Children

But, how do children fulfill this unique vocation to learn? Here, of course, we come across a central problem — children cannot fulfill this calling without help from adults. They are by their very nature dependent creatures, especially during the early stages of their development, and it is most important here to keep in mind the different stages of child development. To do justice to the topic of fulfilling the vocation of the child to learn, we need to begin with the child at birth. I want to suggest that there is a tendency, among scholars in the philosophy of education, to skirt the question of what it means to educate children during the early stages of their development. The reason behind this tendency to overlook the early years of a child's education, I would suggest, is that educationalists find it somewhat embarrassing to admit to the obvious. Children learn from adults. Learning in childhood consists of initiation, absorption, and socialization.

I will say more on this shortly, but first I want to highlight the embarrassment of philosophers of education and contemporary educationalists with regard to the uniqueness of childhood and childhood learning. Again and again in the literature, we find that children are not treated as children. Instead, they are treated as though they are already adults.[1] One sees this, for example, in defenses of children's rights in relation to education. Brian Crittenden traces the origin of the movement for children's liberation to the 1960s when various established patterns of authority, including the family, were challenged severely.[2] This movement relied heavily on the language of rights, and in the 1970s the defense of children's rights flourished.[3] John Holt, for example, in his 1974 publication *Escape from Childhood: The Needs and Rights of Children,* argued that children should be able to choose their own guardian and have the right to control their learning.[4] More recently, James Dwyer has taken a radical position in relation to children's rights, which he uses as an argument against religious schools.[5] Dwyer objects to "adult-centered approaches" that have dominated the discourse on educational rights, and argues instead that "the only rights we should recognize in the law governing child rearing are rights of children themselves."[6]

1. Vigen Guroian, in his chapter in this volume, makes essentially the same point when he argues that all too often in academic literature, the child is discussed in isolation and not in relation to parents (or guardians).

2. Brian Crittenden, *Parents, the State, and the Right to Educate* (Carlton, Australia: Melbourne University Press, 1988), 81.

3. Crittenden, *Parents,* 81.

4. (New York: Dutton, 1974).

5. James G. Dwyer, *Religious Schools v. Children's Rights* (Ithaca, N.Y.: Cornell University Press, 1998). Dwyer's position on religious schools is somewhat ambiguous (1). He is not opposed to religious schools as such. His main concern is with the failure of governments to regulate such schools (2). He admits, though, that his proposals would "so radically alter" the nature of religious schools "as to make them unrecognizable as Fundamentalist or Catholic" schools (180). He declares this to be "cause for celebration, because any form of schooling that systematically violates the rights of children should not exist" (180). For a careful critical review of Dwyer's book, see Stephen G. Gilles, "Hey, Christians, Leave Your Kids Alone! Review of James Dwyer, *Religious Schools v. Children's Rights,*" *Constitutional Commentary* 16, no. 1 (1999): 149-211.

6. Dwyer, *Religious Schools,* 4, 178.

An even more recent expression of this failure to take seriously the unique status of the child is found in Rob Reich's *Bridging Liberalism and Multiculturalism in American Education.*[7] Reich devotes a chapter to a discussion of conflicts that arise over educational authority.[8] What is unusual about Reich's treatment is that he focuses on home-schooling, because, according to Reich, this phenomenon throws the questions concerning conflicts over educational authority "into sharpest relief."[9] The phenomenon of home-schooling is also significant for the purposes of my chapter because it overcomes the tendency to think of a child's education in terms of two stages that are typically sharply separated — nurture in the home and school education. Reich has some serious reservations about home-schooling and in the end advocates stricter state regulations of home-schooling. Reich's fundamental concern about home-schooling has to do with the failure of parents to foster the development of autonomy in their children. Reich is careful, though, to try and distance himself from an unrealistic Kantian ideal of autonomy and opts instead for what he calls a "minimalist autonomy."[10]

It seems to me, however, that Reich runs into problems when he applies this supposedly more realistic notion of autonomy to children. He cites this example: "It is possible for my proselytising parents to compel me to devote myself to God. But we would not say that the person who unhesitatingly and unthinkingly followed the advice or exhortations of others was autonomous."[11] Then this: "What matters for minimalist autonomy is that the decision to lead a life of any sort — liberal or traditionalist, agnostic or devoted, cosmopolitan or parochial — be reached without compulsion from others and always be potentially subject to review, or critical scrutiny, should the person conclude that

---

7. Rob Reich, *Bridging Liberalism and Multiculturalism in American Education* (Chicago: University of Chicago Press, 2002).

8. Reich, *Bridging Liberalism,* 142-72.

9. Reich, *Bridging Liberalism,* 144.

10. Reich, *Bridging Liberalism,* 98. Reich acknowledges that there is widespread disagreement as to what autonomy means, and so he spends a good deal of time unpacking his broader ideal of children developing into "adults capable of independent functioning" (154). He claims it involves two things. First, children need to develop "baseline . . . competencies" that include "things like the need to acquire reading skills and basic mathematical literacy so that as adults they can do things as mundane as read street signs and as important as fill out a job application" (153). Secondly, education must aim to give to children at least a "minimalist" level of autonomy (92). Reich defines minimalist autonomy as a person's ability to reflect independently and critically upon basic "commitments, values, desires, motivations, and beliefs," be they chosen or unchosen, and to enjoy a range of meaningful life options from which to choose, upon which to act, and around which to orient and pursue one's life projects (92, 102).

11. Reich, *Bridging Liberalism,* 102.

384

such a life is no longer worth living."[12] These passages are somewhat vague as to the age of the persons being compelled. Later Reich is clearer on this point. What minimalist autonomy as an educational ideal requires is that "a child be able to examine his own political values and beliefs, and those of others, with a critical and sympathetic eye. And . . . a child be able to think independently and subject his ends to critical scrutiny, enabling autonomous affirmation or autonomous revision of these ends."[13] But surely this is completely unrealistic with regard to the capabilities of a young child. Perry Glanzer, in commenting about these passages, aptly makes this suggestion: "One cannot help but wonder if Reich is envisioning a Stanford liberal-arts education instead of a primary and secondary school education for a 'child.'"[14] The problem here again is that the child is not being treated as a child.

I want to boldly suggest that much of this talk about children's capabilities and responsibilities and even rights with regard to learning is patently absurd. A young child is not in a position to critically review his or her political values! A young child is not able to think independently about ends, nor is a child able autonomously to affirm or revise these ends. Young children are not in a position to choose who influences or teaches them. They are stuck with "fate," if you will, or a "divine lottery" if you prefer religious language. The learning vocation of the young child is really very much out of his or her control.

Lest I be misinterpreted, let me add that I am not rejecting everything that is being said by advocates of children's capabilities, responsibilities, and rights. I am sympathetic with John E. Coons's emphasis on a child's responsibility to give trusting obedience to the authority she deems most likely to present her with the real good. I further concur that as children mature, they can and should take on more responsibility for their learning. I also believe that there is something very healthy about an emphasis on children's rights. Children need to be cared for and loved.[15] They need to be treated as persons. Each child is unique. Each child needs to be helped to grow toward maturity and independence.[16] And I would

---

12. Reich, *Bridging Liberalism*, 102.

13. Reich, *Bridging Liberalism*, 162.

14. Perry Glanzer, "Rethinking the Boundaries and Burdens of Parental Authority over Education: A Response to Robert Reich's Case-Study of Homeschooling," *Educational Theory* (forthcoming).

15. Reich worries about vague terms like "general welfare" or "best interests" of the child (*Bridging Liberalism*, 150). He tries to solve this problem by suggesting that adults are responsible for more clearly defined developmental needs (e.g., shelter, food, protection, nurture, affection, and love). However, he maintains that this line of argument does not in itself give parents "any corresponding interest in control over educational provision" (151).

16. Here Reich agrees with me, but strangely gives to the parents *and* the state the interest "that children develop into adults capable of independent functioning" (*Bridging Liberalism*, 154).

even agree that these parental duties toward children can be translated into correlative rights for children. But all this is rather self-evident. Thanks to maternal and paternal instincts, which are natural to parents, these responsibilities are by and large carried out on behalf of their children.[17]

All I am objecting to is the refusal to really face the unique status of young children with regard to learning. When we talk about the vocation of the child to learn, it is fundamentally mistaken to treat them as though they were adults. Children simply are not autonomous. They need to grow toward autonomy. Contrary to Reich and Dwyer, children are not adults, and it is foolish to try to treat them as such.[18] Children do not have the resources to choose the kind of education they should get. They first need to acquire these resources. Until then, someone will necessarily have to choose for them — parents, guardians, society, or the state.

Here let me interject my own interpretation of what I believe underlies a preoccupation with children's rights and the failure to take into account their dependence on adults. All too often such emphases are, unfortunately, an escape from parental responsibility and accountability. Someone has to assume pedagogical responsibility for children, and it is an awesome responsibility. One way to escape this responsibility is to put the onus on children themselves. Such a move, however, is dishonest: an example of what Sartre called "bad faith."[19] Children simply are not adults who can make important decisions re-

---

17. Dwyer is forced to admit that the vast majority of parents do genuinely love their children and will therefore take care of their fundamental needs (Dwyer, *Religious Schools*, 89). Crittenden further argues that there is something counterintuitive about the claim that for many centuries parents were generally indifferent if not harsh to their children. From the viewpoint of biological survival, adults must care for their young. Even animals do the same (Crittenden, *Parents*, 32-33).

18. Dwyer underscores as a basic assumption of his analysis, "that children are persons and that morally they are equal persons" (Dwyer, *Religious Schools*, 67, 121). But Dwyer's argument plays on an ambiguity in this claim. While he is quite right in insisting that children ought to be treated as persons, and that they are equal to adults in terms of having rights as moral persons, they are *not* equal to *adults* in terms of their ability to be self-determining and to take on certain responsibilities. Yet his whole argument hinges on treating them as *adults*. For example, he repeatedly stresses that no person has the right to control the lives of other persons (67-68, 100). But while this principle might apply to adults, though even here it is problematic as many relationships quite legitimately involve some degree of control over the other person, as Dwyer is forced to admit (72), this principle simply cannot apply to children, as they are not *adults*, as again Dwyer is forced on occasion to admit (64, 73, 85, 107). Indeed, to treat children as adults is to beg the question from the start. Further, there is a vagueness inherent in the very notion of "control," and Dwyer's failure to define the term more precisely really undermines his entire argument.

19. Jean-Paul Sartre, *Being and Nothingness: An Essay on Phenomenological Ontology* (New York: Philosophical Library, 1956), 48.

garding their education. To claim that children should be able to choose their own guardians, as some writers suggest, is just plain silliness.

Initiation as Part of the Vocation of the Child

Earlier I referred to a collection of related notions: initiation, absorption, and socialization. More needs to be said about these notions as we try to understand the learning vocation of the child. It will be helpful here to examine more closely some classic descriptions of education as initiation.[20] Michael Oakeshott, for example, has described education as initiation into the conversation of civilization.[21] In another essay, "Learning and Teaching," Oakeshott writes: "Every human being is born an heir to an inheritance to which he can succeed only in the process of learning."[22] But this inheritance is not what we usually think of, according to Oakeshott.

> What every man is born an heir to is an inheritance of human achievements; an inheritance of feelings, emotions, images, visions, thoughts, beliefs, ideas, understandings, intellectual and practical enterprises, languages, relationships, organizations, canons and maxims of conduct, procedures, rituals, skills, works of art, books, musical compositions, tools, artifacts and utensils — in short, what Dilthey called a *geistige Welt*.[23]

Again Oakeshott reminds us that "this world can be entered, possessed and enjoyed only in a process of learning."[24] And again he explains why he calls this world our common inheritance, "because to enter it is the only way of becoming a human being, and to inhabit it is to be a human being."[25] Oakeshott goes on to reflect on the central theme of this chapter, learning and teaching, and then introduces a word that is the central focus of this section of my chapter, "initiation." "It is into this *geistige Welt* that the child, even in its

20. This section draws on my earlier work on the nature of liberal education. See Elmer John Thiessen, *Teaching for Commitment: Liberal Education, Indoctrination, and Christian Nurture* (Montreal: McGill-Queen's University Press; Leominster, England: Gracewing, 1993), 42-44, 92-98.

21. Michael Oakeshott, *Rationalism in Politics and Other Essays* (London: Methuen, 1962), 199.

22. Michael Oakeshott, "Learning and Teaching," in *The Concept of Education*, ed. R. S. Peters, 156-76 (New York: Humanities Press, 1967), 158.

23. Oakeshott, "Learning and Teaching," 158.

24. Oakeshott, "Learning and Teaching," 158.

25. Oakeshott, "Learning and Teaching," 158.

earliest adventures in awareness, initiates itself; and to initiate his pupils into it is the business of the teacher."[26]

Unfortunately Oakeshott makes some errors in his otherwise insightful description of what it means for a child to learn and to become human. For one, he assumes too much by way of what initiation can accomplish. Initiation into our common inheritance might be the only way of becoming fully human, but surely it is not the only way of becoming human. Further, Oakeshott contradicts himself when he talks about the child initiating itself.[27] For several pages Oakeshott discusses the role of a teacher doing the initiating; however, Oakeshott does say: "It is into this *geistige Welt* that the child, even in its earliest adventures in awareness, initiates itself; and to initiate his pupils into it is the business of the teacher." I think Oakeshott is stressing "world" when he discusses the child initiating. We see here the error I have already referred to — a refusal to face the unique status of the child. The child does not initiate itself. It is a parent and/or a teacher that must initiate the child into the common inheritance that Oakeshott describes so carefully and accurately. Indeed, Oakeshott goes on to emphasize the indebtedness of children to the Sage or the teacher for initiating him or her into the inheritance.[28] I would suggest that his passing reference to the child initiating itself is perhaps a slipup. What Oakeshott might have in mind here is a child's interest or willingness to learn. But to talk of a child initiating itself is an error, which I believe reflects the common error made by so many today as they refuse to face the awesome responsibility of helping children to fulfill their vocation to learn.

I move on to a second classic description of education as initiation, given by R. S. Peters, the father of modern analytic philosophy of education.[29] Peters was in fact influenced by Michael Oakeshott's earlier description of education as initiation. Peters describes education as involving the development of the mind, and by taking such a developmental approach he is able to take into account what is involved in helping the very young child to learn, thus avoiding Oakeshott's error. According to Peters, this development of the mind is not a product of individual experience as the empiricists held. Instead, it is "the product of the initiation of an individual into public traditions enshrined in the language, concepts, beliefs, and rules of a society."[30] Peters also criticizes

26. Oakeshott, "Learning and Teaching," 158.
27. Oakeshott, "Learning and Teaching," 157-58.
28. Oakeshott, "Learning and Teaching," 159.
29. R. S. Peters, "Education as Initiation," in *Philosophical Analysis and Education,* ed. R. D. Archambault (London: Routledge and Kegan Paul, 1965), 87-111, here 102-10; Peters, *Ethics and Education,* Keystones in Education Series (London: George Allen and Unwin, 1966), 46-62.
30. Peters, *Ethics and Education,* 49.

Kant and Piaget for not recognizing "the extent to which the development of the mind is the product of initiation into public traditions enshrined in a public language."[31] There is a "social dimension of the development of mind," and this is why it is appropriate to compare education to a process of initiation.[32] Peters even suggests that because all education involves initiation into public traditions, it can be regarded as a form of "socialization."[33]

These "public traditions" include the traditional subject areas such as science, history, mathematics, religion, and aesthetic awareness.[34] These "forms of knowledge" are viewed as "a public inheritance" that parents and teachers are inviting the child to share and into which he or she is again "initiated."[35] The process is picturesquely described in terms of transforming children who are like "the barbarian outside the gates. The problem is to get them inside the citadel of civilization."[36]

But, how exactly does initiation work? First, we should note the authoritative nature of the initiation process. It is the parent, the teacher, and society, not the child, who determines what inheritance the child is initiated into. The child is simply not given a choice. Here it is interesting to note that Peters is not entirely consistent on this point. Peters explicitly justifies his use of the term "initiation" to describe education by comparing it with typical initiation rites and ceremonies of, say, the Native American.[37] Such initiation rites open up, to the young, mysteries to which they have not as yet been exposed. In making this comparison Peters goes on to argue that such initiation rites presuppose that the initiate has freely chosen to be initiated.[38] It is here where I believe he runs into some problems because there are some real difficulties in describing paradigm cases of initiation as voluntary. In typical "rites of passage," it is precisely the initiation process that transforms immature adolescents into responsible adults. Young adolescents do not choose to belong to their particular tribe. Nor do they choose to be initiated into the particular customs they will have to adopt after initiation. Here we find that Peters, like Oakeshott, succumbs to the error of assuming too much autonomy on the part of the child. Children do not choose to be initiated. Adults choose to initiate children into an inheritance that children themselves do not choose.

31. Peters, *Ethics and Education,* 49.
32. Peters, *Ethics and Education,* 54.
33. Peters, *Ethics and Education,* 81, 253, 257.
34. Peters, *Ethics and Education,* 49.
35. Peters, *Ethics and Education,* 53.
36. Peters, "Education as Initiation," 107.
37. Peters, *Ethics and Education,* 54.
38. Peters, *Ethics and Education,* 54.

A second aspect of initiation that I want to deal with is the role of tradition. The child is initiated into "public traditions," Peters tells us. There are several things we need to note about these traditions. They are viewed as absolute in some sense by Peters. The barbarian is introduced to the "citadel of civilization," and it seems as though there is only one such citadel. Young children will and can only be initiated into our traditions. And in the process of initiation, these traditions will be viewed as fixed and ultimate truth, at least from the point of view of the young child. Of course, we as adults realize that our public traditions can evolve and change. But young children cannot understand the possibility of evolution and change in the public traditions they are taught. Initially the traditions are received and understood as fixed and absolute, and are accepted in an unquestioning manner. Only after children have been initiated into the public traditions can they begin to evaluate them critically.[39] But here we are focusing on what happens before children reach the questioning stage; there is an aspect of the learning process that involves simple trust and unquestioning belief. Indeed, as Peters notes, in referring to Piaget's research, it is doubtful whether most people ever emerge entirely from this stage of unquestioning belief in the public traditions they are taught.[40] Even adults have a need for "plausibility structures" that reinforce tradition.[41]

A final aspect of the initiation process is its nonrational character. Peters is well aware that initiation depends on mechanisms of imitation and identification; those who make the education process entirely child-centered overlook the way, "from time immemorial, most beliefs and forms of conduct have been learnt by the human race, namely by picking them up from the example and instruction of more experienced people who rank as authorities or experts in a community."[42] But the processes of learning by example, imitation, or identification cannot themselves be described as rational processes. Here we must be careful to distinguish between what is being imitated or identified with and the actual mechanism of imitation. I am not denying that the content being imitated might be intelligible and even rational. But the process of imitation itself is not one of reasoning and autonomous critical judgment. Indeed, imitation is largely an unconscious process.

I believe that the notion of initiation is very helpful in understanding how a young child learns. But, as we have seen, the child is not in charge of this initi-

39. Oakeshott, "Learning and Teaching," 162.

40. R. S. Peters, *Education and the Education of Teachers* (London: Routledge and Kegan Paul, 1977), 81.

41. Peter L. Berger, *The Sacred Canopy: Elements of a Sociological Theory of Religion* (Garden City, N.Y.: Doubleday, 1967), 50.

42. Peters, *Education and the Education of Teachers*, 83; cf. Peters, *Ethics and Education*, 60.

ation process. Fulfilling the vocation of learning for a child entails submission to authority, both of persons and of traditions, and it is essentially a nonrational process. But to describe the learning vocation of the child only in these terms is incomplete. Thus, in the following section I talk about the goals of such initiation, taking into account the development of a normal child.

Initiation and Normal Autonomy

Sometimes it is important to state the obvious. A child does not remain a child.[43] The vocation of the child includes growth and development. But what exactly is the goal of such growth and development, specifically with respect to learning, which is the focus of this chapter? And how is the initiation phase of a child's cognitive development related to the eventual goal of his or her development?

The vocation of the child is to grow and develop and become a mature adult. This much can surely be said without encountering too much opposition. To return to some theological considerations, Jesus "grew in wisdom and stature," we are told in the Gospel of Luke (2:52). Eventually he functioned as an adult, making independent decisions, even to the point of challenging his mother and distancing himself from his immediate family (John 2:1-11; Matt. 12:46-50). While I believe there is fairly widespread agreement on this "natural" understanding of what it means to be an adult, significant differences quickly emerge when it comes to spelling out exactly what is included in the ideal of adulthood.

Since the Enlightenment, the ideal of "autonomy" has gained widespread acceptance as a way of describing what it means to be an adult. The following ingredients would seem to be essential to the modern liberal notion of autonomy as found in various treatments of this concept in educational writings: freedom, independence or authenticity, self-control, competence, and rational reflection including the ability to be open-minded and critical. As I have argued elsewhere, there are some fundamental problems with this liberal ideal of autonomy.[44] I believe this ideal fails to do justice to human interdependence and human finiteness. This ideal is also unrealistic as to the level of independence, rationality, open-mindedness, and critical thinking that can be achieved by

---

43. It might seem that Vigen Guroian, in a chapter in this volume, disagrees with me, but this seeming disagreement turns on two different meanings of "child." See 123 above. I quite agree that in one sense a person always remains a child of a father and a mother. "Child" here is a relational term. But children do cease being children in terms of maturity.

44. Thiessen, *Teaching for Commitment*, 117-43.

"normal" human beings. Following Haworth,[45] I defend an ideal of "normal autonomy" as the goal of education. Normal autonomy is more realistic about the level of independence, rationality, and critical openness that we as human beings can achieve. My ideal of normal autonomy is also similar to Reich's notion of "minimalist conception of autonomy," although I don't think he does justice to the fact of human interdependence.[46]

Human beings are obviously not born autonomous.[47] Children, however, should grow toward normal autonomy. One could even say that they have a right to have their capacity for autonomy developed.[48] While children are not born autonomous, they certainly have the capacity and natural impulse to become so. And yet, they also need to be helped to move toward this goal. Here there needs to be a blend between nature and nurture.[49] Children cannot grow toward autonomy on their own. They are again very dependent on adults to help them become autonomous. They need to be nurtured and educated toward autonomy.[50] We must therefore determine what will help children to fulfill this part of their vocation.

I want to argue that initiation is essential to helping children grow toward autonomy. Indeed, rather than being embarrassed about the need to initiate children into the language and understanding of the adult world, we should see such initiation as an essential ingredient to helping children grow toward autonomy. Various philosophers have introduced the notion of a "primary culture" as a way of describing the initiation component of a child's education. These writers have stressed the need for a stable and coherent primary culture

45. Lawrence Haworth, *Autonomy: An Essay in Philosophical Psychology and Ethics* (New Haven: Yale University Press, 1986).

46. Reich, *Bridging Liberalism,* 92, 98.

47. Children may display autonomy in a very minimal sense, but certainly not at the level of normal autonomy expected of adults (Reich, *Bridging Liberalism,* 2, 55). John E. Coons, similarly, in his chapter in this volume, wants to give children some responsibility, but he himself admits that the status of a child prior to consciousness of duty to seek content of an authoritative order of truths and goods remains a mystery. See 80 above.

48. Thiessen, *Teaching for Commitment,* 117-43, 243-77; Crittenden, *Parents,* 99, 116, 203; William A. Galston, *Liberal Purposes: Goods, Virtues, and Diversity in the Liberal State* (Cambridge: Cambridge University Press, 1991), 252; Stephen G. Gilles, "On Educating Children: A Parentalist Manifesto," *University of Chicago Law Review* 63, no. 3 (1996): 941, 945; Eamonn Callan, *Creating Citizens: Political Education and Liberal Democracy,* Oxford Political Theory (Oxford: Clarendon, 1997), 190; Haworth, *Autonomy,* 127; and Reich, *Bridging Liberalism,* 156.

49. Here I am taking a middle position similar to that of Guroian, who, after contrasting two theories of childhood (developmental and postmodern, constructivist), opts for a middle position.

50. R. T. Allen, "Rational Autonomy: The Destruction of Freedom," *Journal of Philosophy of Education* 16, no. 2 (1982): 199.

for children to develop toward autonomy.[51] This need for a stable and coherent primary culture would suggest that children must not be exposed to too many ideas or too much uncertainty too soon. While an infant may learn English or Urdu or both, there are limits to the cultural diversity he or she can confront without losing a sense of the meanings that the noises and motions might ultimately signify. "Exposing children to an endless and changing Babel of talk and behavior will only prevent the development of the abilities he requires if he is ever to take his place among the citizenry."[52]

There is in fact abundant psychological support for this position. R. S. Peters, for example, draws on various findings in developmental psychology to show that a secure and nonpermissive environment is essential to nurturing autonomy.[53] Autonomous adults seem to emerge from homes with a warm attitude of acceptance toward children, "an attitude . . . which encourage[s] trust in others and confidence in their own powers."[54] Children also need a "firm and consistent insistence on rules of behaviour" and "a predictable social environment."[55] This will encourage them to reflect on the consequences of their behavior and to develop self-control, both of which are essential for autonomy.[56] Peters also draws on the work of Piaget and Kohlberg and their theories of moral development, which maintain that autonomy can only be achieved by children first passing through the earlier stages of moral development, i.e., "good boy" and "authority-oriented" stages.[57] So again it would seem that children need a nonpermissive environment where they learn to obey in order to develop toward autonomy.[58]

---

51. Bruce Ackerman, *Social Justice in the Liberal State* (New Haven: Yale University Press, 1980), 139-67; Doret De Ruyter and Siebren Miedema, "Denominational Schools in the Netherlands," in *Spiritual and Religious Education,* ed. Mal Leicester, Celia Modgil, and Sohan Modgil (New York: Falmer, 2000), 139; T. H. McLaughlin, "Parental Rights and the Religious Upbringing of Children," *Journal of Philosophy of Education* 18, no. 1 (1984): 78-82; Brenda Watson, *Education and Belief* (Oxford: Basil Blackwell, 1987), 58-59.

52. Ackerman, *Social Justice,* 141.

53. R. S. Peters, "Freedom and the Development of the Free Man," in *Educational Judgments: Papers in the Philosophy of Education,* ed. James F. Doyle (London: Routledge and Kegan Paul, 1973), 119-42.

54. Peters, "Freedom," 130.

55. Peters, "Freedom," 130.

56. Peters, "Freedom," 130.

57. Peters, "Freedom," 132.

58. These conclusions are confirmed by others working in the fields of developmental psychology and psychiatry, such as Michael Rutter and Urie Bronfenbrenner, to name only two. Michael Rutter, *Maternal Deprivation Reassessed* (Harmondsworth: Penguin Books, 1972); Urie Bronfenbrenner, *The Ecology of Human Development: Experiments by Nature and Design* (Cambridge: Harvard University Press, 1979).

Here I want to stress once again that it is parents or other adults who will be doing the nurturing toward autonomy. Not only do they have a responsibility to provide their children with a stable and coherent primary culture, which is a condition for development toward normal autonomy, but they also have a responsibility to gradually push their children toward growing independence. To fail to do so is a serious failure in child rearing on the part of parents and adults. Indeed, such a failure can properly be described as indoctrination, as I have argued elsewhere.[59]

At the same time, it needs to be stressed that providing children with a narrow upbringing, or a stable and coherent primary culture, should not in itself be condemned as indoctrinating. It is only if parents or adults attempt to stop growth toward autonomy on the part of their children, if they are trying to keep their children as perpetual children, that they should be accused of indoctrinating. In the same way, initiating or socializing children is not in itself indoctrination, as some assume.[60] Indeed, much of the discussion of indoctrination by educationalists is fundamentally misguided precisely on this point.[61] It is only if we fail to give children the tools to critically evaluate that into which they have been initiated that we should be accused of indoctrinating.

Christian Nurture and the Ideal of Autonomy

It is time now to apply all this specifically to a Christian upbringing. Here it will be necessary, first of all, to deal with a couple of widely held objections to the very possibility of Christian nurture promoting growth toward autonomy. The first objection can be dealt with quickly because I have already touched on it. Many critics of Christianity would argue that Christian nurture cannot aim for and promote growth toward autonomy because autonomy itself is not a Christian value. My response: it all depends on what is meant by autonomy. If autonomy is understood in its traditional sense (freedom, independence, rationality, critical openness, and competence), and if these ingredients are understood in a strong, and idealistic sense, then yes, Christian nurture is incompatible with the goal of fostering autonomy. But, as I have already argued, this Enlightenment ideal of autonomy is itself problematic. However, if we adopt instead the

59. Thiessen, *Teaching for Commitment*, 232-41. McLaughlin similarly suggests that indoctrination "constitutes an attempt to restrict in a substantial way the child's eventual ability to function autonomously" (McLaughlin, "Parental Rights," 78).

60. Tasos Kazepides, "Programmatic Definitions in Education: The Case of Indoctrination," *Canadian Journal of Education* 14, no. 3 (1989): 387-96.

61. For an extended argument of this point, see Thiessen, *Teaching for Commitment*, 221-32.

ideal of "normal autonomy," which acknowledges human limitations and inter-dependence, and is more realistic in its expectations of how independent and rational we can be, then Christian nurture is compatible with the goal of foster-ing autonomy.

Normal autonomy is very much a Christian value, as has been argued by Lois Walker.[62] Various scriptural passages could be cited that support the key elements of normal autonomy. The individual person is given value, dignity, and worth (Gen. 1; Pss. 8; 139; Matt. 6:25-34; John 10). Ultimately it is the individual who is called to respond to God and is held accountable by God (Ezek. 3; Matt. 16:24-28), and the individual's right of refusal is respected (Luke 9:5, 55). This emphasis on the individual is of course balanced with an equal emphasis on our collective identity — the community and people of God as a community (Luke 10:25-37; Exod. 19:4-6; 1 Pet. 2:9). But the emphasis on the individual still stands. There is also an emphasis on rationality, knowledge, and the development of the mind, as I argued earlier. Even critical openness (the ability to be critical and open-minded about one's beliefs) is supported as an ideal, though as John Hull comments after a review of the New Testament on this topic, "The kind of critical openness which flows from Christian faith has many links with the secular educational ideal of autonomy, and yet, . . . it has distinctive flavour and colouring."[63]

I return to the central questions of this section: Can Christian nurture be linked with the goal of fostering growth toward normal autonomy? If so, how? Clearly, Christian nurture also aims at conversion and edification in the Chris-tian faith. And here seems to be the rub. Does not the specific intention that children are to grow up to become Christians rule out the possibility of pro-moting growth toward autonomy? I want to suggest that those who see a prob-lem here commit the either-or fallacy. We are not necessarily stuck with a choice between intending to convert a child or intending to foster autonomy. We can intend to do both.

McLaughlin defends the coherence of this two-pronged intention by distin-guishing between the long-term and short-term aims of religious parents.[64] "Their long-term, or ultimate, aim is to place their children in a position where they can autonomously choose to accept or reject their religious faith. . . . Since, however, these parents have decided to approach the development of their child's autonomy in religion through exposing them to their own particular religious faith, their short-term aim is the development of faith; albeit a faith which is not

62. Lois H. Walker [pseud.], "Religion Gives Meaning to Life," in *Philosophy: The Quest for Truth*, ed. Louis P. Pojman, 6th ed. (New York: Oxford University Press, 2006), 551-54.

63. John Hull, *Studies in Religion and Education* (London: Falmer, 1984), 190-95, 207-25; cf. Isa. 41:21; Rom. 12:1-2; Phil. 1:9-11; 1 John 4:1.

64. McLaughlin, "Parental Rights," 79.

closed off from future revision or rejection. So a coherent way of characterizing the intention of the parents is that they are aiming at autonomy via faith."[65]

McLaughlin's distinction between long-term and short-term aims is helpful in that it takes into account the fact that autonomy develops in stages. This "psychogenetic perspective" in the development of autonomy is missed in some accounts of autonomy, according to Haworth.[66] McLaughlin worries that religious parents "might not be committed to autonomy in a sufficiently strong sense to satisfy liberal demands."[67] Indeed, one of his critics has argued that few religious parents would adopt McLaughlin's prescriptions for promoting autonomy.[68] The basic problem here is that both McLaughlin and his critics fail to distinguish between the traditional liberal ideal of autonomy and the ideal of normal autonomy that I have defended in this chapter. Christian parents will probably not be committed to autonomy in a sufficiently strong sense to satisfy traditional liberal demands, but this ideal is philosophically unsound. The ideal of normal autonomy is both defensible and consistent with Christian principles. Therefore it is coherent to say that Christian parents and teachers can aim for "autonomy via faith."

No doubt some critics will remain unconvinced by the above, and thus someone like Gardner argues that Christian parents and teachers claiming to aim for autonomy are being "hypocritical or disingenuous."[69] Unfortunately, this comes dangerously close to being an ad hominem argument that civilized people, especially philosophers, should never use. I would be so bold as to suggest that Christian parents and teachers (and religious parents and teachers generally) who frankly admit that they want their children to grow up to become Christians are perhaps more honest than their detractors. After all, how would a liberal agnostic parent really feel if his child autonomously chose to become a committed Christian? And how about the atheistic parent who, in the interest of a liberal upbringing, faithfully brings his child to Sunday school so she can choose for herself? But of course, this parent never enters a church door himself. What message does the child really get? We all know that actions speak louder than words. What are the real intentions of this parent, particularly from the child's perspective? I would suggest that there is a certain "evangelistic" intent in all forms of upbringing and teaching. It is just that religious parents are a little more honest about their intentions.

65. McLaughlin, "Parental Rights," 79.
66. Haworth, *Autonomy,* 19.
67. McLaughlin, "Parental Rights," 79.
68. Peter Gardner, "Religious Upbringing and the Liberal Ideal of Religious Autonomy," *Journal of Philosophy of Education* 22, no. 1 (1988): 98-99.
69. Gardner, "Religious Upbringing," 102.

Who Helps the Child to Fulfill His/Her Vocation to Learn?

There is a final question that needs to be addressed. I have argued that children are unable to fulfill their vocation to learn on their own. They are very dependent on adults both in terms of initiation into the conversation of civilization or the public traditions enshrined in the language, concepts, beliefs, and rules of a society, and in terms of encouraging growth toward autonomy. Thus far I have spoken variously of parents, teachers, or adults as taking on this responsibility. It is now time to become a little more precise as to who exactly takes on this awesome responsibility.

I maintain it is the parents of a child who have the primary responsibility for helping the child to fulfill his or her vocation to learn. In an earlier work I argued for the primacy of the rights and responsibilities of parents in nurturing and educating their children, focusing particularly on being able to choose the kind of education their children should receive in schools.[70] However, I maintain that these arguments apply more generally, and that they can also be applied specifically to the nurture, training, and education of children in the home before they reach school age. Hence I included a treatment of Reich's discussion on home-schooling.[71] There is something very arbitrary about making a sharp distinction between the education the child receives at home and the education a child receives in school. Indeed, I believe the argument of the primacy of parents' rights to choose the kind of education their children receive in schools builds on the more general argument that parents have the primary responsibility to help the child to fulfill his or her vocation to learn. Thus it is appropriate to review my earlier argument in relation to the topic of this chapter. Here I will merely provide a brief outline of six arguments for the primacy of the rights and responsibilities of parents to help their children to learn.

1. Biblical argument: I begin with a theological argument, though I want to

---

70. Elmer John Thiessen, *In Defence of Religious Schools and Colleges* (Montreal and Kingston: McGill-Queen's University Press, 2001), 63-79. My defense of the primacy of parental rights draws particularly on the writings of Crittenden and Gilles. Crittenden, *Parents, the State, and the Right to Educate;* Gilles, "On Educating Children," 937-1034; Gilles, "Liberal Parentalism and Children's Educational Rights," *Capital University Law Review* 26, no. 1 (1997): 9-44. Here it should be noted that I prefer to talk of both rights and responsibilities. With Locke, I would argue that parental authority over children is in a large measure grounded in parental obligations to children. John Locke, *Second Treatise of Government* (London, 1689). It is unfortunate that discussions about authority over education tend to be expressed in the language of rights. The language of rights tends to be rather absolutist, and therefore not too helpful when conflicting rights emerge. A greater focus on responsibilities to the child in the area of education would, I suggest, ameliorate some of the apparent conflicts that now dominate discussions.

71. Reich, *Bridging Liberalism and Multiculturalism in American Education.*

stress that the remaining arguments are also compatible with the teachings of the Bible. The Scriptures begin with God and creation. God created a structured world, not only physically, but also in terms of the way in which human beings should interrelate and fulfill their various tasks. To Adam and Eve God gave a command, "Be fruitful and multiply, and fill the earth and subdue it" (Gen. 1:28). To fulfill this cultural mandate, man and woman would have to engage in a rich diversity of social tasks. This has led Christian thinkers of both Catholic and Protestant orientation to adopt a social philosophy of structural pluralism that recognizes that there are multiple spheres of social activity.[72]

One of these spheres is the family, which is foundational in a society, according to a Christian social philosophy. Children are God's gift to parents (Ps. 127:3). Parental care for children is assumed (Deut. 1:31; Matt. 7:9-11). And parents are given the responsibility to educate their children (Deut. 6:4-9, 20ff.; Prov. 22:6; Eph. 6:1-4). The primary authority of parents to educate is natural and part of the creation order.[73] Reference to God's creation order explains why this religious argument for parental rights concurs with the "secular" arguments I will review below. A proper regard for nature, with or without reference to God, will yield similar arguments. This is in keeping with a long-standing natural law tradition in ethics, most often expressed in Roman Catholic writings.

2. Biological argument: from a biological perspective, the most obvious answer to the question, "to whom does the child belong?" is that the child belongs

---

72. For a clear statement of the biblical foundations of structural pluralism, see Rockne McCarthy, Donald Oppewal, Walfred Peterson, and Gordon Spykman, *Society, State, and Schools: A Case for Structural and Confessional Pluralism* (Grand Rapids: Eerdmans, 1981), 145-68.

73. There are many people today who would object to any appeal to nature, with or without its theological overtones. The family is viewed as an artificial construct, just as the state is most often seen as a product of a social contract. Crittenden himself, though defending a position similar to mine, explicitly rejects an appeal to nature when he maintains that "marriage and the family are cultural and social designs, not natural necessities" (Crittenden, *Parents*, 48). But Crittenden contradicts himself when he goes on to say that marriage and the family "are anchored in human dispositions and needs that are fundamental in the life of individuals and the species: sexual relations between male and female, the conception and procreation of human life, the care of helpless infants, the socialization and education of children, the companionship of a man and woman, membership of an intimate and personal community that has identity over generations" (48). Crittenden fails to see that to appeal to universal dispositions and needs is to appeal to nature. To those who claim that the nuclear family is a passing phenomenon, I would suggest that historical evidence is against them. Crittenden reviews the evidence and concludes that the institutions of marriage and the family "have proved to be remarkably enduring and resilient" (48). Such continuity provides some justification for claiming that the family is a natural institution, and that education as a parental responsibility is also natural.

to its parents. The child owes its existence to its mother and father. Procreation is generally seen as the "basic ground on which the responsibility of caring for a child can reasonably be assigned, and on which freedom from interference in the rearing of a child can be claimed."[74] While we must be careful not to regard children as mere possessions of their parents, or simply an extension of them, the biological relationship would seem to confer special custodial rights onto parents. Even critics of the primacy of parental education rights are generally forced to concede the biological argument for such rights, at least in part.[75]

It might be argued that other adults could satisfy the needs of children as well as, and sometimes better than, their parents. I grant this, but it is surely rather arbitrary to prevent parents who were responsible for giving birth to a child from being the primary agents of its further development — assuming, of course, that they are willing and able to provide the care and affection needed.[76]

3. Children's interest argument: parents naturally love their children and therefore have strong incentives for looking out for their best interest. True, there are some parents who do not care enough for their children and some who even abuse them, but this is the exception rather than the rule, and might at most call for a selective departure from the principle of giving parents primary educational rights.[77]

Dwyer, despite his opposition to parental rights, makes implicit appeal both to the biological argument and to the children's best interest argument

74. Crittenden, *Parents,* 68. Crittenden devotes a section to reviewing writers, both ancient and modern, who have used the biological relationship itself to confer certain moral rights on parents over their children (55-61). Various writers have also extended the biological argument by appealing to maternal and paternal instincts (73; cf. Locke, *Second Treatise of Government,* #56, 67).

75. Hobson, in objecting to the biological argument, maintains that the mere fact of giving birth to a child does not give a parent moral rights over it. Peter Hobson, "Some Reflections on Parents' Rights in the Upbringing of Their Children," *Journal of Philosophy of Education* 18, no. 1 (1984): 64. But in the next paragraph Hobson argues that "[t]he only rights that parents have by virtue of giving birth to a child flow from duties that this gives rise to" (64). But this is to concede the very point he seems to be arguing against! (this might be an overstatement because Hobson seems to argue that parental rights flow from duties owed to children).

76. Crittenden, *Parents,* 71. There are other problems with transferring parental rights to other adults. How would decisions on the placement of children be made? What criteria would be used to decide when a child should be put into the care of others? Can we measure adequacy of care accurately enough to make decisions like this? Administrative problems such as these lead Gilles to conclude that the "rejection of special custodial rights for biological parents . . . seems unjust but imprudent" (Gilles, "On Educating Children," 961).

77. Gilles draws a useful analogy pointing out that "[w]e don't abandon the principle of adult self-governance just because many adults mistreat, abuse, or even kill themselves" (Gilles, "On Educating Children," 954).

when he concedes that in many aspects of children's lives we should support "a presumption of parental decision-making authority" because parents love their children and are in the best position to know what they need.[78] Similarly Reich is forced to concede that parents are best situated to promote their children's welfare.[79]

4. Parental interests argument: a fourth argument rests on the value of personal relationships. Parents generally take a special interest in their own offspring and find much satisfaction in giving them life. Further, parenting, nurturing, and educating one's children are generally tasks that parents take great delight in.[80] Even liberal writers who place more importance on children's rights or state rights are nevertheless forced to concede that parenting is of paramount importance to most individuals.[81] Given the importance that individuals place on parenting, and given liberalism's aim of enabling persons to satisfy their basic needs, it would seem to follow that parents' desire to shape the education of their children should be respected.

5. Primary culture argument: my fifth argument can be seen as growing out of the previous two arguments. There is a good deal of research highlighting the importance of family as a means of satisfying children's basic needs for

78. Dwyer, *Religious Schools*, 81-90. Indeed, Dwyer's frequent claim that parents should be seen as having only the "privilege" rather than the right to make educational decisions, begs the question as to why they should have this privilege in the first place (4-5, 47, 92, 119). This privilege, which in fact sounds suspiciously like a right, Dwyer's claims to the contrary notwithstanding (46-47), is based on the fact that it is in the best interests of children to give this right to parents. Dwyer raises one important objection to this argument: "There is no self-evident connection between parents' religious beliefs and children's temporal interests" (82). But this rests on Dwyer's grossly exaggerated assessment of the harm that religion does to children, and on an arbitrary limitation to temporal interests. There are studies to show that religion has temporal benefits. George H. Gallup and Timothy Jones, *The Saints among Us* (Harrisburg, Pa.: Morehouse, 1992).

79. Reich, *Bridging Liberalism*, 150.

80. Crittenden refers to research by Brigitte and Peter Berger showing that the family was regarded as the most important personal value by 92 percent of the adults surveyed. Crittenden, *Parents*, 283 n. 30; Brigitte Berger and Peter L. Berger, *The War over the Family: Capturing the Middle Ground* (Garden City, N.Y.: Doubleday, 1983; Harmondsworth: Penguin Books, 1984); Callan, *Creating Citizens*, 144.

81. White, for example, stresses children's rights but admits that becoming a parent and bringing up a family is something that most people want to devote a good part of their lives to and gives them considerable satisfaction. Patricia White, "Parental Choice and Education for Citizenship," in *Parental Choice and Education: Principles, Policy, and Practice*, ed. J. Mark Halstead (London: Kogan Page, 1994), 85. However, White stops at using the language of rights here, though she gives no reason for doing so. Reich similarly talks about the "self-regarding interests" of the parents, where children are seen as linked to the parents' conception of the good life. Reich, *Bridging Liberalism*, 149.

close personal relationships and achieving a sense of identity.[82] As I have already argued, a stable and coherent primary culture is also necessary as a foundation from which children subsequently develop into autonomous adults. This need for stability and coherence gives parents the right to determine the character of the "primary culture" for their children, without undue interference from other individuals or agencies. Such interference would prove harmful to a child's development.

What does this need for a primary culture mean for the family? It entails that sharing beliefs and values, influencing and educating children, is an essential element of the common life of the family. Indeed, all this is inescapable. It is not possible for parents merely to expose their children to their beliefs, as Callan maintains.[83] Infants aren't merely "spectators" as Callan has to assume — they are necessarily totally immersed in their parents' life, language, and culture.[84] To negate the parents' right to influence and educate would in effect destroy the family, with all its benefits. The family could no longer function as a small and intimate community if parental influence were denied.

6. Argument from liberalism: the primacy of parental rights can also be defended on the basis of generally accepted premises of liberalism. A basic liberal value involves treating adults as self-governing persons entitled to choose and pursue their own "reasonable" conception of the good life, unless it rejects a basic moral or liberal-political norm on which there is a general consensus among reasonable people in a society. This principle would suggest that parents should enjoy the authority to educate their children in accord with their own conceptions of the good life, unless these conceptions are plainly unreasonable.[85]

---

82. On the child's need for the family, Crittenden refers to Fraiberg, as well as to a study by Rossi (1977, 15-16) summarizing research showing the difficulties in communal child rearing. Crittenden, *Parents*, 283 n. 31; Selma Fraiberg, *Every Child's Birthright: In Defense of Mothering* (New York: Basic Books, 1977); Alice S. Rossi, "A Biosocial Perspective on Parenting," *Daedalus* 106, no. 2 (1977): 1-31. Even Dwyer, despite his strong attack against parental rights, concedes that "optimal upbringing for a child involves an intimate, continuous relationship with a single set of parents that is largely insulated from interference by third parties" (Dwyer, *Religious Schools*, 81). However, in another place he suggests there is no empirical evidence for the need of a primary culture (145). I would say: no empirical evidence regarding the harm children face from exposure to differing belief systems. The facts are otherwise, and this contradicts his earlier claim.

83. Eamonn Callan, "McLaughlin on Parental Rights," *Journal of Philosophy of Education* 19, no. 1 (1985): 111.

84. T. H. McLaughlin, "Religion, Upbringing and Liberal Values: A Rejoinder to Eamonn Callan," *Journal of Philosophy of Education* 19, no. 1 (1985): 122.

85. Another, simpler variant of this argument involves an appeal to the liberal/democratic value of freedom and personal autonomy. White reviews several writers who have defended pa-

It can further be argued that parental educational rights should be seen as an extension of the right to free speech.[86] Parents should be free to communicate their values to their children directly as well as through the speech of teachers and schools as their chosen agents. I therefore concur with Gilles that liberal statecraft should not only merely tolerate the primacy of parental rights in the area of education but also "should encourage and rely" on it.[87]

This completes my review of the central arguments for the primacy of parents' rights and responsibilities in helping their children fulfill their vocation to learn. Here it should be noted that I am disassociating myself from an extreme position held by some Christians that defines parental rights in the area of the education of children in exclusive terms.[88] This extreme position holds that parents alone have the right to determine the kind of education their children receive. By contrast, I am only arguing for the *primacy* of parental rights and responsibilities. This position still allows for the sharing of responsibilities for the education of children among parents, a larger family or cultural group, teachers, and the state. While such rights are shared, I still believe that parental rights and responsibilities are primary.

It should further be noted that my position on the primacy of parental rights and responsibilities does not in and of itself negate the importance of children's rights. As I have already pointed out, children do have some important rights — the right to have their basic developmental needs met (shelter, food, protection, nurture, affection, and love), as well as the development of "baseline competencies" and the nurturing of growth toward autonomy.[89] But

---

rental rights simply in terms of the democratic right of citizens to personal autonomy. White, "Parental Choice," 84-85. Crittenden similarly argues that the right "to direct the upbringing of one's children is a distinct moral right that derives from a more general right protecting freedom of action" (Crittenden, *Parents*, 66).

86. Gilles, "On Educating Children," 1012-33.

87. Gilles, "On Educating Children," 941.

88. For an example of this position, see Thiessen, *Defence of Religious Schools*, 65-66.

89. Crittenden, while admitting that there is some dispute as to what to include in a list of goods that children require, suggests that the following surely can be safely included: "survival and healthy physical growth; affectionate care by [their parents]; . . . a sense of identity and worth"; and education. Crittenden, *Parents*, 101, 116. My list of basic needs draws on Reich's unpacking of what is in the "best interests" of children. Reich, *Bridging Liberalism*, 151-54. Strangely, Reich limits parental responsibilities to the basic developmental needs, and excludes "any corresponding interest over educational provision," which he gives to the state (151). I would suggest that this is quite arbitrary, and simply reflects Reich's bias toward state authority in education. Concern: Reich seems to be arguing that parents do have responsibility over education and is investigating how much discretion should be allowed by comparing state, parental, and child's interests. See p. 148.

talk about children's rights is problematic, in that they are not in a position to demand the satisfaction of these rights. As I have already argued, children are dependent on someone else for the satisfaction of their needs. Here I want to suggest that the affirmation of children's rights in education at the expense of the primacy of parental rights often rests on an assumption that these two options are mutually exclusive. It is either one or the other. But both can be affirmed at the same time.[90] The "best interests" of the child, an ideal so dear to child-rights advocates, is perfectly compatible with a healthy affirmation of the primacy of parental rights. Indeed, caring parents have the best interests of their children in mind.

I further acknowledge that when parental care is obviously lacking and even harmful, and when educational choices are plainly unreasonable, then the state (or a teacher on behalf of the state) is justified in intervening.[91] My position is similar to that of Gilles, who gives it the label "liberal parentalism."[92] This position is liberal, Gilles argues, "both because it sharply limits the state's role in the upbringing of children, and because it limits parents' educational and custodial authority over them. Parents may not abuse or neglect their children, or deprive them of a basic education; and de jure parental control ends when the child becomes an adult."[93]

The latter point deserves more comment. Exactly when does parental educational and custodial authority over children end? Almost everyone would agree that children are better off when caring adults make major choices for them until after adolescence. The optimal age of general or educational emancipation is ultimately an empirical question. Evidence from the social sciences suggests that adolescents lack self-control, underestimate risks, and make decisions without due regard for their long-term self-interest. Given that this pattern of unreliable decision making extends to educational choices, a good case

90. Callan, for example, has recently argued for a strict equality of parental and children's rights. Callan, *Creating Citizens*, 144-45. He quite correctly points out that to appeal only to the interests of parents is despotic (144). But to maintain that only the interests of children really count merely inverts the despotism (144-45). Like me, Callan wants to avoid exclusive claims with regard to educational rights. We need to affirm both parental and children's rights. I would, however, disagree with the egalitarianism of Callan's treatment, because parental rights need to be given primacy.

91. Here it should be noted that I take strong exception to Rob Reich's position when he puts the burden of proof for adequate teaching and care on home-schooling parents instead of the state. Reich, *Bridging Liberalism*, 169. Surely, as Perry Glanzer points out, home-schooling parents should be seen as innocent until proven guilty (forthcoming). To put the burden of proof on parents opens the door to state authoritarianism.

92. Gilles, "Liberal Parentalism," 9.

93. Gilles, "Liberal Parentalism," 9.

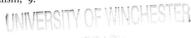

can be made for keeping educational authority in parents' hands until after adolescence. As children mature, they will and should have increasing voice and influence in decision making in the home, but ultimate authority should still rest in the parents.[94] Here, of course, we need to take into account the fact that children mature at different rates.

In summary, while recognizing the primacy of parental rights, I am suggesting that there is a multiple basis for authority and rights in education and that it is wrong to locate this authority in any single institution, person, or group of persons.[95] Such a multiple basis for authority and rights in education is in fact a key to avoiding the dangers of exclusive authority in this area. By giving parents primary authority, I also overcome the potential problem of a conflict when it is claimed that several parties have equal rights to educate children. There is still a need to show exactly how educational authority is to be shared among parents, citizens, and professional educators, while at the same time protecting the rights of the children to ensure that their best interests are maintained. It is beyond the scope of this chapter to provide a careful delineation of these rights and responsibilities. However, I will outline the rough boundaries of these rights and responsibilities, extending this also to education in schools.

The primacy of parental rights and responsibilities entails that parents should be able to home-school or send their children to schools that reflect their own ideological (secular or religious) outlook. Parents, however, must always also have the good of the child in mind. As already pointed out, children have the right to have the basic human goods provided. The education of children should be in their long-term interest, and, as has already been argued, this includes fostering growth toward normal rational autonomy. This also means that as children mature, parents (and teachers) need to adjust their level of in-

---

94. Gilles proposes an experiment to put his position on educational emancipation to the test — give adolescents the financial means to make educational choices entirely on their own. He suggests that few defenders of child rights would really be willing to put this to the test, because of the fear that it would result in significant harm to adolescents who disagreed with their parents (Gilles, "Liberal Parentalism," 43-44). Therefore, parental educational rights should be extended even to adolescence.

95. Here it should be noted that I am fully in agreement with Rob Reich, who acknowledges that there are multiple interests in the education of children, and that "a theory of educational authority that claimed only the interests of one party mattered could potentially establish a kind of parental despotism, state authoritarianism, or child despotism" (Reich, *Bridging Liberalism*, 158). But strangely Reich comes very close to advocating a kind of state authoritarianism in the area of education, as has been ably argued by Perry Glanzer (forthcoming). On this point of the need for multiple authority in education, I also agree entirely with Amy Gutmann, *Democratic Education* (Princeton: Princeton University Press, 1987), 42. However, I disagree with Gutmann when she fails to give parents the primary authority.

put in making educational decisions to the children's developing capacity for independent judgment.[96]

Clearly children do not only belong to parents. They also belong to an extended family, a cultural group, and to society. Thus society as a whole has some interest in educating its citizens. I therefore also believe that the state, as a representative of society, has some jurisdiction in the area of education. In broad terms, the primary function of the state is to promote justice. In relation to education this means that the state should defend by its legislation the primary right of parents to educate their children.[97] Given the pluralistic nature of a society, I believe that this also entails that the state should ensure that a system of confessional pluralism exists in the school system. In other words, there should be a variety of schools within a society, reflecting differing worldviews so that parents can make a genuine choice as to the kind of education their children will receive.

As I have already argued, the state also has a duty to protect the rights of children when these are neglected or violated by parents.[98] The state also has a right to ensure that all children get a certain minimal level of education, and to ensure that all children have equal access to a good education.[99] A liberal state further may insist that all children be given an education that will develop the basic skills and competences necessary for normal human development and liberal citizenship. Here again, I concur with Reich, who argues that the state has an interest that children receive a civic education.[100]

Teachers too have certain rights and responsibilities, but always within the context of parental control of the overall direction of education. If we keep this important qualification in mind, it can then be said that decisions on issues that are specifically academic should be made by teachers and other educationalists. This involves particularly such items as the "formal content of the curriculum, teacher certification," and measuring student achievement.[101]

96. Ackerman argues this point as one element of his liberal educational principles: "As the child gains increasing familiarity with the range of cultural models open to him in a liberal society, the choice of his curriculum should increasingly become his responsibility, rather than that of his educators" (Reich, *Bridging Liberalism*, 158; see also Crittenden, *Parents*, 98).

97. Crittenden, *Parents*, 164; cf. Gilles, "On Educating Children," 941.

98. Crittenden, *Parents*, 164, 174.

99. Crittenden, *Parents*, 194-98.

100. Reich, *Bridging Liberalism*, 154.

101. McCarthy et al., *Society, State, and Schools*, 167.

Conclusion

Let children be children — that has been a central theme of this chapter. Young children are nearly completely dependent on their parents in order to fulfill an important aspect of their vocation — learning. For parents this is an awesome responsibility. They in fact determine the bulk of the content and the direction of their child's learning. As children grow, other adults become more significant in terms of what and how they learn. But children must be helped to fulfill their vocation to learn.

I conclude with a somewhat speculative practical observation about contemporary society. It seems to me that today parents and more generally the adult community are all too often failing in taking on this awesome responsibility of helping children fulfill their vocation of learning. I believe that this failure is in a large part due to confusions that arise because of the increasing pluralism of our societies and also the pervasive relativism that seems to evolve out of such pluralism. Thus, Christina Hoff Sommers, in an article entitled "How to Teach Right and Wrong: A Blueprint for Moral Education in a Pluralistic Society," raises the following question: "Why should we be the first society in history that finds itself hamstrung in the vital task of passing along its moral tradition to the next generation?"[102] Stanley Hauerwas, in a similar vein, says, "Morally, our children are suffering because we do not have the courage of our convictions."[103] Hauerwas goes on to give an example. He says that, morally, he is convinced that Christians are "committed to the ethic of non-resistance."[104] Yet he confesses that he resisted the temptation not to teach for commitment in this area.[105] He admits to being reticent in teaching this ethic to his son. Why? Both Hauerwas and Sommers point to pluralism and relativism as the reason for our failure to pass on to the next generation the convictions that we have.

This is a serious failure, in my opinion. By failing to teach our children, we are in fact making it impossible for them to fulfill their vocation to learn. The prophet Isaiah, in analyzing the corruption of his age, talks again and again of problems of leadership (Isa. 3). Within this same context he talks about the young rising up against the old, and even of youths oppressing the people (Isa. 3:5, 12). And then this: "I will make boys their officials; mere children will govern them" (Isa. 3:4, 5). Clearly this is seen as unnatural. This situation is described in terms of disobedience against God. It is portrayed as a form of wick-

102. *Christianity Today,* December 13, 1993, 33.
103. Stanley Hauerwas, *A Community of Character: Toward a Constructive Christian Social Ethic* (Notre Dame, Ind.: University of Notre Dame Press, 1981), 173.
104. Hauerwas, *A Community of Character,* 173.
105. Hauerwas, *A Community of Character,* 173.

edness. Children are not meant to lead and to teach the old. The old are meant to teach the young. And yet today, we seem to have a reversal of this natural and God-ordained order of things.

The disciples of Jesus at one point rebuked parents who were bringing their babies to him (Luke 18:15). Jesus instead welcomes the children and blesses them. A little earlier, Jesus issues a stern warning — whoever causes one of these little ones to sin, it would be better for him to be thrown into the sea with a millstone tied around his neck (Luke 17:1-2). There are of course many ways in which one can cause a child to sin. One way, I suggest, is to fail in helping children to learn and thus to fulfill their calling and vocation. We need to heed Jesus' stern warning.

15. The Best Interests of the Child: Modern Lessons from the Christian Traditions

Robert K. Vischer

In today's culture war cacophony, no battlefront is more stridently contested than the socialization and value-inculcation of children. Some children's rights advocates have cast a skeptical eye toward the unfettered enjoyment of parental authority in this arena, insisting that children themselves, or the state acting on children's behalf, must be empowered to serve as bulwarks against exercises of parental prerogative that threaten the child's "best interests." And a child's "best interests" increasingly are identified and pursued without reference to the parents' understanding of those interests. The trend toward an individualistic conception of children's interests has exacerbated the cultural fault lines between secularists and religious believers, as the latter strongly associate state incursions into the family as direct threats to the maintenance of religious identity across generations.

Unpacking the concept of the child's vocation thus requires us not only to articulate the substantive ends of childhood categorically, but also to identify who is best equipped to direct a particular child's development in the light of those ends. While mining Christianity for insight on the child is essential, we must acknowledge that Christians are not the only participants in this conversation, even to the extent that the conversation bears on their own children. Advocates of an increasingly prominent rights-based conception of the child claim a stake in the upbringing of all children.

Recognizing that Christian teaching stands in tension with a rights-based conception of the child is a useful first step in placing the child's vocation within its current sociopolitical context, but the articulation is unhelpfully vague when it comes to facilitating Christians' engagement of the rights-based conception. The vagueness emanates from the failure to discern that Christians do not encounter the law's treatment of the child from a common starting point. Christians reject this emerging modern conception of the child's "best interests" from a variety of theological premises regarding childhood, and these premises have diverse implications for the roles of individual autonomy, parental authority, and community identity in the realization of the child's "best interests."

Of course, conceptions of the child's spiritual "best interests" within a faith tradition do not translate directly into conceptions of the child's earthly "best interests" within a pluralist democracy. Christians may observe certain theological truths without replicating those truths in secularist presumptions that operate in the legal sphere. But currently the lines of demarcation remain murky because the points of commonality and divergence between religion and law in this area are left unspoken and unexplored, and the neutral values to be fostered by the liberal order are beginning to resemble more closely the normative values of religious belief. To foster productive conversations on the legal status of the child across the culture war divide, the multiple points of overlap and conflict between the various Christian approaches to childhood and the modern children's rights paradigm must be brought to the foreground.

Accordingly, this chapter will trace the contours of the three primary conceptions of the child in Christian thought and their relationships to the legal understanding of the child reflected in recent children's rights advocacy. Because the rights-based conception of the child is framed in terms of the child's secularly accessible "best interests," the chapter outlines the relationship by articulating the prevailing Christian understandings of the foundational element of the child's "best interests" — i.e., the child's salvation — in the sacramental, conversional, and covenantal traditions. And to ensure a manageable scope, the inquiry will focus on the development of baptism doctrine seen in the work of a leading figure within each tradition. To provide the background for comparison, the chapter will begin by bringing the secular side of the inquiry into focus through an analysis of the presumptions about children underlying two archetypes of modern liberal thought in this area: first, the United Nations Convention on the Rights of the Child; and second, persistent calls by political and legal theorists to impose more stringent state limitations on parental discretion in shaping the education of their children. Taken together, these examples reveal that while Christians' resistance to a rights-based conception of the child is broad and deeply rooted, the tools of resistance are not uniform within Christianity.

Modernity and the Child

A long-standing trend toward individualism in modern liberalism's[1] stance toward family relations has culminated, over the past few decades, with the elevation of individual autonomy as the child's primary path of salvation.[2] Liberal theorists do not argue that children should be independent actors with the same legal rights and privileges as adults, but they do seek to guard against parental actions that threaten to hinder the child's future exercise of autonomy. And the benchmark of individual autonomy, under this view, is a freely chosen life path made possible by exposure to a variety of worldviews and values, fostering a critical distance between the child and the tradition into which she was born. An uncritical inculcation of religious beliefs by parents over the course of childhood is a leading concern underlying calls for new limits on parental authority. Thus understood primarily as either an obstacle to or an instrument of autonomy, childhood tends to be defined "apart from serious reflection on the meaning of parenthood,"[3] and "family" as an entity is dismissed as "a legal fiction that may have an ancient pedigree but [that] has hidden a multitude of wrongs."[4]

In the legal sphere, one ramification of the focus on a child's autonomy is to see the constitutional right to privacy as applying only to individuals, not families. As leading family law scholar Barbara Bennett Woodhouse urges, state intervention into the family unit should not be blocked by legal doctrine because the family's dominant member is thereby given license "to engage in clearly (although not grossly) wrongful conduct while the dependent members are compelled to suffer it."[5] Even if privacy is understood as a "right to caretaker autonomy," the notion "runs counter to the principle of public responsibility and public accountability."[6] While state intervention into the parent-child relationship should not be precluded legally, according to Woodhouse, it

---

1. By "modern liberalism," I mean to signify the political framework in which individual rights have taken on increasing importance, often with a corresponding skepticism toward the authority of groups.

2. The trend toward individualism has long been recognized. As far back as 1861, Henry Maine observed that "[s]tarting, as from one terminus of history, from a condition of society in which all the relations of Persons are summed up in the relations of Family, we seem to have steadily moved towards a phase of social order in which all these relations arise from the free agreement of individuals" (Henry Maine, *Ancient Law* [1861], 165).

3. Vigen Guroian, "The Ecclesial Family: John Chrysostom on Parenthood and Children," in *The Child in Christian Thought*, ed. Marcia J. Bunge (Grand Rapids: Eerdmans, 2001), 61.

4. Barbara Bennett Woodhouse, "The Dark Side of Family Privacy," *George Washington Law Review* 67 (1999): 1251-52.

5. Woodhouse, "The Dark Side," 1255.

6. Woodhouse, "The Dark Side," 1260.

should be rendered unnecessary by making sure that families follow "a clear set of social and legal expectations so that adults will be educated in their 'responsibility' and will be deterred from misusing their powers over children."[7]

To pass muster, limitations on a child's autonomy thus must be justified rationally, not by invoking tradition or biology. Philosopher Gareth Matthews explains society's embrace of children's rights as arising from a vision of "authorities in our society as rational authorities, people who, even if they first come to occupy their positions of authority by biological accident, can be appropriately called upon to justify their exercise of authority, and justify it in the presence of their children, as soon as those children are capable of making reasonable judgments about their own interests."[8] The emphasis on rationality is evident even among liberal theorists who defend some semblance of parental autonomy. Emily Buss, for example, defends limited parental autonomy because "we can expect the heavily invested parent to do a better job than the state would do, and under most circumstances, we will have no way of knowing when this will not be so," but cautions us to keep in mind that the focus should remain on the "relative competence" of parents and the state.[9] The state's "special competence," on this score, includes its ability to shape children "to become citizens capable of meeting the demands of a successfully functioning society," to "identify behavior that the majority of citizens considers harmful to children, no matter what the circumstances," and to "impose some negative limits on the parents' exercise of developmental control."[10]

When parental authority to direct the child's development is conditioned on parents' rationally accessible, context-specific competence, the authority effectively exists at the behest of the state. Woodhouse makes the state's predominance explicit, asserting that "power over children is conferred by the community, with children's interests and their emerging capacities the foremost consideration," and that parental rights of "[s]tewardship must be earned through actual care giving, and lost if not exercised with responsibility."[11] Her approach "would place children, not adults, firmly at the center and take as its central values not adult individualism, possession, and autonomy, as embodied in parental rights, nor even the dyadic intimacy of parent/child relationships," but instead "would value most

7. Woodhouse, "The Dark Side," 1256.

8. Gareth B. Matthews, *The Philosophy of Childhood* (Cambridge: Harvard University Press, 1994), 80.

9. Emily Buss, "Allocating Developmental Control among Parent, Child and the State," *University of Chicago Legal Forum* 27 (2004): 32.

10. Buss, "Allocating Developmental Control," 32-33.

11. Barbara Bennett Woodhouse, "Hatching the Egg: A Child-Centered Perspective on Parents' Rights," *Cardozo Law Review* 14 (1993): 1814-15.

highly concrete service to the needs of the next generation, in public and private spheres, and encourage . . . collective community responsibility for the well-being of children."[12] If parental authority is grounded in rights rather than "demonstrated responsibility," it "constitute[s] a form of bondage."[13]

Even this cursory sketch of the theoretical underpinnings of liberalism's skepticism toward parental rights gives rise to two disturbing implications for those whose religious worldview presupposes a foundational role for the family unit. First, when parental or family autonomy exists only to the extent that it supports the child's individual autonomy, the state has already inserted itself into family life because some degree of intrusion is necessary to judge the acceptability of the relationship between a specific exercise of parental authority and the child's prospects for autonomy. Second, autonomy is not a self-defining concept, and the law's pursuit of autonomy as an ultimate objective of its treatment of children requires the state to supply autonomy's content with normative claims that will invariably be contested by a significant portion of the families affected.

Both of these implications mean very little in abstract discussions of authority allocations between parents and the state, but they become clear upon reading the United Nations Convention on the Rights of the Child, a treaty that has been ratified by every nation in the world except for Somalia and the United States. Given that American opposition to the Convention emanates in significant part from religious groups, the Convention provides a useful vehicle for elucidating the practical dimensions of modern liberalism's conception of the child as a precursor to exploring the competing Christian conceptions.

The Convention on the Rights of the Child, adopted by the UN General Assembly in 1989, is a sweeping attempt to encapsulate children's well-being in a rights-based framework consisting of fifty-three separate articles. Most are relatively uncontroversial to anyone who embraces even a modicum of legal protection for children, including measures designed to protect family integrity, such as Article 11, which requires signatory states to "take measures to combat the illicit transfer and non-return of children abroad." A bevy of provisions enter murkier waters, however, as the Convention enshrines a substantive vision of human rights beyond any that had been seen in international law, even as applied to adults. For example:

- Article 13 grants the child freedom of expression, which includes the "freedom to seek, receive and impart information and ideas of all kinds, regard-

12. Woodhouse, "Hatching the Egg," 1815.
13. Woodhouse, "Hatching the Egg," 1816.

less of frontiers, either orally, in writing or in print, in the form of art, or through any other media of the child's choice."

- Article 14 grants the child freedom of thought, conscience, and religion, and instructs that parents' rights to direct the child in the exercise of these rights should be respected "in a manner consistent with the evolving capacities of the child."
- Article 16 gives the child "the right to the protection of the law against" interference with the child's privacy.
- Article 17 requires states to "ensure that the child has access to information and material from a diversity of national and international sources, especially those aimed at the promotion of his or her social, spiritual and moral well-being and physical and mental health."

Provisions such as these bear out the characterization offered by the Convention's supporters that "[i]nstead of merely picturing the child as a being in need of services, the Convention depicts the child as an individual with the right to have an opinion, to be a participant in decisions affecting his or her life, and to be respected for his or her human dignity."[14] Put simply, the Convention "[moves] beyond protection rights to choice rights for children."[15]

The Convention's embrace of the child's "choice rights," even at the expense of parental authority, is key to understanding the autonomy-driven conception of the child. "Protection rights" — including rights to property, to physical care and security, and to procedural due process — had been the focus of the children's rights movement for much of the twentieth century because such rights do not depend on a minimum level of decision-making capacity. Choice rights, by contrast, "grant individuals the authority to make affirmative and legally binding decisions, such as voting, marrying, making contracts, exercising religious preferences, or choosing whether and how to be educated." Denying these rights, as it has traditionally been understood, "is not a way of discriminating against children, but is a way of protecting them," for "[t]o confer the full range of choice rights on a child is also to confer the burdens and responsibilities of adult legal status."[16]

The underlying premise of all such provisions can be found in the Conven-

14. Cynthia Price Cohen and Susan Kilbourne, "Jurisprudence of the Committee on the Rights of the Child: A Guide for Research and Analysis," *Michigan Journal of International Law* 19 (1998): 637-38.

15. Bruce C. Hafen and Jonathan O. Hafen, "Abandoning Children to Their Autonomy: The United Nations Convention on the Rights of the Child," *Harvard International Law Journal* 37 (1996): 450.

16. Hafen and Hafen, "Abandoning Children," 461.

tion's Article 3, which provides that "[i]n all actions concerning children, whether undertaken by public or private social welfare institutions, courts of law, administrative authorities or legislative bodies, the best interests of the child shall be a primary consideration." The "best interests" standard thus is elevated to the status of nonnegotiable norm to be imposed globally through a framework of choice rights on both private and public actors in their dealings with children. For the law to impose this standard across the board, a degree of uniformity is required, which means that the content of the child's "best interests" will be supplied, at least in part, by the state.

The embrace of the "best interests" standard, in conjunction with the panoply of substantive rights offered in service of that standard, begins to bring into relief the extent to which the legal protection of the child's well-being is disconnected from the parents' understanding of the child's well-being. The disconnect is made more stark by the realization that, even when parents are not acting as impediments to the child's "best interests," they are permitted by the Convention only to "direct the child" as prudent in the light of the child's "evolving capacities." The operating presumption is that when the state deems the child old enough to act for herself in a particular context, the parent is erased from the equation, even if there is no apparent conflict between the parents' wishes and the state's understanding of the child's "best interests." According to the UN's own description, the Convention "promotes a 'new concept of separate rights for children with the Government accepting responsibility [for] protecting the child from the power of parents.'"[17] In the case of the UN Convention, the quest for autonomy has led to a legal posture toward children that increasingly stands for "the right to be left alone, even within the family structure."[18]

While the Convention reflects the legal embodiment of the norms underlying the emerging liberal conception of the child, the battle over education regulation is one in which autonomy-driven norms have held sway primarily in academic circles. One reason is that challenges to parental authority in the realm of education encounter significant obstacles in American jurisprudence, most notably a long-standing triumvirate of Supreme Court cases. In *Meyer v. Nebraska*,[19] the Court struck down a state law banning the teaching of foreign languages to students before they graduated from eighth grade, reasoning that there was insufficient justification for state interference "with the opportunities of pupils to acquire knowledge, and with the power of parents to control the

---

17. Hafen and Hafen, "Abandoning Children," 450.
18. Hafen and Hafen, "Abandoning Children," 452.
19. *Meyer v. Nebraska*, 262 US 390 (1923).

education of their own."[20] In *Pierce v. Society of Sisters*,[21] the Court held that the state could not require parents to send their children to public schools, for "[t]he fundamental theory of liberty upon which all governments in this Union repose excludes any general power of the state to standardize its children by forcing them to accept instruction from public teachers only."[22] Finally, in *Wisconsin v. Yoder*,[23] the Court repelled the state's efforts to compel high school education for Amish children on the ground that such efforts threatened the group's religious liberty, recognizing that a "State's interest in universal education" must be balanced against the reality that "the values of parental direction of the religious upbringing and education of their children in their early and formative years have a high place in our society."[24] Taken together, these cases establish the right of parents to direct the education of their children.

But the cases do not completely foreclose state regulation of a child's education, even if the education is pursued in private schools, and the skeptics of parental authority concentrate their advocacy efforts on creating more space for such regulation based on both the state's interest in producing an educated citizenry and the child's interest in acquiring an education sufficient to allow her full exercise of autonomy. For example, given the rare cultural separation achieved by the Amish community, *Yoder* does not pose a problem for the broad enforcement of state compulsory attendance laws, nor is there a constitutional impediment to states requiring that private schools teach certain core subjects in order to satisfy those laws.

Notwithstanding this regulatory window, criticism of the triumvirate abounds. The deference to parental authority underlying *Meyer* and *Pierce*, for example, is accused by Barbara Woodhouse of being animated by "a conservative attachment to the patriarchal family, to a class-stratified society, and to a parent's private property rights in his children and their labor," reflecting a "narrow, tradition-bound vision of the child as essentially private property."[25] And *Meyer* in particular is seen as having "announced a dangerous form of liberty, the right to control another human being."[26] The legal recognition of parental authority in such cases generally underscores the "bias towards adults' possessive individualism," which "objectifies children and places physical con-

20. *Meyer v. Nebraska*, 401.
21. *Pierce v. Society of Sisters*, 268 US 510 (1925).
22. *Pierce v. Society of Sisters*, 535.
23. *Wisconsin v. Yoder*, 406 US 205 (1972).
24. *Wisconsin v. Yoder*, 213-14.
25. Barbara Bennett Woodhouse, "'Who Owns the Child?': Meyer and Pierce and the Child as Property," *William and Mary Law Review* 33 (1992): 997.
26. Woodhouse, "Who Owns the Child?" 1001.

trol and possession of the children, rather than demonstrated service or shared concern for their well-being, at the center of controversy."[27]

Given the state of constitutional law, a rights-based conception of the child drives an effort aimed not so much at overturning parental authority in the education arena as at chipping away at its practical import. A primary avenue for doing so corresponds with the expanding school choice movement, whereby government funds are made available for families to choose among a variety of public and private schools. James Dwyer, a leading children's rights scholar, welcomes the rise of school choice, as he sees government funding as the perfect vehicle to justify more intensive regulation of private schools, which can ensure that children are not precluded from meaningful self-development simply by the accident of their birth into a family that rejects the educational promises of modern liberalism. Dwyer urges states implementing voucher programs to attach to the vouchers "whatever regulatory strings are needed to ensure that children in all private schools receive a good secular education," and if this means that "some parents cannot use their children's schooling to proclaim the 'good news,' because in the state's judgment the parents' news is not so good, then so be it."[28] This translates into proposals to regulate the content of private school curricula, stamping out even subtle forms of discriminatory and biased content that could result, for example, in "diminished self-esteem, inhibited cognitive development, passivity, reduced aspirations, and lower achievement on the part of female students."[29]

Emily Buss starts from the same premises as Dwyer, but arrives at a different regulatory target: the makeup of student populations at both private and public schools. Buss insists that "a state interest in fostering the capacity for independent thought in its children could justify policies encouraging and even, perhaps, compelling some amount of exposure to ideologically unlike peers," especially among older adolescents.[30] When a family chooses a school based on a student population that reflects the family's values or worldview, the state may be justified in stepping in to avoid the resulting compromise of the child's autonomy, at least as that autonomy is understood by Buss. She argues that peer relationships that reinforce the child's existing value structure are actually doing a disservice to the child:

27. Woodhouse, "Hatching the Egg," 1811.

28. James G. Dwyer, "School Vouchers: Inviting the Public into the Religious Square," *William and Mary Law Review* 42 (2001): 963, 1005.

29. James G. Dwyer, *Religious Schools v. Children's Rights* (Ithaca, N.Y.: Cornell University Press, 1998), 10.

30. Emily Buss, "The Adolescent's Stake in the Allocation of Educational Control between Parent and State," *University of Chicago Law Review* 67 (2000): 1233.

While these relationships with like peers still offer the child an opportunity to "try on" an identity by acting independently of parents and reflecting on that identity through peer interactions, this opportunity for exploration will be more narrowly circumscribed. The child's choice of friendships may offer some range in personality types, but not in value structures or long-term ambitions. The child's conversations with friends may allow her to understand her own value structure better, but they will be less likely to push her to question her own choices because they will not offer her alternative values and plans to compare with her own.[31]

In these terms, the child's "best interests" require separation from the child's family-formed identity, and that separation is important enough to justify state intervention into the family's effort to protect and maintain the identity, regardless of whether or not the child objects to such efforts.

Many proposed private school regulations have already emerged from this conception of the child, and several have already been adopted in districts implementing school voucher programs. Some suggested regulations seem relatively innocuous, such as mandating certain curricular elements, requiring teachers to be state-certified, ensuring that religious instruction or services are optional for voucher students, and prohibiting the use of religious criteria in the admission of students. Such measures still act as constraints on a school's efforts to remain accountable to parents rather than the state, and other proposals are even more problematic, most notably the state power to censor the transmission of illiberal religious teachings. Whatever our view of a particular regulation's reasonableness, the content is not as significant as the underlying notion that the state is equipped to define and pursue collectively the child's autonomy-centered interests, even if it negates the efficacy of parents' child-forming decisions.

The UN Convention, the push to regulate private schools, and the academic theories underlying the children's rights movement evidence a distinct conception of the vocation of the child. For our purposes, the relevant characteristics are threefold: first, the optimal childhood will pull a child inexorably toward the attainment of individual autonomy at the earliest practicable age and to the fullest possible extent; second, the child's autonomy requires cognitive separation from the cultural or religious traditions in which the child has been raised; and third, the child's "best interests" are a universalized construct — articulated in the same terms for all children everywhere, grounded in self-reflection and independence from whatever particular social milieu has shaped the pre-autonomous child.

---

31. Buss, "The Adolescent's Stake," 1233.

None of this is meant to question the many laudable achievements that have resulted from greater public accountability for parents' treatment of their children. Christians' skepticism toward the children's rights movement is well grounded, but it should not be unlimited. Certainly, adequate food, clothing, and shelter are nonnegotiable elements of any meaningful definition of a child's well-being. And many instances of emotional abuse, neglect, and absence of meaningful access to education should trouble any fully formed conscience, Christian or not. But the categorical expansion of the very concept of childhood "best interests" should be troubling, especially as the expansion proceeds to define the concept without reference to family or faith tradition.

Christianity and the Child

So what does Christianity say in response? A glimpse of the tension between the rights-based and Christian views of childhood is found in Christ's caution that "whoever does not receive the kingdom of God like a child shall not enter it."[32] An authentic encounter with God, we are told, requires us to trust God as a child trusts her parents. The child is vulnerable, dependent, and does not purport to function as an atomistic, self-sufficient being. Christianity does not approach relationships of trust as obstacles to be surmounted, but as opportunities to live out the gospel's ethic of sacrificial love and devotion. This recognition does not tell us how the state should respond when parents do not prove to warrant a child's trust, but it should frame the Christian's search for an answer. The search is complicated, though, by the fact that the Christian traditions have developed starkly different conceptions of the child and her spiritual "best interests," as evidenced by their divergent beliefs regarding the function and purpose of baptism.

The Child in the Sacramental Tradition

The sacramental tradition teaches that God's grace is imparted to individuals through their participation in certain church sacraments such as baptism and the Eucharist.[33] The baptism of infants is essential to the sacramental tradition because baptism is seen as a necessary means of grace that sets an individual free from sin. The key intellectual figure in this doctrine's development is Saint

32. Luke 10:15.

33. Baptism and the Eucharist are the two that are common to every branch of Christianity within this tradition.

Augustine, whose fifth-century teachings continue to influence modern sacramental practice.

Infant baptism had been a well-established Christian practice when Augustine began his ministry, but he provided its theological justification through his work on the doctrine of original sin,[34] a concept invoked by Augustine to refer to all humans' participation in Adam's sin.[35] He famously spoke of his realization of original sin in observing "the jealousy of a small child: he could not even speak, yet he glared with livid fury at his fellow-nursling."[36] Observing that "there is no difference between children and adults" in terms of nature, Augustine concluded that "[n]o one is innocent."[37]

Augustine's emphasis on original sin also was grounded in his real-world experience of suffering. Original sin becomes a necessary doctrine once one is exposed to the suffering of infants, which "would certainly not be imposed upon God's image under the just and omnipotent God, if those infants contracted no evils deserving punishment from their parents."[38] A suffering infant with an omnipotent, omniscient, and loving God became impossible for Augustine absent original sin. William Harmless explains that original sin could pass generation to generation because, in Augustine's portrayal, it had "the chemistry of a congenital disease, not of a voluntary sin."[39]

Augustine's conviction in original sin's validity became a springboard for his powerful defense of infant baptism, for, as Martha Stortz puts it, if "all of Adam's progeny were born into the one mass of sinning," it would thus be cruel "to exclude infants from baptism: they too needed access to baptism for the forgiveness of sin."[40] Augustine taught that the corruption of original sin means that infants "are held captive under the power of the devil,"[41] and thus they must be baptized "in order that Christ the redeemer might set them free from sin and incorporate them into his body."[42] He relied on the image of Christ the

---

34. O. M. Bakke, *When Children Became People: The Birth of Childhood in Early Christianity* (Minneapolis: Fortress, 2005), 241.

35. Margaret Bendroth, "Children of Adam, Children of God: Christian Nurture in Early Nineteenth-Century America," *Theology Today* 56 (January 2000): 496-97.

36. Saint Augustine, *Confessions* 1.7.11 (quoted in Bakke, *When Children Became People*, 90).

37. Bakke, *When Children Became People*, 93-94.

38. Bakke, *When Children Became People*, 100 (quoting Saint Augustine, *De peccatorum meritis et remissione* 3.10.18).

39. William Harmless, S.J., "Christ the Pediatrician," in this volume, at 142.

40. Martha Ellen Stortz, "'Where or When Was Your Servant Innocent?': Augustine on Childhood," in *The Child in Christian Thought*, 91.

41. Bakke, *When Children Became People*, 100 (quoting Saint Augustine, *Contra duas epistulas Pelagianorum* 4.4.7).

42. Bakke, *When Children Became People*, 100; see also Stortz, "Augustine on Childhood,"

Physician, who heals infants from the spiritual ravages of a death-plagued world.[43] As the means of sin's remission in a child, baptism, in the Augustinian view, is a precondition to salvation.[44]

Roman Catholic teaching on baptism has evolved over the centuries — notably taking a more hopeful view of the unbaptized infant's fate upon death[45] — but it remains informed to a significant degree by Augustine's understanding of original sin.[46] The *Catholic Catechism* instructs, for example, that "[b]y Baptism all sins are forgiven, original sin and all personal sins, as well as all punishment for sin," and that "[i]n those who have been reborn nothing remains that would impede their entry into the Kingdom of God, neither Adam's sin, nor personal sin, nor the consequences of sin, the gravest of which is separation from God."[47]

This is not to suggest that baptism represents a stand-alone or self-contained path of salvation. Baptism is "the sacrament of faith," but as the *Catechism* puts it, "faith needs the community of believers," and "[i]t is only within the faith of the Church that each of the faithful can believe."[48] In other words, baptism is a necessary gateway into the communal, lifelong faith journey through which the grace transmitted through baptism will be lived out:

> For the grace of Baptism to unfold, the parents' help is important. So too is the role of the godfather and godmother, who must be firm believers, able and ready to help the newly baptized — child or adult — on the road of Christian life. . . . The whole ecclesial community bears some responsibility for the development and safeguarding of the grace given at Baptism.[49]

---

96 (explaining Augustine's view that "the rite of baptism signified first and foremost Christ's repossession of the child" from "the grasp of Satan").

43. See Harmless, "Christ the Pediatrician," 83, in this volume.

44. Bakke, *When Children Became People,* 103. Saint Augustine also found a scriptural basis for infant baptism as a precondition of salvation. He looked to John 6:53's caution that Christ's flesh was given for the lives of little ones, "and if they have not eaten the flesh of the Son of Man, they will not have life either." So, in Augustine's view, "since little children must take part in the Eucharist in order to receive eternal life, they must also be baptized, since the Eucharist presupposes baptism" (250).

45. See Anthony Kelly, "Hope for Unbaptized Infants," in this volume, at 218 ("Not only has there been a development of doctrine, but an expansion of hope"); Patrick Brennan, "Children Play with God," in this volume, at 211 (exploring Jacques Maritain's espousal of Limbo as the eternal destination of unbaptized infants, a place of "pure nature raised to its highest degree").

46. Lutheran and Anglican teaching on baptism have shifted even more.

47. *Catholic Cathechism,* par. 1263.

48. *Catholic Cathechism,* par. 1253.

49. *Catholic Cathechism,* par. 1255.

But this communal, gradual unfolding of baptism's grace does not eviscerate the centrality of baptism to salvation,[50] as children who die without baptism are entrusted "to the mercy of God."[51] Children who have been baptized, by contrast, have been "freed from the power of darkness and brought into the realm of the freedom of the children of God, to which all men are called"; as a consequence, "[t]he Church and the parents would deny a child the priceless grace of becoming a child of God were they not to confer Baptism shortly after birth."[52]

Baptism is not just a path to salvation, though. The act of baptism itself works a fundamental change in the person, making her a "new creature"; indeed, "the whole organism of the Christian's supernatural life has its roots in Baptism."[53] And for purposes of our inquiry, it is crucial to recognize that, by incorporating infants into the universal church, the new spiritual identity brought about by baptism transcends the particular circumstances of our temporal existence: "From the baptismal fonts is born the one People of God of the New Covenant, which transcends all the natural or human limits of nations, cultures, races, and sexes: 'For by one Spirit we were all baptized into one body.'"[54]

As a broad characterization, the child's spiritual well-being within the sacramental tradition centers on the communal implementation of a universal norm. Regardless of family origins or parental faith-forming initiatives, baptism, at least as embodied in the line of thought represented in Augustine and today's catechism, is the nonnegotiable entryway to the communal membership on which salvation rests.[55] This is not to say that salvation is impossible outside the Catholic Church, but rather that the only certain path of salvation revealed to humankind proceeds through baptism. Baptism's salvific efficacy operates independent of the parent-child relationship; in this sense, the child's "best interests" can be defined without reference to the parents. But the parents occupy an integral role in directing the gradual unfolding of grace that baptism initiates.

---

50. *Catholic Cathechism*, par. 1257 ("The Lord himself affirms that Baptism is necessary for salvation. . . . God has bound salvation to the sacrament of Baptism, but he himself is not bound by his sacraments").

51. *Catholic Cathechism*, par. 1261.

52. *Catholic Cathechism*, par. 1250.

53. *Catholic Cathechism*, par. 1266.

54. *Catholic Cathechism*, par. 1267.

55. Cf. Kelly, "Hope for Unbaptized Infants," 238 above ("To hope for the ultimate reconciliation of all with God is to find oneself in good company, as an illustration of the axiom *lex orandi, lex credendi* — the way faith prays is the way it believes. A parent's prayer for a child dying before it could be baptized is a manifestation of the prayer of the whole church").

So while the sacramental tradition and a rights-based conception of the child share a universalized conception of the child's "best interests" that can be defined without reference to the parents' understanding of those interests, there are two key distinctions: first, the sacramental tradition does not contemplate that realization of the interests requires separation of the child from parental influence and presumptive worldview; and second, the full realization of the child's interests within the sacramental tradition requires a life embedded in a broader faith community — with the family being the foremost example — thereby eschewing the atomistic understanding of "best interests" entailed by modernity's relentless focus on individual autonomy.

The Child in the Conversional Tradition

Members of evangelical traditions like Baptists and Methodists have a much different view of baptism's function and salvific efficacy. These branches practice believer's baptism based on the view that baptism brings no spiritual benefit — much less an ontological change in the baptized — but simply symbolizes the spiritual rebirth that has already occurred through the individual's volitional decision to accept Christ as savior. As a result, the evangelical pursuit of a child's spiritual well-being places the emphasis almost entirely on a conversion experience, even for children born and nurtured in a Christian home. This understanding is the most recently developed of the three traditions. While it was foreshadowed by the sermons of Jonathan Edwards,[56] the conversional approach to children's salvation reached full bloom in the nineteenth-century ministry of famed British preacher Charles Spurgeon.

One of the most controversial episodes in Spurgeon's long public career stemmed from a sermon in which he railed against the Church of England's teaching that baptism makes a person "a member of Christ, the child of God, and an inheritor of the kingdom of heaven."[57] Relying principally on scriptural references linking salvation to an individual's belief, Spurgeon argued that "persons are not saved by baptism."[58] To believe otherwise is to "make salvation

---

56. Edwards warned children to remember their mortality: "'Tis not likely you will all live to grow up," so "If you should die while you are young, and death should come upon you and find you without any love to Christ, what will become of you?" Catherine A. Brekus, "Children of Wrath, Children of Grace: Jonathan Edwards and the Puritan Culture of Child-Rearing," in *The Child in Christian Thought*, 316 (quoting Jonathan Edwards, manuscript sermon on 2 Kings 2:23-24).

57. Lewis Drummond, *Spurgeon: Prince of Preachers* (Grand Rapids: Kregel, 1992), 790.

58. Drummond, *Spurgeon,* 792.

depend upon mere ceremony," which is "out of character with the spiritual religion which Christ came to teach."[59] Thereby disconnected from salvation, baptism is simply "to the believer a testimony of his faith; he does in baptism tell the world what he believes."[60]

Replacing baptism at the center of Spurgeon's salvation theology was the individual's moment of decision to accept Christ. The instantaneous, self-contained, and self-executing quality of the decision is obvious from Spurgeon's own account of his childhood conversion experience:

> The clock of mercy struck in heaven the hour and moment of my emancipation, for the time had come. Between half-past ten o'clock, when I entered that chapel, and half-past twelve o'clock, when I was back again at home, what a change had taken place in me! I had passed from darkness to marvelous light, from death to life. Simply by looking to Jesus, I had been delivered from despair, and I was brought into such a joyous state of mind that, when they saw me at home, they said to me, "Something wonderful has happened to you," and I was eager to tell them all about it.[61]

It is important to recognize that this path to salvation had no correlation with Spurgeon's upbringing in a Christian family. Indeed, his entire life experience up until the moment of decision is dismissed as damnable, as seen in this passage written six months after his conversion:

> Sixteen years have I lived upon the earth, and yet I am only — scarcely six months old! I am very young in grace. Yet how much time have I wasted, dead in trespasses and sins, without life, without God, in the world! What a mercy that I did not perish in my sin.[62]

Spurgeon portrayed a conversion experience that was not embedded within the child's community of origin, but required the child to be drawn out of that community. In one letter to a friend's child, he emphasized that "[t]here is no way of salvation but Christ; you cannot save yourself, having no power even to think one good thought; neither can your parents' love and prayers save you; none but Jesus can."[63] And after he heard other ministers pray for their own children, instead of encouraging the ministers in their faith-formative

---

59. Drummond, *Spurgeon,* 792.

60. Drummond, *Spurgeon,* 800.

61. *The Autobiography of Charles H. Spurgeon,* ed. David Otis Fuller (Grand Rapids: Zondervan, 1946), 41-42.

62. *Autobiography of Charles H. Spurgeon,* 45.

63. *The Letters of Charles Haddon Spurgeon* (Harrisburg, Pa.: Good Books Corp., 1923), 174.

parenting, Spurgeon wrote to the children directly to "try to make them think about Jesus" and "while yet a child to be saved by the Lord Jesus."[64] In a letter to another child, he warned that:

> You do not intend to cause grief to dear mother and father, but you do. So long as you are not saved, they can never rest. However obedient, and sweet, and kind you may be, they will never feel happy about you until you believe in the Lord Jesus Christ, and so find everlasting salvation.[65]

So, absent the conversion experience, the child is actually pitted against the parents, cast as a source of their suffering and grief.

Further, the preconversion child is pitted against God in Spurgeon's portrayal, as eternal damnation threatens any individual who has not made the conscious decision to accept Christ, regardless of the faith formation that may have occurred on other fronts. In a letter to residents of his orphanage after one of the orphans had died, Spurgeon asked hauntingly: "Are you all prepared, if he should shoot another arrow into one of the houses, and lay another low? I wonder who will be the next! . . . If you are not saved, you are in great danger, in fearful peril!"[66]

The conversional tradition's conception of the child's "best interests" is disconnected from parents completely, centering on the individual implementation of a universal norm. Resting salvation on childhood conversion brings a remarkable degree of uniformity to the content of the child's spiritual well-being. Regardless of upbringing, parental efforts at faith formation, or the child's involvement with a broader faith community, the child's spiritual well-being is secured only by her deliberate decision to accept Christ as her savior. For most groups within this tradition, there is no possibility of salvation absent conversion once a child has reached the age of accountability, creating an insatiable drive for childhood evangelism, directed even at the children of believing Christians. Roughly identical experiences must be undergone by all children everywhere.[67] And the conversion moment is a self-contained path of individual salvation, obviating the need for any sort of

---

64. *Letters of Charles Haddon Spurgeon,* 179.

65. *Letters of Charles Haddon Spurgeon,* 180.

66. *Letters of Charles Haddon Spurgeon,* 181.

67. Explanations of what is required for conversion generally focus on derivations of the "sinner's prayer," as exemplified by one popular form: "God, I know that I am a sinner. I know that I deserve the consequences of my sin. However, I am trusting in Jesus Christ as my Savior. I believe that His death and resurrection provided for my forgiveness. I trust in Jesus and Jesus alone as my personal Lord and Savior. Thank you, Lord, for saving me and forgiving me! Amen!" http://www.gotquestions.org/sinners-prayer.html (last visited March 1, 2006).

communal context.[68] There are thus two striking similarities between the conversional tradition and the rights-based conception of the child: both require the child's individual exercise of autonomy to secure the child's "best interests," and both contemplate that the realization of the interests has little to do with the parents.

The Child in the Covenantal Tradition

In the covenantal tradition, embodied in today's Reformed and Presbyterian churches, baptism is understood to be the confirmation of the new covenant between God and his people. Unlike the sacramental tradition, it does not constitute the necessary means of salvation, but unlike the conversional tradition, it is more than symbolic, for it serves as the sign and seal of God's promise of salvation. Infant baptism is an integral part of the covenantal tradition, but its practice emerges from different theological premises than those operating in the sacramental tradition.

In its relationship to the new covenant, baptism is the Christian equivalent of circumcision. Circumcision signifies God's covenant with Abraham and his descendants, a tangible individual expression of a community's commitment to follow God's ways and receive God's blessings across generations.[69] Baptism has a similar function in the covenantal tradition. The theological views of sixteenth-century reformer Ulrich Zwingli held that Christians' "new covenant was in substance continuous with the covenant of Abraham, since both pointed in different ways to the same Christ," and consequently "God's command that Abraham's children be circumcised was sufficient reason for Christians to baptize their children."[70] Significantly, the baptism flowed from the faith identity that the child already possessed by virtue of her parents' faith; essentially, "since children were included in the covenant with their parents, there was no reason to deprive them of the sign of that which they already possessed."[71] And the faith of the parents, in Zwingli's thought, linked the infant to the broader faith community.

In this sense, covenantal baptism does not serve to impart grace from God

---

68. Of course, some sort of faith community is needed under the conversional approach in order to facilitate further spiritual development, but the community has no role in the attainment of salvation.

69. See Gen. 17.

70. E. Brooks Holifield, *The Covenant Sealed: The Development of Puritan Sacramental Theology in Old and New England* (New Haven: Yale University Press, 1974), 6.

71. Holifield, *The Covenant Sealed,* 6.

to the individual, but brings the infant into the grace that has already been imparted to the community through covenant, just as the faith sealed by circumcision was not an individual faith, but the faith of God's chosen people.[72] So there is a function to covenantal baptism not present in the merely symbolic quality of conversional baptism and unlike the salvific entry into the faith community performed directly by baptism in the sacramental tradition. For those in the covenantal tradition, "baptism marks the formal recognition of the child in a community of covenant to which he or she already completely belongs."[73]

The linchpin figure in the covenantal tradition, particularly as to the development of the theological underpinnings of infant baptism within the tradition, is Richard Baxter, a seventeenth-century British Puritan. He drove the public debate on infant baptism, and his work provides key insight into the sharp demarcations between covenantal, conversional, and sacramental conceptions of the child.

On the question of original sin, Puritans espoused a federal theory under which Adam acted as a representative of the entire human race, and thus we all share his responsibility for the first sin. In sharp contrast to Augustine's argument that parents biologically transmitted original sin to their offspring, though, we are not deemed to have directly participated in the first sin.[74] But by no means does Adam's function as representative diminish the parents' influence on the child's standing before God. While the seed of original sin was not literally transmitted across generations, "[c]hildren may be said to will the actual sins of Adam and of their nearer parents because those sins are reputatively theirs."[75]

Crucially, it is not just the consequences of sin that are bestowed by parents, but the benefits of faith.[76] Baxter writes:

72. Holifield, *The Covenant Sealed,* 6: "Zwingli strongly emphasized the communal character of sacraments, being careful to point out that the faith sealed by circumcision (Rom. 4:11) was not the 'trust and faith that every individual has in his heart,' but rather the faith of the church."

73. Barbara Pitkin, "'The Heritage of the Lord': Children in the Theology of John Calvin," in *The Child in Christian Thought,* 193 (discussing Calvin).

74. Bendroth, "Children of Adam," 496-97 (arguing that the federal theory "softened the Augustinian argument that all of humanity had directly participated in the first sin and that, with each act of concupiscence, parents passed on to their offspring both the penalty and the original guilt for Adam's transgression").

75. Hans Boersma, *Richard Baxter's Understanding of Infant Baptism* (Princeton: Princeton Theological Seminary, 2002), 62.

76. Boersma, *Richard Baxter's Understanding,* 62 ("Infants may be said to have faith reputatively, because of the faith of their parents").

God joyneth children with their Parents *(variatis variandis)* under the Covenant of Grace, and we are in infancy de jure the better or worse for what our Parents were, are, or did. And that not to be healed, not to be justified and saved, is not now to infants a penalty of Adam's sin alone, but of those Parents (or pro-Parents) in whom the Law of Grace doth judge the infant to have been, or done, or not done what was necessary.[77]

And the guilt flowing from original sin has a "remedy at hand, which [Adam's] had not that he knew of, we being under a pardoning covenant."[78] An individual's birth into the covenantal community gave rise to an entitlement to baptism: "Infants had a right to the baptismal covenant seal because they had been 'entered into covenant' by their parents, who possessed 'so much interest in them and power of them, that their act [could be] esteemed as the infant's act, and legally imputed to them as if they themselves had done it.'"[79] Just as our law empowers parents to act on their children's behalf in areas such as health care and education, covenantal theology empowers parents to act on their children's behalf in claiming the benefits of the covenant.

In contrast to those who see the path of salvation as lying wholly separate from the parent-child relationship, Baxter uses the centrality of that relationship as his primary defense of infant baptism, as "the Infants case much followeth the case of the Parents, especially in benefits."[80] Those who would deny infant baptism, according to Baxter, "do plainly play the Devils part in accusing their own Children, and disputing them out of the Church and House of God, and out of his Promises and Covenaut [*sic*], and the privileges that accompany them; and most ungratefully deny, reject and plead against the mercies that Christ hath purchased for their Children, and made over to them."[81] In other words, according to Hans Boersma's summation of Baxter's work, "[i]nfants are included with their parents and can be baptized on account of their parents' faith."[82]

While affirming the appropriateness of infant baptism, Baxter acknowledged the power of the arguments offered in opposition, especially the assertion that a justifying decision of faith should be a requirement of baptism. Baxter did not ignore the need for personal faith, but he did not view it as a prerequisite to begin the faith journey. The benefits embodied in the covenant

---

77. Boersma, *Richard Baxter's Understanding*, 36 (quoting Baxter, *Two Disputations*, 16).
78. Boersma, *Richard Baxter's Understanding*, 37 (quoting Baxter, *Two Disputations*, 147).
79. Holifield, *The Covenant Sealed*, 93.
80. Boersma, *Richard Baxter's Understanding*, 61 (quoting Baxter, *More Proofs*, 111-12).
81. Boersma, *Richard Baxter's Understanding*, 51 (quoting Baxter, *Plain Scripture Proof*, 13).
82. Boersma, *Richard Baxter's Understanding*, 61.

were naturally available to the child by virtue of her birth into the covenant community, and they would naturally be claimed by the child as her own as she matured. The baptism, thus, seals what has transpired already (the fact of the covenant) and what is to come (the child growing within the covenant and claiming its underlying tenets as her own).

But not all children will come to affirm the faith promises of the covenant. Baxter emphasizes that parents do not:

> promise absolutely that it shall come to passe [*sic*]; but we engage [the child] to it as his duty by covenant, (which also would have been his duty, if he had not covenanted:) and we promise that he shall perform the conditions as a means to attain the benefits of the Covenant, upon this penalty, That if he perform them not, he shall lose the benefits of the Covenant, and bear the punishment threatned. So that we only promise that he shall keep the coveuant [*sic*]; or if he do not, we leave him liable to the penalty.[83]

In other words, parents' faith is imputed to their children until children have matured to the point where they can be expected to claim it as their own, but once children come of age, "the condition of faith can no longer be performed by the parents on behalf of the children," and then "the act of faith is required of the mature children themselves."[84]

It is important to recognize, though, that the child starts from within the faith community and must decide to reject the community's claims and conditions in order to lose her standing, rather than starting from outside the community and needing to gain standing through affirmative acts of membership. For Baxter, it is not simply a question of whether "the infants of believers have a right to baptism," but whether "they have a share in the covenant and its blessings," a question on which turns the very "hope of salvation for one's children."[85]

The figure of Baxter, while essential to the development of a covenantal theology of children, must be supplemented, at least in passing, with a reference to his theological descendant, Horace Bushnell. In response to the dramatic nineteenth-century shift toward emphasizing children's salvation based on conversion, the Congregationalist minister Bushnell struck a deep public chord by mining the covenantal tradition. His thoughts illuminate several of the earlier covenantal themes, though expanding them in a way that was eminently appealing to more modern views on the sacredness of the nuclear family.

83. Boersma, *Richard Baxter's Understanding*, 63 (quoting Baxter, *Plain Scripture Proof*, 113-14).

84. Boersma, *Richard Baxter's Understanding*, 63.

85. Boersma, *Richard Baxter's Understanding*, 65.

Bushnell's famous synopsis of a child's faith formation was that the child should "grow up a Christian, and never know himself as being otherwise."[86] Under Bushnell's view, according to Margaret Bendroth, parents should "envelop the child in Christian love from the point of birth" because "parental love was itself salvific."[87] Bushnell insisted that:

> [T]he aim, effort, and expectation should be, not, as is commonly assumed, that the child is to grow up in sin, to be converted after he comes to a mature age; but that he is to open on the world as one that is spiritually renewed, not remembering the time when he went through a technical experience, but seeming rather to have loved what is good from his earliest years.[88]

The child may be born into her parent's sin, but to Bushnell that reality at the "precise point of birth, is not a question of any so grave import as is generally supposed; for the child, after birth, is still within the matrix of the parental life," and the "parental life will be flowing into him all that time, just as naturally, and by a law as truly organic, as when the sap of the trunk flows into a limb."[89] There is a functional justification to Bushnell's parent-centered approach: the only genuine teaching, he emphasized, "will be that which interprets the truth to the child's feeling by living example, and makes him love the truth afterwards for the teacher's sake."[90] Of course, even among those who applauded Bushnell's approach as a prudent remedy to individualism, he was subject to criticism on the ground that "[a] home can never play the role of the church . . . and parents can never play the part of priests for their children — this is the job of the wider church."[91] But by building on Baxter's work, Bushnell even more clearly elucidated the differences among the three competing Christian conceptions of the child's spiritual well-being.

The covenantal tradition closely connects parents to the realization of the child's "best interests." Baxter did not presume that parents will be a source exclusively of blessings and benefits; sin also comes across the generational link, but that does not negate the fact that the source of redemption lies across the same link. In contrast to the rights-based conception's insistence, the covenantal understanding of the child's interests does not render those interests fungible across families — the interests are wrapped up within the child's par-

---

86. Horace Bushnell, *Christian Nurture* (New Haven: Yale University Press, 1967), 4.
87. Bendroth, "Children of Adam," 502.
88. Bushnell, *Christian Nurture*, 4.
89. Bushnell, *Christian Nurture*, 19.
90. Bushnell, *Christian Nurture*, 318.
91. Bendroth, "Children of Adam," 504.

ticular family. Much less does the covenantal tradition contemplate separation between the child and parents as a precondition of achieving the child's autonomy-centered interests; the child grows into authentic personhood not by escaping the parental purview, but through its nourishment.

Conclusion

The understandable temptation to equate a child's legally enforceable "best interests" with a particular substantive outcome places tremendous tension on the family unit. General concepts like individual autonomy threaten the child-forming identities of families whose ultimate objectives are not coextensive with individual autonomy. This threat becomes even starker when individual autonomy is defined in the narrowing terms of free speech, privacy, access to information, and unfettered conscience. As such, it is no surprise that the UN Convention on the Rights of the Child uses lofty legal aspirations to mask a multitude of divergent and defiant cultural claims. David Smolin presciently points out that if the Convention "were to become a legal document subject to adjudication and enforcement, then its abstract resolution of protection and autonomy would instantly dissolve into thousands of specific cultural conflicts."[92] An equally stultifying sameness underlies calls to bring private schools in line with government orthodoxy, as dissenting worldviews are effectively trumped by the rush toward facilitating a child's "one-way journey into self-creation."[93]

Justification for this top-down imposition of universalized norms lies in the modern view of childhood as a form of cultural migration, which purportedly should facilitate the child's cognitive separation "from the parents' morality, from the authority of meanings the parents have assigned to behavior, even from the parents' religion and their other group identities."[94] This view claims to be agnostic as to whether the child eventually embraces her parents' worldview, but the pre-embrace separation is essential. One way to facilitate the separation is to break down the legal relevance of the family structure, overcoming the obstacles posed by a legal system that supports and protects the family as an independent entity. Martha Fineman's work has been instrumental in this effort, as she calls for "[t]he intergenerational, nonsexual organization of

92. David M. Smolin, "A Tale of Two Treaties: Furthering Social Justice through the Redemptive Myths of Childhood," *Emory International Law Review* 17 (2003): 977.

93. Michael Scaperlanda, "Realism, Freedom, and the Integral Development of the Human Person," *Journal of Catholic Legal Studies* 44 (2005): 83.

94. Kenneth L. Karst, "Law, Cultural Conflict, and the Socialization of Children," *California Law Review* 91 (2003): 991.

intimacy" to be "protected and privileged in law and policy." She urges that the mother-child relationship, not any broader arrangement of roles and relationships, should function as "the base entity around which social policy and legal rules are fashioned."[95] Legal autonomy for a larger set of relationships is rendered superfluous, if not counterproductive, once we conceive of the child's "best interests" in terms of individual autonomy.

All three of the Christian traditions discussed here will resist the rights-based conception of the child, but they bring different resources to the task. Covenantal language provides particularly helpful imagery for engagement because of its explicit linkage between the child's "best interests" and the parent-child relationship. The sacramental view contemplates a supportive role for parents and the surrounding community, even though the child's interests are not secured by the fact of the parent-child relationship. The conversional view offers a markedly reduced role for parents, as salvation flows not from any family or community function, but from the child's own conscious decision. All three traditions, though, will oppose any suggestion that the value of the parent-child relationship is a function of the degree to which it fosters the child's own autonomy.

Ensuring that parents remain at the center of efforts to define and protect the vocation of the child requires that faith communities offer a prophetic voice to the broader society. The promise of Christianity's engagement with today's autonomy-driven approach is that the role of parents is not elevated as a naked power grab, but as the most natural vehicle for promoting authentic childhood flourishing. To the extent that the sacramental and conversional traditions can supplement their theological understandings of the child's vocation with imagery grounded in the covenant, our cultural conversations on the law's treatment of childhood will be that much richer.

95. Martha Fineman, "Intimacy outside of the Natural Family: The Limits of Privacy," *Connecticut Law Review* 23 (1991): 971.

Index of Names

Index of Subjects

Abuse: of children, 243-44, 271, 280, 367, 399, 403, 405, 418

Accountability: of general public, 410, 418; of parents, 43, 94, 386; of schools, 417

Act of existence, 191-92

Adam and Eve: and childhood innocence, 122, 137, 232; compared to infants of Eden, 170, 182; compared to Jesus Christ, 232, 235; corresponding age in Isidorean life cycle of, 156; creation of, 66, 106; original sin or sins of, 119, 127, 137, 141, 150, 167, 232-33, 419-20, 426; women as compared to, 285

Adolescence: during medieval period, 155, 256, 265; growth and development during, 204; possibility of being saved from, 208; as social construct, 297; social science research on, 403-4

Adoption, 250

Adults: as autonomous, 391, 401; and demands of work and family, 297-98; relationship of, with children, 61, 73, 198, 302, 382; vocation of, 54, 73. *See also* Parents

Angels. *See* Guardian angel

Authority: of adults or parents, 41, 44, 65, 89, 92-95, 97, 99-103, 105, 272, 281-82, 298, 400-401, 404, 408-9, 411-12; as authentic, 76; challenges to, 43, 45, 286, 338, 350, 383; of correct conduct, 96; as

creative, 50; function or purpose of, 92, 99-100, 103; gnostic implications of, 84; justifications of, 94-95; model of, 235; parental limitations on, 43-45, 93, 101-2, 256, 270, 288, 403, 410-11, 413, 415-17; of parents in ancient Rome, 245, 250, 257; Plato on, 93-94, 96-97; recognition of or obedience to, 76-77, 92, 224, 391; reconstruction of, 352-54; Rousseau on, 93-94; and school or education, 93, 98-103, 350-51, 374-75, 384, 405

Autonomy: of children, 64, 75, 327, 386, 411-13, 417, 425, 430; as compatible with Christian ideals, 394-96; as gained by growth and development, 108-9, 263, 392-93, 396; "minimalist" notion of, 384-85, 392; parental role in developing, 394, 397, 401-2, 404; of parents, 391, 401, 411-12; of religious faith, 395-96; and salvation, 410; and school or education, 384, 392

Baptism: Augustine on, 137, 225; and calling or vocation, 53, 58, 73; crying as request for or resistance of, 148-49, 153; as cure for original sin, 128-29, 139, 147, 217, 418-20, 427; death prior to, 79, 143, 211-13, 216-18, 224-27, 233, 236, 238-39, 420-21; emergency, 143-46, 149, 153, 217; and God or Jesus Christ, 115-16, 120,

301; children without or excused from completing of, 295-96, 321; as child's contribution to family, 296, 310; economic and spiritual value of, 311, 315, 317, 323; gender segregation of, 319; meaning or significance of, 301, 307-9, 311; social research on, 306-9, 311-12, 317, 322; as vocation, 296, 310-12, 314-15, 317, 321-23. *See also* Domestic roles and work

Church: as Augustinian "emergency room," 129, 145-46, 148; baptism as mission or doctrine of, 226-31, 236; and children's rights or welfare, 51, 244; as mother, 146-48, 237

Correct conduct, 76, 78, 83, 87-88, 95-96

Daughters: being good, 60, 64-65, 73; as family's property, 277-78; limited vocational possibilities of, 283; office of, 57, 59

Death: Aristotle on, 173; causing desire for salvation, 231; causing grief, 225; and infanticide, 145, 152, 223, 245-46, 248-49; and infant mortality rate, 144-45; in original sin, 229; prior to baptism, 79, 143, 211-13, 216-18, 224-27, 229, 233, 238-39, 420-21

Destiny, 226

Discipline: of children as parental duty, 33, 176, 187, 280-81, 290; as alternative to or distinguished from punishment, 45, 285; as lacking in children, 110; as learned through chores and duties, 320; in schools, 367

Divine: calling, 53-54; economy, 211, 214; gift of children, 290; governance, 192-93; grace, 68, 112; intervention, 261; lottery as to child's influences, 385; summons as distinct from vocational calling, 57-58; youth as paradox and mystery, 107

Domestic roles and work: as altered by changes in education and labor laws, 297, 299-300; and division of labor within family, 304, 310, 314, 318-19, 232;

and family's need for help, 310-11; having both economic and spiritual value, 232, 311, 315, 317; history of, 298-99; as outside realm of traditional economy, 314-15, 317; as shaped by childhood, 305; social science studies on, 296, 305, 314, 317; theology on, 296; of women, 300-301, 315. *See also* Chores

Duties: of children to parents and families, 266, 269-76, 278-79, 288, 290, 320; of daughters, 284; and office or calling for, 104, 272; of parents to children, 276-79, 282, 290, 386

Economics and economy: and child's changing role in household, 300-301, 308, 322; and cost and benefits of children, 297, 303-4, 312; of divine grace, 191, 317; and gender-stratified jobs and labor, 306; of household, 296, 299, 301-3, 306; and spiritual value of chores and domestic work, 232, 311, 315, 317; and welfare of family, 298, 313-14; women as invisible in, 315

Education: of children, 36-37, 48-49, 51, 93, 191, 253; and Coleman's study, 100; as collective effort, 402, 404; as commercial venture, 56; contemporary theory on, 383; as distinguished from instruction, 350-51; of girls or daughters, 37, 284, 287, 334, 336, 351; homeschooling and, 384, 397, 404; humanist reforms of, 37; Lasallian tradition of, 358-75, 378-79; Locke on, 285; Luther on, 36-37, 49, 56, 333-34; Maritain on, 199-200, 203-6, 210; and parents, 37, 48, 95, 99-102, 206, 285, 290, 334, 345, 354-56, 387, 397-402, 404-6, 409, 414-15, 427; as preparation for entry into workforce, 322; and religion, 34, 100, 331-34, 336, 345-46, 348-51, 357-66, 374, 377, 379, 383, 417; of Roman children, 247; Rousseau on, 286, 340; schoolchoice or voucher movement, 416-17; and social classes, 99, 214, 336, 342, 344, 346-47, 349, 351, 354, 358, 360-64, 369,

education, 97-98, 243, 329-31, 333-34, 337-38, 340-52, 354, 384, 387, 402-3, 405, 415-16, 430
Stereotypes, 318

Teachers: and duty to initiate child, 387-94, 396-407; five basic human dispositions in Lasallian schools, 358-75, 378-79; parents acting as, 382-88, 396-407; and preparing students to win their personality and freedom, 203-4; as substitutes for parental authority, 102-3, 350-56; to be encouraged by, 204; and variance in curricula or moral pedagogies, 97-98. *See also* Education; Schools

Vocation: applying to adults and children, 32, 39, 223, 318; Christian theologians' work on, 32, 104, 296; in Christian tradition, 39, 54, 104, 295, 381; in contemporary culture, 31; as chores or domestic work, 310-12, 314, 317, 321-23; discernment or realization of, 67, 71, 291; as divine call, 53-54, 57-58, 379; as God's work, 32, 104, 317; interrelated with summons, 58; as literacy, 335; as love of God, 55, 316; Luther on, 35-37, 39, 56, 297, 316; Maritain on, 213; as mutual and coexisting, 318; of parents or adults, 54, 73, 290, 381; as problematic or dangerous concept, 54; and projects distinguished from situation, 58; restrictions on possibilities of, for females, 283, 318; second good as, 87; of

self, 54-55, 58, 61, 71, 73; specific distinguished from general, 32, 55, 104; as subjective and individualistic, 104
Vocation of the child: and abilities, skills, or interests, 282-83; Aquinas on, 187; Augustine on, 127, 136; as autonomous but with best interests, 317; chores and domestic work as, 296, 312, 314-15; as duty to be loved, 268, 276-77, 290; as duty to love, 268-69, 273-74, 277, 290-91; eight dimensions of, 40-52; and expansion of female possibilities, 284-85; as free choice, 81, 265; as growth and development, 391; household manuals on, 267-92; in Lasallian tradition, 357-58, 362-63, 369-70, 376-77, 378-80; as learner, 381-82, 386, 388, 391, 397, 406-7; as lifelong process, 35, 41; as method for challenging conception of children, 34; as neglected or problematic concept, 34-35, 61, 64; and parental resistance, 261-62; parental or adult role in preparing child for, 165, 267, 277, 282-83, 290, 388, 392, 397-402, 406, 430; and role of self, 59, 71, 73; sociopolitical context of, 408; through social grace and good manners, 376; and unbaptized children, 216, 224

Welfare: of children, 93, 244, 400, 412, 414; of child's spirituality, 421-22, 424, 429; of family, 296, 298, 310, 314, 320-21
Winning of personality and freedom, 190-91, 196-99, 203-4, 206-7, 213-14